REAL ESTATE
FINANCE & INVESTMENT
MANUAL

Works by Jack Cummings

The Complete Handbook of How to Farm Real Estate Listings and Sales, published by Prentice Hall, 1973.

The Venture, a novel published by Charterhouse, 1976.

The Ultimate Game, a novel published by Major Books, 1978.

The Complete Guide to Real Estate Financing, published by Prentice Hall, 1978.

Lauderdale Run, a novel published by Manor Books, 1979.

Building Your Wealth through Creative Real Estate Investing, published by Pierce, 1980.

Successful Real Estate Investing for the Single Person, published by Playboy Press, 1981.

Cashless Investing in Real Estate, published by Playboy Press, 1982.

$1,000 Down Can Make You Rich, published by Simon & Schuster, 1985.

The Real Estate Financing Manual, published by Simon & Schuster, 1987.

The Business Traveler's Survival Guide, published by John Wiley & Sons, 1991.

The Guide to Real Estate Exchanging, published by John Wiley & Sons, 1991.

The Real Estate Investing and Financing Manual, published by Simon & Schuster, 1993.

The McGraw-Hill 36-Hour Real Estate Investing Course, published by McGraw-Hill, 1993.

The Real Estate Investor's Answer Book, published by McGraw-Hill, 1994, second revised edition published in 2005.

The Real Estate Finance and Investment Manual, published by Simon & Schuster, 1997.

Investing in Real Estate with Other People's Money, published by McGraw-Hill, 2004.

Commercial Real Estate Investing 12 Easy Steps, published by John Wiley & Sons, 2004.

The Tax-Free Exchange Loophole, published by John Wiley & Sons, 2005.

The Real Estate Investor's Guide to Cash Flow and Equity Management, published by John Wiley & Sons, 2006.

REAL ESTATE FINANCE & INVESTMENT MANUAL

NINTH EDITION

JACK CUMMINGS

WILEY

John Wiley & Sons, Inc.

Published by John Wiley & Sons, Inc., Hoboken, New Jersey.

Published simultaneously in Canada.

For general information on our other products and services or for technical support, please contact our Customer Care Department within the United States at (800) 762-2974, outside the United States at (317) 572-3993 or fax (317) 572-4002.

Wiley also publishes its books in a variety of electronic formats. Some content that appears in print may not be available in electronic books. For more information about Wiley products, visit our web site at www.wiley.com.

Library of Congress Cataloging-in-Publication Data:

Cummings, Jack, 1940-
    Real estate finance & investment manual Jack Cummings.—9th ed.
      p.   cm.
    ISBN 978-0-470-26040-1 (pbk.)
      1. Real estate business—Finance—Handbooks, manuals, etc.   2. Real estate investment—Finance—Handbooks, manuals, etc.   3. Mortgage loans—Handbooks, manuals, etc.   4. Mortgages—Handbooks, manuals, etc.   I. Title.
II. Title: Real estate finance and investment manual.
   HD1375.C854   2008
   332.7'20973—dc22
                                                                            2008002757

Printed in the United States of America.

10 9 8 7 6 5 4 3 2 1

*This book is dedicated
to the many thousands of real estate investors
who have already had the opportunity
to read earlier editions and who,
by their messages to me,
have attested that much of their
success is due to my showing them
the elements of successful real estate investing.
In addition, to the many new investors
who will become true and successful "insiders"
to this field because of this book.*

TABLE OF CONTENTS

Introduction—xxxv

Chapter 1
*How Real Estate Investing Goals Help You Formulate
Effective Financing Strategies—1*

Chapter 2
*How to Set Effective Goals for Successful Real
Estate Investing—23*

Chapter 3
The Power and Art of Effective Negotiating—40

This chapter shows you how a win/win strategy begins with your goals firmly in focus and ends with helping the other party to the transaction move closer to their goals.

Chapter 4
How Leverage Affects Risk and the Value of Real Estate—61

This chapter illustrates the mechanics of leverage and shows you how its magic can generate enormous increases of investment yield and property value when used wisely and correctly.

Chapter 5
Conventional Financing:
Where to Find It and How to Negotiate the Best Terms—83

This chapter introduces you to conventional forms of real estate financing.

Chapter 6
Use Creative Financing to Maximize Benefits—125

This chapter opens doors and your eyes to opportunities available to you by increasing your investment techniques and strategies, enabling you to maximize your benefits and help you to attain your investment goals.

Chapter 7
How to Use Government-Insured Loans to Finance Real Estate Purchases and Sales—142

This chapter gives you a solid working knowledge of several different types of loans that are a function of one or more departments of the U.S. government.

Chapter 8
How to Get Land Development and Construction Loans—186

This chapter introduces you to the initial world of development, land acquisition, and development loans.

Chapter 9
How to Get the Most Benefit from Blanket Mortgages—214

This chapter enables you to adjust financing and shift equities by spreading the lender's risk over more than one property.

Chapter 10
Gain Leverage on Existing Financing with a Wraparound Mortgage—225

This chapter acquaints you with the wraparound mortgage.

Chapter 11
The Sale-Leaseback: An Investment Tool That Works for Both Buyer and Seller—259

This chapter is designed to expand your knowledge of mixed-use strategies that can be effective in reaching certain goals.

Chapter 12
The Last Loophole: IRS Section 1031
Real Estate Exchanges—278

This chapter raises the curtain on the most important benefit that real estate investors have at their disposal.

Chapter 13
How to Maximize Your Use of Pyramid Financing—321

This chapter shows you an exciting technique that allows you to shift equities in such a way that it becomes possible to purchase a property and to obtain new financing that may exceed the actual cost of the property.

Chapter 14
The Discount Sale and Leaseback and Buyback—355

This chapter continues to give you investment alternatives.

Chapter 15
How to Profit with Discounted Mortgages—368

Chapter 16
Two Prime Insider Techniques:
Preferred Income Sweeters and Options—393

This chapter introduces two highly effective negotiation strategies that can help you close transactions whether you are the buyer or seller.

Chapter 17
Five Powerful Secondary Financing Techniques That Effectively Close Deals—420

This chapter introduces five powerful closing techniques that are effective.

Chapter 18
Eleven Creative Financing Techniques That Make Your Transactions Fly—442

This chapter continues to expand your "out of the box" thinking when it comes to real estate investing.

Chapter 19
Four Techniques:
Where You Keep Part and Dispose of Part—478

This chapter illustrates that it is not essential to sell, lease, or otherwise dispose of 100 percent of your real estate to reach your desired goals.

Chapter 20
Using Your Talent and Hidden Benefits to Barter Your Way into Real Estate—494

This chapter reinforces your use of your own natural or learned talents and abilities as well as the hidden benefits of properties you own or will acquire as a method to help solve problems, yours and the other party to your negotiations, by the use of barter.

Chapter 21
Nine Important Stages of Successful Real Estate Transactions—515

This chapter provides you with a fine-tuned checklist of critical stages that are important to the process that begins with finding a property to buy and successfully closing on it.

Chapter 22
The Six Most-Asked Questions about Real Estate Financing—557

This chapter gives you the answers to six of the most-asked questions about real estate financing.

Chapter 23
Keeping the Wolf from the Door—575

This chapter quells any apprehension you may have about foreclosure.

Chapter 24
How to Effectively Develop and Implement
Your Comfort Zone—587

This chapter illustrates the procedure to use to develop and then implement your investment comfort zone effectively with the maximum benefits.

Appendix
How to Use the Constant Tables—607

The purpose and goal of this Appendix is to give you three simple to use and easy to understand financial tables that will assist your problem solving when dealing with virtually any facet of mortgage financing.

Index—649

INTRODUCTION

Are you confused, disappointed, or even financially challenged by the turn of events in the real estate market?

Welcome to the world of opportunity.

And welcome to this new and greatly expanded and revised edition of the single most important book about real estate you may ever embrace. It is one that has passed the test of time, having been purchased, read, and used as a guide to successful real estate investing by thousands of people over a span of over 30 years. This edition contains solutions to virtually every important or difficult problem that faces real estate investors. It is filled with easy to follow examples, and it breaks down the toughest problem into the simple events that have caused the problem in the first instance.

As its author, I naturally am biased on its contents, so let me explain to you why I feel so confident in telling you that this book will serve you for many years to come as a guide and reference tool that will come in handy no matter what you do in real estate. I suppose that the most critical aspect of this book is that I have lived with it for a very long time now, and it has gone through an evolution that has kept it up to date with events, circumstances, and current changes in the problems to be faced, and the solutions to those problems. As a successful real estate investor as well as a realtor and author of many books on this subject, this book has remained the flagship of my real estate investing books. Over the years, I have had the honor to be called the Renaissance Man of real estate investing. Many real estate students, as well as other long-term investors have commented on how they have gained renewed confidence in their abilities to overcome the many roadblocks that lay in wait to the unsuspecting real estate investor, who, like me, had to learn much of their ability the hard way, by making the mistake, recognizing the mistake and what could have been done to avoid the problem in the first place. But there will always be some problems that will occur that seem to have simply snuck up on you from behind. In those situations, the best way around them is to have such a depth of knowledge that almost instinctively you will know what to do, or where you can quickly find the solution. Interestingly, you may even discover that the problem you might have is really your attempt to attain the wrong goal.

One element of this book that you will discover immediately is that I believe you must have sound and clearly understood goals that you can keep in focus. To do that, you must work at your goals because they are your plan for the future. Your goals drive you, keep you on a path, and often send you signals that you have strayed from the path and that you must make an adjustment to those goals.

It is all too easy to become overconfident (even before you have completed this book!) that you know so much more than other real estate investors you meet, that you can make mistakes. Sometimes those mistakes come from what I call "the greener grass syndrome," which strikes like a bolt of lightning and causes you to want to buy something that looks so good you just cannot pass it up. Those episodes occur when we are not in our comfort zone. And yet, the correction to that mistake is also easy because all that is necessary is to expand your comfort zone.

Once you have a goal, you can build your own comfort zone, and this book helps you accomplish that far easier than you ever thought possible.

I believe in getting right to the point, tackling the problem before it has the opportunity to block your moves. To do that, I have continued to build this book into what some call the "bible" of real estate investing. To be a success in real estate investing, you should keep the following tenets in mind:

1. Formulate goals you want to achieve.
2. Establish then implement an investment plan to take you where you want to go.
3. Learn how to maximize your bottom line, take-home profits.
4. Continually reduce your risk while increasing your exposure to opportunities.
5. Develop an exit strategy that will complement your plan and goals.
6. Establish timetables and deadlines to reach your goals.
7. Do not rationalize why you did not achieve them, learn from your errors and move forward.
8. Reach self-established plateaus, then pat yourself on your back.
9. Then set higher plateaus and more worthy goals and work for them.
10. Achieve financial independence.

Armed with this book, you can attain all of this.

This book is devoted to every aspect of real estate investment. It is designed and written to give readers a single one-stop source for the best real estate investing advice and information possible. This book, and its hundreds of financing and investment strategies and techniques, is specifically written for real estate investors, developers, bankers, buyers, sellers, tenants, salespeople, mortgage brokers, land planners, lawyers, and other professional advisors.

The material contained in this book is offered so that each chapter can be used as a stand-alone reference guide for the specifics that are covered within that chapter. This enables you to turn to that chapter or chapters that can provide a source for solutions to existing problems as they occur. In this way, the book becomes an instant tool. As a total source of information, the book is compiled in such a way that you can build your knowledge of real estate investing and financing in a smooth progression of information. As with any comprehensive book, you will find that an initial reading of the entire book will enable you to obtain maximum use of the material for many years to come.

This book will become indispensable to buyers and sellers who are looking to improve their chances in the marketplace. It gives each side of the real estate transaction all the elements that are essential to a successful conclusion of a transaction. Best of all, this book shows you how to become the expert within your own comfort zone, and how to get the edge in the market and keep it.

The hundreds of examples contained within are to spark your own imagination. Every kind of transaction from the purchase of a timeshare week, to the financing of a multimillion-dollar shopping center are covered. The simple strategies that have worked for others are here, waiting for you to discover just how simple it is to become a true real estate investment insider.

In writing this book, I have looked back over my past thirty-plus years as a real estate investor, broker, and developer. I have reviewed mistakes I have seen other people make, and those which I have made along the path to success. I can tell you that the cliché of learning from the mistakes of others is a sound bit of advice, and this book offers you a shortcut around the pain and financial disaster of having to make your own mistakes.

As the author of many books on the subject of real estate investing, brokerage, and financing, I have been able, while drafting this new edition, to bring to the forefront the best of the techniques and strategies that have been presented in my earlier books. As an avid reader and constant student of just about everything dealing with real estate, I have made sure that the material contained in this book is fresh, full of concepts that work and techniques that can make a beneficial difference in your investment plan, which you will be able to implement immediately. Any single chapter of this book can give you a positive edge in your investment plan. Just one of the hundreds of techniques and strategies I have presented can give you financial success.

Have you ever wondered why some people seem to excel at everything they do? Have you wanted to know how some people seem to find success in every real estate investment they make? The answer is one of the first elements of this book you will discover. You will succeed because you learn how to maximize the bottom-line, take home profits, and you reduce risk in your investments because you have discovered how to recognize opportunities.

This book is easy to use. Study it from chapter to chapter and you will be well on your way to being one of the most knowledgeable real estate investors in town. All you will need after that is to begin to implement your own plan, which this book will help you design. Or, use the book for the chapters that interest you the most. This book is, after all, structured for that purpose, too. Take any chapter that fits your current needs and refresh yourself with what you need to get and keep the upper edge in each kind of transaction.

Everything from wraparound mortgages to very creative 1031 real estate tax-free exchanges is at your fingertips. The chapter on goal setting, that starts you on the right track for success, will put everything you do into proper perspective.

The goal of this book is to help you get the most from your efforts and hard-earned money. Each of you, depending on your specific goals or real estate aspirations, will find a wealth of material to fit your own specific needs.

REAL ESTATE INVESTORS

No matter how much experience you have, this book offers you a keen insight on how to increase your productivity, reduce your risk, and maintain your edge even when you sell in a buyer's market or buy in a seller's market. Dozens of checklists help you quickly and simply calculate data that you might have been missing before, or which came in too late to be of any real use to you. This book shows you how you can anticipate which property is going to go up in value, and even better, which properties are going to go down in value, then turn up again. If you already consider yourself a successful real estate investor, then get ready to get some insight into your system that will take you to higher plateaus.

DEVELOPERS

You are special to the real estate market. You make the market out of nothing, but you can also get caught in a down-turning trend over which you have no control. This book shows you that even in the worst market there is a way to find success. All it takes is understanding your goals and applying the techniques and strategies offered to you in this book. In this book, you will find many key elements to solve your specific problems. Because financing is often the most elusive factor for the real estate developer, you will discover this book will be indispensable to you in your next project, and the potential sale, at even bigger profits than you anticipated, of your last project. Much of this book is devoted to obtaining financing in real estate transactions. This means everything from learning how to improve your chances at the local savings and loan association, to cutting a great deal with a seller who, because you are now thinking more creatively, agrees to a proposal you make.

BANKERS

Bankers and loan officers will find that this book offers them a very special look at what's beyond the other side of the fence. This book helps anyone who is in the business of making loans, either for or as a part of a major institution or for his or her own private account. As a lender you will develop a new understanding of what it takes to do deals that work for both parties, and how to take creative concepts and apply them to very sound transactions.

BUYERS

The ultimate profit of every deal depends on an initial purchase that fits the investor's plan. This does not mean that your ultimate success is attained by beating the seller over the head to the point that you walk away from the table with a bargain. Bargains are obtained by knowing what will work for you. This book shows you that to get the edge in the deal does not pit you against the seller. Often, you and the seller have the same goals in mind. You want to buy, and the seller wants you to buy. By creative and constructive use of financing, and incorporating many other aspects of investment strategies, both you and the seller can come out winners, every time. You must open the door to what you need to do to make the deal work for you. This book is your key to that door.

SELLERS

Over the long haul, the seller is the king of the game. You are in possession of the property, and can, if financially strong enough, keep the property. However, buyers often control the market because when you need to sell, nothing happens until you find a buyer who wants your property. When there are fewer buyers than sellers the marketplace can be very slow. Often values have very little to do with this concept. This book shows sellers how to overcome a buyer's market and achieve your goals. Do this once and this book will be worth many hundred times what it cost you. All you have to do is to read on, build a plan that fits your needs, and go for it.

TENANTS

Most real estate investment books don't say much about tenants. As a rental property owner, I can tell you that were it not for tenants there would not be much of a real estate market. The key for you as a tenant is to be able to ascertain when you should buy, and when you should rent. The key to both situations is found in this book. You will find many examples of how to maximize lease terms to your favor, and many special lease terms that you will want to insist on in your next lease.

SALESPEOPLE

If you sell real estate, you know how tough the profession is. As a realtor for over 30 years, I know how the market can rise and fall. In some parts of the country, there seem to be more real estate salespeople than trees. To become a top real estate salesperson in any part of the world means you have to be the best, and offer your clients the best service possible. This book will open your eyes to how you can be of greater service to your buyers and sellers. If you can accept the fact that by helping your buyers and sellers attain their goals, you will be successful as a salesperson, then this book is for you. The idea is to expand your own reference point so that you are better able to put yourself into your clients' shoes. This will enable you to see beyond the standard way of doing things, and be creative in many new ways not possible before. By the way, creative financing often scares people. That is because the word "creative" is often confused with the word "complicated". Creativity really just means keeping your eyes and mind open to new ideas and concepts, and understanding where and when they fit to help someone. Take advantage of the tools contained in this book. Your clients will be glad you did.

MORTGAGE BROKERS

Mortgage brokers all find this book to be a great tool in building a stronger client base. As a reference work, it will be your guide to how to build better presentations, and how to apply simple and creative techniques to make the loan package stronger. We are all in this boat together, and the more the mortgage broker knows about what the real estate investor needs, the greater the success for each of us.

LAND PLANNERS

Every real estate investor and for that matter, just about anyone connected with real estate will feel the touch of the city, county, or state land planning staff, at one time or another. My own experience in this direction is considerable. I have had the experience of making hundreds of presentations before planning boards and city commissioners on subjects that deal with planning and ordinance matters. I have found that the more knowledgeable the planner is about the needs of the real estate investment community, the closer the two sides can work together. This book is a unique tool to aid all land planners.

LAWYERS AND OTHER PROFESSIONAL ADVISORS

Law, tax matters, accounting, and estate planning, just to name a few important factors that demand specialization, continue to become more and more complicated and diverse. No single person in any profession can be expected to know everything about his or her own field. That is why the best advisors read a lot. When it comes to matters dealing with real estate techniques, FHA mortgages, wraparound mortgages, exchanges, including the Starker tax-free exchange and so many other complicated financing techniques, this book will become an extraordinarily useful resource. Scan the Contents and you will quickly discover that this book will be indispensable to any transaction that deals with any aspect of real estate, both your clients' and your own portfolio.

Everyone has a need for this book. At present, you either own or rent. It is likely that in the near future you may make a change in your current status. When it comes time for you to sell, you will be faced with many decisions you need to make. Buyers are faced with many different kinds of decisions that can have a major impact on the future of their investments. Some of these decisions are shared by both buyer and seller, such as the tax basis of a new property, or the correct way to formulate a Starker exchange so that the IRS will not disavow the 1031 tax-free exchange status. This book will help you make the right decision no matter what the problem is that faces you. For the U.S. senior population, one of the most important aspects that need be considered is the tax liability that we will be faced with in an ultimate sale, or in establishing an estate. This book deals with this aspect in detail, and gives you many different strategies that are designed to reduce or eliminate the tax you may otherwise pay in a sale. The IRS will not tell you that you could have legally avoided paying them all that tax, but this book will. Not only that, I will show you, in clear, easy-to-follow examples and checklists, how to beat the IRS at its own game.

Very simply, you should own this book; it is an essential "cooking" book of real estate. It is filled with recipes for success.

Chapter 1

HOW REAL ESTATE INVESTING GOALS HELP YOU FORMULATE EFFECTIVE FINANCING STRATEGIES

GOAL OF THIS CHAPTER

The goal of this chapter is to impress on you the importance of establishing worthy and measurable goals to which you can direct your investment efforts. Because real estate is such a versatile method of investing, the most effective method of buying, holding, and later selling differs among investors with different goals, but similar properties. A goal without a method of measurement leaves investors adrift in a sea of doubt as to where they are in respect to the attainment of their goals. A goal is reached by interim steps or interim goals that lead to the desired results.

Most real estate investors struggle through their initial investments. Although this is a common situation, it does not have to be a normal one. It is possible to avoid the difficulties of establishing an effective investment strategy, which is an essential step to your ultimate success in the quest to attain your desired goals. The very mention of the need to obtain effective methods should be etched into your mind as one of the critical keys to achieve success in any task.

TO BE EFFECTIVE, FOCUS ON RESULTS

To be effective, you must know what the results should be in very specific ways so that you can remain focused on those desired results. Effective strategies are not fixed, however, and it is essential that, in real estate investing, likely mistakes are acknowledged, and that corrections in the investment plan be implemented.

The typical investor often uses what I call the "shotgun" method of investing: Their time, energy, and financial resources are spread over a wide range of tasks. This is a system of default, that is, one arrived at because of a lack of knowledge about how to design an effective program. These investors waste resources by learning about the wrong kind of investments for their desired results, often concentrating on investment tactics, and are not productive in maximizing those desired results. This improper use of time and effort diverts the progress toward their goals and can postpone or even halt achievement of those goals.

Have Clear Goals

Much of this book is devoted to helping you achieve your goals, so one of the first steps is to embrace the concept that through a clear understanding of your goals you will have a running start to attain them.

There are eight simple and undeniable factors that will lead you to success in real estate investing. They are:

1. Know what you want to accomplish: Your goal.

2. Ascertain what you need to maximize your abilities and to overcome your deficiencies. Establish your interim goals.

3. Put a timetable on your success in completing an interim goal: to measure where you are in your journey.

4. Find the specific type of real estate that will take you to your goal: Your vehicle.

5. Learn everything you can about that kind of property in the areas you want to own it: Master the vehicle.

6. When you find the property that seems to meet your investment criteria, tie it up: Take action and gain control.

7. When you have entered into a contract that binds the seller to terms you think will work for you, spend time and effort to ascertain if this is truly the property for you to purchase: Conduct due diligence.

8. If you discover anything that suggests the property will not meet your goals, then either withdraw from the transaction, or adjust the price and/or terms to the point where the transaction will meet your original criteria: Final decision time.

While these eight elements may appear to be very basic and overly simplified, they are a specific and important part of real estate financing. These eight elements are so important they should be the essence of every chapter in any book written about real estate investing.

ESSENCE OF ACCOMPLISHMENT

Ultimate success in real estate investing depends on a clear focus of the desired result. As an example, a hotel developer who wishes to own a chain of hotels must first understand what it takes to own and operate such properties. This requires a total commitment to every aspect of hotel operation, starting with what kind of location will best fit the specific type of hotel to be developed. A great location for a convention hotel may not be good at all for a budget "stop-for-the-night" kind of hotel/motel property. However, operational aspects are just a part of the overall picture, and the hotel developer must continually be cautioned to avoid being sidetracked to the green pastures of another category of real estate development. Hotel development requires a very specific and dedicated approach to the economics that make that type of real estate venture work. The same specific knowledge will apply to every category of real estate from rental apartments, shopping centers, mobile home parks, and so on.

Don't Stray from the Right Path

In my more than 30 years as a broker and developer, I can attest to the fact that truly successful investors are those who stay firmly within a narrow focus of interest and knowledge. They are the shopping center giants who do nothing but develop, own, and operate regional malls, or the rental apartment owners who dominate a local or national market. However, size and importance of investment has little to do with this idea. Success is a function of focus that is directed to becoming an expert in the category of real estate desired and to the precise location where the investor wants to own. For the residential rental investor this means knowing what is available, what prices are offered, and how to deal with residential rentals in any given area of the country.

LOCATION, LOCATION, LOCATION IS NOT THE ANSWER

This introduces the critical factor of location. By location, I mean the specific and well-defined area chosen. The less than perceptive investor will quickly discover that to accept the Wall Street definition of real estate as being a universal commodity is a mistake. Wall Street likes to compare every investment to stocks, which can be treated as universal in nature. However, real estate cannot be so easily defined, so what happens in San Francisco will not equally happen in Miami, or New York, or anywhere else. To forget this is a tragic mistake. Although there will be some events that will be similar in the diverse real estate market, real estate is essentially a local commodity that will rise and fall in long-term value based on what goes on in that very local market. Only then will you begin to see opportunity surfacing long before other, less knowledgeable investors recognize a good buy from a relatively poor one.

Real Estate Is Not Universal

The trick is to recognize that real estate is universal in nature, but its value orientation trends, which seemingly follow a similar pattern from area to area, are really very local in nature. This paradox occurs because real estate is not as dependent on national trends as many investors believe. What causes real estate to go up or down in value may be something occurring in or around the location of the real estate and may be created by a much longer process than is apparent. Such events would include elements of financing, taxation, recession or legal impediments, which effect real estate in a national and international way.

What may appear to be a sudden jump in the value of vacant commercial land may really be the long-term effect of continued down-zoning by local building and zoning departments, which have caused a shortage of such zoning. This is an important factor in both the purchases and financing of real estate.

For this reason, it is important that you develop a system or operating procedure that allows you flexibility. With a set program, you can move quickly and decisively when you recognize a property that fits your investment criteria. In addition, be ever vigilant on governmental intervention in land use because simple changes in use ordinances can have a major impact on land values in the future.

Your Secret Weapon Is the Local Building and Zoning Department

Because many local building and zoning departments are often directed by local governmental departments that are antigrowth, it is not uncommon for building regulations and restrictions to continue to change and together with zoning ordinances become more restrictive. These tightening of rules can quickly take away development rights you thought you had purchased a few years earlier. You need to be ever vigilant of what goes on in your local government. This includes all levels of your city, county, and state governing bodies.

BE AT THE RIGHT PLACE AT THE RIGHT TIME

Just about every person has made this comment at one time or other: "Boy, that person sure was lucky to be at the right place at the right time." Timing is very important to just about every decision you can make, and when it comes to investment decisions, timing is generally the most important aspect of the entire process. However, for timing to work there must be recognition of opportunity. Unless you see a way to reach for your goals, the right time just never seems to come around. As for being at the right place, that is up to you. Your gold mine is likely to be found wherever you want to look for it—that is, if you truly want to take the time and effort to learn everything you can about the kind of property you want to buy in that chosen location.

Without Action, the Best Time and Place Are Lost

To benefit from being at the right place at the right time you must act. You must make a decision to move forward in a decisive way. For a pilot, the act of taking off requires a decision to pull back on the yoke before arrival to the opposite end of the runway. Fortunately, the real estate investor can act without having to make an all-or-nothing decision. But there is a right way and a wrong way to go, and unfortunately, the vast majority of real estate buyers or sellers only think they are acting decisively. In reality, they make decisions by default, or they spend time trying to decide what to do without having control over the situation.

GET THE OTHER PARTY TO COMMIT FIRST. The key to having control over the situation is to get the other party to commit to deal with you prior to your being locked into the deal. This kind of strategy sounds simple and it is how smart investors function. Only by locking up a deal as early as possible will you have extra time to do due diligence, obtain ideal financing, and decide if that investment truly fits into your investment portfolio prior to that final decision moment.

Who Is More Motivated?

Sellers are generally the more motivated of the two sides of any transaction. They are, after all, fixed to one action: to dispose of that property. The buyer has the luxury to buy that property or to go on to another one. Sellers will commit to a price, terms that seem to work for you, and while they are bound to those terms, buyers are still are not firmly committed to the transaction.

As a buyer, it will be up to you to discover the important facts about the property and to make educated investment decisions accordingly. In real estate terms, you negotiate a contract to purchase the property that gives you time to conduct and approve all the due diligence, elements you believe are necessary. Only when you have completed these inspections and investigations can you be expected to make an informed final decision. That decision may be to move forward to close on the contract, to walk away from the deal, or to seek to modify the agreement by adjustment in price, time, or terms—or all three. The key is to obtain the time that allows you to control the deal until you are comfortable to continue to invest time and money in the deal.

Know What Is Important

Timing plays its most important role in the step that comes just before your gaining control over the situation. For example, suppose you have made a decision that rental apartments are what you want to buy. Your goal is to own enough rental apartments to allow you to hire full-time outside management to professionally and effectively manage and operate the investment. This is your choice because it fits the kind of lifestyle you want for yourself and your family. You have hired a good real estate lawyer and a good tax accountant to advise you on those specific matters. Your lawyer has given you a good purchase agreement that allows for adjustment to different situations, but that covers all the possible due diligence you would want to accomplish. This means full property inspections. These inspections will include all building elements, such as plumbing, electrical, structural, roof, foundation, termites, radon gas, and most important of all, environmental problems.

CAREFULLY INVESTIGATE EXISTING LEASES.   Added care must be given to a complete review of all existing leases, if any exist, to be sure that the revenue potential has been properly stated by the sellers and that you do not become saddled with a rent roll full of holes. It is not uncommon for sloppy management to fall down on lease control and the tenants you ultimately inherit may have you over an economic barrel.

BUYERS NEED A CITY CODE VIOLATION INSPECTION.   In addition to these situations, your due diligence provisions should give you the right to request a city code violation inspection. Most cities will send out a code enforcement inspector to decide if there are any building code violations. You will also want to check out all other governmental restrictions such as zoning, environmental issues, and possible limitations due to platting or possible building moratoriums. These situations all require time to check.

DUE DILIGENCE CHECKLISTS.   Remember this simple statement: There is no set or specific list of due diligence items you need to include that will cover you in every category of real estate for every location. Every property and every location has different factors that need to be checked. The list that served you so effectively in Miami may overlook a lot of critical factors you need to check when buying a property in Seattle or Chicago. Time and money are spent in accomplishing these studies, and they should be done only if you have the property locked up; that is, have the seller firmly tied into a deal while you spend the time and money to properly make a decision.

Your private due diligence checklist must be compiled locally to fit your specific category of real estate and your own needs. Local inspection companies, your realtor, your lawyer, and individuals in the construction trade (who know the area and the kind of real estate you want to buy) can be helpful in compiling your specific due diligence checklist.

Once you are armed with the knowledge that allows you to recognize a potential opportunity, you are at the right place and now are the right time. You should act by moving quickly to tie up the property. After all, if the property looked good to you, it may also appeal to other prospective buyers.

Because there may be other possible buyers who are about to come to the same conclusion, you do not want your indecision to cause you to lose the opportunity. You act, and now that the property is in your control, you can spend the time and money to make your thorough inspections before making the final decision. All of this assumes that you are acting with a goal in mind. A clearly seen goal is the destination to all your effort and will allow you, or force you, to stay on the right road as you head toward the goal. Not all investors have the same result in mind, and your own goals are likely to vary over a period of time. Therefore, it is important to recognize that ownership and debt structure may also vary. These changes may allow goal adjustments without having to deviate from the actual type of property chosen in the first instance. Any specific property can help its owner attain different goals, depending on the structure and the terms of that debt. This chapter is designed to help you develop a clear understanding of the relationship between financing and the attainment of your financial goals, as they relate to real estate. The financing tools and techniques described in this book will help you enhance your success in real estate investing.

BEGIN WITH YOUR GOALS

All success must begin somewhere, and in real estate financing, it begins with the 11 goals of financing. You will find that you can approach any problem using these 11 goals to decide whether financing can provide a solution or direction to attain your specific goals. If, after reviewing each goal and applying it to a given situation to achieve a desired result, no benefit or clear direction can be obtained, you can stop looking to financing as the source of the solution.

To help you decide how to use financing as a purchase or sales tool, review the 11 goals of financing. As you continue through this book and learn the many different financing techniques, you will see how each technique benefits the buyer or seller in different ways, depending on how they are applied. The idea is to gain as much flexibility in moving closer to your desired investment goal or strategy. Financing is more than obtaining a mortgage. Any time you are able to structure a transaction that uses any technique other than 100 percent cash as the payment, you have used a financing technique. You will discover many different financing techniques as you progress through this book. They include steps such as first and second mortgages, deferred payments, split payments, land leases, exchanges, sweat equity transactions, and options just to name a few. By the time you reach the end of this book, you will have a vast tool chest at your disposal as you move on to build your wealth in real estate.

The 11 goals of effective real estate financing are:

1. Enhance the value of a property.
2. Consolidate existing debt into more manageable debt.
3. Attract more buyers to a property for sale.
4. Increase the market potential of a property.
5. Increase the return on cash invested in income properties.
6. Generate immediate cash that is often tax-free.

7. Maximize equity build up of a long-term investment.

8. Help solve tax problems.

9. Create tax-deferred transactions.

10. Open new doors for the investor to expand an investment portfolio.

11. Provide a professional touch to a good marketing plan.

Review each of these goals carefully. It is important to realize that the improper use of any financing tool can negate the positive result needed. It is important to look at all the different techniques that this book provides so that you can select the best approach to solving the problem and to attainment of the desired goal.

Enhance the Value of a Property

When properly used, financing can enhance the value of a property to the owner or buyer. From a buyer's standpoint, financing should provide the best terms that fit the ownership goals. These terms can vary between different owners and buyers, dependent solely on what they expect from that investment. It is possible that for one buyer or owner the best terms may be a high beginning interest rate that declines over the mortgage term. Another investor may find a mortgage with a deferred payment plan where either interest, or interest and principal are reduced during the initial payment term of the mortgage. A third investor may want to incorporate a land lease as part of the financing strategy for reasons that are unique to his or her situation.

Whatever the situation, the amount of principal payments could be the same; the only difference may be the adjustment of when the actual payments are made and what they are called (principal, interest, rent, percent of gross sales, and so on). You should recognize that while the total payments may not vary for one party (either paying or receiving), the benefits or penalties could differ for the other party. Interest and rent may be tax deductible for the payer, but taxable as income for the receiver.

The term *value* is relative to the goal one wants to attain. From the seller's point of view, the financing that attains the seller's most important goal works best and establishes the highest *value* even if the monetary amount is less. If the seller needed to attain the highest possible market price for tax or other reasons, the terms the seller provided to the buyer may soften the economic impact to counterbalance the high price. This could occur by a lower than market interest rate or another condition of the payback. Because the concept of best value is likely to differ between the parties, the method of financing used often helps bring the two parties together to maximize mutual benefits. The compromise aspect of negotiations is enhanced when each party has a wide range of options to view.

The buyer or seller who has only one fixed agenda in drafting a contract will not be as successful in attaining his or her investment goals as the investor who has a strong understanding of the tools of finance. When the market is buyer driven, which is to say, a buyer's market, the most important goals are the buyer's goals. However, when the market is strong and there are more buyers than sellers, then the seller can call the shots. In a seller's market, the seller's goals receive the highest priority.

Usually, the market is rarely oriented exclusively to the buyer or the seller. Savvy investors understand this and, no matter if they are buyers or sellers, they try to make the terms of the deal work for each party. Real insider buyers recognize the value of this well-worn adage: "I'll pay your price, if you'll take my terms." In other words, price can often be a fluctuating factor, solely dependent on the terms of the sale.

It should be clear that a property could be difficult to sell if the seller feels that he or she must receive all cash to agree to the sale. There is, however, a potential market for the property at an all-cash price. Yet, the seller usually does not want to reduce the price to that level. This is a typical situation that often can be solved by a hard look at the seller's most important goals. By doing this, it may be possible that the original plan of action was not the best one to follow. In Chapter 2, you will see more on this aspect of goal orientation and investment strategy achievement.

As a buyer, it is critical to realize that the importance of the cash to the seller may be more critical than the highest possible price. Yet, it is equally critical to recognize that some sellers will find their goals are better attained if they get less cash at closing, and a higher price. It is important for sellers to understand that there are reasons for this disparity in payment schedule and in price determination. Often transactions are lost because none of the parties to the deal—buyer, seller, or brokers—could grasp this truth.

Therefore, using the tools of financing to solve their problems, all parties involved should look at the principal goals more closely. The final aspect of this goal is that the technique used enhances the idea of value that is important to the buyer and seller.

Consolidate Existing Debt into More Manageable Debt

Financing can be used to consolidate existing debt that is overburdening the owner of a property. The goal here is to reduce the total annual (or monthly) payment of the existing debt or the combination of all forms of debt on the property. When this is the desired result, it is necessary to examine the owner or buyer's options. You may discover that by using one or more financing techniques, you can find several potential solutions to the problem.

The simple refinancing of a property can work wonders in a market where interest rates have dropped. In this situation, the owner or buyer may find the opportunity to convert a high-interest loan into a newer, more affordable loan. If there has been an increase in the value of the property, the added value may also provide the opportunity to increase the loan amount, without a reduction of the bottom-line benefits of the property.

For example, a buyer purchases a 10-unit apartment complex for $500,000. There is an existing first mortgage of $250,000 with an annual debt service of $41,240 (principal and interest as would result with a 12-year term at 13 percent interest). The buyer obtains a new loan of $350,000 payable over a 20-year term at 8.75 percent interest. The new annual payment on the new mortgage would be $37,117.50.

Two important things have happened. First, the investor has obtained an additional $100,000 over the previous debt, which could be used to pay off other debt. That other debt might have been the down payment needed to give to the seller. Second, by refinancing at a lower overall payment, additional cash flow has resulted. This additional cash in the pocket of $4,122.50 ($41,240.00–$37,117.50) may be the single element that makes this transaction work. An important benefit in this transaction is that the additional $100,000 comes to the mortgagor tax-free.

Consolidation of debt extends beyond real estate investing and should be an important part of anyone's personal financial planning. We live in an age of high credit charges. It is not very smart to carry high cost credit card or installment loan interest rates. Such rates can cost in excess of 18 percent. This is not a good idea especially when you have the potential of refinancing your real estate through more modest rates. In the early 1990s, there was a rash of refinancing. It was not uncommon for people to have refinanced their homes several times between 1989 and 2006. The key here was to be tuned into what was going on. Even a small gain obtained through a refinanced loan, such as the reduction of a monthly payment, or amortizing the new loan quicker for less than the old loan, can be smart investing. Those investors who kept putting that off waiting for the rates to drop even more than they had suddenly came up against a hard brick wall. It was called 2007. A bubble in the lending market burst, for many reasons, and I will touch on them as you go through this book. But don't worry, if there is one constant in the real estate market, it is that both good times and tough times come around from time to time. You must look at the overall picture to see if there is any real benefit.

The interest rates are not the only criteria to examine when you are looking into total debt payments. You may owe on several different loans at various repayment terms. The most specific item to note is the combined constant rate of payment of the loans. The term *constant rate of payment* is used within the lending industry, and you should become aware of what it means and how it is used. In Chapter 3, I provide you with details of how to use the constant rate of payment in analyzing mortgage situations.

Consolidation of debt has many different benefits, as you will see when you combine its effects with some different financing tools illustrated in this book. The key to using any of the consolidation techniques is to make sure that you keep your ultimate goal in clear focus. For example, if you simply want to reduce your monthly debt payments that currently satisfy several loans (home, car, credit card company, and so on), you could consider refinancing your home to produce the added cash to retire all outstanding loans. This may look attractive at first, but it is important that you look at other alternatives. One of the most basic forms of reduction of debt payments, often overlooked, is to pay off the overburdening debt. One way to do this is to refinance at a lower constant payment rate. This could be accomplished by obtaining a lower interest rate or a longer amortization term or a combination of both. Other more creative forms of financing, such as an interest-only schedule or deficit payment loan, can provide some debt relief. From a financial point of view, this may be nothing more than sound economic practice. In essence, do not overextend your ability to pay off debt.

Of course, this is often easier said than done, and once you are in the trap of consumer debt (high interest rates), the solution can be hard to come by. The critical point to consider in any form of consolidation is to take a hard look at how the remedy will affect your long-term goals. If a longer payback at lower interest rates benefits you in comparison to paying off debt, then the proper thing to do is to look to consolidation. On the other hand, a very low rate existing loan may be kept in place if the new real estate loan that replaces it produces a greater payback, even if the monthly payments seem lower. For example, you have a total of $20,000 in short-term consumer loans at an interest rate of 18 percent. At the same time, you owe $120,000 on a first mortgage on your home, at 7.5 percent interest per annum. If current new rates on real estate loans were higher than your present 7.5 percent, say 9.5 percent, you may not find any benefit to a refinance and consolidation of the two debts. This would be the situation even though the consumer debt was more than double the interest rate of the potential of your new loan. Review the current payments: Interest on the $20,000 consumer loan is 18 percent of $20,000 or $3,600 per year. Interest payment on the real estate loan is 9.5 percent or $9,000. This gives you a total current interest obligation of $12,600. If you refinanced, with the idea to consolidate your debt, so that you could cover your loan cost, and then pay off the existing consumer loan, you may discover that your new loan balance is $141,500 ($120,000 existing loan, and $20,000 consumer loan, and $1,500 in loan origination cost and out of pocket). If the interest rate on this new loan was 9.5 percent, then your interest cost the first year would be over $13,000. The general result is not favorable. On the other hand, if the $20,000 is due now, or there is some other pressing need for cash, refinancing, even if it increases the previous payment schedule, may be the only solution. If this is the case, you should review all the different possible refinancing tools available to you. You must look at the total picture.

KEY POINTS TO USING CONSOLIDATION TECHNIQUES

1. There is a need to reduce existing debt payments through the refinancing of any or all of the existing debt so that the total future payments will not exceed those payments under the old finance situation.
2. There is an inability to meet current debt payments, and refinancing is the only way to meet the current payments, though the total payments will exceed those of the current debt structure.

3. The property is not readily marketable with the present financing structure. A change in this situation through refinancing may provide a more favorable result in the marketplace.

4. A cash-out situation is needed in which the owner can mortgage above the present financing levels and put cash in his or her pocket. This must be done so that the property will not become overburdened.

5. There is the immediate need to create cash, and no other option is presently viable.

6. There are many ways to consolidate existing financing. Almost any form of financing will lend itself to consolidation of an existing debt. Naturally, some forms of financing will give better results than others.

Attract More Buyers to a Property for Sale

One of the major aspects of financing is the ability to make property more salable. This goal may seem to be the same as Goal 1, but through a careful analysis of the former, you will see some very important, though subtle differences. After all, your initial goal in buying and financing a property may be to maximize either your cash flow or your equity build up of the property. You may not be purchasing for a quick flip or turnover of the property. But then, perhaps that is exactly what you want to do. The flip-artist will look to either temporary or ready to flip type of financing, both of which will not stand in the way of a quick sale. The investor looking for a longer hold time, to either enjoy the investment or to give more time to bring out the full potential of the property for enhanced profit will want to use financing that uses the full benefits of the cash flow or equity build up form of financing selected.

In the real-life approach to the sale of real estate, creative financing may be the only way to take a property that is difficult to sell into the marketplace. The actual contract of sale may contain more than one form of financing to bring the buyer and seller together. For example, consider a sale then leaseback. Here the seller holds secondary financing (with or without additional security for the lease). This reduces the buyer's risk and is an example of multiple techniques that can be used to simplify the sale. In this and every other situation, the goals of both the buyer and the seller are weighed, then balanced on which is the most critical to solve.

Even great properties are difficult to sell because of high interest rates in the finance market or low buyer demand. In these circumstances, the seller must find techniques to make his or her property stand out as a property that is both attractive and affordable. For example, to get the buyer in the door of a model apartment or home, it is not unusual for a builder to offer mortgage financing at well below the marketplace interest rate and at attractive principal payback for the first several years of the mortgage. Once the buyer has been attracted to the property, the buyers may discover (or be led down the path by the seller) that if they can pay more cash up front they can get a better price (use of the first goal).

We are all accustomed to the leader ad that brings us to the store. Financing terms attract buyers to cars, computers, and homes. The importance, when it comes to real estate, is that you recognize that when the seller offers great terms, that this is a seller who understands the concept of good marketing. This is the right kind of seller to be, and to deal with, if you are a buyer.

In commercial real estate, there are many different techniques that can be offered that look more attractive than they actually are. If you keep your own goal firmly in focus you can be more likely to stick to the techniques that take you closer to your goal rather than farther away. The key to this is to keep your goal clearly in your mind and not to deviate from any technique that will lead you away from the ideal. While you may give in or compromise in the end, it is best to leave that concession to the final moment. You should attempt to visualize the entire deal before you need to learn exactly where to make compromises.

Increase the Market Potential of a Property

This is another seller-oriented financing benefit. Here, the idea is to expand the market potential of the property, which is more than just making the property more salable. It is possible, of course, that by doing one you will also do the other. Review the following case study.

Mr. Wallace wanted to sell his 25-unit apartment house for a price of $500,000. He had an opportunity to buy another property in another town and needed the cash for that purpose. The price he was asking was within the market range with a net operating income (NOI is gross rents less operating expenses, which does not include any debt service) of $53,000 out of a gross rent roll of $76,000.

However, the city was about to launch a major road and sewer project right in front of the apartment house, and it was likely that the apartment complex would lose all of its tenants for part of the year. Once the work was finished, there would be a newly planted median with wide sidewalks where none had previously existed. This kind of improvement could cause the value of the apartment complex to quickly recover as well as substantially increase.

For Mr. Wallace, the approach to his first goal (to sell his existing property) was to find a solution to the pending problem of the loss of tenants. A simple answer was for Mr. Wallace to indemnify a potential buyer for any possible loss of revenue during the construction period. This was accomplished by establishing a format for a sale and lease-back for one year. Wallace became the master tenant, with the existing tenants his subtenants. By assuming the risk for the year during which the roadwork was to take place, the seller was taking no greater risk than if he put the building up for sale and was unable to sell it during the same time period. As the specific need of the seller was to sell the building, holding onto the building was a hardship that he could not afford to take because he was sure to lose the opportunity to buy the other property. By offering an indemnity, a buyer would not suffer from any loss of tenants, and Wallace would only be liable for any lost rent. Wallace calculated that the maximum rent he would have to make up would be around $40,000. He calculated this amount based on the idea that if he cut the monthly rent to the tenants, some of them would tough out the construction mess.

Thus far, the goal served was to help make the property salable. Now the task was to increase the market potential for the property.

To this end, Mr. Wallace could have taken a number of directions. Keep in mind that one form of increasing the market potential of a property is to make it available to more ready, willing, and able buyers. As seller of the apartment building, Mr. Wallace could have turned the building into a condominium or a cooperative apartment building, seeking 25 different buyers at much reduced prices. In some market areas, this has been the direction that many sellers have taken, producing a greater sales price than would have been realized had the building been sold to a single investor.

Another way to increase market potential is to be more flexible in the terms he is willing to accept in the sale of the property. This flexibility is difficult for many sellers to attain because they have not properly established their own investment goals. If you have clear goals and know exactly where you want to be at any given time in the relatively near future, and you constantly review those goals, you will begin to realize that it is the attainment of the goals that is important, not the attainment of any specific terms of a sale.

Let's go back to our apartment building seller, Mr. Wallace. If part of his long-term goal was to retire to the mountains of North Carolina with a nice cabin and 10 acres of apple trees, he might look for an exchange that would take him directly to that goal. It is possible that somewhere in the North Carolina mountains there is a property owner who would like to own the Wallace apartment complex. Of course, Mr. Wallace may not like the cabin offered, if indeed any were offered. However, by offering the apartment complex for exchange, he might be offered something other than a cabin in North Carolina. Something that he would be willing to take as a small part of the overall transaction, for example, a nice vacant lot overlooking Grandfather Mountain.

No matter what Mr. Wallace's long-term goal is, by viewing it clearly, he will begin to see that there are additional ways to help him entice more buyers to his apartment building. At the same time, these ways or avenues of approach would accomplish the critical task of "getting rid of the apartment building" while moving Mr. Wallace closer to his long-term goals.

Meet the Tax-Free Exchange

By utilizing Internal Revenue Code (IRC) Section 1031 (also called the *tax-free exchange provision*), a buyer or seller may enter into an agreement that will have more specific benefits than a more conventional transaction because of the reduced tax liability to one or more of the parties. This option is open to you only if you know how it works and how it fits into your goals. Chapter 12 illustrates the strategic moves you can make as a buyer or seller (or broker) to use IRC 1031 tax treatment to obtain marvelous benefits.

Mr. Wallace decided that another available option was to reduce the amount of cash needed to take control of the property. With his accountant, he worked up an attractive package that, when coupled with the sale-leaseback technique, would allow a buyer with little cash to purchase the property. This technique enticed more buyers and produced the desired results of selling the property.

Increase the Return on Cash Invested in Income Properties

This goal is usually the most important goal for owners or potential buyers of income property. Due to its importance to buyers, it also becomes an important criteria of market appeal to sellers. The potential effect of financing on cash flow can be very important to the ultimate success in the sale of a property. For example, consider an office building that is free and clear of any debt. The NOI is $90,000. If the current market for such properties required that the invested capital give the buyer a 9 percent return, then an all-cash purchase price would require the buyer to come up with $1 million in cash. In essence, the return of $90,000 on the cash invested ($1 million) would be 9 percent per annum. Now consider the effect of financing. Assume the buyer could borrow (or the seller arrange for it as a part of the offering package) new financing of $800,000 on the property at a constant rate (the combined rate which is interest and principal repayment) of 8 percent interest per annum over the next 30 years. This kind of financing may be easily found and would ensure that by the end of the 30-year period the debt will have been fully paid off.

Now, during these 30 years of ownership, the investor would have a constant annual debt service of $64,000 (8 percent × $800,000 = $64,000). Deducting this from the present NOI of $90,000 results in a cash flow of $26,000. Remember, the debt service in a mortgage with both principal and interest payments is calculated to include both the principal and interest portion of the mortgage. In this way, although each monthly payment will have a slightly different mix of interest and principal, the total for the year will be $64,000. The resulting $26,000 is the return that the investor would obtain on his or her investment of $200,000 ($1,000,000 less the new debt of $800,000 = $200,000).

A $26,000 return on an investment of $200,000 is a return of 13 percent per annum. This is a substantial increase over the original return of 9 percent. By using financing, the buyer has caused an instant increase of new value (value that is above the amount of debt created in the deal). How did this happen? If the market supports a return of 9 percent, the $26,000 cash flow is a 9 percent return on an investment of $288,888. So, by using this simple financing technique, the buyer is $88,888 richer. There is a longer-term benefit here that should not be overlooked. This debt will eventually be paid off over the next 30 years. If the strategy the investor was striving for was to maximize this investment as a retirement vehicle, look what happens at year 31. Assume a modest 3 percent compounded each year of NOI. This means 3 percent × 30 years × $90,000 will be the actual increase in the cash flow once the debt has been paid off. This means an average of 3 percent of increase each year, until the final cash flow equals the original $90,000 plus an additional 90 percent of that amount (3 percent × 30 years = 90 percent). The grand total is $180,000 per year of cash flow, with no debt to pay.

If cash flow is the desired effect, the investor's goal is to maximize immediate return instead of equity build up or other benefits, then an increase of cash flow will appeal to that investor. All things being equal, a cash-oriented buyer will pay more for a property that produces a greater cash flow, whereas an equity-motivated buyer will adjust financing (on this same deal) to maximize debt pay-off and equity enhancement. The bottom line, which is so important to most investors, is clearly a function of the kind of financing that is placed on the property.

If local or currently available financing is not viable at the best rate or terms, then the ultimate payments would reduce the potential cash flow that the investor could realize. This would indicate that more creative measures might be necessary to sell the property.

Most creative financing tricks learned by real estate investors are designed to soften the overall blow of the property debt. There was a time, not so long ago, when it was deemed that the ideal situation for an investor was when the investor could buy a property without putting up any of his or her own money. This use of other people's money (OPM) would create a deal that was 100 percent financed, or at least 100 percent purchased, without the buyer digging around for cash.

Before you jump to conclusions that such a transaction can be counterproductive to your healthy attitude about buying or selling real estate, let me state that buying real estate without putting up any cash is not difficult to do. The hard part is being able to make money doing it. In any city in the world, there are sellers of real estate who would gladly accept a solid promise of payment as a down payment to a property that they could not sell, or that was grossly overpriced. Let this statement be a warning to you before you rush out and invest in a quick way to fame and riches as promised by some promoters of investment programs who tell you that your only way to success and wealth in real estate is through investing with 100 percent of other people's money. Having just said that, let me also encourage you to learn as many of the techniques that allow you to get the maximum benefit out of the investment capital you have. Remember too that there are many assets at your disposal other than cash. Your ability to create instant value (we just saw $88,888 worth of instant value) which can create investment value to the lender or to the seller in your ability to structure additional financing for the transaction.

As the goal to increase cash flow from marginal properties serves the buyer best, it is essential that you recognize that buying from a seller who is inflexible and who only wants cash over his or her existing mortgage may not give you much room to be creative. In these circumstances, and assuming that you want that property and none other, it may be that the brick wall in the way of the deal is that the seller is ignorant of the benefits of creative financing. As a broker, I have had to educate many sellers to the benefits of using sound economic investment planning that saved them money and time, and produced the desired result: the sale of their property. This is important for every potential seller to review because there are important tax and reinvestment criteria that should be considered. Buyers and/or brokers often must help educate stubborn sellers.

Investors will look for sellers who are flexible and with whom the investor can mix and match one or more of the techniques that will be discussed in detail in this book.

Generate Immediate Cash That Is Tax-Free

Often this goal is overlooked. Since the principal owed in existing mortgages may decline over the years, and the value of the property may increase, generally it is possible to refinance and obtain additional cash after repayment of the old loan. This becomes very attractive when this can be accomplished without affecting the cash flow on a property. For example, the mortgage payment for $150,000 over 15 years at 9.5 percent per annum is $1,554 per month. If a new mortgage can be obtained at 10.5 percent per annum but the term is 25 years, the same payment of $1,554 would allow the owner to get $179,275. This would produce $29,275 (less loan costs) in immediate cash. Naturally, if the interest rate was lower, the benefits for refinancing would be greater. For example, a loan payment of $1,500 per month on a 25-year schedule would allow a mortgage of $194,384 at 8 percent to produce an excess of $44,384 (less loan cost) at a slightly lower mortgage payment schedule than the existing 15-year loan.

While this may not appear to be dramatic, if cash is essential at that moment, the opportunity to get cash and use cash may be worth the increased term and interest in the debt payment. While the amount paid each month has not increased, the investor has an additional term of years to make those same payments.

When a borrower obtains money through financing, such as getting a loan from the local lender, there may be no income tax liability on that money. In essence, the money was not "earned" but borrowed. The borrower can in many circumstances renew loans from time to time, increasing amounts borrowed as the values of the real estate go up, pulling out capital that is tax-free, at least for the moment. When the borrower ultimately sells the property, an adjustment would be made to determine what amount of the loan still outstanding exceeded the basis (book value) of the property. This excess would be treated as earned income at that time and taxed accordingly. Under present IRS rules, the real estate investor is able to deduct the interest paid on many real estate loans, which makes this technique a very positive approach to real estate investing. For example, if you refinanced a property you had depreciated down to $100,000 but was actually valued by the lender at $500,000, you might be able to borrow $350,000 or more on that property. If the actual loan was $350,000, your loan is $250,000 more than your book value (depreciated basis). If you sold the property for $500,000 any time prior to repayment of the loan to a level below your basis, the IRS will calculate that the excess funds are now taxable. While this may not be a problem, it needs to be considered before you end up selling with a down payment that does not provide sufficient cash to pay your taxes. If you sold for $500,000 and took a $50,000 down payment, and held onto the balance in the form of a wraparound mortgage, you would think you had an installment sale (an IRS-approved method of spreading tax over a period of years—which will be covered in detail in Chapter 13). As an installment sale, there may be little or no initial tax to pay on principal except as the buyer makes payments of principal owed to you. This is a common error that sellers make. Because you borrowed money above your tax basis (book value), and the funds borrowed were tax-free at the time of the loan, it becomes taxable the year you close the sale. Your tax liability on this borrowed money could be over $75,000. This simply stresses the need to examine all potential costs that may diminish what looks like a windfall profit. Pulling out tax-free cash can have a penalty later on, but even that can be part of the overall investment strategy and needs to be considered in your long-range planning.

Your use of financing to produce cash in a transaction will depend on your ultimate goals and what it is that you are trying to accomplish at the time you desire this cash. As you learn more of the creative techniques of financing, you will discover that getting cash in refinancing is not always the most productive or best route to take. For example, also in Chapter 13, you will learn about a technique called *pyramiding*. With it, you will be able to take the cash needed to buy property from the first property you own by giving the seller of the second property a second mortgage on the first property. You will do this, and variations thereon, at interest rates well below those offered by the institutional lenders in your marketplace. Do not jump to conclusions that because I used the word *pyramid* I am suggesting anything illegal. In real estate investing, where real equity that is genuinely creating new value is pledged for future investments, it is not only legal, it can also be a beneficial form of buy and sell for both parties involved. More on that subject in Chapter 13.

Maximize Equity Build Up of a Long-Term Investment

Financing has the ability to maximize equity build up when the investor structures the debt in such a way that there are funds that are continually used to improve and enhance the income of the property. By allowing a steady growth of the NOI of an income property, the long-term value is one of the beneficial results. This usually is done at a sacrifice of the cash flow, so this has to be considered and become a part of the long-term outlook for that investment. I often suggest that investors look to long-term enhancement of value by a well thought out landscape plan for their real estate investments. Twenty years of mature tree growth can turn an apartment complex into an attractive garden that not only provides beauty to the renters who live there, but shade and privacy as well.

Help Solve Tax Problems

This goal serves two masters: the buyer and the seller. When you use a form of financing to solve a tax problem, you often create a problem for the other party to the transaction. The most critical item that comes into play is the motivation of the parties. If the most motivated party is the seller and his or her goals are better met by selling the property, the transaction may be slanted to the buyer in tax benefits and still be able to close. However, if the most motivated party is the buyer, there may be an opportunity for the seller to find additional solutions to his or her tax problems. On some occasions, both parties can gain benefits from careful review of the transaction and the tax laws.

The items to review will vary, depending on the circumstances and needs of the parties. However, there are 10 items that should be part of your checklist when either buying or selling real estate. A review of each item with careful attention to your own goals and circumstances will aid you in determining if there are any tax advantages you need to consider prior to either making the offer or at least prior to closing.

TAX ADVANTAGES CHECKLIST

- ✓ What items are to be depreciated within the investment property? Buyers generally want maximum values established; sellers often want lower values set. In exchanges, both parties may want to have the depreciable items considered with different base values.

- ✓ Should you take title to land and building and personal property equally? There are advantages to taking it differently if it fits your circumstances.

- ✓ On what date should you close? This can have a specific advantage to one party or both if the date can be split between two tax years.

- ✓ How should an option payment be established? This can create cash to the seller that is not taxed right away and can be highly effective in nailing down a deal.

- ✓ Review the advantages of the wraparound mortgage because it might apply to the transaction contemplated.

- ✓ In an IRC 1031 exchange, should the replacement property's values be directed against the land, the building, or both?

- ✓ What are the one-time capital gains exclusions available to you under the current tax laws?

- ✓ If the seller is to hold financing, should part of the down payment include the maximum advance interest allowed by the IRS? (The maximum allowed as of this writing is the interest that would be earned during the balance of the year.)

- ✓ Should the buyer buy the property or the personal interest in a corporation or trust that owns the property? This and similar questions about form of ownership can give the investor a lot to think about when he or she buys so as to establish the best form of selling interest.

Create Tax-Deferred Transactions

Sometimes, the only major benefit from a financing technique might be to pass on the possible tax consequence to some future date. There are, of course, other nonfinancial options available to the investor that may have similar results. The idea is to examine what benefit the investor or the seller may have and at what cost. For example, if the technique used by a buyer was to acquire a property by entering into a long-term lease with an option to buy, the seller would not have a capital gain tax to pay until the sale took place. If part of the rent paid was money that was paid each year or month to the seller to keep the option to buy alive, it may not be taxable until the actual sale closes. As long as that money was to be applied toward the ultimate purchase, it is possible that some or all of the option money would not be taxed as income or as capital gain until the sale actually took place no matter how many years in the future that was.

In the IRC Section 1031 exchange mentioned earlier, it is possible to have a lifetime of investing and still not trigger any capital gains tax; with an installment sale provision you can sell a property and only pay the gains tax on the portion of the actual gain you get, and in the year you get it. Both the exchange and the installment sale allow creative tax planning, and as with any provision that deals with the Internal Revenue Service (IRS) Codes, you must make sure that you have gotten the most recent up-to-date advice possible. All IRS rules and regulations are subject to change and different interpretations to what appear to be similar transactions. While this often intimidates people, you should not let fear of the IRS stand in your way of using totally legal and often creative means to build or keep your wealth.

Keep in mind that many techniques have an effect on the benefits of real estate and change the long-range tax, which may be payable at some time in the future. The more you know about your own tax consequences and your future goals, the better you will be at using the laws and finance tools to your best advantage.

Open New Doors for the Investor to Expand an Investment Portfolio

As a real estate investor, you would learn quickly that profit in real estate is not a function of buying real estate. It depends on use and utility of the property and the final disposition of the property.

This signifies that to be successful in real estate investing, you will benefit the most when the complete plan fits the goal. You will not succeed in investing by buying this and/or that without knowing what to do with the property after you have acquired it. There is no doubt that with sound study of the area and with the development of expertise, you could recognize opportunities that other people would overlook. Soon you will be able to take advantage of those properties. In those cases, the use or utility of the property is simply that of a sound investment spawned out of your unique knowledge in the area and your grasp of the opportunity.

The more you understand about the tools of financing, the better equipped you will become to use them to expand your portfolio. In developing your knowledge, you are reducing your risk in the investment game. Some of the benefits of finance are to assist in the sale or disposition of property. Through your knowledge of these tools, you will move through your portfolio to other properties and investments.

Risk, which will be discussed in greater detail throughout this book, is similar to the term *value*. Both risk and value are relative to the investor's ability and capability. Savvy investors make things look easy because they recognize opportunity, therein reducing or removing the aspect of risk. They create value because they know what they want, and where they are going.

Provide the Professional Touch to a Good Marketing Plan

In selling your most difficult property, the maximum appeal to the marketplace and the maximizing of your goals will be in covering all possible bases. Investors who look after details are generally the most successful investors. Your devotion to the use of the tools of finance will demand that you anticipate your ultimate marketing plan, which should include various financing approaches to suit the probable investors who will buy your property.

When the time comes for you to "need" heavy financing for a large transaction or the development of some upcoming project you have wanted to build, success could well depend on your past history of dealing with lenders.

KNOW THE LIMITATIONS OF THE TOOLS OF FINANCING

The preceding 11 goals are the keys to your use of financing as a problem solver. Yet from time to time, there will be situations that you cannot solve by using any of the financing techniques. In fact, at best you will simply maintain the status quo by using these tools. In the worst case, you can ruin the property and the investment by applying the wrong technique.

The knowledge that you develop of the financing techniques covered in this book cannot be considered absolute. There will be many tips and suggestions to help you expand your knowledge, and you should recognize that there is no single source of knowledge in any field.

In the chapters to come, I show many different investing techniques and list some of the advantages and disadvantages as they are applied to the buyer and seller of any property. In your review of these different points of view, you should ask yourself how you would approach a particular technique in your own circumstances. If you are reviewing this book to brush up on some of these techniques in anticipation of some specific transaction you are trying to nail down, I recommend that you also review the Contents to become aware of other techniques as well.

It is rare for a real estate investor to use any single technique offered, countered, or refined in the final document of sale. One party buys hoping to have made the best investment possible, and another sells with a similar hope in mind. Each party to the transaction may have still held onto a card that he would have thrown into the pot to sweeten the transaction were it necessary. But no more cards were required, so the deal stands as executed.

Some important points to remember when approaching a situation that you feel may be solved with one of the financing techniques covered in this book are discussed next.

Six Tips to Solving Real Estate Financing Needs or Problems

At least one of the 11 goals described in this chapter should be met for financing to have any real benefit to the parties involved. The following six tips will help you relate to the needs of the other parties and attain your own goals while establishing a win/win result:

1. Different points of view will be held by the buyer and the seller in their interpretation of these goals.

2. The results of the form of financing used often will affect these two parties differently.

3. Theories that work on paper are valid only if they work in real life.

4. There often are many parties to a transaction even when only two or three are apparent. The visible ones are the buyer and seller, and often the broker. The not-so-visible ones are the lawyers, wives, boyfriends, bankers, bartenders, and so on; each party has some relationship to the deal.

5. Each party has to be dealt with when he or she impedes the desired results of a transaction.

6. To achieve constant success in real estate investing, stay as close to your long-range goals as possible.

Since so much does depend on this goal-setting ability, I have provided a detailed chapter on goal setting and development of your comfort zone. Each chapter will become a foundation to your future as a real estate investor. If your role in the game of financing is that of a real estate broker, you will have the added burden of acting as fiduciary in the transaction. However, you will also have the advantage in the investment game and will find that all of the techniques covered in this book will become useful tools in helping you buy and sell properties.

Chapter 2

HOW TO SET EFFECTIVE GOALS FOR SUCCESSFUL REAL ESTATE INVESTING

GOAL OF THIS CHAPTER

This chapter walks you through the goal setting process.

The importance of setting your own investment goals is critical to getting the maximum benefit out of your time and effort. Once you have your goals firmly established, every decision you make about your investments will be directed to one ultimate result: the attainment of your goals. Because real estate financing has an immediate as well as a long-term effect on those investments, clear goals help you select the best financing tool to get the most out of the investment. Because the actual goal selection process is so important, I have devoted an entire chapter to this topic.

Word of Caution about Goal Setting

A cliché suggests that you should be careful what you ask for because you just might get it. So it is with goals. Set your sight for an improperly established goal and it is entirely possible that you will end up with something you asked for, but which was not what you really wanted in the first place. So, let's approach goal setting with a clear understanding that it is not an easy task to accomplish. If it were, why would so many people avoid the task?

I have a very good answer to that aspect of goal setting, which is important to consider. With many years of experience in managing salespeople, I know that one reason people tend to avoid goal setting is that they fear they will not achieve the goal they set and would rather not have to deal with that kind of failure. They rationalize that by not setting a goal at all, they have no destination they will ever have to reach.

Whatever your situation, it is likely, as with most people, your own goal setting has not produced the desired results or that your goal plateaus have been rather lackluster. Proper goal setting is difficult and should not be contemplated halfheartedly, but instead should be given thought and deliberation. Above all, the one person you must be honest with is yourself. Understand that no goal is fixed and the path to those goals should come under constant review, and you should not hesitate to alter or revise your goals once you are sure they need changing. Resist, however, the urge to make a change in a goal just because you are having difficulty reaching it. It could be that the method you are following is faulty, or you are moving in the wrong direction although the goal is a good one. Most failure to achieve a success toward a goal centers on the intermediate steps that have been planned to reach that goal and then carry the individual forward.

THE CHICKEN OR THE EGG?

Consider that every pilot about to take off in an airplane has the same goal: To become successfully airborne before reaching the end of the runway. That is fine, but what about the preliminary and secondary steps that go along with that goal? Does the pilot have the forethought to check the fuel level to support that intended plan? Does the pilot know how to land the plane when the more critical stage of this goal process is completed?

The fact that you may set goals does not ensure success or happiness. Some people attain wealth and happiness without having gone through any specific goal-setting process. Yet, motivation within these people often is at a very high level. While they may not have made a conscious effort to set goals, they often are driven by high ideals or are out to prove something to someone.

Having said that, if you look at the truly successful people around you who are in the news, you will find one trait that links them all. The ability to stay focused on a task. That kind of focus allows the person to have an actual vision of what the results will be. This is not easy and is not something people are born with. It requires work and self-confidence. You will discover that your level of self-confidence will begin to climb once you start setting goals that you then attain.

The kind of goal setting that I refer to relates to the prudence of setting your priorities straight. You would not get much out of training to be an Olympic swimmer by spending all your energy on the ski slopes. It is the same with any business or investing arena. A computer designer needs to establish a foundation that will build to the result that person is shooting for. A real estate investor needs to set a foundation of knowledge and experience in much the same way, but directed to a different topic and different result in mind.

The management of your time and the acts that will be required of you to achieve the most basic goal will depend on your knowing what the desired results should be and what you need to do each step of the way. The goal of this chapter is to help you find and set goals that will work for you. Keep in mind that the progression of setting and then attaining goals is a multiple, step-by-step process.

Before You Can Get to Your Destination, You Must Decide Where You Want to Go

It is similar to going on a vacation by car. You have to make the following determinations:

- Where do you want to go?
- Do you know the direction that will get you there?
- Do you have some mode of transportation in mind?
- Do you know how to operate that vehicle?
- Do you have the staying power, both physical and economic, to keep it on the road?
- Do you have the willpower to avoid being detoured from your desired destination?
- If you take a wrong turn and get lost, do you know how to find your way again?
- Will you recognize when you have arrived at your destination?
- Will you set new destinations and start over again?
- Will you give up and go back to where you started or to what you were doing before?

The foregoing sequence should be easy to follow. It is all a matter of goal setting and then formulating the plan to get you to your goals. It starts with the selection of the destination. Let us begin there.

Develop a Vision of the Future

In one of my all-day seminars, I go through the following exercise: It is important that you relate to my definition of a goal. It must be worthy; by this, I mean that it should be worthwhile for your overall happiness and financial independence. It should also be measurable. This means that it should have a clearly readable timetable that will allow you to ascertain how far you have progressed toward that goal. That is the gauge that will help you make adjustments if you get sidetracked. Read over the following material and then let your mind take over. Better yet, have someone read this section to you.

LEARNING TO VISUALIZE YOUR GOALS.   First: Get comfortable. Find everything about your position that is not comfortable and change it. Then, when you feel you have a comfortable position, tense every muscle in your body in any random order that works for you, then, one by one tell each muscle to return to that comfortable position. Do this for about thirty seconds, and then relax.

Now close your eyes and have someone read the following to you:

I want you to clear the slate in your mind. I want you to think only about the things I tell you to think of, remembering things from your past only to make the scenes I describe more vivid to you.

Erase the mixture of colors in your mind, just as a child would wipe the blackboard with a dusty eraser. Now, all you see is that misty white slate; a white mist fills your mind. Unlike dusty chalk, the mist is cool, damp, like a friendly fog rolling in off a calm lake.

You will relax even more now. See the cool, fresh-smelling milky white fog in your mind as it changes from the white on the blackboard to a misty morning. You are somewhere where it is cool and pleasant, you are very relaxed, your mind very clear, and you now see clearly that the mist is over a lake or pond. The water is very still, and you are very relaxed. You are thinking at this very moment how relaxed you are. You are very relaxed.

You are actually in a time machine, and you are passing ahead into the future. Somewhere below as you are flying through this cool, pleasant mist, you see things going on. It is as though you are in the clouds and cannot quite see what is going on below you.

It is clearing now and you realize that you are beginning to see where you are. You look around within your mind. You see yourself and you note on the wall there is a calendar. The date is nearly 10 years into the future. You look around and see what is going on.

Take careful note as to what you are doing, who you are with, where you are. What kind of clothes do you have on? When you are satisfied that you can fully describe the setting, you will return to the mist and return to the present.

When I finish this, I let everyone relax for a few minutes. Then I ask several of them to describe to me, and to the others, what it was they saw.

When you look into your future like this, you have the tendency to see your own self-image of your future. To some degree, it might be the dream of what you want or hope for in the future. These are the natural goals that live within you. Like computer programs that can be altered, these goals may well be the default parameters that drive you.

The critical part of these visions is that they are not accepted by you as goals but as dreams. For some people, these visions are not pleasant at all, as if some more dramatic force were taking them into the future without much hope, without much self-esteem.

Visualizing the Future Is Essential to Sound Goals

Every athlete knows the power of visualizing winning. The runner who is able to demonstrate that he or she "sees" him or herself winning can demoralize an opponent. Likewise, the salesperson who "sees" the sale being closed and assumes that his or her efforts will be rewarded knows that his or her success in selling will be increased. So it is with goals. If you cannot clearly see the end result, you may never attain the desired goals or, at best, you will not attain them with the ease and satisfaction that comes through goal setting.

ARE YOUR GOALS REALISTIC?

Proper goal setting is critical because it is easy to "see" the wrong future. You must realize and accept the fact that you can change your self-image, and can set your own goals. You are not bound by the vision you first saw when you looked into the milky mist.

Is What You See What You Want?

In this new point, there are elements that you will want to work on. It is critical that you constantly recall this vision because you will be making changes as you get closer to it. However, the most important aspect to pay attention to is the vision, and not the specifics as to how you got to the vision.

Most people have the wrong concept about goals, and when they set them, they look more to the mode of transportation rather than to the destination itself. For example, if your vision is of you and your family living on an island paradise with dozens of close friends around you at all times with nothing to do but lounge around, the first element you would establish as your goal would be the money it will take to buy this lifestyle. Money is the mode of transportation, not the destination. The goal of having lots of money, "I want to be a multimillionaire," is an improper goal because it directs you to the vehicle of transport rather than to the lifestyle you think money will buy.

Mind you, money and the desire for it are very strong motivators and can drive many people to get money but little else. It is far better for you to understand that there are people so motivated and to use their motivation for your own benefit. Money is relative and its worth changes as you attain it. The amount of money you think it might take to attain your goals can be much more than your goal actually requires.

To understand this last statement, you need only look at what has happened to the value of money in some countries. If you were looking into your own vision 20 years ago in Turkey, your concept of the amount of money needed to become "independent" would just about buy you breakfast today. In the early 1930s in Germany, boxes of money would not buy you the boxes the money was in.

The best goals are those that follow these guidelines:

Tips to Help You Set the Right Kind of Goals

• DEFINE YOUR GOALS IN TERMS OF WHAT YOU WANT TO ATTAIN, WHERE YOU WANT TO BE, WHAT KIND OF LIFESTYLE YOU WANT TO LIVE. Avoid establishing a monetary value to either the effort or the results. The true value of a goal is successfully attaining it. The money aspect of goal setting will play its part later on.

- MAKE SURE THAT YOUR GOALS FIT INTO YOUR ABILITIES OR THE ABILITIES YOU PLAN TO ATTAIN. It should be obvious that if your vision has you doing heart transplants and you are not yet out of high school, you have a lot of work ahead of you and you must plan accordingly. But do you understand what it will take to obtain the abilities to move on to the next step? That is, in itself, your next goal.

- GOALS SHOULD BE SET IN STAGES. You will have to establish these visions in increments of future time zones. In other words, the greater the distance you put between now and your first vision, the tougher it will be to attain that goal. It is far better to establish deadlines that are closer together and work for those intermediate goals, then attain them and move on toward the greater goal down the road. For example, for a car trip to the West Coast from New York City, you want to know exactly where you want to go (say, Beverly Hills, not just California), but equally important, you want to know you need to stop for gas along the way, and where you plan to stop for the night. Investing, just like this car trip, will come easier if you do not push either. Plan ahead, and attain each step along the way before going on to the next. If it takes a bit longer to get halfway, do not worry about it; after all, you have already attained that part of the goal, and that is worth your own pat on your back before you move forward.

- ACCEPT THE FACT THAT FAILURE IS ESSENTIAL TO SUCCESS. This is important because it is a realistic view of life. You have to plan for setbacks so that when they occur you will be able to move on without becoming disillusioned about your ultimate success. Learn by your failures to the extent that you review your own goals to make sure they are attainable. Remember that if your goals are too distant, it is very difficult to be able to find the opportunity to adjust in midstream. Failure is not the opposite of success. Failure is the sweetener of success.

- CONTINUE TO FINE-TUNE YOUR VISION OF YOURSELF IN THE FUTURE. This will be a constant ongoing process. The clearer your vision, the easier it will be to attain that image. You will modify and enhance the goals as you advance toward them.

- BE SO SPECIFIC THAT YOU CAN WRITE DOWN THE SIGNIFICANT ELEMENTS OF YOUR GOALS AS YOU VISUALIZE THEM. This is important because it will later give you proof that you have attained your goals. Nothing is better for your self-esteem than the personal satisfaction of attaining something you have set out to obtain. The written-down evidence is important because it is too easy to remember a goal slightly less than or greatly more than its actual realization. Some people always believe they are right on target when they are way off base, and others continually fail because they are too harsh on themselves. Be honest with yourself and write down the goal.

- WHEN YOU HAVE ATTAINED THE GOAL, CELEBRATE. You will enjoy the success more this way and let these moments offset the temporary disappointment of failure you are bound to encounter along the way.

Your Goals Will Help You Properly Finance Your Real Estate Investments

Let us tie everything together and make sure we keep the continuity of goals with the concept of using the tools of real estate finance to make for better real estate financing.

As you develop goals, you will begin to visualize how the other side of the forest should look, even while you are still deep in the woods. This ability allows you to anticipate what you will need to do, what abilities you will have to attain, and just how much money you may need to accomplish the current and upcoming tasks. You will also begin to see other ways to obtain your desired goals without using cash.

Take Stock of the Assets at Your Disposal

Let me give you an illustration of how this can work for you. Assume that you are a fresh-out-of-law-school graduate who has just started to work for some big law firm in Miami, Florida. You have worked hard to get where you are at the moment, and you want to build a future for yourself using all of your abilities. This includes taking the plunge into real estate investing.

EXAMINE ALL OF YOUR ABILITIES AND LIABILITIES.   One of the first stages in setting your goals is to look at exactly what you are good at and what you might want to be good at (and therefore could take a course to learn). As a budding lawyer, you might have made the following list:

ABILITIES
- Good at law.
- Can study well.
- Know and enjoy working around the garden.
- Have painted inside and outside houses before.
- Can come up with $10,000 in cash to invest.
- Can carry a moderate mortgage (rent?) payment of $1,000 per month.
- Have a high energy level.
- Have weekends partially free for other self-investment work.
- Want to specialize in real estate law.
- Need to develop contacts in all real estate areas for your legal work.

As the list is being composed, your mind is running on the back lot side of the fence. When the abilities list is completed, you begin to look at your liabilities:

LIABILITIES

- Have to be very conservative because of the new job and lack of security.
- Can only spend a few hours per weekend to look for or keep up investments.
- Have car payments.
- Have a six-month lease I cannot get out of.

EXAMINE ALL OF YOUR WANTS.   Once these two elements have been taken care of, you then sit back and let yourself be immersed into that milky-white substance of the clearing of the mind. You work on your vision for several weeks and decide that your destination in about 10 years involves:

WANTS

- Own my own office building and law practice.
- Own my own home, somewhere in the Boca Raton, Florida, area.
- Have a 40-foot (or better) sailboat.
- Be financially set for life.

In a review of these four goals, you notice that you have not been specific enough concerning the levels of debt that might occur. Owning an office building, home, sailboat, and being set for life are relative to how much you want to owe (in order to buy them) and what you mean by "set for life." So, you sharpen your pencil and come up with these more specific goals:

FINE-TUNING GOALS FROM THE WANT LIST

- Owning an office building where I can have my own offices without expense, sufficient income to support any debt on the building, and a minimum of a current market rate of return on my cash invested.
- Own a home on the water in Boca Raton where I can dock a boat and own the home free of any debt.
- Own a 40-foot sailboat free of any debt.
- Have sufficient outside income to support all insurance needs, and all costs to keep and maintain a home.
- Begin to build a portfolio of real estate investments designed to support myself and my family at retirement by the age of 55.

Set Intermediate Goals

Once the revised goals are established, you can set your intermediate goals to guide you along the way. These intermediate or interim goals may include a number of items that may not be necessary at first, but may at the outset go down on the list. Your preliminary list of interim steps to attain your goals could look like this:

STEPS TO ATTAIN GOALS

1. Need to build a specialty in your law field that will support your other interests. This specialty should be within the real estate field in the geographic areas in which you want to live and invest.

2. Need to develop insight into the techniques of investing in real estate and specific contacts in the area where you want to live and invest.

3. May want to buy some vacant land on which you can build your office building and/or home in the future.

4. Learning how to operate a 40-foot sailboat.

5. Your first step is to stop renting and start owning and building equity.

6. Begin by going to the town building and zoning public meetings.

Your approach to setting your goals should follow similar stages in real life. This need not be an overnight event, and if you are married or have dependents, they should be a part of this process.

Who Do You Share Your Goals With?

Your goals have to be your own goals and not your friends' goals that have been superimposed on you. This goes for your family goals, too. But what then? Whom do you entrust with this personal information? Whom do you let know your secret?

The answer is: Keep your goals to yourself and only the most important members of your "advancement" team.

DEVELOP AN ADVANCEMENT TEAM. Every person who has a plan should have as part of that plan an advancement team. This team is made up of people who can advance your interests toward your goals. The available members to the team are many, and best of all their services may be free. Others may charge you only for their performance, while others will charge you by the hour. In any event, to attack a future without an advancement team is foolhardy.

YOUR ADVANCEMENT TEAM CONSISTS OF THE FOLLOWING PEOPLE:

General Team Members	Specific Team Members
Partner	Spouse or life partner
Realtors	Your specific and loyal lawyer
Bankers	Your own true-and-true accountant
Insurance companies	Your own banker
Loan officers at savings and loans	A trusted financial advisor
A repairperson you know and trust	
Local governmental officials	

Of these advancement team members, you entrust your goals only to specific team members. The general team members should be told only what they need to know, as they need to know it. (It is like sending them behind the lines; you never know whether the enemy will get to them.)

Get Your Goals, Team Members, and Your Abilities and Put Them to Work

The total picture now comes together: You have your goals, you see your abilities and your liabilities, and you begin to develop your team members and your techniques at the same time. The only thing that is keeping you from success and attainment of your goals is fear of failure, or just fear itself. There is still one element you need to attend to. It is the development of your comfort zone. Once you have finished this last task, risk will be minimized and success is just around the corner.

PROFIT IN REAL ESTATE THROUGH YOUR COMFORT ZONE

The *comfort zone* is a category of knowledge and ability that is directed to any given task. In the case of real estate, it will become a geographic area where the type of real estate you plan to invest in will be found. The real estate comfort zone will be your specific niche in which you will live and invest. It is your zone of reference, your zone of total comfort and knowledge. It will be within this zone that you will reduce or eliminate all risk in an activity. It will become your financial security blanket.

Why Is a Comfort Zone Important?

Every form of investing or activity has its comfort zone. If you were to make your fortune investing in stamps or coins, you would have to have an area of interest and expertise. Just as in other fields, people first become proficient and then expert in any specific talent. The singer, the dancer, and the pilot—each requires something unique, something oriented to one area of risk. To intrude into another's field can be highly risky, even deadly. For the jazz singer to try to sing hard rock could be suicide, as could be true for the Sunday afternoon pilot who tries to land a 747.

All forms of investing have comfort zones in which the participants succeed once they understand the rules, the regulations, and most importantly the pitfalls of what they are doing. Just as the windsurfer makes that sport look easy (when in reality it is almost impossible until you have spent many hours of practice), the investor with a comfort zone can create the illusion that making money is easy and simple.

What is simple is the technique. What is easy is the concept of how to make money. What is fun is the development of the comfort zone. What is difficult is making money without knowing what you are doing.

The Comfort Zone Will Make You Successful

Nothing lends itself to a comfort zone as much as real estate. Of course, you can develop a comfort zone in any field or interest, but when it comes to making money in your backyard, real estate is it.

Basically, the reason the comfort zone works so well for real estate investing is this: Real estate is local in nature. Local real estate has very little relationship to long-term real estate trends that are going on across the country or in another, distant town. Even though this may seem to be the case when there is a widespread buyer's or seller's market, and financing suddenly seems to be universally impossible to get, this kind of event is temporary, and is still not uniform in every market. Real estate is specifically here and not there. It has appeal because of that fact. Its value or lack of it is due solely to where it is located. It is said that "location, location, location" are the three most important aspects of real estate. While this statement is not entirely true (as you will discover later on), location plays a very important role in the importance of real estate. Remember what I said in Chapter 1: Value is a relative aspect of real estate. This is where location comes into the picture. Real estate value is less dependent on the actual location as it is on the value of that location to you. Your intended need for a tract of land, for example, may allow you to pay much more for a main intersection of two highways than another investor would be willing to pay. Alternatively, that other investor may place a greater value on a different location for reasons that pertain solely to the use that investor has for the other site. Value is a function of how important a location is to the investor who is ready, willing, and able to buy it at any given moment of time.

That location is important only if the local zoning ordinances, rules, regulations, and all governing authorities allow you to do what you want with that property. The best site in the world for a fast-food restaurant, for example, will not be worth you investing your life's savings so that you can own a Burger King if the zoning says no to that request. Both the site and the zoning rules are strictly local.

Due to real estate's purely local nature, you cannot devise an accurate national statistic on what is going on in the market. The only important fact to keep in mind about national statistics and real estate is to understand that some people will believe a national statistic that is published in the newspaper. Take, for example, a headline that indicates a major drop in housing starts. This is a popular statistic that may have importance to the lumber industry more than it will to the values of property in your neighborhood. But, people become intimidated when they hear such news. Perceptive investors take advantage of this and make their move. If you have been watching what is going on in your neighborhood, you know that values are going up or down all the time. Act on what is real in your area, and not some national trend. Having just said that, I caution you to pay close attention to factors that are truly national, or even international in scope and impact (i.e., war, terrorism, the cost of oil, recession as the result of any cause, and the collapse of some critical economic factor). We have seen the impact all of these have on real estate, cost of living, and unemployment. The collapse of the savings and loan industry in the 1970s and the overlending practices in the subprime loan market of the late 1990s through 2008 contributed to a decline in real estate values. It is interesting to note that in both examples, the ease of lending fed a boom in real estate development that expanded to overdevelopment which exceeded demand. In the end, however, lack of prudence on the part of the investors who rushed into the market of the early 1980s and again in 2006–07 added to the difficulties the subprime lenders encountered. Like a virus, the problems spread through the lending system on a grand scale. So, even though each marketplace experienced different levels of impact, not all real estate values declined in all markets. You must always be cautious of borrowing more than you can pay back. Real estate is not a commodity that you can sell tomorrow (like stocks or even your two-year-old car); it is not a question of biting the bullet and taking a loss, rather; it is how long you can hold on to that property until you find a buyer.

The stock market expert can watch the market and become the national expert in gold, silver, or pork bellies. But someone in Chicago can never be an expert on Asheville, North Carolina, real estate unless that town is part of his or her comfort zone. Only in real estate can you become an absolute expert in what you want to buy and sell in record-breaking time. In fact, you can become so expert in such an area that very few of the other investors you will compete with for properties in that area will be as knowledgeable as are you.

There can be a million experts in real estate, each having a different comfort zone, each knowing more about a particular area than any other person, and yet none of them ever infringe on the others. Your comfort zone is the totality of where you are comfortable in the opportunity to use your techniques and abilities within the real estate game. Some of you will become multinational investors who think nothing of building high-rise buildings, while others will be single-home investors who never buy any further than two miles from where you live. The whole idea is to be pleased with yourself, to have confidence in what you are doing, to achieve the goals you set for yourself, and to sleep soundly at night.

Building Your Comfort Zone

The rest of this chapter is an introduction to building your comfort zone. The last chapter of this book is a more defined look at all the steps you will take. However, do not jump to that chapter yet. There is much to do to get ready to start building your comfort zone. However, I do want you to have a brief look at the benefits of this process so that you will be encouraged to build that foundation. Your goals are critical. Without a clear set of goals, you will not be able to formulate or benefit from your comfort zone properly.

To establish your comfort zone, begin with your goals. Remember when you role-played the lawyer, the list of four goals were the office building, the home, the sailboat, and economic freedom. A comfort zone should be devised to help you attain those goals. However, in getting started, the comfort zone may have little relationship to the final product.

If you, as a young lawyer, began at a stage in your life where you wanted to buy office buildings and have waterfront homes in Boca Raton, Florida, you would develop as your comfort zone the specific areas that contain exactly the kind of property that you want to buy. This means that you would geographically locate a zone or territory that consists of office buildings and waterfront homes in Boca Raton.

You then would define that area in specific terms. It might be all the property along three main commercial streets in town, or all the waterfront properties along five or six canals. Whatever the area, it would begin small and work into a comprehensive area. However, because you are just starting out, you may begin with your more immediate needs, your intermediate goals. To this end, you still devise a geographic area, and you will follow the same techniques you will use later as you advance to the higher, more specific areas of your dreams and goals.

How to Get Started with Your Comfort Zone

You might want to establish your first ownership of real estate or find a good investment in apartment buildings. The types of properties that you decide you want to buy should take you closer to your final goal.

First, you have to learn how to set your priorities to the kind of property you want to own within the geographic area we now call your comfort zone. Since you cannot know everything about every area of town, you need this specific area to be well chosen and clearly defined. So, decide right now that you will never stray from your comfort zone.

This "never stray out of the comfort zone" rule is not a limiting element. The concept is that you must start somewhere, and that as you develop the comfort zone, you will be adding to your own confidence and therefore reducing your risk. As this process develops, the comfort zone is expanded little by little. So, instead of being limiting, it is constantly allowing you to expand your opportunity awareness safely.

This Concept Works Well for Investors and Real Estate Salespeople

Using the comfort zone concept, you can actually feel the power gained through knowledge. Knowledge, by the way, is the same kind of foundation that makes one real estate salesperson stand out over another. Smart real estate salespeople will learn all that they can about the area in which they want to list and sell real estate. Their demonstration of being experts in the geographic area enables them to dazzle owners into the realization that the best person to list and sell their property is someone who knows the property like the back of his or her hand.

The investor who has established goals, has picked out a comfort zone, and is proceeding to become an expert in the area will equally demonstrate to the participants that he knows what he is doing.

The effect of all of this is multi-level. Not only will sellers be more receptive to buyers who are so knowledgeable, but lenders also will lean toward doing business with this kind of person. Much of the art of using the tools of finance depends on your being able to convince the other side of the deal that what you propose is sound, good business for all persons involved, and should be accomplished.

The prospective investor who shows up at the local savings and loan without confidence in himself and without assurance that he can back up the property will not be well received.

We Live in a World of Nameless, Faceless Neighbors

The comfort zone works simply because people have a tendency to live in a world in which they keep to themselves. We don't know the names of our neighbors, we don't know values across the street, and we don't even care if the house down the block is rented, or if so, for how much. Investors buy for many reasons, often taking the word of their realtor or salesperson as to what is going on in the area. This fact may not hamper their success—in fact, many investors succeed with this tactic of investing.

However, this involves taking more risk than is necessary for the majority of investors, and most certainly for the investor who doesn't have a lot that can be placed at risk. The lack of knowledge that most people have of where they live and invest can then work for the investor who has developed his or her own comfort zone and works it properly.

Make Your Comfort Zone Work with Creative Tools

Once your goals are firmly established in your mind and you are under way with your plan, the critical steps are just around the corner. You must implement your plan with the financing techniques, and how you use them will become an important aspect of your success in real estate investing. All the financing techniques and tips described in this book can be utilized in combination with each other, giving you endless opportunities to best solve a problem at hand or seek the best format to buy or sell your real estate to take you closer to your desired goal. The subtleties of these techniques will begin to become evident as you use them. Each will have a slightly different effect on each deal and for each user. A sale-leaseback in one transaction could work wonders for you, whereas in the next deal it could be the least attractive format.

You should approach each real estate investment with the question, "Do I need to buy this?" If the answer is yes, your whole approach to the transaction may be greatly altered. In essence, you would be "forced" to find a technique that solves that basic need (to buy that property), with the secondary benefit of doing so at the best terms possible. However, if the answer is no, and you would buy it only if it was clearly a good deal, you can be far more selective in the use of your financing techniques. It will be much easier to walk away from those deals that cannot be made on terms that enable you to "own" that property in such a way that it moves you closer to your desired goals.

Keep your goals constantly in your mind. Review them, update them, and work toward them. They are what will help keep you out of trouble. Your goals will keep you on the right track. The following list will show you many opportunities to the end result of disposing of real estate. Review this list from time to time to remind yourself that disposition of real estate is not just selling, and in some cases not even a transfer of title. Real estate ownership can be considered the use and benefit of the real estate as much as the holding of a fee simple title:

METHODS FOR OBTAINING OR GETTING RID OF REAL ESTATE

1. Acquisition (of additional property).
2. Adverse possession.
3. Bankruptcy.
4. Build to suit.
5. By will.
6. Charitable contribution.
7. Chattel.
8. Condemnation.
9. Conversion.
10. Demolition.
11. Development.
12. Discount sale with leaseback.
13. Discount sale with recapture.
14. Easement lease.
15. Easement sale.
16. Eminent domain.

17. Escheat.
18. Exchange all the property.
19. Exchange a portion of the property.
20. General corporation.
21. Gift.
22. Joint venture.
23. Holding company.
24. Improvement of building.
25. Insurance lease.
26. Insurance mortgage.
27. Lease of air rights.
28. Lease of all rights.
29. Lease, Sub.
30. Limited partnership.
31. Mortgage out, foreclose.
32. Option-lease.
33. Option-sale.
34. Partition sale.
35. Prescription.
36. Pyramid.
37. Reclamation.
38. Refinancing.
39. Rent.
40. Rezoning.
41. Sale, Air rights.
42. Sale, Auction.
43. Sale, Improvements only.
44. Sale, Land only.
45. Sale/Lease riparian.
46. Sale, Leaseback with a recapture.
47. Sale or lease of leasehold.
48. Sell option back.
49. Subdivide.

50. Subordination.

51. Subordination of the mortgage.

52. Syndicate.

53. Tax sale.

54. TIC (tenant in common venture).

55. Timeshare.

56. Trusts.

All of the foregoing methods to obtain or to dispose of real estate can be accomplished using the techniques in this book. Once you have finished this book, plan on going over this chapter again to remind you of the importance of goals and your comfort zone; you will use Chapter 24 as your constant guide to developing an effective comfort zone. Let it help you build that tower of wealth and financial independence on the foundation you have thus far undertaken to build.

Chapter 3

THE POWER AND ART OF EFFECTIVE NEGOTIATING

GOAL OF THIS CHAPTER

This chapter shows you how a win/win strategy begins with your goals firmly in focus and ends with helping the other party to the transaction move closer to their goals.

There are many different ways to establish a meeting of the minds. This is especially so when it comes to purchasing real estate. There is, however, considerable pressure applied to both sides of a transaction. After all, that may be the largest single purchase or sale that either party has ever made. This pressure can cause deals to be quickly made, or even more quickly lost. Good salesmen know this, and the best of them do everything possible to help the deal-making process along before indecision or transaction breakdown occurs.

DECISION TIME—YOURS OR THEIRS?

Buyers come face to face with the bottom-line decision of should they go forward or not. They may even ask themselves questions such as: "Am I doing the right thing here? Am I about to pay too much for this property? Can I afford this property? Will my friends think I was stupid?" Whatever those questions are, it is likely that the single most important question goes unasked by either the buyer or seller. "Is this transaction going to move me closer to my intended goal or not?" This is the critical point to which Chapters 1 and 2 of this book have been focused. I am not talking about failure to buy at the lowest price or to sell at less than the buyer would pay. A few dollars here or there really should not matter if the goal is coming closer to your reach, or even within your grasp at last.

40

Success in real estate investing is touted in every media. Paid advertisement television shows you testimonies of buyers who have made their fortunes in real estate; books, even this one, show you the techniques to attain such successes; and radio shows are full of rich people telling you that real estate made them so. All of this simply enhances the pressure that falls on the shoulders of the buyers and sellers out there who really just want to attain a goal.

DARTS-ON-A-MAP TIME IS OVER

There was a time, not too many years ago, when buying real estate, and making money doing it, were as simple as throwing a dart at a map of the area. This is not the way it is now. Now you have to be on your toes from the day you pick up the map of the area until you close on the transaction. What has happened over the years to turn real estate investing into the bundle of bureaucracy it has become? People who moved to the town before you even were born. They had it easy because the rules of the game were far less complicated. Why, you didn't even have to ask anyone if you could chop a tree down (to make your log cabin). Now, in some communities, you can't chop a tree down until you have done a tree survey together with an environmental study to make sure you don't chop down the habitat of a pink and yellow dwarf tree frog or something like that. Oh, and yes, those people who got there first, they are the very ones who have voted in that save-the-frog rule so that you don't mess up their little bit of paradise.

As a city grows, so does the local government. City, county, and state ordinances become less developer-friendly. Land planners, straight out of the State University system, want to practice what they have been learning while in college, and that generally means putting the clamps on growth. Then scores of different environmental groups and protection laws that look good on paper all want to save what is there, no matter if you are being eaten alive by mosquitoes on a nice summer evening because no one can drain the swamp behind your house. Zoning ordinances, the backbone of real estate use, have become the ever-changing, rarely constant, wishy-washy way which city council members demonstrate their power over developers. Real estate is becoming a complicated place, so out with the darts thrown at a city map. Such tactics to choose your next real estate acquisition are no longer valid.

However, this is the good news of the story. The tougher it is to deal with the bureaucracy, the less competition there is for great deals. There is even better news, too. Each city comes with its own set of building codes and city ordinances, and each city council is manned by people who are usually not really professional at what they are expected to do. This means that to survive in the resulting turmoil that can (and frequently does) occur, you can develop a great edge over your competition by doing one simple thing. What is that simple thing? Establishing your comfort zone as I discussed in Chapter 2. All you have to do is to specialize in one or two towns. Get to know everything and everyone that is important to what makes real estate go up or down in value in those towns. Those elements will be covered in this book, so just be patient. Quickly you will have the edge on any outside buyers. Better yet, with a little effort, very quickly you will know more about what is going on in the community than most of the players you meet—even the real insiders who are making the decisions that cause things to happen. This means you know and understand more about property values than most real estate brokers in the area do as well as the majority of sellers. By following a comfort zone program as was discussed in Chapter 2 and augmented throughout this book, you will start to see opportunities popping up all around you.

Timing is everything when it comes to getting the best deal. This means being early to spot the opportunity and take control of the property, before you actually close on the transaction. The steps that fall between each of those two events are the subject of this chapter. The goal of this chapter is to introduce you to some of the critical aspects of what it takes to take control of the property. The key word in this process is control: You want to be in control before you actually must commit to buy. The reason for this is simple. You want to have control to allow you time to make a complete inspection of the property and all possible elements that affect the property. To spend the time, money, and effort on this kind of detailed due diligence without being in control is a waste. To get into control takes a combination of talents. These talents combine to describe the art of negotiating. The route to success in real estate is through good negotiating. Nothing happens within the closed doors of bankers, buyers, sellers, and developers that is not won or lost by the finesse of the participants to negotiate properly, or, for that matter, to negotiate at all.

When it comes to being a success in real estate, you must develop good negotiating skills, or find someone who can do that important task for you. This is as important to a buyer as it is to a seller.

Timing, by the way, has little to do with the clock or a date on a calendar. At any given moment, the motivations of a buyer or a seller can change. This change can be so dramatic that an opportunity is born. Many buyers fail to grasp this concept of good timing. I have seen buyers turn down a property that truly suited their investment portfolio because it had been on the market for a long time. They were confusing timing with the lapse of time. "How can this be any good?" they would argue. "Look at how long the seller has tried to sell this property. Why, everyone in the world has turned this down." Suddenly, there is a change that makes the property more attractive. It might be the announcement of a new bridge over the river that has separated the property from the mainstream of commerce, or the development of a major employer in the area, or just a softening in the seller's motivation to sell. The buyer who grasps that there is a positive change and also recognizes how that change can affect the value of the property is the person in the right place at the right time.

However, all the best timing will not put you into control unless the negotiation to purchase or to sell is effective and produces a meeting of the minds. Keep in mind that this chapter is not meant to teach you all you could learn about the art of negotiation.

However, this chapter and this book are more than a first-aid course that can only save your life in an emergency. This chapter and this book will give you the knowledge of what to look for and how to develop critical insight into what motivates the other party. Start with the understanding that you will win in negotiations if you approach every contract confrontation with the idea that you will succeed only if you help the other party attain all or most of his or her goals. Sound revolutionary? Just wait and see how this works.

STEPS TO SUCCESSFUL NEGOTIATING

This chapter guides you through the early stages of getting your act into proper gear so that you can present your case in a businesslike way, and move into the close of the transaction. You will find that the most essential part of any negotiation is to have an absolutely clear vision of your goal. If you don't know what it is you are negotiating for, your end result is apt to be far different from your original desire. Also critical is your understanding that winning doesn't mean coming out ahead of the other party. Winning is achieving your goals. Win/win situations occur when each party attains a substantial percent (not necessarily 100 percent) of their critical goals.

The best part of negotiating is that you don't require a college degree in the art of negotiation or any education other than the ability to demonstrate empathy and to keep your cool. The homework that you may need to do from time to time will be easy, and there will be many people ready to help you. Sometimes the most help comes from the other side.

The two most important elements to start with are the basis of the transaction and doing effective homework. Look at each of these elements in detail.

Basis of the Transaction

The first step in any negotiation is to review your goals, or if you are negotiating for someone else, make sure you have a clear understanding of the goal desired. Each situation may present a different set of circumstances, but the end result should be clearly in mind. Assume, for example, that you are in the hospitality business, and want to add to your existing holdings of hotel properties. Long before you sit down with a seller of a property you want to buy, you must be sure you understand what kind of property and the criteria of that property that will work for you.

If the property must be purchased to allow redevelopment of an adjoining property, there will be different tactics used in the acquisition of the site than if the goal was to land bank a future development site. Write down the goal, and the way in which a successful negotiation will help attain that goal. This will help you stay on track during the negotiation process.

Suppose you want to buy an apartment building for yourself. Within step 1 of negotiating, you must examine the various elements involved: What is the long-range goal you plan to reach through the purchase or acquisition of the apartment building? Is it to buy the property for a potential conversion to a condominium or other use some time in the near future? Or do you want to maximize equity build-up and plow as much of the cash flow back into the property to attract a wealthy prospect? The investment plan is important because this will dictate the direction you go in developing the financing for the acquisition. Both the long-term and short-term goals are important, and must be kept clearly in sight. It is too easy to overlook the original objective and to attain the desired result in such a way that you jeopardize your long-term position.

Assume that your long-term goal is to establish a steady income at the end of a 15-year period and that the apartment complex will fill that need by paying off its debt by then. Once the total goal is seen, visualized, and written down, you can move deeper into the basis of the transaction in preparation for your negotiations. One of the next stages is the review of options open to you to meet this goal. How many apartment buildings have you seen? Where do you want your apartment building to be? Each move toward the end result will take you deeper into more alternatives that can sway you from your intended path. It is important that you be flexible so that as you move into this jungle you won't overlook the fact that other pathways that present themselves to you might improve your chances of realizing your goals. However, do not let the greener grass syndrome take you into an ambush by the local natives (brokers or other sellers). Many a would-be investor has lost his or her head over something that looked too good, too easy, and too quick.

Review the Alternatives

Look at and examine the alternatives. If you have an effective comfort zone system in place, you will know the marketplace and focus on what works for you. It is this thought process that has led you to this property in the first place. Still, you will want to ask yourself these questions prior to entering into negotiations:

Does this property appear to meet or exceed my minimum criteria?

Are there circumstances that suggest that this represents an opportunity?

Have I arrived at the point in time that I need to take control of this property?

Will this property help me achieve my investment goals?

Is this property in my comfort zone? Or do I need to change my goals or expand my comfort zone?

All investors who succeed ask themselves these questions over and over again. They listen to the answers, and then act.

You are ready to proceed to the next step in negotiating when you are comfortable that you know just how far you are willing to go in the acquisition of the property. Even at this stage, you must be flexible. The other participants may have some elements available that you don't know about, and these elements might get you where you want to go quicker than you thought. But remember this word of warning: The best negotiator is the one who makes you believe that you have just won when in fact you both have.

BASIS OF THIS TRANSACTION

- Meets your predetermined criteria for the kind of real estate you want to own.
- Fits to move you closer to your goals.
- Appears to be within your economic and management abilities.
- Has potential (for your abilities) for the creation of new value.
- Your decision-making players are in agreement to move forward on this deal.
- Get ready to move to the next step to get control of the property.
- Once under control, be aggressive with the due diligence to fine-tune the economics of the transaction.
- Review the findings of the due diligence studies.
- Extend, conclude, modify, or terminate the transaction.

Some of the best examples of real estate investors who follow all of these elements are the national fast-food franchises. They know what works for them, what they need, and generally must act quickly when they decide to saturate a market area. But not all national companies are so smart. Poor long-range planning and the inability to make a decision often cause many investors to lose.

Doing Effective Homework

Every transaction requires different levels of homework in preparation for the negotiation stage of this transaction. Remember, you have not tied up the property at this stage, and need to limit the amount of time and effort you spend on the deal until you are in control. The bulk of this work comes early, often before you have even seen the property you are now negotiating to purchase. That homework is associated with your comfort zone. The actual negotiating homework will vary dependent on which kind of negotiating you are engaged in. There are two basic types—blind and open.

BLIND.   This is the most common kind of negotiation. Blind is when you have no idea who you are dealing with, and make little or no effort to find out the motivations that steer the other side of the deal. Blind negotiations occur much of the time because of blocks in the way of your finding out anything about the other side. Real estate brokers or salespeople are one such roadblock. In real estate transactions, they frequently represent the sellers and like to keep control of the situation. They want to keep the buyer and seller apart and generally feel that each party should know as little about the other party as possible. This situation is founded on the premise that many transactions are lost when the buyer and seller get together. This is a very valid basis, too, because most buyers or sellers let personality get in the way of sound negotiations. "What do you mean who picked out that carpet? I did." Just about every real estate broker who has been on the job for a couple of weeks can tell you horror stories of buyers and sellers going at each other viciously.

However, it is a good idea that you know as much as possible about the other party, whether you are the buyer or the seller. This will help you put together a deal that will work. If you want to let the broker keep you apart, that's just fine. There is a school of international negotiations that is sometimes called the English School of Negotiation that works very well in real estate transactions. The theory is that, blind or open, it is critical that the negotiator be talking with someone who can make a decision. In real estate terms, this might be the actual buyer or seller. However, the negotiator is not someone who can make decisions. This kind of negotiation is difficult, and the negotiator must be very calm under stress. The key to success is that one side is always committing to each point discussed, whereas the other side must always go back to the principal, to get confirmation. "My brother has controlling interest" is a more Americanized version of this same tactic where no matter if you actually have control of the deal, you always imply that there is always someone else who has to make the decision. Many an only child has used this tactic.

Blind negotiation is not a waste of time, however. The speed with which you can make an offer makes blind negotiation work when speed is the most critical element of the transaction. If you know your comfort zone well and recognize that the property offered is a bargain, you have already done your homework and that additional information on the other party may not be necessary. This points out the importance of knowing all you can about the property you want to buy or the market in which you want to sell. That homework is the most essential.

OPEN.   This form of negotiation involves a lot of homework. The idea is to know as much as possible about your counterpart so that when it comes time to make the deal you won't have any surprises or anything outstanding to keep you from closing the transaction. In essence, you have made the decision this is a deal you want and that you will do all you can to make the deal within reason and legality. This kind of negotiation isn't as difficult as it might seem. Most of the homework you can and will do will fall into your lap, if you let it. Of course, you should rely on the help of your broker, lawyer, or accountant whenever he or she can be of assistance. Let me give you an example of one such transaction where the homework made the difference.

Charles wanted to own a home that he saw on Center Avenue. It was just a few blocks from the beach; he could walk to his office on nice days, and he liked the look of the house from the street. After only two blind offers, the seller stood firm at a price that Charles didn't think was realistic. In essence, price was standing in the way of the deal. Instead of giving up on the transaction, Charles decided to ask the broker to look into the motivations of the seller. Keep in mind that the broker worked for the seller, so he already knew some things about him.

Charles was interested in knowing what would turn the reluctant seller into a willing participant to the transaction. This was the critical stage of the transaction because the broker didn't want to betray any secrets, but at the same time, he wanted to make a deal.

Charles wants to buy the property, the broker wants him to buy the property, and the seller wants someone to buy her property. But, so far, neither the seller nor any buyer has been able to get together to make the deal work. Charles knows that in good negotiations there is always a way to make a deal if one side makes a greater effort than the other does. Since Charles is a good businessman, he knows that there is a limit to the economic cost of the transaction for the deal to make sense to him, and he would like to get in as inexpensively as possible. Therefore, Charles wants to discover if there is some factor that will help put the deal together. Sometimes the roadblocks to putting a deal together is that one side or the other cannot see how to attain his or her own goal other than by proceeding in one direction. In Charles' case, it might be that the seller needs to be shown some alternative directions that will achieve the seller's goals.

The homework Charles must consider may take a different tack than that which you may require to make your next deal. But all homework must be comprehensive and to the point.

FACTORS THAT MAKE DEALS COME TOGETHER

Why Does the Other Party Want to Buy or Sell?

Simple logic will tell you that this is the toughest question to answer. If you are the buyer, you want to know the reason the seller wants to sell. The reason the broker comes up with is apt to be a figment of the broker's imagination or the seller's invention. You need to look deeper. Do some homework. Find the answers to questions such as: What are the economic factors of the property? Is there a mortgage foreclosure, are there liens filed against the property or the people? Has the owner lost his job? What is it that occurred that causes this property to be up for sale?

This is an overall review of the circumstances: The seller just bought a new home. He just divorced his wife. He lost everything he owned in the storm and wasn't insured. He drew into an inside straight. He just doesn't know what he is doing. Or whatever. If you are the seller, knowing why the other party wants to buy is helpful, too. The answer to this question is a bit more difficult to find since the motivations of those who have money or who are in the "taker" position might be more difficult to inspect. However, there are very obvious reasons some buyers want to buy. The fast-food franchise company that needs a location in the area, the hospital next door that wants to expand, and so on. When you have this kind of insight, you can act accordingly. Generally, sellers can get sufficient information about the buyer by finding out who the buyer is.

Much of the homework you do is a matter of being aware of what is going on around the transaction. That information must then be tied into the form of negotiations you devise to meet any objection that stands in your way of successfully concluding the transaction. Other parts of the homework fall into the comfort zone that we have discussed in earlier sections of this book. So far, each of these two tactics is a question of awareness and comfort. The facts are often public knowledge and easy to obtain once you know how to find them.

For example, in your community there are sources of information that can tell you a lot about the person with whom you are dealing. Some of these are:

• A CITY CROSS-REFERENCE DIRECTORY: This is a book much like a telephone book but it contains other data, such as place of employment, name of spouse and children. You also can check addresses to match phone numbers if you have one and not the other. Once you know where your counterpart lives and works, you can go deeper into the background of that person.

• A CITY/COUNTY SOCIAL DIRECTORY: If you are dealing with one of the social elite, you can bet that he or she will be listed in the social directory. This book often tells you things such as the clubs the person belongs to, the name of his or her yacht, the person's summer or winter address, the names of children, where the children are going to school, and so on. A check of some of these key items can be rewarding.

• COUNTY COURTHOUSE/CITY HALL DIRECTORY: Here, you can find a great deal of information about many people in your community. What real estate do they own, how much tax do they pay, what did they pay for the real estate they own? Do they have mortgages on their real estate? Is there a foreclosure in the wings? How much? Have they been sued? When and for what? Are they divorced? Married? And so on.

• CREDIT REPORTS: You can obtain a credit report on almost any company. Look in your phone book for companies that provide this service. If you are a member of Dun and Bradstreet, this is a good place to start. But be careful of the institutional kind of report. It often only shows up the shine, and unless the company had a lot of bad news lately, that part may not be available for the usual Dun and Bradstreet report.

• BETTER BUSINESS BUREAU: Give this organization a call if your counterpart in the deal is a businessperson in the community. What about his or her reputation anyway? If you find a long list of complaints, be warned that you may soon be following with one of your own.

• BUSINESS ASSOCIATES: If the party is in business, why not check with other people in the same line of business? "Oh, by the way, do you know . . ." can be a simple way to open the conversation. Perhaps members of your investment team know of this person, and can help you find other doors to open.

Relying on reports such as those mentioned will give you some insight into the person and the potential problems you might have. But by themselves, they will not make your deal for you. You will have to make your deal based on the final play of this game as it develops. Homework only gives you the edge; the actual play is up to you.

Who Is He or She Trying to Impress?

Almost everyone has someone he or she is trying to impress. The loan officer wants to impress his boss, the guy down the street wants to impress his wife or his girlfriend, and your next-door neighbor may want to impress you. Whom do you want to impress?

While you may never discover the person the other party is trying to impress most, it should be obvious to you that knowing that information would be very important. For example, some people want to impress their parents more than anything else in the world. Other people want to impress their bosses, or employees, while others are constantly trying to impress their husbands or boyfriends. Possessing this information would allow you to present an offer that would allow the person to impress that person most. If it was the mother, a casual remark made in front of the party, such as, "I'll bet your mother would be proud of your making a deal like this," would do no harm.

Try to find out something about the other party if you can. Sometimes you can get enough insight from the real estate broker who represents the seller, or if the deal is big enough, and important enough, some homework in the way of research into the other party's motives or interests will help. Knowing who the other party wants to impress, and why, could be the difference between a closed deal and wasted effort. There is a negative part of this situation. You do not want to make a mistake and say something like "Only your mother could be so bossy."

Know the Timing of the Transaction Better Than the Other Party Does

How much can you know about the time elements that the other person must face up to? Time often gets in the way of many deals. If it is the loan officer: When does she have to meet her quota? If it is the seller: When does he have to own up to his foreclosure? Or the buyer: When does she have to move out of her current home? Or office? When must she meet some deadline? Find out the deadline of the other person by asking the following types of questions:

"When do you need this property?"

"Is the first of March okay?"

"Can you get an okay by June 15?"

By itself, the time element is not critical unless there is a specific urgency, such as the buyer's lease is up on the first of next month. What is important is acknowledgment of the transaction. Any statement, either positive or negative, may be a buying or selling acknowledgment. Time is no exception. For example, if the buyer asks, "Can you move out by the first of next month?" then the seller should ask, "Can you close on the title that soon?" If the buyer replies positively then the contract may be all but signed. If the buyer replies negatively, "You're right, that might be too soon for me to come up with the money" the deal is still on track, and you know what factor to work on.

Any time urgency works in favor of the opposing party. The party with the time urgency will make a deal that is realistic, even one that costs more than he wants to pay or gets him less than he wants to get. However, some participants will end the deal if they feel they are being delayed: "Look Mr. Broker, I can't fool around with that seller any longer. Get me another deal, even if I have to pay a little more. Okay?"

In negotiations with a loan officer, there are some important facts to know. These include the time periods for submission to loan committees, quotas that the loan officer has to meet, and other time traps that affect you in your need for money. For example, a 90-day delay while your credit is being checked, or the 90-day down time to have an appraisal made when you only have 60 days to meet some contract provision to keep your deal alive can be disastrous.

Verify the Facts

This sounds like good, sound business practice. However, you would be surprised to learn that most deals are completed without the major factors being tested out. In many transactions, the end result is that those factors might not have mattered anyway. However, if you are trying to make the best deal you can, you owe it to yourself to make sure that the following items are verified.

TIPS FOR THE BUYER

Price

Is the price quoted to you the lowest price quoted in the most recent period? Sometimes brokers get old brochures; in reality, the price may have gone down. I don't ever recall a seller telling the offering party that he had just reduced the price from $300,000 to $250,000 when the would-be buyer has just offered $275,000. Make sure your broker has double-checked the price the day you go to make the offer. While on the price issue, it is becoming more and more important to be cautious of hidden costs that can come with the transaction due to factors over which you have no control—like getting a building permit, for example. What used to be a relatively simple process as long as the property was properly zoned for the construction use now can deteriorate into months, if not years of expensive battle with planning and zoning boards, and other governmental agencies. This occurs even though you thought the approval would be a simple "review" and stamp indicating APPROVED. Some planning and zoning departments and city council boards have invoked such vague ordinances that are so complex and interconnected that it becomes next to impossible to do the logical. For example, in Fort Lauderdale the city commission regularly votes "no" on beautiful new developments to urban renewal areas that are on their way to becoming slums because the development rules state that the new projects must be compatible with the community. Now tell me, what is compatible with a slum? Another slum?

Legal Description

The legal description can be, for example, "Lot 1, Block 7 of the Cummings Plat Number 1" (often followed by other information such as a tax folio number to make it easy to find the property through tax rolls). Be sure that the legal description you put in the offer is in fact the property you want to buy. This error sometimes occurs, and people have bought the wrong property. It is critical that you do this for vacant land and improved property. In addition to any legal description, I suggest that the property be described in lay terms as well: "That property located at 2671 East Commercial Blvd., Fort Lauderdale, Florida 33308, a two-story office building consisting of 3,100 square feet on a lot sized 36' frontage on East Commercial Blvd., at a depth of 150' to an alley to the north, which are the present offices of Cummings Realty, Inc." It would be difficult for a problem to arise if you take this simple step. There is one additional step to add to this protection: "As is shown on the attached survey and plat map."

To illustrate what can happen if you don't pay attention, let me give you an example. I purchased a vacant lot (and later built a home on it) in Fort Lauderdale. The property was the last vacant lot in an area of homes that fronted canals leading to the ocean. It was very odd to find a vacant lot in this area, and on walking the lot, I realized that the reason it had remained vacant was its odd shape and the small amount of water frontage it had on the canal. The lot seemed unattractive due to vegetation on two sides of the lot (the lot itself was a corner, so it had streets on two sides, and neighbors on two sides, with a fifth side facing the canal). Along its northern boundary were a massive hedge and a tree line that ran down to the canal retaining wall to a point where there was a marker nail driven into the concrete with a yellow circle around it. The amount of canal frontage that seemed to belong to this lot was only about 20 feet, whereas all of the neighbors had 100 feet or more of dock space. However, on reviewing the plat, it turned out that the lot actually was larger than it appeared and had about 60 feet of canal frontage with riparian rights that gave the lot an ideal dockage for boats up to 70 feet long. Also, all of the hedges, trees, and barbecue, and most of the lawn sprinklers and yard of the home to the north belonged to this lot, which I bought.

I also discovered that the home to the north had gone through five owners in the past seven years. I surmised that owners made the discovery of just where their south lot line really was located and sold out to someone else.

The current owner of the property to the north had no idea, of course. When he purchased the property, he asked his lawyer to check the title, plat, and survey of the lot. The only problem was the lawyer failed to do the most critical check of all. Neither the attorney nor the current owner had walked the property with a tape measure to locate the actual corners and side boundaries and to compare them to the descriptions in the title, plat, and survey. Had either of them done so, they would have known that the nail and yellow circle were the figment of an overly anxious seller.

The lesson learned here is to be sure of everything that relates to the specific property in question.

Mortgages

Whether you are taking out or assuming a mortgage, be sure you understand all of its terms. The mortgage documents should be in your possession prior to your final acceptance of any offer, and your lawyer should go over the mortgage with you to explain it fully. Do not let him or her slip by a clause by saying, "That's common." You should know what it means, and be sure you will agree to its terms.

For new mortgages, you will be able to negotiate some terms and conditions. You should question any part of a mortgage you don't like or that sounds unfair. If it doesn't sound fair, it probably isn't.

Many mortgages have clauses and conditions that can be confusing to anyone, including wise and educated lawyers and real estate brokers. These clauses include, but are by far not limited to, the following:

- What are the terms of payment? How many payments?
- Can the mortgage be paid off ahead of schedule?
- Is it principal plus interest, or interest and principal?
- How is amortization calculated?
- Are the payments monthly, or what?
- Are there balloon payments? One balloon or two? When? How much exactly?
- Is there a formula to calculate the balloon in the event of an earlier prepayment?
- Can assumption be made by other parties?
- Is there a pay-off penalty?
- Are there provisions for acceleration?
- What is the form of payment? In U.S. dollars?
- Does the monthly payment include principal and interest?
- Is the escrow included or added in a lump?
- What are the escrow terms? Why? How much? Exactly what is included?

- Is insurance included or required? Can you get your own? Why is it required?
- What are the terms involving the title insurance? Can you provide your own and co-insure the lender?

What Is Included with the Property?

Is a comprehensive inventory attached to the contract, or do you at least have the right to make up an inventory and approve it? If you don't approve it, can you get out of the deal prior to the closing? If not, you may be making a bad deal. The only time you will get everything you think you are getting is to have it in writing. Make sure that you get an inventory that is specific: not just chairs and tables and beds, but specific chairs and tables and beds. A good idea is to go through the property with a red marker and number each item of furniture and each fixture (provided the mark does not detract from the value of the property). If you cannot mark the property itself, place a stick-on tab on the item with your initial and that of the seller. Then make a detailed list of each item. The hazard of not doing this early in the negotiation or shortly after the contract is that items will disappear and/or will be replaced with less valuable items.

The same goes for the landscaping. If there are valuable plants in the garden and you want to make sure that they remain, do an inventory of the gardens (preferably with a camera). I can tell you many sad stories of sellers taking plants with them.

Are There Environmental Problems?

This requires professional help. It is very critical to include in a contract a clause that the seller warrants there is no environmental problem at all. Most people think that it is the law for sellers and brokers to disclose this and other kinds of known problems. In reality, this may not be the case at all. If you ask the question, however, and the seller, broker, or any other party to the deal says there is not a problem, they will have broken the law if you can prove they did know.

Are There Code Violations?

This is a simple item to check if the local building department has a program in place where they will make an inspection of the property for this purpose. If not, double check your property inspection company (there will be several in your area you can choose from) and go over their checklist in careful detail. What you want to know is not just what they check, but what do they not check. Some inspection companies are strictly building oriented and they do not check code violations at all. This can be very important if you have to replace all the electrical work done by a moonlighter without a permit—you can be in for a hefty expense.

TIPS FOR THE SELLER

When Will the Closing of the Transaction Occur?

If you think that the closing date is the one that is filled into the blanks following the words, "The closing will occur on the _____ day of _____ in the year 201_ ," then you might be in for a surprise. Sharp buyers have a tendency to insert provisions in the agreement that may, at their option and often at their control, delay the closing well beyond the established date indicated on the contract. You should examine the agreement carefully to determine whether such conditions exist and what delays they may cause. One safe thing to do is to put an outside date in the agreement with wording such as: "All parties agree that under no circumstance whatsoever shall the closing occur after the following date, providing the seller is not in default in this agreement and has used due diligence to meet all obligations herein contained, and that if the buyer elects not to close on that date and the seller does not extend the closing date then this agreement will terminate and any and all deposits placed in escrow pending the closing will become liquidated damages to the favor of the seller." Keep in mind that this is just a part of what you will need in your agreement. The wording is not as critical as the effect.

How Is the Price Determined, and Exactly How Much Is It?

I have seen agreements that showed a price that the seller would never get due to other conditions that took away from that price. If the agreement calls for you, the seller, to pay certain costs; cover certain expenses; make repairs, additions, refurbish; give credit for changes; allow for interest to be included; have moratoriums on interest or principal or both, these are all deductions from the price.

As long as you agree with these deductions, there is no problem; but watch out if you don't. By the way, don't assume that your lawyer will tell you about these items. He is apt to look at the agreement with a legal eye instead of a business eye, thinking that whatever terms or conditions are contained in the agreement are acceptable to you. What are you selling? For the same reason the buyer wanted to know what he or she was buying, you need to check very carefully what it is you are about to sell. I can tell you from firsthand experience that it is easy to slip up in this area if you own a lot of property or have complicated legal descriptions on the property being sold. The solution to this problem is exactly the same as what was provided for the buyer. Review that section once more.

How Are the Mortgages to Be Paid?

The same situation that befalls the buyer will befall you; only you as seller have other considerations to consider. If you have a large taxable income or capital gain as a result of this sale, the method of payment of the mortgage could have a major impact on your tax considerations. You may want to make some adjustments in that area prior to final agreement.

Get Started on the Right Foot

In the art of negotiation, it is important to begin properly. You should establish, right up front, the tone of the negotiation and the pattern you wish to follow. This will be your game plan, and like all good game plans, it will be flexible enough to allow you to make adjustments along the way to meet any objections.

It is my opinion that in buying real estate a direct confrontation between the buyer and the seller is not wise. Now by this I do not mean that the buyer and the seller should not know each other, or that they should not be in communication during the negotiation process. I mean that all confrontation should be left to intermediaries. This works for both the buyer and the seller.

GETTING STARTED

1. If you already know the other party, maintain the same relationship as before if it is friendly. If it is not friendly, do nothing to aggravate the circumstances. Don't make any rash changes in the friendship. Under the circumstances, you are apt to appear to be insincere and this may discredit your proposal or counterproposal.

2. As a buyer, do not criticize the property or give it praise. Be polite in complimenting the owners on their good taste, beautiful view, and other obvious elements of the home just as you might had you been invited to tea that afternoon.

3. As a seller, do not knock yourself out to sell the property. You have a salesperson or broker to do that. If you are called on to give information, do so without adding postscripts: "Yes, but you know . . ." Too much talk by either party kills deals.

4. Do not criticize the agents or brokers representing the deal. You never know whether the agent is the other party's brother- or sister-in-law, mother, or friend. Even if he or she is not, there is no reason to find fault with the people the other party has hired as representatives. Some buyers do this in the belief that they can divide the broker from the seller and therefore achieve some advantage.

5. Explain why you want to buy or sell the property if you can do this without disclosing any secrets or important strategies. "I want to acquire a vacant tract to build an industrial park. I have had this dream for several years now and believe that now is the time for me to act on that goal. My timing is such that I wish to have a property under contract within the next 30 days so that I can lock up my financing, get my building permits, and start construction as soon as possible." How the other party responds to a statement like this can give you some clue if you are dealing with a seller who will be receptive to your offer, or not.

6. Do everything you said you would do on time, or sooner. If you promised the seller that you would have your lawyer call his lawyer by Friday, make sure the call takes

place on Thursday. If you said you would be there at 3:00 PM be there by 2:55 PM at the latest. This sets a theme that you value your time enough to get things done and that you value other people's time so as not to waste it. This is the single factor where many buyers go wrong. When you promise you will deliver an offer by Friday, and Wednesday of the following week rolls around and you have not even bothered to make a phone call to explain the reason for the delay, you are jeopardizing the future of these negotiations. This is true even if there is a very good reason for the delay. Many institutional buyers are the worst violators of this simple rule. Remember that by doing what you say, when you promised it, you are establishing a good example for more important things later on such as "Sure, I'll pay off the $5 million in two years, no problem."

7. Critical elements to remember:

- Avoid using the other party's phone or taking calls that are about other business while in the presence of the other party. If you are at a place of business or home of the other party or his lawyer, and you must use the phone for some other business, wait until you have concluded your business with that party.
- Do not say, "We are tired of dealing with people who waste our time. I want you to know we aren't like that," or any other statement that only your actions can prove.
- Do not praise yourself. However, feel free to let others mention your past successes or point out your professionalism. All you have to do is be professional.
- Do not lie. If you can't think of any good truth, say nothing. Many people lie and never get caught. However, it is the quickest way to end a negotiation or, at best, discredit everything you have said.

Understand the Essence of Negotiation

Communication becomes a step to understanding any form of negotiation. Like an argument, it is very difficult to have lasting problems if there is no communication. It is the same in negotiations. It is better to have no communication at all than to have no understanding, or bad communication. But, you must get your point across. You do that by demonstration more than by talk. Talk is the murderer of negotiation.

How then do you negotiate? As a buyer of real estate, you do it through an offer to buy, or a letter of intent to buy. In essence, no talk until there is a basic form of contact, which shows your intent. To be effective that intent should be in writing. Actual counter and counter-counter negotiation can take several forms that include writing and personal meetings, but always be the first to put what you say down on paper.

Talk is cheap and memory of what was said often varies between the parties. Only clearly stated terms written down can move the process forward. This occurs after you have concluded many elements of the transaction that less informed people want to "negotiate" their way through. It is easy to overlook the original object of the negotiation, which is from the buyer's point of view to get into a position of control without being 100 percent committed. Sellers who do not understand the need for a buyer to be in this position and who continue to jockey for a similar right (to back out of the deal) will have a very difficult time selling their property. The best a seller should negotiate is to limit the time that the buyer has a "lock" on the deal. That "lock" should be reasonable, under whatever the circumstance of the transaction. A land deal where the buyer wants to build a shopping center may require a long process where the buyer ultimately obtains local approvals, perhaps even a building permit. The sale of a condo may require approvals by the condo board, over which neither the buyer or seller may have any control or influence. Most deals that require new financing for the buyer to be able to close will require a period of 30 to 90 days and perhaps longer for these approvals to be obtained. Because there is always a "hidden cost" in many of these factors, buyers generally want to be able to withdraw if one or more elements of their due diligence prove to be unsatisfactory. What makes them unsatisfactory may be the expense in dealing with the situation.

Confrontation Before Negotiation

The actual negotiation need not occur until there is a confrontation. After all, if you offer $100,000 on a property that the seller has been asking $200,000 for, there is nothing to negotiate if the seller accepts. (Except you won't sleep well wondering if he would have accepted $90,000.) Only when the other party balks at your offer does negotiation begin.

Take into consideration the other form of buying and selling. In bartering, where one person asks (talks), "Would you take $100,000," the rest of the conversation might go like this:

"Are you offering $100,000?"

"No, just wondering if I did, would you take it?"

"If I said yes, would you want to buy it?"

"If you said yes, I'd think about it."

"So why not offer the $100,000 then?"

Nothing is going on here that resembles negotiation, yet each party thinks they are negotiating pretty well.

CARPET MERCHANT STYLE NEGOTIATION.   Some years ago, I was in a rug merchant shop in Tangier, Morocco:

I asked, "Would you sell that for $200?"

"Would you like to own this rug?" was the reply.

"I might if you'd sell it for $200."

"Do you want only one?"

"Yes. One is all I can afford at the moment."

"Will you take it with you, or must I ship it to you?"

"I'll take it with me."

"You have very good taste, sir. And for only $200 you have made a very good buy."

How I love to meet good salesmen like that! Not only is he negotiating pretty darn well, he lets me sell myself by giving me simple decisions to make. Every time I respond positively, the sale has moved closer to a closed transaction.

Know who the enemy is in the game. Both the buyer and the seller are actually on the same side. They both want the same ultimate goal: the sale of the property. The enemy includes following:

SEVENTEEN ENEMIES TO EVERY TRANSACTION

1. Taxes.
2. Death.
3. Government.
4. Rejection.
5. Hate.
6. Fear.
7. Failure.
8. Desire for immortality.
9. Intimidation.
10. Indecision.
11. Emotion.
12. Envy.
13. Inability to understand.
14. Inability to communicate.
15. The phantom.
16. Greener grass.
17. Greed.

Win by Knowing the Other Players' Weaknesses and Goals

To win any game, you must know whom you are playing against, so try to let other game players help you rather than block you. It's like having your star player on the bench right when you need him or her in the game. The only thing you have to remember to do is not let on that you know the others are really on your team; better to let them think you are on theirs.

Winning in negotiation is not a matter of intimidation. Intimidation is one of the enemies to establishing good rapport in any kind of negotiation process. It is poise, diplomacy, charm, courtesy, that keep you on the right track, and it is action and decision that win the game. All participants in the game of negotiation want to feel that they are the winners. Good participants know just how far they can go to get the points they feel are essential and still let the other side walk away satisfied.

It is possible to nail someone's back to the wall when all their chips are down, or to play a dirty game putting them into a position where there are no other participants. I won't judge you nor will I claim there is a special morality in the matter of business or negotiation that you are required to follow. Each player must find the kind of game they want to play. I have known very successful businesspeople who are ruthless and cunning, who had no friends, and who won their business deals by pushing their counterparts to the wall. Some of these "successful" people have hung themselves, filed bankruptcy, or fled to Rio, and they are usually sad cases. Were they successful? Only in their minds.

BUILDING TRUST IS BUILDING A NETWORK FOR SUCCESS

In the real estate field, success tends to be related to fair dealing. Much of what really goes on between the people who will help you occurs without contract, and without obligation, because all of us need people we can trust. So you will spend much of your business life finding out who you cannot trust and therefore cannot deal with. Some of the difficult-to-negotiate-with people are just frightened or unsophisticated men and women who are in trouble and don't know who to turn to for help. These people don't want to appear to be frightened or unsophisticated, so they delay, balk, or just become uncommunicative. You may batter down those kinds of doors, but it can be a very slow and unpredictable process. Sometimes the best negotiator has to throw in the towel and give up. If you do enough deals, there will be some failures. The key to the failures is to size up the deal as soon as possible and not waste time in closing down the negotiations. Just remember to do so without burning bridges in case the roadblock suddenly comes down due to something unexpected that happens.

HOW SWEET IT IS

It is a good idea to remember that the sweetener of success is failure. After all, without failure there would be no pleasure to success. I call this to your attention because in any negotiation you will be under the pressure of "failing" at your intended task. In the case of real estate investment, the task is generally to make the best investment possible to meet or take you closer to your desired goals. To do this requires you to: (1) find properties you would want to own which serve your needs, and (2) make offers and attempt to negotiate the acquisition of those properties. Having said this, it is critical that you understand that all successful real estate investors fail at step 2 some of the time. Failure in this task should not discourage you, nor deter you from moving along to another property. You should fail from time to time in step 2 because, if you don't, you are doing one of two things:

1. YOU ARE BUYING PROPERTY ON TERMS THAT ARE NOT FAVORABLE TO YOUR GOALS. This could be because of your inexperience, or lack of clear understanding of your goals.

2. YOU AREN'T MAKING ENOUGH OFFERS TO BUY PROPERTY. If you pick the property, and stick to terms that you know will help you reach your goal, you will not be able to buy every property you find. Not all sellers will be that cooperative.

Analyzing your failures will help you improve your future negotiations. Never avoid a conflict because you fear you cannot succeed. However, never let a failure go by without it being a learning process.

Chapter 4

HOW LEVERAGE AFFECTS RISK AND THE VALUE OF REAL ESTATE

GOAL OF THIS CHAPTER

This chapter illustrates the mechanics of leverage and shows you how its magic can generate enormous increases of investment yield and property value when used wisely and correctly. Leverage used incorrectly, however, can waste capital, reduce property value, and make investments unprofitable as well as unsalable. This chapter provides you with the tools to maximize the benefits that come from leverage of debt over equity, and shows you how to effectively use an often-misunderstood friend of the real estate investor: inflation.

DEFINITION

Leverage is a measure of the positive or negative benefits of financing that are obtained as a relation to the interest gained (either through income or appreciation) and the interest lost through payment of debt. It comes in two forms: positive leverage and negative leverage.

Positive Leverage

Positive leverage occurs when you borrow money at a lower interest rate than the return you get on the amount of cash that would otherwise be invested in a transaction out of your own pocket. For example, if you are purchasing an office building that has a net operating income (NOI) of $150,000 and the purchase price is $1,500,000, then you will make 10 percent on the investment of $1,500,000 each year. However, if you can borrow

$1,200,000 at 8 percent interest, your cost to carry that $1,200,000 is only $96,000. Yet, you still earn 10 percent on that part of the office building. Your cost of $96,000 reduces your cash flow from $150,000 down to $54,000 but the amount of the mortgage reduces your cash requirements to acquire the property down to $300,000. Your cash flow is now $150,000 less $96,000 or $54,000 and your invested cash is $300,000. Your return is a hefty 18 percent ($300,000 × 18 percent = $54,000). This is one of the magic elements that happen when you borrow at marginally lower (2 percent in this case) interest than what you earn.

What started out to be a good 10 percent yield has turned into a whopping 18 percent bonanza. Not only has this positive leverage increased the cash flow, look what it potentially does to the value of the property. If a new buyer comes along and is satisfied with a 10 percent return on his invested capital, how much would he pay for a property that produces an NOI of $54,000 and can be purchased subject to an existing mortgage of $1,200,000? My calculation is a sum of $540,000. If you did not do anything to the property to increase rents, cut expenses, or anything, you could sell the property, get your $300,000 back, plus another $250,000. See how quick it is.

Negative Leverage

Negative leverage is the other side of the coin and, as you will learn, it has a place in real estate investing, too. Here is how it works: You are not a buyer who, in the previous paragraph, had the opportunity to borrow money for less than he would earn. Your credit score is a bit off the mark. Yet, you have some ready-to-spend cash, and you want to purchase the office building. At $1,500,000, you are satisfied it is a steal. However, the best you can get is a $1,100,000 loan, but it will cost you 11 percent interest. Even with interest only, your annual cost would be $121,000 ($1,100,000 × 11 percent = $121,000 for the year). Your cash out of pocket to meet the required down payment is $400,000. Your original NOI of $150,000 is now reduced down to $29,000. This means that your investment return on the cash investment of $400,000 is reduced to 7.25 percent. Is this terrible? It might be a return that is less than you would want, but wait a moment. You could not borrow any more than the $1,100,000 anyway. Moreover, you did not (or should not have, at any rate) buy this building because of the existing economics, you bought the building because you knew you could increase the rents and do better than a $150,000 NOI. Therefore, as you look at the two examples, one of positive leverage, and one of negative leverage, each had its place. Each technique worked for the investor. Which would you elect? The answer to that question would be positive leverage, but in the second example that was not an option. The option was to buy or not to buy.

Every form of finance has an effect on the return you get on the cash you invest. When more than one form of debt is used simultaneously, as would be the situation with a combination of mortgages, it is possible that there will be both positive and negative leverage in the mix. The overall cost of debt will determine if there is positive or negative leverage present. In the second example, where we saw negative leverage, you would benefit from the acquisition more than from the increase of yield (which actually went down). If you were right, and in a relatively short period were able to increase rents and increase the NOI of the property, say to $170,000 before debt service, the cash flow would now be $49,000 ($170,000−$121,000 which is the 11 percent interest on $1,100,000). This is a 12.25 percent return on your $400,000 invested. This is now a positive leverage situation as the 11 percent interest would be less than the new return.

Leverage then is the effect of financing on any investment. When used properly it can increase the yield on cash invested. It is an important factor in real estate financing. With it you can reduce investment risk, adjust a transaction to better fit your goals, and ultimately change the value of the property. This chapter shows you how these three elements can dramatically be altered by the structure of the financing of a transaction.

ROLE OF RISK IN LEVERAGE

Risk is present in any and/or all investments. Most certainly, any real estate deal can fail to achieve its projected end result. This does not mean that the transaction fails completely or at all. Failure to achieve goals can mean the goals were overly optimistic. Falling short on a timetable can be a fault of the business plan, and not the goal. Most real estate investments are inherently risky because of the investor's inability to properly assess the needs of the investment. Management of the investment is one of the major factors that can determine if the investment will be a success or not. The lack of good management skills often appears when an investor acquires a property and is thrown into on-the-job-training.

The sudden requirement to deal with tenants, lease difficult-to-rent property, fight with the city over rising taxes, and so on can require skills that most investors do not instantly have. Therefore, risk is present for many reasons, and different financing techniques may not have a direct solution. Yet, anything that can soften the drain on cash will buffer the loss of capital and can buy time for the investor to graduate from that on-the-job-training university.

Within the scope of financing, the level of risk is important to at least two parties in the transaction: the buyer and the lender, and often the seller as well. The buyer looks at the level of risk to define in what jeopardy he or she has placed the invested capital. The buyer would view a purchase with only 10 percent down as highly leveraged. The lender looks at the level of risk in a repayment of the loan. In this situation, a 90 percent loan is seen as a highly leveraged transaction and therefore a more risky loan than if the borrower has more equity in the deal. Sellers can have a stake in the success of a venture, too. You will see later on in this chapter that the difference of point of view between these parties can shift between what might be highly leveraged for the buyer and not be highly leveraged for the primary lender.

Relativity of Risk

Lenders associate risk differently than the owner of the property would. For example, the most important element of security to a lender is the combination of value plus owner strength. Lenders disagree on which of these two factors is the most important. Some lenders look to the loan-to-value ratio as a primary criteria to making a loan. For example, if the value of a property is a conservative $100,000 and the lender's loan-to-value comfort level is 80 percent, then the lender may look harder at the borrower. Larger loan amounts usually cause the lenders to look more to the owner's strength, and may require additional security or collateral.

Review the following examples.

EXAMPLE 1.   Winkle wants to purchase a small apartment building that contains five apartments. The value that would be accepted by a lender is $400,000. Winkle has an agreement to purchase at a price of only $380,000, provided he pay the seller $320,000 in cash of which only $20,000 comes from his pocket, Winkle expects to get a first mortgage of $300,000 plus give the seller a second mortgage for the balance of $80,000.

EXAMPLE 2.   Jones wants to purchase an office building that any lender would value at $1 million. His purchase agreement requires him to pay $800,000 in cash, and the seller will hold additional financing for the balance ($200,000).

Can you tell what the level of risk is for the buyer, seller, or lender in either example?

EXAMPLE 1: REVIEW.   If the seller were to hold an $80,000 second mortgage on the five apartments Winkle is buying, it is very doubtful that any lender would loan him the $300,000. Why? Because the total price is made up of a first mortgage and a seller-held second mortgage, which is a total combination of financing that equals 100 percent loan-to-value ratio. Not impossible, mind you, but the lenders (both the first and second mortgage lenders) would be looking to the strength of the buyer as the primary security to the deal.

If this was your first real estate transaction, and unless you could meet the obligations the lender might impose on you, this transaction might slip past you. After all, from the lender's point of view, the prospect of a 100 percent loan to value has increased the lender's risk for repayment considerably. The seller is in a secondary position and has the majority of the risk, but even the first mortgage holder would feel uneasy.

Risk for the buyer is another thing altogether. Unless there is a requirement of personal obligation on the loan, the actual risk to Winkle is limited to his time and effort to put the deal together and keep it together as he meets the obligations of the mortgage. If he is confident in that ability and has a sound plan for the property, which will allow him to increase rents, thereby increasing value, that risk may fade away to little or none.

If the seller recognized that he or she would be in a risky position with the $80,000 second mortgage, Winkle may have to sweeten the deal. One creative approach, and this book will give you many, would be for Winkle to increase the security to the seller by giving him an $80,000 first mortgage on another property. As long as the property was worth more than $80,000, the seller would have improved his position.

In doing this, the first mortgage lender's position has improved dramatically. Now a loan-to-value ratio of 75 percent ($300,000 loan, $400,000 value—but remember Winkle's contract is for $380,000) will allow the lender to make the loan of $300,000. Carry this one step more, Winkle can ask for a new first mortgage of $320,000, which is a loan-to-value ratio of only 80 percent. At this point, what has happened is Winkle's deal is now 100 percent financed. He has a good first mortgage of $320,000 which goes to the seller, the seller holds the balance of $80,000 on another property Winkle owns, and Winkle can put $20,000 in his pocket, or spend it to upgrade the property. A truly nothing-down deal where everyone wins.

EXAMPLE 2: REVIEW.   Jones has the similar opportunity to obtain 100 percent financing. All he has to do is to get the seller to shift the secondary financing to something else, or to take an exchange in lieu of the added payback in the form of a mortgage. If the seller were to accept other real estate worth $200,000, then Jones has invested the real equity into the property and the only debt he would have to pay back would be the $800,000. While Jones did not pay the $200,000 out of pocket, the new first mortgage lender would treat this as cash invested and would look at the new $800,000 loan as a loan-to-value ratio of 80 percent. If this loan-to-value risk was acceptable to the lender, then the loan would be obtainable. For Jones, this deal has more risk than Winkle's example. Winkle did not invest any cash. His sole investment was the promise to pay back, putting the property he purchased, and perhaps his own personal signature, on the line.

Each of these examples shows varying levels of leverage in action. If Winkle was able to get a lender to make loan without the need for personal signatures, then Winkle's actual risk would be limited—high leverage without great financial risk. Jones' deal equally could end up high leverage, but if he gave the seller another property (worth $200,000), then his deal is zero cash, with moderate leverage.

Introduce Leverage into the Equation

As simple as leverage is, it is still one of the most misunderstood factors of real estate financing. I am convinced that the confusion many investors have about leverage comes because investors often relate high loan-to-value ratios to high risk—that the greater you have of one, the greater you have of the other. But as with Winkle's example, this is not always the case. In fact, once you realize just how leverage works, you will see that if this financing tool has been used to its maximum benefit, the greater the leverage the lower the risk.

The concept of highly leveraged properties as being risky will continue to be seen as investments to avoid. When you run into this kind of viewpoint, you will know that you are dealing with someone who operates under the myth rather than the reality of this factor of financing.

Desirable leverage results from borrowing money at a constant rate lower than the net operating income rate generated by the property. If the property is not income producing but is going up in value at an establishable rate, then the benefit or disadvantage of leverage can be applied. In general, however, leverage works best when lenders can see income from the property as a source to repay the loan. For example, suppose you buy a small shopping center. The store price is $400,000 and because it is owned free and clear (free of any debt), the seller wants all cash. The net operating income is $44,000 each year; you would have a return on your investment, prior to income tax computations, of 11 percent of your cash invested. Any debt you can obtain to help you reach the needed $400,000 cash to close the transaction, which could be borrowed at a cost to you of less than 11 percent, will generate a positive leverage situation for you. Clearly, if you borrowed $380,000 at 10 percent constant rate (principal plus interest), your cash flow would be $6,000 for the year on your investment of only $20,000. Your return, therefore, jumps from 11 percent to 30 percent. More important, which will become more evident as you progress through this book, you will have discovered the magic of using other people's money (OPM)—in this case, the lender's funds—and the debt will eventually get paid off, not by you, but by your tenants.

EXAMPLE 3.   You purchased a modest shopping center: Price paid: $1,000,000. Cash return before taxes: $110,000. Return on your invested cash: 11 percent per annum.

Because there is no mortgage in this deal, there is no financing effect (either beneficial or otherwise). Without financing, nothing is leveraged. Leverage only occurs when there is borrowed money.

If you purchase this same property using one or more of the financing tools available to you, there would have been one of three possible results from leverage: positive leverage, negative leverage, or no yield leverage at all. However, for every dollar of financing, you decrease one dollar of your cash invested. So, you are increasing your ability to acquire property—either more expensive properties than you may otherwise be able to afford or more properties by reducing the needed capital expenditure for any individual transaction. An investor with a total of $1,000,000 to spend can purchase one property for $1,000,000 or five such properties by putting $200,000 down on each and financing the balance.

Assume that you put $200,000 down on this strip store, and obtain a total of $800,000 in financing. This financing might be in one new mortgage obtained from the First Forever Savings Bank, or a combination of mortgages you finesse out of the transaction. The transaction might have one mortgage that is held by the seller in the amount of $800,000. The terms of this mortgage are one annual payment per year of $82,240 until the mortgage is paid off. This payment of $82,240 per year now represents a constant annual payment of 10.28 percent per annum. (Remember, the constant payment takes into consideration both principal and interest, and the rate is an initial percentage, which reflects the payment in relation to the original amount of the principal owed.)

Since the total purchase price is $1,000,000 and the net operating income is $110,000, if you now have a mortgage payment of $82,240, there will be a sum of $27,760 left over after all expenses and debt payments.

The leverage factor is viewed as follows: In this case, we have a debt of $800,000 that has a constant payment of 10.28 percent, or $82,240 per year. The net operating income is $110,000 when based on free and clear property; this would give a return on the all-cash investment of 11 percent of the purchase price. When financing is introduced into the investment, there is a change in the interest yield of the cash invested.

In the financed deal, you paid $200,000 down (assume that came from your savings), and had a cash flow (gross income less all expenses and all debt service payments) of $27,760. You have a cash yield on cash invested of 13.88 percent. You have also obtained the benefit of borrowed money in the amount of $800,000 to make the purchase. So, in this deal you have leveraged on your cash and have also created positive leverage by increasing your yield. This increase has come solely from the effect of the financing applied. It is possible that you may have created even greater increase in yield through the use of other financing techniques. There are many different kinds of financing that you could apply in a situation such as this previous one.

However, as attractive as high leverage is, the maximum effect may not be to create the highest possible leverage. You will soon see that overleverage as the result of borrowing so much that your margin of cash flow needed to meet your debt service is so thin that one or two vacancies in your rent roll can create negative cash flow. Worse still would be that negative leverage, which may seem acceptable because you have high hopes of increasing revenue to the point where you can overcome a lower than desirable cash flow (or even a negative cash flow), can accelerate your losses in this investment with a very small reduction of rental income. What you want to do is use the highest leverage that allows you to meet your goals, while at the same time keeping the financial obligation of the investment within your control. Investments that are very highly leveraged may reduce the investor's risk because there is a smaller percentage of investment to risk. But if there is negative leverage present, the available cash flow may erode away if the business plan to increase rent and decrease vacancy does not work out.

In the balance of this chapter, I delve into leverage to show you how to put it to work. I also cover the elements of overleverage. As in all aspects of anything good, there are pitfalls that must be discussed, such as overextension.

EFFECT OF CONSTANT RATE ON CASH FLOW

The effect of leverage is always examined with its relationship to the constant rate of the mortgages and the constant cash flow rate of the net operating income. As has been mentioned, the combined principal and interest payments of the total mortgages make up the *constant rate*. This constant rate is fixed at the time of the mortgage for that investor.

For example, if you bought a rental home and had one loan for 30 years, with an interest rate of 8.47 percent per annum and the principal balance of the mortgage at the closing of the purchase was $175,000, your annual payment would be $16,000, with a monthly payment each month for 30 years of $1,333.33. The constant rate would be found by dividing the total annual payment by the amount of principal owned ($16,000 ÷ $175,000 = 0.0914). To show this as an interest rate, move the decimal two places to the right to get 9.14 percent.

Learn the Effect of Constant Rate Financing

The constant rate is important as a way to gauge the overall effect of financing. Since interest rates only tell you the economic cost of the money you have borrowed, they cannot be the final criteria in the overall cash payment. As the constant rate contains both interest and principal payback, its rate is an effective guide to determine your final cash-flow circumstances.

The constant rate is a function of time and interest, and, as one changes, the constant rate changes. As shown in Table 4.1, a $100,000 loan has a combination of constant rates, depending on the functions of time and interest.

You quickly notice that while the lowest interest rate is 8 percent, due to the short payout of four years, it has the highest constant payment and therefore the highest constant payment rate.

When refinancing older properties, it is common to discover mortgages that can be assumed at rates well below the current market conditions. These mortgages may be attractive to assume on first glance at their interest rate. Yet, when you discover the actual cost, the sacrifice to get the attractive interest rate may not be worth the loss of cash flow due to the excessive constant rate.

Table 4.1
Examples of Constant Rates for a $100,000 Loan

Interest (%)	Years	Monthly Payment ($)	Annual Constant Rate (%)
10	25	901.13	10.814
11	30	943.65	11.324
9	10	1,256.93	15.083
8	4	2,423.76	29.086

Your review of the options available to you, and the creative way in which you reduce the overall constant rate, can mean additional cash flow to you and increased value in the property. Each of these two elements satisfies financing goals covered in Chapter 1 of this book.

Value and Risk in Leverage: The Bottom Line Can Be the Most Important Criteria to Determine Both Value and Risk

Income-producing real estate properties generally are valued by the cash flow they produce. A buyer will pay a price based on the yield he or she gets from the cash invested. If the risk demand for the investment for this investor is 10 percent, the maximum amount of money the investor may be willing to spend would be the amount that would then earn that desired rate.

While the amount of cash flow is not always the most important economic criteria for an investor, it is generally the safest guide to market value for income-producing properties. Some investors want fast debt reduction and sacrifice cash flow for some other benefit because it fits their business plan. Low or even zero cash flow would be the case of an investment in vacant non–income producing or low-income property. Because there is little or no income to be leveraged into a higher yield, the relative yield must be based on the potential increase in value when the property is either sold or developed. In the meantime, debt and holding costs must be met by reaching into your own pocket. If the property were to be developed within a year or so, short-term financing costs may be absorbed into the transaction even though it might have an excessive constant rate in comparison to the actual market conditions of financing.

You purchase a lot on which you plan to build a fast-food restaurant for a national company. It has signed a triple net lease (where the tenant generally pays all expenses including real estate taxes, insurance, and maintenance). The period of time you pay the debt and carrying cost out of your own pocket or finance them into a final development loan should be considered as part of the gross investment. Any tax advantage you may obtain by deduction of interest and so on may lessen that financial drain. In this kind of situation, a very high negative leverage would result, but would not be detrimental to the deal if you have the financial staying power. The end result (the goal is to build a fast-food restaurant) should have a positive leverage once rents begin to come in. If the leverage still shows as negative (in comparison to a free and clear ownership), then you need to rework the plan, or reassess your goals.

KEY FACTORS IN REAL ESTATE LEVERAGE

Structure of Financing Affects the Amount of Leverage You Receive

A short payout of a mortgage may have a very high constant rate and may eliminate the cash flow. However, an interest-only mortgage will reduce the constant rate to a lower level for the early term of the loan, even though it may create havoc in the cash flow of later years.

The goals of the investor form the basis of the way to establish the leverage best suited for the transaction if the investor has the option available to alter the financing at all.

Leverage Calculations Are Merely a Comparison of the Yield Changes

The actual amount of yield that is increased or decreased is not the specific criteria for the use of the financing tool. However, it is helpful to see how the leverages can be increased or decreased, and know what element is affecting the outcome. Some of the discount transactions you will have available to you will enable you to increase the amount of the loan at zero or very low constant rate. This kind of financing can enable you to average out very low rates.

Maximum Leverage May Not Be Possible in All Situations

Maximum leverage may not be the most advisable option either. The options available to the buyer or to the seller in the actual structure of the deal are limited by the circumstances and the goals of both parties. In the give-and-take of the negotiations, each party may give in to some demand of the other party. In addition to these demands, the lender may require some changes in the overall deal. It is generally the buyer who is the lender's target, and buyer's flexibility is increased tremendously when the lender is the seller.

In the trade-off between obtaining the maximum benefits of price and terms, the buyer should consider the following elements.

APPRECIATION.   Appreciation is the increase in the value of a property over a period of time. The methods used in financing an acquisition can have a sudden and dramatic effect on appreciation. We have seen this where an increase in cash flow yield obtained solely through use of a financing technique has jumped the amount a buyer would reasonably pay for a property. So financing has more than a passive effect on appreciation, and this effect is very real. Because income properties are valued as per their income based on the desired yield, a mortgage or set of financing tools that reduces or eliminates the increase of income, the appreciation of this property would be slowed or eliminated. Some financing tools can maximize the immediate cash flow and hold back future increases of value. If the immediate cash flow was the most important aspect of the purchase, that loss would not be a sacrifice at all.

For some investors, appreciation is the most important aspect, and whole estates are planned on the ultimate growth of a portfolio.

EQUITY BUILDUP.   This is the slow-and-steady payoff of the principal owed on the debt against the property. An interest-only mortgage would have no principal payback and would therefore have no equity buildup at all. Other mortgages that have a negative payment, which is one where the monthly payment is not sufficient to pay the interest due, so unpaid interest is added to the principal owed, actually reduce equity by building on to the amount owed. This kind of financing is good only where the need for cash and the assumed appreciation of the property support taking out the future equity now through greater cash flow.

CASH FLOW.   This usually is the desired goal for many investors. However, when the existing financing is at a low interest rate, despite the high constant rate of a short-term payback, the sacrifice might well be the cash flow to obtain greater yields later on by increasing the equity buildup for the early years.

TAX CREDITS.   Some investors want greater tax credits and lower immediate cash flow. These investors would want to see financing tools that would provide for maximum tax credits at a sacrifice of cash flow. Some of the tools that increase cash flow have the effect of reducing tax credits. This is all part of the balance between these four elements.

USE OF FUNDS AVAILABLE.   The maximum use of your investment funds may demand that you get the highest mortgage you can and invest the least cash possible. This frequently is done with the idea that eventual income levels can be increased. This causes investors to go in on a shoestring. Great fortunes can be made this way . . . and lost.

Nonetheless, if you know your comfort zone and have strong and visible goals, you will find that the risk you would have on such an investment may be well below that of the typical investor in the marketplace.

Amount of Leverage Generated Is Not the Final Criteria

Remember, while you can make a marginal deal acceptable, you may not be able to turn a bad deal into a good deal. Overworking a transaction generally means you are looking for some rationalization to enable you to make the investment. While it may be okay for you to make the investment, do not kid yourself that something that looks good on paper (using figures you have forced) is a good deal after all. This points out the importance of having good facts on which to base your final decision. In all my 35-plus years as a commercial real estate broker, I stress to buyers that the only economic figures of a transaction that they can rely on will be the ones they arrive at through effective due diligence and the application of their own experience. This is not because sellers lie about the data, although many do, but the simple fact that the present owner may be running the property (or business) to a different drummer than you would.

Investment Leverage Available to Real Estate Investors Is Maximum

There are few investments available where the investor is able to establish a long-term payback at a moderate cost (interest charged). This is due to the ease and acceptability of real estate as a collateral for mortgage financing. However, we often take this for granted without realizing that in many areas of the world, long-term loans on real estate are unheard of. In some countries, the land and real estate is state-owned. In other countries, much of the land is "leasehold" and all users are tenants on land owned by the Crown, state, or old families who have handed down townships over generations. In other parts of the world, land and other real estate may be private ownership but have no value as a security on a mortgage due to the lack of confidence the banks would have in "taking that land" as a security.

Real estate in the United States normally is considered as the single most secure form of security for a loan. For this and other reasons, institutional lenders have no hesitation making a loan based on some reliable estimate of value. This fact has given rise to a strong secondary market for real estate loans. Of all the secondary loan markets, the best for the buyer, and often the most motivated to make the loan, is the seller.

This often easy-to-obtain debt is relative to the marketplace, and often that market becomes distorted. We have seen this happen a number of times in recent banking history. What occurs is a flushed banking system that has access to more cash than they know what to do with. This cash accumulates in banks because the owners of that cash cannot find "safe" investments as alternative parking places for the money. The banks, anxious to put the cash to work, lend it wherever they can. This tends to be real estate and credit card debt. The real estate loans, often sub-prime, are combined into bundles of investment packages that are sold to insurance companies, mortgage companies, and so on. The original bank may continue to service the loans or may sell those rights to service companies.

Somewhere along the way, greed enters this scenario and mortgages are offered to borrowers who are not truly qualified to repay those loans, certainly the case when adjustable rate mortgage terms suddenly are adjusted and the repayment amount increases substantially. This most recently describes the financial condition that befell the lending market in 2004/2008. Subprime loans became a household term and foreclosures rocketed the market from coast to coast. This condition was not limited to the United States, and much of the real estate industry worldwide experienced to one degree or the other the effect of real estate following a trend of what goes up must also eventually go down.

Leverage Is a Function of Financing and Can Be Seen as a Gauge of How One Investment Strategy Compares with Another

Understanding financing means understanding the overall picture of what happens when mortgages are paid down and equity is built up. As the term suggests, leverage is a fulcrum where the weight of the loan offsets the absence of weight of the investment capital. Many multimillionaires are defined as people who owe millions of dollars.

Pitfall of Leverage: Overextension

Overextension occurs when the cost of the debt exceeds the abilities of the borrower. This event can occur with the most conservative approach to a mortgage on one property when the borrower has gotten in over his or her head on another property. In fact, this seems to be true for many foreclosures.

In the case of income properties, the proper approach to financing is to try not to overexpose the ability of that property. Naturally, there are times when you are looking for increases in rents to support the added debt to the property, and sometimes those increased rents just do not occur.

While there is no single test for you to use to keep from going in deeper than you can swim, there are some guidelines you can follow that would help you stay out of overextension:

SEVEN GUIDES TO AVOID OVEREXTENSION

1. Make sure you are investing within your comfort zone. This means a comfort zone you have been working and know like the back of your hand. The fastest way to become overextended is to buy something out of your comfort-zone area.

2. Be very sure the investment will move you closer to your goals. That means do not fool yourself. Does the purchase of that property bring you closer to your goals? Can you write down why?

3. Is it within your physical abilities? Do not take on anything that you cannot handle just because it looks good. Many people are drawn to things they like, without any understanding of how to make it work.

4. Have you "worked" the purchase negotiations? This means: Have you been a part of the transaction, or was it brought to you? If you have worked it or have been involved with the transaction for a while, it is likely you will have a better understanding for items 1, 2, and 3.

5. Can you carry the property for the estimated time plus an additional 50 percent of the estimated time needed to generate the income it would take to support the property 100 percent? In short, a low down payment and tons of leverage will not help if you promptly go bankrupt because it took nine months to get the tenants you anticipated you would have in six months.

6. Are you jeopardizing everything for this one deal? If so, you had better make sure you are all set on items 1, 2, 3, 4, and 5.

7. If things go astray, be sure you do not hold onto the sinking ship for too long. Too many investors fail because they tried to save something they were incapable of saving. If they had simply stepped out of the deal at the time they knew the ship was actually going to sink, they would have been a lot wiser.

Final Element: How Leverage Affects the Increase of Value in Real Estate

There are eight reasons property values go up. Often more than one of the eight factors is working at the same time, some to a positive way, others negative. Each of the following eight factors can be enhanced or detracted from by the total effect of financing. First look at the eight factors that cause real estate values to increase:

1. Inflation.
2. Improved infrastructure.
3. Government control and regulation changes.
4. Neighborhood sizzle.
5. Economic conversion.
6. Increased bottom line.
7. Capital improvements.
8. Supply and demand.

We review each of these factors in detail next.

INFLATION.   Inflation increases the monetary value of a property by the effect of two different, but related events. The first is the general decline of the buying power of money, also referred to as the effect of the increase in the cost of living. The increased cost of living is a widely studied economic circumstance that is the result of many different things. The end result is that the same item that cost $10 a few years ago may now cost $30. The cause of inflation is the trend for more complicated and sophisticated apparatus to be a part of our lives. The equipment we take for granted such as Boeing 747s, mainframe computers, widescreen television sets, ultra-sophisticated life-saving equipment, and so on—all are far more expensive than what our grandfathers were used to. We actually develop a need for things that cost more because they do more. This is the price we pay for having a high standard of living.

Income property has the potential of offsetting the effect of inflation. This single factor can make a real estate investment worthwhile even if there is no immediate cash flow return. The investor's opportunity to enhance this potential even more, through positive leverage or other beneficial financing techniques, can turn a modest investment into a real winner. The following is an example of how inflation and financing techniques affect the value of an investment.

EXAMPLE 4: HOW INFLATION AND LEVERAGE CREATE VALUE.   Frank York has owned a 20-unit apartment building for the past 25 years. The original purchase price was $200,000. He was able to obtain new financing when he purchased the building in the amount of $160,000 and invested a total of $40,000 in the down payment. The mortgage payments over those 25 years consisted of approximately $14,000 per year, payable in monthly installments of $1,166.67. Over the term of the loan (25 years), he has paid $370,480 in total payments, around $210,480 of which was interest, and the balance was principal.

The first year of his ownership Frank pocketed around $6,000 in cash flow after making all payments for operations and debt. This was a 15 percent annual return on his $40,000 investment. Actual return would be found by the formula: $6,000 (return) divided by $40,000 (investment) equals 15 percent (yield).

Over the years, the monthly rents outpaced the cost of living and what began as $150 per month is currently $550 per month. Gross rents increased from $36,000 per year to $132,000. The annual operational expenses also rose, keeping pace with the cost of living, averaging 40 to 45 percent of gross revenue. Current net operating income is $72,600.

If Frank had purchased this property using 100 percent cash, his return would have been 10 percent of his investment from day one. If the increase in income and the increase in expenses had just kept pace with the rise in the value of the building, at any given point of time the property would have been giving Frank a return of only 10 percent, and not the 15 percent bonus he actually had.

Because Frank had borrowed $160,000 to purchase the property, he benefited in two ways over an all-cash buyer. First, he was able to buy a property he might not have been able to afford otherwise. Second, he let his tenants pay off the $160,000 so that at the end of the twenty-fifth year he now has a property that is worth over $700,000. His investment never changed. The yield on that $40,000 grew each year until presently with a $72,000 net operating income and zero mortgage payments, the yield on cash invested (with no other things taken into account) is 180 percent. Now that's how to make money.

The effects of the cost of living for Frank were buffered by this steadily increasing spendable cash flow. As has been my experience in similar investments, the rental income increase from $150 per month to $550 per month could easily more than counterbalance other costs, say Frank's health insurance, or real estate tax on his home, or his monthly electric bill at his own home. As this is the way it works, for Frank, his electric bill for his home has actually not gone up over the past 25 years because one apartment's rent covered it. For Frank and other income property owners, this is a considerable benefit. As all benefits contribute to value, this is one of the best sources of wealth you will ever find, and it occurs because of the very enemy we tend to fear. That enemy we feared is inflation.

In this instant, inflation is the real estate investor's ally. Coupled with a fixed-rate mortgage, the largest single expense Frank has to pay each year is his mortgage payment. As we have seen, that payment is actually made by his tenants through Frank's monthly deduction of the payment he sends to the lender. However, the rent paid by the tenants has increased over the period of his ownership of this property. Yet the mortgage payment remained the same and never increased.

This ability to borrow money with a long-term payback at a set and never-changing annual cost is part of the magic of having leverage and inflation work for you. You will see this wondrous thing at work throughout this book. Learn to use it wisely.

IMPROVED INFRASTRUCTURE. Changes in the infrastructure within a community can produce a very predictable effect on the value of real property. Not all of these effects are beneficial.

Community infrastructure is a combination of many different things. New roads, bridges, new hospitals, water systems, schools, and so on, all contribute to the infrastructure within a city or area. Some of these elements are publicly built and financed, others are privately owned and financed. Each can have an immediate impact on the value of a property. Each can present an investment opportunity by pointing to a time and place to buy, or signal an urgent need to sell.

Positive impacts of improved infrastructure are relatively easy to anticipate, when you look at a long time period. Immediate or short-term benefits may not materialize, however, and some values may go down, only to recover dramatically later on. This dive-and-recovery of property values is an important factor, and many savvy investors look for these situations.

For example, a new bridge is planned to replace an old one. The approach roads from both sides will be widened. The reasons for the new bridge and widened road system are to meet the growing traffic demands for the next 20 years or more. The logical long-term benefits would include increased values of some of the property on both sides of the bridge. However, not all property is likely to go up in value, and some may actually go down in value, with no short-term recovery possible. Other property will drop in value for a short time, then recover nicely.

Consider a potential of 18 months of construction time. During that period, there is likely to be a considerable amount of roadwork, noise, detours, dust, and so on. This often causes major disruption in the existing commercial properties along or near the work area. Even prior to the construction actually beginning, a year or two of preliminary work may have occurred. This may include the taking of additional road right-of-way, and condemnation of properties for new approach ramps and other needed land areas to support the new bridge. Tenants may have run for the hills in search of new sites for their businesses. Few companies and businesses can weather this kind of storm. And what about the property owners who own the commercial properties? Don't they have mortgage payments to make?

The argument that all they need to do is hang in and wait out the construction until the values go up may not be good enough for every property owner. These properties might be ripe picking for the investor who has a new use for the property to take advantage of the soon-to-be-increased traffic flow.

New roads may cut off entire sections of the previous subdivision. This might cause one part of the area to suddenly be the prime spot, whereas the other part may now be hard to get to, or suddenly on the wrong side of the tracks, and it may go down in value.

As a seller, you want to be very alert to any changes that are going on that have any effect on property you own, no matter how small the effect might appear to be. Very small changes from the previous status quo may be the start of a trend of changes. As a buyer, being alert to these same potential changes on a broader scale will lead you into investment potential.

Virtually every change in infrastructure requires a long lead time. Government projects might be in planning for years; city and other local development follows long-range planning and often the need to have special public ballots prior to funding. The majority of people are not aware of even very major construction or other changes to their city or neighborhood until the work actually begins. Apathy about what is going on in your backyard will cost you dearly, and you will miss many opportunities to sell before the crash, or buy before the jump in values.

Your approach to either situation may require some fancy footwork and creative financing strategies. As a seller, the key is time. Get the property sold prior to the bottom dropping out. As a buyer, make sure you take into account that there may be a delay in the rise of values.

GOVERNMENT CONTROL AND REGULATION CHANGES.   When there are positive factors taking place in government control or regulation changes, the real estate community can see sudden increases in value. The kind of controls or changes I am referring to are those that improve communities, cause urban renewal, and enhance the ability to benefit from capital that flows into an area that is investor friendly and seeks to improve the lifestyle of a community. These controls or changes can, when properly applied, create job opportunities to entire states through an aggressive economic growth department. Real estate investors should always look to the temperament of local government to ascertain if it is friendly toward new investment or anti-growth. But remember, all it takes is one election process to change local government from one mode to another.

NEIGHBORHOOD SIZZLE.   Most communities have one or more areas that sizzle. Real estate values are higher there, and the neighborhoods seem to sparkle. This occurs because of a number of elements that have taken place at the same time, such as crime watch, sidewalks, pride in landscape, pride in maintenance of homes and buildings in the area, and a willingness of the people in the community to commit to improvement of their own property.

ECONOMIC CONVERSION.   Economic conversion occurs when there is a change in the use of a property. If you cause the change to take place, then this is voluntary economic conversion. For example, you buy an old home that is in an area where the zoning permits professional offices (or you get the zoning changed). Your economic conversion would happen when you convert the old home into offices. If the change is involuntary, as might occur with a government action, such as rezoning, or the taking of part of the land (to widen a road or other use), then the present use must be changed.

Voluntary economic conversion is the best immediate real estate investment strategy available to investors. It is immediate because you generally don't do it until you are ready to act. This is the opposite of buying vacant land to sit on for the next 10 years. Because it is immediate, every decision you need to make can be based on facts as they actually will affect what you want to do. Rental market studies, construction costs and zoning rules and regulations, for example, will apply today to what you are doing. Planning to do the same thing some time in the future can be met with a future of changes that may prevent you from following your desired plan.

Mostly economic conversion is creating something new from something old. This has certain appeal because the key word "new" seems to bring with it added value. This concept spills over into the financing aspects of the property or venture. Because you are approaching a property with change in mind, the prefinancing package or loan presentation will need to demonstrate the soundness of the plan. This is where your homework will pay off handsomely.

INCREASED BOTTOM LINE.   The value of every income-producing property is greatly affected by small changes in certain aspects of the property. The increase in the bottom line, or cash flow of any property, either before or after taxes, is one of the important criteria to the investment. Your specific goal may not depend or even require an increased cash flow. Yet, because cash flow sets the cash on cash yield (the return on your actual cash invested in the deal), anything that increases the cash flow will generally increase the value of the property.

STEPS NECESSARY TO INCREASE CASH FLOW.   You can increase cash flow by doing any of the following. The steps shown may be combined or acted on individually. It is possible that the result will be immediate with some, and slower in coming with others. To accomplish some of these, such as increasing rent, you may have to spend money on improvements and maintenance to upgrade the property. Each of the following four items may be within your control:

1. Increase collected revenue.
2. Reduce operating expenses.
3. Reduce fixed expenses.
4. Reduce cash invested.

INCREASE COLLECTED REVENUE

- INCREASE MONTHLY RENT. If you study your competition closely, you may discover that your rents are lagging behind. Stay up with the market whenever possible.

- INCREASE OCCUPANCY. Be aggressive in looking for good tenants, even when you do not have a vacancy. You may help a would-be tenant plan for a scheduled vacancy you will have coming up in the near future.

- INTRODUCE ADDED INCOME. With residential income properties, you can introduce add-on rents for services or benefits, a supplement for pets, kids, extra cars, cable TV, and so on. Social functions can prove to be profitable, too. In commercial properties, these extra services might include security alarms and service, janitorial, executive services, and the like.

- ENFORCE RENT PENALTIES. Many landlords overlook or forgive the penalties that are built into the leases. When tenants are late or damage a property, they should be held accountable. Failure to collect can come back and punch you in the nose by encouraging people to get away with violations.

REDUCE OPERATING EXPENSES

- GET COMPETITIVE PRICES. If you have a lot of services, then get competitive prices from different providers.

- CHARGE THE TENANTS FOR SOME OF THE "FREE" SERVICES. If you do not have a common area maintenance (CAM), then add it. It is always quoted extra from rent and may vary according to the actual common area expenses.

- PRACTICE PREVENTATIVE MAINTENANCE. Major repairs and replacements may be cut down dramatically by having better preventative maintenance. Good planning generally is the key to getting more out of your appliances, roof, air-conditioning equipment, and so on.

REDUCE FIXED EXPENSES

- REDUCE ANNUAL REAL ESTATE TAXES. Appeal to the taxing authority and request a reduction in the tax assessment. There are companies you can hire who will charge you only a percentage of what you save.

- REDUCE YOUR DEBT SERVICE. This may be nothing more than refinancing to a lower interest rate, or if your existing loan is two-thirds into its term of years, then a new longer-term loan may reduce your monthly payments even if the interest rate is higher than the existing one. Remember, it is the constant rate that you need to look at.

REDUCE CASH INVESTED

- TAKE OUT CASH. The key word here is tax-free cash. If you can refinance the property, you may find that by increasing the debt you can pull out some of your investment. If nothing else changes, if you cut your previously invested cash in half, you will have doubled your cash yield.

• BRING IN A PARTNER. The partner may not get the same split for his or her half of the cash as you do.

• SELL OFF PART. This technique is often overlooked. You might find that a sale and leaseback of part or all of the property can free up capital, get your investment back, and still give you cash on top of that. If you do not need part of the property at all, then sell it, or find a way to get income from it.

CAPITAL IMPROVEMENTS.   While not all capital improvements increase in value overnight, you will find that any capital improvement that allows you to accomplish one of the previously mentioned items will increase value. Capital improvements that are nothing more than catch-up of poor maintenance may not have any immediate benefit to value.

A sound investment plan will include a schedule of capital improvements that are designed to enhance and upgrade a property. One of the most productive forms of improvement to a property is decorative landscaping. Because landscaping will vary in price depending on the age and size of the plants when they are purchased, the sooner the plan gets under way, the less expensive the ultimate five-year goal can be. One word of warning about landscaping: Get professional help in the plant selection, time of the year to plant, and overall design. Good landscapers are worth their fees.

When you purchase any real estate, the future capital improvements you anticipate might be included in the initial financing package. Instead of putting off improvements that will increase revenue, get the money up-front and get the work done sooner, rather than later. To accomplish this may not require you to add any more invested capital because the projected new or increased income may warrant the purchase moneylender to add it to the loan. Keep in mind that the key word is "new" because new implies more income and greater value.

SUPPLY AND DEMAND.   When there are only one or two vacant corners in town where the zoning will allow a gas station to be built, then the reduced supply of such sites is bound to increase the value. When the demand for fast-food locations is high, any kind of property that will fit that need is going to be priced at a premium. The other side of this equation dictates that when there are a thousand residential lots or condominiums on the market and few buyers, the values will come down, or at least not go up, unless one of the other factors works its magic on the situation.

Often, the only way to deal with a big supply and a low demand is to try to get the property out of the category that is not in demand. This is where well-informed investing comes in handy, and the knowledge of the local market is important. When there is a large supply of something—say, for example, old homes—but a short supply of nice professional office space, find an old home that can be converted into a nice professional office building. This is very simple economics that, best of all, actually works.

Moving from one kind of property that is a buyer's market to another that is a seller's market may not be possible when there are few alternatives to follow. When your options are few, and you are a seller, then the only thing you may have going for you is to change the direction you are going; that is, stop being a seller and become a buyer.

How can you sell a property in a buyer's market by becoming a buyer? I realize that this appears to be a paradox, but in reality, it is simple. Take, for example, a really strong buyer's market for exactly the same kind of property you need to sell. You have toughed out the market, endured bottom-scraping offers that just did not work, and are ready to make a change. Remember back in Chapter 1 where I stressed the importance of knowing where you want to end up? Remember your goals? Now is one of those times you can put them to use.

Selling a property is less an economic benefit than it is the attainment of some other need or goal. This does not take away from the fact that money may be at the center of your motivation. Yet, often the need for money, or for that matter, the need to sell the property is because you have not reviewed all the other alternatives open to you. This frequently is because you do not have a clear goal in mind. Assume the goal is to maintain or improve your present living standard while living within your fixed income. Presently, you are living in a 4,500-square-foot apartment that is double the living area you actually need or think you can afford and you believe that one step to your goal is to downsize your living accommodations. Sell the big place, move into something smaller. By doing this, you should have some cash left over to invest to increase your income. Not a bad approach either: save money on expenses and have more money to invest. The only problem might be that for the moment big apartments are very hard to sell, and there are few buyers in the marketplace.

Become a buyer. Turn the tables on the poor market to sell your apartment and start looking for a purchase that can help you get closer to your goals. Remember, attaining your goal is what is important, not just the idea of selling the apartment.

One of several approaches would be for you to start looking for an investment that would strengthen your annual income. To acquire this new investment, you will want to incorporate the equity you have in your apartment. If the value of the apartment is $800,000 and it is free and clear, it is likely that you could purchase a property worth well over $2,000,000. If your total down payment was $800,000 this would indicate that to borrow the balance would create a loan-to-value ratio of only 60 percent (60 percent of $2,000,000 is a $1,200,000 loan with your equity of $800,000 as the balance).

A $2,000,000 income-producing property might have a viable NOI of around $220,000. If you could get a loan or combination of first and seller-held second loans of a payback with a constant rate of 10 percent, your total debt payment would be $120,000 per year. This would give you a cash flow of $100,000. This additional income may allow you to go back to the marketplace and buy a new place to live. You are benefiting because it is a buyer's market in all instances. Your large apartment becomes a part of a bigger deal, and may actually help the seller of the income property you acquire by taking that person closer to his goal.

Leverage is like the foot in the door for the encyclopedia salesperson. It gives you opportunity. It is not a reason, by itself, to make the purchase, nor is it a solution to any specific problem, if the deal is a bad deal to begin with. You will maximize its benefits only when you use it to move closer to your goals.

Chapter 5

CONVENTIONAL FINANCING

Where to Find It and
How to Negotiate the Best Terms

GOAL OF THIS CHAPTER

This chapter introduces you to conventional forms of real estate financing. This form of financing constitutes the vast bulk of capital that is available for real estate owners and investors. This is the form of finance available all over the world. However, there are some unique aspects to its availability and payback terms in its use within the United States. This chapter gives you the edge in finding the best mortgage to fit your specific needs. It will show you where to go and how to negotiate the best terms available in the market at the time you need the loan.

THE NEIGHBORHOOD LENDER IS AS
CLOSE AS YOUR COMPUTER

We live in a world that is fast becoming dominated by the Internet. It is not uncommon for a child to learn some of the basics of computer operation before attending kindergarten. Those skills may be necessary to conduct virtually any kind of business in the very near future. One business that has fallen into the clutches of the Internet is conventional financing. It is nearly impossible, in fact, to escape the Internet advertisements for mortgages that flood television, as well as your computer screen.

UNVEILING THE MORTGAGE

Because many of you may never see a real live mortgage broker or mortgage consultant, this chapter will be more important than ever. Much of the financing world used to be found on the local level, perhaps down the block from where you lived or worked. Local banks made those loans. Now, because of the ease of doing business on the Internet, the money can come from anywhere. Unfortunately, a financing package that may look the same as a dozen you have already seen may be considerably different due to a few, often hard-to-spot, phrases. A mortgage is the document you execute and give to the lender when the lender gives you money. It can be a very complex document. It is evidence that you have put something up (your home, office, shopping center you just bought, or whatever) as collateral for that loan. If you don't live up to the obligations covered in the mortgage note, which spells out how much you owe, what interest you must pay, when you have to make those payments, and other terms as well, you might find yourself losing your collateral. So, getting a mortgage in exchange for money is serious business, and should be treated that way.

CONVENTIONAL FINANCING

Conventional financing is obtained from commercial banks as well as savings banks (likely former savings and loan institutions), pension funds, insurance companies, and other similar institutional lenders. However, conventional financing terms can be from any other source that will lend on the same terms and standards as these institutions.

For this reason, the term *conventional financing* is misleading. Conventional need not be institutional. It simply must be a loan along the same general terms and conditions as one provided by one of the institutional sources. This factor in itself is not that significant, unless the purchase agreement requires that you obtain financing from an "institutional lender." In that situation, you would be excluded from finding the funds from a private source, even if the private loan had better terms and conditions than an institutional lender.

INSTITUTIONAL LENDERS

Whenever a seller anticipates holding secondary financing to facilitate the transaction, and the buyer will take out a new first mortgage to cover all or part of the balance due, that seller should be specific on the type of financing the buyer will obtain. I recommend sellers require the buyer to use "institutional loan sources." This would be especially important if the seller was to hold a substantial second mortgage, or offer a subordinated land lease that tied him or her to the deal after the closing. Forcing the buyer to go to a local savings bank, for example, may offer some insurance to the seller that the buyer and the lender were dealing at arm's length.

Less than arm's length deals have happened. For example, a buyer offers an above-market price and gets the seller to take back a very large second mortgage subordinated to new financing. The buyer goes to his brother-in-law (or someone else in on the caper) and borrows more than the purchase price. A year later, the buyer lets the loan go into default. The brother-in-law (and his partners) foreclose on the loan, all according to their original plan. The seller has to step in and cover the excessive loan or lose his position. This kind of ruse *should* never happen and will not happen if the seller is careful and has good legal advisors on his investment team. But, be aware: those kinds of things *do* happen.

Different Types of Institutional Financing

This chapter covers the different types of first mortgages offered by the institutional lenders and examines some of the advantages of dealing with private conventional sources over lending institutions. In all instances, however, there are different techniques and strategies in dealing with the different kinds of lenders. I give you a full and comprehensive procedure to follow that will aid you in obtaining any kind of a first mortgage.

When Is a First Mortgage a First Mortgage?

A first mortgage, or first deed of trust, as it is called in some states, is a document that gives the lender a right, or lien, to the title of the property that is pledged as security to the loan. These rights, by the way, are an application of law, which may vary slightly from state to state.

The mortgage document itself is not evidence of the amount of money owed—it is only the evidence of the security to the mortgage. As mentioned earlier in this chapter, the document that describes the amount of money owed, the method of payments, and other terms of payback is called the mortgage note (or just note) and is sometimes attached to the mortgage document. If you are doing due diligence on a property you want to purchase and do not find the mortgage note, then you will not have the complete picture of what the lender expects. The review of both the mortgage *and* the mortgage note of any existing debt on a property you are about to purchase is essential. Some of these documents may contain provisions that can be violated by your purchase agreement and can cause the transaction to fail to close, or become an otherwise very expensive proposition. One such problem can be that your purchase agreement carefully spells out that you are purchasing the property subject to the existing financing. You might have planned on that event and have made arrangements to meet your cash-down obligations only to find (at the closing table is when this comes out when you do not have proper closing representation), that the existing first mortgage has a clause that says the mortgage cannot be assumed. There are many other provisions a mortgage can contain, and they likely carry greater legal implications and position than anything contained in your purchase agreement. The fact that the seller has told you, "Don't worry, my friend, you can assume my existing debt, which will save you a bundle in new mortgage costs," may be just another of his newly discovered lies.

STEPS TO OBTAINING A MORTGAGE

I will assume that by the time you are going to apply for a mortgage you will have read this book from cover to cover. That will ensure that you have the knowledge available to you that you need. I will also assume that you are as adept at working a computer as any 14-year-old is, which is likely to be pretty darn good.

There is no computer that you can negotiate with. It is simply a tool that will make your life a breeze (most of the time). But, to negotiate anything, you need to be face to face with a person who can make decisions, or at least work between you and the decision maker to fine-tune details of the loan. And yes, as this paragraph suggests, loans and their repayment terms are fully negotiable.

But, where do you go to get the best terms for that maximum loan? Do you want to use the Internet as a sounding board? If your loan is a basic one, say for the purchase of a home or small investment property, you can go online with a number of mortgage sources and make your needs known. Those sources may in turn pass that information on to the actual money source and reply to you as to what loan terms are available. You may eventually get to a person with whom you can hopefully fine-tune the loan package.

The initial information you have to divulge to process the loan application consists of the following data:

- Your employer
- Salary
- Position or title
- How many years tenure
- Your social security number
- A net worth statement showing assets and liabilities
- Details on what the loan is to be used for
- The property to be pledged as collateral for the loan
- Its address, description, and other data including an appraisal

Loan Origination Costs and Fees

If the lender approves the loan application, a commitment of the lender's willingness to make the loan is given. This loan commitment generally contains the full terms and conditions of the loan and the payback terms of that loan. Some lenders will not issue a loan commitment unless the borrower has paid a *loan origination fee*. This fee may have many different names, and will range from a very small amount to cover credit reports, to as much as two or three points of the total loan requested. The term *points* is just another way of saying "interest percent." Two points of $50,000 is $1,000 ($50,000 × 0.02 = $1,000).

If the borrower needed $3 million for a first mortgage on a commercial building, the commitment fee could be $60,000 or more. If the borrower was not a triple prime borrower, then the commitment fee, or loan origination fee, may be much higher. The lender will tell the borrower that if a loan is offered along the terms requested, then the fee will apply to the closing of the loan. In some situations, this fee may be built into the loan or added on top of the amount required by the borrower. This is to ensure that the project or purpose of the loan will not be diluted. Also it will ensure to the lender that the fee for making the loan will be covered.

Construction and Development Loan

If there is new construction or development involved, there are often two different loans. The original construction loan covers the cost of the actual acquisition and development. Then, within a prescribed period of time, sufficient to allow development and rent-up or resale of the proposed development, the construction loan would need to be paid off. Prior to actual issuance of the construction loan, the lender usually requires the borrower to have a take-out loan, or a permanent loan commitment already arranged.

Take-Out or Permanent Loan

The take-out loan may come from a completely different lender, or be made by the same lender, but through another department of that same institution. This loan will step in and pay off the construction loan and become the first mortgage or financing of record. As indicated, each of these two loan types may come from the same lender, or two or more different lenders may participate to make this all happen. These two elements, the construction loan and the permanent take-out loan, are separate because the construction loan is made with a series of payments being made to the borrower to cover the actual development as it takes place. The construction loan may also include partial or complete acquisition of the site on which the development is made. This is called an acquisition and development loan package. The word "construction" could be also used in place of the word "development." The actual ceiling amount of the loan, the $3 million or whatever the loan amount is to be, only reaches that amount at the last payment to the borrower. The permanent loan pays off the construction loan at the prescribed moment, and repayment of that loan begins over the terms of the permanent mortgage note.

Mortgage and Mortgage Notes

At the closing of the loan, the lender advances the money, and the borrower executes the mortgage note and the mortgage. The lender will generally require that the title of the property that is the security to the loan be rechecked by a title company and/or lawyers working for the lender prior to releasing any funds. This title is frequently checked prior to the issuance of the loan, and then once again after the mortgage document and note have been executed (and/or recorded). This final check is to ensure that the borrower has not managed to "hit" several lenders using the same property as security on several loans. Until the lender is secure that such an event had not happened, it will generally hold up giving the borrower the proceeds of the loan. This is critical because until the mortgage documents have been recorded, any other loan document recorded ahead of this acquisition and development loan will precede it in its claim of the security.

Title Retained by the Borrower

Because title has not passed to the lender, the borrower still owns the property and has full use of it. The lender, however, has obtained the right or lien against the property, and should the borrower default on the note the lender can exercise its rights as would be provided for in the mortgage and by state and federal law. The rights to foreclose or to accelerate the demand of repayment are two of the rights the lender has to govern the force it can exert on the borrower to recover its money back.

Contract for Deed

There is one form of mortgage agreement where the title is retained by the lender. This is generally a seller-held mortgage, although sellers sometimes sell these mortgage agreements to third parties. This type of mortgage is the "contract for deed," sometimes called a "land contract" if the property is vacant land and no development has occurred. There could be other terms used by sellers or realtors in your area that would in fact create the same kind of mortgage. No matter what it is called, if it fits the example I will give in the next paragraph, be aware of its conditions.

The contract for deed or land contract occurs when the seller and the buyer enter into an agreement where the buyer puts a down payment in the hands of the seller, and then makes a series of payments over a set period of time. At the end of this payment period, the amount owed on the purchase price would then be paid up and the property title would be delivered to the buyer. This resembles the mortgage you might get if you bought a home and owed the seller for the balance of the purchase price after making a down payment. The difference is who holds the title of the property. In the contract for deed or land contract, the seller retains title to the property until the terms of the sale have been met. In a mortgage situation, the borrower holds the title and pledges that title as security. In the contract for deed the buyer only gets the actual title when all the payments have been made, according to the terms of the agreement.

Some states have specific laws that deal with this kind of contract because it has been a favorite kind of sales agreement by land developers and timeshare sales efforts, two kinds of development and sales operations that often have specific laws that govern sales practices to protect buyers. Because of this, you must be especially careful when this kind of mortgage or purchase/sales provision is used.

Most investors would avoid the contract for deed because it has a number of problems that become more evident the longer the term of payment. Sellers might "sell" bulk packages of collections ($1 million or so worth of contracts for deed) or simply go out of business. If the buyer was still making payments for another 15 to 20 years, it is possible that when the loan was paid off, there would be no entity to get the title from. Private deals using the contract for deed and short payoff may be okay as long as you follow the advice of your lawyer. It is sound practice to keep the payback term to fewer than five years. Even in those instances, as a buyer, you would want to limit this technique to vacant land. Because you don't get title until the last payment, you do not want to put capital into land by building a building, or other equity, unless you are very sure you will eventually get title. Be sure to use a very good real estate lawyer who knows about this kind of agreement as local laws apply.

Mortgage Satisfaction

A conventional first mortgage can be satisfied simply by paying off the amount owed plus any interest or other assessments that are due. When the mortgage is paid off, the lender gives the borrower (or whomever holds title to the property at that time) a document titled "mortgage satisfaction," or "notice of satisfaction of mortgage." It is up to the borrower to be sure that he or she gets this document from the lender and that it is properly executed by the lender. The borrower then has the document recorded in the county records, where the property is located. Unless this satisfaction of mortgage is recorded, there could be a cloud on the title at a later date as to the status of this mortgage. A cloud on the title is any possible glitch that shows up in the title. This can be an outstanding judgment against you, or some previous owner, or some other problem that suggests or illustrates that the present owner does not have all the rights to the title that are possible. Some clouds exist that may be okay—for example, a utility easement or drainage ditch. In the case of the missing mortgage satisfaction, unless there is clear evidence that a mortgage was actually paid off (as the recorded mortgage satisfaction would illustrate), a prospective buyer or future lender would insist that such evidence be produced. This can be a costly circumstance several years later if the principals to the loan have died, or cannot be found, or take the position that the loan has never been repaid.

Grace Period

The grace period is the few days provided for within the mortgage note during which the payment is due, but not yet in default. Not all mortgages have a grace period, so do not assume that one exists. If the borrower fails to make payments to an existing mortgage on time, nothing happens until the grace period has expired. This grace period can be any time period that the parties establish, but in general use it is 5 to 20 days. Remember, there may be no automatic grace period in your state, and while mortgages often provide for such a period of grace to take into account delay in mail, or other reasonable events, you can be held accountable if you do not pay on time.

If the payments due are not made by the last day of the grace period, the mortgage is in default and subject to the wrath or pleasure of the lender. Chapter 23 of this book discusses what can be done to delay the unpleasant steps a lender can take. I suggest it as required reading. In this chapter, I comment only briefly on foreclosure.

Foreclosure is very cumbersome and expensive for lenders. Usually a lender will avoid taking a borrower into foreclosure if at all possible. It is not uncommon for an institutional lender to let their borrowers get behind in their payments prior to actually filing foreclosure documents. Nonetheless, as the final step they will do all they can to collect the amounts owed. No lender likes foreclosure, but they all have gotten so they can do it with the least possible inconvenience. Still, almost all of them will work with the borrower who is in trouble and who comes to them and presents his or her case and can demonstrate the ability to catch up delinquent payments. But remember, that nice loan officer who processed your loan may no longer work at that institution. More likely, the bank may have packaged several million dollars of their loans from that week into a portfolio of loans that have been sold to a pension fund or insurance company. The bank you dealt with might have acted as collection agent, but then sold that "job" to an agency that specializes in such collections.

Loan Position—Right to Lien

The position the lender has in a first mortgage exceeds any right of any other lender. This is the primary loan. Secondary loans are loans that are made behind the rights of the first mortgage or that were actually made prior to the first mortgage but subordinated to the rights of the lender. Subordination is the circumstance where one person agrees to let the rights of another person (or entity) move ahead of his or her rights. An example follows.

SECONDARY POSITION.   I sell you a property and you give me a mortgage that I now hold that creates a mortgage on the property. While my mortgage is a first mortgage simply because there is no other mortgage yet recorded, I can give you the right to go to another lender to borrow more money and let the rights of the other lender move ahead of my former first mortgage. Secondary financing of any nature has more risk to it than the primary loan. This is because these second loans are junior to the rights of the first mortgage. In the event of a foreclosure against the borrower, the primary or first loans get paid off first, and the junior or secondary loans come next, in their order of rank (second, third, fourth, and so on). If there is not sufficient equity or value in the property, it is possible that all junior mortgages will go unpaid. Even some first mortgages may not be fully paid. This assumes that the borrower has not filed bankruptcy, which would upset this sequence, and in those events the end result may be that a court decides who gets what.

The position of the mortgage with respect to this junior or superior rank is not always what appears and should be examined carefully. For example, the document that says "This is a first mortgage" is not always a first mortgage. The rank of a mortgage with respect to the position of rights of the lender has to do with the time of recording and possible subordination provisions.

Recording Mortgage Documents

When a mortgage is executed, the lender will take that document, along with the mortgage note, and record it in the county or township of the state where the property is located. The intention of the lender may be to have a first mortgage; however, if the borrower has given another mortgage to another party (thinking it was a second mortgage) and the mortgage that was to be the second mortgage was recorded ahead of the mortgage that was to be the first mortgage, the time of recording becomes the critical element and not the intention or the title of the document.

Review of Lien Position Is Essential

In taking back a mortgage, as a lender (if you were to sell your own property or to make a loan to another party), you would want to be absolutely sure that the mortgage is indeed what it has been reported to be. In short, no matter how much you trust the people, make sure that the actual recording dates are verified. Errors by lawyers, title companies, or county recording offices could have positioned another mortgage ahead of that "first mortgage" you thought you were holding. This situation explains the requirements of most lenders to check the title of a property after they have actually made the loan, but prior to funding the money.

WHO IS THE MORTGAGOR AND WHO IS THE MORTGAGEE?

The *mortgagor* is the person who gives the mortgage document to the lender. The lender is the *mortgagee*. The mix-up in these words comes from the common practice of saying, "I will go to the bank and get a mortgage." In actual fact, you go to the bank to "get money" and by doing so to "give a mortgage." The key to this and any other "give" or "take" terms is that any words that end in "-er" or "-or" generally denote the "giver of the item." For example, the mortgagor, lender, grantor, lessor, and so on, are all people who have given something to someone else. That someone else—the "-ee," of the same term: mortgagee, lendee, grantee, lessee, and so on—is the person who "gets" the item. So the mortgagee is the person who gets the document called a mortgage . . . and in return is the grantor or lender of the funds, therefore, the person or institution that gives the mortgagor the money.

Still not clear? Okay, think of it this way: When you borrow money from a lender who demands security in the form of a mortgage, you give that lender a right to your property by giving the lender a mortgage document. By giving the lender the mortgage, that act makes you the mortgagor. That document says that if you don't make your payments on time or default in any other way, you risk actions by the lender that are not pleasant and where the end result is that you can lose your property. In essence, you pay up on time "or else." Remember that you are the mortgagor when you get money, and all else will fall into place.

STANDARDS THAT MAKE A LOAN CONVENTIONAL

When you are dealing with the conventional loan market, you will find a standard that tends to prevail throughout the country. There is little variance in the basic format of the loan once you are within the same category. However, many aspects of the loan can differ between states and even within the same city. Lending is a business, and a very big business at that. The people who make loans and the organizations who provide money are open to negotiation. If you know what you want and what the competition is offering, you usually can improve your position.

It may be as basic as understanding the difference between government restriction and lender policy. Each aspect is critical so that you know just how far you can go in hammering out good terms. Start with the fundamentals. The lender's policy is the flexible part of the equation. The inflexible part of any institutional transaction lies within governmental restrictions.

All lending institutions that function as a bank are governed by either state or federal regulations or both, and these regulations may restrict the percentage to a category of loan the lender can give. The restriction will not hamper your ability to negotiate with the lender as long as it still has room to make the loan within its portfolio requirements. However, when the lender is nearly out of its allocation for commercial loans, things begin to get tough for that lender. When things are tough, the lender begins to get very picky about where to place funds.

To improve your success in loan presentations, make sure the lender has money to lend prior to knocking yourself out to win one or two points. Remember the old vaudeville phrase, "Yes, we have no bananas"? The fundamentals are simply that yes the lender will loan you money at the best rate and terms, but no they don't have any funds available at the moment.

POLICY, RISK, AND CREDIT HISTORY.   Other restrictions that affect you, as a borrower, are the percentage of loan-to-value ratio that the lender is allowed to lend. This percentage depends on the kind or category of loan and may vary between lenders. For example, most savings banks (both state and federal) are allowed to lend up to a set amount that is determined by a percentage of the appraised value of that property. But, and most important, most of these institutions have internal limits that they set on their own lending practices that generally limit those amounts to a lower amount. This may depend on the borrower's credit history and credit scores. There are many things you can do to improve your credit history. The most important of all is to simply pay off your obligations in full, or at least meet all your scheduled payments on time. Credit card debt is the major reason that people have a poor credit history, mainly because it is promptly reported by the credit card companies and banks that issue these items. Make it a point to enquire what the specific policy is at any lending institution from which you may be seeking a loan. The policy may also qualify borrowers by category of the kind or category of property that will be pledged as collateral. Clearly, a $5 million, fully occupied class A office building would be a better security than a $5 million home. They may both have the same appraised value, but the cash flow on the office building has an appeal that the home rarely has. You will discover that most lenders have a preference for certain types of property. They also have a "burned fingers" attitude about other types of real estate. Learn their preferences, approach to risk, and lending policy before you ask the wrong lender for a loan on a property they hate.

Use every meeting as a learning session. If you sincerely approach every contact as if he or she can teach you something, you will be giving a compliment while at the same time establishing good rapport. A secondary benefit is that you will get updated data on these regulations and policies at the same time. Remember, the key to this exercise is to discover the policy; it is here that you will be able to win points and obtain better loan conditions and terms from one lender over the other. But you must know the lender's policy. For example, the regulation may limit the maximum investor-nonresident owner loan on a single-family home to 80 percent of the value of the property, yet the loan officer may tell you that the maximum the bank will loan is 75 percent of the loan value. In this case, the policy is 75 percent, not the regulation. Policy can be negotiated, whereas regulation is fixed. Another element of this example is the loan value percentage. The regulation generally states that the percentage of the loan is based on the value of the property. Value is somewhat of an opinion, and to help smooth out this potential problem, many lenders temper this regulation and add policy that should be something like the following: ". . . and value will be determined as the lower of the contract price or the appraisal." The wording can be rephrased a thousand different ways, but the idea should be clear to you: The lender wants to see your contract of purchase and will reserve the right to use its price as the value.

Yet, you know that loan percentages are dependent on value and not price so you can push the lender to make the loan based on real value and not a contract price on a property you are buying. If you bought the property for a song, you should be able to utilize the real value for the basis of the loan and not the contract value as the limitation to the deal. After all, if you already owned the property (say you bought it 10 years ago), the actual price you paid would have no bearing, would it?

EXAMPLE: 100 PERCENT FINANCING USING REGULATIONS AGAINST POLICY. I was reviewing the needs of a friend and client one day when he told me that he wanted to buy a small industrial building in Fort Lauderdale, Florida. He was very familiar with the building because he had worked as manager of an industrial parts distribution business that had occupied the structure for nearly seven years. The owner of the distribution business (who was at that time the owner of the building) acquired another company in Miami and moved the distribution business to that city. In the meantime, he leased out the Fort Lauderdale building to another firm, which was about to move out, leaving the building vacant. The owner had no real interest in owning the Fort Lauderdale building, and he did not want to get into the problems of management at a distance.

My friend suggested to the owner that he sell the building to him. He would then relocate the business that had moved to Miami back into the building and operate as the firm's representative rather than as a company-owned outlet. The concept made economic sense to the owner. As a seller, he could rid himself of a real estate problem and at the same time remove the management headaches of the company store in Miami.

With my help, my friend worked out a contract to buy the building for what was a very good price—$305,000—which was actually the true value of the land under the building. In a review of the capital needs of my friend, we determined that he would need all of his capital to get the business going and would not have sufficient funds to pay the $305,000 price unless that sum could be financed. From the way the numbers looked, I didn't think there would be any problem financing not only the purchase price, but the loan costs and some improvement money as well.

To accomplish this, I developed a pro forma and an evaluation of the building as it would be at the time of sale. I was not interested in the actual current value of the building, only what the value would be under the upcoming circumstances and use.

In doing this study, my back-up material showed that the value of this building, after the sale and with the fix-up intended and the new use of the facility, would be $525,000. I followed the mortgage request outline beginning on page 121. I was satisfied that I had sufficient material to support the following request:

Loan requested: $355,000

Use of the funds:

To seller	$305,000
Remodel	25,000
Loan costs	8,550
To borrower	16,450
Total of loan	$355,000

Loan-to-value ratio = $355,000 ÷ $525,000 = 68 percent

What I had not anticipated was being thrown out of the first two lenders because the loan officer could not understand how he could request a loan based on value and not just the contract price. The end result: My friend got his building without having to spend any of his own money, and the lender got a good deal. The value of the building was as it had been represented, so the parties made a very good loan-to-value ratio. Once the contact had been made with the loan officer at the lending institution, it was a matter of "educating the lender" as to policy versus regulation.

No matter what your current needs in real estate financing, if you plan to become an investor, you will need to shop for a loan. Since lending is a very big business, you will want to have friends in as many places as you can find to ease your way into the loan committee's good graces. Visit several potential lenders now and make the proper contact well before you need it.

MAKE CONTACTS WITH LOAN OFFICERS AND MORTGAGE BROKERS

One of the best ways to obtain information about the policy of a lending institution is to sit down with one or more loan officers within a lending institution or local mortgage brokers who may represent a number of lenders. They can explain the different rules, regulations, and policies of the lenders available locally (see Table 5.1). You may discover that the loan officers are learning about these rules and regulations at about the same time you are, because policy is regulation to the employees and they often don't attempt to distinguish between the two until someone else forces the issue.

MODIFICATIONS LENDERS FREQUENTLY IMPOSE ON LOANS

- Almost all loans over 80 percent of loan monthly payments include principal, interest, and a pro rata buildup for an escrow of taxes and hazard insurance. If the property is a residence of the borrower (and therefore qualifying for a better term mortgage),

Table 5.1

Loan Conditions Generally Common to Commercial and Savings Banks

Maximum Loan (%)	Term (Years)	Type of Property	Conditions
90	30	Single family and condos	Loan is based on the contract amount or an appraisal, whichever is the lower amount.
95	30	Single family and condos	Same as above, except private mortgage insurance is required. These loans usually are below $40,000.
80	30	One to four multifamily dwelling units	Appraisal value will take market conditions of rental area and vacancies into account.
75	25	Five or more units commercial real estate	Greater emphasis on the person behind the loan. Appraisals will also be more detailed and the term of years reduced.
75	3	Developed lots	Terms for builders of more than two lots.
	5	Developed lots	Terms for individuals are longer. Usual provisions on which the lots are built within the term of loan.
100	12	New mobile homes	Based on invoice price.
100	8	Used mobile homes	Wholesale value.

there must be a certification that the property will indeed be the borrower's home. Most lenders will limit the years and offer more restrictive interest rates and payback terms on investment property.

- At the time of the loan, no secondary or junior loans can be made or placed on the property. This is standard for all primary lenders, but is more policy than regulation. Creative investors know that you can have secondary financing that makes the deal work, if the secondary loan is on another property. Land leases are a common form of secondary loan that is actually on the same property which secures the primary loan, provided that the loan is either subordinated, or of such a long term that the lender is comfortable with the loan situation.

- Depending on the market, many lenders seek to shorten the payback terms of loans. It is not uncommon for these repayment terms to be 5 to 10 years. The lender wants to shorten the exposure to the property and market conditions by having this short repayment term. To encourage the borrower to agree with this shortened term, a lower interest rate may be offered.

• Most institutional lenders will offer a variety of repayment programs. In Chapter 6, a number of these different programs are discussed. They include straight amortization, where the loan is repaid over a term of years, where equal monthly payments will satisfy the loan by the end of the term. Shorter payback schedules, but with a long amortization schedule require a balloon payment to retire the still outstanding debt at the end of the term. These are just two of the many different repayment schedules that may be offered.

All lenders will negotiate any term or condition it considers reasonable or obtainable in the market. Banks and other lenders are in the business of providing loans to borrowers for a specific business reason: profit. If the lending institution cannot make a profit, it is apt to slip slowly but surely into the oblivion of bankruptcy. Because any business can go out of business, it should not be a surprise if a lending institution that uses poor judgment about whom it makes loans to also fails to remain profitable itself.

The effect of competition on the borrower's ability to obtain loan terms that are better from one lender to another is something that has been around for a long time. One of the goals of this book is to assist any lender to recognize what the options are in seeking these better terms, and how to distinguish what is better instead of just different.

INTEREST, POINTS, AND COST

Interest rates are not regulated except by state law, which establishes the maximum rate that can be charged. Interest charged is generally somewhat competitive, and on the surface it may not seem to vary much between lenders. However, the jargon of finance is somewhat concealing, and the total outcome of one loan that looks close to another can be more costly in the end.

The actual cost per $1,000 loaned is the best way to determine the overall cost of the total term of the loan. By comparing overall cost to actual cost, you gain a composite view of the potential economic picture. I say potential picture because some loan terms are not possible to forecast accurately. For example, if you take out a loan that is adjustable in the future, the lender has a formula that allows him to adjust the interest charged against the outstanding balance owed. This adjustment is frequently tied to the interest charged on an average of the U.S. Treasury Bills, or a specific "T" Bill rate. If this is the case, the interest can go up or down (but generally up) from the original loan rate. Some lenders attract borrowers to their institutions by offering interest rates below the market for the first year or so and then count on the adjustment being sufficiently beneficial to the lender to make up for the "come-on" rate. In this ploy to lend money, different lenders will offer different packages in their adjustment loan package. Maximum adjustments each year, or over the life of the loan, as well as different terms for adjustments do more to confuse the borrower (and make it far more difficult to calculate the actual cost in comparison to another lender) than to serve the public. One way to combat this is to take a "best" and a "worst" appraisal of specific loans. In essence, look at the actual cost to you if the loan rates are adjusted to the maximum rates. This will then give you the parameters for any specific loan and the absolute comparison between different loans. Adjustable rate loans often begin with a rate that is truly below the market at the time. This attracts borrowers who may also be enticed to max out the loan because they are told they can always "refinance" at any time. That opportunity may come at a high cost, however, or may not be possible if the market slips down a bit. It is easy for a property to drop below a favorable loan-to-value ratio. The lending crisis that began in the early 2000s is a good example of how quickly things can escalate. While real estate is a very local market, lending is a worldwide venture. Therefore, what happens in London from a real estate point of view is not the same as what goes on in San Francisco or Detroit. However, because lenders bundle and then sell their loan packages on a worldwide market, when that market gets into trouble it will have an impact on real estate lending opportunities and practices.

Fixed-rate loans were once the only kind of loan available. However, even then the kinds of fixed interest rates were varied. For example, automobile loans often are quoted at an "add-on" interest rate and the final cost of an add-on rate is nearly double that of the same rate on a common interest loan. The reason for this is the way interest is calculated. In a typical real estate mortgage or loan, interest is quoted as an annual percent charged against the amount of the loan (the principal) outstanding for the term that the interest is paid.

For example, if the principal of a mortgage was $100,000 at the start of the year, and no payments were made to reduce the principal during the year, and there was an annual interest payment due at 12 percent per annum, at the end of the year the interest due would be $12,000. If the interest payments were due each month, the borrower would owe $\frac{1}{12}$th of the interest rate monthly, which in this case would result in 1 percent per month being due. In a mathematical sense, the monthly $1,000 appears equal to the annual $12,000, but economically it is not. As a borrower, you would find it to your benefit to pay annually at $12,000 rather than monthly at $1,000. You could take the $1,000 each month and put it to work for you at the same interest rate of 12 percent; at the end of the year, you would have accumulated $682.25 of interest. If you then made your mortgage payment, you would pay a net of $11,317.75 because the interest in your account goes to you and not the lender. The actual cost of the annual payment (if you can earn 12 percent) of this mortgage is not 12 percent but only 11.31775 percent. Any interest you can earn on the monthly installments of $1,000 would be to your benefit. While this may not sound like a lot of difference, it can add up.

On the other hand, the way the game is played by lenders is reversed. Lenders want interest as often as once a month. As you saw in this example, your bank account earned interest of $682.25 by your paying the interest annually; therefore, the lender will be able to earn that rate instead of you. So the lender gets your 12 percent in this example, plus a bonus of $682.25. Because the amount of the principal has not changed due to the lack of principal payments, the bonus is 0.68225 percent for the year. In real terms, the lender makes 12.68225 percent on the loan in comparison to your paying 11.31775 percent on an annual payout.

Let's review the mathematics involved: $682.25 interest divided by the principal of $100,000 equals 0.0068225, or 0.68225 percent. Remember that whenever you divide dollars, you will get the mathematical percentage and not the actual rate, which first must be multiplied by 100. Equally, when you want to multiply a number, say $50,000, by 12 percent, you must first translate that percentage to the decimal number by dividing by 100 to make it 0.12.

The relation to the interest you pay and the method of payment should be clearly understood. Only by having it clear in your mind will you be able to make maximum use of the loans offered, and obtain the best terms to suit your goals.

Negotiate Interest and Term of Repayment

Interest is another of the elements of the mortgage that can be negotiated between the borrower and the lender. Not just the rate of interest is involved, but how it is paid. As we have just seen, the frequency of payment during the year has a relationship to the total cost of the mortgage. This cost should be considered in the complete relationship of the circumstance.

For example, if the interest is a deductible expense and will reduce another out-of-pocket cost, such as income tax, then the increase of the interest cost, if offset by some other element, may cause the borrower to give in on the higher interest (thereby increasing the yield to the lender at no net cost to the borrower). An example of this would be in a tradeoff to a lender who might be holding out for some other factor besides the interest. One such factor is participation in the transaction. This hidden interest is commonplace in large commercial transactions where the lender not only gets paid in interest, but also takes a percentage of ownership of the property or a percentage of gross income from the venture.

If this were the case, the wise borrower takes a hard, cold look at the potential cost of that participation and calculates the overall cost of a higher interest rate, which will have a definite termination point: that being when the mortgage is finally paid off, whereas the participation may be for the duration of ownership of the property. Another example of a tradeoff in which the tax advantages of higher interest may be desirable is in situations where the amount of the loan is higher than that loan possible at a lower interest rate. The borrower again has to weigh the cost of the money, and in this case the use of the funds, or the need for the funds to complete the transaction at hand.

Interest and Principal Payments Combined

As interest rates increase, the combined effect of interest and principal makes for high monthly payments. To counterbalance this, lenders have come up with a form of mortgage that has negative amortization. Amortization is that element of a mortgage that is the reduction of the principal owed. In most mortgages, the monthly payment does not change during the base term of the mortgage.

If the mortgage had a 25-year term with no balloon payment due, over the period of 25 years, which may be seen as 300 months, the monthly payment would contain two amounts of money that would total one steady monthly payment. For example, if the amount of the loan was $100,000 and the rate of interest was 12 percent per annum, over a 300-month mortgage with regular amortization, the payment would be $1,042.79 per month (a total of $312,837 over 300 months).

If the lender was unable to lend sufficient money to meet its lending requirements with these terms, it could reduce the payback sum by either reducing the interest or increasing the term of the loan to cut the payments and therefore attract more borrowers. However, by increasing the term from 25 to 35 years, the payment only drops to $1,005.49.

This would mean that the borrower would pay back a total of $422,307.82 if he or she lived those 35 years and still owned the property. As you can see, spreading out the total term doesn't help, and the lender will not want to reduce the interest if there is another alternative. Thus, the negative amortization mortgage was born (Table 5.2). In this kind of mortgage, the payment is set at an attractive amount. How about $600 per month for the first two years, $700 per month for another two years, and so on, increasing the monthly payment every few years until the mortgage reaches the end of the tenth year, at which time the whole thing balloons?

Table 5.2
Negative Amortization Mortgage Table

Principal at the start of the term: $100,000.
A 10-year mortgage with 12 percent interest and the monthly payments shown.

Year	Monthly Payments ($)	Unpaid Interest Added to the Principal ($)	Principal at the End of the Year ($)
1	600	4,996.91	104,996.91
2	600	5,630.64	110,627.55
3	700	5,063.81	115,691.36
4	700	5,706.03	121,397.39
5	800	5,148.77	126,546.16
6	800	5,801.76	132,347.92
7	900	5,256.63	137,604.55
8	900	5,923.37	143,527.86
9	1,000	5,393.60	148,921.46
10	1,000	6,077.64	154,999.10

Total payments made over 120 months equal $96,000 on the $100,000 loan and the borrower still owes $154,999.10 because each payment was short of an interest-only payment. Note that Table 5.2 does not show each month's calculation but has all 12 payments for each year lumped into a single deduction of the payments and the amount of deficit interest for the year added to the principal owed.

Lenders discovered that with this kind of lending two catastrophic things often occurred. The first was that many borrowers found that they were obligated to a debt greater than the property would support. The second event was that the property often didn't keep pace with the increased principal owed on the mortgage. If the original loan had been at a 90 percent loan-to-value ratio, the original value would have been $111,111 (90 percent of $111,111 is $100,000 rounded up one cent). At the end of the third year, if the actual value of the property had not increased, the borrower would have no "profit" in the property and foreclosure by the lender would soon follow. Many investors operate by spending the cash flow, and almost no one builds a reserve for replacements anymore.

The concept of reserves for ultimate replacements is a sound accounting practice, when used. However, most investors simply go back to the lender to get the needed funds, when replacements are needed. This works too, but can have major setbacks if the lending market dries up just when you need to make some major replacements. The negative amortization compounded this potential problem.

In looking at negative interest mortgages, you must be critically aware of the overall effect. If you take all of these elements into consideration, you will then be able to proceed to make value judgments that will direct you closer to your goals.

When we get to secondary financing, I will show you how many of these aspects discussed will be put into play to give you the advantage as either buyer or seller. When you are dealing with the institutional market, and therefore the conventional form of financing, you have less creativity available to you in private dealings.

Points and Closing Costs

All lenders seek to cover their expenses in any transaction. The first line of defense of such costs and expenses comes in the way of points. The origin of the points that lenders charge was to discount the amount lent so that when you paid back the total amount, the lender would get an additional yield. For example, if I borrow $10,000 and the lender charges $500 in points (5 percent of the amount borrowed), I only get $9,500 but have to pay back the $10,000. All interest is calculated on the $10,000, so you can see the lender's advantage.

When we get to FHA loans, you will see that the points charges have this effect. The lender gets a higher yield because FHA charges the seller for some of these points. This cost is the seller's expense because the seller can sell his property with a lower interest rate than available from the general market.

Points have become so commonplace in the conventional market that it has become a situation of the lender getting back from the borrower as much as it can to increase its yield and to make the interest rate appear lower. Points are an up-front deduction or expense from the borrower. If the lender wants five points and the loan is $1 million, we are talking about a lot of money. However, most lenders will talk about reducing their points just as they will talk about other factors of their loans with which they have some leeway.

Out-of-Pocket Expenses

Another cost for conventional lenders and secondary lenders are *out-of-pocket expenses.* In essence, lenders make a list of expenses they have incurred over the past year and charge it to you as out-of-pocket expenses. So far, competition in the industry has kept this list to a minimum, but you should question every item that is going to be charged to you prior to signing the mortgage and note. The list is apt to include items such as the following:

- Abstract or title review
- Credit report
- Document preparation
- Environmental inspection and review
- Field investigation
- Legal expenses
- Loan origination fee
- Miscellaneous expenses
- Mortgage insurance
- Postclosing title review
- Postrecording title check
- Preloan title check
- Property inspection
- Recording of title and other documents
- Review of credit report
- Staff review of documentation
- Survey check
- Title insurance

Many of these items are duplicates of other things you may be doing through other activities of the transaction. You need to ask about each item because the lender's list may have some very creative titles to describe some of the expenses. You will end up paying for most of the expenses the lender wants to charge. However, there are apt to be some expenses that will save you money if you know about them in advance, and others that may be eliminated.

For example, lenders often charge you for a title insurance policy to cover the amount of the loan. If you are not careful and observant you could end up paying for two policies: one for the lender, which would be insufficient to cover the total value of the property, and a separate one in a greater amount to cover the amount of your investment. The proper and least expensive way is to make sure you get one policy to cover the value of your investment, and provide (at a small expense) for a coinsured provision in the policy to cover the lender.

Find out all of the items the lender wants to charge you for. Ask if you can have them done elsewhere, and then get a price quote from several other sources. You might find that the lender is the best price around, or the worst.

Some lenders try to sell you all sorts of other insurance. Extra insurance comes in two forms: Hazard insurance covers the property against storms, fire, and other disasters, and mortgage insurance pays back the lender should you die before the mortgage has been paid in full. Mortgage insurance is usually very expensive for what you get, and you may already have life insurance that can be partially assigned to the lender in the unlikely event of your death. Even if you don't have any other insurance, make sure to ask an independent insurance agency for the price of life insurance that will pay off your mortgage, if necessary.

Another factor that comes into play in these costs is the loan-to-value ratio. This is one of the strongest factors in lending. Is the loan 50 percent of the value, or 95 percent, or somewhere in between? The lender likes a large spread in the loan-to-value ratio. If you have done your homework well and utilized all of the steps provided in this book, you can maximize your loan and at the same time minimize the payback cost of the loan by showing a low loan-to-value ratio. One step in that direction will be to do all you can to show the maximum value of the property you are buying. Remember the industrial building that was discussed. Your contract doesn't establish the value of the property, and you must provide backup data to support the real value, which you believe to be higher than your contract price (if it is a new property), or provide as much detail to support the appreciated value if you have held the property for some time.

Later in this chapter, you will find an outline for a loan request. Follow it for all loans except for development loans, which are discussed in Chapter 8.

WHERE DO CONVENTIONAL LOANS COME FROM?

You will find conventional loans from the following sources:

- Savings banks
- Thrift savings associations
- Credit unions

- Commercial banks
- Mortgage bankers
- Mortgage brokers

How to Determine Which Source to Approach

Which lender in your area will be the best for you? That is a difficult question to answer. The economic market in lending fluctuates greatly from time to time, and the lender with the best secondary market going for it will be apt to be the most liberal lender. The majority of the money that you borrow comes from the secondary marketplace. The lenders sell their loan packages to this market.

THE BEST SOURCE WILL BE THE ONE THAT LIKES YOU MOST.   In all business dealings, the element of like and trust mean a lot. Naturally, there must be good, sound business principles at work, and in the moment of compromise between you and someone else, the soundness of the loan might weigh more than friendship. However, never underestimate the power of your contacts. What this means, of course, is if you do not have any contacts you had better start establishing them. Your contacts should not be only in the banking field, but in all fields.

THE PERSON YOU TALK TO IS NOT LOANING YOU HIS OR HER MONEY.   You will rarely, if ever, sit down with someone who will give you money out of his or her own pocket in the conventional mortgage market. You will be dealing at a distance through the institution's agents, employees, or whatever. Eventually, even if you start online with the Internet, you will be dealing with people, and no matter what the institution is, the person you meet face to face is an obstacle on your way to a loan.

It is rare for any mortgage or loan board in any institution to grant a loan that gave the loan officer a "funny feeling." Somewhere along the way between your first encounter with the institution and that person, you will be judged in a variety of ways. Many of these judgments will have nothing to do with your ability to pay back the loan. Some simply are personal; others are purely business or even based on envy, jealousy, or hate.

It's a people business: the attitude one person has toward another, or how well a prospective borrower is prepared to meet any objection the loan officer can throw his or her way. Power players in any game or business abound. These people will cause or invent problems to test and pressure you. For example, your loan officer might try to improve the loan-to-value ratio, thereby increasing the security to the lending institution, and to test your vulnerability he might spring something like this on you: "You know, Mr. Cummings, in the preliminary review of your loan request several questions came up that centered on the magnitude of your request. Do you suppose you could reduce your request by $1 million?"

There are several reasons for this kind of approach; one is as I suggested and another is to set me up for some other term consideration that I would not want to give in on unless absolutely necessary, such as, "Of course, Mr. Cummings, I realize how important it is for you to keep the loan at the requested amount. I offered one suggestion as a compromise to the committee. What do you think, Mr. Cummings, of a $300,000 reduction instead of $1 million, and you accept a small increase in the interest rate to 11 percent?"

You will be better equipped to handle this type of approach by the time you finish this book. You must understand that all of the people whom you deal with need to have some personal satisfaction from their job, just as you must from yours. It is not critical that you understand what position the other person has taken in his or her own mental game, but only that you do not infringe on that position.

We all play some kind of mental game in our business dealings, and while some of us are quarterbacks in that game, others are owners of the team. Loan officers are not the owners of the team, but they often act as though they are.

The reality is that in the lending business, loan officers get many red marks when loans they have recommended go sour. It does not matter if the reason for the loan going sour had nothing to do with them. They get the red marks just the same. They will avoid red marks whenever possible and will do everything they can to show that they did everything they could have (or should have) to make a loan that should not have gone bad.

However, loan officers must make loans because they also get red marks when they are not doing the business for which they are hired. When the institution is flush with money and word has come down to lend out the money, the loan officer is anxiously looking for you to help him or her avoid red marks. You will do that by knowing how to deal with different institutions, and what it is that they need.

Part of your success then will be in making sure that you have developed some kind of relationship that is on the professional and business level. You can socialize with the loan officer, but if you had to socialize with anyone at the bank try the president first, vice presidents second, and so on. Remember that the higher your contacts, the easier it is in dealing with the lower echelons.

Dealing with the Local Lenders—Savings and Commercial Banks

When you are in the market for a first mortgage, the first source you should turn to is the local savings or commercial banks in your area. We have already discussed some of the basic restrictions of the savings and commercial banks; however, as mentioned earlier, it is the bank's policy and appetite for loans that will affect you the most. Remember, they have to like you and like the category of real estate you are about to mortgage. Pick the closest lender to either you or the property.

If you do not already know anyone there, do not worry. That might actually be an advantage because they will not know you either, and all banks like to take a new customer away from a competitor. Walk right up to some employee other than the person seated behind the desk that says "Information" and ask where to find the president's office. The reason you do not go to the information person is that the sign is only to mislead you. The person sitting behind the "Information" sign is really a traffic cop. His or her real job is to direct you to the person he or she wants to send you to, no matter who you want to see. Information people will not send you to the president except as a last possible choice. On the way to the president's office, ask someone else the name of the president's secretary. Armed with this information, you are on your way to making your first and most effective contact: the secretary of the president of the institution.

SIX ADVANTAGES IN DEALING WITH A NEIGHBORHOOD BANK

1. LOCAL IN NATURE: Unlike some sources, the savings banks or commercial banks are local in nature. Granted, the bank may have branches all over the country, but the office you deal with is on the spot. The loan officers are on the spot, too, and you will find them easy to get to and for the most part very helpful. You usually have direct contact with the loan official and are not dealing through some other party, such as a real estate broker or mortgage broker. If you develop a success pattern, this local aspect of the bank will be far more visible than at a more distant lender. It is critical, however, to make sure that the decisions for the loan are as local as possible. With the branch banking that is found in most states, the savings bank two blocks away from the home you want to buy could be in the direct control of an institution 3,000 miles away. This may not work against you, but your approach and the details you provide would be different if you knew that. As you shop for a loan, make sure that none of the lenders you visit are controlled from a great distance. Find out by asking the direct and obvious question: "Where is the loan committee, who sits on it, and are they all from this area?"

Like most local businesses, the savings banks and commercial banks like to pride themselves on community spirit. You can and should take advantage of that whenever possible and whenever there is something unique about the loan request that has some specific benefit to the community.

In rough times, lenders do not like to spoil their community spirit and friendly neighbor image. If you keep your rapport with the institution, it can be most understanding. This is one of the most rewarding advantages and one of the reasons for its success. You will find great differences in personnel, attitude, and service. However, if it is truly local in thought, policy, service, and attitude, find a loan officer in that institution with whom you can work. Because many banking institutions have more than one office in a community, it is not unusual for some of the smaller branches to have limited services. Because of this, you may enter a branch that does not have any loan officers present. Instead of your finding the president of the institution, you may only have a branch manager available to help you. If this is the case, find out if they also handle loan requests, or should you make an appointment with a loan officer. You may have to go to the main branch to get that service, or the loan officer may make the rounds, so to speak, and meet you at the branch.

2. INEXPENSIVE APPRAISALS: This is a side benefit of the local nature of a local lending institution. Since it is in the community, it usually has its own appraisal division or department. This department keeps up-to-date records on what is going on in the community and on the evaluations of property in that area. However, more than that, it is aware of what is happening with future growth, new developments that you may not be aware of that can have some positive effect on your loan. You will note this difference far more positively when you deal with a distant lender who knows nothing about your area (or assumes it does not) and needs to be taught everything that is going on. Appraisals to satisfy these lenders can be expensive and long in coming. Naturally, the accuracy of the appraisal can work against you if it lowballs their proposal. Give it all necessary data. This will only lend credence to the fact that you are on top of the game.

3. CONFIDENCE IN AREA: Lenders must have confidence in the growth potential of an area. In essence, they are forced into this confidence. Remember, the lender exists because of the need to loan money. Naturally, areas can change, and more than one savings and loan was closed due to bad loans and a declining number of depositors. Like all businesses, savings and loans are not immune to failure, and they can and do go out of business. Nonetheless, their desire to be in business works for you.

4. ATTRACTIVE TERMS: For all lending institutions, the amount of competition for borrowers will vary with the circumstances of the market. In the middle 1980s, for example, the lending business grew with a multitude of companies vying for borrowers. For the first time in a long while, there seemed to be competition for the lenders. Along with competition usually come benefits for the consumer in the form of lower prices or, in the case of lending, better borrowing terms, so shop around not only between the savings and commercial banks, but with other lenders as well.

5. BETTER LOAN-TO-VALUE RATIOS IN THE FAVOR OF THE BORROWER: With the exception of government loan programs such as VA and FHA loans, 90 percent to 95 percent of the value that can be borrowed on many types of property and circumstances is most attractive to some borrowers. Keep in mind that the maximum loan from any institution or any lender will generally carry with it a penalty of higher interest than a lower loan-to-value ratio. This is because of the added risk to the lender, or to cover the insurance the lender puts into the transaction to cover the upper limits of the loan in the event of a default. This added risk or cost gets passed on to the borrower, who may, as many do, still find that loan to be the one that enables him or her to reach his goal.

6. LOWER QUALIFICATION STANDARDS: Among local S&Ls, there seems to be a drive to provide loans wherever possible, often making the local savings bank the most lenient of all sources. However, I do expect this to change and for lenders to pay much more attention

to the credit of their borrowers and to the appraisals and evaluations of the properties they take as security on their loans in the future. From the middle 1970s to early 1980s, S&Ls lost money with some of the creative lending techniques they devised that did little more than encourage borrowers to maximize their loans. The lending institutions took the blunt of a decline in growth in many areas and a real decline in property values in some parts of the country. Does any of this sound familiar? A similar event unfolded over the years 2000 to 2008.

The overly aggressive lending posture by many mortgage brokers and loan companies was fueled by some of the lowest interest rates in the past 40 years of conventional financing. This, coupled with a booming real estate market, partially encouraged by those low interest rates and a sluggish stock market, was a new gold rush into real estate as the way to make a quick million or two. Real estate investors could do no wrong, the buyers flocked to anything they could buy, and the cheap money was there for the taking.

People would finance, and as the rates continued to drop, refinance. Lenders began to get lax about their policy to make good loans to creditworthy borrowers. What did they care? They simply packaged loans off to insurance companies, pension funds, and other investors who liked the idea of spreading the risk over hundreds of individual loans. Then the crunch began to hit the entire industry. To some degree, it was the fault of the lenders for their aggressive and perhaps even cavalier way of conducting their business, but so too the fault lay with investors who thought the crest of the wave would never stop building. Flip a condominium before you have to close, buy two more in a new building, and repeat the success of the first one. Then BANG! Everyone suddenly began to listen to the media, and the balloon burst. History does repeat itself.

ELEVEN EFFECTIVE STEPS TO APPROACHING AND DEALING WITH LENDERS

1. GET TO KNOW THE SAVINGS AND COMMERCIAL BANKS IN YOUR AREA. This should include mortgage brokers. Begin by looking in the Yellow Pages to get the names of the institutions and their branch offices. Make note of those that are closest to your area, keeping in mind that any of the institutions in your county and most in the state may actually be able to serve your needs. However, you will begin with three different institutions and follow each of the next 10 steps with them until you have a working relationship with a minimum of three such savings and commercial banks.

2. MAKE YOUR INITIAL CONTACT THE MOST IMPORTANT ONE. This means you should call on the president or manager of that association. Find out the person's title by calling the bank and asking the receptionist to connect you with the secretary for the president of that facility. Be sure to ascertain first that you have reached the facility you want, and not a central phone number that was answered five hundred miles away. This can happen, and it is very frustrating when it does. It only demonstrates a slipping away from the local, friendly neighbor policy most institutions have prided themselves on over the years.

Although the ultimate contact is, of course, the president or general manager of the bank, from a practical point of view, it is the secretary of the president that you want to win over to your side. We shall assume that by going to the top of the line with bosses, we have also gotten to the best secretary available for the position. Once you take that position and treat her accordingly, you will find that no matter how slight your relationship with the president, you will have access to him or her through the secretary.

Your quest to know the president should not be more than a professional visit. Its goal is simply to meet the person and make sure that he or she knows who you are. Call, make the appointment (through the secretary), and introduce yourself as a real estate investor who plans to buy property in the area. State that you have been told (by me) that meeting the president would be productive for you both. Oh . . . no, you do not have an account at that bank just yet. Perhaps that can come later, if there is to be a mutual understanding. (If you have a small savings account and do not have much action in the deposit side, why have that prejudice the loan officer when he wants to know about your account history?)

Begin at the top, but move quickly into the ranks because it is here that you will find the loan officer who will help you get the money you need. To keep you from wasting time, ask your friend, the president's secretary, if she could recommend one of the loan officers that she feels would be good for you to meet.

Word from the secretary, no matter if it is to the president of the United States or the manager of the branch office, has a sting that is not unlike that of the top person him or herself. After all, who passes on the president's words if not his secretary?

A call from you to "Fran," with a simple request that sounds like this, is very effective: "Oh, Fran, seems like I remember you liked concerts. Well, could you do me a favor? My wife and I cannot make the concert next week, and I am going to drop two tickets to the concert in the mail. Please see they get used, would you? Oh yes, Charles (the president) said I should call if you could help with any introductions. Anyway, I would like to meet with one of the loan officers. You know, Fran, I like dealing with an officer who is not one of the old-timers or the new person in the department. Who would you recommend I meet with?"

When Fran comes up with a name or two, follow up with: "Fran, look, I don't want to bother Charlie about this. Would you please call this fellow you just recommended and ask him when it would be convenient to meet with him? I've got next Tuesday at 10 or Wednesday at 2 open. Can I call you back on this tomorrow?"

What happens now is Fran will call the loan officer she recommended, and her request to meet with you will sound like an absolute order directly from the president of the association himself. This is all rather simple. The next part of this step is to make the meeting and find out for yourself if this is indeed someone with whom you can work. If for any reason you feel uncomfortable with the loan officer, give your friend, the secretary, a call: "How was the concert?" Thank her for setting up the meeting and let her know that you would now like to meet another loan officer so that you can meet as many officers in the institution as possible to better determine which would work well with you.

Finally, make sure you have at least two meetings with the loan officer of your choice. It will be in these meetings that you set the foundation for the loan requests you may submit in the future.

3. LEARN THE PROCEDURES OF THE INSTITUTION. The procedures of each bank will vary slightly. Some require very detailed forms to be filled out for any loan request; others are less complicated. Collect all of the forms you must ultimately fill out and go over them so you understand exactly what the institution wants, and why. You will want to know:

- How often does the loan committee meet?
- What day do they meet?
- What is the deadline to get a request in any meeting?
- Does the association do its own appraisals?
- If not, who does?
- What are the current loan rates, terms, and policy?
- What kind of property does the association *not like* to lend on?
- What kind of property does the association *like* to lend on?

You will collect considerable data by visiting the institution. As you make calls on several lenders, you will find you are receiving quite an education. In fact, it is a good idea to make two practice calls on S&Ls that are on the other side of town to get the feel for things. Ask the loan officer to explain anything and everything until you are absolutely sure you understand the terms he or she is using and the reasons behind everything.

4. WHEN YOU GET READY TO ASK FOR A LOAN, PLAN YOUR SUBMISSION WELL. Later in this chapter, you will find an outline for a loan request. It contains all of the information the lender would need to know about you and the property except some minor details it may want to know just because of some local quirk. You should have already discovered through your contacts with the loan officers what data that association will look at most. If one institution looks very hard at the loan-to-value ratio, it is critical that you pay more attention to that aspect of the request.

Another loan officer may have told you that the economics of the transaction and pro forma are the key factors for the kind of property you know you want to buy. It is important, however, that you pay some attention to all of the items in the loan request. In the lending business, it is impossible to provide too many answers. Remember, the more detailed your request and back-up data, the heavier your report, the more time you have spent on specifics and background, the better your loan officer will feel about backing you in the loan committee. Don't forget that the loan officer doesn't want to get red marks, and the best way to avoid this is to give the impression that he or she did the job, so do yours.

5. MAKE YOUR LOAN REQUIREMENTS KNOWN. You should be able to support that request fully, of course, but be as specific as possible, and have a margin for negotiations in the request: small, but some margin.

You have to ask for an amount of money and show the terms you expect to be able to pay based on the project or property. For example, you might ask for $500,000 with a payback over 18 years, with a monthly payment not to exceed $4,375. In this way, you have established what would be an 8 percent mortgage for 18 years with a normal payback to amortize the mortgage for that term. The lender has room to match many of the criteria of the mortgage and still better its position if it can and if you will let it. For example, if the lender said okay to the monthly payment and total amount of the loan, but that at the end of the 18 years you will have a balloon of $50,000, the lender has, without saying so, disagreed with the interest level you had proposed (even though you did not specify it in your request). This balloon may not mean that much to you since you don't plan to keep the property for the full 18 years anyway, and by keeping the constant payment rate the same for the term you may agree to that slight increase in interest.

As you go through this book, you will see that it is designed to allow you to use it continuously as a reference tool. You will become aware that the more you know about the functions of finance and where the tradeoffs lay, the better you will be at developing more attractive loan portfolios for yourself and your property.

6. DON'T RUSH THE LOAN COMMITTEE. You will know from earlier contacts its schedule and the general policy with which it functions. Plan your submission well and submit it on time so you don't have to use up any of your "credits" by asking the loan officer to "please get this processed for me." The presentation is important also. If your package is complete and up to date, and you have anticipated all of the loose ends that might occur, the approval will be faster. Loan requests often are held up due to many items that the applicant could have taken care of in the beginning. The loan officer will have to go back and ask an applicant repeatedly for this or that document that is lacking in the files. Don't let that happen to you. If you do leave out something, make sure that you take care of it the moment it comes to your attention.

7. NEVER TAKE NO FOR AN ANSWER. Not everything you do is going to succeed. The same is true with loan requests. If the loan committee comes back with a direct turndown on a request, which is unusual, go back to the loan officer and ask if the head of the department could sit in on the meeting to explain what happened and why the loan was turned down.

As I said, a direct turndown is unusual. Generally, the loan officer will come back to you with some change in the terms you requested. It might be a decrease in loan amount, an increase in interest rate, a shorter term, a balloon payment, or all of these changes. Some loan officers will give you an idea about what went on in the committee. Just before leaving his office, you might turn to the loan office and say, "I have a lot of confidence in you, Frank. Let me give this some thought for a couple of days. I know you have spent a lot of time and effort on this, and if there is any way we can work something out we will."

As you start to leave, turn to him and say, "Only it's hard to understand how your institution could be so much below the others," and slowly let the door close.

Some lenders just won't make the loan no matter what. It might be that they don't have the funds or that they have filled that kind of loan in their portfolio for the month. Most likely, it is that they must change to meet the needs of their secondary market.

If the lender won't give you the loan, don't beat a dead horse. It is far better just to shop around for another lending institution. There will be another time you may want to ride this horse.

8. Use your influence. You either already have some, or you can develop some quickly. If you don't now belong to some success-oriented kind of organization, take a look at the partial list below and select one that sounds good and is located in your area. Pay it a visit. You will find that within these organizations are the leaders of the community or the future leaders of the community:

Toastmasters International	SME International
DECA	Junior Achievement
Junior Chamber of Commerce	United Way
Lions Club	Other charitable organizations
Rotary	

Of course, there are many other organizations, which are social or fraternal organizations, and they are important, too. However, if you want to develop influence and do it in a hurry, pick one or several of the organizations listed, or one that is especially active in your community to get things moving. If more than one such club exists in your area, pick the one that meets for breakfast. Remember the adage: The early bird gets the worm.

As you develop your comfort zone, you will be following a pattern also designed to expand on your potential influence. One of the steps in comfort zone development is attending city and county council meetings, and going to the city hall, courthouse, and building departments to meet key people. As you are doing this, you should also be making sure that the people you meet are also meeting you. Through proper follow-up, you will find that they will remember you, so if you have left a good impression you're on your way.

Be careful not to abuse your hospitality or influence. If you work for a company that has an account with a potential lender, don't threaten to remove your company's account unless:

- It is absolutely the final straw and you are so burned up you don't care about burning your bridges, or

- You are so secure in your position that you don't care what your boss thinks about that threat.

9. REMAIN CALM. It is not the end of the world, and there will be other opportunities. There are times when you have to step back and take a hard, cold look at what it is you are trying to do. One turndown doesn't mean you need to make any changes, but if you are consistently being turned down, then something you are doing isn't winning people over to your cause. So back off. Don't push the cause until you have the opportunity to sift out the bugs. Your friendly loan officer should help here if he or she can and will. Ask. If you're turned down, he or she should be replaced.

However, never fade into the background. Send a thank-you note to the loan officer and anyone else who worked on your project. Tell them you appreciated their sincere help and that you are sorry things didn't work out with that lending institution on that project (never admit that you were wrong or that you failed in getting the loan somewhere else). Tell them you will keep in touch and that because of their efforts you will contact them on your next transaction.

10. KEEP UP YOUR RAPPORT WITH THE INSTITUTION BETWEEN LOAN REQUESTS AND PROJECTS. Maintain some kind of contact from time to time: a lunch, a note in the mail, a copy of a book you have read about the decline of the savings and loans, whatever might give you the opportunity to keep your name in front of the people who may help you out when you need it.

11. AVOID DIRECT CONFRONTATION AND COMPARISON OF ONE LENDER TO THE OTHER. There is a temptation to invent offers that you have had from other lenders, such as, "Yeah! Well, you know that American National Federal has offered me $500,000 at 7 percent?"

However, as long as you have made it clear in a sound business way that you are talking to at least one other lender, you will keep them on their toes. If you are talking with 20 lenders, don't let that get around. In fact, talk about your loan with no fewer than four lenders, but do not let them know you are dealing with more than two. You don't want to give the impression that you fear the failure of one lender, but simply that you want to get the best terms from the best lenders around.

These 11 steps are easy to follow and apply to other kinds of lenders as well. As you follow the 11 steps, you will learn more about the lending business than you could in any book. Best of all, you will be giving yourself a better foundation to deal with other aspects of the real estate finance and investment arena.

As you progress in this book and in your own experiences in real estate investing and financing, you will discover that the creativity of bankers and lenders is often quite shallow. Perhaps that was not a fair statement because you will find several bankers or lenders who are progressive and most astute at what they do. However, they must limit that progressive and astute behavior to their own industry. As an independent investor, you have far more tools at your disposal to attack the problem of financing or investing. Your creative power and finesse then will exceed the ability of many lenders to provide compatible responses to your circumstance. This is not to be viewed as a detriment to you, but as a challenge for you to expand on your own opportunities. Do your best to take advantage of those opportunities. You must be open to all of your options and attempt to utilize a particular tool or option that is best suited to take you closer to your goals. By becoming proficient with the 11 steps in approaching lenders, you will see that there are ways to use the institutional lender to the maximum benefit.

For example, one financing tool we have not yet covered, but will in great detail, is open to you through the very best lender of all, the seller. As we get into seller-held financing, you will see that there are times when you can utilize the institutional lender with a conventional loan and the seller to provide you with more money than you need to acquire the property.

Several years ago, I helped a client of mine do exactly that when he was buying an expensive single-family property. The property consisted of two oceanfront lots in Fort Lauderdale, Florida. On the two lots, there was one single-family home. The home was livable, but was 55 years old and in great need of remodeling. The most conservative cost estimate to put the home into livable shape was $650,000.

The buyer was very well qualified financially and had a good personal statement; however, he wanted to keep his cash in reserve for his business and for any unforeseen event. His intention was to build a modern home on the same location as the existing one, either through extensive remodeling or new construction. He had correctly concluded that the $400,000 price he would pay for the property was a good value just for the lots. Like many homebuyers, my client owned another home that he was living in at the moment. His existing home was to go on the market for $850,000. Because that home had a first mortgage of $230,000, he had $620,000 of equity in his present home. After the sale and deduction of all expenses, he could count on a profit of about $685,000.

His need at the moment was to buy the oceanfront property without putting any cash into that deal, sell his existing home, and prior to moving rebuild the oceanfront property for his own use. Since he didn't know at this time how extensive the remodeling or construction would be, he could not apply for a development loan.

The lender he had a good relationship with had indicated that it would lend 75 percent of the contract price now, and when he knew what his plans would be, it would renew the loan to include the new construction.

This 75 percent loan would account for $150,000 of the purchase of the oceanfront land, but my client still would have to come up with $50,000 out of his own pocket, and he didn't want to part with that cash. Therefore, in the negotiations with the seller of the oceanfront property, the following deal was worked out.

The seller agreed to sell the oceanfront property for $200,000, taking a $100,000 cash down payment at the closing. The balance of $100,000 was to be held by the seller in the form of a second mortgage secured by my client's existing home. There was a stipulation that on the sale of the existing home, the $100,000 second mortgage would be paid off.

Now we went back to the lender and borrowed the $150,000 that they said they would lend in the first place. They had the first mortgage on the oceanfront lots, and out of the proceeds of the mortgage my client gave the seller of the lots $100,000, paid the lender for the costs involved in the mortgage, and had about $46,000 cash to go toward design plans for the new oceanfront home.

Everything about this transaction was legal and ethical. However, the lender that ultimately made the loan had first objected to the concept. When I pointed out that they did have the first mortgage on the oceanfront property and that there was no secondary financing on that property, they realized that they had made a good loan.

In a follow-up some eight years later, my client decided that living on the ocean was nice, and he and his wife loved the new home they had built there. However, he wanted to move to a waterfront location on one of the Fort Lauderdale canals. In the eight years that had gone by, the values had gone up substantially and he ended up selling the home for over $1,800,000.

Disadvantages of Dealing with Commercial Banks for Conventional Loans

1. Commercial banks are older than savings banks and thrift institutions and often have a more conservative approach to lending. This conservatism can present some distinct disadvantages to the borrower. Some of the more pronounced are:

   - A low loan-to-value ratio. The bank will look hard at the loan and examine the value of the property very carefully. It would rather be conservative and lose the loan than produce a high loan-to-value ratio and risk taking back a property.
   - Commercial banks do not like to lend their own funds above the 75 percent loan-to-value ratio. Of course, when it comes to FHA- or VA-insured loans, that is another matter and the bank will go all the way on those.
   - They generally require that the borrower be a client of the bank. This sometimes means that the borrower also has to keep a substantial deposit in the bank during the term of the loan. This goes back to the concept that if you have it, you don't need it so that's when we'll give it to you.
   - Interest rates can be higher than current rates from other sources. However, as the commercial bank is usually the fastest lender on any kinds of properties, the extra interest paid can be worth the cost later on down the line.

2. Prepayment of mortgage loans will generally carry a penalty or some other stipulation that limits the amount of principal that can be paid off at any given time or during any year. This may not seem to be a problem. However, you may want to sell the property in a few years. If the new buyer had to refinance to make the transaction, a penalty to get the old loan off the books can get in the way of a successful closing or can come out of your pocket.

3. The term of years a mortgage is amortized is generally shorter with commercial banks than with savings banks. For example, this means that even though the loan looks as though it is good for 25 years, the lender or the company that the lender has sold the mortgage to can call the loan at the end of seven years.

Dealing with the Mortgage Broker

Mortgage brokers and mortgage bankers can be worth their weight in gold. It is a very good idea to have at least one or two contacts with a mortgage brokerage firm in your area. These companies either act as a "finder" for money for you or actually bank the loan with their own sources. They deal with many of the prime money sources around, with which you would have no direct contact were it not for these brokers or bankers. These sources are the pension funds, insurance companies, large out-of-the-area commercial banks and savings banks, offshore money, real estate investment trusts, and so on.

When you deal with a mortgage broker, it is similar to going to a real estate broker who'll find you a house; only the mortgage broker finds a lender who will make your loan for you. Since the mortgage broker shops around for you, you sometimes can save time and effort by using his or her services. However, any benefit can come at a high penalty because you may be lax in seeking other sources for the funds. You may find in the end that the mortgage broker was unable to make your loan or does, in fact, place it with the lender around the corner from where you work.

However, there are many loans that cannot be made without the help of a good mortgage broker. So make a contact with a mortgage broker in the same way you would with a loan officer of a commercial bank. Do it before you need to borrow the money.

PRIME SOURCES FOR CONVENTIONAL LOANS

The following sources for conventional money may or may not be available to you on a direct basis. Most often, the following lenders are buyers of mortgage packages from savings banks, commercial banks, or mortgage bankers. However, sometimes you do have access to them, and if that is the case these lenders can offer the very best terms for your borrowing needs.

Insurance Companies

Insurance companies are a good source for funds and supply a major amount of cash outside the governmental reserves into the conventional lending systems. Unless you are a major borrower (in need of $1 million or more), it is unlikely that you will have a loan directly placed with an insurance company. However, some insurance companies will look at smaller loan requests through their representative mortgage brokers and mortgage bankers.

Insurance companies have very strong motives to lend out money if they have it. Like savings or commercial banks, insurance companies have their own cash and they must put it somewhere. The investments the insurance companies make include a wide range of items, of which mortgages are just a part. However, if you need a lot of money, this is usually where you will get it.

Dealing through a representative, such as with the mortgage broker, is different than dealing with the loan officer at the local commercial or savings and loan association. Because the lender is usually distant from you and your property, loan committees generally require far more details and information than the local lender.

There are several drawbacks in dealing with insurance companies other than their distance. These drawbacks may not be a problem for you, and if it is not, you should make sure that your mortgage broker has included one or more insurance companies in his or her search for a lender to take your loan. Naturally, this assumes that your loan request meets the minimum loan requirements by the specific insurance company.

The most notable drawback is the problem of good news–bad news. Since insurance companies are a good source for major loans, they frequently have many requests for the funds available. This enables the institution to be selective, and that makes their money difficult to get at times. This also leads to a time element that can be the killer for most borrowers who have a need to get the funds relatively quickly. Of all lenders, insurance companies can be the slowest to approve a loan. Of course, this time factor varies between different lenders and projects, but when you consider the extra data needed, frequently the requirement of having an MAI appraisal in addition to all the other back-up material, plus a 30- to 60-day shuffle through a loan committee, you can see that the commercial bank or savings bank can be a good alternative.

Real Estate Investment Trusts

There are three basic types of real estate investment trusts (REITs):

1. THE EQUITY REIT: This is similar to a mutual fund except the investors own an interest in whatever real estate the organization acquires. The form of ownership is like a corporation, only the income and losses are treated, for the investor, as though this were individual ownership of that percentage of the transaction. The equity REIT is a major buyer of office buildings, shopping centers, and the like. It takes part in joint ventures, develops, builds, and otherwise is involved in many forms of real estate investing.

2. THE MORTGAGE REIT: This form of real estate trust is designed for lending. They vary in size but are potentially in the lending game. They got into trouble in the early 1970s by being overly zealous with their lending practices. Many of their loans went bad, and they ended up owning property through foreclosures. Some of the mortgage REITs found themselves in irreversible trouble as they made construction loans on projects that failed prior to the permanent loan paying off the REIT. As the earlier mortgage REIT

based its success on a shorter duration loan, that is, the development loan, it was not a surprise that these REITs have undergone the greatest change over the years. Where they still exist, they are more often found as a part of the third form of REIT.

3. THE HYBRID REIT: This is a mixture of the two earlier forms of REITs. Some of these REITs were formed by accident, others by design. They have found the best and worst of both worlds, but in a counterbalance they seem to now make up the majority of REITs. Hybrids generally participate in the project, lending money and taking a percentage of ownership or override on income.

REITs fall into the same category of lending institution as insurance companies in that they are prime sources for funds, but their access is generally remote and distant unless you are a major borrower or developer. Nonetheless, keep them in mind. When they have money to lend, they can be very aggressive in lending it. As a joint venture partner, the REITs can be one of the first lenders to call.

Pension Funds and Credit Unions

These organizations collect massive amounts of funds and then make investments to suit their charters and goals. They act much like insurance companies but are often more accessible to fund or union members than other larger lenders. For example, if you are a member of a credit union, there are many services that organization can provide to you besides lending money. Pension funds vary in the services they offer their members; find out what services they offer, if any.

Wall Street and International Security Markets

Many large commercial transactions are financed in part by stock market venders. These large financial institutions may include banking groups as well as stockbroker houses. They are found around the world and often are truly international in scope. Their sources are generally a combination of joint venture and loan. They like to become partners in very large transactions and frequently do so by funding 100 percent of a project. Unless you are a big borrower, they may not be attracted to you. However, if there is an attraction, then be ready to accept a partner in your business and investment portfolio.

General Comments about Institutional Lenders

The whole finance game seems to revolve around major lenders. The secondary market buys packages from savings banks and commercial banks. The U.S. government plays a big role through the Federal Reserves monetary policy.

The economics of government intervention in the free enterprise system is subject to argument by just about any economist you will find. The problem seems to be that no two economists may agree as to the exact definition of the problem or its potential solution. The theory of control by the government to provide checks and pushes to the nation's economy is based on the principle that if nothing is done, things will work out.

The U.S. government is both a lender and a borrower. It is a lender in that its insurance to banks, and for FHA and VA loans, makes a marketplace for borrowers that may not exist otherwise. The money borrowed through the sale of bonds and the like is a real debt that is repaid through new loans made (more bonds sold).

If You Are a Big Borrower, the Pension Fund May Be the Only Way to Go

No one will disagree with this statement, except the other lenders hoping to make the same loan. The only answer, of course, is to shop around and find out for yourself just who is the best source for you at the time you need the money (see Table 5.3).

Table 5.3
A Summary of Advantages and Disadvantages of Loan Sources

Loan Sources	*Advantages*	*Disadvantages*
Savings banks and thrift or credit unions	Local and on the spot Know property and area Have confidence in area Long payout High percent of loan to value More lenient in qualifying both the property and the borrower	High points Personal liability Nonassumable at times Prepayment penalty
Commercial banks	Local and on the spot Know property and area Have confidence in area Lower points Construction and land loans	Low percent of loan to value Want other business Higher interest rate Sometimes prepayment penalty Shorter term of years
Insurance companies	Have ample money Like big borrowers Lower interest rate Low points Permanent loan usually not personally guaranteed	Not local Can be impersonal Highly selective Demand greatest qualification on property and borrower Long processing time
Real estate investment trusts (REITs)	Same as insurance companies Less conservative Loan terms more flexible	Not local Can be impersonal Generally short-term lender Long processing time

Table 5.3 (continued)

Pension funds	Same as insurance companies	Same as REITs
Stock market sources	Same as insurance companies	Want a piece of the action
Sellers	Depends on the situation and the seller No points at all Usually best rate No processing time to worry about	Seller may be limited in the amount he or she can hold Term usually shorter

THE SELLER IS OFTEN THE BEST (AND MOST MOTIVATED) SOURCE

One of the best sources for first mortgages is the seller. There are many advantages to this source, and oddly enough it is the seller that is often the first source that is overlooked. The biggest advantage to you is that there is no middleman. You are the intermediary, and the saving of loan points and time are valuable to all parties of the transaction. This chapter does not deal with the methods of approaching the seller. Other chapters cover this aspect in greater detail. Yet you should never overlook the seller as perhaps the best source of all.

Private Money: Where It Is and How to Find It

Because private money is not institutional, it is often not classified along with conventional financing. However, because conventional financing is a type of loan and not limited by the source, I have chosen to include a brief section on private money. Because the use of private money varies greatly in its advantages and disadvantages, it is safe to say that it can have both the advantages and the disadvantages of all other sources.

Each private lender is an independent lender, and reacts to a loan request by seeking the most profitable deal based on what the market and his or her requirements dictate. In general, rates will be the highest and the amounts limited. Some private sources seem to be well financed, but these are few.

However, finding the private money is easier than getting it. A look in the Yellow Pages or newspaper classifieds will be a good start. Many mortgage brokers and stockbrokers know of private money. Deal with private money very carefully. It is best to have any and all mortgage documents examined by an attorney.

PUT TOGETHER A LOAN INFORMATION PACKAGE

Whenever you have a loan request in excess of $100,000, and always when you are putting a commercial venture together, you should develop a loan request package. The lending institution will use this information to help justify the loan. The approach is to demonstrate your professionalism. Every point you can win up until the final vote of the loan committee will be a point in your favor. Give them something they can look back at that will make them feel good about their decision to give you the money.

The information you provide should be data already known to you. Your investment team should be alert to the need for a pending loan request and start obtaining the necessary information the moment you begin planning for the purchase or the project.

Table 5.4 is an outline that you can follow in the preparation of a Mortgage Loan Request. The request you formulate should be as complete as possible. Because the outline can become the index to all your loan applications and requests, you should make several copies of this outline. Highlight the sections that your different investment team members need to work on. A review of the first five chapters of this book might be excellent brush-up before any formal presentation is presented.

Table 5.4
Outline of a Mortgage Loan Request

I. The Property
   A. General description
   B. Legal description
   C. Location
   D. Location sketch
   E. Aerial photo
   F. Location benefits
   G. Location drawbacks
   H. General statistics
      1. Demographics
      2. Average rent
      3. Traffic counts
   I. General site data
      1. Legal
      2. Size and square feet of land and site coverage
      3. Use of site
      4. Zoning
      5. Utilities

Table 5.4 (continued)

6. Access
7. Sketch of lots sharing building location
8. Survey

J. Land value
    1. Estimated value of site
    2. Comparable land sales and values

II. The Improvements

A. Description
B. General statistics
    1. Date built
    2. Year remodeled
    3. Type of construction
    4. Other structural and mechanical data
    5. Floor area
    6. Parking
    7. Other data
C. Sketch of ground floor
    1. Show tenants
    2. Show square feet
    3. Show approximate sizes
    4. Building plans (if new building, if lender is not in area, or if requested)
D. Sketch of second floor
    1. Show tenants
    2. Show square feet
    3. Show approximate sizes
    4. Building plans (if new building, if lender is not in area, or if requested)
E. Sketch of third floor
    1. Show tenants
    2. Show square feet
    3. Show approximate sizes
    4. Building plans (if new building, if lender is not in area, or if requested)
F. Personal property
    1. Inventory
    2. Value
G. Statement of condition of property
    1. Copies of general inspection reports
    2. Copies of environmental inspections and recommendations if any.

H. Replacement cost of structure
   1. Original cost
   2. Replacement cost
I. Comparable sales of improved property of similar nature in the area
J. The economics (actual)
   1. Income
   2. Expense
   3. Net operating income
   4. Economic value
   5. Rent roll
   6. Sample lease
   7. Past records of income and expense
K. Opinion of economics
   1. Relationship to average square-foot rent for area
   2. Average of square foot for this building
   3. General opinion
   4. Estimated future income
L. General summary of value
   1. Land values
   2. Replacement value
   3. Personal property value
   4. Estimated present value
   5. Economic value at present income
   6. Comparable value
   7. Contract price
   8. Copy of contract
   9. Value justified

III. The Borrower

A. Name
B. Address
C. Occupation
D. General data
E. Net worth
F. Supporting documents
   1. Net worth statement
   2. Schedule of assets
   3. Schedule of liabilities
   4. References
   5. Position of employment

Table 5.4 (continued)

6. Verification of salary
7. Estimated annual earnings
8. Credit report of applicant
9. Other forms supplied for application

IV. The Loan Request
A. Amount
B. Terms and conditions

Note: If there are environmental problems, you need to address these with a business plan, which covers how they will be dealt with, cost estimates from reliable contractors experienced in dealing with cleanup or treatments, and so on.

FOUR KEY STEPS IN FORMULATING THE LOAN PACKAGE

1. Keep your sales material up to date and accurate. This will mean knowing all there is to know about the property you are to sell or buy.

2. Accumulate the various sketches, photographs, past records, and other supporting documents you will use. These are shown in the Presentation Index as you go from listing to marketing.

3. Develop an understanding with the lenders you will approach to make sure what parts of the presentation they want emphasized. Remember, some lenders pay more attention to the person, others the property. You will want to know just how far you should go with the economics on the property. I prefer to limit the economic data to a minimum. Past records going back two or three years are helpful, and of course current data is a must. Expenses are almost more important than income and should be realistic. In most cases, you will have to increase the expenses the seller gives you. Avoid pro forma showing the next five years or more. Some of the new computer printouts enable you to run a 10-year, or longer, projection of income and expenses. This is a waste of time on two counts. First, no one will read them with any real belief that they are correct. Second, they will not be correct. You cannot effectively project into the future, so don't go beyond one or two years at most.

4. Get into the habit of using the package on all your loan applications.

Chapter 6

USE CREATIVE
FINANCING TO
MAXIMIZE BENEFITS

GOAL OF THIS CHAPTER

This chapter opens doors and your eyes to opportunities available to you by increasing your investment techniques and strategies, enabling you to maximize your benefits and helping you to attain your investment goals. This chapter expands and reinforces much of the information provided in Chapter 5.

MAXIMIZE CLOSED TRANSACTIONS

Deal making in real estate is closing transactions. Making successful investments in real estate is a combination of events, which will happen only when the property you want to buy passes your due diligence inspections and fits your investment needs. If you walk out of the closing room with a deed in your hand but your investment plan runs into a snag, everything can be in jeopardy unless your financing strategy works to move you closer to your desired goals.

Move Closer to Your Investment Goals

With this in mind, it is important that you understand at least some of the many creative ways in which you can nail a deal together. Some of the creative techniques that I will teach you bring the seller around to sign the kind of deal that makes the investment work for you. At the same time, these investment strategies work for the seller because they take the seller closer to his or her desired goals as well. Remember, sellers want to sell. You should never forget the most basic of all motivations, no matter what the underlying cause, is the need or desire to sell. Having just said that, there is a pitfall in that motivation that many sellers never grasp. Sometimes the goal to sell the property is not the only, or even right path the seller can pursue. Equally, often the method of selling that the seller believes he must take is not the only way to achieve his main goal.

Creative Strategy Means Examining All Opportunities

For example, I recently had a call from a real estate developer from Michigan. He asked my opinion on how he was handling a financing situation. It seems that he borrowed $950,000 on a development tract of land located on Lake Michigan. The lender, a local bank, wants him to pay off the loan and has called his note (to call a note is bankers' jargon for requiring you to pay off the outstanding balance). This has frustrated his plan, which was to construct a luxurious lakefront home for resale. His problem now is the land has slipped in value and if he had to sell it today, he would not get more than $820,000. He rationalizes that if he can borrow sufficient funds to build the home, he can rent it out, and in a few years when the real estate market has recovered, sell it at a big profit and be in good shape. However, he has a problem with obtaining the financing to build the home. He needs an additional $450,000 to construct the home on the tract.

I asked him if he could go to the lender and get them to finance the construction of the home, and he replied that he had burned that bridge and was negotiating with a new bank. Burning bridges with your lenders is not a wise thing to do, and he now realizes that. Nonetheless, I suggested that he go to that lender and present them with a detailed plan whereby they and he could benefit. In essence, either they now own the lot, worth $820,000 if they can find a buyer, or they collaborate with him to build the new home. They should see the lightbulb turn on above their head to replace that dark cloud of a pending foreclosure where they end up with the lot in a down real estate market.

Too Narrow a View

Often a seller sees one avenue and no other. A client of mine owned a motel across from the beach in Fort Lauderdale, Florida. It was an old building that was a liability to the prime dirt on which it sat. The value of the land far exceeded the motel, yet he continued to pour money into the buildings in the hopes that it could produce enough income to support the value he thought was in the business. He failed to grasp that his plan was misdirected and that he would be better off selling the property or developing a new hotel on the site. Instead, he eventually went broke, could no longer make his mortgage payments, and lost the property in foreclosure.

Do Not Get Locked into a Single Strategy

Sellers sometimes overlook the fact that one of the best strategies to sell a property, especially in a buyer's market, is to become a buyer using their "for sale" property as a part of a purchase of another property. That tired old motel owner might have been able to do that himself, exchanging the equity in the land for something else. Oh, I know what he would say about that plan: "What would I exchange for anyway?"

The reality is that anything would have been better than where he ultimately ended.

Creative deal making can become a learning process for sellers you run into in your journey to build a real estate empire. Your knowledge and experience in use of the creative techniques contained in this book may help them conclude a successful real estate transaction with you for a truly win/win deal.

FINANCING IS A SHIFT OF EQUITY

Real estate financing can be much more creative once you are outside the box of conventional financing. Your success in dealing with conventional financing will often be by using it with one or more of the unconventional techniques discussed in this book.

Unconventional real estate financing consists of elements that often appear not to be financing at all. For example, land leases rarely are considered a financing technique; likewise, few bankers would call timesharing a hotel a financing tool. Nonetheless, both of these two methods of shifting equities are exactly that: financing tools that are available to you when the right moment comes along.

Once you understand the idea of shifting equities, you will have a much easier time using the more complex techniques displayed in this book. Best of all, you will find that you will begin to combine different techniques to fit your specific situation and transaction.

If you owned a home that had no mortgage and was worth $290,000, your total equity would be $290,000. If you go to a local lender and give them a mortgage, and they lend you $200,000 against your home, your equity is still $290,000. You have shifted part of it ($200,000) into your pocket as cash. The remaining equity of $90,000 is still in the house. This means that if you do not count the cash in your pocket, your home equity is only $90,000.

For example, assume that you want to acquire a small farm on the outskirts of town. When you meet the seller's broker, you discover that the seller may be interested in taking your mortgaged house as partial payment against the farm. The farm is priced at $270,000. You have $90,000 equity in your home (value $290,000 but there is an existing mortgage of $200,000). To balance this exchange, you would owe the seller $180,000.

The seller indicates he will lend you the $180,000 by taking a mortgage back from you secured by your equity in the farm. What happened to your original $290,000 equity?

Nothing, except that it has been divided and spread around. You have $200,000 cash, and owe $180,000 on the farm that is worth $270,000. Your $90,000 equity in the farm and the $200,000 in cash means your original equity of $290,000 is still in place. However, because your goals were to sell the house and purchase a farm, you have moved toward that goal in a very positive way.

The critical part of this example is that you must keep all of your options open and available to you if you expect to use financing to your best benefit. You will find that you can shift equity and ownership at the same time to get closer to your goals. Alternatively, you could have taken a different tack, such as a land lease with option to recapture. Using a combination you give up ownership, but keep the use of the property until you decide if you want ownership back again. All of this is shifting equity.

One reason this concept is important is that many people look at it as a two-sided affair. You buy it, and you sell it. Many people think that the immediate step to buying one property is to sell the property they currently own. For many people, they should follow this exact pattern. There are other ways to attain your goals than just selling one property to be able to buy another. I will show you techniques that will help you buy two properties easier than you could buy one, and other techniques that help you get the maximum value out of your investments.

Most new single-family financing is through conventional lenders. The money market favors single-family homes because institutional lenders can sell these loans to larger investment banks or funds. Portfolios of several million dollars worth of loans are packaged together with loan service included in the deal. In this way, the banks or other lenders can make loans, make a profit on selling the loan package, and retain an annual servicing fee. These loan packages must meet the institutional buyer's criteria, and for the moment, all loans that fall into this category are first mortgages, with the vast majority on single-family owner-occupied homes and condominium apartments.

RANKING OF MORTGAGES

As we get into the nonconventional financing arena, we will find that we for the most part are now dealing with a mixture of first and second mortgages. This topic has been touched on in the previous chapter, and will be brought up when it is important in later chapters. There will be times when the mortgage looks like a conventional mortgage and appears to be a first mortgage just as its institutional lender's counterpart would be. However, if you go by the label and you are the seller in the situation, you might find yourself on the losing end of that deal.

As you develop the basics of secondary and other creative financing, look at how mortgages are ranked and the significance of those rankings.

A First Mortgage Comes First, but It Isn't Always

The rank of a mortgage is its position to the other mortgage liens recorded against the property. The important word here is *position*. When a mortgage is given to a lender, it is taken down to the courthouse and the document is recorded as a lien against the property.

For example, you have just sold your home for $300,000, and after getting $130,000 cash at the closing, you took back a mortgage for the balance of $170,000. The buyer had the standard forms, and the document said "first mortgage" right on the top line. In fact, the buyer was so nice that he said he would drop the papers off at the courthouse for you. He did so the day after he recorded his title, and he took out another mortgage for $80,000 from his brother-in-law. If the brother-in-law is able to get his mortgage document recorded prior to yours, he would have the first mortgage position and you would have a second position.

AVOID SUBORDINATION TO A LATER RECORDED MORTGAGE. This following example is not the only scenario in which this problem can occur, but it is a frequent pattern. Assume that there are several mortgages on a property. This is the order in which they were recorded:

1. A $30,000 mortgage.
2. A $25,000 mortgage.
3. A $50,000 mortgage.

Because the recording was in the order indicated, the first mortgage is the $30,000 mortgage, unless something else had also happened; that something is subordination.

REVIEW SUBORDINATION. Subordination has been mentioned earlier in this book, but as it can cause very serious problems to the security of a mortgage, I will discuss it here and in other chapters so that you can see how easily it is slipped into a deal. Subordination relates to holding rank in order of time recorded in the public records, to such an extent that one mortgage is given priority over others that would normally have superior rank. For example, at one time there was only one mortgage on the above property. When the property was sold to Mr. Smyth, it was done so on the specific terms that he could get a total of $25,000 in additional financing, which would be ranked ahead of the existing mortgage. This change of rank does not mean that the $25,000 would actually become a first mortgage, only that it would have the power and lien rights of a first mortgage. (Naturally, either this provision would have to be already in the existing mortgage terms or the mortgagee would have to agree to its conditions in the agreement with Smyth.) The $50,000 mortgage may have been put on the property later when Smyth sold it to a third party.

The significance of this subordination is the position of the mortgages and to illustrate that in some circumstances the position and rank can change. The $30,000 mortgage was a first mortgage at one time, and it was ranked ahead of any other mortgage until the subordination provision was inserted. When the second mortgage was recorded for $25,000, it actually took over the rights of the first mortgage even though it is technically a second mortgage. The last mortgage remained the third mortgage. However, the wording of the subordination provision could have been something like the following:

> and the mortgagee does herein agree that during the life of this mortgage and until such date that all principal and unpaid interest shall be satisfied to the benefit of the mortgagee. This mortgage will be, at the option of the mortgagor or his successors in title, subordinated to a debt of up to but not to exceed $25,000, provided that the payment of that debt shall not be at an interest rate to exceed ___ percent per annum, with total payments of interest and principal per year not to exceed $____ in any given year.

It is not the form of the statement that is important. What you want to look for is an open-ended form of subordination. What would happen here is that if the second-recorded mortgage of $25,000 was to be paid off, an amount of $25,000 of what was the third-ranked mortgage could then take over the lien rights of the first mortgage. The point is that rank can change because of the terms and conditions in other mortgages no matter what is said within a specific mortgage.

Knowing the whole story when you buy or sell property or deal in discounting of mortgages (which will be a separate chapter in this book) is critical for you.

Please make careful note: Never rely on the mortgagor or the mortgagee to give you the whole story or even the truth when it comes to the terms and conditions of a mortgage that person, company, or bank may be holding. It has been my sad experience that lending institutions give out information about mortgages they hold and the information they give you is very often wrong, misleading, incorrect, and, in general terms, a lie.

That is a strong statement, but it has been true in the majority of situations and circumstances involving my clients. There are reasons for this that do not include intent to commit fraud, such as inexperienced staff, change in loan policy and loan forms, the deneighborhoodization of the institute or bank so it is possible that the forms are a thousand miles away, and so on. However, if you have not read the actual terms and conditions of any mortgage (or any legal document for that matter), get them, read them, and make sure you understand how they impact you.

Make sure your lawyer has read them, too. In addition, be sure he has understood what they said. There are many ways to write mortgage terms, and those terms can sound so similar to methods used by lawyers that they too could overlook the change.

SECOND MORTGAGE FINANCING IS A DEAL MAKER

In a purchase or sale, it is not unusual for a seller to be asked to take back a second mortgage. This second mortgage, in its usual form, is nothing more than an additional mortgage that runs concurrent to the existing financing. This mortgage must, however, be allowed for it to be properly made. An existing first mortgage or a purchase money first mortgage the buyer takes out to finance the acquisition may have a provision that does not permit secondary financing without express permission of the mortgagee.

When secondary financing is permitted by an existing mortgage, it will be the terms of the secondary mortgage that give you the flexibility in the overall financing to maximize the benefits of the investments so that it fits your needs. The secondary financing that you develop will follow the same techniques that will work for first mortgages or in conjunction with several techniques. It could well be that you establish both conventional and secondary financing at the same time.

I WILL PAY YOUR PRICE IF YOU ACCEPT MY TERMS

By adjusting the form of financing you use in your offers to acquire or in the methods used to negotiate to sell your own, you will find that price can be the least important aspect of a transaction. Many transactions have failed to achieve agreement even though both the buyer and the seller already had a meeting of the minds; only they did not know it.

For example, Bob has made up his mind that he will never take less than $100,000 for a vacant lot he wants to sell. Along comes Charlie who has made up his mind that he will not pay more than $90,000 for the property. However, out of this seemingly impossible situation, Bob has indicated that one or more of the following factors apply to the deal.

1. He wants to take $50,000 of the sale and travel around the world on a cruise ship with his wife.

2. Since he paid only $5,000 for the lot five years earlier, he will have a heavy gains tax to pay and needs some tax planning.

3. He plans to buy a boat with the balance of the cash, expecting to add more money to that transaction if necessary.

4. Or, he will take as little as $10,000 down and get the balance over a period of up to 15 years (putting that in the bank for his grandson's future college education).

Working with any of these factors would have made this transaction work. Let's look at each one in more detail:

1. Charlie gets additional information from the broker about the desired cruise. Charlie then goes to a wholesale cruise agency and makes the following deal with the owner.

"I plan to buy a property by giving away cruises that you sell. I want you to pay me a top commission. Please give me a list of cruises that pay maximum commissions." The travel agent shows Charlie some cruises that would earn Charlie a 25 percent commission. Charlie picked out a couple of around-the-world voyages and booked space in the name of Bob and his wife. These cruises ranged from $50,000 to $90,000 (for double occupancy). He then makes his offer to Bob showing that he will pay cash over and above the price of any of the cruises to match Bob's asking price of $100,000. Bob says okay and picks a $50,000 cruise package. Charlie now closes the deal with the travel agent to lock in the deal and closes with Bob. The actual commission Charlie gets is $12,500, so he writes out two checks, one to the travel agent for $37,500 and the balance to the closing agent on the vacant lot of $50,000. This means that the transaction will now close with Charlie actually paying only $87,500 while Bob got his full value of $100,000.

2. Realizing that the seller has a capital gains problem, the buyer approaches the situation with an installment sale. This is a provision where the seller takes the purchase price spread over more than one year. He saves on tax as he does so since the total gain does not increase his income to the point that his overall tax rate is increased excessively.

   This technique can be coupled with the "split payment" method, where the actual price is shown as $100,000 but the payments are divided into several years. Assume the buyer split the purchase into the following payments: $20,000 down, and eight annual payments of $10,000 each, the seller would be able to spread the capital gain over a total of nine years. Assume that there was zero interest in those payments, so the buyer benefits, the seller gets his price, and so does the buyer. If the buyer's cash can earn him extra dividends elsewhere, the ability to spread the total payment of the purchase over the additional years may make up part or all of the $10,000 over the desired payment of $100,000, and the seller may well end up the slightly better than he would getting all cash at closing.

3. The boat deal is even easier to handle than the cruise around the world. The buyer pays a visit to one or more boat brokers or companies and makes a deal to "sell" one or more of their boats. The buyer puts $50,000 in the bank, and whenever the deal goes through, he can collect the $10,000 or more that would be his commission from the yacht deal.

4. Any time a seller indicates that he or she will hold secondary financing and spread the payments on the balance over time, he tells the buyer that the most critical aspect of the deal is the price, but that the terms are somewhat flexible.

   Because financing is simply an adjustment of values to interest rates over time, the buyer can make up his needed $10,000 discount over a 10- to 15-year term. In fact, this could be done in a much shorter time period.

For example, an $80,000 mortgage at 6 percent interest per annum over 10 years (120 months) will have a monthly payment of $888.16. A $70,000 mortgage for 10 years at 9 percent has a monthly payment of $886.73. The buyer can rationalize that he negotiated this deal the way he wanted it, and why not? A deal was made when it might not have been made otherwise. The basic structure of the financing technique used should then be devised to meet your goal and close the transaction.

All Transactions Should Have a Proper and Satisfactory Close

Investors who build substantial wealth through their investments know that there is a time and place for talk, and a time for action. Between the two, it will be action that closes the deal, not talk. Too much talk makes a deal drag along until all parties lose interest. Reluctant sellers and difficult situations that cannot be resolved simply or quickly, or buyers who cannot make up their minds, cause more deals to be lost than any single deal breaker.

Real estate salespeople know the power of "now" and act to nail down deals while the decision process is working. In any secondary financing, a good salesperson will help you take advantage of this power, whether you are the buyer or the seller.

ADVANTAGES AND DISADVANTAGES OF SECOND MORTGAGES

This is how second mortgages look to lenders and borrowers:

Institutional or Private Lender	Borrower
The higher the risk, the higher the position (second mortgages more than firsts, third mortgages more than seconds, and so on).	Can reduce equity in the property and leverage the return.
The higher the risk, the higher the rate.	Can mean a high rate on the money borrowed.
Borrower should be strictly qualified.	May be hard to get.
Keep the term short.	Term too short to make a reasonable payment schedule.
Obtain other security.	Other security can tie up other property.
Be quick to foreclose.	Even slight default can bring pressure.

A lender will examine all superior financing when considering making a loan on a property. The value of the property and the percentage of existing financing will dictate the amount of risk he or she is taking. Obviously, the lower the percentage of existing financing to total value, the lower the risk to the lender. If the property is valued at $50,000 and the first mortgage is $20,000, a second mortgage of $10,000 is a fairly safe gamble for the lender. The rate and term of years can be adjusted to account for the level of risk.

Lower-ranking mortgages, such as third or fourth mortgages, will command even higher rates as the risk increases and as the position or rank decreases. From a practical point of view, there are few institutional or private money sources that will lend on third or fourth mortgages.

When Secondary Loans Are Needed

Because not all transactions involve the use of secondary financing, it will be helpful for you to know when you should look to this form of financing as a deal maker. The first step in ascertaining when the secondary form of financing is needed is to fully understand what the second loan can do:

1. It can enable the buyer to structure the total financing so that he or she can afford the required equity down payment. Because the terms of the secondary financing may vary, the overall debt service may require lower monthly payments due to the combined financing, when compared to other alternatives. Of course, there are times when the new first mortgage money market will not permit the loan-to-value ratio needed, and the secondary financing may be the only way to achieve that ratio.

2. It can increase the cash flow yield on the cash invested in an income property transaction by reducing the amount of cash to be invested, and by establishing a constant rate of payment on the secondary financing which is lower than the prior cash flow yield, then the new cash flow yield will be increased.

3. It can leverage a seller's return on the paper. If the seller were to receive $50,000 in cash, where could (or would) he or she invest the sum or money and at what interest rate? Alternatively, if the seller were able to obtain a 15 percent return or better from a secure second mortgage on previously owned property, he or she might be interested. The wraparound may do this, and is one of the better forms of secondary financing.

4. It can spread risk and separate values. Because secondary financing covers such a broad spectrum, it includes such creative forms of financing as land leases, wraparound mortgages, blanket mortgages, cross-collateralized purchase money financing, subordinated interest, interest-only payments, moratorium on all payments, percentage override sale of divided interest, and on and on. Various techniques that are covered in this book are used mostly in secondary financing. You will be able to sell a building, for example, but keep the land, which is then leased to the purchaser (this is a form of secondary financing).

5. There may be a limit to other choices. If the new money market is tight, seller-held secondary money may be the only possibility for structuring a high loan-to-value ratio.

6. The secondary loan can substantiate value. If the seller will hold a substantial second or third mortgage, at good terms, a sale at a higher price may be attained. There is

normally a trade-off in this situation. The seller accepts lower than current interest over the term of the mortgage and the buyer pays more for the property than he or she might have if more cash were invested. The judgment of which is better for the buyer or the seller depends on the alternatives that are actually present. It will do no good to assume it would be better to take cash instead of a mortgage, unless someone actually is offering cash and someone else is offering a mortgage.

Of the six things that secondary financing can do, not all may be present in every situation. In fact, to have two or three would be exceptional. Now that you have seen what secondary financing can do, look at the circumstances that will cause you to look to it as the most effective method of financing a transaction.

When to Use Different Types of Secondary Mortgages

EXAMPLE 1. New money is tight and expensive. Closing costs and points are high, and loan-to-value ratios are 75 percent or less. The property has an existing financing that totals 50 percent of the property value and has a reasonable constant rate of payment. The buyer has a limited amount of cash to invest and must raise the loan-to-value ratio.

EXAMPLE 1—TYPES OF SECONDARY FINANCING TO USE

- Start with seller-held secondary financing. If the seller won't hold a normal secondary loan, then approach him with a wraparound structure.
- A land lease subordinated to existing financing will separate values and reduce the cash needed for the down payment.
- If the seller will not take the paper, look to other markets for the secondary loan.
- Possible cross-collateralization of other property may provide sufficient equity to support the loan for the seller or other lenders.

EXAMPLE 2. New money is tight and expensive as in the previous situation. Loan-to-value ratios are not sufficient to give the amount of financing needed, and the lender will not permit secondary financing on the property. The existing mortgage is very low (below 30 percent of value) or the property is free and clear.

EXAMPLE 2—TYPES OF SECONDARY FINANCING TO USE

- Use other property the buyer has for the security of the secondary financing and go into the new money market for a first mortgage.
- In some situations, the lender will not look at a land lease that is subordinated to the first mortgage as secondary financing, and this alternative can be used.
- Leaving the seller in the deal with a right to buy him or her out in the future is a form of secondary financing.

- Establishing a royalty fee on overages of income can provide income to a seller and will not affect the lender's restrictions on new money.

EXAMPLE 3.   New money is available at reasonable rates. Loan-to-value ratios are high, and the property is free and clear or has a low percentage of existing financing. However, the buyer still needs extra financing.

EXAMPLE 3—TYPES OF SECONDARY FINANCING TO USE

- Look to the seller as the prime secondary lender.
- If the amount of the secondary financing needed is small and the commission substantial, the broker will often hold the paper.
- The land lease and other provisions mentioned earlier may be useful in this type of situation.

The above situations are the ones most frequently encountered. There are many variations, of course, and secondary financing can be used in any deal. However, there are times when secondary financing is not effective and you should be aware of these:

- Avoid using secondary financing when the buyer is financially weak and the transaction must be forced to meet his or her economic ability. If a buyer is putting down a last dime on an income property, he or she may be destined for trouble. Overextension of loan-to-value ratios will create debt service that may be more than the property or the buyer can handle.
- Avoid seconds if the new money market is good, the existing financing on the property is low, and the equity needed with this type of financing is available from the buyer. Do not use secondary financing simply to increase this extension at the sacrifice of leverage. You should, however, first analyze the leverage and extension of a property to be sure you are arriving at a debt that you can reasonably repay.
- If a property has several existing secondary loans, you may still use secondary financing, but see if it is possible to eliminate some of the current loans with the cash down or by refinancing the entire package with a new first mortgage.
- Avoid a package of combined financing that has a constant rate which is more than 3 points above the possible existing financing, unless there is a good reason (such as an existing mortgage that is to retire in a few years, and the current cash flow can be sacrificed for the period of time in exchange for future gains in the form of appreciation).

Remember that the greater the percentage of loan-to-value ratio, the more risky the secondary loans become. There are exceptions to every rule mentioned about secondary financing. The needs of the parties involved, their capabilities, and their willingness to risk capital need to be considered.

FINDING SECONDARY FINANCING

The few sources of secondary financing are:

• THE SELLER: The best. (See sections of this chapter that follow for more detailed information.)

• COMMERCIAL BANKS AND SAVINGS BANKS: These sources are available for secondary financing in the form of home improvement loans. These loans should not be overlooked because the buyer often anticipates additions to a property and plans on using cash after the sale for these improvements. Transfer cash to the down payment and finance the improvements with a home improvement loan. Some commercial banks are good sources for personal loans secured by real estate. This is a changing market, however, and will depend on the bank and the person.

• MORTGAGE COMPANIES: Most communities have several mortgage companies that deal in the secondary loan market. They are effective, although often expensive. Check your area to locate them. Then use the same methods of establishing rapport with them as you would for a lender (discussed in the previous chapter).

• PRIVATE INVESTORS: This source is hard to find, and often there are investors that deal with the mortgage companies. Sometimes, however, you will find them advertising in the classified section of the local newspaper. They should be found before you need them. Your commercial bank may know of some. Many mortgage brokers have a list of private investors who supply funds for loans. Make a few calls to some of the local mortgage brokers and inquire what private funds they might represent.

• THE REAL ESTATE BROKER: In the large commercial transactions, brokers are often asked to hold a part of the risk in the transaction by holding some of the paper. Some brokers will, and others will not.

Dealing with Secondary Loan Makers

Each of the five sources will require a slightly different approach. Not all five will be available for all transactions. The banks, for example, will not be very useful in secondary financing over a first mortgage that represents at least 75 percent of the value. The effectiveness of mortgage companies diminishes when there is existing financing of at least 80 percent of the value.

Therefore, in the order of their acceptability to the transaction, look at the major sources of secondary loans and learn how to deal with them.

DEALING WITH THE SELLER ON SECONDARY FINANCING. The seller is the most motivated of all possible lenders. When you deal with the seller, you don't have to justify the value or pay points. But sellers require special handling.

Third-party loans, made by outside lenders, banks, or private parties, are not highly negotiable. The end result will be a loan in the amount and at the terms the lender feels he or she can live with. The seller, on the other hand, is not bound by the same restrictions and can be more flexible. Some brokers mistakenly feel that the sellers who don't need the money (wealthy sellers) are the best candidates for purchase money secondary financing. Naturally, these sellers are good sources and are often receptive to this form of financing. However, they can sometimes be very independent. They may take the attitude that they will hold out until a cash buyer comes along. Wealthy sellers sometimes expect all buyers to have money.

The seller who doesn't have money and needs money from the transaction is generally the one who is most motivated to take the secondary financing. Why? Look back at the motivation. If he or she needs money, the sale of the property becomes the important aspect. It could be that the person is being transferred, or just cannot afford to keep the home or property being sold. The desire to get money (that seller's goal) may really be the need to get off the current debt. The transaction can provide some of both benefits. By selling there are no more debt payments to make, and a small down payment with secondary financing provides sufficient cash to meet that part of the deal. In this situation, the need to make the sale will motivate the seller to hold some reasonable paper. Many sales are lost because the broker assumes the seller will not hold secondary paper. The fact may be that the seller cannot afford not to be flexible.

Laying the Groundwork for Secondary Financing to Be Held by the Seller. First make sure you know the difference between the goals and the needs of the seller. If the seller needs a quick sale or money in a hurry, then your entire marketing program may take on a different approach than if he or she was not pressed. You may find secondary financing becomes more important and crucial as the motivation of the seller increases. However, because most people associate needs as their goals, the direction the seller (or buyer, for that matter) follows may be shortsighted to attaining the real goal. Remember that either party may not know or understand how to use the different creative financing tools, or realize there are different benefits that can be obtained. This is one of the reasons a broker or other intermediary is worth its weight in closed deals.

Examine the property carefully. If you believe the first or existing financing is good and adds to the salability of the property, start talking about the possibility of the seller holding paper or other forms of secondary financing rather than new financing. When the money market does not provide suitable or reasonable terms for new financing, then seek a form of secondary financing as a solution to the marketing problems. Remember, the seller is the best such source.

Know the options you have in providing secondary financing. Do not forget that it is not a first mortgage; it is a secondary or junior loan, and secondary financing is not just mortgages. It can be a land lease or building lease. The combinations are many, and you can utilize this book as a reference source for reviewing those options.

DEALING WITH COMMERCIAL BANKS FOR SECONDARY FINANCING. There are usually two forms of commercial banks in any area, state and federal. There are slightly different regulations that govern each of them, and the individual bank policy on secondary financing may vary widely. It is necessary, therefore, that you review the following guide in order to obtain good secondary financing from these institutions.

Institutional savings banks, many of which were more formally called Savings and Loan Associations (S&Ls), also follow similar guidelines, so you may consider this section as a combined guide for both these institutions. Many of these former S&Ls are still chartered under the savings and loan format and regulations. However, since the demise of many such institutions and the federal government's bailout by way of the Resolution Trust Corporation (RTC), the title "Savings and Loan Association" has a sour taste in many people's minds. Most of these institutions were either merged, purchased by commercial banks, kept their identity but dropped a portion of their original name, or simply closed their doors and disappeared. Those still in business under the catchall name of "bank" look and function more like a regular commercial bank.

For this reason whenever you hear the name "savings and loan," simply think of them as a bank. Keep in mind, however, that each loan situation is different and, as with all loans, one bank or association will look for different criteria in its analysis of the risk.

FIVE IMPORTANT LENDING GUIDELINES

1. Know the policy of the institution before you go in to talk about a loan.

2. When you make a loan presentation, have all the necessary back-up material you know the institution will require in order to reach a decision.

3. Precondition your buyer to the possibility that he or she may need a cosigner for the note. Sometimes a relative will be glad to do this.

4. Do not approach this form of secondary financing unless you could not arrange satisfactory financing with the seller or get new money.

5. Find out, ahead of time, what additional collateral your buyer has that can be used as security on the loan needed. Often, stocks can be pledged, eliminating the need for a second mortgage on the property, or at least assuring the availability of a second mortgage.

DEALING WITH MORTGAGE COMPANIES. Mortgage companies are also regulated, but not to the same degree as normal banks or S&Ls. These companies are either private firms or credit institutions. They may be a branch of a union dealing primarily with its own members, or backed by insurance companies or trust funds. Their interest rates vary from higher than any other source to lower.

The first step is to locate them, and the best place to start is the Yellow Pages of your phone book. They will be listed under "Mortgages," "Loans," and sometimes "Trust

Funds–Credit Unions." If you fail to locate any this way, contact your commercial bank and ask if it has a list of the public as well as private mortgage companies that are in the area.

Once you have found them, learn what their lending policies will be in various types of deals. Some of these lenders will not touch anything but single family, while others will go into hotels and other commercial transactions.

This source is large and seems to have a lot of money most of the time. However, before you deal with any such lender, do the following:

- Sit down with one of its representatives and find out how the operation works.
- Ask if he or she will give you information on the company.
- Get a list of references.
- Check out the references given, but also ask others about them.
- A check with the Better Business Bureau may disclose some interesting facts about the firm.
- Get a clear understanding of its charges and interest rates.
- Be sure that the mortgage company is indeed reputable.

FINDING PRIVATE LENDERS AND DEALING WITH THEM.   This is the most difficult source of all to find, but can be one of the best. These investors are usually wealthy persons who have substantial cash and/or the ability to borrow cash at better rates than you can. They will then lend the cash out at a higher rate, picking up the leverage. Secondary loans that are secure are a good form of investment for many people, and those who are in that field seem to do well. It is not, however, a market for the occasional investor, and you should avoid the casual investor who says he or she will take a second mortgage on a property if it is exceptional. Look for the full-time investor.

These investors are found in the most unlikely places. They will normally deal with mortgage brokers or mortgage lenders to some degree, but the mortgage broker or lender will guard the identity of this investor and you will not find out who he or she is. Sometimes they work from leads they cultivate with commercial banks, and this contact is more accessible to you.

Some private lenders advertise in the newspaper, usually in the classified section under "Venture Capital" or "Capital Available." Various newspapers have different headings for this type of ad, so look around. You can, of course, advertise for this source yourself, but this is rarely very productive. About the only way is to keep your eyes and ears open and to ask your commercial bank president and other lenders.

Because the private lender uses a lawyer in closing transactions, you may find that if you send a letter to attorneys in your area, asking them if they know of private investors dealing in first and second mortgages, you may locate this elusive investor.

The private lender has an advantage over you and your buyer, and takes advantage of that situation. After all, this is often the last person you and other borrowers will turn to. Because of this fact, the private lender will either take the loan or not, and the initial presentation is critical. The terms and conditions the lender offers will depend on many different aspects, of course. Some private lenders stick to one type of property, while others are less selective. The harshness of the terms will depend mostly on the general market for other investments. If the investor is able to obtain investments that have little risk elsewhere at a good rate, then the rate he or she will demand on a second loan will be considerably higher, depending on the risk involved. You can do very little to change the outcome of a loan from such a lender. Nonetheless, you may find that the need for the money will be great enough to warrant the cost.

There are times when the private lender will lend at comparative terms when all things are considered. Usually, the closing costs are a fraction of those available from commercial banks and mortgage companies.

When dealing with private lenders, keep in mind the following two warnings:

1. Be sure the lender's attorney does not represent you (as the borrower) in closing the transaction.

2. Have your own attorney go over the loan document before you sign it.

WHEN AND HOW THE BROKER CAN HOLD SOME OF THE PAPER

If the transaction has a substantial commission, and the buyer is just a little short of cash to close the deal, the broker may be asked to take some of the paper as a deferred commission. Of course, this situation can come up in almost any transaction, and this becomes an individual matter that some brokers will agree to do while others will not. It is important, however, that certain factors be understood about deferred commissions:

- If the broker takes a note or other form of loan equivalent to a deferred commission, it is likely the IRS will tax the full amount of the commission the year the note was taken, rather than in subsequent years when payment is received.

- A fee conditioned on the future collection of a debt held by the seller may avoid the tax situation shown above, as the future payments are in a sense based on continued performance.

Chapter 7

<hr>

HOW TO USE GOVERNMENT-INSURED LOANS TO FINANCE REAL ESTATE PURCHASES AND SALES

GOAL OF THIS CHAPTER

This chapter gives you a solid working knowledge of several different types of loans that are a function of one or more departments of the U.S. government. These loans fall into two categories: Federal Department of Housing and Urban Development–sponsored programs (HUD at www.hud.gov) and the U.S. Department of Veterans Affairs (VA at www.va.gov).

Each of these programs is amazing in the depth of benefits that are offered. HUD in particular is a trove of treasure for many real estate developers who have found a niche in their investment endeavors by taking advantage of the benefits provided to such developers. For the real estate investor, both buyer and seller, there are many opportunities to buy right and to help entice a buyer even in the toughest of times.

Because these programs are always changing, I give you a comprehensive look at only the most interesting of programs and benefits. First there is a brief description, followed by a paragraph or two on how the program works. The last paragraph tells you who is eligible to apply for the program. You will, however, leave this chapter with a greater respect for the U.S. government, when you first see these programs, then realize that there is no other country in the world that has so many beneficial programs available to real estate investors. Although many of the programs are cumbersome to operate, the people who administrate them are patient, and if you have the time, they will help you with the paperwork. Keep in mind that as with any government operation, these programs are apt to be altered, dropped, or replaced by new programs at any time.

DEPARTMENT OF HOUSING AND URBAN DEVELOPMENT PROGRAMS

One- to Four-Family Home Mortgage Insurance (Section 203(b))

Federal mortgage insurance helps finance homeownership and the construction and financing of housing.

Homebuyers may obtain Federal Housing Association (FHA) mortgages from HUD-approved lenders to purchase houses with low down payments. By insuring commercial lenders against loss, HUD encourages them to invest capital in the home mortgage market. HUD, through the FHA and/or Fannie Mae and Freddie Mac mortgage programs, insures loans made by private financial institutions for up to 97 percent of the sales price with terms for up to 30 years. The loan may finance homes and small multifamily properties in both urban and rural areas. The maximum mortgage amounts vary across the country, and specific dollar floor and ceiling can be found by going to the following web pages to obtain the data that was released in early March 2008, as a result of the Economic Stimulus Act signed into law by President Bush on February 13, 2008.

For FHA, Fannie Mae, and Freddie Mac conforming loan limits visit https://entphud.gov/idapp/html/hicostlook.cfm. When you get to that page, you can select the state and county to ascertain the limits for your area. *Note:* The term "FHA Forward" in the limit-type drop-down box is what HUD calls the temporary FHA loan limit. It is not necessary to fill in the other boxes, so click on send at the bottom of the page and receive your requested data. You can also go to the FHA and Fannie Mae–Freddie Mac loan limit page at realtor.org by using the following link: http://realtor.org/GAPublic.nsf/files/chart_hud_loan_limits_08.pdf/$FILE/chart_hud_loan_limits_08.pdf. The resulting information automatically shows you the many different counties for each state.

The new loan limits for FHA, Fannie Mae, and Freddie Mac are now calculated at 125% of the HUD published median prices, with a floor of $271,050 and $417,000 respectively, and not to exceed $729,750. Higher limits also exist for two- to four-family properties. The loan limits change annually, based on home price estimates. The limits are benchmarked to the loan limits of the government-sponsored Fannie Mae and Freddie Mac. The mortgagee collects from the borrower an up-front mortgage insurance premium payment, which may be financed, at the time of loan closing, as well as monthly premiums that are not financed, but included in the regular mortgage payment.

Any person able to meet the cash investment can apply.

Mortgage Insurance for Disaster Victims (Section 203(h))

This federal mortgage insurance is designated for victims of a major disaster who have lost their homes and are in the process of rebuilding or buying another home.

This program helps victims in presidentially designated disaster areas recover by making it easier for them to obtain mortgage loans and become homeowners or reestablish themselves as homeowners. The program provides mortgage insurance to protect lenders against the risk of default on loans to qualified disaster victims. Individuals are eligible for this program if their homes are located in an area that was designated by the president as a disaster area and whose homes were destroyed or damaged to such an extent that reconstruction or replacement is necessary. Insured loans may be used to finance the purchase or reconstruction of a one-family home that will be the principal residence of the homeowner. This program resembles the Section 203(b) program (Mortgage Insurance for One- to Four-Family Homes), FHA's basic mortgage insurance program.

Section 203(h) offers features that make homeownership easier. For example, no down payment is required. The borrower is eligible for 100 percent financing. Closing costs and prepaid expenses must be paid by the borrower in cash or paid through premium pricing by the seller, subject to a 6 percent limitation on seller concessions. Mortgagees collect from the borrowers an up-front insurance premium (which may be financed) at the time of purchase, as well as monthly premiums that are not financed, but instead are added to the regular mortgage payment.

As mentioned earlier, any person whose home has been destroyed or severely damaged in a presidentially declared disaster area is eligible to apply for mortgage insurance under this program, even if they were renting the property. The borrower's application for mortgage insurance must be submitted to an FHA-approved lending institution within one year of the president's declaration of the disaster.

Rehabilitation Loan Insurance (Section 203(k))

This program insures loans to finance the rehabilitation or purchase and rehabilitation of one- to four-family properties.

HUD insures rehabilitation loans up to approximately 98 percent of the lesser of appraised value before rehabilitation plus rehabilitation costs or 110 percent of appraised value after rehabilitation. A loan can be used to (1) finance rehabilitation of an existing property; (2) finance rehabilitation and refinancing of the outstanding indebtedness of a property; and (3) finance purchase and rehabilitation of a property. An eligible rehabilitation loan must involve a principal obligation not exceeding the amount allowed under Section 203(b) home mortgage insurance.

Any person able to make the cash investment and the mortgage payments can apply.

Single-Family Property Disposition Program (Section 204(g))

This program disposes of one- to four-family FHA properties in a manner targeted to expanding homeownership opportunities.

The purpose of this program is to dispose of properties acquired by the Federal Housing Administration (FHA) through foreclosure of an insured or Secretary-held mortgage or loan under the National Housing Act. Foreclosed properties generally contain one to four units. Listings of properties in inventory are available on the Internet. Individual parties may submit an offer through a real estate broker over the Internet. Awarded bids are announced through Internet posting and notification to the selected bidder. Nonprofit and government entities may purchase properties at a discount through a lottery system without a real estate broker.

Individual bidders are eligible to apply if they can finance their home purchase and provide an earnest money deposit with their bids.

Mortgage Insurance for Older, Declining Areas (Section 223(e))

Mortgage insurance is available to purchase or rehabilitate housing in older, declining urban areas.

In consideration of the need for adequate housing for low- and moderate-income families, HUD insures lenders against loss on mortgage loans to finance the purchase, rehabilitation, or construction of housing in older, declining, but still viable urban areas where conditions are such that normal requirements for mortgage insurance cannot be met.

Properties must be in a reasonably viable neighborhood and acceptable risk under the mortgage insurance regulations. The terms of the loans vary according to the HUD/FHA program under which the mortgages are insured. HUD determines if the loan should be insured pursuant to Section 223(e) and become an obligation of the Special Risk Insurance Fund. This effectively allows HUD to manage the greater expected risk in these loans. The insurance premium is 0.5 percent per year on the outstanding loan balance.

Home or project owners who are ineligible for FHA mortgage insurance because property is located in an older, declining urban area can apply.

Mortgage Insurance for Condominium Units (Section 234(c))

This is federal mortgage insurance to finance the purchase of individual housing units in proposed or existing condominiums.

HUD insures mortgages made by private lending institutions for the purchase of an individual family unit in housing projects under Section 234(c). A project must contain at least four dwelling units; they may be in detached, semi-detached, row, walk-up, or elevator structures. The maximum mortgage amount for a unit mortgage insured under Section 234(c) is the same as the limit for a Section 203(b) mortgage in the same area.

All FHA-approved lenders are eligible who may make condominium loans in approved projects for any creditworthy owner-occupant.

Graduated Payment Mortgage (Section 245(a))

The graduated payment mortgage (GPM) enables a household with a limited income that is expected to rise to buy a home sooner by making mortgage payments that start small and increase gradually over time.

This program targets early homeownership by helping first-time homebuyers and others with limited incomes, particularly young families who expect their income to rise, but may not yet be able to handle all of the upfront and monthly costs involved in buying and owning a home.

The GPM works in times of high interest rates when first-time homebuyers cannot meet the standard mortgage payment, but expect their incomes to increase substantially in the next 5 to 10 years. The GPM (a form of deficit amortization) accrues negative amortization so that the borrower's initial mortgage payments are made at a nominally discounted interest rate from the standard prevailing rate. The difference is then added to the principal balance. The GPM program offers five different plans varying in length of time and rate of increase of nominal interest rate. It is anticipated that when the interest rate, and thus the mortgage payment, increases with time the borrower's income also will have increased to accommodate the higher payments. Larger than usual down payments are required to prevent the total amount of the loan from exceeding the statutory loan-to-value ratios. Down payments required for GPMs vary in proportion to interest rates on the loans. In all other ways, the GPM is subject to the rules governing ordinary HUD-insured home loans.

All FHA-approved lenders may make GPMs available to persons who intend to use the mortgage property as their primary residence and who expect to see their income rise appreciably in the future.

Adjustable Rate Mortgages (Section 251)

Under federal mortgage insurance for adjustable rate mortgages (ARMs), the interest rate and monthly payment may change during the life of the loan. The initial interest rate, discount points, and the margin are negotiated by the buyer and lender.

The one-year Treasury Constant Maturities Index is used for determining the interest rate changes. FHA lenders may offer ARMs that have interest rates that are fixed for the first 1, 3, 5, 7, or 10 years of the mortgage. The interest rate for 1-year and 3-year insured ARMs may not be increased or decreased by more than 1 percentage point per year after the fixed-payment period is over, with a maximum change of 5 percentage points over the life of the loan. For 5-year, 7-year, and 10-year ARMs, the interest rate may change a maximum of 2 percentage points annually and 6 percentage points over the life of the loan.

Lenders are required to disclose to borrowers the nature of the ARM loan at the time of loan application. In addition, borrowers must be informed at least 25 days in advance of any adjustment to the monthly payment.

All FHA-approved lenders may make ARMs; creditworthy applicants who will be owner-occupants may qualify for such loans.

Home Equity Conversion Mortgage Program (Section 255)

The Federal Housing Administration (FHA) mortgage insurance allows borrowers who are at least 62 years of age to convert the equity in their homes into a monthly stream of income or a line of credit.

Reverse mortgages can provide a valuable financing alternative for qualified homeowners. Any lender authorized to make HUD-insured loans may originate reverse mortgages.

Borrowers may choose from among five payment options: (1) tenure, by which the borrower receives monthly payments from the lender for as long as the borrower lives and continues to occupy the home as a principal residence; (2) term, by which the borrower receives monthly payments for a fixed period selected by the borrower; (3) line of credit, by which the borrower can make withdrawals up to a maximum amount, at times and in amounts of the borrower's choosing; (4) modified tenure, by which the tenure option is combined with a line of credit; and (5) modified term, by which the term option is combined with a line of credit.

The borrower retains ownership of the property and may sell the home and move at any time, keeping the sales proceeds in excess of the mortgage balance. The borrower cannot be forced to sell the home to pay off the mortgage, even if the mortgage balance grows to exceed the value of the property. An FHA-insured reverse mortgage need not be repaid until the borrower moves, sells, or dies. When the loan is due and payable, if the loan exceeds the value of the property, the borrower (or the heirs) will owe no more than the value of the property.

All borrowers must be at least 62 years of age. Any existing lien on the property must be small enough to be paid off at settlement of the reverse mortgage.

Manufactured Homes Loan Insurance (Title I)

This is federal loan insurance to finance the purchase of manufactured homes.

HUD insures loans to finance the purchase of manufactured homes or lots. The loans are made by private lending institutions. The maximum loan amount is $48,600 for a manufactured home, $64,800 for a manufactured home and a suitably developed lot, and $16,200 for a developed lot. The maximum limits for combination home and lot loans may be increased up to 85 percent in designated high-cost areas. The maximum loan term varies from 15 to 25 years, depending on the type of loan. Most manufactured home loans are financed through purchases by lenders of retail installment contracts between homebuyers and manufactured home dealers.

Any person able to make the cash investment and the loan payments can apply; however, the home must be the principal residence of the borrower.

Property Improvement Loan Insurance (Title I)

This is federal loan insurance to finance property improvements.

HUD insures loans to finance improvements, alterations, and repairs of individual homes, apartment buildings, and nonresidential structures, as well as new construction of nonresidential buildings. Loans on single-family homes (except manufactured homes) and nonresidential structures may be for up to $25,000 and may extend to 20 years. Loans on apartment buildings may be as high as $12,000 per unit, but the total for the building cannot exceed $60,000, and the loan term cannot exceed 20 years. A loan on a manufactured home that is classified as real property may be for up to $17,500 with a maximum loan term of 15 years. Loans on other manufactured homes are limited to $7,500 and a maximum term of 12 years. A property improvement loan may be a loan from the lender to the borrower or a retail sales installment contract (purchased by a lender) between the borrower and the contractor or dealer providing the materials or services.

Loans over $7,500 must be secured by a recorded mortgage or deed of trust on the improved property.

Any person who is able to make loan payments and has at least a 50 percent ownership in the property to be improved can apply.

Counseling for Homebuyers, Homeowners, and Tenants (Section 106)

Housing counseling is available for homebuyers, homeowners, and tenants.

HUD is authorized to counsel current and prospective homebuyers, homeowners, and tenants. HUD provides the service through approximately 1,700 HUD-approved counseling agencies. These agencies are public and private nonprofit organizations with housing counseling skills and knowledge of HUD, VA, and conventional housing programs. HUD awards housing counseling grants on a competitive basis to its approved agencies when Congress appropriates funds for this purpose. The funding helps the approved agencies partially meet their operating expenses. The objective of the counseling is to help homebuyers, homeowners, and tenants to improve their housing conditions and to meet their responsibilities.

Homeless individuals and families, potential renters, renters, potential homebuyers, homebuyers, and homeowners may seek the assistance of a HUD-approved housing counseling agency to meet a housing need or resolve a housing problem.

Good Neighbor Next Door

This program provides law enforcement officers, teachers, firefighters, and emergency medical technicians with the opportunity to purchase homes located in revitalization areas at significant discount.

HUD wants to make American communities stronger and build a safer nation. The Good Neighbor Next Door program promotes these goals by encouraging persons whose daily professional responsibilities represent a nexus to the needs of the community to purchase and live in homes in these communities. This program makes homes in revitalization areas available to law enforcement officers, teachers, firefighters, and emergency medical technicians. Each year, HUD sells a limited number of properties from its inventory at a 50 percent discount from the list price to eligible persons in the above professions. To make these homes even more affordable, eligible program participants may apply for an FHA-insured mortgage with a down payment of only $100. Because homes sold through this program are located in revitalization areas, there may be additional assistance from state or local government sources. If the home needs repairs, the purchaser may also use FHA's Section 203(k) mortgage program. The Section 203(k) program provides financing for both the purchase of the home and cost of needed repairs.

Purchasers must be employed as a full-time law enforcement officer, teacher, firefighter, or emergency medical technician, and must certify that they intend to continue such employment for at least one year following the date of closing. The eligible purchaser does not need to be a first-time homebuyer. However, the purchaser (or spouse) cannot have owned another home for one year prior to the time a bid for purchase is submitted, and the purchaser must agree to live in the HUD home as the principal residence for three years after move-in.

Legal Authority: Section 204(g) of the National Housing Act (12 U.S.C. 1710(g))

Regulations are at 24 CFR part 291, subpart F.

Energy Efficient Mortgage Insurance

This is federal mortgage insurance to finance the cost of energy efficiency measures.

A homebuyer may obtain an FHA mortgage that exceeds the normal maximum loan limits if the mortgage includes an amount for the purchase of energy-efficient improvements made or to be made to the property. The borrower does not have to qualify for the additional money nor make a down payment on it. The borrower must make a 3 percent cash investment in the property based on the sales price. One- to four-unit existing and new properties are eligible. The cost of the energy improvements and estimate of the energy savings must be determined by a home energy rating, which may be financed as part of the cost-effective energy package. Energy improvements to an existing home may be installed after the insured loan has closed—within 90 days of closing unless the loan is insured under Section 203(k), in which case the improvements must be installed within 180 days. Energy improvements to a newly constructed home must be installed prior to closing. The lender will place the money in an escrow account, to be released to the borrower after an inspection verifies that the improvements have been installed and the energy savings will be achieved.

The maximum mortgage amount for a single-family unit depends on its location and is adjusted annually. The cost of the eligible energy-efficient improvements is added to the mortgage amount. The final loan amount may exceed the maximum mortgage limit by the amount of the energy-efficient improvements.

Insured Mortgages on Hawaiian Home Lands (Section 247)

FHA insures loans made to native Hawaiians to purchase one- to four-family dwellings located on Hawaiian homelands. Regulations pertaining to these loans are fundamentally the same as regular Section 203(b) loans except that they are only available to Native Hawaiians on Hawaiian homelands.

Because a mortgage is taken on a homestead lease granted by the Department of Hawaiian Homelands, many lenders have been reluctant to finance housing. With FHA insurance, the lender's risk is minimized, and this program increases the availability of mortgage credit to Native Hawaiians to live on Hawaiian homelands. FHA's low down-payment requirements and flexible underwriting standards increase the ability of Native Hawaiians to meet the requirements for the loan. A Native Hawaiian is defined as any descendant of not less than one-half part of the blood of the races inhabiting the Hawaiian Islands before January 1, 1778 (or, in the case of an individual who succeeds a spouse or parent in an interest in a lease of Hawaiian home lands, such lower percentage as may be established for such succession under Section 209 of the Hawaiian Homes Commission Act, 1920, or under the corresponding provision of the constitution of the State of Hawaii adopted under Section 4 of the Act entitled, "An Act to provide for the admission of the State of Hawaii into the Union," approved March 18, 1959).

Insured Mortgages on Indian Land (Section 248)

FHA insures loans made to Native Americans to buy, build, or rehabilitate houses on Indian land. These loans are fundamentally the same as regular Section 203(b) loans except that they are only available to Native Americans on Indian land.

Native Americans are the most poorly housed sector of the U.S. population. FHA's mortgage insurance provides opportunities for low- and moderate-income Native Americans to purchase a home in their communities on Indian land. Because of the complex title issues on Indian land, many lenders have been reluctant to finance housing. With FHA insurance, the lender's risk is minimized, and this program increases the availability of mortgage credit to Native Americans living on Indian land. FHA's low down-payment requirements and flexible underwriting standards increase the ability of Native Americans to meet the requirements for the loan.

Any Native American wishing to live on Indian land and intending to use the mortgage property as the primary residence is eligible to apply for mortgage insurance.

HUD MULTIFAMILY HOUSING PROGRAMS

Supportive Housing for the Elderly (Section 202)

This program provides assistance to expand the supply of housing with supportive services for the elderly.

Capital advances are made to eligible private, nonprofit sponsors to finance the development of rental housing with supportive services for the elderly. The advance is interest free and does not have to be repaid so long as the housing remains available for very low-income elderly persons for at least 40 years. Project rental assistance covers the difference between the HUD-approved operating cost of the project and the tenants' contributions toward rent (usually 30 percent of monthly adjusted income).

Private, nonprofit organizations and consumer cooperatives may qualify for assistance, and may partner with private, for-profit entities as long as the sole general partner is a nonprofit organization that meets the statutory requirements. Occupancy is open to very low-income households that include at least one person 62 years of age or older.

Assisted-Living Conversion Program

This program provides grants to private nonprofit owners of eligible developments to convert some or all of the dwelling units in the development into an assisted-living facility for the frail elderly.

The Assisted-Living Conversion Program (ALCP) provides funding for the physical costs of converting some or all units in an eligible development into an assisted-living facility (ALF), including the unit configuration, common and services space, and any necessary remodeling consistent with HUD's or the state's statute or regulations (whichever is more stringent). ALFs are designed to accommodate frail elderly and people with disabilities who can live independently, but need assistance with activities of daily living (e.g., assistance with eating, bathing, grooming, dressing, and home management activities). Under this program, ALFs must provide supportive services, such as personal care, transportation, meals, housekeeping, or laundry. The facility must be licensed and regulated by the state (or, if there is no state law providing such licensing and regulation, by the municipality or other subdivision in which the facility is located).

Private nonprofit owners of Section 202, Section 8 project-based (including Rural Housing Services Section 515), Section 221(d)(3) Below Market Interest Rate, and Section 236 housing developments that are designated primarily for occupancy are eligible to apply.

Emergency Capital Repairs Program

This program provides grants for substantial capital repairs to eligible multifamily projects with elderly tenants that are needed to rehabilitate, modernize, or retrofit aging structures, common areas, or individual dwelling units. The capital repair needs must relate to items that present an immediate threat to the health, safety, and quality of life of the tenants. The intent of these grants is to provide one-time assistance for emergency items that could not be absorbed within the project's operating budget, and where the tenants' continued occupancy in the immediate future would be called into question by a delay in initiating the proposed cure.

Private nonprofit owners of eligible multifamily assisted housing developments designated for occupancy by elderly tenants are eligible to apply.

Manufactured Home Parks (Section 207)

This is federal mortgage insurance to finance construction or rehabilitation of manufactured home parks.

HUD insures mortgages made by private lending institutions to help finance construction or rehabilitation of manufactured home parks consisting of five or more spaces. The park must be located in an area approved by HUD in which market conditions show a need for such housing.

Investors, builders, developers, cooperatives, and others meeting HUD's requirements may apply to an FHA-approved lending institution after conferring with the local HUD office.

Mortgage and Major Home Improvement Loan Insurance for Urban Renewal Areas (Section 220)

These are federally insured loans used to finance mortgages for housing in urban renewal areas, areas in which concentrated revitalization activities have been undertaken by local government, or to alter, repair, or improve housing in those areas.

HUD insures mortgages on new or rehabilitated homes or multifamily structures located in designated urban renewal areas and areas with concentrated programs of code enforcement and neighborhood development. HUD insures supplemental loans to finance improvements that will enhance and preserve salvageable homes and apartments in designated urban renewal areas.

Investors, builders, developers, individual homeowners, and apartment owners can apply.

Multifamily Rental Housing for Moderate-Income Families (Section 221(d)(3) and (4))

This program provides mortgage insurance to finance rental or cooperative multifamily housing for moderate-income households, including projects designated for the elderly. Single Room Occupancy (SRO) projects are also eligible for mortgage insurance. Section 221(d)(3) and (4) are HUD's major insurance programs for new construction or substantially rehabilitated multifamily rental housing.

HUD insures mortgages made by private lending institutions to help finance construction or substantial rehabilitation of multifamily (five or more units) rental or cooperative housing for moderate-income or displaced families. Projects in both cases may consist of detached, semi-detached, row, walk-up, or elevator structures. SRO projects may consist of units that do not contain a complete kitchen or bath.

Currently, the principal difference between the programs is that HUD may insure up to 100 percent of replacement cost in the case of new construction under Section 221(d)(3) for public, nonprofit, and cooperative mortgagors, but only up to 90 percent under Section 221(d)(4), irrespective of the type of mortgagor.

Section 221(d)(3) is available to public, nonprofit, and cooperative mortgagors. Section 221(d)(4) mortgages are available to profit-motivated sponsors.

Existing Multifamily Rental Housing (Section 207/223(f))

HUD insures mortgages under Section 207 of the National Housing Act pursuant to Section 223(f) of the same Act to purchase or refinance existing multifamily projects originally financed with or without federal mortgage insurance. HUD may insure mortgages on existing multifamily projects under this program that do not require substantial rehabilitation. A project must contain at least five units, and construction or substantial rehabilitation must have been completed for three years or more.

Investors, builders, developers, and others who meet HUD requirements may apply.

Mortgage Insurance for Housing for the Elderly (Section 231)

To assure a supply of rental housing suited to the needs of the elderly or handicapped, HUD insures mortgages made by private lending institutions to build or rehabilitate multifamily projects consisting of five or more units. HUD may insure up to 100 percent of the Federal Housing Commissioner's estimate of value after completion for nonprofit and public mortgagors, but only up to 90 percent for private mortgagors. Congregate care projects with central kitchens providing food service are not eligible.

Investors, builders, developers, public bodies, and nonprofit sponsors may qualify for mortgage insurance. All elderly (62 or older) or handicapped persons are eligible to occupy units in a project insured under this program.

New Construction or Substantial Rehabilitation of Nursing Homes, Intermediate Care Facilities, Board and Care Homes, and Assisted Living Facilities (Section 232); Purchase or Refinancing of Existing Facilities (Section 232/223(f))

HUD insures mortgages made by private lending institutions to finance construction or renovation of facilities to accommodate 20 or more patients requiring skilled nursing care and related medical services, or those in need of minimum but continuous care provided by licensed or trained personnel. Assisted living facilities and board and care facilities may contain no fewer than five one-bedroom or efficiency units. Nursing home, intermediate care, and board and care services may be combined in the same facility covered by an insured mortgage or may be in separate facilities. Major equipment needed to operate the facility may be included in the mortgage. Facilities for day care may be included. Existing projects are also eligible for purchase or refinancing with or without repairs (and not requiring substantial rehabilitation) under Section 232/Section 223(f).

Developers, private owners, and private nonprofit corporations or associations, and public agencies (nursing homes only), or public entities that are licensed or regulated by the state to accommodate convalescents and persons requiring skilled nursing care or intermediate care, may qualify for mortgage insurance. Patients requiring skilled nursing, intermediate care, assisted living, and/or board and care are eligible to live in these facilities.

Supplemental Loans for Multifamily Projects (Section 241)

HUD insures loans made by lenders to pay for improvements or additions to apartment projects, nursing homes, hospitals, or group-practice facilities that already carry HUD-insured or HUD-held mortgages. Projects may also obtain FHA insurance on loans to preserve, expand, or improve housing opportunities, to provide fire and safety equipment, or to finance energy conservation improvements to conventionally financed projects. Major movable equipment for nursing homes, group practice facilities, or hospitals also may be covered by a mortgage under this program.

Qualified owners and purchasers of multifamily projects and owners of health-care facilities (as specified above) are eligible to apply.

Hospitals (Section 242)

HUD insures mortgages made by private lenders to facilitate the construction or renovation of acute care hospitals. Clients range in size from large urban teaching hospitals to small rural hospitals. Critical Access Hospitals (hospitals with 25 beds or less which have received designation by states and the Department of Health and Human Services) are also eligible. Facilities must be properly licensed, provide primarily acute patient care, and be able to demonstrate the need for the project. Key program criteria include a maximum loan-to-value of 90 percent, a loan term of 25 years, and funding of a mortgage reserve fund. The term of the HUD-insured mortgage for hospitals cannot exceed 25 years.

Public, proprietary, and nonprofit acute care hospitals licensed or regulated by the state are eligible to apply.

Multifamily Mortgage Risk-Sharing Programs (Sections 542(b) and 542(c))

Two multifamily mortgage credit programs under which Fannie Mae, Freddie Mac, and state and local housing finance agencies share the risk and the mortgage insurance premium on multifamily housing.

Section 542(b) of the Housing and Community Development Act of 1992 authorizes HUD to enter into reinsurance agreements with Fannie Mae, Freddie Mac, qualified financial institutions (QFIs), and the Federal Housing Finance Board. The agreements provide for risk sharing on a 50/50 basis. Currently, only Fannie Mae and Freddie Mac have active risk-sharing programs with HUD.

Section 542(c) enables HUD to carry out a program in conjunction with qualified state and local housing finance agencies (HFAs) to provide federal credit enhancement for loans for affordable multifamily housing through a system of risk-sharing agreements. Agreements provide for risk sharing between 10 percent and 90 percent.

Fannie Mae, Freddie Mac, QFIs, HFAs, and the Federal Housing Finance Board can apply.

Mark-to-Market Program

This program preserves long-term low-income housing affordability by restructuring FHA-insured or HUD-held mortgages for eligible multifamily housing projects.

The Multifamily Assisted Housing Reform and Affordability Act of 1997 (MAHRA) authorized a Mark-to-Market program designed to preserve low-income rental housing affordability while reducing the long-term costs of federal rental assistance, including project-based assistance from HUD, for certain multifamily rental projects. The projects involved are projects with (1) HUD-insured or HUD-held mortgages; and (2) contracts for project-based rental assistance from HUD, primarily through the Section 8 program, for which the average rents for assisted units exceed the rent of comparable properties. The program objectives are to (1) preserve housing affordability while reducing the costs of project-based assistance; (2) restructure the HUD-insured or HUD-held financing so that the monthly payments on the first mortgage can be paid from the reduced rental levels; (3) reduce the costs of insurance claims; and (4) ensure competent management of the project. The restructured project is subject to long-term use and affordability restrictions.

A public agency (including a state housing finance agency or a local housing agency), a nonprofit organization, or any other entity, or a combination of such entities that meet the requirements of Section 513(b) of MAHRA can apply.

Self-Help Housing Property Disposition

This program makes surplus federal properties available through sale at less than fair market value to states, their subdivisions and instrumentalities, and nonprofit organizations.

The property must be used for self-help housing for low-income persons. Residents of the property must make a substantial contribution of labor toward the construction, rehabilitation, or refurbishment of the property. HUD has the right to take the property back if it is not used in accordance with program requirements.

State and local governments can apply.

Renewal of Section 8 Project-Based Rental Assistance

Through Project-based Section 8, this program assists more than 1.3 million low- and very low-income families in obtaining decent, safe, and sanitary housing.

HUD renews Section 8 project-based housing assistance payments (HAP) contracts with owners of multifamily rental housing. The project-based rental assistance makes up the difference between what a low- and very low-income household can afford and the approved rent for an adequate housing unit in a multifamily project. Eligible tenants must pay the highest of 30 percent of adjusted income, 10 percent of gross income, or the portion of welfare assistance designated for housing or the minimum rent established by HUD.

Originally, the assistance was provided in connection with new construction or substantial rehabilitation or to support existing projects. Authority to use project-based rental assistance in connection with new construction or substantial rehabilitation was repealed in 1983. While funding is no longer available for new commitments, funding is available for the renewal of Section 8 HAP contracts for units already assisted with project-based Section 8 renewal assistance.

Project sponsors are private owners, both profit-motivated and nonprofit or cooperative organizations. Very low-income families whose incomes do not exceed 50 percent of the median income for the area are eligible to occupy the assisted units. A limited number of available units may be rented to low-income families whose incomes are between 50 percent and 80 percent of median income for the area.

HUD PROGRAMS FOR PUBLIC AND INDIAN HOUSING

Housing Choice Voucher Program

Through tenant-based vouchers, this program provides rental subsidies for standard-quality units that are chosen by the tenant in the private market.

Key features include targeting and eligibility. At least 75 percent of the families admitted to a public housing agency's (PHA) Housing Choice Voucher program during the PHA's fiscal year must have income at or below 30 percent of the area median income. In general, eligibility for vouchers is limited to:

- Very low-income families.
- Low-income families previously assisted under the public housing, Section 23, or Section 8 project-based housing programs.
- Low-income families that are nonpurchasing tenants of certain homeownership programs.
- Low-income tenants displaced from certain Section 221 and 236 projects.
- Low-income families that meet PHA-specified eligibility criteria (see Section 8(o)(4)).

Revitalization of Severely Distressed Public Housing

The goal of this program is eradication of severely distressed public housing. The Urban Revitalization Demonstration (URD) program, or HOPE VI, is a program that was born out of the Commission's work. Since 1993, this program has been an important part of the transformation of public housing by encouraging public housing agencies (PHAs) to seek new partnerships with private entities to create mixed-finance and mixed-income affordable housing. In 2003, the HOPE VI program was expanded to assist local governments in the production of affordable housing in Main Street rejuvenation projects. The activities permitted under HOPE VI include, but are not limited to: the capital costs of demolition, major reconstruction, rehabilitation, and other physical improvements; the provision of replacement housing; management improvements; planning and technical assistance; and the provision of supportive services (including the funding, beginning in Fiscal Year 2000, of an endowment trust for supportive services).

The HOPE VI program was modified and extended by HUD appropriations acts, commencing in 1994 through the present. In 1998, Section 535 of the Quality Housing and Work Responsibility Act of 1998 (Title V of Public Law 105–276) amended the U.S. Housing Act of 1937 to establish a new Section 24 in the U.S. Housing Act of 1937 that addresses demolition, site revitalization, replacement housing, and tenant-based assistance grants for projects. The HOPE VI Program Reauthorization and Small Community Main Street Rejuvenation and Housing Act of 2003 (Title IV of Public Law 108–186, approved December 16, 2003), amended Section 24 of the U.S. Housing Act of 1937 by extending the program until September 30, 2006.

The program allows HUD to provide competitive grants to PHAs to carry out HOPE VI–eligible activities. PHAs provide matching contributions in amounts at least equal to 5 percent of the grant amount.

Public housing agencies and, for Main Street Grants only, "smaller communities" as defined in Section 24(n) are eligible to apply for this program.

Indian Community Development Block Grant (ICDBG) Program

This program provides federal aid for Indian tribes and Alaska Native Villages to develop viable Indian communities.

The program offers grants on a competitive basis to eligible Indian tribes and Alaska Native Villages to improve the housing stock, provide community facilities, make infrastructure improvements, fund microenterprises, and expand job opportunities. Eligible activities include housing rehabilitation, acquisition of land for housing, and assistance for homeownership opportunities for low- and moderate-income persons. Grantees may also use funds for construction of single- or multiuse facilities, streets, and public facilities, as well as for economic development projects, especially those sponsored by nonprofit tribal organizations or local development corporations. Funds may not be used for constructing or improving government facilities, for new housing construction (unless carried out by an eligible nonprofit organization), for general government or income expenses, for operating or maintenance expenses, for political activities, or to purchase equipment.

Indian tribes, bands, groups, or nations, including Alaskan Indians, Aleuts, and Eskimos and Alaska Native Villages that are eligible for assistance under the Indian Self-Determination and Education Assistance Act or had been eligible under the state and local Fiscal Assistance Act of 1972 can apply.

Federal Guarantees for Financing for Tribal Housing Activities (Title VI)

HUD guarantees loans for financing eligible affordable housing activities and affordable housing-related community development activities. This program authorizes HUD, through the Office of Native American Programs, to guarantee obligations issued by tribes or tribally designated housing entities (TDHEs) with tribal approval, to finance eligible affordable housing activities under Section 202 of the Native American Housing Assistance and Self Determination Act (NAHASDA) and housing-related community development activities consistent with the purposes of NAHASDA. No guarantee could be approved if the total outstanding obligations exceed five times the amount of the grant for the issuer, taking into consideration the amount needed to maintain and protect the viability of housing developed or operated pursuant to the U.S. Housing Act of 1937.

The program requires issuers to pledge current and future Indian Housing Block Grant (IHBG) appropriations to the repayment of the guaranteed obligations. The full faith and credit of the United States is pledged to the payment of all guarantees.

HUD may not guarantee obligations exceeding $400 million for each of Fiscal Years 1997 to 2007, with a cumulative cap of $2 billion for the 11-year period. Once 50 percent of the authority has been committed in any year, HUD may limit the amount of guarantees any one tribe may receive in any fiscal year to $50 million or request an increase in the statutory dollar limitations. HUD may enter into commitments to guarantee loans for any fiscal year only to the extent that funds have been appropriated.

Indian tribes and tribally designated housing entities that are IHBG recipients can apply.

Loan Guarantees for Indian Housing (Section 184)

Home loan guarantees are provided for Indian families, Indian housing authorities, and Indian tribes. Section 184 of the Housing and Community Development Act of 1992 established a loan guarantee program for Indian families, Indian housing authorities (IHAs), and Indian tribes. The purpose of the program is to provide access to private mortgage financing to Indian families, IHAs, and Indian tribes that could not otherwise acquire housing financing because of the unique legal status of Indian lands. The loans guaranteed under the program are used to construct, acquire, refinance, or rehabilitate single-family housing located on trust land or land located in an Indian or Alaska Native area. The program authorizes Indian tribes to assume responsibility for federal environmental reviews. This guarantee authority is freestanding and has its own guarantee fund. HUD may enter into commitments to guarantee loans for any fiscal year only to the extent amounts have been provided in appropriations acts.

Indian families, Indian housing authorities, and Indian tribes are eligible.

HUD PROGRAMS FOR FAIR HOUSING AND EQUAL OPPORTUNITY

Fair Housing Act (Title VIII)

This program investigates, conciliates, and charges cases of housing discrimination prohibited under the Fair Housing Act of 1968 (Title VIII). The Fair Housing Act prohibits discrimination in housing based on race, color, religion, sex, national origin, disability, or familial status (includes individuals or families with children less than 18 years of age and pregnant women). The Fair Housing Act applies to almost all housing in the country.

The Fair Housing Act prohibits discrimination in residential real estate transactions and makes it illegal to coerce, intimidate, threaten, or interfere with people exercising their rights under the Act, or assisting others in exercising their rights.

To comply with the Fair Housing Act, a seller, landlord, lender, insurance agent, realtor, and so on may not:

- Deny housing, offer different terms and conditions to an applicant, or refuse to rent, sell, or negotiate with an applicant because of one or more of the prohibited bases cited above.

- Use discriminatory advertising or make discriminatory statements in connection with housing.

- Falsely deny that housing is available.

- Deny access to or membership in a multiple-listing service or real estate broker's organization.

- Discriminate in making loans for, or secured by, residential real estate.

In addition, landlords, condominium boards, homeowner associations, or other entities that exercise control over individual residences or common spaces within a development may not:

- Refuse permission for residents with disabilities or their families to make reasonable modifications to housing, at their own expense, if the changes are necessary for a resident to enjoy his or her premises. However, in some instances, the resident may be required to restore the property to its original condition before moving out.

• Refuse to make reasonable accommodations in rules, policies, practices, and services to provide equal opportunity to residents with disabilities to use and enjoy their homes, so long as it does not interfere with the rights of others to use and enjoy their homes.

Communities should not adopt and enforce discriminatory zoning and land use ordinances.

Familial status protections do not apply to certain housing for older people. Such housing is exempt under the law if it is intended for, and solely occupied by, residents 62 years of age or older, or if 80 percent of the units are occupied by at least one person 55 years of age or older, and the housing facility or community publishes and adheres to policies and procedures that demonstrate this intent to be housing for older persons.

Since March 13, 1991, most multifamily dwellings of four or more units have been required to be designed and built so that the units are accessible to people with disabilities.

In addition to nondiscrimination, the Fair Housing Act also provides that HUD must administer all of its programs and activities in a manner that affirmatively furthers the policies of the Act.

Anyone who believes that he or she has been discriminated against can file a complaint with any HUD office in person, by mail, or by telephone within one year after the alleged discrimination has occurred. HUD or an equivalent state or local agency will investigate and attempt to conciliate the complaint. If it is not conciliated and it appears that discrimination has occurred, then HUD will issue a charge. A HUD administrative law judge (ALJ) will hold a hearing unless either party chooses to take a case to federal district court.

Equal Opportunity in HUD-Assisted Programs (Title VI, Section 504, Americans with Disabilities Act, Section 109, Age Discrimination Act, and Title IX)

These programs assure equal opportunity to participate in and benefit from HUD-assisted programs or activities without regard to race, color, national origin, disability, or age, and, in some instances, religion or sex.

HUD determines the extent to which its programs comply with federal laws prohibiting discrimination in federally assisted programs or activities. Section 109 also has a provision that includes religion and sex as prohibited bases for discrimination in the Community Development Block Grant program. Under Title II of the Americans with Disabilities Act, HUD is designated as an agency to investigate discrimination complaints.

The Office of Fair Housing and Equal Opportunity investigates complaints and conducts compliance reviews to eliminate discrimination by entities receiving HUD assistance. Policies are developed to make HUD-assisted activities available to protected classes and to promote nondiscriminatory participation by persons in those protected classes.

Technical assistance is available to state and local agencies with civil rights problems in HUD-assisted programs. Recipients that are in noncompliance are given the opportunity to achieve voluntary compliance. If this fails, federal assistance for the program may be refused, terminated, or suspended. HUD may refer the matter to the Department of Justice for enforcement if efforts to achieve voluntary compliance are unsuccessful.

Any HUD-assisted program or activity, except contracts of insurance or guaranty, is subject to Title VI, Section 504, and the Age Discrimination Act. CDBG recipients are also subject to Section 109; HUD-assisted educational programs are also subject to Title IX. Any person or group suspecting discrimination in any HUD-assisted program because of race, color, national origin, age, or disability (and religion in the Community Development Block Grant program, and sex in HUD-assisted education programs or activities) may file a complaint.

GOVERNMENT NATIONAL MORTGAGE ASSOCIATION (GINNIE MAE)

Ginnie Mae I Mortgage-Backed Securities

This program expands affordable housing in the United States by linking global capital markets to the nation's housing market. Ginnie Mae guarantees investors (security holders) the timely payment of principal and interest on securities issued by private lenders that are backed by pools of Federal Housing Administration (FHA), Veterans Affairs (VA), Rural Housing Service (RHS), and Public and Indian Housing (PIH) mortgage loans. The full faith and credit guarantee of the U.S. government that Ginnie Mae places on mortgage-backed securities lowers the cost of, and maintains the supply of, mortgage financing for government-backed loans.

In the Ginnie Mae I program, all mortgages in a pool are fixed-rate, single-family mortgages with the same interest rate. The mortgage interest rates must all be the same, and the same lender must issue the securities. With the exception of Ginnie Mae I pools that are used as collateral for state or local bond financing programs (BFP) for which Ginnie Mae provides special consideration, Ginnie Mae I securities have a servicing and guarantee fee that totals 50 basis points, and the minimum pool size is $1 million.

To issue a Ginnie Mae I security, an approved lender applies for a commitment from Ginnie Mae for the guaranty of securities. The lender originates or acquires mortgage loans and assembles them into a pool of mortgages. The Ginnie Mae I program permits lenders to issue securities backed by pools of single-family, multifamily, and manufactured housing loans where the interest rate is the same for each loan in the pool. The lender decides to whom to sell the security and then submits the documents to Ginnie Mae's pool processing agent. The agent prepares and delivers the Ginnie Mae–guaranteed security to the investors designated by the lender. The lender is responsible for selling the securities and servicing the underlying mortgages. Issuers of Ginnie Mae I securities are also responsible for paying security holders on the 15th day of each month.

To be eligible, a firm must be approved as an issuer based on capital requirements, staffing, experience criteria, and infrastructure. The firm must also be an FHA-approved lender in good standing.

Ginnie Mae II Mortgage-Backed Securities

This program expands affordable housing in America by linking global capital markets to the nation's housing markets. The Ginnie Mae II program complements the Ginnie Mae I program.

Ginnie Mae guarantees investors (security holders) the timely payment of principal and interest on securities issued by private lenders that are backed by pools of Federal Housing Administration (FHA), Veterans Affairs (VA), Rural Housing Service (RHS), and Public and Indian Housing (PIH) mortgage loans. The full faith and credit guarantee of the U.S. government that Ginnie Mae places on mortgage-backed securities (MBS) lowers the cost of, and maintains the supply of, mortgage financing for government-backed loans.

In the Ginnie Mae II program, one or multiple lenders may pool mortgages in the same pool, which in turn allows for larger and more geographically dispersed pools. The Ginnie Mae II program also allows securities to be issued with smaller numbers of mortgage loans than the Ginnie Mae I program, and allows ARM loans to be pooled. Wider ranges of mortgage interest rates are permitted in a Ginnie Mae II MBS pool (lenders are permitted servicing and guarantee fees ranging from 25 to 75 basis points). With the exception of Ginnie Mae II pools that are used as collateral for state or local bond financing programs (BFP), for which Ginnie Mae provides special consideration, the minimum pool size is $250,000 for multi-lender pools and $1 million for single-lender pools.

To issue a Ginnie Mae II security, an approved lender applies for a commitment from Ginnie Mae for the guaranty of securities. The lender originates or acquires mortgage loans and assembles them into a pool of mortgages. The Ginnie Mae II program permits lenders to issue securities backed by pools of single-family or manufactured housing loans where the interest rates can vary within a fixed range. The lender decides to whom to sell the security and then submits the documents to Ginnie Mae's pool processing agent. The agent prepares and delivers the securities to the investors designated by the lender. The lender is responsible for selling the securities and servicing the underlying mortgages. Issuers of Ginnie Mae II securities are responsible for paying security holders on the twentieth day of each month.

To apply, a firm must be approved as an issuer based on capital requirements, staffing, experience criteria, and infrastructure. The firm must also be an FHA-approved lender in good standing.

Ginnie Mae Multiclass Securities Program

In 1970, Ginnie Mae made history when it pooled government mortgage loans together and created the first mortgage-backed security (MBS). Ginnie Mae and the capital markets have evolved since 1970, and now play a pivotal role in improving the affordability of housing for all Americans by increasing the availability of investment capital to the housing sector. In 1994, Ginnie Mae broadened its investor base for MBSs with the introduction of an innovative and more efficient vehicle, the Real Estate Mortgage Investment Conduit (commonly known in the industry as a REMIC). The mortgage market has matured to include a variety of REMIC securities, each with a broad array of features and each with a different risk-return profile. In July 2004, Ginnie Mae complemented its REMIC product line with the launch of its stripped mortgage-backed securities (SMBS) Trust vehicle. The SMBS Trust product adds another investment type to sophisticated investors in Ginnie Mae MBSs seeking better market liquidity and management of MBS prepayment risk. Callable securities, another one of Ginnie Mae's Multiclass Securities products, give investors the option to redeem previously issued securities, allowing greater hedging flexibility.

The Ginnie Mae Multiclass Securities program is a vehicle that increases the liquidity of Ginnie Mae MBSs and attracts new sources of capital for federally insured or guaranteed loans. A REMIC is a type of pay-through bond characterized by a multiclass or multitranched serialized structure. REMICs are partitioned into several tranches of bonds of serialized priority by which the bonds are redeemed. Ginnie Mae REMICs are collateralized by Ginnie Mae MBSs, which are in turn backed by FHA, VA, RHS, and PIH mortgage loans.

Ginnie Mae REMICs direct principal and interest payments from the underlying MBSs to classes (tranches) with different principal balances, interest rates, average lives, prepayment characteristics, and final maturities. This enables investors with different investment horizons, risk-reward preferences, and asset-liability management requirements to purchase mortgage securities that are tailored to their needs.

While REMICs add the flexibility for dealers to tailor cash flows to investors with duration concerns, the SMBS Trust product allows sophisticated investors to reduce (or increase) prepayment risks by isolating and combining various interest only (IO) and principal only (PO) cash flow components.

Callable securities are structured through a Grantor Trust vehicle and consist of the following classes: Class A is the callable class that receives the pass-through cash flow; and Class B is the call class that can call Class A securities and exchange them for the underlying collateral at any time after the lockout period.

Ginnie Mae is a government-owned, publicly managed corporation that has never failed to fulfill its responsibility as guarantor of its securities. Ginnie Mae's obligations are backed by the full faith and credit of the United States government. Nevertheless, investors considering an investment in a Ginnie Mae REMIC should read the related offering 110 circular and offering circular supplement, and consult their investment advisors to ensure that they fully understand the risks, particularly the prepayment and market risks associated with an investment in a REMIC security.

A dealer must meet the following six requirements to participate in the Ginnie Mae Multiclass Securities program:

1. Apply and be approved;

2. Demonstrate to Ginnie Mae's satisfaction its capacity to accumulate the eligible assets needed for a proposed structured securities issuance;

3. Meet the minimum capital requirement of $250 million in shareholders' equity or partnership capital, evidenced by the dealer's most recent audited financial statements, which must have been issued within the preceding 12 months;

4. Demonstrate good standing with, and have been responsible for, at least one structured transaction with Fannie Mae or Freddie Mac, or demonstrate to Ginnie Mae's satisfaction the capability to consummate a structured transaction;

5. Represent the structural integrity of the proposed issuance under all cash flow scenarios and demonstrate to Ginnie Mae's satisfaction its ability to indemnify Ginnie Mae for a breach of this representation; and

6. Comply, and obtain compliance from the participants that it selects, with Ginnie Mae's participation requirements and policies regarding participation by minority- and women-owned businesses.

HUD'S FEDERAL HOUSING ADMINISTRATION (FHA) SINGLE FAMILY HOUSING PROGRAMS

Housing in Military Impacted Areas (Section 238)

This program provides federal mortgage insurance for housing in areas affected by military installations. Insurance is available, but there is little activity in recent years.

Growing Equity Mortgage Insurance (Section 245(a))

This program enables the homeowner to apply scheduled increases in monthly payments to the outstanding principal balance of a mortgage and thereby considerably shorten its term. This program has had little activity in recent years.

FEDERAL HOUSING ADMINISTRATION'S MULTIFAMILY HOUSING PROGRAMS

Multifamily Rental Housing (Section 207)

This program provides federal mortgage insurance to finance construction or rehabilitation of a broad cross section of rental housing. Privately owned new construction and substantial rehabilitation of multifamily rental projects are generally insured under Section 221(d)(4), because it is more advantageous to the developer.

Mortgage Insurance for Single-Room Occupancy Projects (Section 221(d)) pursuant to Section 223(g)

Mortgage insurance is available for the new construction or substantial rehabilitation of single-room occupancy (SRO) facilities. The SRO program without subsidies has not been used in recent years. The more active program is Section 8 Moderate Rehabilitation Single Room Occupancy.

Congregate Housing Services

This program provides federal grants to eligible housing projects for the elderly and disabled. No activity in recent years except to extend previously funded grants.

Flexible Subsidy (Section 201)

This program provides federal aid for troubled multifamily housing projects, as well as capital improvement funds for both troubled and stable subsidized projects. No new commitments are being made.

FEDERAL HOUSING ADMINISTRATION'S PUBLIC AND INDIAN HOUSING

The following programs remain as some old projects still exist. However, as of this writing no new funds have been authorized for new projects. Because it is possible that new funds may become available in the future, they have not been eliminated from the list.

Section 8 Moderate Rehabilitation Program

This program assists very low-income families in obtaining decent, safe, and sanitary housing in privately owned, rehabilitated buildings.

Section 8 Moving to Work Demonstration

This program allowed public housing agencies to design and test ways to promote self-sufficiency among assisted families, achieve programmatic efficiency and reduce costs, and increase housing choice for low-income households.

FHA/HUD POLICY DEVELOPMENT AND RESEARCH

Doctoral Dissertation Research Grant Program

This program provides competitive grants to PhD candidates to enable them to complete their dissertations on research issues related to HUD priorities.

Early Doctoral Student Research Grant Program

This program provides competitive grants to PhD candidates early in their studies to complete their research manuscripts on issues related to HUD priorities.

HUD Urban Scholars Fellowship Program

This program provides competitive grants to PhD candidates early in their academic careers to undertake research on issues related to HUD priorities.

HUD Regional and Field Offices

To access HUD and FHA offices by state please use the following web address (see www .hud.gov/localoffices.cfm). Or phone: 800-CALL-FHA or (800-225-5342) Monday–Friday, 8 AM to 8 PM ET; TDD: 877-TDD-2HUD or (877-833-2483).

FEDERAL DEPARTMENT OF VETERANS AFFAIRS

For all Veterans Administration (VA) benefits, including medical and income please go to: www.va.gov.

The following deals with VA loans (also called GI loans):

ARRANGING FOR A VETERANS GUARANTEED LOAN

1. Find the property suitable for your needs.
2. Go to a lender and apply for a loan.
3. Present your discharge or separation papers relating to latest period of service and/or a Certificate of Eligibility.
4. Property must be appraised by approved appraiser.
5. Estimate the property's reasonable value.

If application is approved, you get the loan. VA loans offer the following important features:

- Ensure that all veterans are given an equal opportunity to buy homes with VA assistance, without regard to their race, color, religion, sex, handicap, familial status, or national origin.

- No down payment (unless required by the lender, the purchase price is more than the reasonable value of the property as determined by VA, or the loan is made with graduated payment features).

- A freely negotiable fixed interest rate competitive with conventional mortgage interest rates.

- The buyer is informed of the estimated reasonable value of the property.

- Limitations on closing costs.

- An assumable mortgage. However, for loans closed on or after March 1, 1988, the assumption must be approved in advance by the lender or VA. Generally, this involves a review of the creditworthiness of the purchaser (ability and willingness to make the mortgage payments). Be sure to see section entitled "Loan Repayment terms."

- Long amortization (repayment) terms.

- Right to prepay without penalty (lenders may require that any partial prepayments be in the amount of at least one monthly installment of principal or $100, whichever is less).

- For houses inspected by VA during construction, a warranty from the builder and VA assistance in trying to obtain the builder's cooperation in correcting any justified construction complaint.

- Forbearance extended to VA homeowners experiencing temporary financial difficulty.

What the Veterans Administration Cannot Do

The VA cannot guarantee that the house you buy, whether it is new, or previously occupied, will be free of defects. The VA appraisal is *not* intended to be an "inspection" of the property. It is in your best interest to seek expert advice *before* you legally commit yourself in a purchase agreement, particularly if you have any doubts about the condition of the house. Most sellers will permit you, at your expense, to arrange for an inspection by a qualified residential inspection service and negotiate with you concerning repairs to be included in the purchase agreement. Such action can prevent later problems, disagreements, and disappointments. In brief:

- VA guarantees only the loan, not the condition of the property. It is your responsibility to be an informed buyer and assure yourself that what you are buying is satisfactory to you in all respects.

- If you have a home built, VA cannot compel the builder to correct construction defects or otherwise live up to the contract. VA authority is limited to suspension of the builder from participation in the VA Loan Guaranty program.

- VA cannot guarantee that you are making a good investment or that you can resell the house at the price you paid.

- VA does not have the authority to provide you with legal services.

Requirements for VA Loan Approval

To get a VA loan, the law requires that:

- You must be an eligible veteran who has available home loan entitlement (except in the case of an interest rate reduction-refinancing loan—see "Interest Rates").

- The loan must be for an eligible purpose. The purchase price should not exceed the appraised value. Otherwise, you will have to pay the difference from your own resources.

- You must occupy or intend to occupy the property as your home within a reasonable period of time after closing the loan.

- You must have enough income to meet the new mortgage payments on the loan, cover the costs of owning a home, take care of the obligations and expenses, and still have enough income left over for family support (a spouse's income is considered in the same manner as the veteran's).

- You must have a good credit record.

The Guaranty

VA-guaranteed loans are made by private lenders such as banks, savings and loan associations, or mortgage companies. To get a loan, you apply to the lender. If the loan is approved, VA guarantees the loan when it is closed. The guaranty means the lender is protected against loss if you or a later owner fails to repay the loan.

THE FIVE MOST ASKED VA LOAN QUESTIONS AND THEIR ANSWERS

1. HOW MUCH IS THE GUARANTY? VA will guarantee up to 50 percent of a home loan up to $45,000. For loans between $45,000 and $144,000, the minimum guaranty amount is $22,500, with a maximum guaranty of up to 40 percent of the loan up to $36,000, subject to the amount of entitlement a veteran has available. For loans of more than $144,000 made for the purchase or construction of a home or to purchase a residential unit in a condominium or to refinance an existing VA guaranteed loan for interest rate reduction, the maximum guaranty is the lesser of 25 percent or $89,912, which is 25 percent of the

Freddie Mac conforming loan limit for a single family residence for 2005. This figure will change yearly. (For information about entitlement see "Service Eligibility.")

2. Is $36,000 the biggest loan a veteran can get? No. You may generally borrow up to the reasonable value of the property or the purchase price, whichever is less, plus the funding fee, if required. For certain refinancing loans, the maximum loan is limited to 90 percent of the value of the property, plus the funding fee, if required. To determine the reasonable value, VA requires an appraisal of the property. (Also see "Down payment Requirements.")

3. What is the maximum VA loan? There is no maximum VA loan, except that the loan cannot exceed the lesser of the appraised value or purchase price, plus VA funding fee and energy efficient improvements, if applicable. However, lenders usually won't make a no-down-payment loan larger than $359,650 due to secondary market limitations.

4. Must the loan be repaid? Yes. A VA guaranteed loan is not a gift. It must be repaid, just as you must repay any money you borrow. The VA guaranty, which protects the lender against loss, encourages the lender to make a loan with terms favorable to the veteran. But if you fail to make the payments you agreed to make, you may lose your home through foreclosure, and you and your family would probably lose all the time and money you had invested in it. If the lender does take a loss, VA must pay the guaranty to the lender, and the amount paid by VA must be repaid by you. If your loan closed on or after January 1, 1990, you will owe the government in the event of a default only if there was fraud, misrepresentation, or bad faith on your part.

5. Does VA make any loan directly to eligible veterans? Yes, but only to Native Americans on trust land or to supplement a grant to get a specially adapted home for certain eligible veterans who have a permanent and total service-connected disability(ies). For information concerning direct loans to Native American Veterans See VA Pamphlet 26-93-1, which can be found on the Internet at: www.homeloans.va.gov/VAP26-93-1.htm. See VA Pamphlet 26-69-1 for information concerning specially adapted housing grants.

Service Eligibility

As military actions around the world continue to occur, VA eligibility is continually extended to cover veterans of those conflicts. Currently you are eligible for VA financing if your service falls within any of the following categories:

Wartime service: If you served any time during:

- World War II (September 16, 1940, to July 25, 1947).
- Korean Conflict (June 27, 1950, to January 31, 1955).

- Vietnam Era (August 5, 1964, to May 7, 1975), the Vietnam Era begins February 28, 1961, or for individuals who served in the Republic of Vietnam.
- Persian Gulf War (August 2, 1990, to present [requires service for two years or the full period for which called to active duty, except that exceptions applying to service between September 7, 1980, and August 1, 1990, also apply to Persian Gulf War]).
- You must have served at least 90 days on active duty and been discharged or released under other than dishonorable conditions. If you served less than 90 days, you may be eligible if discharged because of a service-connected disability.

PEACETIME SERVICE: If your service fell entirely within any one of the following periods:

- July 26, 1947, to June 26, 1950.
- February 1, 1955, to August 4, 1964.
- May 8, 1975, to September 7, 1980 (if enlisted), or to October 16, 1981 (if officer), you must have served at least 181 days of continuous active duty and been discharged or released under conditions other than dishonorable. If you served less than 181 days, you may be eligible if discharged because of a service-connected disability.

If your entire period of service was between September 7, 1980 (enlisted), or October 16, 1981 (officer), and August 1, 1990, you must have:

- Completed 24 months of continuous active duty or the full period (at least 181 days) for which you were called or ordered to active duty, and been discharged or released under conditions other than dishonorable.
- You may also be determined eligible if you were discharged for a service-connected disability, or you were discharged for the convenience of the government after completing at least 20 months of a two-year enlistment, or you completed 181 days of active duty and:
  - Were discharged because of a hardship, or
  - Were determined to have a service-connected compensable disability, or
  - Were discharged or released from active duty for a medical condition which preexisted service and has not been determined to be service-connected, or
  - Received an involuntary discharge or release from active duty for the convenience of the government as a result of a reduction in force, or
  - Were discharged or released from active duty for a physical or mental condition not characterized as a disability and not the result of misconduct but which did interfere with your performance of duty.

Note: During the Persian Gulf War, the foregoing exceptions to the two-year requirement apply, except that 90 days of active duty is sufficient in lieu of 181 days.

- ACTIVE DUTY SERVICE PERSONNEL: If you are now on active duty, you are eligible after having served 181 days (only 90 days during the Gulf War), unless discharged or separated from a prior qualifying period of active duty.

- MEMBERS OF THE SELECTED RESERVE: Individuals who are not otherwise eligible and who have completed at least six years in the Reserves or National Guard, or been discharged because of a service-connected disability, and have been discharged with an honorable discharge, or have been placed on the retired list, or have been transferred to an element of the Ready Reserve other than the Selected Reserve, or continue to serve in the Selected Reserve are eligible for a GI loan.

Other types of service personnel who are eligible include:

- Certain U.S. citizens who served in the armed forces of a government allied with the United States in World War II.

- Unmarried surviving spouses of the above-described eligible persons who died as the result of service or service-connected injuries. (Children of deceased veterans are not eligible.)

- The spouse of any member of the Armed Forces serving on active duty who is listed as missing in action, or is a prisoner of war and has been so listed for a total of more than 90 days.

- Individuals with service as members in certain other organizations, services, programs, and schools may also be eligible. Questions about whether this service qualifies for home loan benefits should be referred to the Loan Guaranty Division of the nearest VA regional office.

Obtaining a Certificate of Eligibility

VA determines your eligibility and, if you are qualified, a Certificate of Eligibility will be issued.

ACE (AUTOMATED CERTIFICATE OF ELIGIBILITY). In some cases, veterans can obtain the *Certificate of Eligibility* from a lender. Most lenders have access to the ACE system. This Internet-based application can establish eligibility and issue an online Certificate of Eligibility in a matter of seconds. Not all cases can be processed through ACE—only those for which VA has sufficient data in our records. However, veterans are encouraged to ask their lenders about this method of obtaining a certificate. If the certificate cannot be issued by ACE, you can request it from VA, by completing VA Form 26-1880, "Request for a Certificate of Eligibility." The form should be submitted along with either the originals or legible copies of your most recent discharge or separation papers covering active military duty since September 16, 1940, which show active duty dates and type of discharge. This form may be obtained from any VA office or at www.va.gov/vaforms/. If you were separated after January 1, 1950, you must submit your DD Form 214, Certificate of Release or Discharge From Active Duty.

In addition, if you are now on active duty and have not been previously discharged from active duty service, you must submit a statement of service that includes the name of the issuing authority (base or command), and is signed by or at the direction of an appropriate official. The statement must include date of entry on active duty and the duration of any time lost.

Since there is no uniform document similar to the DD214 for proof of service in the Selected Reserve, a number of different forms may be accepted as documentation of service in the Selected Reserve. For those who served in the Army or Air National Guard and were discharged after at least six years of such service, NGB Form 22 may be sufficient. Those who served in the Army, Navy, Air Force, Marine Corps, or Coast Guard Reserves may need to rely on any of a variety of forms that document at least six years of honorable service. Often, it will be necessary to submit a combination of documents such as an Honorable Discharge certificate together with a retirement point's statement. It is the reservist's responsibility to obtain and submit documentation of six years of honorable service.

The Request for Certificates of Eligibility, VA Form 26-1880, should be mailed to one of the two Eligibility Centers. Generally, veterans in the western half of the country mail applications to the Los Angeles Eligibility Center, P.O. Box 240097, Los Angeles, CA 90024 (888-487-1970). Veterans in the eastern half of the country mail applications to the Winston-Salem Eligibility Center, P.O. Box 20729, Winston-Salem, NC 27120 (888-244-6711).

VA ENTITLEMENT QUESTIONS AND ANSWERS

1. WHAT SERVICE IS NOT ELIGIBLE? You are *not* eligible for VA financing based on the following:

- World War I service.
- Active Duty for Training in the Reserves.
- Active Duty for Training in the National Guard (unless "activated" under the authority of Title 10 U.S. Code).

2. DOES THIS KIND OF SERVICE PROVIDE ENTITLEMENT TO ANY OTHER VETERANS' HOME LOAN BENEFIT? Yes. World War I and Active Duty for Training service may qualify you for a HUD/FHA veterans' loan. Under the National Housing Act loan program, the Federal Housing Administration of the Department of Housing and Urban Development administers a loan program for veterans. Financing under this program is available under slightly more favorable terms than those available to nonveterans. VA's only role in this program is to determine the eligibility of the veteran and, if qualified, issue a Certificate of Veteran Status as evidence of entitlement to HUD/FHA loan benefits for veterans. You may get a Certificate of Veteran Status by completing VA Form 26-8261a, Request for Certificate of Veteran Status, and submitting it with the attachments listed in the instructions to any VA regional office or center for a determination of eligibility. This form may be obtained from any VA office or at www.va.gov/vaforms/.

All veterans discharged under other than dishonorable conditions from at least 90 days of service that began before September 8, 1980, are eligible. Veterans of enlisted service in a regular component of the Armed Forces, which began after September 7, 1980, or officers or reservists who entered on active duty after October 13, 1982, must have served at least 24 months of service or the full period for which called to active duty or Active Duty for Training before being discharged, unless the discharge was for hardship or disability.

3. WHAT CAN A VETERAN DO WHO HAS LOST HIS OR HER ORIGINAL DISCHARGE PAPERS AND DOES NOT HAVE A LEGIBLE COPY? The veteran should obtain a Certificate in Lieu of Lost or Destroyed Discharge. Any VA Veterans Benefits Counselor at the nearest VA office will assist a veteran in obtaining necessary proof of military service.

4. DOES A VETERAN'S HOME LOAN ENTITLEMENT EXPIRE? No. Home loan entitlement is generally good until used. However, the eligibility of service personnel is only available so long as they remain on active duty. If they are discharged or released from active duty before using their entitlement, a new determination of their eligibility must be made, based on the length of service and the type of discharge received.

5. HOW MUCH ENTITLEMENT DOES EACH VETERAN HAVE? Originally, the maximum entitlement available was $2,000; however, legislation enacted since that time has provided veterans with increases in entitlement up to the present maximum of $36,000 (or up to $89,912 for certain loans over $144,000). The $36,000 may, however, be reduced if entitlement has been used before to get a VA loan. The amount of remaining entitlement can be determined by subtracting the amount of entitlement used from the current maximum available entitlement of $36,000. (See question 8 for information on using remaining entitlement.)

6. DOES VA HOME LOAN ENTITLEMENT PROVIDE CASH TO THE VETERAN? No. The amount of entitlement relates only to the amount VA will guarantee the lender against loss.

7. CAN A VETERAN GET USED ENTITLEMENT BACK TO USE AGAIN? If you have used all or part of your entitlement, you can get that entitlement back to purchase another home if the following conditions for "restoration" are met.

- The property has been sold *and* the loan has been paid in full.
- A qualified veteran-transferee (buyer) must agree to assume the outstanding balance on the loan and agree to "substitute" his or her entitlement for the *same* amount of entitlement you originally used to get the loan. The buyer must also meet the occupancy and income and credit requirements of the law.
- One time only if you have repaid the prior VA loan in full, but have not disposed of the property securing that loan, the entitlement you used in connection with that loan may be restored.
- Any loss suffered by VA as a result of guaranty of the loan (e.g., a claim paid to a lender if a loan goes to foreclosure) must be repaid in full before the entitlement used on the loan can be restored.

- Restoration of entitlement is not automatic. You must apply for it by completing and returning VA Form 26-1880, "Request for a Certificate of Eligibility" to one of the Eligibility Centers.

8. IF THE REQUIREMENTS FOR RESTORATION CANNOT BE MET, IS THERE ANY OTHER WAY A VETERAN CAN OBTAIN ANOTHER VA LOAN? Yes. Veterans who had a VA loan before may still have "remaining entitlement" to use for another VA loan. The current amount of entitlement available to each eligible veteran is $36,000 ($89,912 for certain loans over $144,000). This was much lower in years past and has been increased over time by changes in the law. For example, a veteran who obtained a $25,000 loan in 1974 would have used $12,500 guaranty entitlement, the maximum then available. Even if that loan is not paid off, the veteran could use the $23,500 difference between the $12,500 entitlement originally used and the current maximum of $36,000 to buy another home with VA financing.

9. MAY SEVERAL VETERANS USE THEIR ENTITLEMENT TO ACQUIRE PROPERTY TOGETHER? Yes. The guaranty is based on each veteran's interest in the property, but the guaranty on the loan may not exceed the lesser of 40 percent of the loan amount or $36,000 ($89,912 for certain loans over $144,000).

10. IF BOTH A HUSBAND AND WIFE ARE ELIGIBLE, MAY THEY ACQUIRE PROPERTY JOINTLY AND SO INCREASE THE AMOUNT WHICH MAY BE GUARANTEED? They may acquire property jointly, but the amount of guaranty on the loan may not exceed the lesser of 40 percent of the loan amount or $36,000 ($89,912 for certain loans over $144,000).

11. MAY A VETERAN JOIN WITH A NONVETERAN IN OBTAINING A VA LOAN? Yes, but the guaranty is based only on the veteran's portion of the loan. The guaranty cannot cover the nonveteran's part of the loan. This does not apply to a loan to a veteran and spouse when the spouse is not a veteran. (Consult lenders to determine whether they would be willing to accept applications for joint loans of this type.)

12. DOES THE ISSUANCE OF A CERTIFICATE OF ELIGIBILITY GUARANTEE APPROVAL OF A VA LOAN? No. The veteran must still be found to be qualified for the loan from an income and credit standpoint.

Eligible Loan Purposes

You may use VA-guaranteed financing:

- To buy a home.
- To buy a townhouse or condominium unit in a project that has been approved by the VA.
- To build a home.
- To repair, alter, or improve a home.
- To simultaneously purchase and improve a home.

- To improve a home through installment of a solar heating and/or cooling system or other energy efficient improvements.
- To buy a manufactured (mobile) home and/or lot.
- To buy and improve a lot on which to place a manufactured home which you already own and occupy.
- To refinance a manufactured home loan in order to acquire a lot. (See VA Pamphlet 26-71-1, on the Internet at: www.homeloans.va.gov/VAP26-71-1.htm, for more information about manufactured home loans.)

VETERANS ADMINISTRATION DOWN-PAYMENT REQUIREMENTS

Traditional Fixed-Payment Mortgage, Buy-down Loans, and Growing Equity Mortgage

VA does not require a down payment if the purchase price or cost is not more than the reasonable value of the property as determined by VA, but the lender may require one. If the purchase price or cost is more than the reasonable value, the difference must be paid in cash from your own resources.

Graduated Payment Mortgage

The maximum loan amount may not be for more than the reasonable value of the property or the purchase price, whichever is less. Because the loan balance will be increasing during the first years of the loan, a down payment is required to keep the loan balance from going over the reasonable value or the purchase price.

Interest Rates

The interest rate on VA loans can be negotiated based on prevailing rates in the mortgage market. Once a loan is made, the interest rate set in the note will stay the same for the life of the loan. However, if interest rates go down, and you still own and occupy (or previously occupied) the property securing a previous VA loan, you may apply for a new VA loan to refinance the previous loan at a lower interest rate without using any additional entitlement.

Closing Costs

The cost of obtaining any mortgage can be high. VA regulates those closing costs that a veteran may be charged in connection with closing a VA loan. No commission or brokerage fees may be charged to you for obtaining a VA loan. However, you may pay reasonable closing costs to the lender in connection with a VA-guaranteed loan. Although some additional costs are unique to certain localities, the closing costs generally include VA appraisal, credit report, survey, title evidence, recording fees, a 1 percent loan origination fee, and discount points. The closing costs and origination charge may not be included in the loan, except in VA refinancing loans. In addition to negotiating the interest rate with the lender, veterans may negotiate the payment of discount points and other closing costs with the seller.

Often, sellers will consider paying some or all of the discount points required by the lender in order to complete the sale. This can have a big impact on the amount of cash you must pay out of pocket in order to complete the purchase. If the seller will not consider paying points, the veteran may be able to negotiate an interest rate with the lender that is sufficient to avoid the need to include any discount points in the transaction.

Funding Fee

In most instances, veterans must also pay a VA funding fee at the time of loan closing. The fee may be included in the loan and paid from loan proceeds.

State Benefits

Another area to be explored is the existence of state benefits. Many states offer housing programs that are independent from federal programs. The programs and benefits, as well as the qualifying criteria, may differ from one state to the next. Information on state programs may be obtained from state officials or from the local VA regional office.

LOAN GUARANTY SERVICE REGIONAL OFFICE ADDRESSES LIST

Alabama
VA Regional Office
345 Perry Hill Road
Montgomery, AL 36109-4541

Alaska
VA Medical and Regional Office
Center
2925 Debarr Road
Anchorage, AK 99508

Arizona
VA Regional Loan Center
3333 North Central Avenue
Phoenix, AZ 85012-2402

Arkansas
VA Regional Office
PO. Box 1280
Bldg. 65, Ft. Roots
N. Little Rock, AR 72115

California
Oakland VA Regional Office
Federal Building, 1301 Clay Street
Oakland, CA 94612-5209

Los Angeles VA Regional Office
Federal Building, 11000 Wilshire
Boulevard
Los Angeles, CA 90024

San Diego VA Regional Office
8810 Rio San Diego Drive
San Diego, CA 92108

Colorado
VA Regional Office
155 Van Gordon Street
Lakewood, CO 80228

Connecticut
VA Medical and Regional Office
Center
450 Main Street
Hartford, CT 06103
*Note: Loan Guaranty consolidated with
Manchester, NH*

Delaware
VA Medical and Regional Office
Center
1601 Kirkwood Highway
Wilmington, DE 19805
*Note: Loan Guaranty for Wilmington,
DE, consolidated with Philadelphia, PA*

District of Columbia
VA Regional Office
1722 I Street, NW
Washington, DC 20421

Florida
VA Regional Office
9500 Bay Pines Boulevard
St. Petersburg, FL 33708

Georgia
VA Regional Office
1700 Clairmont Road
Decatur, GA 30033-4032

Hawaii
VA Medical and Regional Office Center
Loan Guaranty Office
459 Patterson Road
Honolulu, HI 96819-1522

Idaho
VA Regional Office
805 W. Franklin Street
Boise, ID 83702-5560

Illinois
VA Regional Office
536 S. Clark Street
P.O. Box 8136
Chicago, IL 60680

Indiana
VA Regional Office
575 North Pennsylvania Street
Indianapolis, IN 46204-1581

Iowa
VA Regional Office
210 Walnut Street
Des Moines, IA 50309

Kansas
VA Medical and Regional Office Center
5500 E. Kellogg
Wichita, KS 67218-1698

Kentucky
VA Regional Office
545 S. 3rd Street
Louisville, KY 40202

Louisiana
VA Regional Office
701 Loyola Avenue
New Orleans, LA 70113

Maine
VA Medical and Regional Office Center
Route 17 East
Togus, ME 04330
*Note: Loan Guaranty consolidated with
Manchester, NH*

Maryland
VA Regional Office
Federal Building
31 Hopkins Plaza
Baltimore, MD 21201
*Note: Montgomery and Prince George's
counties are under the jurisdiction of
VARO Washington, DC*

Massachusetts
VA Regional Office
John F. Kennedy Federal Building
Government Center
Boston, MA 02203
*Note: Loan Guaranty consolidated with
Manchester, NH*

Michigan
VA Regional Office
Federal Building
477 Michigan Avenue
Detroit, MI 48226

Minnesota
VA Regional Office and Insurance
Center
One Federal Drive
Fort Snelling, MN 55111

Mississippi
VA Regional Office
1600 E. Woodrow Wilson Drive
Jackson, MS 39216

Missouri
VA Regional Office
400 South 18th Street
St. Louis, MO 63103-2271

Montana
VA Medical and Regional Office Center
Fort Harrison, MT 59636
*Note: Loan Guaranty consolidated with
Denver, CO*

Nebraska
VA Regional Office
5631 S. 48th Street
Lincoln NE 68516

Nevada
VA Regional Office
1201 Terminal Way
Reno, NV 89520

*Note: Loan Guaranty consolidated
with Oakland, CA. Loan Guaranty
activities for Clark and Lincoln counties,
NV consolidated with Phoenix, AZ*

New Hampshire
VA Regional Office
Norris Cotton Federal Building
275 Chestnut Street
Manchester, NH 03101

New Jersey
VA Regional Office
20 Washington Place
Newark, NJ 07102

New Mexico
VA Regional Office
Dennis Chavez Federal Building,
U.S. Courthouse
500 Gold Avenue, SW
Albuquerque, NM 87103-0968

New York
New York VA Regional Office
Federal Building, 245 West Houston
Street
New York, NY 10014

Buffalo VA Regional Office
103 S. Elmwood Ave.
Buffalo, NY 14202-2478

North Carolina
Winston-Salem VA Regional Office
Federal Building, 251 North
Main Street
Winston-Salem, NC 27155

North Dakota
VA Medical and Regional Office Center
2101 Elm Street
Fargo, ND 58102-2498
*Note: Loan Guaranty consolidated with
St. Paul, MN*

Ohio
  VA Regional Office
  Anthony J. Celebrezze
  Federal Building
  1240 East Ninth Street
  Cleveland, OH 44199

Oklahoma
  VA Regional Office
  125 S. Main Street
  Muskogee, OK 74401

Oregon
  VA Regional Office
  Federal Building
  1220 Southwest 3rd Avenue
  Portland, OR 97204

Pennsylvania VA Regional Office
  VA Regional Office and Insurance
    Center
  1000 Liberty Avenue
  P.O. Box 8079
  Pittsburgh, PA 15222
  5000 Wissahickon Avenue
  Philadelphia, PA 19101

Puerto Rico
  VA Regional Office
  GPO Box 364867
  150 Charden Avenue
  San Juan, PR 00936

Rhode Island
  VA Regional Office
  380 Westminster Mall
  Providence, RI 02903
  Note: Loan Guaranty consolidated with
    Manchester, NH

South Carolina
  VA Regional Office
  1801 Assembly Street
  Columbia, SC 29201

South Dakota
  VA Medical and Regional Office Center
  P.O. Box 5046
  2501 West 22d Street
  Sioux Falls, SD 57117
  Note: Loan Guaranty consolidated with
    St. Paul, MN

Tennessee
  VA Regional Office
  110 Ninth Avenue, South
  Nashville, TN 37203

Texas
  Houston VA Regional Office
  6900 Almeda Road
  Houston, TX 77030-4200

  Waco VA Regional Office
  One Veterans Plaza
  701 Clay Avenue
  Waco, TX 76799

Utah
  VA Regional Office
  P.O. Box 11500
  125 South State Street
  Salt Lake City, UT 84147

Vermont
  VA Medical and Regional Office Center
  White River Junction, VT 05001
  Note: Loan Guaranty consolidated with
    Manchester, NH

Virginia
  VA Regional Office
  210 Franklin Road, SW
  Roanoke, VA 24011
  Note: Arlington, Fairfax, Loudoun, Prince
    William, Spotsylvania, and Stafford coun-
    ties and the cities of Alexandria, Fairfax,
    Falls Church, and Fredericksburg, VA,
    are under the jurisdiction of VARO
    Washington, DC.

Washington
   VA Regional Office
   915 Second Avenue
   Seattle, WA 98174
   Note: Clark, Klickitat, and Skamania
      counties are under the jurisdiction of
      VARO Portland, OR

West Virginia
   VA Regional Office
   640 4th Avenue
   Huntington, WV 25701
   Note: Loan Guaranty consolidated with
      Roanoke, VA

Wisconsin
   VA Regional Office
   Building 6
   5000 West National Avenue
   Milwaukee, Wl 53295

Wyoming
   VA Medical and Regional Office Center
   2360 East Pershing Boulevard
   Cheyenne, WY 82001
   Note: Loan Guaranty consolidated with
      Denver, CO

HOW INVESTORS USE THESE GOVERNMENT SERVICES AND BENEFITS

The United States government provides these insurance and lending programs that will help you buy and sell your properties. These programs vary tremendously and are available in every state. They help buyers who do not have the larger down payment required for more conventional loans. Equally, these loan programs aid sellers who may not be able to sell their properties were it not for this easy-to-come-by financing. When it comes to providing options to finance your investments and to aid in the sale of your properties, you will want to learn as much as you can about government-insured loans and programs.

The VA and FHA have loan programs for single-family homebuyers. However, government loan programs are wide reaching and take into account a substantial amount of loans for many different kinds of residential and commercial ventures.

To Get Effective Benefits Use a Qualified Mortgage Broker Dealing with These Types of Loans

When it comes to government programs, you will want to deal with a good mortgage broker who is up to date in this kind of market and who deals with the specific type of loan you may want or that will best suit your needs. The information provided in this chapter is as up to date as possible, and while there may be no changes by the time you read it, government loan programs are constantly reviewed for alterations. Generally, the changes that may be enacted will improve the programs since the loan amounts are revised upward on a frequent basis. The first step, however, is to have a general understanding of what the government programs do and how you can benefit from them.

Keep in mind that you should think of two factors of each loan program: (1) how it will help you to buy a given property, and (2) how you can use that technique to sell a property you own. Since not all of the loan programs are applicable to everyone, it is possible that you cannot use some of the loan programs offered. However, as a seller, many of your properties will find an increased market through the VA or FHA programs previously described.

Once you have reviewed this chapter, find a good mortgage broker who is familiar with these types of programs. You will find mortgage brokers listed in the Yellow Pages or by simply searching the Internet. Say, for example, search "FHA Loans in New York" or wherever your needs may be. Take a look at the questions and kinds of answers that will help you find the right broker.

Questions and Answers to Find a Qualified Government Loan Mortgage Broker

Q.1 Does your company have a loan officer who specializes in FHA loans, VA loans?

A.1 Yes. (If any other answer is given, you need to call another broker.)

Q.2 (To that specialist.) Do you specialize in single-family loans and investment loan programs within the VA and FHA programs?

A.2 Yes. (Or better: No, I specialize only in the single-family loans. Mr. Jones of our office is the government loan specialist for investments.)

Q.3 I would like to sit down and discuss my investment needs. Would there be any charge for the opportunity to discover if you can help me?

A.3. No. When would you like to get together? If you want to include investments as well as single-family homes, I'll ask Mr. Jones to join us.

You will find that while there may be programs on the books that look as if they are exactly what you need, the actual availability of that program will depend on the determination of the area's needs and the amount of money that has been allocated to that specific area of loan assistance. For example, there are loan programs that are designed to assist in the construction of low-cost housing for the poor or the elderly. These programs open and close for specific areas of the country based on the needs for housing in those areas. Some builders and investors follow these programs around the country, looking for opportunities when they open up.

Remember: Government Programs Provide Insurance, Not Loans

The first thing you should know about government loans is that in most instances the government does not make the loan. Instead it merely insures a portion of the loan, thereby reducing the risk to the lender who actually provides the funds. This insurance then makes more money available from conventional lenders for these programs since the loans are more secure than uninsured loans in the same category.

In addition, since such loans are less risky, the lender is willing to increase the amount of the loan. Some government loans provide 100 percent of the funds needed for the buyer to acquire the property. In turn, this increases the number of ready and willing buyers, which enables many real estate developers to find an easy market for their properties. As a buyer, this is good news if you can qualify for the program; as a seller, this is great news if your property meets the requirements for the program.

The insurance premium is paid by the buyer. The mortgage insurance premium (MIP) was implemented as a lump sum in 1983, and two methods of payment are allowed. One hundred percent of the payment can be financed, or the borrower can pay a percentage of the premium in cash at the closing, with a monthly add on paid over a period of years. This period of years will vary depending on the initial up-front payment and the loan-to-value ratio (LTV) of the loan.

How Do the Investors Make Out?

The lender or investor who buys the loan portfolio finds that usually it is going to benefit from ownership of the loan in two areas. First, a contract rate is paid by the borrower to the lender. This rate usually is slightly lower than the same conventional rate that would have been offered for the similar loan. However, as the risk is less, some investors feel this rate, and the next item to come, makes these loans very attractive investments. When the loan is made, a discount is paid by the seller. This discount is a cost that is required to be paid by the seller and adjusts the yield to the lender to increase the actual percentage earned by the lender above the contract rate. For example, if the contract rate were 10 percent on a loan of $80,000, the interest paid by the buyer the first year would be approximately $8,000. On this same loan, the seller may have paid a discount (points) of 4 percent, or $3,200, which would have reduced the actual amount of the funds provided by the lender by the same amount. The lender then actually paid out only $76,800. However, the loan is set at a contract rate of 10 percent on $80,000. In this case, the actual interest yield to the lender is about 10.54 percent if the loan was a 25-year loan and was not prepaid. Since the lender gets an additional bonus if the loan is prepaid, and as most loans are prepaid within 7 to 12 years, the lender could earn an average yield of 11 percent or more on this example.

When you review the chapters on mortgage discounts and wraparound mortgages, you will find other examples of how this discount can be put to use.

Keep in mind that the entitlement is not the loan amount, but the insured amount. Lenders look at the entitlement as the top portion of the loan and will issue loans in multiples of this amount. In general, the lender will advance a loan equal to four times the entitlement. The VA loan can be used for a variety of real estate ventures and is not limited just to single-family homes.

Income Requirements to Obtain a Loan

The VA has set a basic qualification formula that must be met by every applicant for a GI loan. This formula sets the maximum loan available in most cases. The essence of this formula is to assure the lender that the borrower has reasonable income and credit to repay the loan. Therefore, in addition to being declared eligible for a GI loan based on his or her period of service, the veteran must meet the requirements of the governing law in respect to income and credit. This income and credit takes into consideration more than the property and the respective mortgage payments that will become due as a result of the financing. It also takes into account other obligations confronting the veteran, which include dependents and other expenses that he or she may have. At the time an applicant is filing for a loan, the pertinent data will be used in the final calculations as to the credit of the borrower. The wife or spouse's income will also be included in the total family income. Prior to going for an interview for an application, there is some specific information that you should have available.

DATA NEEDED FOR ANY VA MORTGAGE APPLICATION

- The veteran and spouse's name and current address.
- Entitlement amount. (Obtain through the VA office.)
- Entitlement certificate. (Obtain through the VA office.)
- Place of employment for veteran and spouse, with name for verification.
- Internal Revenue Service 1040 or other form for the last two years.
- All sources of income, with documentation.
- Bank, savings and loan, investment brokerage account, thrift institution address, and account number, and exact name on the account.
- Loan information, lender's address, amount owned, and loan number.
- Credit card numbers.
- List with values of all major assets, and amounts owed against each.
- Total (with breakdown) of all loan payments.
- Details on any unusual expenses, which may be temporary or permanent.

The Procedure with a VA or GI Loan

Under the current law, there are several elements about the GI loan that both the buyer and the seller need to be aware of. The VA is very specific about what costs the veteran can pay and which costs he or she is not allowed to pay. The importance is that the seller is required to pay certain costs with respect to a sale to a veteran through the GI loan.

The seller's cost is limited to 4 percent of the loan amount. It is critical that the seller understand that if the contract calls for the veteran to pay for cost the VA will not allow him or her to pay, the contract will not close in accordance with its provisions. At or prior to the closing, the parties will have to have an understanding based on the following items:

Veterans/Buyers Can Pay	Veterans/Buyers Cannot Pay
The veteran's lawyer	Discount (points)
Title insurance (if no charges for abstract)	Photographs
Survey	Preparation of deed
Credit report	Surtax on deed
Appraisal (if obtained in his or her name)	Assignment of mortgage
Intangible tax on mortgage	Mortgage satisfaction
State stamps on note, if any	Recording of mortgage satisfaction
Repairs	Documentary stamps on deed
Funding fee	Inspections
Appraisal in another's name	

All veterans need to understand that when they take out a GI loan, they are on that loan until either it is paid off or they are replaced by another veteran. The significance of this is that loan remains as an outstanding liability to the original veteran no matter how the loan is assumed on the specific property. If the buyers are not veterans, or if a buying veteran has no entitlement to replace the original, then the vet is there for the duration. This may not present any economic hardship for anyone, but when the veteran sells the property he or she would be best advised to sell to another veteran who can remove him or her entirely, and thereby restores and reinstates the entitlement back to the original veteran.

How to Use the FHA Programs to Maximize Sales of Your Inventory

The FHA covers far more ground than the VA. Therefore, it will offer more opportunities; however, there are some ups and downs for the seller. The seller takes the big bite when he or she pays the discount on the VA-FHA loan. A minor disadvantage comes in taking the property off the market while the appraisal is made and the buyer is undergoing the qualification process. Time thus becomes the major nonmonetary stumbling block for the seller. Nonetheless, the sale via VA or FHA may still be the best way to go, or the only way to go. The arguments made by the seller over discount are usually unwarranted, since he or she would have dropped the price anyway. But this usually means that sellers increase the price to cover the cost. Of course, the appraisal should include this price, and history has indicated that it generally does.

The biggest problem for the seller in this whole transaction is the waiting period, or worse, having taken the property off the market when the market is hot while the buyer is going through the approval period. In addition, the seller will not know the exact amount of the discount at the times he or she places the property on the market, nor know the totality of repairs that the VA or FHA appraisal will indicate must be made.

The advantage to the seller is the obvious expansion of the marketplace for this property. Many buyers would not qualify for any other form of loan except the VA or FHA loan, and if that is the only way to sell that property, then there are no drawbacks, only benefits.

Chapter 8

HOW TO GET LAND DEVELOPMENT AND CONSTRUCTION LOANS

GOAL OF THIS CHAPTER

This chapter introduces you to the initial world of development, land acquisition, and development loans. This adds an important dimension to your financing capability. Land loans and land development represent a special area that brings new problems to the mortgage situation. New problems can mean additional risk. However, as risk is relative to your abilities, by becoming familiar with development loans you may actually reduce your risk as you move into this area of real estate. You will level the playing field with this added knowledge.

Development Is the Wave of the Future

The thought of real estate conjures up visions of endless tracts of homes or new buildings replacing tired old slums. Real estate is development and something new to replace the old, even in cities where something old might be a couple of thousand years old, and urban renewal is saving the façade of a building but removing everything else because 200 years ago, when the building was constructed, the craftsmanship that went into that can no longer be replaced. The United States is new and thrives on more and more new coming online.

To a degree, the essence of real estate depends on the development of land and new construction of buildings. When this sector of the real estate market is not doing well in the marketplace, the entire real estate market is in trouble. The very hint that housing starts have dropped for three months in a row can send shivers up and down the spines of the people and industries that depend on a continued and healthy statistic of housing starts and building permits. Land development and the construction of buildings on that land create different financing problems that are not present in typical conventional loans to finance acquisition of existing property. Yet, just as the old question of which came first, the chicken or the egg, the following two loans are the foundation of real estate development. They are the land development loan and the construction loan. Each of these loans is similar to the other in many respects, yet in some critical aspects, each differs greatly. Each of these loans is generally tied to a third loan: the permanent loan.

In this chapter, we examine each of the three loan formats to illustrate how each type of loan is obtained and what you can do to maximize your ultimate result to best fit your needs and goals.

Those three loan formats are:

1. Land development loan.
2. Construction loan.
3. Combined loan.

Land Development Loan

The land development loan is obtained by a property owner or developer for the specific purpose of development of that property. This kind of loan is unique to the development of vacant land, or redevelopment of existing properties that are first removed to create vacant land. In the process of development, this loan will be similar to the construction loan once development of the basic infrastructure has been completed and actual buildings begin to rise.

Land development has been one of the greatest areas for an investor to build wealth. However, taking a vacant tract of land and turning it into home sites or industrial sites or whatever is not easy and it is growing to be next to impossible to achieve in the same timetable of 20 years ago. The bureaucracy that has sprung up causes delays that can stretch into very long periods of time. While these delays may not be the reason a project fails, simply running out of time to complete due diligence in a timely manner may defeat development. At best, in many cities, a plan from "remove the farm" to "turn on the city lights in the new neighborhood" can take years. Obtaining permission to do what the local zoning ordinances already indicate can be done can involve major roadblocks. When it comes to major developments, just a delay of a few months can add thousands if not hundreds of thousands of dollars to the total cost of the project. Much of the delay comes before the project has even been approved. This means that a developer may have no prior knowledge if his project will ever be approved until he has already invested considerable time and lots of money into the deal. Because so much time is eaten up in this process, sellers, who have not closed on their land yet, may sit and wait for months past what was anticipated as a closing date. They may actually sit and watch as the city turns down the proposed development and see the value of their land slip into the toilet.

I have been through many large commercial development projects where the developer has tossed in the towel and walked from the deal. Some of them have even walked from the state. In the period of time between 2004 and 2008, many fortunes were lost because developers were still riding the crest of an earlier boom in real estate. These developers had new projects on the planning board. They had a lot of capital invested in what looked like a sure thing, only to find that the time it was taking was carrying them closer to the rocky beach. Lenders who were waiting to move forward with funding on these projects withdrew from the deals and left the developer holding a dying project. Sellers who were counting on the profits from their sides of these deals are not part of the real estate decline of 2008.

However, land development is a sure way to wealth if it goes well, and if approvals can be obtained, and the market stays strong between the start and the cashing of the last closing check.

Real estate development is vibrant, exciting, and fresh, and when it is hot, one must make the most of it. All real estate categories have their cycles. The cycle may last 10 to 15 years, and will vary in any given market as to what is hot and what is not because all categories of real estate may not be on the same cycle. There will be different timetables in different areas of the country. Some areas may escape harm altogether, while others seem to suffer together at the same time.

The financing techniques and strategies that are used in this sector of real estate vary from the source of funds that the developer seeks. Some of the largest "national" developers such as Trammel Crow Residential (TCR) look for Wall Street or insurance companies as partners in their deals. In this way, TCR does not risk much if any of its own money. In a trade off, it builds and owns thousands of apartment complexes around the country, most of which are ultimately sold to more sedate investors, such as insurance companies or pension funds or REITs or condominium developers who convert rental apartments into a for-sale product. The profits are divided between the money partners in a formula that is more protected than Paris Hilton's phone number.

There are many different steps that frequently come up between the idea and the last sale of the last site. To illustrate this process, review the following example.

EXAMPLE: LAND DEVELOPMENT PROJECT FROM START TO FINISH.   Oscar owned 224 acres of prime timber land about 45 miles west of Boston, Massachusetts. The timber had not been fully cut in over 30 years, and except for one time about 10 years ago when Oscar had all the soft wood culled out for pulp, no trees had been taken.

Due to the property's proximity to Boston and the nature of the surrounding area, Oscar decided he would develop the land into two-acre single-family homesteads. He would then sell the sites to Bostonians who would like to have a retreat a short drive from the city. He was sure this was going to be a quick deal. After all, for years local real estate brokers have been trying to get him to do exactly this.

To help finance the cost of development, Oscar planned to sell most of the hardwood on the land. By being selective with the cutting he would, however, maintain a heavy growth on the property. With this in mind, he contacted several hardwood buyers who dealt with the furniture industry. They were all interested until they found out that Oscar wanted to be very selective in the cutting. This would increase the cost to remove the trees, and would require a longer cutting period for the amount of board feet that would be removed. This added expense to the hardwood buyer meant a lower price for Oscar. Yet the deal still looked good on paper, so Oscar moved forward.

Oscar got a good price for the hardwood, even though it was much less than he had hoped. Economic reality was beginning to set in, as Oscar realized that for this project he would need additional funds to develop the land to a stage where sales could start.

Oscar also discovered that development of his land was going to be much more expensive than he originally anticipated. The local building department told Oscar that they were going to insist on paved roads connection to city water and sewer, which meant upfront costs that he could recoup from later sales. Higher development cost meant a greater need for funds. This translated into higher interest cost, and the bottom line would be that the sales price for the home sites needed to be higher. Would the sites be too highly priced to sell? Doubt added another problem. To make sure the sites sold a bit more infrastructure would be added. "Give them a good deal," the brokers said, "and you will succeed every time." This meant a higher price, or lower profit. Oscar found that the days of taking a tree farm, cutting some dirt roads through it, to sell off home sites was a day of the past.

Putting Together a Presentation to the Lender. Oscar reviewed what he needed in the way of funds:

1. Roadway costs	$ 475,000
2. Power line costs	248,000
3. Sales brochures	18,000
4. Interest on loan needed during selling time	162,000
5. Miscellaneous costs	195,000
6. Reserve for contingencies	150,000
7. Sales commissions and other sales costs	650,000
8. Total development cost not including the land	1,898,000
9. Less the net from the timber sales	–75,000
10. Total cash needed	1,823,000

The cost of the land has not been calculated into this transaction. Oscar had owned the land for over 17 years, and his actual cost was only $50 per acre. A more realistic value of the land today would be $7,500 per acre. This matched the current sales of similar raw land in the area. To provide values in the project that relate to the profit from the development and not profit from appreciation of the land, Oscar set up a development corporation that would handle all development, sales, and the like. In essence, he "sold" his land to that new company at $7,500 per acre, or a total of $2,247,500. This value would show Oscar an appreciated gain in the land of $2,236,300.

The sale to the new entity could be accomplished by many different means. One might be a joint venture with an arm's length developer; another could be that Oscar contributed the land to a limited partnership of which he had part or full control and ownership. Each strategy would have a different result and/or benefit to Oscar and his family.

Review Potential Sales. From the 224 acres, he expected to obtain 112 tracts at an average of 2 acres in size including the roadway access, which would be kept private and not become a public dedicated way. Oscar had decided to keep the roadways private for two reasons. First, he did not want the public having access to the area; second, by keeping the roadways private, he did not have to build a roadway to the local road department's higher, public way specifications, which would have more than doubled the cost of the road.

Oscar looked at the market to determine what other similar products were available to investors in an attempt to price his tracts. He discovered that there was nothing around that would compare with his end product, especially when he took into account the beauty of the hardwood trees, which was unique to his site. Nonetheless, there was other property available that people from Boston and surrounding towns could buy, so Oscar determined that the maximum price he could ask would be $80,000 per two-acre tract.

ECONOMICS OF OSCAR'S DEVELOPMENT

Gross sales ($80,000 per each of the 112 tracts)	$8,960,000
Total cash spent	−1,823,000
Net revenue from sales	$7,137,000
Cost allocated to land cost	−2,236,300
Anticipated profit	$4,900,700

Amount of Money to Borrow. The estimated cash to be spent is $1,823,000, but because it is an estimate and does not take into consideration any remuneration for Oscar while the development is taking place, it would be wise for Oscar to request a higher amount. He does not have to draw on any of the funds until they are needed, so he will not have added interest to pay unless he needs the extra funds. Oscar has substantial equity in the land that he can substantiate to be $2,236,300.

The best result for Oscar could be to take the majority of the land purchase out of sales, rather than out of the loan proceeds and to hold his loan-to-value ratio as low as possible. Because his sell-out estimate is $8,960,000, he would have a draw capability of at least 50 percent of that amount. This would mean his loan request could be as high as $4,480,000. This would allow Oscar to get some up-front cash toward the initial sale of the land. The balance could come from sales.

The actual percentage of up-front money that can be borrowed in the land development loan will depend on the lender, the interest rate, and the payback terms. The more that Oscar is willing to wait for a return of the capital investment of the land (either as developer or as seller of the land), the less risk the lender has; therefore, the easier the terms of the loan.

This example is a relatively simple land development loan that does not require later construction loans or permanent loans; there would be no need for Oscar to do anything else. However, if Oscar wanted to provide potential buyers end loans or permanent loans, he would need to locate a source. The same land development lender or a local bank would be a good source for these loans. Oscar would contact these lenders, explain what he was about to do, and ask if they would preapprove the project. By doing this, a prospective buyer interested in obtaining such financing would apply to a single lender for that financing.

If Oscar wanted to build homes on these home sites, he could take care of the second loan format that we will discuss next. This would be the construction financing which would allow individual homes to be developed. The construction phase of the project could be based on one home at a time, or several homes all at once. When homes were sold, the buyer would take out the permanent loan (already set up, or through their own lending source), and the construction loan on the home sold would be paid off. The amount Oscar owed on the total construction loan (assuming there were more than the one home to secure the loan) would be reduced by the release price of the home sold. This release price would be an amount stipulated by the lender, to which Oscar had already agreed when the loan was set up.

Each lender will look at the ultimate sales figures and make its assessment of a prudent loan-to-value ratio. Oscar's logical approach would be to be conservative in his loan amount and in the cost to develop and to sell. This would require him to anticipate a loan larger than he would hope he would need, if he did not draw down or draw against the loan (get the money from the lender as he needed it) to the full extent of the loan requested and approved. This way he would always have something in the bank as a pillow to fall back on, if plans and timing did not work out right.

A review of Oscar's situation and how it was handled may give you some ideas of how you might have handled it differently. There is no doubt that the pattern could have been different, and the end results better suited to your own specific needs and goals. The lessons to be learned from Oscar's example are the need to examine all potential problems and to look beyond the basic idea to find methods that get you to your desired location quicker, and with fewer problems.

Construction Loan

To explain this second format, let's continue the example. Bill, who is a general contractor of large office buildings in the Boston area, wants to buy one of Oscar's lots so he can build a small home away from the big city. He makes his deal with Oscar and puts down $40,000 on the tract he is buying. He gets Oscar to subordinate his remaining interest to a construction loan to finance the cabin. Bill plans to replace the construction loan with a permanent loan from one of the banks in the area as soon as he is finished building the cabin. That, at least, is his plan.

So far so good, and there is no problem with Oscar. He gets sufficient money out of the down payment to release the development loan he has to pay off, and does not mind holding the balance owned on the land since Bill is paying good interest.

Then the plan goes wrong. Bill discovers that he cannot get a regular construction loan as long as there is secondary financing in the deal. Because he still owes Oscar $40,000 for the tract, the bank wants to see more equity put up to secure the loan. Even though they have the full value of the home site, they are apt to shy away from the high leverage of the deal.

Bill comes up with a potential solution and gives Oscar a first mortgage for $40,000 against another property Bill owns. Now the home site purchased from Oscar has been paid for in full (as far as the bank is concerned) and it is free and clear of any secondary debt. Based on this, the lender approves the construction loan, and the permanent end loan. As long as Bill can build the home for what he thinks it will cost, he knows that once the job is completed he will be able to obtain a permanent loan for enough to pay Oscar the amount still owed to him, which is secured by the other property Bill owns.

Combined Loan

The majority of all construction loans are combined loans. The combination of a construction and a permanent loan is in reality a circumstance where the lender advances the funds for the construction. When the property has been completed, the loan automatically converts to a long-term loan (either the same lender holds both, or two separate lenders are tied together). The ideal source for this kind of loan is the local banks or thrift organizations, but because lending habits are quickly changing, these loans can be found from almost any lender.

The straight construction loan and the combined loan differ only in the effort it takes to nail them down. Combined loans are generally smaller than divided loans, where the construction loan is obtained from one source and the permanent loan is obtained from another source. For that reason, combined loans are often much easier to get when the amounts of the loan are modest. With jumbo loans of $3 million or more, it begins to make sense to look for two separate lenders. The extra cost and time to deal with double paperwork usually does not make good economic sense for the smaller loan amounts.

Fortunately, there are lenders for both, and often the same source of money will fund both. For example, many insurance companies buy commercial paper from banks that support construction loans and at the same time buy long-term paper from savings banks and commercial banks.

Keep these factors in mind as we look at the ways in which you will deal with lenders to maximize your loan proceeds while minimizing your costs and interest.

These forms of financing are important because they form the basis for all new development. Very few projects will get off the ground unless the cost of development can be financed. It is necessary, therefore, for you to understand the workings of these types of financing and how to find lenders willing to look at your presentation.

The ability to provide for development loans is also important. If you are a real estate broker you will be able to sell properties when you know funds are available for specific projects. If you know in advance what lenders want to lend on, you will have a jump that may be sufficient to put you ahead of your competition. Naturally, this advantage will come as good news to your clients, both buyers and sellers. As a buyer or seller, this advantage will work to your favor too. Buyers find it much easier to invest in the kind of property that lenders like. To work against this trend, that is, to try to buy property the lenders do not like is clearly an uphill battle.

Sellers of property that local lenders favor as collateral for their loans will have a much easier time and get top dollar as opposed to when lenders will not touch your property. You need to remember the condition of the market and risk. If the lender can get a good interest return without taking much if any risk, then he or she is apt to follow that line of action.

Before we get to the fine points for developing this advanced knowledge, let us examine the end loan or the permanent loan.

The Development or Construction Loan Usually Relies on the Permanent End Loan

The permanent or end loan is the final mortgage that will be placed on the property. This loan may have a term of 20 years or as long as a 40-year amortization schedule for payback. The longer the term of years of an amortization, the lower the constant payment.

Keep in mind that lenders often quote loans on a long-term amortization schedule, but balloon the payment on a much shorter time period. Compare the following three loans.

The property is a triple net-leased retail building. The price to the investor is $1,430,000 with the buyer putting $430,000 down. The annual NOI (all income less all operating expenses), is $171,600. In each of the three loan situations assume a loan origination fee of $30,000.

LOAN 1: $1,000,000

Interest rate: 9 percent interest per annum

Amortized over 25 years

The monthly payments are: $8,391.70

Total payments to be made over the term: (25 × 12 × $8,391.70) is $2,517,510

LOAN 2: $1,000,000

Interest Rate: 9 percent interest per annum

Amortized over 10 years

The monthly payments are: $12,667.50

Total payments to be made over the term: (10 × 12 × $12,667.50) is $1,520,100

LOAN 3: $1,000,000

Interest rate: 9 percent interest per annum

Amortized over 25 years with a balloon payment at the end of 10 years

The monthly payments for 10 years are: $8,391.70

Balloon payment at the end of the 10 years: $827,369.90

Total payments to be made over the term including balloon (10 × 12 × $8,391.70 plus $82,736.99) is $1,834,373.99

Reflect on these three loans for a moment. The first is the old style loan that was commonly made, and can still be found from some lenders. This kind of loan is more attractive to major institutional lenders who want to lock up a portfolio for a long term, and not have to deal with shorter-term loans. Security is the key, and the lender will often want a slightly higher interest rate than for a shorter loan term. Note that in the examples all three loans are at 9 percent. In a real situation, the actual parity between lenders and loan interest may vary. This kind of loan is good for borrowers because they can count on this loan until it self-amortizes. This means that as long as the monthly payments are met, the loan will eventually pay off sometime in the future.

When other people's money (remember OPM) is paying off your debt, the key is that you do not have to reach into your pocket to meet those obligations. Because the loan began as a loan-to-value percentage, and because income and expenses usually maintain a similar increase, your bottom-line cash flow will increase in relation to the original investment. This loan has a constant rate of 10.07 percent of the original loan. The investment property generates a net operating income of 12 percent of the purchase price, so the loan with a constant rate of 10.70 percent will allow very good leverage for the investor.

The net operating income is $171,600, which is 12 percent of the purchase price of $1,430,000. Deduct your debt service of $100,700 and you are left with a cash flow of $70,900, as you paid $430,000 down, plus an estimated loan fee and out of pocket of $30,000. Your actual invested capital is $460,000, and the $70,900 cash flow represents 15.413 percent of it (divide the cash flow of $70,900 by the invested capital of $460,000). Leverage from this financing has increased the NOI return of 12 percent to 15.413 percent. This is good news for real estate investors and is one benefit of a fixed-rate, long-term amortized loan. For many investors this is the best way to go, unless terms and conditions lead you to another loan.

The second loan is the kind of loan the lender might like to make: shorter term, in this case 10 years, but the lender might offer a term of five or seven years. The loan is self-amortizing and will pay itself off over 10 years. If the income is sufficient, and the situation right for the investor, there is nothing wrong with this kind of loan. However, it is a very high constant rate of 15.2 percent of the loan amount per year. Because the NOI is $171,600, there will be sufficient funds to meet the monthly loan payments, but just barely. At the end of the year, the cash flow on this loan will be $19,600. Your cash flow return on the cash investment of $460,000 is 3.673 percent. That is not very good, and it is the result of the negative leverage present. This may not be the wrong loan for you if this kind of situation fits your overall needs. After all, this loan will pay off in only 10 years, and if you wanted to put yourself into good financial shape at the end of 10 or 12 years, just in time for retirement, or have a child in college, or whatever, then you can trade off cash flow for equity build up. There are some very good reasons that this loan can work for you. It might be there are no other loan formats offered to you at the time.

The third loan is a middle-ground loan and gives the lender the short-term payout, and the borrower the leveraged income for the first 10 years of the loan. Clearly at the end of the 10 years, the borrower will have to either pay off the loan or make some other disposition of the property. The proper use of any of these three loan situations depends on which fits your needs, and which is available. The disadvantage of a balloon mortgage is that the borrower may be caught with a property that is no longer in the lender's eye. Trends change, and it is possible that 10 years from now, when that $827,369.90 balloon must be paid off, the new loan to finance the payoff will be either very expensive, or not available at all.

Any of these permanent loans are made by commercial banks, credit unions, insurance companies, REITs, pension funds, and other sources. These loans are the pay-off for the earlier development and construction loan. Although the borrower may have a commitment for the end loan, it is not placed on the property until construction is completed.

The timing works like this. Development and construction loans start with the actual development or building. The borrower takes down or is given advances from the lender as the money is needed. Interest begins to accrue on the amount of the loan being used. If the construction loan follows a development loan, then the development loan agreement must be fully met. In this situation, there is apt to be a combination of construction and permanent loan to follow the development loan. Although the permanent loan is the last in the sequence, it has a major effect on the amount of the development or construction loan.

Development and construction loans are predicated on the amount of the final permanent commitment. If you are going to build 100 apartment units and you obtain a commitment from one or more lenders for a permanent loan, to lend $8.5 million, provided the final product meets the specifications of your submission, you will find the maximum development or construction loan available will not exceed the $8.5 million. In fact, it will generally be below that amount, depending on the size of the project and cost overrun averages for the area no matter how much profit is anticipated in the deal.

Because the permanent financing has such a profound effect on the nature and amount of development and construction funding you may obtain, we will look at the proper way to examine new developments:

1. Feel out the market to see what permanent lenders favor. Once the lender's criteria and favorite categories of loans are understood, you can move forward to build or develop the kinds of investments where financing is available. For this example, if you find major permanent lenders are looking favorably at single-family homes in the $340,000 range, shopping centers located in new growing suburban areas, and mobile home parks that have a density no greater than six sites per acre, then look for those kinds of projects in which to put your investment capital.

2. Smart developers follow big money. In the example shown in Step 1, the favorites for lenders are single-family projects, shopping centers, and mobile home parks. There may be many other areas that will be open to funding, and it is natural for lenders to disagree on their favorite type of project. What is hot in one area of the country may be cool to cold in others. As with almost everything in real estate, you must look to the local aspect of the market and not national trends. "National trends" is a media concept, and not an investing concept. What goes on in your backyard will affect you the most, so pay attention to local trends first. National trends are important only in how the uninformed investor or lender views the market. This can be a factor you may need to deal with when it comes to very large loans you need to get from lenders who look at the big picture first.

3. If you have flexibility to move from one endeavor which is out of favor to another in vogue, you will do better in the end than the investor who will only build warehouses, whether they can be financed or not. Our ideal investor has flexibility and looks to either mobile home parks or single-family projects as a potential.

4. Once you are armed with advance knowledge of the type of project a lender favors, you should look to the geographic areas that lenders prefer. Remember, in looking for the construction loan you are still concerned with finding the permanent lender. By dealing with local mortgage brokers, loan officers, and other loan officers, you will shortly discover that lenders tend to specialize in areas of a community. Because real estate is geographic, so are lenders. For one reason or other, which you will ultimately discover when you talk to the loan officers, certain lenders will favor specific criteria as to location, or even more

specifically, certain precise areas of town. You will be surprised to find that many lenders maintain comprehensive statistics on the growth of areas in which they invest their funds.

5. You may not know which of the several types of projects to consider, or you may have narrowed it down to single-family homes. If you have picked one of several favored lender properties, then you should start to look for the best location in town where the lenders are apt to lend the most. In a couple of days of talking to loan officers and/or mortgage brokers, you will be able to ascertain the type of property and general location where the best loans can be obtained. Now you are ready to start putting your talents and this knowledge together. Real estate brokers and salespeople, mortgage brokers, real estate lawyers, and anyone else interested in the real estate market should pay attention to this stage. Remember "Location, Location, Location" are not the three most important criteria of real estate. As I have pointed out earlier: It is the *importance of the location.* This means that use of a location is the most important factor to value, when everything else comes together for you. The use, which is generally governed by a combination of zoning ordinances and building rules and regulations used to be pretty much an automatic thing if you could meet all those rules and regulations. However, and I will repeat this throughout this book: *Take nothing for granted when it comes to your rights to build or use the property until you have local government approvals.* Because of this, the three most important elements in real estate are Location, Use, and Approval—in that order. Your goals must be the most important end result of any investment, and if you need financing, then the lender's goals must be considered if you expect to get a loan. If you are beginning to understand that real estate investing is a tradeoff between goals you are catching on. The concept is very simple: Work with the flow, not against it.

6. Okay, you have a lender-favored property in mind, and you know the general locations of town where lenders go top dollar. Now find a site that works for what you want to do. A site is selected and negotiations begin. The first rule of any real estate investor (once you have reached this state) is to tie up the property. You will spend many hours leading up to this point in your investment strategy, so once you think you have found a property that works for you, in an area of town lenders like, and of an end use lenders favor, then tie it up. As I have mentioned before and will again, do not waste your time and effort, at this stage, unless you can get the seller to agree to basic terms and conditions that should work for you. The exact conditions you would put into the agreement would depend on the actual transaction. However, you need a reasonable due diligence period to check out the details of the property. With that information behind you a firm decision should be available to you. To move forward without having the transaction firmly tied up can be a waste of time, money, and credibility. One method to tie up a property is to contract for option to buy. You put up a deposit pending some inspections, with the stipulation that if the inspections are okay (to your satisfactory approval) then you have a period of 90 days to act (buy) or not. Keep in mind that the actual time you might need will depend on

local conditions and lender preferences. If you must ask for changes in local ordinances or zoning changes, then this will require a longer time period. Even getting the final building permit in your hand can be timely. Many developers have underestimated the time it would take to achieve the necessary approvals. Until they are in your hand there will be no loan, no closing of the real estate transaction. If you run out of time with your purchase agreement, you may find yourself having to renegotiate the purchase of the property at terms much less attractive than when you started. Whatever it takes, this book will give you the proper strategies to follow.

7. When you have a loan commitment in hand, you can nail down the development or construction lender. At times, the permanent lender will also make the interim loans leading up to the permanent loan. In this case, a combined package of construction and permanent loan can be arranged. However, more often than not, there will be two different lenders on the large projects. Keep in mind, however, that on small projects requiring less than $2 million, the local lender can compete favorably with other lenders by making a package development and permanent loan.

8. In most commercial projects where the investor is also a final owner, rather than a builder/seller, this stage would begin with negotiations on the terms of the construction loan. If, for example, you had a commitment for an end loan of $3 million, you would take this commitment to several commercial banks in the area and shop for the best terms on the construction loan. Because the terms of the end loan may call for placement not earlier than 24 months from the present date to no later than 36 months, you would look to the longest take-out construction loan possible, in this case 36 months. Many permanent end loans committed to income property projects have a floor loan amount and a maximum amount. The spread between the two sums is generally based on the break-even rent roll as projected. The lender will calculate the projected break-even rent schedule, then deduct a percentage the lender anticipates is reasonable for the market conditions. Based on the resulting net operating income, a floor or lowest loan amount available will be established. The maximum amount of the loan will be paid if a percentage of net operating income, as determined by the lender and agreed to by you, is met. There is generally a time period to allow you to meet rent roll. Fail at that goal and you will only get the lower amount of permanent loan. Because construction lenders look at all the terms of the permanent loan, any such variance in top or bottom loan amounts will force the construction lender to lend at the lower of the two amounts. This spread in the two sums often leaves the builder short of loan funds to finish the job. This creates a gap in the transaction.

9. This is where *gap financing* comes in. This is another part of the development and construction loan process and is often referred to as *mezzanine financing*. The gap loan is a secondary form of financing that is used to literally fill the gap between the floor amount of the loan and the maximum, or the construction loan amount and the permanent loan.

The source of these loans is often a mortgage banker or private party. At times, commercial banks will take up the call here but these loans are often very expensive for builders and should be used only when absolutely necessary. The only redeeming factor on a gap loan is that it is usually for a short term. This means that even though the interest rate is high, it will not last for long.

Moving Forward

With the end loan commitment obtained, the construction loan set, and the development loan tied down, the builder can now proceed with the expectation that he or she will not need any other financing. The project gets started and, as one loan is paid off by another, the progression of financing from development loan to end loan takes place.

The foregoing nine steps cover an ideal situation. All aspects of this development seemed to go smoothly. They often do, and when you are dealing with professional mortgage people all the way down the line, you will usually have a smooth transition.

However, if one barrier in a long progression of steps appears, a mess can result. These barriers appear with amazing speed and never seem to disappear. They take the form of title problems, legal hassles, attorney's errors, and nitpicking; fights over wording in legal descriptions (the legal direction and identity of each property is different), contracts, mortgage documents, or releases from mortgages; delays caused by documents lost in the mail, pages missing from loan commitment letters, or documents not properly signed or witnessed. There is no doubt that if things do not go right, it can be a mess.

The fact that all goes smoothly at first does not mean it will stay that way from the day construction starts until the day the end loan is placed. In the first place, the terms of the commitment must be met. That means that the building to be constructed must be exactly as the plans and specifications indicated when the commitment was issued. Any changes must be approved by the lender. This is where many loans have gone astray. A lender who wants to withdraw from a loan he or she committed to two years earlier when interest rates were 2 points lower than the current rate will look very hard to see if there is a way to get out of it.

The construction lender gets very anxious about this type of talk from permanent lenders. The construction lender is in the project for a short time, he hopes, and enjoys the high interest rate he gets on the construction loan. However, he is not ready to take over a project that fails to close on the end loan. If the end loan does not close because you did something wrong, you will have made an enemy.

Getting a Development or Construction Loan without an End Loan

This was very popular at one time, and as you might suspect, due to its dangers, has lost the favor it once had. This type of financing gained support when the permanent market all but dried up. Builders, sensing that the money market was very tight on a long-term loan but still relatively soft in the construction money market, went out on a limb and started projects without effective end loans.

Not many lenders would make development loans without the end loan commitment first. Then, some of the big builders persuaded their banks to go with them on the idea that by the time construction of a big project was finished one, two, or three years later, the permanent market would be back in the swing of things and that type of money would be available again.

Other builders took advantage of commitment letters from mortgage brokers, bankers, and other sources, which in effect sold these letters to the builders. In essence, the commitment letter would state that an end loan was available. This would satisfy the construction lender and the loan would be made. However, these commitment letters were for throwaway loans. The terms of the end loan under many of these letters were so onerous that to take the loan would have been a financial disaster.

The idea was this: Pay for the letter to satisfy the construction lender that an end loan was available, then wait for better years ahead in the long-term end-loan market. Even the best-laid plans do not always work out, and the commitment letter format was not very effective. The permanent money market remained firm and the commitment letters were called to take out the construction loans. In some cases, the commitment letters were found to be worthless and projects got into trouble one after the other.

The lesson to be learned is simple and sweet: There are few reasons to obtain a construction loan without having an end loan. It is much better to have a binding end loan commitment from a lender known to be reputable before you start.

Project Size Doesn't Matter

The size of the development or construction project is not the main criterion for understanding and using this form of financing. It is natural, of course, that in projects under $2 million the local lender may compete favorably with a two-part loan, where the construction loan is replaced by the permanent loan. The combined package loan that most savings or commercial banks as well as other lenders offer puts both aspects of the two separate loans into one document. Still, builders of single-family homes will operate with separate construction loans rather than have this combination package of end loan and construction loan as an automatic event.

Using the Development or Construction Loan to Make Sales

Putting the whole ball of wax together may be your role. If you are dealing in developable types of land, the redevelopment of urban areas, or in any type of real estate that calls for some form of development or construction, then you must have a working knowledge of this tool.

To be specific, the ability to package a deal will require a considerable amount of expertise in many areas. In some of these areas, you need only have the sense to get someone else on your team. Planning and engineering, for example, will no doubt be beyond the scope of most salespeople. To be sure, moving from a listing to a sale can be an immense task for some salespeople on some properties.

EXAMPLE: A $4 MILLION DEAL. Jackson owned a very interesting property in Fort Lauderdale. The site was about 15 acres of prime, business-zoned land located on a major highway. Its uniqueness was that it was the largest vacant property in the city that had deep-water access to the Atlantic Ocean. The site was located in a high-income area of town and adjoined a major shopping center.

The drawbacks in marketing the property were the general economy and the price. The economy was not as strong as it was two years earlier. The price Jackson felt he could get—$22 per square foot—was higher than realtors had predicted a buyer would pay. The price was not high when compared to other smaller sites in comparable locations. In fact, smaller lots similarly zoned had sold for over $35 per square foot. However, the size of this tract and the fact that it could not be subdivided made prospective buyers scarce.

It was clear to Jackson that what was needed to entice an investor was an economic use. A use that could not be financed was not going to be productive, so Jackson had to find a use that could be financed. Jackson tried to list all the possible uses the site could be put to. He and others made a list of all the possibilities no matter how silly they sounded at the time.

Armed with this list, Jackson approached several lenders and mortgage brokers that he had dealt with in the past and presented the problem to them. He was not asking for money, only assistance in solving a problem. What were the possible uses for the tract, which could be financed? Several new possible uses were added to the list by the lenders. Then Jackson put this question to each of them: "Of all the possible uses on this list, which is most financeable assuming that the economics work out?" Many of the suggested uses were eliminated. Some sound ideas were cast off as being overbuilt for the area or impractical for other reasons. The list was narrowed down to five possible uses that could be financed if the economics did work out.

A Conservative Approach. Jackson knew that for the economics to work out, a conservative approach to development, income, and expenses would have to show the project to be profitable. Once he had some possible lendable projects, he went to work to see if the numbers would work.

One by one the projects failed to work out on paper. Then two concepts began to make economic sense. Jackson took his numbers to a mortgage broker. The mortgage broker went over the numbers and made some changes and suggestions, then sat back and agreed. It did look as though there were two types of projects that might work economically.

Jackson did not stop there. He went to his builder and management friends and smoothed out the figures even further. With the refined projections, he returned to the mortgage brokers. Several brokers got excited about the two concepts. They could see the possibility of making a nice loan fee, so they in turn talked to several of their lenders. Before Jackson knew it, lenders were hot to go. He knew that his job was now almost completed.

The result of Jackson's efforts was that the property was sold. He had developed two concepts that in turn attracted lenders and buyers' interest in the property. The lenders' interest was prequalified as they were able to recognize the proposals were sound and feasible. What Jackson sold was not the land but the concept.

How to Increase the Amount of Money You Can Borrow on a Development Loan

It is possible to obtain 100 percent of the funds needed for the development and construction of many projects. In many cases, you can even include the land in this mortgage amount and enter into a development with little or no cash. Your ability to do this depends on several simple factors. Experience by the way, is not necessarily one of these factors. The following list outlines the factors, which must be developed in order to obtain the highest possible loan:

1. SEEK THE LENDER'S FAVORITE TYPE OF PROJECT. Follow Jackson's example of finding out what the lenders like and then go for that type of loan.

2. DON'T JUMP IN TOO SOON IN ASKING FOR THE FUNDS. Plan out your project. Some lenders will ask for a feasibility study if you move too quickly. Wait until you have done your own study. If you have done it well enough you may not need a feasibility study.

3. HAVE THE RIGHT NUMBERS. Do not take one person's advice on what rent you should be able to collect on a proposed office building until you have checked out the actual market as it now stands.

4. HAVE THE PROPERTY TIED UP. If you do not own it already, be sure you have some tie on it. You have a lot of work ahead of you, and unless you can hold onto the land you may end up with a commitment and then be unable to buy the property or have to pay more than you expected.

5. WHEN READY, ACT FORCIBLY. Bravado is important in asking for money, so have plenty of it (bravado is a nice word for guts). Do not, however, try to cover up lack of knowledge with smugness. Point out good features instead.

6. LEAVE INEXPERIENCE AT HOME, YOURS OR YOUR CLIENT'S, WHATEVER THE CASE MAY BE. What are important are the project, the numbers, and ability. Note the word "ability" and not "experience." The fact that it may be your first shopping center or strip store, or ten times larger than anything you have ever built, is not important.

7. NEGOTIATE FOR MORE. Your lender will usually offer less than you ask for. Hold firm if you can try to get what you feel you need. Remember, if you say you must have $5,000,000 you may then have to explain why you are willing to take $4,250,000.

8. OFFER INCENTIVES TO THE LENDER. When the need for venture capital is overwhelming, you may have to resort to trade outs with the lender. In order to increase the loan amount closer to 100 percent, you may often have to give the lender a percentage of the action. This can occur in many ways, which will be covered later in this chapter. Be careful, however, since the lender knows all the tricks and controls the purse strings.

PUTTING TOGETHER A PRESENTATION FOR A DEVELOPMENT LOAN

In Chapter 4, the basic loan presentation was outlined. This format should be used in all loan presentations that cover existing properties. Its adaptation so it can also be used for presentations on proposed projects is covered in this chapter. In essence, greater detail must be included to cover the potential of the project. You cannot rely on past performance, which in the case of a new development does not exist.

The presentation itself takes on the aspects of a feasibility study. It is often thought that all feasibility studies ascertain the best use of a given site. However, this is only one type of feasibility study. More commonly, a lender may request that a study be made to indicate the potential for success a given project may have. The lender's reason for requesting this study is to use the data obtained to help the money managers come to a decision as to whether the money requested should be lent.

Unfortunately, the whole system of feasibility studies has gone somewhat astray. There is the classic story of a major lender from the Northeast. This lender was presented with a well-planned hotel project that looked fantastic on paper. The developers were experienced, the designers were well qualified, and all the right things had seemingly been done. However, the lender needed a third-party reference, so the loan was not going to be granted unless a feasibility study was made. At considerable cost, therefore, such a study was hastily ordered and sent to the lender as soon as it came off the press.

The loan was made. Nevertheless, after several years of development, and one failure after another, the project developers went into bankruptcy. The lender had to take the project into his portfolio and finish the construction. Sometime later, a bright young lawyer in the lender's office read the feasibility study. The study had predicted that the project had merit and, based on the then-present statistics of competition, would be successful. However, the study continued, there were over 47 similar ventures currently on the drawing boards, which would no doubt enter competition around the time of the proposed hotel development. The study went on to disclose the statistics, the number of projects, and their locations.

The mistake in this situation is obvious. The venture under consideration was a hotel, and the existing hotels in the area would not be able to handle the demand for rooms that the future Disney World complex would provide. So, what else but a hotel would be a good idea? Unfortunately, what is good for the goose is not always good for the geese. The lender was anxious to make the loan, and once the study came in it was most likely glanced over and then filed. In reality, he had paid for a study that recommended that the project not be started in the first place.

How to Approach a Feasibility Study

In many respects, the feasibility study is similar to the loan request shown in Chapter 4. However, the differences are sufficient for you to follow the modified outline in Table 8.1.

Table 8.1
Feasibility Study Outline

I. The Project
  A. General description
  B. Site plan
    1. Breakdown of project to square footage of improvements
    2. Use of project
    3. Stages to be built or developed
  C. Economics of project
    1. Cost estimates
      a. Builders' bid on other supporting data
    2. Operating expenses
      a. During development
      b. Marketing expenses
      c. Preleased agreements (if applicable)
    3. Cash flow, expense versus income chart
  D. Feasibility of project
    1. Economy of area
      a. Aerial photo showing location of similar projects in competing area
      b. Description of competing projects
      c. Economics of competing projects
      d. Future growth proposed and documented
      e. Future demand on type of project (including supporting documents)
      f. Summary of economics of competing projects
    2. Opinion of use based on area economics
  E. Value of completed project
    1. Estimated potential cash flow on finished project (if the property shows operational statement, 12-month estimate after project completed)
    2. Market value based on cash flow (capitalized at current investor demand rate)
    3. Value of existing projects of similar nature (refer to same projects covered in earlier description of competing projects)

II. The Property
   A. General description
   B. Legal description
   C. Locations
   D. Location sketch
   E. Aerial photo
   F. Location benefits
   G. Location drawbacks
   H. General statistics
      1. Demographics
      2. Average rent
      3. Traffic count
   I. General site data
      1. Legal
      2. Size and square feet of land and site coverage
      3. Use of site
      4. Zoning
      5. Utilities
      6. Access
      7. Sketch of lots sharing building location
      8. Survey
   J. Land value
      1. Estimated value of site
      2. Comparable land sales and values

III. The Developer
   A. Name
   B. Address
   C. Occupation
   D. General data
   E. Net worth
   F. Supporting documents (not included, but will be on forms the institution supplies)
      1. Net worth statement
      2. Schedule of assets
      3. Schedule of liabilities
      4. References
      5. Position of employment
      6. Verification of salary
      7. Estimated annual earnings
      8. Credit report if applicable
      9. Other forms supplied for application

Table 8.1 (continued)

IV. The Loan Request (for End Loans)
  A. Recap value of finished product
  B. Recap development cost
  C. Add land cost to development cost
  D. Show relation to total estimated value and total cost to develop
  E. Amount of loan requested
  F. Terms and conditions requested (for construction or development loan)
    1. Recap value of finished product
    2. Recap development cost
    3. Add land cost to development cost
    4. Show relation to total estimated value and total cost to develop
    5. Copy of end loan commitment
    6. Amount of construction or development loan requested
    7. Terms and conditions requested
V. Supporting Documents
  A. Full set of working plans (if available)
  B. Topography (if needed)
  C. Preleased documents (if applicable)

WHERE TO GET A DEVELOPMENT OR CONSTRUCTION LOAN

Many lenders will provide such funds, and for the most part all normal institutional leaders have involved themselves from time to time in this type of financing. However, some sources are better than others, depending on the size of the loan and the nature of the project.

The best places to go for any development loan will be to lenders who are actively lending on other developments nearby. Most of these developments are highly visible, and often the lender advertises that the loan was placed through them.

Mortgage brokers will be an initial place for you to go, and if they are into this size of loan they should already know which lender would like or dislike your project. It is likely that a local commercial bank with national recognition also can be a good place to go to discuss your needs. If the commercial bank has been burned with construction loans, they may not be ready to jump back into that market. Nonetheless, commercial banks tend to be the better source for short-term construction funds.

Never forget the private money sources. These funds can be available when all other sources dry up. In essence, they are costly monies to borrow, but can compete favorably in a very tight money market. When you have to borrow to protect already invested capital, the cost may be immaterial.

Seven points to remember in negotiations with the lender or the lender's agent are:

1. DISTANCE REQUIRES MORE SUPPORT. The farther you get from the lender in the chain of command, the more the decision to lend is based on the opinions of other people. This is human nature. The loan officer will act without having to check with as many people as the mortgage representative at a major insurance company a thousand miles away. Because of this, try to obtain as many outside opinions yourself. Then document them in your presentation. These outside statements of market conditions, rental pro forma, expenses, and operating costs can be found without much effort. Fellow brokers, banks, property managers, owners of similar properties, and so on will often be glad to help. When you do get information from them, do not just refer to the facts; put a copy of the memo they sent you or the letter from the property manager in your report. This padding will become third-party support material that people who make the final decision can hang their hats on.

2. YOU CAN'T REALLY LOSE. Do as much of the initial work as you can yourself. The first time you make one of these studies you will be amazed at how little you knew about the area, the project, and your perseverance. By the time you have finished the study, you will know more than much of your competition about this type of property and development. That is not a bad side benefit, no matter what happens to the development. After you have gone through several such studies you will have the formula down pat.

3. CONTINUE TO EXPAND YOUR ABILITIES. At first, there will be some aspects that you may need assistance with. If you are dealing with a mortgage broker, he or she can usually provide help. Brokers are often able to go over the numbers with you, and once they see a feasible project they will get excited as hell. If they can make the loan, then everyone will benefit.

4. BE READY TO NEGOTIATE FOR THE MONEY. When money is tight, lenders will take advantage of the scarcity of funds to make as favorable a deal as they can. This may mean they will demand a percentage of the action, which can take many forms. The most usual are shown here:

- *An override:* This form of percentage of the operation is based on the lender receiving a preset percentage of all income that exceeds certain amounts. For example: A $10 million loan on a shopping center has a provision that the lender will receive 5 percent of gross income on excess of $2 million. Once the loan is satisfied, this provision does not continue.

- *Land ownership:* The lender takes title to the land and leases it to the developer. The lease may be reasonable, and in essence the lender becomes a partner in the venture. The loan covers the development of the land. Once the loan is paid off, the land lease still goes on. This way the lender continues to benefit even though the loan has been satisfied.

- *Co-venture:* This can take many forms. The percentage of co-venture will depend on the lender and the deal. It is not uncommon that a lender will put up all the money and then take a substantial percentage of the venture. Usually, only builders of outstanding reputation can get these deals. However, when money is flowing, these builders can make deals without having to give up a percentage to a lender, or at most very little. If you do negotiate a joint venture, remember that everything is open for negotiation.

5. DON'T TAKE "NO" FOR AN ANSWER. For the most part, you are dealing with very conservative people. They take lending the money of their employers very seriously. Therefore, you may get a "no," especially if you approach the lender prematurely. Therefore, if you think you have a hot item, hang it on the possibility of getting the money. However, do not be overly pushy.

6. BOUNCE RIGHT BACK FROM A DEFEAT. Nothing should keep a good person down for long. When you have made your most fantastic presentation for the greatest project you have ever thought of and on the hottest site in town, and can't get a lender to sound interested, try to find out why. One mortgage broker I have dealt with in the past may smile if he is very excited. The rest of the time he speaks of doom as though it came two hours ago. He tells me this is his way of maintaining his sanity in the business he is in. From your point of view, negativism can sound like lack of interest. If one mortgage broker or lender gets to you in this way, go on to another. Always be ready to accept the fact that your idea is not sound. In addition, if it's not, find one that is.

7. WATCH OUT FOR TOO MUCH PRAISE. This is the one thing that concerns me. If all I hear is good news about a project I am working on, I start to worry. (I call my mortgage broker friend from item 6 and know he will have something bad to say.) You need to find someone you can count on to cut the project you are working on to ribbons. You won't get ahead riding the crest of disinterested praise.

FINE-TUNE YOUR FINESSE IN THE USE OF CONSTRUCTION AND DEVELOPMENT LOANS

There are many techniques that you can apply to development and construction loans to make them easier to obtain and to keep down their overall costs. The goal of most of these techniques is: Buy the property right. Thus far in this book, I have emphasized the need for proper attention to your own goals and abilities. When you are able to approach the buying moment with the end result in mind, you will be far more successful at attaining your desired goal.

However, from a practical viewpoint, things don't always work out that way. Keep your long-range goal in sight, of course, but if you are watching your comfort zone correctly, you will find it too difficult to pass up "bargain" property, even though you may see no benefit from the property that would blend with your goals.

Later, as you are proven right about the "bargain," you may want to develop the property. At this time, the need for development of construction money may arise. If you try to take this potential need into account, no matter how remote it may be, you can be successful at obtaining your needed financing without excess cost.

You need to look at many factors in any transaction where there will be a future need for development or construction loans. Begin with the following 12 factors.

Key Factors to Watch for in Existing Financing

Make a chart of all of the existing financing on the property and make sure you have all the answers to these questions:

1. WHAT IS THE TERM OF THE LOAN? This is important simply because it is the most basic of all elements of the mortgage. Some mortgages seem to have a term of one set of years due to a statement in the mortgage document that looks like this: "And the mortgage will be paid out over a 25-year amortization schedule." At this point, you might think you have a 25-year term. Then, three pages later there is a paragraph that has this phrase or something like it imbedded in the fine print: ". . . and at the call of the lender, to be given at any time at the option of the lender following the seventh year with a 90-day notice, the loan is to be due and payable in full." This loan could last for only seven years.

2. WHAT IS THE EXACT DATE OF THE LAST SCHEDULED PAYMENT? This can be a minor issue. However, sometimes mortgages are so devised that this date is never specifically shown. When a property is closed, the people taking care of these details often don't have the necessary equipment on hand (a math table and calculator) to show the amortization properly. Therefore, there can be a difference between a stated amount that should retire a loan within the desired and thought-to-be term between the parties at hand. When a third party enters the picture, there is a sudden remembrance of the incorrect math that set up a mortgage that will take another five years to pay out. This can be absolute death to any refinancing ideas since the amount to pay off the mortgage at any given moment will also be incorrect.

3. IS THERE A BALLOON ANYWHERE IN THE PAYMENT, AND HOW MUCH IS IT? Much the same is true with balloon payments as with other terms in the mortgage. The words used might not be the words you are accustomed to. For example, "ending the 50th quarter of the formation of the lien, its full and complete satisfaction to the mortgagee is herein demanded." Interpretation: A balloon payment is due at the end of 150 months. This might make what would look like a subordinate mortgage useless.

4. WHAT IS THE INTEREST CHARGED? There are many ways to increase interest without the mortgagee realizing what is happening. Penalties, increases due to "adjustments to the All Items Index as published by the U.S. government," would be just one way. If any such

provisions exist, make sure you know what they are and how they can affect you. Any description of a formula should contain an example that applies the formula to a hypothetical, but realistic situation.

5. DOES THE INTEREST CHANGE AT ANY TIME? If so, how and when? Most modern mortgages have provisions that will limit the long-term obligation of the lender if you sell to someone else. In the mid-1970s and early 1980s, lenders began to enforce provisions that gave the lender the right to change the interest rate charged when a property was sold or leased on a long-term lease. Many property owners tried to get around these provisions, but most failed in the attempt.

6. CAN YOU PREPAY PRINCIPAL WITHOUT PENALTY? If not, what is the penalty? This single element has ruined many potential new loans, which can of course include construction and development loans. One very good rule to follow is: Don't accept a loan that has a penalty for any prepayment, and if you are buying a property that has a mortgage with that kind of provision either get it removed (you don't care if the seller has to "pay" to have it removed) or build the penalty into your offer.

7. IS THERE ANY SUBORDINATION AVAILABLE IN ANY OF THE FINANCING? If so, what, where, when, how much, and for what? Subordination is that event where the mortgagee has agreed to a provision that would permit some lien not yet in existence to be placed above the position of the mortgage, or if there were existing liens that were behind the rank of the mortgage, to move ahead. This increases the risk in all loans, and while warranted some of the time and essential for many investors, the provision itself may not provide what you think. When buying a property with the idea of future development and the seller is holding paper, try to get the seller to agree to allow new financing above that mortgage. For example, you could state that new financing and the remaining balance owed to the seller would not exceed a specific percent of loan to appraised value of the property.

8. WILL THE MORTGAGE PERMIT THE SECURITY TO BE CHANGED? This is a sliding mortgage technique that would allow you to move the security for the note to another property. In our earlier example of Oscar's sale to Bill, had Bill made this kind of provision with Oscar he would have been able to shift the mortgage to another property. The advantage to this is it will "free and clear" the specific property on which you plan to place a construction or development loan. This makes the task of getting good terms that much easier.

9. CAN YOU SELL OR REPLACE ANY OF THE ASSETS OF THE PROPERTY FREELY? Sometimes an existing loan will have a chattel as additional security. This has the effect of locking in different assets such as furniture, fixtures, equipment, and so on. Sometimes the chattel is so poorly drafted that it will not allow for replacement of the item. This requires careful attention if you plan to remodel a property completely and throw out all the old equipment and furniture.

10. IS THERE A RELEASE PRICE OF PROPERTY FROM THE MORTGAGE? If so, what, how, what pattern, what conditions, what payment? In the development of a property or construction

on part of a property you have just bought or currently own, you must have the right to separate that property from any other mortgage prior to placing a new first mortgage on the property. If the underlying mortgage does not have provisions that allow releases, you must attempt to have the mortgage modified. Otherwise, you will be faced with having to pay off a mortgage at the very moment you might need available every penny from the construction loan; or worse, because of the added economic drain you may not be able to get the financing at all.

11. IS THE LENDER LOCAL, A PERSON, OR AN INSTITUTION? Where the lender is based has become critical. The more remote the home office is from the branch office, the more difficult it will be to get facts straight. It is unfortunate that in an age of computer data it has become impossible to communicate from Florida to California to get the current pay-off or terms to a specific mortgage and feel you have the right data. When it comes time to ask for any modification of any mortgage, you will find that the private party will be the best to deal with. He may extract some penalty or ask for some benefit given in exchange for what you ask, but that is far better than to find out that they have sold your mortgage along with several thousand others to an insurance company located in Mexico City.

12. KNOW WHAT THE LAWS ARE AND HOW THEY MAY AFFECT YOUR PROJECT AND/OR ANY FINANCING IN THE TRANSACTION. This is an essential step and should not be overlooked. I have seen projects that were ready to go, funds committed (but not yet paid out by the lender) come to a sudden halt because someone forgot to double check something. It might have been a document that the seller did not sign, or that the seller's wife withheld signing, a lost wire of funds from Germany, or a law that prohibits the South American buyer from transferring funds from Venezuela without government approval. When you are all through with the first 11 factors, run through them again looking for something that did not happen as it should have. If you find nothing, then you can count your blessings.

Buying any real estate that you plan to develop or on which you are going to build requires your attention to these 12 factors whenever there is existing financing or the seller will be holding the financing. Remember the following phrase: Assume that your future goals are unknown—plan for everything. You should anticipate the need for as much flexibility as possible. It will not do you any good later on if you have overlooked one of these twelve factors.

The Borrower's Credit

Another element to the development and/or construction loan is your credit. This is something about which you can plan and improve. All lenders want you to have good credit and to provide them with good business references. The lender must be able to "check" on your credit and your references, and credit checks cannot be performed unless you leave some history of credit. In addition, the idea is to leave good history. References should be cultivated, and they should know that they are your references. To build good credit and excellent references, follow these steps:

1. OBTAIN SEVERAL CREDIT CARDS AND USE THEM. Credit cards are not as difficult to obtain as some people think. Start with local shops, oil companies, bankcards, and so on. Work up to one or two cards that you use most of the time, taking advantage of the "credit payment plan" offered for a month or two. Then pay off the balance. Once you have done that with your bankcard (or American Express or another similar card), write and ask for an increased line of credit. Find out the maximum credit offered and work up to that. Always pay early, since you want to build a history of responsibility. Keep in mind that you must be careful not to miss a payment. Credit card companies like to offer you a very low interest on your "financed" portion of your bill, but only if you are never in default on anything. If you are ever in default on one card, your other cards may have a provision that allows them to call you in default on their cards too. Watch for that initial statement when you just receive your new card. There is usually a charge that covers the annual use of that card. Overlook that and when you get the next statement you will have lost your low introductory rate for "financed" balances, and may lose your rights with other cards as well.

2. MEET YOUR COMMERCIAL BANK PRESIDENT. Make sure that he or she knows you. Keep in touch with this person and inquire about what loans are available. Start with a small loan, even if you don't need the money. You can pay it back early, and the small cost will be worth the effort since it will build more good history into your credit check.

3. DO BUSINESS WITH PEOPLE ON A REGULAR BASIS. Make sure you know the owner or manager of the business and that he or she knows you are a regular client. If the business has "charge accounts," get one, ask for the maximum line of credit, and always charge, and then pay early.

4. TELL EVERYONE YOU DEAL WITH FROM ITEM 3 THAT YOU ARE GOING TO BE TAKING OUT A LOAN SOON AND THAT YOU WOULD LIKE TO USE THEM AS A CREDIT REFERENCE. Ask them to respond to any inquiry as promptly as possible since it may mean the difference between your getting the loan and not getting it.

5. WRITE A SHORT PERSONAL REFERENCE LETTER. It should touch on those aspects that are critical to the potential loan, as well as give your personal background: where you live, who your wife and kids are, what school you went to, and so on. Everything in this personal reference letter should be positive.

6. GIVE THIS LETTER TO THOSE PEOPLE WHO MAY BE CALLED ON TO BE YOUR CREDIT REFERENCES. This letter will also improve your relationship with these people as they will find out things about you they didn't know.

7. BUILD A LIST OF CREDIT REFERENCES. This list should include all your business contacts indicated in item 3 as well as your CPA, banker president friends, professional associates, and so on. It should not be a Christmas card list, but a solid and impressive list of

known businesspeople in your community. If you do not know any such people, go to the library and get a copy of the local social register book. Make a list of people you recognize, and make a point of meeting them. References must be cultivated, for if you neglect them, they will be worthless.

8. ADD THE LIST OF CREDIT REFERENCES TO YOUR REFERENCE LETTER. Update them each time you can add something important to the list. Each new person sees that he or she is in good company on your list.

9. GET A LETTER OF RECOMMENDATION. This is a letter from your selected reference that tells whom it may concern that you are a highly trustworthy and honest person who is respected in your community. Get this letter by sending your public relations (PR) package to this person and asking for a letter of introduction or recommendation because of an upcoming business deal with important people out of town (the big lender in far-off lands). Your PR package is made up of your personal reference letter, your list of references, and a sample letter of introduction. In your letter, mention that you know their time is valuable, so you have enclosed a short sample letter indicating what you need. It is important that each sample letter you send is different and as personally oriented as possible. The sample letter should give the impression that it has been written specifically by that person. For example: "As State Representative from Florida, I can introduce and recommend Mr. Cummings with the clear conviction that he is one of the leaders of the South Florida community. Having served with him on a number of local committees . . ." It is important to be specific and that each letter drafted in a unique style to avoid obvious multiple copies of the same attributes. It is likely the letter will come back to you, signed as you hoped, and exactly as written.

10. GET A NEW LETTER FROM THE SAME PERSON EVERY COUPLE OF YEARS. If there has been a change in your biography or reference list, send it along, and attach to your new sample letter a copy of the last letter. Make the new letter a little more favorable than the last. Obtaining the maximum loan at the most favorable terms is now a matter of good planning and sound business practice. If you are to succeed at both, you should start to fill in any of the missing blanks in your plan. Learn the things you don't know, improve on those you do. Moreover, remember, when it comes to loans, a full, complete package wins out in the end.

Chapter 9

HOW TO GET THE MOST BENEFIT FROM BLANKET MORTGAGES

GOAL OF THIS CHAPTER

This chapter enables you to adjust financing and shift equities by spreading the lender's risk over more than one property. This creates a highly flexible mortgage technique that can be very useful in maximizing debt while at the same time reducing cash requirements to zero.

DEFINITION OF A BLANKET MORTGAGE

A blanket mortgage is any mortgage that has more than one property as security to the debt. This type of financing may also be called a *congruent loan.* For example, Janette wanted to borrow $250,000 to purchase a studio for her art class, but the lender she was talking to told her that the loan-to-value percentage was too high for the value of the property. She told the lender that she would add a first position on a vacant lot the owned to the security of the mortgage. The lender was satisfied with the loan-to-value ratio now that there was additional security to the loan. Janette purchased the studio.

A blanket mortgage often is mistaken or confused with the wraparound mortgage, which is covered in Chapter 10. Blanket mortgages and wraparound mortgages are two very distinct tools that have some similarity, but serve to achieve different goals. As stated, blanket mortgages are mortgages where the security to the loan is more than one property. This means that there is one lender, and one loan that needs to be repaid, but the borrower has given the lender two or more properties to secure that loan. The wraparound mortgage is a mortgage on one or more properties that wraps around other mortgages. In the wraparound mortgage, the mortgagor generally pays on one mortgage amount, while there are actually several mortgages, often each with different terms and conditions.

USING BLANKET MORTGAGES

After reading this chapter, you should be comfortable with some of the many different ways you as either a buyer or a seller can use the blanket mortgage.

Any basic form of mortgage, including a wraparound, can be used to encompass more than one property. The moment more than one property is security for the mortgage, you have created a blanket mortgage. For example, an investor I knew owned three duplexes that were side by side. He wanted to refinance the mortgages on two of them, but found it was to his advantage to refinance all three under one mortgage. The resulting mortgage was a blanket mortgage. The lender received greater security for the loan made, and was therefore enticed to reduce the interest rate.

As you read this chapter, you will begin to see the many advantages of the blanket mortgage. We will also examine the drawbacks.

Who Can Utilize This Mortgage?

The criterion for using a blanket mortgage is easy enough. You must have at least two parcels of property. It helps if they are adjoining or in the same area, but this is not necessary. A home and a lot, an apartment building and a warehouse, or vacant land and a duplex are some of the many combinations of dissimilar properties that can be combined in a blanket mortgage. Some blanket mortgages can include dozens of properties.

Most investors seeking to obtain maximum leverage will find the blanket mortgage helpful in obtaining the highest yield on their invested capital. Let's look at other benefits that can be derived from the blanket mortgage:

• PROVIDE MAXIMUM FINANCING. Generally, if you can include more than one property as security for a loan, it is possible to borrow in excess of the value of a part of the total security. With this in mind, blanket mortgages can provide 100 percent financing for new ventures and throw off cash to boot. In the refinancing of several properties, the combined effect of the security can make the package presented to the lender more secure and thereby increase the amount of the mortgage.

• ALLOW THE MORTGAGOR TO OBTAIN BETTER TERMS AND CONDITIONS ON THE LOAN. It follows that if the loan is more secure, then you have room to bargain for better terms. Of the terms to be considered, the interest rate and annual payment will be most important. If you can decrease the percentage of the loan-to-value ratio, thereby decreasing the lender's risk, you will find the terms should ease considerably. For example, Simon, a local investor, wanted to purchase a 10-unit apartment house fairly priced at $745,000.

The property had a low first mortgage of $230,000. The seller indicated he would hold up to $200,000 in a second mortgage, and wanted cash above that. Simon discovered that within the new money market, the best he could come up with, after mortgage cost, was $500,000. This left him short the difference needed to buy the property, even if the seller held the $200,000 paper. The best terms available from a local lender were 24 years at 8 percent with two points closing costs. However, he did own a small lot that was across the street from the apartment house. It was free and clear and he hoped to build on it one day. Its value was $125,000. He went to the bank again and offered to put the lot up as additional security on the loan. The lot was appraised at the $125,000 value. Thus, a total value of the apartment building at $745,000 and the lot of $125,000 was $870,000. The bank then offered Simon $609,000 on the package but they would not allow any secondary financing on the apartments. The most Simon could come up with toward the balance was $100,000 so he went back to the seller and explained the situation. Because Simon was still short $36,000 and because the seller had offered to hold as much as $200,000 second, they agreed that Simon would give the seller a personal note for the $36,000 due and payable at the end of five years, with interest-only payments in the meantime. Because this was not a second mortgage, the bank loan was approved. Simon also got the bank to put a provision in the blanket mortgage that would allow him to obtain a release of the vacant lot with a principal payment to the bank of $50,000. This would allow Simon to sell or even develop on the lot at a future date if he so desired.

• CONSOLIDATE PROPERTIES. Some investors have put together a considerable array of properties over the years. Mortgages have different payment schedules and termination dates. Sometimes it is feasible to add several properties to a refinancing package of another property to provide a larger base and reduce the overall loan-to-value ratio. In this type of blanket mortgage, the properties should be similar types of realty when dealing with institutional lenders. However, private lenders may not care. For example, a local investor, Aston, had nearly a dozen small warehouses across town. Each of them was fully rented and none of the buildings had a mortgage greater than 50 percent of its value. Two of the larger warehouses had mortgages that were at very high interest rates as compared to the present market with only a few years remaining. This gave those mortgages a very high constant rate for debt they supported. Aston decided to refinance them all under one blanket mortgage. He obtained an excellent commitment from one of the local commercial banks in the area, and another almost equally good from another local commercial bank.

I had the opportunity to see Aston just before he made his deal with the lender. In looking over the package, I discovered he had two warehouses that had 5.5 percent loans. While these loans had a low loan-to-value ratio, their term was still 14 years to go. (They may have been FHA or VA in origin.) I suggested he keep these loans and let the lender hold second position on those two warehouses. This would lower the overall payment and probably not affect the amount of money lent. One bank did not go along with that idea, but the other bank did. The total loan was far in excess of the payoff of the existing financing, and Aston withdrew nearly $275,000, which was not taxable as it was borrowed funds. His annual payment increased only $5,000 over his previous debt service on the earlier financing although the total number of years for the repayment also increased.

• LOCK IN THE PROPERTY. This can be an advantage as well as a disadvantage. In the previous example, if Aston had ideas of selling some of the warehouses in a few years, he would have to have release provisions as a part of the mortgage terms. Some lenders will go along with this, but others will not. However, if you are selling property, the features of the blanket mortgage can be made to work for you if you are asked to hold paper. You can have the buyer include other properties, which will become security to the transaction. This becomes both a buyer and a seller provision, depending on the circumstances and point of view.

• LOCK IN OTHER ASSETS. There is no reason that the blanket mortgage should be limited to real estate. As in the previous situation, the buyer or seller can offer or require other assets to be pledged as security. A liquor license, for example, may be tied to a bar in this way. Stocks or other collateral can be given as additional security via the blanket aspects of the mortgage.

In these examples, the assets can be pledged by the mortgagor or a cosigner. For example, Walters wanted to buy a home that had existing financing of $150,000 and $140,000 in equity. He had no cash to put down, but he did have a father-in-law anxious to see his daughter move out of the guesthouse and into her own home. The father-in-law offered a second mortgage on his own home as additional security to the seller. In the end, the seller took a blanket second mortgage on the home being sold, with a second position on the father-in-law's home. The total equity was more than enough, which saved the deal.

WHERE TO GET BLANKET MORTGAGES

Not all lenders will approve a loan that requires a blanket provision in the final mortgage. However, the big lenders, such as insurance companies and REITs, have made such loans. In addition, many of the local lenders, such as commercial banks and mortgage bankers, will frequently lend with blanket provisions. The whole idea of blanket provisions is to make the loan more secure, and virtually all lenders will make blanket loans given the right circumstances. Although there are some complications in the deal, such as two or more titles to check and additional paperwork, any loan that is more secure to the lender is a better loan.

The best place to look for money when you are willing to offer additional property as supplemental security is to the seller. The increased equity gained by virtue of this form of financing often can sway the seller into holding large amounts of paper. Other private sources, such as investors, private lenders, and mortgage brokers, also like the blanket mortgages and should not be overlooked.

WHEN TO USE A BLANKET MORTGAGE

When you are considering the use of a blanket mortgage, reexamine the five things it can do:

1. Provide maximum financing.
2. Provide a stronger position for negotiating the terms and conditions of the loan.
3. Consolidate properties.
4. Lock in the property.
5. Lock in other assets.

Situations that call for blanket financing require the satisfaction of one or more of these five items. Because items 1 and 2 are rather general, it is important to remember that there are many different forms of financing that can accomplish these two desired goals. However, when the best form for the borrower is unacceptable to the lender, a blanket mortgage may be the answer.

Providing maximum financing may not be worth the cost or the disadvantages that result from both excessive leverage and overextension. Because of this, the use of blanket mortgages must be compared to the other alternatives. Once you have a basis for determining which form is the most advantageous to you, you can proceed to see if you can work out the transaction on those more favorable terms.

DETERMINING THE ACCEPTABILITY OF A BLANKET MORTGAGE

The acceptability of a blanket mortgage can be seen from both sides of the transaction. As in all forms of mortgages, the effect may differ from transaction to transaction and from buyer to seller. Unless you can pinpoint what makes the blanket mortgage acceptable, you may not know when to use it.

Blanket Mortgages as Seen from the Buyer's Point of View

The buyer must understand that in order to use this form of financing, it is necessary to encumber more than one piece of property. If the transaction itself contains these separate properties, there may be no reason to hesitate, providing the buyer can obtain releases that may be necessary (such as purchasing four lots from one seller). It is usual for the buyer to add security to the blanket mortgage from property already owned.

The majority of blanket mortgages do occur with this extra outside security as a part of the transaction. The buyer uses equity in other property to assist in new financing. To some degree, it is seen in pyramiding and other forms of high leverage and extension buying. Nonetheless, the buyer must understand the disadvantages, as well as the advantages, of this format, and must weigh these in determining whether it is wise to use a blanket mortgage.

DISADVANTAGES OF BLANKET MORTGAGES FOR BUYERS

- These place a burden on other properties. Whenever a second property is pledged as additional security on a blanket mortgage, that property is in jeopardy if the mortgage falters.

- These can make a separation difficult or impossible. Of course, this will depend on the terms of the blanket mortgage. However, to some degree, the mortgagor is hampered in his or her ability to sell the other properties. A buyer can, however, purchase the property subject to the blanket mortgage, and if the principal of the mortgage is less than the amount of financing held there is no disadvantage.

- Assets can be locked in. This works as both an advantage and a disadvantage. In this instance, the combined effect of tying two or more assets together can cause unforeseen hardships in the future if the mortgagor needs to separate those assets.

- You can see that the main disadvantage is the combining of other properties with the inability to separate them when or if the need arises. With this in mind, you can then look to the blanket mortgage as a useful tool when the criteria, which follow, can be met.

BUYERS' CRITERIA FOR USING BLANKET MORTGAGES

- Other properties exist which have sufficient equity that will be accepted by the seller or mortgagee as additional security to arrange the financing required.

- Total income generated from all properties covered with the blanket mortgage is sufficient to meet the payout requirements of the debt service to be created. A reasonable leeway should provide for a drop of income before the break-even is reached. This will depend on the situation of course. Some transactions may be approached with a deficit, the mortgagor coming out-of-pocket for a time until new income from the property can be generated (as in the case of a new development, construction, or other income-increasing methods).

- The mortgagor can project that he or she will not need to separate the properties from the mortgage in the relatively near future. Even if he or she has release provisions, they will no doubt be costly, so it may be dangerous to enter into a blanket mortgage if it is anticipated that early separation will be necessary. This will not be the case if the mortgagor is anticipating a complete refinancing of the property, and has confidence he can recast the mortgage and obtain separation in that way. Nonetheless, the risk remains and it may be costly to obtain separation.

- Effort by the mortgagor to find another solution other than adding additional debt to the transaction has failed. These other solutions may have included the exchange of another property owned by the buyer, or using sweat equity to pay off the seller with something other than cash.

In summarizing the blanket mortgage from the buyer's point of view, if the buyer can meet these criteria and understands the disadvantages of this form, he or she can use the mortgage.

Blanket Mortgages as Seen from the Seller's Point of View

Like the buyer, the seller and other mortgagee should know all the ins and outs of the blanket mortgage. Yet, because this format is designed to increase the security, the advantages are more often weighted in the seller's and the mortgagee's favor. However, disadvantages do exist.

OVEREXTENDED DEBT.   The blanket mortgage may cause an overextension of the debt against the properties. This can lead to the inability to meet the debt service. This is a potential problem whenever debt reaches high loan-to-value ratios. The mortgagee (seller or someone else) can take all the precautions possible to ensure that this does not happen. However, if the investor has little capital invested, the security may disappear relatively quickly. For example, Curtis purchased a 15-unit apartment house that had a fair market value of $800,000. Already in existence was a first mortgage of $550,000 held by a former owner. To close the deal, Curtis offered a second mortgage in the amount of $250,000 that would be secured by his remaining equity in the 15-unit complex he was purchasing and a second position on a vacant tract, which Curtis valued at $150,000. That property already had an existing first mortgage of $75,000.

Quick Trip to Foreclosure. As it turned out, Curtis had purchased the lot a year earlier for $80,000, giving the seller a timeshare week that Curtis owned in Orlando as the down payment. A conservative present-day value of the lot was about $100,000. True to his nature, Curtis milked the apartments for a few years, got behind on his mortgage payments, and then walked away from a foreclosure. The seller had to step in and rescue the 15 units from the first mortgage, and spend several thousand dollars as well to repair them.

LITTLE OR NO CASH AT CLOSING. Blanket mortgages generally reduce the cash at closing. This happens because the blanket aspect is used to supply additional security to a mortgage greater than the seller is willing to hold otherwise. The effect is to reduce the amount of cash he or she will receive. All things being equal, this in itself is not a disadvantage, but merely a characteristic of this form of financing. However, all things are rarely equal, and equity rarely equals cash.

Despite the examples shown here, the error made is letting the buyer take title to a property without checking the details on the additional collateral supplied. In most all situations that I have experienced, as either a seller or broker, neglecting or having an inability to do a full investigation of those values and other potential debt against them was generally the case. This, ironically, points out the main advantage of using a blanket mortgage: When used properly, they can increase the equity brought to the table. I have found that most lawyers are able to draft a blanket mortgage that will adequately protect their clients. I suggest, however, that you always have the lawyer for the seller draw up the mortgage documents. Once drafted, each party should have separate legal representation for this and all mortgage and closing documentation.

Criteria for Mortgagees Holding Blanket Mortgages

Sellers who hold the blanket mortgage:

- Must have strong motivation to sell or hold the blanket mortgage. It is possible that the blanket is solid, and more than provides the security. Usually, the overwhelming motive by most sellers in this instance is the need to be relieved of superior debt, or is sick to death of the property.

- The security checks out. The combined equity, which secures the blanket mortgage, should be well over the principal amount of the mortgage itself. This will vary depending on the type of property and the existence of superior mortgages. Do not rely on the value as stated by the buyer or agent. Seek an independent appraisal, or at least ask the advice of other realtors in the area.

- Some cash can be a part of the deal. All buyers should put some cash into a transaction. Of course, the amount depends on many factors. However, it does have a solidifying effect.

Third-party lenders who hold the blanket mortgage must answer these questions:

- Is the security good, sound, and acceptable?
- Are the terms of the loan good, sound, and acceptable?
- Is the return on the mortgage good enough, nonusurious, and acceptable?
- Is the mortgagor's credit good, sound, and acceptable?
- Have all details of the property pledged as security been thoroughly investigated?

USING A BLANKET MORTGAGE TO HELP SELL YOUR PROPERTY

Blanket mortgages have a function as a sales tool in some types of transactions. If you are selling property from a large inventory within the same owner's portfolio, such as tract lots or other subdivided property, the seller can offer packages of lots or parcels to investors with the blanket mortgage. In this way, the buyers would have two or more pieces of land covered by one mortgage. The seller would agree to release some of the lots as the buyer paid part of the outstanding mortgage. The release would be the same kind used in any form of financing that might provide for the division of a property. The actual wording of the release could be predetermined by the seller to afford him or her maximum protection in this type of transaction.

The advantage to the seller in this type of mortgage is mainly the increased sales potential. The risk to the seller over other forms of financing is negligible, if the land in question is substantially worth the price. The buyer can compare the blanket mortgage to other forms of financing to see how it will affect him or her. In the following example, you will find one such comparison.

McMoore was a land developer who had more than 50 lots remaining in his most recent subdivision. He was not a builder, so he preferred to sell the lots rather than get into the housing business. While homes were moving at a fair pace, he could not attract private buyers, and homebuilders were not interested in his normal sales terms. McMoore had been selling his finished lots at a rate of about one a week and was asking $62,000 for each one. In the past, McMoore wanted and had gotten $15,000 down and was holding the balance for up to four years at 8 percent interest only. Some buyers had paid cash, financing the paper with their own sources. McMoore's broker, who had sold him the raw land nearly three years previously, suggested that he make a quick deal for a sellout and move onto the next land development program they had been working on. The broker reasoned that if the proper terms were given, they would be able to get some homebuilders to buy the remaining lots. They came up with this plan: The lots would be put into groups of five. This meant they had 10 packages to offer to the local builders or investors. The average price per package was $300,000. The down payment, however, was $60,000. The mortgage balance of $240,000 (per package of five lots) was held by McMoore at 7 percent interest per annum for three years. Each builder could release a lot from that mortgage with a payment of principal for $50,000 (the last lot would only be $40,000). That release provision would allow a builder to deliver finished houses to buyers without having to pay off the entire mortgage. This marketing of the package was bound to produce the desired results. McMoore knew this and wanted to make sure he was secure in the transaction. Each builder had three years to build before the balloon came due on the unpaid balance.

This Transaction Appealed to Buyers

It was a good deal. McMoore had priced the lots fairly and the housing market was strong enough to warrant tying up the initial cash. McMoore had also made the down payment reasonable, so once the builders had invested the $60,000, they could move forward with preparations to build. They would arrange construction financing through local lenders to cover the cost of the home (plus a little overage). The excess of the loan, if any, would help pay off the lot. When they were ready to go, the lender would advance $50,000 for the first lot and the lot would be released from the blanket mortgage McMoore held.

Security Is the Key Motivation for the Lender

The real key to this formula was simply the security for the seller. The blanket formula of holding all the unreleased lots into the mortgage was part of the security. The idea of adding the second mortgage on each new home as it was built, releasing the previous one, put the icing on the cake for the seller and did not affect the buyer.

SUMMARY OF BLANKET MORTGAGES

The concepts inherent in blanket mortgages are also found in other forms of equity liens. If you remember that the ability to add other assets in order to bind the mortgage is the concept behind the blanket mortgage, you can apply this idea to leases as well.

In the lease, the term used to cover this concept is *cross-collateralization*. The main use of the blanket lease is in the sale-leasebacks. In this situation, the seller of a property becomes the lessee to the buyer. If the seller holds a mortgage as part of the sale (e.g., sale price: $150,000, seller holds $50,000 in paper and takes $100,000 down), the mortgage may be given as additional security on the lease. This has a very strong effect in securing the lease.

Blanket mortgages can be in any position on the scale of superior or junior liens. The mortgage can actually take different positions on the various properties it covers. Usually, however, the same position on all the properties is attained, but the fact that this is not necessary is most important.

It is always possible to hold individual mortgages instead of a blanket. From the seller's point of view, if the two mortgages were offered at the same term, interest rate, and principal, then the only advantage in the blanket would be the lock-in provision. This would depend on the situation and what assets or property the seller wanted to use as additional collateral to the mortgage.

Buyers use this form of financing to cover a down payment. However, even the buyer can take the alternative route and offer secondary paper on the existing property. Usually, the blanket mortgage is used in circumstances when the buyer is looking for the combined effect of one seller-held mortgage that is supported by his or her equity in other property, other than an exchange of equity by virtue of paper offered on something else. It is a matter of negotiation. In addition, it often sounds better to offer a blanket mortgage secured by the purchased property and the buyer's equity in a vacant lot, instead of a mortgage to the seller and a mortgage on the lot. Of course, if several additional properties are used to add security, the blanket mortgage is easier to work with.

Chapter 10

GAIN LEVERAGE ON EXISTING FINANCING WITH A WRAPAROUND MORTGAGE

GOAL OF THIS CHAPTER

This chapter acquaints you with the wraparound mortgage. This form of mortgage is a unique strategy to use to increase your leverage, convince a seller to help you by holding secondary financing, and close more transactions by using wraparound mortgages when they help move you to your goals.

DEFINITION OF A WRAPAROUND

A wraparound mortgage is a highly effective seller's tool that buyers often introduce into a transaction to help sway a reluctant seller to accept the terms offered. The reality of a wraparound or wrap mortgage, as it is frequently called, is that it can benefit both sides of the transaction.

A wraparound mortgage is a new mortgage that has one or more properties as security to the amount of the loan, and the total amount of the loan is a combination of the new loan and one or more existing loans. This type of loan is generally held by a seller, which is then called a purchase money wraparound mortgage.

Example: Sam and Bruce. Sam is negotiating a sale of a warehouse he owns for $250,000 to Bruce. Bruce wants to put $75,000 down. He also wants to structure the financing so that his annual payments on the balance owed of $175,000 do not exceed

225

$22,000 per year. The current market rate for new financing on this older warehouse is around 9.75 to 10.75 percent per annum. Bruce is willing to accept such financing as long as there is at least 10 years of fixed payments before a balloon payment would be due. There is the following existing financing on the property:

- A first mortgage for $50,000 that was the original mortgage Sam had when he purchased the property 15 years earlier. This mortgage will amortize in full in eight more years at $706.83 per month. The interest rate on this mortgage is 8 percent per annum.

- A second mortgage for $90,000 Sam obtained five years ago. This mortgage is at 8.5 percent per annum and will amortize in 10 years with monthly payments of $1,115.85 per month.

Sam tells Bruce that he will create a purchase money wraparound mortgage in the amount of $175,000 that will have monthly payments of $1,822.68 ($21,872.16 per year), at an annual interest rate of 9.75 percent per annum. Bruce will make those payments directly to Sam, who will hold the mortgage. This mortgage will be in effect for 10 years, at the end of which time there will be a balloon payment of (approximately) $94,065.00. Sam will take those payments and will make the first and second mortgage payments as they come due.

In this example, it will take 100 percent of the payment that Bruce makes Sam to meet the obligations of the two existing first mortgages.

First mortgage of $50,000 has a monthly payment of	$ 706.83
Second mortgage of $90,000 has a monthly payment of	1,115.85
Total monthly payment	$1,822.68

This means that until the first mortgage is paid off, by the end of eight years, Sam will not get any money in his pocket. Then, for two years, he will be able to put into his own pocket the portion that was previously going to the first mortgage. This is $706.83 per month × 2 years (24 months), or a total of $16,963.92. Then, at the end of the 10-year payment schedule that Bruce is obligated to, there is a balloon payment due of $94,065.00.

Sam ends up with:

Payments for years 9 and 10 after first mortgage is paid off	$ 16,963.92
Balloon payment (because second mortgage was fully paid off)	94,065.00
Total payments to Sam by the end of 10 years	$111,028.92

Remember that the portion of the $175,000 mortgage that consisted of Sam's equity in the mortgage was only $35,000. ($175,000 − $50,000 [first mortgage] − $90,000 [second mortgage] = $35,000).

This means that for a $35,000 investment, Sam would have a return of over $111,028.92. I can say "over" that amount because I can assume that as Sam begins to collect the monthly payments in years nine and ten (of $706.83 per month), that he could put that money in a savings account and earn some additional interest.

The actual yield on the $35,000 invested by Sam in this mortgage was leveraged up by the spread between the existing mortgages (which were 8 and 8.5 percent per annum, respectively). The simple approach to find the yield would be to assume that Sam did not get anything until the end of the tenth year. The compound interest it would take to increase $35,000 to $111,028.92 would be approximately 12.24 percent per year. Because Sam did get some of the return (almost half of the original $35,000) earlier, his real yield would be considerably higher. While Sam will end up with a leveraged return, Bruce has not been penalized. He got a mortgage that was at or below what he might have gotten at current interest rates. In addition, he did not have to pay mortgage points to a lender, and was able to make the deal at a price and terms he was comfortable with.

BASICS OF THE WRAPAROUND

Because wraparounds are misunderstood by many buyers, sellers, and real estate lawyers, the format of the mortgage is often used incorrectly. There are some important factors about the wraparound that you need to understand to protect you from using the wraparound incorrectly or in a situation that will not be beneficial to you. At the same time, you should not be detoured from using the wraparound when one of your advisors tries to steer you away from the technique. That may happen just because they do not understand the benefits of this tool.

Often, as a buyer, you realize that the wraparound mortgage may enable you to purchase a property. However, the seller does not know or understand how the wraparound can help. In this circumstance, you may have to assist that seller in making a proper and educated decision. This chapter should help you accomplish that task.

Because the wraparound does provide sellers with an opportunity to shift assets to later years, it can become a highly creative technique to build wealth. Your own retirement and/or future education of a child are just two reasons the wraparound can make that shift. However, its biggest benefit to both buyers and sellers is that it can provide a creative way for the deal to come together. There are several elements that buyers and sellers need to be acutely aware of, but once you understand how and why it works, you will find that it will facilitate many difficult transactions.

I have provided several examples of wraparound mortgages that demonstrate the major elements of the technique. As with all tools in this book, I frequently use a technique in conjunction with other forms of finance without re-explaining elements of a transaction contained in other chapters. I mention this because you will find examples of other wraparound transactions in other chapters where the wraparound was combined with financing strategies that are the subject of that chapter. To find all the different examples of where a wraparound has been used as a part of a financing package, please check the index.

This chapter deals with the mechanics of the wraparound. There is no simple way to explain some of its workings other than by example, and there is no simple way to calculate the yield except by following the method contained herein. Some handheld calculators have programs to calculate wraparound mortgage yields. Unfortunately, not all of these programs are accurate. If you are using one such program, I recommend you check it by comparison to the example later on in this chapter.

As you know by now, there are several different kinds of yields available in wraparound mortgages. The average yield is the usual one that computers give, but that is not the most effective yield. When you get the average yield, you have found nothing useful. Let us take a look at another example of a wraparound mortgage.

EXAMPLE: BOBBY AND JEFF.   Bobby wants to buy Jeff's condominium apartment for $220,000. There is an existing first mortgage of $150,000, which is payable over the remaining 18 years at a fixed interest rate of 6.5 percent per annum, with monthly payments of $1,198.75. At the time Bobby would close on this transaction, that mortgage would have a constant rate of 9.439 percent (see Table A in the Appendix, look at 6.5 percent interest, in the "18 years remaining" column multiply the constant by the principal of $150,000 then divide the answer by 12 to get $1,179.87). For the sake of this example, let's round this off to $1,180.00 per month.

Bobby offers Jeff a down payment of $25,000 cash and a second mortgage of $45,000 at an interest-only payment of 9 percent for 10 years with a balloon payment at that time, plus his assumption of the existing mortgage. Under these terms, Bobby would have a combined monthly payment for the two mortgages of $1,517.50.

Jeff counters by offering to take the $25,000 down payment and hold a $195,000 wraparound mortgage with a 9 percent interest-only payment each month for 10 years with the principal amount of the mortgage coming due (ballooning) at the end of the 10 years. In these terms, the payment Bobby must make is only $1,462.50. Calculate 9 percent of $195,000 (195,000 × 0.09 = $17,550.00 ÷ by 12 = $1,462.50 per month) because this amount is less than the payment in his own offer, Bobby accepts Jeff's deal. Both sides have won.

As far as Bobby is concerned, the wraparound that Jeff is holding is really one mortgage in the amount of $195,000. However, from Jeff's point of view, there are three mortgages:

1. An existing mortgage of $150,000 that has a mortgage payment of $1,180.00 per month for the next 18 years.

2. The wraparound mortgage in the amount of $195,000, which Bobby pays to Jeff for 10 years at $1,462.50 per month.

3. The seller's equity in the wraparound mortgage is the difference between the existing and the wraparound mortgages, less any cash paid.

The wraparound mortgage of $195,000 less the existing first mortgage of $150,000 and the cash gives Jeff a difference of $45,000. This difference is Jeff's equity position in the wraparound mortgage at the date of closing.

In reality, Bobby is paying as if he held the single $195,000 mortgage that was interest-only for 10 years. At the end of that term, if he still owns the property, he will pay off the amount in full ($195,000). In the meantime, Jeff continues to make payments on the existing financing, and puts the leftover money in his pocket. Because he collects $1,462.50 and pays out $1,180.00, he has $282.25 left over each month for himself. That amounts to $3,390.00 per year. This amount ($3,390.00) is Jeff's cash flow on the equity portion of the wraparound. This is 7.533 percent on the $45,000 difference ($3,390.00 ÷ $45,000 = 7.533 percent).

However, since the wraparound mortgage paid by Bobby is interest only, and the existing mortgage is being paid off by Jeff, at the end of each year Bobby still owes Jeff $195,000; however, Jeff's outstanding balance on his $150,000 mortgage will continue to decline each year. At the end of the 10 years, the balance Jeff owes will be $88,114.50. We find this by looking at Table A, under 6.5 percent interest for the eight years remaining. Remember, the mortgage had 18 years to go at the closing and now, 10 years later, still has eight years left. Therefore, the question is: What principal amount will be retired in eight years at 6.5 percent interest per annum with a monthly payment of $1,180.00? The constant rate (at 6.5 percent in the eight years column) is 16.063 percent. Therefore, annualize the monthly payment of $1,180.00 by multiplying it by 12 months to arrive at the yearly total, which is $14,160. Then divide that by the constant rate you found in Table A of 16.063. By dividing $14,160 by 0.16063, you will get $88,152.90 as the principal, which Jeff still needs to pay off. Of course, he will collect $195,000 from Bobby. Therefore, at the end of the 10 years term of the wraparound mortgage, Jeff will pay off that amount ($88,152.90) and have $106,847.10 left over. Of that amount, $45,000 was his equity in the wraparound, so his bonus earnings will be the difference ($106,847.90 − $45,000 = $61,847.10). This $61,847.10 is the unpaid interest on the combination of the original principal ($45,000 plus each year of unpaid interest added to the growing principal). In effect, the $45,000 was compounding at an unknown interest. I say unknown because if there is an early repayment of the debt, we do not really know what the bonus will be without calculating that at the time it occurs. Do not let that statement bother you. It will come together in a moment. It is like a discounted mortgage really. The earlier it is paid off, the greater the final yield.

Yield on Jeff's Invested Equity in the Wraparound Mortgage. It will be a combination of two amounts.

First the cash flow yield, which was what was left over from the two payments (what Bobby paid, less what Jeff paid on the first mortgage). That amount was $3,390.00 for the year ($3,390.00 ÷ $45,000 = 7.533%). Therefore, of the equity that Jeff held in the wraparound mortgage, his cash flow was equal to a 7.533 percent return. This part of the yield would occur no matter when the total was repaid.

Second is an amount that we still need to calculate. It is the amount that began as $45,000 but had no direct payment made for over the 10 years, which accumulated to a total of $106,847.90. One quick way would be to look at the compounding effect of the $45,000 at an unknown amount of interest. This is where Table C in the Appendix will come in handy. This table takes into account the compounding of a principal amount. To use this table, all you need to do is look at what you know is the time period the amount was compounding and the final amount of the combined principal plus interest. So, if in 10 years $45,000 compounded annually to reach $106,847.90, let's discover the interest rate that caused that to occur:

- If the mortgages continue to final pay off at the end of 10 years, Jeff will collect $106,847.90, and get his $45,000 back plus a bonus of $61,847.10 on his original principal of $45,000. In essence, we can say this is exactly what would happen if he put the money in a CD that was compounded each year at X percent interest. While you do not know what the interest is, you do know that the final compounded amount is $106,847.90.

- The answer is found in two short steps. First, you divide $106,847.90 (the payoff) by $45,000.00 (the original investment). The answer 2.374398 is your target to find in Table C under the 10-year column. The closest you will find will be 9 percent, which shows 2.36736. As that does not quite reach the target, Jeff's yield to the bonus is just slightly above 9 percent but less than 9.25 percent—call it 9.12 percent.

- Take the two returns, 7.533 percent and 9.12 percent, and you can see that Jeff will have the total return of approximately 16.653 percent return on his invested $45,000. I have not taken into account what interest Jeff might have made had he reinvested the annual cash flow that he did put into his pocket, and neither should you as we are arriving at the annual yield and not an internal rate of return. The importance at this point of a discussion on wraparound mortgages is to understand what is going on between the different mortgages. Clearly, Bobby is paying a higher interest on a greater amount than Jeff is retiring at a lower interest rate. In the example, the bulk of Jeff's return will not come until there is a payoff of the wraparound. His return, however, will be considerably higher than the contract rate of the wrap (contract rate is the interest rate stated in the mortgage note).

Think about this problem for a moment: What if Jeff decided to extend the wraparound mortgage for another eight years. What would the payoff be? What is the bonus above the original "difference" of $45,000? What is his final yield?

Another Win/Win Situation. Bobby won because he decreased his debt service, and Jeff won because he increased his overall effective yield on the wrap. Other things occur, too, but we discuss those factors later in this chapter.

Most Important Factor about Wraparounds

If there is a single, most important factor about wraparounds, it is that a wraparound mortgage is just a tool. Depending on your knowledge of the tool and your goals, it has many uses; it can be the best thing for your situation, or it can do nothing at all to take you closer to your goals.

What the Wraparound Is Not

To get a good grasp of what the wraparound is, it might be helpful to see what it is not:

1. IS NOT A CURE-ALL FORM OF FINANCING. This can be said of any technique in this book. Nothing will do everything, and nothing is so inflexible that some other technique may not work just as well depending on the people, the property, and your needs and goals.

2. IS NEVER IN FIRST POSITION. The very nature of a wraparound mortgage causes the situation to contain existing financing on the property. It could be possible for a mortgage to be called "The First Wraparound Mortgage." Even though this term might be used incorrectly, it could refer to a transaction that had more than one wraparound mortgage in existence on the same property.

EXAMPLE: AL AND ROBERT. Al wants to purchase Robert's property. The current financing consists of the debt Robert has assumed when he purchased the property and is a seller-held wraparound in the amount of $100,000. That mortgage consists of a wrap of $100,000 that encompasses a first mortgage of $60,000, and a difference of $40,000, which Robert owed to the seller when he purchased the property. In addition to the wraparound mortgage, Robert had placed another mortgage on the property several years ago in the amount of $25,000. This would be a third mortgage as the rank of mortgages at this point would be: (1) the existing first mortgage, (2) the wraparound, and (3) the $25,000 mortgage. In Al's transaction, Al wants the seller, Robert, to hold a fourth mortgage for $35,000. The seller could do exactly that, or he would have the following options that would involve new forms of wraparound mortgages.

As the seller, Robert could structure one of the following transactions:

First wraparound	$100,000	($60,000 first plus $40,000 difference)
Third mortgage	25,000	
New difference	+ 35,000	
Second wraparound	$160,000	

If the Robert did this, Al would make one payment on the second wraparound of $160,000 as would be indicated by the terms of that mortgage. In turn, Robert would make payments on the first wraparound (which would include the first mortgage payment and the difference to the holder of that wraparound), and make the payment on the third mortgage, keeping the balance left over as the payment on the new difference.

Alternatively, the seller could create a wraparound mortgage solely around the third mortgage. In this case, Al would make two monthly payments: one on the first wraparound, and a second to the seller on a wraparound at a face amount of $60,000 ($25,000 + $35,000). Out of that payment by Al, the seller would have to meet the obligations of the third mortgage. The seller could also take a fourth mortgage, which Al would pay in addition to the wraparound and the third mortgage.

3. IS NOT REQUIRED TO ENCLOSE ALL EXISTING MORTGAGES. The foregoing example was a good illustration of that. This is important to remember because if you buy a property using a wraparound, you should not assume that there are no other mortgages you need to pay. One of the key elements of any real estate transaction is to know exactly what debt there is against the property you are buying. You will only know for sure by having a title search made by your lawyer, or a title insurance company or escrow company. Even then, as a part of the closing statement, the seller should warrant that there are no hidden loans that may surface later on.

4. IS NOT ALL THE SAME. Since this is a technique and not a specific form that can be bought at a stationery store, you must recognize that this tool is very flexible, and it will be different each time you see it or use it. No matter how similar one form of a wraparound looks, you have to be very careful with the exact terms contained within the document to make sure you understand what is expected of each party. I mention each party because the wraparound has obligations to both the mortgagor and the mortgagee. Later, there will be more on this aspect of wraparounds.

EXAMPLE: THE PAULSEN STUDY.   Paulsen wanted to sell his small mountain cabin and put a price of $155,000 on it. He had an old low-interest existing first mortgage in the amount of $75,000 that had 20 years remaining in its payout at an interest of only 8 percent per annum.

The Offer. Beck, the investor, offers to pay $35,000 down, assume the first mortgage, and let Paulsen hold the balance of $40,000 in secondary financing. Like many sellers, Paulsen balked at that, saying the risk was too high. Beck reconsidered and countered with the following terms:

Price	$150,000	
Cash down	− 35,000	
Wraparound	$115,000	(20-year payout at 10 percent)

Beck's broker presented the new offer. He explained to Paulsen what a wraparound was and went over the advantages to Paulsen in this offer.

The broker showed Paulsen how this wraparound would return a yield of over 13 percent over the term of the mortgage. Take a look at the illustrations the broker used.

Paulsen's Wraparound Mortgage. In the transaction, Beck will make payments on one mortgage: the $115,000 wraparound. It will be set up with a 20-year amortization at 10 percent per annum. The total annual payment will be $13,317.55.

Paulsen will be required to set up a method of collection of that mortgage from Beck so that from Beck's monthly check, the payment required on the existing first mortgage can be made. The required payment on the existing first mortgage is $7,527.75, which is deducted from Beck's total annual payment of $13,317.55. This leaves $5,789.25 per year for Paulsen. This means that Paulsen will get a monthly payment of $482.44 for 20 years (unless he sells the mortgage or uses it in exchange for another property). This payment, on the equity in the wraparound of $40,000, would represent a monthly payment based on a 20-year payout at 14.47312 percent ($5,789.25 ÷ $40,000). However, this is not the interest rate, as this payment will fully amortize the "difference" during the 20-year period. So, the constant rate based on 12 monthly installments each year is 14.47312.

How Was the Yield on Paulsen's Mortgage Calculated? This was a simple calculation on a wraparound mortgage. There was only one existing mortgage, and the wraparound was for the same term as the existing mortgage. In essence, by the end of the term (20 years) each mortgage would be retired. Beck would make one payment each month that would total $13,317.55 per year for 20 years. During this same time, Paulsen or any successor holder of that mortgage would pay the existing payments of $7,527.75 per year and would collect on the difference of $40,000 an annual total of $5,789.25.

To find the actual effective yield on this wraparound for the total term of the mortgage (20 years), you simply need to find the constant rate on the payment toward the difference. As long as the monthly payments of the existing mortgage and the wraparound do not change each month and no interim balloon occurs, the following is a quick math solution to the problem. To calculate Paulsen's return on his invested capital portion of the wraparound (his difference of $40,000), the answer will be found by calculating what interest rate will pay off $40,000 over 20 years if the annual payment (of 12 monthly installments) is $5,789.25.

Find the constant rate of payment on the difference:

Amount owed to Paulsen	$ 40,000
Amount Paulsen gets each year	5,789.25

Formula: Annual payment (12 months total) ÷ Principal

Step 1: Once you have the annual payment of $5,789.25, which you obtained by taking the total payment on the wraparound and by deducting the payment to the existing mortgage, you then go to Step 2 and divide that amount by the total amount owed on the difference (Paulsen's equity in the wraparound). The difference in this example is $40,000 and is found by subtracting the existing mortgage from the gross amount of the wraparound mortgage.

Step 2: $5,789.25 ÷ $40,000 = 0.1447312

Step 3: Convert the answer, 0.1447312, into a percentage amount by moving the decimal two places to the right. The percentage is now 14.47312. This is the constant rate of payment for an amortizing mortgage with monthly payments.

Step 4: Look at Table A in the Appendix in the 20-years column until you find a constant percent that comes closest to the 14.47312.

Step 5: Discover these two percentages, 14.273 followed by 14.488. These correspond to the different interest rates for that term of years:

Percent Interest	20-Years Constant
13.25	14.273
13.5	14.488

As the desired percent is more than that shown for 13.25 percent interest but slightly less than that for 13.5 percent interest, the actual effective interest yield on the difference for the full term of the wraparound would be about 13.45 percent per year. It is sufficient to come to an average interest rate at this point.

What All This Means Thus Far

If Paulsen were to hold onto this mortgage for the full 20 years, his effective yield would be approximately 13.45 percent per year. This is, of course, based on his equity of $40,000 and a full term payout. As real insiders know, mortgages do not always run the full term. If Beck, for example, decided to sell the property in a few years, a new buyer may want to refinance to new terms from an institutional or other lender. This is very good news for any holder of a wraparound mortgage because when a wraparound mortgage is paid off early, there can be substantial bonus to its holder. For additional information about such bonus, look at Chapter 15 that deals with buying mortgages at a discount. For the moment, take a look at the following example to get an idea about early payoff.

EXAMPLE: THE MORTGAGE IS PAID OFF EARLY.   An unusual event happens in wraparounds that gives the holder a bonus when the mortgage is paid off early. Assume for a moment that Beck sells the property at the end of the first year and the new owner refinances the wraparound, paying off the amount then owed. To see what happens, let us first get the facts at the end of the first year:

Facts	*Wraparound Mortgage*	*Existing Mortgage*
Original amount	$115,000.00	$75,000.00
Annual payment	$ 13,317.55	$ 7,527.75
Term	20 years	20 years
Interest rate	10%	8%
End of which year	1	1
Remaining term	19 years	19 years
Amount still owed	$113,100.21	$73,412.81

This last amount is found by finding the constant rate for the remaining term, at the interest rate for the mortgage, and then dividing that rate into the annual payment.

If Beck paid off the wraparound at the end of the first year, it would cost him $113,100.21, out of which Paulsen would have to pay $73,412.81, leaving him a balance of $39,687.39 from the original $40,000 difference. At the end of the first year, Paulsen would have gotten:

In monthly payments	$ 5,789.25
Payoff at the end of the year	+39,687.39
Total paid to Paulsen	$45,476.64
Original principal amount	−40,000.00
Net interest for that first year	$ 5,476.64

Actual effective yield based on an annual return for the first year based on a payoff of the existing mortgage and the wraparound at that time would be found by dividing the original principal amount of $40,000 into the net interest for the year. The sum of $5,476.64 ÷ $40,000 = 13.692 percent per annum.

The point to this illustration—in a wraparound mortgage, the general rule is that the actual effective yield will be higher if the mortgage is paid off early than if it is held to maturity. This mortgage yield went from 13.45 percent to 13.692 percent on the prepayment of the first year. The yield earned at the end of a first-year payoff in a mortgage such as described will be its maximum annual yield. Each year thereafter, the mortgage yield will move closer to the average of 13.45 percent per annum.

Later on in this chapter, when I illustrate the Hodges Shopping Center example, you will see how existing mortgages affect the total wraparound balance and the relationship to the difference.

Keep in mind that in the Paulsen example everything was at its simplest. In the real life use of the wraparound, it is usual to have more than one mortgage and more than one term of years within the existing financing. These factors make the wraparound a rather complicated mortgage to calculate, so do not be surprised if you have to apply some extra thought to this chapter. It will be worth it in the long and profitable run.

MOST COMMON USES OF A WRAPAROUND MORTGAGE

1. Use this tool as a method of leveraging a seller's position upward with the idea of increasing the effective yield earned on the mortgage. The ability to increase the return on funds mortgaged is the primary benefit of the wraparound.

2. Used to induce the seller to hold secondary paper. The benefits of the increased return may help a broker convince a reluctant seller to take secondary paper, or any paper at all for that matter. Many transactions are saved simply because the sellers were made aware of the benefits of this tool.

3. When the existing financing is at a relatively low rate and the constant payment percentage is relatively low, the green flag is out that a wraparound is potentially viable. The key factor here is the constant rate, and the investor's goals. We say more about that later.

4. If the existing financing has any provisions that make prepayment difficult or costly, then the wraparound mortgage may provide an effective solution to the inability to economically obtain new primary financing. When there are several mortgages encumbering a property, there may be one or more with provisions that will create such problems. It is best to consider the wraparound when such conditions are present. Sellers unwilling to approach the wraparound should be made aware of the full impact of their present financing.

5. A nonassumption clause in the existing financing may be an indication that the wraparound mortgage can be used. Institutional lenders almost always use these provisions in their loans. When a property is sold, the buyer must make application to the lender to be permitted to assume the obligation. Some lending institutions have taken a harder stand than others, but most will allow the wraparound if the first is assumed. The lenders, however, generally reserve the right to adjust the interest rate when such a new assumption takes place. Nonetheless, a wraparound mortgage does not require the buyer to assume the existing financing. This is a key factor in the whole structure of the wraparound mortgage, and indirectly has created the difficulty for third parties to lend on the wraparound. When a buyer purchases a property and gives the seller a wraparound mortgage, the existing financing remains the obligation of the seller. The seller makes the payments directly or causes them to be made on the existing mortgages. Some secondary financing, which may be encompassed within the wraparound, may have absolute provisions, which would make the wraparound difficult to accomplish because it may violate terms, which are contained in the superior mortgages of the transaction.

6. The increase of cash flow is a definite benefit, which can be accomplished by using the wraparound. Therefore, when the sale of a property is hampered by a low cash flow,

look to the wraparound as a solution. In essence, there are only a few ways to increase cash flow. Assuming a status quo in all other factors, the increase of income will accomplish this. If this fails, a reduction of expenses will also increase the cash flow. A combined effect of increased income (via more rents, and so on) and lowered expenses often will solve the problem and make the wraparound unnecessary. Normally, however, the seller has already maximized income and minimized expenses. The resulting NOI can only show an increased cash flow based on lowered debt service. The yield resulting from the cash flow, based on the invested capital, must meet the investor's demand rate (at the price the seller is willing to sell at). In the general marketing of an income property, the cash down is often based on the seller holding some paper, or with new financing necessary. The cash flow yield may be too low with new financing at high market rates, to warrant the investment. The wraparound can, and often does, solve this problem nicely.

7. Tight mortgage markets bring out the best need for the wraparound. When you find you are trying to sell a property, which cannot be financed due to the current market conditions, you must look to all the possible alternatives. The toughness of the market need only be relative to the overall rate on the existing financing. This means that if you have a property that has existing financing at very low rates, and the current market is a point or two above those rates, then you should examine the possibility of the wraparound. Of course, the complete inability to refinance for any reason within the economics of the deal will bring the wraparound into play more quickly and with more dramatic positive results.

8. Refinancing costs can sometimes be a major problem, and this factor can be a good reason to look to the wraparound. The overall effect of placing a wraparound mortgage is less costly to administer than new financing. The seller need only charge whatever legal cost is involved in the preparation of the loan document, and this should not be much more than the cost of preparing a standard form for a secondary loan.

9. Multimortgaged properties can often be very difficult to sell or market simply because of the number of mortgages present. If you have a property that has three or more existing mortgages, the wraparound can convert these into one. The buyer, after all, makes only one payment on the wraparound, even though the seller must direct payments out to the encompassed mortgages.

10. A short balloon in existing financing can create many difficulties in selling property. If the property is an income producer and the possibilities of refinancing it to cover the balloon payment are slim, then the wraparound can provide a solution. Naturally, the amount of the balloon must be considered. However, if it is due to close and is not excessive, then the wraparound may work out.

11. Marketing a property with sound financing can bring about a quicker sale and less negotiating of the price. When a property has only a moderate leverage of financing, that is to say a low ratio of the loan to value, the seller's equity will come under attack by buyers

anxious to buy at a lower price. It is obvious that a home offered at $100,000 with an $85,000 mortgage leaves only $15,000 to negotiate whereas a $500,000 property with $100,000 of financing leaves the seller vulnerable to negotiation on his equity of $400,000. Buyers expect some equity, and will haggle on the upper limits of such a transaction.

The seller in such a situation may offer the property with a reduced equity right from the start. The seller quotes to his or her broker a price and terms that include a single mortgage. At this point in there is no need to explain that a single mortgage is really a wraparound mortgage. Say, for example, in a $500,000 property with $400,000 equity, the seller offers the property at the $500,000 price subject to an existing mortgage of $300,000 and a down payment of $100,000. This increasing of the loan-to-value ratio will benefit the negotiations. As the buyer approaches the close of the sale, full ramifications of the underlying mortgages encompassed by the wraparound will, of course, be disclosed. The first examination, however, need only show the higher wraparound.

12. Buyers will look to the wraparound as a beneficial investing tool as often as a seller will see it as a selling tool. The buyers' benefits are in the overall comparison with the existing mortgage market, rather than in seller-held, conventional secondary financing. There are a few examples where the buyer will benefit from a wraparound, such as when the seller will hold a usual second mortgage for the same terms and rates. The seller will, however, hold a wraparound for longer, and often at lower rates than a usual second. Therefore, the buyer can benefit by approaching any situation that may call for refinancing and offer the seller terms only slightly less costly to the buyer in the general lending market. In this way, the buyer obtains better terms from the seller than he or she could at an institutional lender, saves the points, and at the same time passes on to the seller the full benefits of the wraparound.

If the primary reason for using the wraparound is to increase the cash flow on the income property for sale, there may be a sacrifice in some other area. The nature of the wraparound and its effect on the dollar amounts paid and received by the seller or lender should be clearly understood. In the first place, it is normal for the balance of the "difference" (mortgagee's equity), that is owed to increase for a period of time. Remember, the word difference in wraparound terms refers to the amount of the total wraparound mortgage that is left whenever you deduct the then present amount owed on the existing financing. This "difference" is the equity the seller or mortgagee has in the total amount of the wraparound. A wraparound in the amount of $100,000 that encompasses a first and a second totaling $80,000 will have an original difference of $20,000. This term is not universal, and in some areas this amount ($20,000) is called the wraparound difference, the lender's position, or new money, and as I have used, the mortgagee's equity. From this point on, I shall refer to this amount as the difference. This difference will not remain constant throughout the mortgage and normally grows in the early years. In essence, the equity or investment that the mortgagee has in this wraparound will grow as it earns interest that is not paid, and then begin to decline as the principal is ultimately repaid. To best illustrate what happens to this difference, examine the following case history.

The Function of the Amortization and Its Effect on the Difference in Wraparound Mortgages

EXAMPLE: THE HODGES CASE.   Hodges sold a shopping center for $2,500,000. He received $350,000 down and held a wraparound for the balance. The wraparound was for a face amount of $2,150,000, and was payable over a period of 20 years at 9 percent per annum in equal monthly installments that totaled $235,532.50. This wraparound was scheduled to balloon at the end of the 15th year, which was chosen for ease in calculating the yield and would be the year of maximum return to the seller. The existing financing was a first mortgage ($1,200,000) at 7.5 percent with 19 years remaining. Annual payment was $120,492. There was a second mortgage in the amount of $700,000 payable over 15 years at 8 percent. The annual payment was $81,781.

Mortgages	Face Amount	Annual payments
Wraparound	$2,150,000	$235,532.50
First mortgage	−1,200,000	−120,492.00
Second mortgage	− 700,000	− 81,781.00
Original difference	$ 250,000	$ 33,259.50

The foregoing calculation is correct only for the moment the wraparound is made. Each year the balances due on the mortgage will alter. The payment allocation to the difference will also change when the existing mortgages retire.

Here is what occurs by the end of the first year:

	Mortgage Balance— Start of First Year	Total Payment		Balance Owed— End of First Year
		Principal	Interest	
Wraparound	$2,150,000	$42,032	$193,500	$2,107,967
First mortgage	−1,200,000	−30,492	− 90,000	−1,169,508
Second mortgage	− 700,000	−25,781	− 56,000	− 674,219
Difference	$ 250,000	−$14,241	$ 47,500	$ 264,240

What has happened is this: The balance owed on the wraparound has declined by the principal paid of $42,032. However, the existing mortgages have declined $56,273. The total owed or remaining as a principal balance on the wraparound is $2,107,967. If the mortgage were paid off by the buyer at that time and the existing mortgages satisfied, then $264,240 would remain to apply to the mortgagee or the seller. The original amount at the beginning of the year was only $250,000. The $264,240 is the difference at the end of the first year. This is ($14,241) greater than the original difference of $250,000. What happened shows up in the interest column.

The interest on the wraparound mortgage is $47,500 greater than the combined interest on the first and second mortgages. This $47,500 is net interest earned by the holder of the mortgage, but since the holder received only $33,259.50 (see previous chart) the total principal amortized on the existing financing exceeded that amortized on the wraparound. The deficit ($14,241) had to be deducted from the total interest, then added to the balance owed. This constant adding of the deficit interest to the balance applicable to the difference will continue as this mortgage progresses.

The following is what happens by the end of the second year:

	Mortgage Balance—Start of Second Year	Total Payment		Balance Owed—End of Second Year
		Principal	Interest	
Wraparound	$2,107,967	$45,815	$189,717	$2,062,152
First mortgage	−1,169,508	−32,779	− 87,713	−1,136,729
Second mortgage	− 674,219	−27,843	− 53,937	− 646,375
Difference	$ 264,240	−$14,807	$ 48,067	$ 279,048

The holder of the wraparound still only gets the $33,259.50 cash left after the total payment is received less the existing payments on the first and second mortgages (see first chart). In this year, however, the balance applicable to the difference has grown to $279,048.

The reason for this build-up is not simply explained. It is a function of several factors that combine to create the major leverage to the difference. In the first place, leverage is present in the spread of mortgage rates. The interest charged on the wraparound is greater than the combined effect of interest charges against the total existing financing. You should be cautioned at this point not to jump to conclusions that all the underlying mortgages must have interest rates below that of the wraparound. It is the combined effect you must look at. In a multimortgaged property, you may have one or more mortgages with greater interest rates than the wraparound and still have a build-up of difference owed.

Therefore, the function of the amortization on the balance applicable to the difference will generally be that the amount owed will grow each year until there is a satisfaction of at least one existing mortgage. Keep in mind, however, that this is not always the case, and the actual calculation to determine this factor must be done. To recap the amortization of the wraparound in this case study, I have provided a breakdown of the mortgages and the difference throughout the full term of the loan. This breakdown is necessary in the understanding of the effective yield gained on the wraparound and will be used in the larger analysis of this yield later on. The amortization of the mortgages shown in Table 10.1 on page 242 gives the amounts owed at the end of the periods shown. Generally, you are dealing with amortizing loans, which will have one constant monthly or annual payment that includes interest and principal. Because of this, neither the interest nor the principal payments in each period are equal to other previous payments. Therefore, the corresponding balances of each mortgage and the difference must be calculated for each period. In analyzing a mortgage, you can be fairly accurate with year-end totals. Only in this way will you know what the pay-off amount applicable to the difference is at any given point of time.

In Table 10.1, each mortgage is shown with the principal balance outstanding at the end of each period. For example, at the end of eight years, the balance outstanding on the wraparound mortgage is $1,686,446 (Column A), the first mortgage is $881,469 (Column B), the 2nd mortgage is $452,777 (Column C), and the difference has grown to $379,200 in Column E. Note that the difference in Column E continues to increase until the end of the 15th year. When this occurs, it is the best time to have the wraparound balloon when the difference begins to amortize (or drop in value); this is a signal that the yield is at its peak to the mortgagee. It is unlikely there would be an objection to this in any event, and it will simplify the calculation of the yield. I have carried out the mortgage through to the end of the 20th year so that you can see the overall effect of cash flow as the first and second mortgages are retired and paid off in full.

Effective Rate Earned on the Wraparound. The big question is this: What is the real (or effective) return to the holder of the wraparound? As occurred in the earlier examples of wraparound mortgages, the overall yield is a combination of two factors. The cash flow yield which is shown in Columns F and H, and the compound interest factor that you will calculate by using Table C in the Appendix or by using a calculator that will raise a number to a higher power (as will be shown in the following example).

In the Hodges Shopping Center Case Study, the cash flow for the first 15 years remains steady at $33,259.50 per year (based on the total of the monthly installments). Because the mortgagee's equity in the wraparound begins at $250,000, this represents a return of 13.30 percent.

At the end of the 15th year, the difference increases to $512,289, and the mortgage is scheduled to balloon at that time. In essence, the seller of this property has an investment of $250,000 that has been growing at an unknown interest rate for a full 15 years. To discover that interest rate, we need to find a target rate to interpolate the actual interest that has caused the growth:

Table 10.1
Hodges Shopping Center Case Study Analysis

	Wraparound Principal Balance at End of Period					Existing Financing Principal Balance at End of Period				
	A	*B*	*C*	*D*	*E*	*F*	*G*	*H*	*I*	*J*
	Wraparound Mortgage	*First Mortgage*	*Second Mortgage*	*Third Mortgage*	*Difference*	*Total Cash Received on Difference*	*Difference Amortized*	*Retained Interest*	*Annual Interest Rate (%)*	*Earned But Not Retained Bonus*
	$2,150,000	*$1,200,000*	*$700,000*	*$___*	*$250,000*	*$33,259.50*				
	20 Years Rate	*19 Years Rate*	*15 Years Rate*	*Years Rate*	*20 Years*					
	9% Payment	*7½% Payment*	*8% Payment*	*Payment*	*Rate Varies*					
Period	*$235,532.50*	*$120,492*	*$81,781*	*$___*						
0	$2,150,000	$1,200,200	$700,000		$250,000					
1	2,107,967	1,169,508	674,219		264,240	$33,259.50	0	$33,259.50	13.30	$ 14,240
2	2,062,152	1,136,792	646,375		279,048	33,259.50	0	33,259.50	13.30	29,048
3	2,012,213	1,101,492	616,035		294,416	33,259.50	0	33,259.50	13.30	44,416
4	1,957,780	1,063,612	583,828		310,340	33,259.50	0	33,259.50	13.30	60,340
5	1,898,448	1,022,891	548,753		326,804	33,259.50	0	33,259.50	13.30	76,804
6	1,833,775	979,115	510,872		343,788	33,259.50	0	33,259.50	13.30	93,788
7	1,763,283	932,057	469,961		361,265	33,259.50	0	33,259.50	13.30	111,265
8	1,686,446	881,469	452,777		379,200	33,259.50	0	33,259.50	13.30	129,200
9	1,602,693	827,087	378,058		397,548	33,259.50	0	33,259.50	13.30	147,548
10	1,511,403	768,627	326,522		416,254	33,259.50	0	33,259.50	13.30	166,254
11	1,411,897	705,781	270,863		435,253	33,259.50	0	33,259.50	13.30	185,253
12	1,303,435	638,223	210,750		454,462	33,259.50	0	33,259.50	13.30	204,462
13	1,185,212	565,598	145,830		473,784	33,259.50	0	33,259.50	13.30	223,784
14	1,056,348	487,525	75,715		493,108	33,259.50	0	33,259.50	13.30	243,108
15	915,887	403,598	0		512,289	33,259.50	0	33,259.50	13.30	262,289
16	762,785	313,376	0		449,409	115,040.50	62,880	52,160.50		
17	595,903	216,387	0							
18	414,002	112,124	0							
19	215,729	0	0							
20	0	0	0							

Step 1: Divide the Payoff amount by the Original Difference

$512,289 ÷ $250,000 = 2.049

2.049 is the target rate.

Step 2: Refer to Table C and under the 15-year column you will discover that the compounding factor shown for 4.75 percent is 2.00591 and that for 5 percent is 2.07893.

Step 3: You can estimate here that your compounding rate will be slightly less than 5 percent. If you have a handheld calculator that will raise a number to a power (usually shown on the calculator as Y^X), you can test this by doing the following steps.

Step 4: The formula to compound the amount $\times (1 + \text{interest rate})^N$

Where N is the number of periods the amount is compounded.

By arriving at $(1+ \text{interest rate})^N$ you will find the exact number of the table. Because the amount of interest rate you need is not found in the table you could either estimate the rate at 4.9 percent or solve for several different rates to see if you can close the gap.

Clear the calculator.

Test for 4.9 percent by solving the formula $(1 + \text{interest rate})^N$

$(1.049)^{15}$

Enter 1049 (you need to override the computer's urge to round off your answer). You already know your target of 2.049 so you can expect something close to that number anyway.

Press the Y^X key and then enter 15.

Press the equal sign and you should see 2.049428

This is close enough. Your interest rate is 4.9 percent.

Step 5: Combine the two rates:

Cash flow rate:	13.30 percent
Bonus rate	4.90
Total effective rate	8.20 percent

In looking at the Hodges Shopping Center Analysis Sheet (Table 10.1) on page 242, we can see numerous yields. At first glance we see that the seller will receive, after all payments on the existing financing, a balance of $33,259.50, Column H, for the time that the existing mortgage debt service remains unchanged. This amount of return, in cash, represents 13.30 percent of the original balance of the difference, Column I ($33,259.50 ÷ $250,000 = 13.30 percent). However, the balance of the difference does not diminish during the period of full existing debt service. In addition, should the mortgagor pay off the wraparound before any of the existing debt is satisfied, the holder will obtain the full $250,000 plus a bonus of built-up interest, which was earned but not received. This bonus is in addition to the interest of $33,259.50 received or retained. With this in mind then, until the outstanding difference drops below its original sum, we can treat the wraparound as an interest-only return to the mortgagee with the effective yield being this original 13.30 percent plus the bonus rate.

Therefore, when analyzing the wraparound there will be more than one rate, which you must recognize. First, there is the rate on the retained cash. This represents that sum of money that is actually received net of payments on the existing financing less amortization of the difference. In Table 10.1, the total cash received on the difference, Column F, is $33,259.50 for the term of the existing financing. This will increase when the second is retired. As there is no amortization of the difference during this period, the Retained Total, Column H, equals Column F. Since the original investment by the mortgagee is $250,000, and that balance owed remains at or above that sum during the term of the existing financing, then the retained cash is 13.30 percent for that period of time only. This rate becomes the capitalization rate of the difference.

In reference to Table 10.1, you will notice that this annual payment of retained cash changes when the second mortgage is satisfied. All calculations on wraparound effective rates must be broken down to the periods of the existing financing. When there is no amortization of the difference, which generally will occur only in the first period, the cash received will equal the retained cash. In addition to the effective rate of 13.30 percent for the retained cash, a bonus also occurs. This bonus is earned but not retained. It cannot be accurately computed until the mortgagee benefits from that sum at some time in the future.

Finding the Overall Effective Yield of a Wraparound Mortgage

The first step in finding the effective yield of the bonus is to fill out the wraparound analysis chart (Table 10.1). In looking at the amortization chart for the wraparound mortgage and the existing financing, you will be able to note the year in which the build-up of difference stops and amortization of that balance begins. This is significant since it establishes the year the bonus begins to benefit the mortgagee. In the Hodges Shopping Center Case Study (Table 10.1), this occurs in the fifteenth year. When there is a build-up or accrual of bonus, the change generally occurs when all or part of the existing financing retires. In some mortgages, the retirement of one mortgage is not sufficient to increase the payment enough to begin to reduce the difference.

Because the bonus amount is important, and because the data necessary to obtain an accurate effective rate of return is dependent on the Analysis Sheet (Table 10.1), a brief discussion of how to fill out this sheet is in order. Examine Table 10.1. Notice that there are columns A through J. These 10 columns will accommodate a wraparound and three existing mortgages. If you have a situation where you have more than three existing mortgages, you need to add D1, D2, and so on, for each additional mortgage.

Using the Wraparound Mortgage Analysis Sheet

It will be helpful if you make a copy of the Hodges Shopping Center Case Study Analysis as shown in Table 10.1 on page 242 and enlarge it. This larger copy will help you follow the steps as you go through the discussion that follows this paragraph.

COLUMN A.   The basic information needed, which pertains to the wraparound, should be filled in at the top. The term of years, annual interest rate charged, and annual payment of P&I are important for reference. At the end of period 0, you should place the face amount or original balance owed on the wraparound. In the following years, as the column extends down the page, you can put the principal balances owed at the end of each successive year. This is a purely mathematical calculation, which can be done easily with a two-memory calculator or can be obtained from an amortization schedule. It should be noted that the years shown are the end of that period, and in order to find the balance owed at the beginning of a year you need to look to the balance owed at the end of the previous year.

COLUMNS B, C, AND D.   These columns contain the same type of information as Column A, except that they are for the currently existing mortgages. Most sellers will have amortization schedules for this information. In this example D, is omitted.

COLUMN E.   This is the balance owed on the difference and the most important part of this computation. If there is no amortization of the difference, as will usually be the case in early years, this amount will grow. The total in this column represents the net payoff to the mortgagee at the end of any given year. This column will indicate when the difference peaks out and begins to amortize. Subtracting the original balance of the difference from the amount in this column at the end of any year will give you the amount of the bonus thus far accrued (to be shown in Column J).

COLUMN F.   The total cash received on the difference is the amount of net cash left over after the existing mortgage payments are deducted from the payments received on the wraparound. These payments will remain constant for the separate periods of the existing financing. If you have only one existing mortgage that is satisfied before the end of the wraparound, you will have only two periods. This column is very easy to calculate and should present no difficulty.

COLUMN G.   This column will contain amounts only for the years when the difference is declining. These amounts are found by looking at Column E. In Column E you have the amount of the difference as it increases and then declines. You need not be concerned with the increase in the Column G calculation, only the decline. The amount amortized is the amount of decline each year as seen in the reduction of Column E. When the total in Column E does begin to drop, deduct the end of the year amount from the previous year.

COLUMNS H AND I.   It is generally best to do these two columns as one calculation. The Retained Interest and Annual Interest Rate are found as follows: The Retained Interest, Column F (total cash received on difference) less Column G (difference amortized). The result will be the interest portion of the total cash actually received. In most all instances of a wraparound, the amortization, Column G, occurs late in the term.

The annual interest rate is found by dividing the interest received by: (1) In the event of 0 amortization as seen in Column G, by the original balance of the difference; (2) in the event of amortization, by the amount of the difference at the start of that year (end of the previous year). You may have a very low annual interest rate when the total cash received in the early years is just above the existing mortgage payments. Therefore, a low annual interest rate is not unusual.

COLUMN J.   This column need not be filled in completely. Its function is to show the amount of accrual of "extra lending." It represents the amount found in Column E (difference) less the original balance of the difference. You need only put in this calculation the year the difference peaks out. (The year before amortization begins on Column D, as shown in Column G. The amount you will show in Column J is the total bonus for that period. Generally, this is the only bonus you will have for a wraparound.)

In the example given in Table 10.1, you will note that on the line that corresponds to the end of the fifteenth year under Column E the difference peaks out at $512,289. Further review of the remaining payout of the wraparound and the existing financing indicates that the difference amortizes beginning the sixteenth year. The amount of the amortization, Column G, is simply found by subtracting the current year's balance from the previous year's balance. The retained interest total, Column H, is the total cash received, Column F, less the amount of amortization, Column G.

Bonus, Column J, is the accrual of the earned but not retained portion of the difference. Of course, it peaks along with the difference. This bonus can be deemed to become a benefit at the time the difference begins to amortize. In essence, the return to the mortgagee can no longer be treated as interest only, as was done as the difference grew. Instead, the annual interest rate must take into account the bonus. While the difference was growing, the annual interest rate was found by dividing the retained interest by the original difference. Now, as the mortgagee is receiving benefit from a new difference, the annual interest rates, for years when there is amortization, are found by dividing the retained interest by the balance of the difference owed at the end of the previous year. For example: At the end of the fifteenth year the difference was $512,289, Column E. During that year, the difference had grown and there was no amortization.

Because this mortgage balloons at the end of the fifteenth year, there would be the usual payments during the year, but the last payment would include the balance owned on the wrap of $915,887.00. From that amount, the existing first mortgage of $403,598 would be paid off, and the second mortgage completed its amortization during that year.

ADVANTAGES TO THE SELLER OR OTHER MORTGAGEE AND HOW TO CAPITALIZE ON THEM

- EFFECTIVE YIELD INCREASES: This is one of the most important advantages to the wraparound. Great leverages in annual return are commonplace in them. No form of secondary financing can be as productive in increasing yield for the lender.

- DEFAULT NOTICE: When a seller or other mortgagee holds a wraparound mortgage, the owner of the property makes one payment to the mortgagee. From this payment the mortgagee then causes the existing mortgage payments to be made. Because the new owner has no control over this act, his default will come at the level of the wraparound. In other words, if the new buyer falls behind in payments, the wraparound mortgagee is the first to know. Action to collect, and even foreclosure if necessary, can be made at an early date, well before the existing mortgages themselves become overdue or go far in arrears. Of course, the mortgagee can easily step in and pay down the existing financing with no difficulty in the wraparound.

This advantage is considerable. If the mortgagor is going into arrears, it is not unusual for the mortgage having the lowest priority to be the last to be paid. It is possible and quite common, for example, for a new owner of multimortgaged property in financial difficulty to let the last mortgage (the third or fourth mortgage held by your seller) to go unpaid. In the meantime, this mortgagor may keep the first mortgage current for a while, then slip into problems. However, if the seller-held mortgage is sizable, the mortgagor may keep that one current and let the first mortgages go into default. Even with provisions that lenders are to notify the other mortgagees of any default, this may not occur until a bad situation has advanced into a most impossible default.

The wraparound solves this problem nicely. The buyer's broker in the transaction can casually point out the priority of a fourth mortgage to the seller and show him or her the possibility of not knowing about economic problems the new buyer is having until it is too late. With the wraparound he still has the same position against the property, but he gets all the money and makes the payments himself.

- THE SELLING TOOL WORKS FOR THE SELLER: When you are marketing a property and have the ability to provide what appears to be an excellent mortgage, at terms under current rates and years longer than those available at local lenders, you have a good advantage in selling the property. This advantage goes to the seller. It is important to remember that you need not offer alternatives. A buyer may well understand the leverage of the interest on the existing mortgages and may not want to have that advantage pass on to the seller or some other party. In this event, he or she may ask the seller to hold secondary paper at a nominal interest rate and take over or assume the existing mortgages at their lower rate. The fact that the seller will hold a wraparound, however, should become the new financing offered. Hence, the comparison that a buyer must make is not between the wraparound and normal assumption of the existing mortgages and secondary paper, but between the terms offered on it and the conventional terms available at local lenders. The wraparound will compete favorably in almost any market, providing the existing financing can be wrapped around and there is a spread between the constant rates of the existing debt and that of the wraparound. This spread should be in favor of the holder of the wraparound, which should have a lower constant rate even if the interest rate was higher. In other words, when the existing debt is at 8 percent and the wrap is at 9 percent, actual interest charged the overall cost to the buyer is at a lower constant due to the longer payout term of the wrap. However, there are exceptions to almost any statement. If there was a high contract rate, say 12 percent on a first mortgage that would be paid off in a year or two, it would have a very high constant rate, whereas other mortgages in that package could average things out to a more favorable balance. Look at the combined effect of the existing and not any specific mortgage in the package. Do, however, be willing to accept a short term high constant mortgage in the package of existing debt if it goes away quickly.

In marketing a property with the wraparound, you will find it easy to make this comparison: "Mr. Buyer, we have provided terms which are far better than those currently available at the local lenders. This fact, the ease in closing on the property due to this mortgage, and no points are to your advantage." Therefore, while this is a seller's advantage it is a buyer's advantage as well.

• MAINTAIN INSTALLMENT SALE: The wraparound mortgage has a most important use that has nothing to do with leverage on rates or even its use as a marketing tool. When a property that has a very low basis is sold, there is a capital gain circumstance that can often be costly. If the owner of the property for sale has mortgages above the basis, simply to receive a sale, with no money down, can cause tax to be due. For example: Barkley owned a small office building for nearly 20 years. The current tax basis is only $50,000 (the amount over which a sale price would be potential capital gain and taxable as such). However, Barkley had placed new financing on the property a few years ago and currently owes $300,000 on it. Because of this "refinance situation" he has $250,000 of debt on the property that is in excess of his tax basis. There is nothing wrong with this, as pulling tax-free money out of a property by refinancing can be a sound strategy. However, as you will see, it can create a complication to this deal.

Barkley was negotiating with a buyer who said he was to pay $500,000 if he could put $100,000 down and close. Barkley determined that he would have a $425,000 adjusted gain in the sale and over $140,000 in capital gains tax. To make that sale would require him to come out-of-pocket over $40,000, plus fees, commissions, and other closing costs. However, Barkley's accountant pointed out there was a problem in the mechanics of the deal. Because Barkley was mortgaged over his basis, if he had a conventional sale he would be relieved of the debt, and the IRS would want him to pay tax at his earned income rate on the $250,000 excess that he put into his pocket at the time of the refinance. The IRS is not concerned what Barkley did with the money as long as it was used for a legal purpose.

A wraparound mortgage in the form of a contract for deed was established, in the amount of $400,000, payable over 20 years at a nominal interest rate. The contract for deed was a provision that required the buyer to meet certain obligations to the deal in order to have the property deeded to him. The agreement provided that the buyer make payments to Barkley for a period of time, at the end of which the deed would be recorded to the buyer's name (or any other name designated by the buyer). Because Barkley was still on the mortgage and the buyer did not assume the liability, Barkley was not relieved of that amount of debt. The income that came in over the term of the wraparound allowed Barkley to maintain an installment sale since he did not receive more than 30 percent of the principal of the transaction in any year. The capital gains tax was still there, but now it was payable over the term as though a normal installment sale had taken place.

Using a technique such as this will require careful review by your tax advisors. It is important that they have a good understanding of your goals. Your other income and expenses may suggest that a different technique would be better for you. A similar result as that shown above might have been a lease option, where the would-be buyer leases the property for a few years, then exercises the option to buy. In the meantime between the start of the lease and the option to buy, Barkley might be able to establish an IRC 1031 treatment exchange in a proper format that would avoid any immediate tax payment at all. Another direction would be to gift percentages of interest to other parties, say his children, or grandchildren so that by the time the option to purchase came around they would be the fully vested owners of the property.

ADVANTAGES TO A BUYER OF PURCHASING WITH A WRAPAROUND

- THE BEST TERMS IN TOWN: The wraparound is so flexible that a high effective yield can be passed on to the mortgagee even though the buyer has a better rate and years than available elsewhere. The buyer saves on points, and when given no alternative of closing with assumption of the existing financing and the seller holding normal secondary paper, he or she will choose the wraparound. Of course, the wraparound can also offer better terms than assumption and secondary paper. If the existing financing has a low interest rate, but also a short term to go, the annual payment may be just about as high as the buyer can pay or the property can stand. To place on top of that a second mortgage of even the most modest annual payment may be more than either the buyer or the property will pay. The wraparound has the capability of having a very low retained interest on the difference. The build-up of the bonus and its later recovery together with a greater yield are unique to this form of financing. This factor can save many transactions that have a short balloon in one of the existing mortgages by having that mortgage amortized out of the total wraparound and carrying forward the new difference to a later year.

Most buyers are cash flow conscious. They may not pay much attention to the term of the mortgage. As long as they derive the desired cash flow yield on their cash that has been invested into a well-leveraged situation, the 30-year mortgage is simply a mortgage that is 10 years more than a 20-year mortgage, and has a lower payment due each month on the same amount borrowed. When an investor is looking at how much cash he or she gets on the down payment, then the wraparound can keep the debt service at a more constant level, and often much lower than other forms of mortgages.

- INCREASE CASH FLOW: Because the wraparound can provide a lower total annual payment (even though over a longer term) than a combination of existing financing and secondary financing, the advantage to a buyer in the case of income property can be considerable. A property with an NOI of $200,000 and existing annual debt service of $155,000 provides a cash flow of $50,000. If the investor demands a 10 percent cash flow yield (10% interest return on the cash invested) he or she can pay $450,000 cash to the existing financing. However, the seller may want $600,000 to the same amount of existing financing. If the combined cash down and balance owed is within the fair market value range and the seller is firm on the price, the wraparound can provide the answer. The question to answer here is: What total amount of wraparound, at what interest rate, for how long, will cover the existing mortgage and its constant annual payment? Assume that the amount is $1 million at 8 percent for approximately 10 years, and as the annual payment of principal and interest is $150,000, the constant annual payment is 15 percent. Also assume that the investor will pay up to $450,000 cash down. Can you propose a contract that would fit those criteria?

WORK SHEET FOR THE CASH FLOW PROBLEM

A. Minimum price	$1,600,000
B. Maximum cash to invest	− 450,000
C. Amount to be held as wraparound	$1,150,000
D. NOI	200,000
E. Cash return demanded (Line B × Interest rate demanded)	−45,000
F. Amount available for debt service	$ 155,000
G. Constant annual payment percentage (Line F ÷ Line C)	13.479 percent

H. Minimum years possible (total years of remaining payout   10 years on existing mortgage)
  I. Nominal rate on highest existing mortgage   8 percent
  J. Possible terms shown below (1, 2, 3, 4)

	(1)	(2)	(3)	(4)
Nominal rate	8 percent (same as I)	8¾ percent	9½ percent	10 percent
Years	12	12.5	13.5	14.5
Constant shown	13.270 percent	13.471 percent	13.450 percent	13.353 percent
Annual payment	$152,605.00	$154,916.50	$154,675.00	$153.559.60

• EASE OF PAYMENT: In multimortgaged property, nothing can be more annoying than to have to make several payments to different lenders each month. Keeping track of the amortization of each is a problem. With the wraparound, however, the buyer has only one payment to make and can look to one amortization schedule. The form of payment is very important, as this is the area where most objections arise. Because the buyer does not directly make the payments on the existing mortgages, he or she may be most concerned that those payments will in fact be made. There have been many cases of wraparounds where the buyer faithfully made the monthly payment, only to find that the seller, who was collecting payments, did not pay any of the existing mortgages. This is a nasty situation, and people who have experienced it have been needlessly hurt.

PAYMENTS SHOULD ALWAYS BE MADE TO AN ESCROW ACCOUNT. When you set up a wraparound mortgage it is imperative that the payments on it be made to an escrow agency, or collection agency. The agency would then make the existing mortgage payments, collect for taxes and insurance, and disperse the balance to the mortgagee. This makes the maintenance of the wraparound relatively easy for all parties concerned, and assures the mortgagor that the existing payments, which should go to the existing mortgages, are made. This escrow agency, either a commercial bank, savings and loan association, or other third-party service, should be paid by the mortgagee, but it is not unusual that this cost is shared by the mortgagor as well.

HOW TO PROTECT THE MORTGAGOR AND THE MORTGAGEE IN THE ESCROW AGREEMENT. The escrow agent will only do as instructed, so it is important that he or she has complete and comprehensive instructions. The factors that need to be covered in this escrow agreement will be:

• HOW THE FEE IS PAID FOR THE ESCROW SERVICE: The escrow agent will normally deduct his or her fee from the amounts collected. If the mortgagor is sharing this cost, his portion of the fee must be added to the total wraparound payment.

- COLLECTIONS FOR TAXES AND ESCROWS COVERED IN THE WRAPAROUND OR EXISTING MORTGAGES: A first mortgage may have a constant monthly payment added each year to the amortization, which accrues annual taxes, insurance, and other assessments. It is imperative that these provisions be made a part of the wraparound document, and that the escrow agent is instructed to make those payments as well. In the event of a future assessment, or changes in taxes or insurance that would alter this escrow collection, the wraparound should provide for those changes and the agent instructed on how to notify the mortgagor of these additions or subtractions to the total payment.

- PREPAYMENT PROVISIONS: Careful analysis of prepayment provisions in existing mortgages should be made and incorporated in the wraparound. The holder of the wraparound should provide an equal pro rata reduction of both the existing financing as well as the wraparound for all prepayments. For example, if the outstanding balance at the time of the prepayment is shown to be 80 percent to existing financing and 20 percent to the difference, then a prepayment of $200,000 would be divided by that ratio. The 80 percent would then be prepaid to the holder of the existing financing. Of course, the entire 100 percent is reduced from the wraparound balance, and new calculations would occur. The prepayment in full is the same as a balloon with regard to the effective yield rate.

- GRACE PERIOD: There should be a shorter grace period on the wraparound than on the existing financing. This will assist in notification of default ahead of due dates on the existing financing. When there is a very short grace period on any of the existing financing, it may be desirable to allow a build up on one period to accrue in the escrow account in order to advance the lead time on default on the existing financing. For example: If a second mortgage has a 10-day grace period, the mortgagee may find it to his or her advantage to allow collections, less disbursements, to build up to an amount equal to one period payment on that second. If it is a monthly payment, then the grace period allowed to the mortgagee is now one month plus 10 days.

- AUTOMATIC FORECLOSURE BY UNDERLYING MORTGAGES: In a multimortgaged property, the first mortgage may have a provision which provides that it will automatically be in default and become subject to immediate foreclosure in the event that any secondary lender file foreclosure proceedings. There is no real justification in this, but some lenders may have this provision in their loans. It is far more important that the inferior loans have this provision, in the event the existing mortgagee or superior mortgagees file foreclosure. As the mortgagee in the wraparound pays the existing mortgages, he or she knows when a default will occur. However, since the mortgagee has the ability to make the existing payments on the existing mortgages, he or she can keep them current even though the wraparound goes into default. Should the mortgagee file foreclosure proceedings against the mortgagor, and should the existing mortgage have this automatic foreclosure provision in their loan, they too may file foreclosure, even though they are current. In this event, the escrow agent must be instructed not to file such proceedings without obtaining an agreement from the existing mortgage lenders that they will not file as long as they keep current. Most lenders, even if they have this provision of automatic foreclosure, will go along with such a request.

• MAINTAIN INTEGRATED ACCOUNTS: The escrow agent should keep one account for the funds. The account should be in the name of the mortgagee. If the agent is a bank or other lending institution with savings accounts or checking accounts, then all the funds collected should be paid into that account. Then the agent will pay out the funds required for the existing financing. Have your lawyer draw up this escrow agreement. It is a very important part of the wraparound process and is highly recommended. This is not a necessity, yet to have a wraparound without collections made by a third party can be less than prudent for the mortgagor.

Unique Problems for the Third-Party Lender

When a wraparound mortgage is given to a third-party lender, such as a commercial bank or mortgage company, some unique problems occur. Take this situation as an example: Midwest Central Bank examines a potential lending situation that will involve a wraparound mortgage. They have concluded that by lending new money to a buyer of property and wrapping around the existing mortgage they will leverage their yield to above 12 percent. Assume that the new money they lend is $100,000. At the end of the first year of the loan they will receive their total investment of $100,000 plus $12,000. The mortgage they are wrapping around has a one-time payment as follows:

	Face Amount	*Rate*	*Term (Years)*	*Due at End of Term*
(1) Existing mortgage	$400,000	7	1	$428,000
(2) New money	+100,000	?	1	?
(3) Wraparound total	$500,000	8	1	$540,000

Total principal and interest return on wraparound (end of first year)	$540,000
Total payout, First mortgage	−428,000
Total principal and return on new money	$112,000
Original principal on new money	−100,000
Total return on new money	$ 12,000
Effective rate of return on new money (end of first year)	12 percent

The third-party lender has lent only $100,000 in this transaction. The lender has not had any obligation to pay the original first mortgage of $400,000. If he or she makes the wraparound loan with the existing owner and original mortgagor on the existing mortgage, or a new owner that has assumed the first mortgage, he or she is advancing only new money with no liability on the existing financing. Courts have contended that in these situations the return to the lender is 12 percent and if the sum is usurious the loan is not valid.

In the wraparound mortgages we have concluded it is possible to leverage a yield much higher than the 12 percent shown in this example. Nonetheless, in some instances a 12 percent return may be usurious. Therefore, this examination of return must be considered a potential problem for the third-party lender. The real advantages for a third-party lender are the leverage and the increased yield. If in making these loans the courts determine that usury is present, the loan can be null and void and the lender face loss of the sum lent and have a penalty placed on him or her as well.

The face rate of the wraparound is only 8 percent, below usury. However, since the lender has no obligation to pay the existing financing—no risk as it were—the actual yield may be considered, by a court, the effective rate of return.

Usury on Wraparound Loans by Third Parties

The actual answer to this is not clearly defined by the courts. However, it does seem that if the third-party lender can place him or herself in the same shoes, so to speak, as a seller holding a wraparound, then this problem can be averted. To do this will require the lender to assume the full obligation of the existing financing being wrapped around. When the lender has liability against the existing loans, then he or she may well be in the same position the seller would be in by holding the wraparound.

It is hoped that in the near future this matter of possible usury on third-party loans will be more clearly defined by the courts. In the meantime, third-party lenders must accept the advice of their legal advisors on this matter.

Calculating Interest Earned for Annual Income Accounting

It is necessary to know how to account for interest earned in the wraparound for income tax purposes. In essence, the interest earned on the wraparound mortgages will be the interest to be reported as income. Deductions of interest to be reported as income and deductions of interest paid against the underlying existing mortgages will offset that total interest as long as the tax laws permit deduction of interest. For example:

Total interest collected at end of first year on a $500,000 existing wraparound at 8% per year	$40,000
Total interest paid out on existing mortgage, assuming a $400,000 existing mortgage at 7% per year	−28,000
Net difference	$12,000
Income to be reported	$40,000
Interest deduction	−28,000
Taxable to the wraparound lender	$12,000

Note: Watch tax laws that may limit or remove interest deductions on real estate mortgages. If your situation is affected by such laws, then your use of the wraparound may be reduced.

Identifying an Ideal Wraparound Mortgage Situation

There will be definite signs that should indicate to you if a situation is right for the use of the wraparound mortgage. Your ability to recognize these signs will aid you in reaching the conclusion that the wraparound will help achieve the goals of your client. Listed next are some of the primary signs that you will encounter. At times they will present themselves alone, while at other times in combination with each other:

- EXISTING LOAN CONSTANT ANNUAL PAYMENT PERCENTAGE RELATIONSHIP TO MAXIMUM LOAN POTENTIAL. Take a look at the total annual payment of the existing mortgages. Then find the constant payment percentage this represents of the total loan potential. If this constant is below a normal loan constant, you have a prime candidate for a wraparound. For example the total loan payment on three existing mortgages is $15,000 per year starting the first year. The property is priced at $225,000; therefore, a normal loan may be 80 percent of that amount or $180,000. The $15,000 existing loan payment represents 8.33 percent of the total loan potential. A look at constants available in the market for new money may show an 11 percent annual constant to be reasonable. The spread of 2.67 percent in constants for the first year is tremendous. In fact, a spread of only 0.5 percent would be sufficient to warrant a further look to see if the wraparound would be desirable. If you find that the constant annual payment on the existing financing is higher than the present market constant, a wraparound may not be effective unless there are other circumstances present. One of these was discussed earlier: the presence of one or more very short-term existing mortgages that have increased the present debt service, but will shortly disappear as they are paid off.

- A FORCED WRAPAROUND. If you have existing financing that cannot be assumed and a refinancing of the property is not possible due to market conditions or economic cost, then the wraparound sign is very strong.

- REINVESTMENT GOAL OF THE SELLER. The leverage gained on the yield may be most attractive to the seller, and could be a primary sign that the wraparound should be considered. Keep in mind that the constant spread indicated in the first item (previous) should be favorable for the leverage to occur.

Using the Wraparound to Close More Transactions

You should have a good understanding by now what the wraparound will do, should do, and can do. The ability to take this tool and apply it to the selling of property will depend on whether you can sell the concept to the parties involved. The proficiency with which you accomplish this will therefore depend on how comfortable you feel in dealing with this tool. I suggest that the first step is to take several properties you presently have listed and restructure the existing financing via wraparound to see what happens to their marketability. If you see that you can offer a property with better financing and increase the cash flow, you are on the way to having a better inventory and making more sales.

You will have only relative difficulty in selling this concept to the buyer. After all, this depends on the alternatives offered. If he or she can buy with the wraparound, instead of conventional financing, and the wraparound offers better terms than the present market, then the buyer will go with it.

The seller must also see the advantages it has to offer the buyer. This chapter has given you all the ammunition to make that part of the sale easier than it might have been otherwise.

The wraparound is a fine tool in the hands of the real estate broker or associate. It is most effective as a selling tool, and while third-party loans may become more frequent in the future, the major lenders will continue to shy away from this format. Do not let that aspect dismay you, however, since the third-party lender has problems that are unique to the wraparound that the seller does not have. Unfortunately, however, the power third parties exert in the lending area has been to hold down wider use of the wraparound by sellers and brokers.

Remember: The wraparound is merely a tool. It has limitations and drawbacks. The return to the mortgagee is often postponed until the future, and though the yield is leveraged upward, the funds may not be available for use when they are needed. This factor should be considered as the major disadvantage to the wraparound from a seller's point of view.

EXAMPLE: CLOSING A TRANSACTION WITH A WRAPAROUND.   The following is one more example of using the wraparound to close a transaction. In this case Rodger is the anxious seller. Take a look at what often happens when a wraparound mortgage is prepaid. In this example, Rodger sold his office building to Alex for a total price of $1,500,000. At the time of the sale there was a first mortgage in the amount of $700,000 that had been put into place when Rodger had acquired the property 10 years earlier. This mortgage, with a monthly payment of $7,770, still had 10 years of amortization to its final satisfaction and was at 6 percent interest rate, which was slightly below the current market rate for new mortgages, and substantially below the rate generally offered for secondary financing. Assume that Alex wanted to refinance the total purchase so that he could purchase the building using around $300,000 of his own cash. This would require a total of $1,200,000 in new financing (plus mortgage origination and closing costs).

The best that Alex could obtain was from a local commercial bank and their offer was $1,150,000 at 9 percent on a 20-year amortization schedule. This would require a monthly payment of $10,347.13. That part of the offer was okay, even though it meant Alex would have to come up with a total of around $400,000 cash to cover all the costs.

However, the killer provision was the bank wanted the mortgage to balloon at the end of 10 years. That balloon payment would be $816,824.55, and Alex did not want to be forced to refinance the property at that time.

Rodger saw that there was a good chance that Alex would walk away from the deal unless he came up with a way for the deal to work. Rodger suggested the wraparound mortgage with the following terms. He would hold a wraparound in the amount of $1,100,000 and the total that Rodger would have to come up with would be $400,000. The mortgage payment would be $10,253.83 per month on a 20-year amortization and, instead of 10-year balloon, Rodger would offer 15 years. The payment on the slightly smaller mortgage amount included interest at 9.5 percent. As Alex was more interested in the effect on the NOI, the deal closed on that basis.

Therefore, the wraparound held by Rodger was $1,100,000 and consisted of the existing first of $700,000 and the difference held by Rodger of $400,000. (The other $400,000 paid by Alex was the down payment of the deal.) Alex had a monthly payment of $10,253.83, which would total $123,045.96 per year. At the end of 15 years the wrap mortgage was scheduled to balloon in the amount of $488,238.86.

However, events have a way of following a different course than originally planned, and five years later Alex sold the building for $2,250,000. The buyer at that time refinanced the transaction and Rodger's wraparound was paid off. Let us review the mortgage situation and see how it ended up when Alex sold the property.

The payment schedule in the wraparound (looking at annual amounts only) is shown below:

End of Year	Amount Alex Paid ($)	Existing First Mortgage Payment ($)	Amount Rodger Kept ($)	Year End Balance of Existing First Mortgage ($)	Year End Balance of Wraparound Mortgage ($)	Difference to Alex ($)
1	123,045.96	93,240.00	29,805.96			
2	123,045.96	93,240.00	29,805.96			
3	123,045.96	93,240.00	29,805.96			
4	123,045.96	93,240.00	29,805.96			
5	123,045.96	93,240.00	29,805.96	401,896.50	981,932.49	580,035.00
Total annual payments to Rodger			149,029.80			
+ Difference payoff			+580,035.00			
Grand total to Rodger			729,064.80			

Rodger was able to end up with a good deal by using the wraparound, and Alex also benefited from the events. How would you have handled this situation? Can you calculate what yield Rodger obtained from the leverage of the 9.5 percent interest on the wrap over the 6 percent of the existing first?

As you can see, the wraparound mortgage is a versatile form of financing. It works well for both the buyer and the seller when the situation warrants it. You could use it with the blanket mortgage format by encumbering more than one property when the mortgagee requires additional security.

Sellers will find the wraparound to be especially desirable in providing them additional yield on the debt they hold when selling a property. The key here is to make sure that the existing debt allows use of the wraparound. In reality, there is no need to ask the holders of the existing debt this question as long as the mortgage documents do not contain provisions that prohibit secondary financing. If such a provision were to exist in any of the underlying existing debt, permission to use any form of secondary financing would be required. Say, for example, that there were two existing mortgages that had a relatively low interest rate as compared to the rate you could actually establish for a wraparound. As the seller in this situation, you would want to use the wraparound format because it would be able to give you a better return by leveraging over the existing rate.

Because you need not ask the existing mortgagees for subordination to their position (first or second position), your third position within the wraparound remains behind their rights to lien the property in the event of a foreclosure. So, all you need ask for is the right to hold a third mortgage (in this hypothetical example). Disclose to them the amount of that mortgage, but it is not necessary for you to tell them that it will be in the format of a wraparound. Naturally, there may be no reason not to tell them this, but they might block your attempt to leverage over their rate and ask you to modify your terms with them.

Chapter 11

THE SALE-LEASEBACK

An Investment Tool
That Works for Both
Buyer and Seller

GOAL OF THIS CHAPTER

This chapter is designed to expand your knowledge of mixed-use strategies that can be effective in reaching certain goals. One such tool, which is widely used in large real estate transactions, is the sale-leaseback technique of selling a property then leasing it back from the new owner. However, any size transaction can work with this strategy, and this chapter expands on the usual methods used. Investors should always think out of the box and discover new ways to implement strategies to maximize the benefits that can be obtained.

You have already seen several other financing and investing tools and strategies that work to benefit both the buyer and seller at the same time. These win/win techniques all have their special place in your quest to attain certain goals, and depending on how you use them, your benefit may not be at a cost to the other party of the transaction. However, as anyone who has hit his or her thumb with a hammer while driving a nail can understand, any tool can be used improperly. Aim at the right place, but look at another destination and you can end up with a very sore thumb. So, pay close attention to some of the pitfalls in the use of this fantastic technique that is becoming very popular with certain types of investors.

DEFINITION OF A SALE-LEASEBACK

A sale-leaseback is the sale of an interest in realty and the subsequent leasing back of that same realty. For example, Frank owns a hardware store. He is doing very well with the business, but needs capital to expand. He owns the real estate free and clear of any debt,

259

as well as the business, so he decides to sell the property—land and building—to generate the needed capital, and to lease this property back. This act will free up both the capital he originally invested in the property, as well as any appreciation he may recover in the sale. Even though he will have a capital gain in that sale, he has sufficient losses from the sale of other long-term assets that he can take advantage of those long-term losses to offset all or most of his potential gain. He also knows that because he will be both the seller and the tenant, he can make minor adjustments in the sale price and terms to adjust the sale price and the future rent he will be paying.

The sale-leaseback is one of the best tools in moving capital from real estate assets to other uses. It can also support a sales price for the seller when the actual use is worth more than the actual ownership. To get the most benefits from this tool, the seller/tenant must either need to generate capital in a hurry and not have other viable or more effective ways to do that, or have a clear and precise investment plan that will be able to take advantage of the benefits of this strategy. The ultimate success in this quest depends on the actual terms arrived at by the negotiations between the seller and the buyer of the property.

This form of financing may begin as a sale. Frank's investment plan is to franchise his hardware store business, and eventually be out of the day-to-day operation, and simply oversee dozens or (if he is lucky, hundreds) of "Frank's Hardware" stores around the country. Franchise-operated businesses often lease their real estate because it is the business that is important and ownership of bricks-and-mortar and dirt less so. A seller is attracted to this idea and agrees to lease back the property being sold. Sometimes this leaseback can merely be a move to entice the buyer into the transaction. Some investors may see that as a less attractive investment so Frank's business plan makes sense.

Consider Trade-Offs between Lease Terms and Purchase Price and Terms

Leaseback negotiations can jockey back and forth between the price to buy and the amount of rent the seller, now tenant, will pay. The buyer has a targeted investment yield that he wants to achieve. However, these targets have a range of terms that will work to that goal. Frank, as a seller, knows that his pro forma must work if he is going to sell franchises. Future store operators do not want to be saddled with excessive rent, and they will need to be able to find locations for their new franchise stores that also fit the pattern of the original franchise store.

In its most effective use, the sale-leaseback is a technique that allows the seller to generate capital by selling the property, while allowing the seller to maintain the use of the property.

The property being sold can be all of the property. This means it can be land and buildings, or it may be just the buildings or just the land. Each aspect of the sale-leaseback can have different long-range results, depending on what portion of the realty is sold and then leased back. Can you think of other things that Frank could have done to reach his goal? Consider several other strategies also using the sale-leaseback scenario. First, we need to understand precisely what is his goal, and how much capital does he believe he will need to attain it? In addition, what are the existing amounts of equity that Frank has at his disposal? Remember, financing is the movement of equity. If the creation of a leasehold asset instead of a fee simple asset does not balance out, then the form used to achieve the result may not have been effectively used. The balancing factor may be cash, or other benefits received or given up.

FRANK'S GOALS AND EQUITIES AT HIS DISPOSAL

Real estate owned:	
Land value	$120,000
Building value	500,000
Cash on hand	+220,000
Total equity	$840,000
Capital needed to expand to two new locations	$300,000

This $300,000 is over and above his present $200,000. His original plan was as indicated earlier. Sell the land and buildings and lease it back. However, to do that and only generate $300,000 of cash seems a waste. What can he do?

EXPAND ON FRANK'S OPTIONS. Why not do the following: Create two leases. One is a land lease between Frank's Hardware, and Frank LLC (Limited Liability Corporation). This lease could be for any amount but because Frank may want to sell his hardware store at some future date, he wanted to make the lease realistic and balance out the equity with an upside for him at a future date. Therefore, he sets up the lease at an annual rent of $12,000 per year with a cost of living index adjustment every year. The lease is also triple net (NNN), which means that the lessee (Frank's Hardware) pays taxes (on the land) and provides full liability insurance for $5,000,000 for the lessor (Frank LLC). As long as Frank continues to own both entities, the rent payment is simply a movement from one of his pockets to another. He now has the flexibility, however, of opening the door to move equities to other family members by way of gifting (or selling) interests in either the hardware store or the Limited Liability Partnership. He then offers the building for sale (i.e., on the land owned by Frank LLC). The price of the building is $300,000 cash net to Frank Senior (owner of the building). Frank Senior (really Frank himself) sells the building and takes back a $200,000 first mortgage that has a provision that indicates that this mortgage is inferior to the land lease (owned by Frank LLC). The sale is made to Enterprise Ownership, who gets title to the leasehold interest of the building, subject to the land lease they must pay to Frank LLC, and the rent they will collect from Frank's Hardware (and, of course, the long-term lease that is owned by Frank Senior in the operation of the business). Now I know all this sounds confusing, but look at the following outline to see how this shakes out and what flexibility remains. You will see how Frank benefits.

Stage One. Frank Senior owns a hardware store and the land and building that goes with it.

Stage Two. Frank Senior owns a leasehold interest in the hardware store's facilities.

Frank LLC owns the land and collects rent from Enterprise Ownership (who owns the building subject to the land lease obligation).

Frank Senior and Mrs. Frank Senior collect payments on the $200,000 mortgage paid by Enterprise Ownership—say, $20,000 a year interest only for 10 years then a balloon payment in full.

Frank's Hardware has a leasehold interest in the Frank's Hardware facilities, and pays a rent of $60,000 a year and all expenses of taxes and maintenance of the real estate.

Enterprise Ownership owns the facilities subject to their paying the lease on the land, and the right to collect rents from Frank's Hardware. Say the rent they collect is $60,000 a year. From that, they deduct the rent they pay to Frank LLC of $12,000 and the mortgage payment they pay to Mr. and Mrs. Frank Senior of $20,000 a year. Their cash flow is $60,000 less ($12,000 + $20,000) = $28,000 NNN (remember the land lease and building lease are both triple net so all operational costs and maintenance are paid by Frank's Hardware). Because Enterprise Ownership paid $300,000 down to purchase the facility and their net cash flow is $28,000, they have a demand yield on their capital of 9.333 percent. There is a slight negative leverage on the debts, which costs them 10 percent; but remember debt service is paid by the tenant (it is a part of the rent).

Can you think of something that Enterprise Ownership should have done to improve their situation?

Why not negotiate the right to buy the land at a future date? If that were to coincide with their balloon date of the $200,000 mortgage, even at an escalated price they should easily be able to refinance sufficiently to pay off both the mortgage and the land lease.

The emphasis of this chapter is to show you how to use this important technique, as both a buyer and a seller.

STRUCTURE OF THE LAND LEASEBACK

The most basic sale-leaseback is when the land has no buildings or whatever is constructed is going to be removed to make way for a new development. In this kind of situation, the land will be leased by the new tenant, say a new supermarket or a drugstore, and they will build their new facility on that leased land. Often, when they are up and running, they will sell that package to a new investor who will own the building (subject to a ground lease) and in turn lease the package of land and building to the store operator. As you can see, there are a number of interesting combinations that can work here. Many mixed-use development projects, such as large office complexes that also have residential components as well as retail "out parcels," can offer investors or operators a multiple of opportunities. Buy, lease, lease with option to buy, and so on can use many of the different forms of ownership thus far mentioned in this book. All of them can be used in the same project.

It is very common in many parts of the world to have leased land under many types of buildings. These land leases generally began with a sale to one party, who then leases the land back to the seller. Over the years, the owners of the leasehold change, but the lease remains in effect. Naturally, all leases are unique and it is rare that any two leases will have identical terms and conditions. As with any contract, just about everything is open for negotiation. This gives both parties to the agreement flexibility in tailoring the terms and conditions to fit very specific goals.

In all leasebacks of the land, the fee simple title to the realty does not belong to the lessee. All the lessee owns is the leasehold interest. If the leasehold is later sold, the interest passed on is merely the remainder rights in the underlying lease. Keep in mind that some leases may contain provisions that limit this transferability, and it is possible that a new owner may not have all of the rights that the original lessee had. In addition, if the previous lessee was in default, or in any way caused a breach in the lease contract, there may be no rights to be transferred.

Fee simple title is the absolute form of ownership rights of any real estate interest and is held by the grantee or heir of those rights from the previous owner. Those rights remain with that individual or individuals (including an entity), until sold or otherwise passed on to another owner. A leasehold interest has fewer rights than this and has a finite life that is defined by the lease. When the termination date or renewal date arrives, its continuation will depend on the circumstances contained within the lease itself. If there is a renewal condition that must be met, the lessee can opt to abandon the lease and endure any penalties, and to attempt to renegotiate another set of terms altogether. The leasehold interest may be transferable, provided that the lease contains provisions for this event. Generally, this is something that most lessees will insist on, even though the usual provision that both parties can live with is something like: "the Lessor agrees that the lessee may sell or sublet the premises to which this lease pertains; however, the Lessor must agree to this sale or subtenant and the Lessor agrees that said approval will not be unreasonably withheld." Be sure that your lawyer has drafted a successor provision that covers you (as lessor or lessee, depending on which side of the fee you stand).

Leasehold interests then are what the tenant owns. If the lease is a good one, and the cost of the rent no greater than what actual ownership of the property would require, then the value increase or decline of the real estate will be directly transferred to the value of the leasehold, less a calculation for the loss of all that value at some predictable future time.

Clearly, if you were leasing a 10-acre tract for a fixed rent of $5,000 a month, and over the term of the lease that land has become very expensive and as a shopping center site would command rent of $50,000 a month, your leasehold interest could jump from $600,000 or so to $6,000,000. That is based on an investor yield of 10 percent of the value of the land. However, because there is a finite termination of most leases, the longer the lease, the more valuable that ultimate leasehold interest. If your lease at $5,000 a month ends in two years, then you may discover that your leasehold value is not really much at all. It will take that long just to get approval for the shopping center to be developed anyway.

The terms of a lease to a tenant can also create difficulties for the lessee to obtain other or additional financing. Even though some lenders will make leasehold loans, the terms of the lease will dictate whether or not a loan will be offered. If the lease is unsubordinated, that is, the owner of the fee retains a first lein position in the land, he or she would be ahead of any mortgage and it may become difficult to obtain long-term financing. In such a situation, it may become difficult to obtain long-term financing. Even having said that, everything is possible and the amount and length of the loan term and the strength of the borrower will generally be the factors that allow the lender to proceed with such a loan.

Subordinated land leases should not present a major problem provided that the term of the lease is beyond the term of the loan. Some lenders may require longer terms than others so the leasehold owner in need of capital must be ready to shop around for a loan. The following section provides more information about subordinated loans.

The Subordination Factor in a Land Lease

Subordination is an event where one person gives up certain rights to another. In mortgages, this takes many different forms and is not solely an event where there are leasebacks. A simple example is when a seller of a property holds a purchase money mortgage (the type and rank are not critical in this example), and allows the buyer to put a new first mortgage ahead of this financing. In doing this, the new owner of the property can borrow additional financing (if someone will lend to him or her in this situation) and that new loan will come ahead of the seller held purchase money mortgage. In land leases, the lessor (owner of the land) agrees to subordinate the fee simple right to the land by allowing the lessee to obligate the title to the land as security to financing. By doing this, should there be a default on the mortgage, the mortgagee could look to the real estate as collateral for that loan.

A lessor who has allowed subordination and the mortgage, which is now ahead of the lessor's rights, will be forced to make a difficult decision if it goes into default and foreclosure. Pay off the debt, or otherwise continue to make the payments, or potentially lose the real estate completely. Naturally, if the tenant failed to meet the rent payments as well, there would be a legal right for the lessor to seek remedy in court. However, what if the tenant has flown to Brazil or Namibia or just doesn't have a dime to his or her name? One thing for sure, I doubt that lessor would agree to any form of subordination in the future.

Because subordination can be an essential part of any lease, it is critical that all the parties to this transaction—the real estate owner, the lessee, and the lender—pay close attention to what is going on. Most conventional or institutional lenders will not lend on leased land without the title being subordinated to the mortgage. For good reasons, many landowners are reluctant to lease land to someone who requires the title to be subordinated to new financing. Nonetheless, there are thousands of subordinated land leases in the United States and, for the most part, they are viable transactions. However, there can be substantial risk for a property owner to give up first position right to the title. This chapter shows you these risks and steps you can take to lessen them.

When a lessee decides to develop a property he or she is leasing, there will be five ways to obtain development funds:

1. Use all cash with no lien.
2. Obtain a loan without property in question as the security.
3. Find a lender who will treat the leasehold as a fee simple.
4. Obtain a loan with something else as security.
5. Get the owner of the property to agree to subordinate to the required financing.

Review the first way, many builders do just that. They build with their own cash. It may be they have leased the land with options to purchase, and so they build without having to pay the cash needed to buy the land. They pay the nominal rent during construction, and later when the building is finished, obtain a mortgage, pay off the land by exercising an option to buy, and move on to another project. This is done in single-family housing where the builder can and does build the house quickly, and then sells it before many of the outstanding bills on it come due. In those cases, the overall cash outlay by the developer is not as great as if he or she had bought the land for cash.

The second situation requires the lessee to find a lender who will make the loan without taking the real estate (either leasehold interest or fee simple interest) as security. This kind of loan is possible to find, depending on the amount of the loan, and the strength of the borrower. It may be possible to pledge a chattel; that is, give the lender a lien right against something that is not real estate. This might be inventory, or other assets. Any such loans would have no lien against the real estate.

The third situation is more likely, if the lease warrants it. There are lenders who approach the leasehold interest as being similar to fee simple. In some areas of the world, a long-term lease of such a time period as to be beyond the normal life span of the building planned may be accepted as being the same as completed ownership. Some leases that have been in effect for many years have such reasonable lease terms that it is less expensive to lease the property than it would be to buy it. For example, assume there is a tract of land that is located under an oceanfront hotel in Fort Lauderdale. The lease was originally a 99-year lease, initiated in 1961. At the time the lease was negotiated, the value of the property was around $250,000. The lessor, thinking he or she was very smart, set the rent at $30,000 per year. After all, 99 years at this rent would total $2,970,000. With a long time still to go, the rent is still only $30,000 per year. The annual real estate tax on the hotel is over $100,000. Even without subordination, it would not be difficult to find a lender willing to take this leasehold interest as security for the loan. While this fixed lease term was not uncommon in the 1960s, most leases drawn today have provisions to index the payment to a cost-of-living index, or some other benchmark. Leases that have options for the lessee to acquire or buy out the lease (and take title to the real estate) may also index the ultimate purchase price. This indexing may be directly to the same index or benchmark used in rent adjustments, or to a formula, that adjusts the purchase price to a multiple of the index-adjusted rent. I show examples of these situations later in this chapter.

The fourth solution is to put some other real estate up as security for a loan. This may be a combination such as a blanket mortgage where you would pledge your leasehold interest together with some other property. In a pyramid loan, which will be discussed in Chapter 13, the borrower is constantly generating capital from one property to buy or improve another.

The fifth solution is the principal topic of this chapter, subordination. When you can get it, the ability to raise capital is improved. Your chance of convincing the lessor that his or her risk is warranted may depend on your financial strength or the combined strength of you plus a coguarantor. The introduction of a coguarantor into the picture is what makes land leases popular for many different types of businesses that do not need to own their real estate. Fast-food franchise restaurants, for example, are one of these kinds of businesses. While this is a risky business, the solid players are able to substantiate that it is worthwhile for a property owner to lease the ground to a franchisee, or an investor who is going to build for that franchisee. The franchiser often becomes a coguarantor to the lease. This can be risky as often the coguarantor, while seemingly the franchiser, is another corporation of the same name in a different state or country without any real or little net worth. Careful investigation of the net worth of any coguarantor is an absolute requirement. Where these coguarantors are located is also critical. Getting legal service to the president of the corporation who has acted as a coguarantor when that person and the company is located in San Francisco, Paraguay may be impossible.

Leasehold versus Fee Simple Values

Unlike the creation of a normal lease, whether it is land or buildings, the sale-leaseback is unique. The previous owner, or fee owner, becomes the leasehold owner. It is this change of ownership that makes the sale-leaseback both dangerous and quite often rewarding.

A lease is a combination of rent and terms. The value of that lease to the lessor is based on the economic return to the lessor generated by the rent, as well as ability of the lessee to pay the rent or the security he or she offers to support that ability. If the tenant, or lessee, fails to pay the rent, and the security is not sufficient to support the economic base of the property until another lessee can be found, the lease may then become worthless. Of even more consequence, it may cost the lessor money to get the tenant out of the property. If you purchased a property from its former owner, who now becomes your sole tenant and you are forced to seek legal means to evict this tenant who is already five months behind in his rent, whatever bargain deal you thought you got at purchase time may have been a terrible deal.

If the building is a single-purpose structure and the tenant not very strong, then the ultimate ability to pay the lease and the possible long delay in finding another tenant could reflect on the value of the fee simple.

Establishing the Leasehold Value

The terms and conditions of the lease establish the value of the leasehold. It is clear, for example, that two identical parking lots, side by side on leased land, will have values depending on the terms of the underlying land leases. The parking lot that has an annual rent of $1,000 will be of far more value as leasehold than the one that has an annual rent of $3,000. In reverse, the owner of the lots will find the lease which returns $1,000 per year is less valuable than the one which returns $3,000 per year unless the owner of the first lot can find a way to evict that tenant, or at least renegotiate the lease terms. What is shown here is the variable between value of the lease and value of the leasehold. It is important, then, to distinguish these two values in each sale-leaseback situation. The sale-leaseback creates both events: the previous owner of the fee becomes a tenant and now owns a leasehold interest, and the new buyer becomes a lessor and owns the property. The key words in that last statement are both the value of the fee and the amount of the rent to be paid are created to meet the goals of the seller/tenant. If the whole purpose to this end was to sell the property, and the seller created a superficially high rent to justify the sale, then the deal might be a sham.

WHEN A SALE-LEASEBACK IS EFFECTIVE TO THE SELLER

1. When the use of the property has more value than owning the property.

2. To substantiate the value of the fee by creating a fixed return.

3. The need for capital makes the leaseback more economical than other forms of financing.

4. By the creation of several layers of ownership (as Frank did) vis-à-vis a land lease, leasehold interest in the facilities, and a sale-leaseback of the land. In Frank's case he was the entity that owned each element until he sold the facilities and had Frank's Hardware Store take over the obligation ($60,000 a year rent plus triple net maintenance, taxes and other costs). In the end, Frank also ended up selling the business to a new franchise operator who paid him a handsome price and didn't even bat an eye at the $60,000 rent plus other costs because it was the business clientele of the hardware store who really paid that rent and costs. Frank could have walked away from all of this quite well and still be collecting rent on the underlying land.

These four situations cover a lot of territory, and from a practical point of view, the latter two will be seen more often in real life. However, a quick look at the three gives some insight as to the use of the two aspects of this form: the value of the fee and the value of the leasehold.

When the Value of the Use Exceeds the Value of Owning

When you own a property, you have all the usual rights, including expenses and the potential loss of value if the property declines in worth. If you have a long-term lease on the property, your obligations are only those described in the lease. Often there is a value to the lease that is created by improvements made by the lessee, or the relative cheapness of the lease. This is called leasehold equity. For example, you lease a property that you use as a vehicle storage yard and pay $1,000 a month lease to the property's owner. Your lease is for 25 years without any escalation in the lease amount. Ten years ago when you started the lease, the land was worth around $90,000 but today it is now worth $500,000. This rent began a bit high to the land value, but that quickly changed. To rent a tract of land that you can use "as is" that is worth $600,000 and pay only $1,000 a month is giving the owner of that land a 2 percent return on the value of that land. If I needed that land for a similar use, I might offer you $2,000 or more a month to sublease it from you. The difference between what it costs you and what I pay is your profit each year for the remaining term of the lease. The value of that is your leasehold equity. That value, by the way, is relatively easy to calculate. To do this you would first establish an interest return that is realistic to the market. If that is 6 percent, for example, you can consider that for the next 15 years (i.e., what remains on your lease) what I am giving you is much the same as paying off a mortgage to you over 15 years at 8 percent interest. The question then is what principal amount have I given to you that you repay to me plus 8 percent interest over that 15-year term. Look at Table A in the Appendix to find the constant rate of a monthly mortgage at 8 percent with a term of 15 years. What you see is 11.468 which represents the constant rate per year (based on 12 monthly installments per year) for such a mortgage. Because we know that, the total annual amount you would put into your pocket each month for 15 years is $12,000. Divide that by the constant of 0.11468 (changed now from a percentage to a mathematical amount). The result is $104,638.99. Therefore, your leasehold would have at least that value at a sublease of only twice what you are paying. The reality is, because the value of the land has already taken a major hike all the way to $600,000 your sublease potential might be much more than you would ever dream.

Therefore, you turn down my offer to you of $2,000 a month for a sublease. Another year goes by and a new interstate highway is approved which will have a major intersection right at your corner. This land now jumps up to $1,200,000 in value. Your lease still has 14 years to go, and the poor landowner is still getting only a $1,000 per month. To make things worse, along comes the county tax assessor who recognizes that the land value has gone through the roof and increases the tax to an astronomical $25,000 a year. Your lease never said anything about you being obligated to real estate taxes, and when the landowner comes to you and tells you that you have to pay that increase, you tell him you are busy and can't talk to him right now. The fact that he never thought about such an eventuality is something that you now know will never happen to you (when you eventually sublet).

This situation happens rarely and never if both parties have good legal advisors on their team. In addition, when you begin to own real estate that others want to rent, remember this and make sure that any lease terms take into consideration that certain expenses can eat up any rent profits you thought you were going to keep. Of those, taxes and insurance are the two major ones. They do not stay fixed, and the more valuable your property (especially the buildings) the greater those expenses become. However, back to the lease where rent is forced to show a greater value than might be the reality.

Kaiser's Transaction

Let's look at what happened with Kaiser, as this case history illustrates this point. Kaiser had a small restaurant. He owned the land and building free and clear. He wanted to start another restaurant across town, but found he did not have sufficient capital to do this. Naturally, he looked to the normal forms of financing to raise this capital, so he visited the local banks and savings and loans. Even though his past record was good, he found that new restaurants are not easily financed because they are costly to start up. He did find that he could obtain new financing, up to a point, but the balance must be cash out of his pocket. Kaiser counseled with his broker and discovered he could approach an investor to buy his present restaurant to create the new capital. His options on a leaseback showed he could set up a sale-leaseback on the land, or the buildings, or both. The final decision would depend on capital needed, on the value of the property, and the rent he was able to pay.

The value of the land was $135,000. This was based on other similar properties in the area. The buildings had been appraised at $200,000. The new restaurant Kaiser was planning was expected to cost about $400,000.

Kaiser was sure he could support an overall debt service of $35,000 to $45,000 in annual payments with ease, once the second restaurant was built and operating. At present, he was making a good living from the first restaurant by taking home around $90,000 per year. He expected to make the same, or more, from the second one.

If Kaiser were able to sell his first restaurant for $300,000 and lease it back on a net-net lease (he has to pay all maintenance, taxes, insurance, and so on, as well as the lease payments), he should easily be able to borrow the remainder on the new property to finish the construction and provide working capital.

The broker knew that an investor would be inclined to buy the first restaurant since it had a good track record, and Kaiser would be, after all, leasing the property back at a good return to the investor. That return, by the way, is subject to good, hard negotiation.

There are many factors on which to bargain in sale-leaseback, and the buyer and seller can find much to negotiate on before the final transaction is signed and closed.

For Kaiser, the value of owning has taken a back seat position to the value of use of the property. As long as he has control of the restaurant, it may not make much difference if he owns or leases. His leasehold value becomes more apparent after he leases. In this case, the leaseback was $30,000 per year, based on a sale at $300,000 as Kaiser was netting $90,000 before the lease. The $60,000 he will net after the lease becomes the factor in establishing the economic value of the leasehold. As restaurants have an investor demand yield of about 20 percent, the leasehold value is about $300,000. Therefore, if a buyer interested in owning and operating the restaurant came along, that investor may likely pay $300,000 to take over Kaiser's position. This really looked good for Kaiser, because he got $300,000 when he sold the buildings and leased them back, and now he might get another $300,000 when he sells the business. That is all well and good only if the math shown above can be substantiated by reality. In short, can the business support that rent and deliver to Kaiser or a replacement operator a clear $60,000 return at the end of the year.

Substantiate the Value of the Fee by Creating a Fixed Return

In Kaiser's case, he might not want to build another restaurant at all. The fact of the matter could be that business is off, and for the past year the best he was able to take home was $40,000 and that was with him working 12 hours a day, 7 days a week. In this situation, he may want to get as much cash out of the property as possible.

To substantiate the value of $300,000 on the sale, he agrees to lease the property back on a long-term lease. That pleases the investor, until the lease becomes worthless when Kaiser goes off to another state to run a bar. Of course, the title to Kaiser's new bar is in his wife's name.

This would not be a laughing matter to the lender who was pulled into the deal with the promise of making a great return on the sale-leaseback. When the seller becomes the tenant, the motives of the sale should be very carefully inspected. If the seller tells you that he or she needs the capital to make improvements, then it would be a good idea to tie the funds to that end use. This can be done through an escrow account set up with a lawyer or escrow or title company. They would release the money directly to the contractor doing the improvements or to the seller when he produces paid bills.

Use the Sale-Leaseback When Other Forms of Financing Are More Costly

If the money market will support your financial needs at reasonable rates through more conventional forms of mortgaging, there may be no need to look elsewhere. However, due to any number of circumstances, a reasonable or sufficient loan may not be available.

Specialty types of real estate fall into categories that many lenders will shy away from, or at best, they'll quote high interest rates and low loan-to-value amounts. The combined effect of insufficient restructure of existing debt and high constant payments on the borrowed funds may put the borrower in deeper trouble than that in which he currently finds himself.

During this same time when the money market is tight, interest rates tough, and loans low or nonexistent, there may be a solution via the sale-leaseback. Your ability to determine the effectiveness of the sale-leaseback will require you to examine the effect the two forms available have on the situation.

Lloyd's Used Car Lot

For example, Lloyd has a used car lot. He makes a good living from this business, but finds he needs cash to expand his inventory. He has approached a local lender and has found he can borrow only 75 percent of what he needs by placing a first mortgage on the property. Besides the insufficient sum of money available, there is a high point cost and interest is set at six points above prime.

On the other hand, a sale-leaseback may produce 100 percent or more of the cash needed at an overall interest rate that is lower than that charged by the lender. As Lloyd needs the property and has substantial records to show he can support the rent, he may, out of necessity, move in the direction of the sale-leaseback to solve his problems. He recognized that his ability to earn money on the input of new capital is greater than the cost of the land lease. As long as he has a prudent leaseback from his long-term growth, he will make this move.

Of course, he will be forced to look to some other form of financing or capital seeking, if he cannot raise the money in the conventional money market. However, Lloyd should seek conventional sources as possible alternatives to his problem, if for no other reason than as a comparison to the sale-leaseback.

There Is a Risk in the Leaseback

There are valid reasons for the leaseback. However, the risk involved, due to the value adjustments, requires buyers to be rather cautious of overstated values of the fee or of the leasehold.

It is possible for the seller to substantiate the value of the fee by creating the fixed return with a minimum of risk to the buyer. This can be accomplished with lease insurance. The insurance will cover the rent in default should the seller/tenant get into trouble. What could be a bad deal can become a Triple A transaction.

PROPERTY OWNER'S POINT OF VIEW: VALUE OF LEASES DEPENDS ON EIGHT FACTORS

1. THE GUARANTOR TO THE LEASE. Who or what is he, she, or it? What are the past record, financial backing, and motivation? Will they sign personally? Put up corporate backing, find a satisfactory coguarantor? If not, why not?

2. THE USE. Has it been successful? Is the operation well run, managed, and staffed? Is there a future for the present use? Does the use present unusual hazards to the property? Does the use limit the function and flexibility of the property?

3. LEASE CONDITIONS. The term of years: too long or too short? Who pays taxes, utilities, assessments, repairs, maintenance, and other property costs? Is there a provision for increasing the rent due to cost of living increases? What other provisions can affect the future return to the owner (options, provisions for cancellations, and so on)?

4. THE PERFORMANCE. What is the record of the lessee in making rent payments? In new leases, this is a big unknown and only time will tell. What do other landlords say about this tenant?

5. THE PROPERTY. Is the economic life of the property beyond that of the term of the lease? If so, the fact that a new tenant must someday be found or the same tenant enticed to stay can cause a problem in the future. Is the location suitable for the present tenant? Is the tenant suffering because of the property or the location?

6. FEE VERSUS LEASEHOLD. There must be a real value in both. The greater the value in the leasehold, the greater the security for the lessor. In the sale-leaseback, this apparent value in the leasehold should be carefully examined.

7. HAS THE TITLE BEEN SUBORDINATED TO TENANT FINANCING? The terms of such subordination can reduce the risk to the tenant, and at the same time generate considerable risk for the owner. Elements to be watchful for: Does the subordination extend to multiple events? If so, then future new financing can be even more risky than original financing. Can the tenant divide financing over separate parts of the property? This can create a nightmare for the owner of the fee simple.

8. HOW SALABLE OR LEASABLE IS THE FACILITY IF THE TENANT LEAVES? This can be very important because all of the items, one through seven, can come through very positive in favor of making the lease. Often a property is modified by either the owner or the tenant in such a way as to make the use undesirable to another owner or tenant without substantial reinvested capital. If this is the situation, then one or more of the first seven items must counterbalance this aspect.

The value of the lease depends heavily on the use and the user. Artificial value can be generated in the leasehold by the lessee. This artificial value is, in essence, a burden to the property and results from pushing this form of financing.

The Need for Capital

Need necessitates action, and a need for capital is generally the reason for the sale-leaseback. There are many favorable forms of financing which might be adequate for the situation if they could be obtained in the market. For example, there is no real reason why a seller who wants to use the property should take a sale-leaseback transaction, unless the economics of accepting another form are onerous or unavailable.

However, this does not make the sale-leaseback the last resort, and it should not be considered as a step down from something not available or economically unsound. It can be highly advantageous to the seller. If the seller cannot borrow the necessary funds and he needs the use of the property for economic reasons, then the sale-leaseback can solve these problems.

Advantages and Disadvantages of the Sale-Leaseback

To the advantages and disadvantages listed in Table 11.1, you can apply most pro-and-con aspects of any lease. One thing is definite, however. The sale-leaseback is more complicated than it appears on the surface. It requires good, sound legal advice and possible tax consideration. A buyer should never enter into a sale-leaseback unless there is absolute confidence that the transaction is beneficial to both parties. It is far too easy for the seller to boost the value of the property with this form of financing and take advantage of some buyer not aware of the potential danger. Be sure you understand the pros and cons of the leaseback before you establish that transaction.

A Special Warning about Franchisers

The buyer should be especially cautious when the sale-leaseback has been established by a franchiser who has sold the business (not the real estate) to an operator and offers to guarantee or coguarantee the lease payments for a period of time. The franchiser's primary goal was to sell the franchise, and their "name" on the lease may not be worth what you think it is.

Lenders May Initiate Lease backs to Get a Piece of the Action

The leaseback form of financing has a place in real estate. It is used in commercial realty and other forms of development, such as land planning. Lenders find it an ideal for securing their position in large development loans. Here the lender may take a land lease under a project he or she is financing, participating in the overall project to the degree that he or she will always own the land. In many cases, the developer may buy the land back in the future at an escalated price. Since the lender may not be extending more funds than he or she would have on just a development loan, the lender exercises a strong advantage over the developer of the project.

Yet, the developer may not fare too badly either, and can cash out ahead of the project and still have control over the improvements. The cost of carrying the land and paying the portion of debt service that applies to the land lease will never retire any principal, and the ratio of constant to remaining balance of any comparison mortgage will increase faster than in a mortgage without a land lease. However, the developer may not have any of its own capital invested in the land portion of the project, and as long as the rent comes out of rents, well then, it is the tenants that are paying the lease payments.

Table 11.1

Advantages and disadvantages as they apply to both the seller and the buyer

	Advantages	*Disadvantages*
The Seller	Retains use of the property.	Possibly gives up many benefits of ownership of improvements and land.
	Negotiates the amount of the rent by offsetting the sale price.	Loses future appreciation of land.
	Offers more flexible lease terms in the leaseback.	Leasehold value has a shorter life than the property.
	Firms up the price and value.	Declines in leasehold value can be a total loss.
	Gives flexibility to difficult transactions because the land and improvements can be separated.	
	Offers more strength to the seller in dealing on the leaseback terms as the seller is the ultimate tenant.	
	Potentially provides capital when all else fails.	
The Buyer	Makes an excellent tenant.	Either the price or the rent will be to the seller's advantage; often both.
	Offers some flexibility in price versus rent negotiations.	Too hard a push on the seller may give you an investment without a tenant.
	Unsubordinated land offers: (a) low-risk investment potential, (b) future recoupment of improvements, and (c) appreciation of land and improvements.	A leaseback by a nonuser may be a good sign that the income won't support the value.
	Offers an excellent investment potential if very carefully examined and secured.	May have to step into a large mortgage to protect his or her interest in the property.

Public Corporations May Want to Take Real Estate off Their Books

Many public corporations find that ownership of real estate can be less attractive than the use of the property. This is generally a tax consideration and may not provide actual long-term benefits. When a public company is trying to boost earnings, it often gets rid of depreciable assets that reduce those earnings on paper. In those instances, investors find that they have usually found the best kind of sale-leaseback possible.

SETTING UP THE SALE-LEASEBACK

When you are sure the sale-leaseback is the proper way to go, carefully examine the two values involved: The fee simple and the leasehold value.

There will be some flexibility in the adjustment of these two values. This adjustment may have tax-saving results. For example, if the seller has a low base, it may be possible to set a price that is near that base and reduce the rent the seller will pay in the leaseback to offset the reduced price. Remember, the lower the rent paid by the seller the higher the value of the leasehold. Naturally, you cannot reduce the price to a point that is below the market value just to save on taxes. However, there is usually ample room in which to work in order to provide some flexibility in these negotiations.

It may be in the seller's best interest to attempt to establish the lowest value on the sale to reduce gains tax. The rent paid later on the lower base can, over a few years, make up the reduced sales price. On the other hand, if the capital gained from the sale is not sufficient, then the higher price, even with the tax, may be more prudent. Because the sale-leaseback can justify a higher price, the spread in the low-to-high value will be greater than in a normal sale. This high value is said to be somewhat artificial and warranted only based on the leaseback.

Negotiating a Lower Price

This occurs because the buyer recognizes that he or she is buying at a good price and can adjust income accordingly. The buyer should realize that reduced rent and soft terms for annual rent increases increase the value of the leasehold interest for the tenant. These terms may be required to get the tenant in the first place, and if that is the case, do not reduce the value of the property. However, very long terms that favor the tenant can have a great effect on future appreciation of the owner's interest. Yet, from the initial point of view, if the tenant has a high equity in the leasehold, the owner of the property will be more secure in the transaction. This can be a very important tradeoff in the negotiations of a long-term lease. For this reason, early concessions that entice the tenant into the property can pay off later. In the sale-leaseback, the concessions are part of the negotiation in the transaction. Assume the seller (and soon-to-be tenant) is asking $500,000 for a property and he or she then wants to lease it back for $50,000 per year, plus taxes, insurance, and maintenance. If you push to get higher rent that may look attractive from your yield point of view, all that does is reduce the leasehold value, and put the tenant in a position where he or she might start looking for another place to rent. A better approach would be to try to buy for less, but give the tenant an even better deal than he or she was offering.

One approach is to let the tenant have prepaid rent or discounted rent as part of the deal. For example, instead of the $500,000 asking, you offer $400,000 with the initial four years rent to be graduated, with the first year at $10,000, the second at $25,000, the third at $30,000, and the fourth at $35,000. Year five can have a cost-of-living adjustment to bring it up to around $50,000 or so. If you analyze this, you will discover the end results to be much the same as if you had paid $500,000 with an annual rent of $50,000. However, now you get in for less gross price, and let the seller have an easier time to become accustomed to being a tenant.

A buyer will find that the maximum security he can have on a leaseback is the lease insurance. This type of insurance is obtained by the tenant and insures the lessor in the event the lessee fails to pay his rent. It is not easily obtained, however, and is not used too often in sale-leaseback situations. However, if the buyer wants the utmost in security, then this type of insurance will provide it.

If only the land is being leased and there is no subordination, the risk to the fee owner is limited. If the price for the land is realistic and not inflated, then the owner of the realty has a sound investment. There would be little reason to consider insurance with this type of transaction. In limited subordination situations, where the lessee has the right to put on a mortgage of limited proportions, the buyer will find his or her security waning. The amount of the mortgage and its repayment terms as well as the percentage to the value of the property will establish the value of the security. Should the leaseback carry full subordination, the risk to the buyer of the land lease will be predicated on:

- The success of the property.
- The ability of the lessee to pay the rent.
- The value of this asset in ratio to the net worth of the fee owner.

The buyer should realize that in the sale-leaseback the lessee may have made a profit, and may have no actual equity in the property or the leasehold. In this event, the loss to the lessee in a failure to perform on the lease may be small.

We have discussed two values: the fee simple and the leasehold. In fact, there may be a third value—the value of the business itself. A retail shop, for example, may have a business value not dependent on the exact location or improvements. If the lessee can move the business with ease and retain its value, the security to the buyer is reduced unless he or she ties the lessee into the lease more stringently. One way to do that would be to restrict the lessee from opening a similar business within a certain distance from the leased one. Why make it easy for the tenant to do a midnight move?

The ability of the seller-tenant to move the business does not in itself reduce the buyer's security. However, unless the improvements are single purpose, the new owner may find it difficult to rent the space should the leaseback tenant fail on the lease for some reason. The best security for the buyer in the sale-leaseback will always be extreme caution.

SALE-LEASEBACK HIGHLIGHTS

What the sale-leaseback will do:

1. Generate cash.
2. Provide terms on a lease to suit the lessee.

When to use the sale-leaseback:

1. When value of use exceeds value of ownership.
2. To substantiate value of fee.
3. When borrowing to raise capital is not economically effective or available.

What to look for:

1. Seller who has successful use of property.
2. A use that is potentially successful, but may need either time or capital or both.

Negotiating points of a sale-leaseback:

1. Term of lease.
2. Sale price.
3. Other options, such as: (a) subordination, (b) recapture of ownership, (c) subdivision of property to separate lease (land or improvements).

Danger to seller:

1. Gives up advantages of ownership.
2. Loses future appreciation of property.

Chapter 12

THE LAST LOOPHOLE

IRS Section 1031
Real Estate Exchanges

GOAL OF THIS CHAPTER

This chapter raises the curtain on the most important benefit that real estate investors have at their disposal: the Internal Revenue Service (IRS)–approved strategy that allows a real estate investor to acquire real estate and later sell it at a gain, and to be able to avoid paying any capital gains tax on that transaction. The application of the U.S. tax code, under section 1031, is this bonanza; a magical elixir comes to all real estate investors who are lucky enough to be able to take advantage of this provision. In addition, where does this provision come from? Why, the IRS, that's who.

Internal Revenue Section 1031 is the name of a provision that when applied to real estate allows you to build wealth by rolling the gain from one investment into another. There is no limit as to how many times you can do this, and, when properly done, all the gain from each transaction is truly tax free.

This chapter is a comprehensive look at what this provision does, how it works, and how you can make it build wealth for you. However, this chapter is not designed to turn you into the world expert in the use of section 1031. Over the past dozen years, I have written two books on this subject, and I recommend that you add the latest of those two books to your personal investment library. *The Tax-Free Exchange Loophole* (Hoboken, NJ: John Wiley & Sons, 2005) is packed full of helpful tips to maximize the use of this fantastic giveaway program brought to you by the IRS.

However, this chapter tunes you in to the basic mechanics of this program, and by the time you finish it, you will know if you want to learn more about the inner workings of tax-free exchanges.

AN AGELESS STRATEGY—EXCHANGE ONE THING FOR ANOTHER

The whole idea of swapping something you do not want for something else is the magic of this century. It is kind of like a game of dice that always comes up seven, or selecting one unopened box instead of another unopened box to discover that you picked the one with the most valuable items inside. It is American. It is everything you ever thought magic could be. Best of all, for the true insider real estate investor it is a way to build wealth, beat the IRS at its own game, and change a buyers market, when you are a seller, into your own personal limo to the bank.

Fred's Tax-Free Exchange

Let us begin. If you enter into an agreement to trade a property you own, for all or part of the equity in another property, you have accomplished a real estate exchange. For example, Fred owns a residential lot in North Carolina that he purchased on a whim 10 years ago and has not seen since. He paid $5,000 for the lot and recently a local real estate broker in North Carolina told him that presently the lot is worth around $95,000. What Fred wants to own is a small strip shopping center near his home in Naples, Florida. The center is on the market for $650,000 and is free and clear. The center is a bit run down, but Fred knows that if he fixes it up, mostly cosmetic changes, he can improve the rent and double the value of the center in a couple of years.

Fred offers the seller $500,000 for the center. Because the seller's primary goal has been reached, that is, to sell the center and get out of property management, the price is almost acceptable. The seller counters with a price of $625,000. Fred does not respond right away, and lets a week go by. Then he comes back and says that he will go to the $625,000 price, which will be made up of $530,000 cash, and a beautiful mountain lot in North Carolina. The deal is ultimately accepted, and Fred has entered the ranks of real estate exchangers.

Is it that simple? Sometimes it is. There are strange emotions that often occur in real estate exchanges. First is the attainment of the majority of the buyer's or seller's goals. For the seller of the strip stores, the primary goal was to get rid of the property. The amount of cash that was in the deal was substantial, and the idea of owning a lot in the cool mountains of North Carolina was not unattractive. Remember that unseen box behind curtain A.

However, Fred heard about the tax-free exchange concept and became intrigued at the prospect of exchanging an asset that he had all but forgotten about, without paying any tax on the resulting gain. Therefore, when the seller countered at a higher price than Fred had originally offered, he threw the lot into the pot to see what would happen.

From Fred's point of view, he could have approached the deal differently and not offered an exchange at all. However, the lot had only cost him $5,000, and he had only seen it once, so there was no emotional attachment to the lot. He also knew that the final price of $625,000 was a fair price for the strip stores.

Fred ultimately went to a local commercial bank. He showed them a pro forma whereby with $50,000 of cosmetic face-lift, and six months of time he would increase the NOI by $20,000. Using a conservative approach, he believed the center (no longer strip stores now) would be worth $850,000 to $1,000,000. The loan request of $600,000 would cover loan costs, face-lift expenses, and Fred's original capital invested in the North Carolina lot of $5,000. The loan was approved so Fred not only made a qualified section 1031 transaction, he did it without spending any of his own cash. Another OPM deal made good.

THERE ARE DIFFERENT REAL ESTATE EXCHANGES: SOME ARE TAX-FREE, SOME ARE NOT

The IRS looks at real estate exchanges from several different points of view. Under some circumstances, the exchange takes place without any gains tax being paid on the transaction. Look at the following exchange rules as defined by the IRS.

IRS Tax Code Section 1031

This is the last loophole left to real estate investors. This type of exchange is the subject of this chapter, and is a technique that every real estate investor should know and understand. Internal revenue tax code section 1031 provides that under specific circumstances a real estate transaction may be closed wherein a capital gain will not be taxable at the time of the closing. In fact, if the deal is handled properly, any tax on the gain can be postponed indefinitely.

An exchange of real estate may also include other elements that are not real property. For example, if Fred had included a $50,000 diamond ring as part of the transaction and he had a profit of $30,000 from the ring (it had only cost him $20,000) he would have a tax to pay on that portion of the deal.

Section 1031 is not available for any form of real estate that does not fall into the following category: It must be property held for productive use or investment. Review the entire tax code that follows:

§1031. EXCHANGE OF PROPERTY HELD FOR PRODUCTIVE USE OR INVESTMENT

(A) NONRECOGNITION OF GAIN OR LOSS FROM EXCHANGES SOLELY IN KIND

(1) In general

No gain or loss shall be recognized on the exchange of property held for productive use in a trade or business or for investment if such property is exchanged solely for property of like kind which is to be held either for productive use in a trade or business or for investment.

(2) Exception

This subsection shall not apply to any exchange of—

(A) STOCK IN TRADE OR OTHER PROPERTY HELD PRIMARILY FOR SALE,

(B) STOCKS, BONDS, OR NOTES,

(C) OTHER SECURITIES OR EVIDENCES OF INDEBTEDNESS OR INTEREST,

(D) INTERESTS IN A PARTNERSHIP,

(E) CERTIFICATES OF TRUST OR BENEFICIAL INTERESTS, OR

(F) CHOSES IN ACTION.

For purposes of this section, an interest in a partnership which has in effect a valid election under section 761(a) to be excluded from the application of all of subchapter K shall be treated as an interest in each of the assets of such partnership and not as an interest in a partnership.

(3) Requirement that property be identified and that exchange be completed not more than 180 days after transfer of exchanged property

For purposes of this subsection, any property received by the taxpayer shall be treated as property which is not like-kind property if—

(A) SUCH PROPERTY IS NOT IDENTIFIED AS PROPERTY TO BE RECEIVED IN THE EXCHANGE ON OR BEFORE THE DAY WHICH IS 45 DAYS AFTER THE DATE ON WHICH THE TAXPAYER TRANSFERS THE PROPERTY RELINQUISHED IN THE EXCHANGE, OR

(B) SUCH PROPERTY IS RECEIVED AFTER THE EARLIER OF—

(I) THE DAY WHICH IS 180 DAYS AFTER THE DATE ON WHICH THE TAXPAYER TRANSFERS THE PROPERTY RELINQUISHED IN THE EXCHANGE, OR

(II) THE DUE DATE (DETERMINED WITH REGARD TO EXTENSION) FOR THE TRANSFEROR'S RETURN OF THE TAX IMPOSED BY THIS CHAPTER FOR THE TAXABLE YEAR IN WHICH THE TRANSFER OF THE RELINQUISHED PROPERTY OCCURS.

(B) GAIN FROM EXCHANGES NOT SOLELY IN KIND

If an exchange would be within the provisions of subsection (a), of section 1035(a), of section 1036(a), or of section 1037(a), if it were not for the fact that the property received in exchange consists not only of property permitted by such provisions to be received without the recognition of gain, but also of other property or money, then the gain, if any, to the recipient shall be recognized, but in an amount not in excess of the sum of such money and the fair market value of such other property.

(Continued)

(C) Loss from Exchanges not Solely in Kind

If an exchange would be within the provisions of subsection (a), of section 1035(a), of section 1036(a), or of section 1037(a), if it were not for the fact that the property received in exchange consists not only of property permitted by such provisions to be received without the recognition of gain or loss, but also of other property or money, then no loss from the exchange shall be recognized.

(D) Basis

If property was acquired on an exchange described in this section, section 1035(a), section 1036(a), or section 1037(a), then the basis shall be the same as that of the property exchanged, decreased in the amount of any money received by the taxpayer and increased in the amount of gain or decreased in the amount of loss to the taxpayer that was recognized on such exchange. If the property so acquired consisted in part of the type of property permitted by this section, section 1035(a), section 1036(a), or section 1037(a), to be received without the recognition of gain or loss, and in part of other property, the basis provided in this subsection shall be allocated between the properties (other than money) received, and for the purpose of the allocation there shall be assigned to such other property an amount equivalent to its fair market value at the date of the exchange. For purposes of this section, section 1035(a), and section 1036(a), where as part of the consideration to the taxpayer another party to the exchange assumed (as determined under section 357(d)) a liability of the taxpayer, such assumption shall be considered as money received by the taxpayer on the exchange.

(E) Exchanges of Livestock of Different Sexes

For purposes of this section, livestock of different sexes are not property of a like kind.

(F) Special Rules for Exchanges between Related Persons

(1) In general

If—

(A) A TAXPAYER EXCHANGES PROPERTY WITH A RELATED PERSON,

(B) THERE IS NONRECOGNITION OF GAIN OR LOSS TO THE TAXPAYER UNDER THIS SECTION WITH RESPECT TO THE EXCHANGE OF SUCH PROPERTY (DETERMINED WITHOUT REGARD TO THIS SUBSECTION), AND

(C) BEFORE THE DATE TWO YEARS AFTER THE DATE OF THE LAST TRANSFER WHICH WAS PART OF SUCH EXCHANGE—

(I) THE RELATED PERSON DISPOSES OF SUCH PROPERTY, OR

(II) THE TAXPAYER DISPOSES OF THE PROPERTY RECEIVED IN THE EXCHANGE FROM THE RELATED PERSON WHICH WAS OF LIKE KIND TO THE PROPERTY TRANSFERRED BY THE TAXPAYER,

there shall be no nonrecognition of gain or loss under this section to the taxpayer with respect to such exchange; except that any gain or loss recognized by the taxpayer by reason of this subsection shall be taken into account as of the date on which the disposition referred to in subparagraph (C) occurs.

(2) Certain dispositions not taken into account

For purposes of paragraph (1)(C), there shall not be taken into account any disposition—

(A) AFTER THE EARLIER OF THE DEATH OF THE TAXPAYER OR THE DEATH OF THE RELATED PERSON,

(B) IN A COMPULSORY OR INVOLUNTARY CONVERSION (WITHIN THE MEANING OF SECTION 1033) IF THE EXCHANGE OCCURRED BEFORE THE THREAT OR IMMINENCE OF SUCH CONVERSION, OR

(C) WITH RESPECT TO WHICH IT IS ESTABLISHED TO THE SATISFACTION OF THE SECRETARY THAT NEITHER THE EXCHANGE NOR SUCH DISPOSITION HAD AS ONE OF ITS PRINCIPAL PURPOSES THE AVOIDANCE OF FEDERAL INCOME TAX.

(3) Related person

For purposes of this subsection, the term "related person" means any person bearing a relationship to the taxpayer described in section 267 (b) or 707 (b)(1).

(4) Treatment of certain transactions

This section shall not apply to any exchange which is part of a transaction (or series of transactions) structured to avoid the purposes of this subsection.

(G) SPECIAL RULE WHERE SUBSTANTIAL DIMINUTION OF RISK

(1) In general

If paragraph (2) applies to any property for any period, the running of the period set forth in subsection (f) (1) (C) with respect to such property shall be suspended during such period.

(2) Property to which subsection applies

This paragraph shall apply to any property for any period during which the holder's risk of loss with respect to the property is substantially diminished by—

(Continued)

(A) THE HOLDING OF A PUT WITH RESPECT TO SUCH PROPERTY,

(B) THE HOLDING BY ANOTHER PERSON OF A RIGHT TO ACQUIRE SUCH PROPERTY, OR

(C) A SHORT SALE OR ANY OTHER TRANSACTION.

(H) SPECIAL RULES FOR FOREIGN REAL AND PERSONAL PROPERTY

> For purposes of this section—

(1) Real property

> Real property located in the United States and real property located outside the United States are not property of a like kind.

(2) Personal property

(A) IN GENERAL

> Personal property used predominantly within the United States and personal property used predominantly outside the United States are not property of a like kind.

(B) PREDOMINANT USE

> Except as provided in subparagraph [1] (C) and (D), the predominant use of any property shall be determined based on—

(I) IN THE CASE OF THE PROPERTY RELINQUISHED IN THE EXCHANGE, THE TWO-YEAR PERIOD ENDING ON THE DATE OF SUCH RELINQUISHMENT, AND

(II) IN THE CASE OF THE PROPERTY ACQUIRED IN THE EXCHANGE, THE TWO-YEAR PERIOD BEGINNING ON THE DATE OF SUCH ACQUISITION.

(C) PROPERTY HELD FOR LESS THAN TWO YEARS

> Except in the case of an exchange which is part of a transaction (or series of transactions) structured to avoid the purposes of this subsection—

(I) ONLY THE PERIODS THE PROPERTY WAS HELD BY THE PERSON RELINQUISHING THE PROPERTY (OR ANY RELATED PERSON) SHALL BE TAKEN INTO ACCOUNT UNDER SUBPARAGRAPH (B)(I), AND

(II) ONLY THE PERIODS THE PROPERTY WAS HELD BY THE PERSON ACQUIRING THE PROPERTY (OR ANY RELATED PERSON) SHALL BE TAKEN INTO ACCOUNT UNDER SUBPARAGRAPH (B)(II).

(D) SPECIAL RULE FOR CERTAIN PROPERTY

> Property described in any subparagraph of section 168 (g) (4) shall be treated as used predominantly in the United States.

Of all the information contained in the tax code, the two elements that seem to give people the most difficulty are: "property held for productive use or investment." Because this code can apply to nonreal estate categories of property, the only element you need to grasp here is that for real estate, the original intent and use of the real estate must be as an investment. This will exclude the home in which you live. It will also exclude that part of a property (such as a multiple family or use property) where you live. The idea that your home is your best investment (whether it is or not) does not wash with the IRS. There are other tax benefits that apply to your home, which I will touch on later. Therefore, if you can show that the intent of ownership at the time leading up to an exchange was that of investment, you should be on good terms with the IRS and Section 1031. The other term that even drives some accountants and lawyers up a wall is the term "exchanged solely for property of like kind." What this means, again as it relates to real property, is that if the property you are giving up in an exchange was held for investment, then you must acquire a property for investment. You cannot exchange your investment rental property for a personal home, for example, even though the rental property would qualify for an exchange to another investment property.

However, remember, there is no criteria which would define either of these situations (tax-free or not) as to which is the better deal. And although the opportunity to use an exchange because there is a potential tax savings is a strong motivation to use this strategy in your real estate investment strategy, such a transaction may not present itself. The lack of a savings on a capital gain may not be a reason to stop you from making an exchange. It might be that $50,000 diamond that turns the deal around and moves it to a closing. *Remember:* Any exchange that moves you closer to your goal may be a great exchange. You do not have to attain 100 percent of your desired goals. Also, never compare two deals when only one is offered to you. I have seen many transactions that would have moved both parties closer to their goals fail because one or both of the parties held out for that ultimate. "Gee, I know the price is good, but a lot in North Carolina is not as good as getting all cash, now is it?" That is fine, and of course all cash might be better, but there is not anyone offering all cash now, is there?

I will show you later that there is a provision in the tax code that will allow you to make that cash transaction and still preserve the tax-free benefits.

NOT ALL EXCHANGES ARE BENEFICIAL

Not every real estate exchange is beneficial. This also means that not all such exchanges will produce tax benefits, even if the property in question would qualify for IRC 1031 rules. To benefit from IRC 1031, you must have a potential taxable gain in the event of a sale to have a benefit from 1031 treatment. It might be that your goal is motivated not solely to shelter the gain from tax, but to transfer that gain to another investment where you increase your tax basis to gain depreciation, which you have used up with the original investment. However, if your investment has not gone up in value and you sell it, there is no taxable gain. If your investment property has gone down in value, you have not depreciated the asset more than this decline in value, and you have not borrowed more than the depreciated basis, then there would be no gain. However, take note, just because you might not have a taxable gain does not mean that the exchange would be without benefits. There are other benefits from a real estate exchange. The rest of this chapter shows you how to maximize those benefits.

Keep in mind that there may be other income tax strategies that may work for your specific circumstance. The use of any single technique may be enhanced by sound economic planning. Be sure to let your CPA or other tax advisors know what your long-term plans are and incorporate those plans with your real estate and other investment goals.

THE BEST BENEFIT OF ALL IS THE TAX-FREE BENEFIT OF SECTION 1031

The potential indefinite postponement of tax on a gain that comes from the use of the IRS tax code section 1031 is limited to investment property or property held for production. This kind of transaction has mistakenly been named the tax-free exchange. It is important that you understand that 1031 provisions can have that end result *only* if the technique has been properly used. The ultimate escape from any gains tax can work as long as you live with proper planning. To be fully free of a gains tax, it is necessary for the owner to die while he or she still owns the property. The 1031 exchange cannot be used if you are selling or exchanging your personal residence.

Later on in this chapter, I discuss the specifics of the 1031 provisions. For the moment, just keep in mind that this tax-free exchange is a viable tool for many investors to use. It is one of the best methods of moving equity and building wealth. However, exchanges are complicated and to use them properly requires care and study on the part of any buyer or seller who finds that his or her benefits are desirable for the situation at hand.

Not all exchanges you may consider or in fact accomplish will qualify for the 1031 provision. For some exchanges that would qualify, it may not be advantageous for you to use the 1031 provision either. It is all a matter of understanding the bottom line and the future you have in mind for that asset, the new asset, or your investment portfolio. For example, if you have very little or no gain at all in the property you want to dispose of, a 1031 provision has little or no effect on your transaction from your point of view. On the other hand, the other side of the deal may find the 1031 provision of postponing tax on a gain to be absolutely critical to the transaction. In fact, it is so critical to that investor that without that benefit there would be no reason to make the deal at all.

Motives and Goals Differ between the Parties of the Exchange

In any exchange, you will find that the motives and goals of the two parties may differ. In addition, as exchanges often have more than two parties in the deal, the motives of three or more owners can be very different indeed. You should look to your goals first as always, and attempt to make the kind of transaction that works best for you. Any give-and-take in the deal format should be counterbalanced by some other negotiated element of the deal.

If you can save money through postponing the tax, then you are ahead of the game by that amount. If you can entice a reluctant seller into a transaction by showing him or her how to save money through the 1031 provision, you may make a deal that would escape you otherwise.

BENEFITS OF THE 1031 EXCHANGE

The IRS Code Section 1031 says that if you make a like-for-like exchange, you do not have to pay the gains tax at the time of the exchange. This is true as long as you have done everything properly, and have not received any boot, nor had net mortgage relief. Let me explain. "Boot" is a form of a pirate's booty. It is anything except real property or fixtures attached to the real estate. Cash is boot; so is a diamond ring or a collection of stamps. All boot will not qualify as a part of any 1031 exchange, so it will be taxable. "Like for like," in this context, simply means "investment for investment." You cannot exchange part of your inventory as a builder for an investment and have a 1031 exchange. Investment for investment is the major thing for you to remember. The major benefit of 1031 is its ability to postpone gains tax, with the ultimate goal of avoiding it altogether.

"Gain" on property is the sum of everything you get in a sale (or exchange) less your adjusted cost. Your taxable gain, if any, is found by using the tax calculations for 1031 exchanges shown in Table 12.5 on page 291. In any sale or exchange, the primary number you will need is your tax basis. The tax basis on a property is like book value. When you buy a property, it has a value. You can add to the value by building something on the property. You can take away from it by certain deductions, such as removing part of the improvements, or depreciating the assets over the years as allowed by the IRS. In the tax law revision of 1986 the depreciation rules were revised drastically to reduce real estate as a major tax shelter for investors.

The tax law also revised the method calculations for adjustment of basis. In essence, when you depreciate a property you artificially reduce its value, and reduce the basis accordingly. In reality, of course, depreciation may have little or no effect on actual value. The IRS allows depreciation to be treated as an actual expense (even though no money was spent) and, as such, in the year-end tax accounting it will reduce actual earnings or profits. As earnings are automatically reduced each year, you pay tax not on actual earnings but the reduced amount. Depreciation is an allowable expense; therefore, it is a legal tax deduction. It is applied to bricks and mortar of buildings and other such improvements within the buildings sitting on the land. Only the value of the land cannot be depreciated. Assume that you paid $2,500,000 for an office building under which the land had a value of $250,000, the improvements would then be valued at $2,250,000 (let's not get into the value of goodwill at this point in time as that is generally a business operation value and can disappear and become a "business loss" which would, in some instances also be a deduction from other gains). The general IRS code allows the cost of these improvements to be deducted from your Income from that property over a set life. This life or term of years is established by the code and is available to you.

To make this discussion easier to follow, let's assume that you were to use a 40-year life at a straight line deduction of a realistic value less salvage value at the end of those 40 years. This would mean that you would assume a salvage value, say, of $200,000 and deduct that from the actual cost of the improvements. Of the remaining $2,050,000 value you then divide by 40, which would give you an annual deduction of $51,250, which would be a direct line deduction from the NOI (net operating income). This deduction would be the same as your insurance, or advertising or salaries paid to operate and manage your rental property. However, that $51,250 is not an out of pocket deduction during that year. Of course, over the 40 years it will amount to a sum close to the actual purchase price of those improvements, but unless you paid all cash for those improvements it is likely you let OPM work for you. Look at this magic as it unfolds. You borrow a high percentage of the capital to buy the property, then most of the portion of that borrowed money (cost of improvements less salvage value) will come back to you tax-free as long as you don't sell the property (as depreciation). Then, if you ultimately conclude a qualified Section 1031 transaction your total gain (which likely includes very valuable bricks and mortar as well as high priced land) you are able to escape paying taxes on that gain.

This has the benefit of allowing you to shelter income because while the taxable income has been reduced, the actual income has not. Assume that last year you had a taxable salary of $65,000, and after all normal allowable deductions had been taken and the tax was paid, you took home $50,000. This year you invested in a small commercial building that generated a net income of $20,000 (gross revenue less all expenses). At this point in time, if your taxable salary has not changed, you would have a taxable income of $85,000. This higher amount would likely put you into a greater tax rate, so your take home spendable cash might be close to $65,000 after tax. However, if you had $20,000 of depreciation on the building for the year, that would be a valid deduction from your income from that building. Thanks to this shelter, you would still have a taxable income of only $65,000 but an actual income of $70,000. Take a look at how this looks at the end of the year (Table 12.1).

Real estate losses are generally passive losses and will offset only passive income, however, when an investor owns, say, 10 percent or more of real estate investments and

Table 12.1
Taxable Income versus Accrual Take Home Income

A. Taxable Income last year	$65,000
B. Take home income after tax	50,000
C. Added net revenue from real estate this year	20,000
D. Without "tax shelter" total taxable income	85,000
E. Likely take home after tax is paid on the $85,000 Take $20,000 of depreciation into account	65,000
F. New Taxable Income (Line D − $20,000 depreciation)	65,000
G. Actual After Tax Take Home Amount (Line B + Line C)	$70,000

actively manages that property. He or she could then apply a passive loss against $25,000 of active income. Continually review the IRS revisions as more changes in the treatment of real estate are anticipated.

For example, if you earn $100,000 this year from a combination of sources, some active and some passive, but have depreciation of $100,000 from your active business, which you manage and operate, your taxable earnings are zero. Of course, in this example, you actually received $100,000 in earnings and did not spend the depreciation of $100,000. As far as the IRS is concerned you did. You would have no tax to pay.

Along with the new depreciation schedules, there has been a change in the accelerated-depreciation rules. In short, now if you take any form of depreciation faster than straight line (27.5 years at straight line), that depreciation cannot be used to create capital gain, and the gain equal to the overage will be ordinary gain.

This means that if you had an apartment building worth $275,000 and a $20,000 lot and you depreciated that building on the straight line over the 27.5 years allowed, you would have $10,000 of depreciation each year. At the end of five years, your adjusted tax basis would be $225,000 plus the lot cost of $20,000, or a total tax basis of $245,000.

If you sold the building and lot for a total price of $345,000, you would have a gain of $100,000 and it would be taxable as income at your earned income rate:

Sales price	$ 345,000
Adjusted basis	−245,000
Capital gain	$ 100,000

Boot is the part of the exchange that will be taxable even in the best-set-up 1031 exchange. Boot is anything other than real estate. If you get $10,000 in cash it is boot. If you get a gold watch, it is boot. A car, boat, airplane, diamond ring are all called boot and are taxable. You can qualify for a 1031 with receipt of boot, but you will still be taxed on the boot portion (Table 12.2).

Use Table 12.3 to check out this exchange: Hugh exchanged an office building to Mike. Mike gives Hugh a prime commercial vacant tract. Here are the details of the exchange: Hugh balances the exchange with cash and a $44,000 sailboat that Mike agrees to take (Table 12.4).

This is not the entire picture of the tax consequences of this transaction. To see this, look at Table 12.5.

Net mortgage relief is something else to look for. When you exchange one property for another and they are both free and clear of any mortgages throughout the exchange,

Table 12.2
Calculating the Amount of Boot

The Calculations	You	The Other Party
Total debt on the property offered to exchange		
Less total debt on the new property		
Net relief of liabilities (cannot be less than 0)		
Less any cash paid		
Less any boot given		
Plus any boot taken		
Net boot received in this exchange		

Table 12.3
Hugh and Mike Exchange Data

Calculating the Amount of Boot	Hugh	Mike
Property value	$600,000	$580,000
Existing debt	−110,000	Free and clear
Existing equity	$490,000	$580,000
Cash given by	46,000	0
Boot given by	+ 44,000	0
Balanced equity	$580,000	$580,000
Original price paid	$400,000	$150,000
Capital improvements made	+ 50,000	+ 0
Depreciation taken	−120,000	− 0
Adjusted tax basis	$330,000	$150,000

Table 12.4
The Boot Received

Calculating the Amount of Boot	Hugh	Mike
Total debt on the property offered to exchange	$110,000	$ 0
Total debt on the new property	− 0	−100,000
Net relief of liabilities (cannot be less than 0)	$110,000	0
Any cash paid	− 46,000	− 0
Any boot given	− 44,000	− 0
Any boot taken	+ 0	+ 90,000
Net boot received in this exchange	$ 20,000	$ 90,000

Table 12.5
Calculating the Tax Consequences of a 1031 Exchange

IRC 1031 Tax Calculations	Hugh	Mike
1. Total debt on the property you offer to exchange	$110,000	$ 0
2. Total debt on the new property	− 0	−110,000
Net relief of liabilities (Line 1 − Line 2, cannot be less than 0)	$110,000	$ 0
3. Cash you paid to the other party	− 46,000	− 0
4. Value of any boot you gave to the other party	− 44,000	− 0
Subtotal		$ 20,000
6. Value of any boot or cash you get	+ 0	+ 90,000
7. Total boot received by you in this transaction	$ 20,000	$ 90,000
Computation of realized gain		
8. Value of property that qualifies as 1031 like kind you receive	$580,000	$600,000
9. Qualified deferred installments	0	0
10. Value of any boot you received from the other party	0	$ 44,000
11. Any cash you received from the other party	0	$ 46,000
12. Amount of the existing debt on your old property	+110,000	+ 0
13. Total consideration you received in this exchange	$690,000	$690,000
14. Adjusted basis in the property you gave up	−330,000	−150,000
15. Any cash you paid to the other party	− 46,000	− 0
16. Any debt you assumed on the new property	− 0	−110,000
17. This is the gain or loss you realized in this exchange	$314,000	$430,000
18. This is the gain recognized and taxable (lesser of line 7 or line 17)	$ 20,000	$ 90,000
19. Gain not taxed in this exchange (greater of Line 7 or Line 17 − Line 18)	$294,000	$340,000

there is no mortgage relief in that there are no mortgages given up. However, when you deal with properties encumbered with mortgages, you need to look for the situation referred to as net mortgage relief.

Assume you have a property worth $100,000, and you owe $55,000 against it. If you exchange for a property worth $45,000, making an even swap (your equity for theirs) you will be relieved of $55,000 of mortgage obligation. You now own a $45,000 property without mortgages. You have had an exchange without any boot, but you have a recognized gain of $55,000 (the amount of the mortgage). You will have a taxable exchange if the mortgage relief is greater than your realized gain by the amount of the mortgage relief. If there is any gain at all, and you have net mortgage relief, you will have some tax in this exchange. Review the calculations in Table 12.5.

The reason for this should be simple to understand. Assume for a moment that today you own the same $100,000 property and it is free and clear. You go down to the local savings and loan association and borrow $55,000 in cash, which you put into your pocket, tax-free. A day later you make the exchange shown above, getting a free-and-clear $45,000 property. As you now have net mortgage relief, you may have a tax because you have already received the $55,000 cash without paying any tax on that revenue.

CALCULATING THE TAXABLE GAIN IN EXCHANGES

Smith and Greenwald are our two owners. Smith owns 100 acres of land. Its value is $200,000. He owns this land free and clear of any mortgages and his tax basis is the $100,000 he paid for the property. The other $100,000 in value is appreciation of more than 12 years of ownership. Greenwald owns a 3-unit apartment house. Its value is also $200,000, and it, too, is free and clear. Greenwald's tax basis is $140,000 (he paid $180,000 but has taken $40,000 in depreciation, Table 12.6). Smith and Greenwald make a trade with no cash paid between them and no mortgages swapped or assumed. It is a one-on-one exchange.

In the second exchange, the two parties are Jones and Blackburn. Jones owns 100 acres of land valued at $200,000 with a first mortgage of $50,000. Jones's tax basis is $100,000. Blackburn owns a 5-unit apartment house valued at $300,000. His tax basis in the apartment house is $125,000 and he owes $200,000. Jones has an equity of $150,000, while Blackburn

Table 12.6
Smith and Greenwald Exchange Data

	Smith	*Greenwald*
Property value	$200,000	$200,000
Tax basis	100,000	140,000
Existing debt	Free and clear	Free and clear

Table 12.7
Jones and Blackburn Exchange Data

	Jones	*Blackburn*
Property value	$200,000	$300,000
Tax basis	100,000	125,000
Existing debt	50,000	200,000
Cash paid	0	50,000

has a $100,000 equity. In order to make the exchange, Blackburn must balance his equity with Jones'. He will do so with a $50,000 cash payment to Jones (Table 12.7).

Table 12.8 shows the tax calculations in these two exchanges. In examining this table, you will notice that in the Smith and Greenwald exchange there will be no resulting tax because the recognized gain for both Smith and Greenwald was zero. However, look what happened to Jones and Blackburn.

Table 12.8
Calculations of Taxable Gain Exchanges

	Jones	*Blackburn*	*Smith*	*Greenwald*
Value of property received	$300,000	$200,000	$200,000	$200,000
Cash received	50,000	0	0	0
Other boot received	0	0	0	0
Mortgage relief	+ 50,000	200,000	0	0
Subtotal	$400,000	$400,000	$200,000	$200,000
Tax basis at time of exchange	−100,000	−125,000	−100,000	−140,000
Amount of mortgage assumed	−200,000	− 50,000	0	0
Amount of cash paid	− 0	− 50,000	0	0
Amount of other boot given	− 0	− 0	0	0
Gain realized	$100,000	$175,000	$100,000	$ 60,000
To compute taxable gain				
1. Total mortgages relieved	$ 50,000	$200,000	$ 0	$0
2. Total mortgages assumed	−200,000	− 50,000	− 0	− 0
(If line 2 is greater than line 1 put 0 amount)	0	$150,000	$ 0	$0
Cash paid	− 0	− 50,000	− 0	− 0
Subtotal	$ 0	$100,000	$ 0	$ 0
Cash received	+ 50,000	+ 0	+ 0	+ 0
Recognized gain	$ 50,000	$100,000	$ 0	$ 0

Note: Taxable gain is the lesser of gain realized or recognized gain.

The next calculation shows the gain, which is not taxed by virtue of the exchange:

Gain realized	$100,000	$175,000	$100,000	$60,000
Taxable gain (recognized)	− 50,000	−100,000	− 0	− 0
Gain saved	$ 50,000	$ 75,000	$100,000	$60,000

You can use the numbers of your own exchanges in place of those shown in Table 12.8 to see just where you will stand in the case of a potential tax. The tax, of course, will be calculated on the taxable-gain portion by using the current calculations. Because these are apt to change from year to year, consult your tax accountant for the current method.

MOVE TO THE ADVANCED STAGE AND LOOK AT THE STARKER EXCHANGE

The Starker Exchanges are a very special area of the IRC 1031. This is an exchange technique whereby you can find a buyer for your property, then go out and find what you want to own, and still qualify for the benefits of the 1031 exchange.

Starker Exchanges are very different from any other kind of exchange and are full of pitfalls that can turn a potential savings of would-be tax liability into a nightmare of audits and future penalties. I say this, not because this is the normal trend for Starker Exchanges, but because too many quasiprofessionals have entered this specialized area of IRS manipulation, and are making a mess of things for their clients.

Definition

A Starker Exchange is an IRS 1031 qualified exchange where the originator of the 1031, say it is you for example, have a buyer for the property. That transaction would, were it not for the Starker rules, create a potential capital gains that would be taxable event in the year of the transaction (unless it also had installment sales treatment).

However, by following the rules of the Starker Exchange, or deferred exchange as it is also called, the proceeds from the sale are placed in the hands of a third party (the facilitator or intermediary) who holds the funds and ultimately uses those funds to purchase a replacement property for you. This replacement property will become the exchange property, which will meet the full test of the rules and regulations of the Starker 1031.

Advantages

The advantage of using a Starker exchange technique is that it can put you firmly into the shoes of a buyer. Consider this: You have been looking for a direct one-on-one exchange for some time and the only thing that has come around is 500 acres in the Sinai. You have identified a dozen properties you would like to buy, and you have been offering to exchange your property for those properties to no avail. Suddenly someone comes along and wants to buy your property. If there is a way that you could accept the deal, despite the fact that the offer is only 80 percent of what you have been asking, you know that you could take that cash and buy exactly what you want. Only, if you were to sell, you believe that Uncle Sam would eat you alive in taxes.

However, if you could keep intact the opportunity to shift your $3 million in gain to some other investment or like kind property you would save on all that tax. This is where the Starker Exchange comes into play. The IRS, after losing a couple of tax cases, has established some parameters that allow you to sell now, and exchange later. Take a look at how these rules and regulations work.

Rules and Regulations of the Starker Exchange

The tax benefits only apply to that portion of the property you give up and the property you take that qualifies as like kind property. As has been stated earlier, the idea of like kind property is not its quality or category, but the intent of ownership. As long as the property (not just real estate) is owned for investment purposes or for use in trade or business, then the IRS says you meet the test. There will be some gray areas in this test, but for the most part, any real estate investment you own that is not your personal residence, that you exchange for some other real estate that will not be your personal residence will qualify. This statement assumes that you are not a real estate developer who is building or developing properties to sell or exchange. Those kinds of property are inventory, and would not qualify as an exchange for an investment property. Keep in mind that when you make an exchange, you can qualify as the giver and receiver of like kind property, even if the other party does not. A simple example of this would be if you exchanged a vacant lot you owned as an investment for a home you planned to rent out. The developer who may have built the home most likely would not qualify, but you would.

You must follow the time rules exactly as they are prescribed. This is the area where most people go wrong in trying to accomplish the Starker. Before I show you these rules, keep in mind that the most important factor in properly following these rules is in the calculation of the time periods and deadlines you need to follow. These calculations begin on the actual date you transfer title to your old property. This date is the actual closing date when you hand over the title to your old property. It is not the date you enter into a contract to sell. The sales contract can be 10 years earlier, for all that the IRS seems to care. They are only interested in the actual day of the month of which year you deed your property to someone else.

Time table of Events

You must identify a potential property you are going to acquire within 45 days of the date you transfer your deed to a buyer.

You must take title to the replacement property within 180 days from the date you transfer your deed of your old property to a buyer. Sounds simple, right? The problem is the first 45 days. You can identify several properties, just in case one or more of them do not work out. Today, this is more often the rule than the exception. By the time you go through due diligence, and discover all the lies the seller told you about the property, you can start eliminating one property after the other rather quickly.

You cannot have access to the money paid to you for your property when you sold it. This violates the whole 1031 exchange process, so you have to be very careful that you set up the procedure correctly. The way the IRS sees this, if you have the money in your hot hands, then no matter what you do with it, the whole deal is off, as far as tax benefits are concerned. This rule also requires you to use a qualified intermediary or facilitator to hold the money, and act on your behalf to contract for and close on the replacement property.

Avoid intimacy in these dealings. This means you should not use your best pal as the intermediary, or even your lifelong lawyer for that matter. Keep everything at arm's length and follow the book from start to finish. To follow the book means not this book because rules and regulations that have anything to do with the IRS are not etched in stone, and are subject to interpretation by courts. In addition, the IRS has a nasty habit of changing things around just when you have properly memorized the routine. The clear and safe method to proceed with anything that has to do with the IRS is to discuss the situation with your CPA or other favorite tax advisor from time to time and, most certainly, just before you actually enter into any contract.

DO YOU REALLY WANT TO USE A STARKER?

My personal experience of dealing with IRC 1031 is that this is a highly effective tool when used properly. The major drawback is the timetable, and the selection process where you have to identify the replacement property during that initial 45 days following the closing of your property in the sale. Many transactions, especially large commercial transactions, may never close within the time span allowed in the Starker. Those 180 days just fly by. The pressure to close within the time period may cause you to make a decision to move to another of your identified properties if your due diligence is not completed or is not conclusive as to which is the better property for your intended use.

The technique works and is necessary when you have a property that you truly need to exchange, and there is a ready and willing buyer who will not wait for you to find another property to exchange. In those very few opportunities, you will have to decide within a short period of time if you are going to let this buyer slip away, or take a shot at using the Starker.

You can use the Starker and be very successful. You can find the right property within those first 45 days after you transfer title and hope you can close on it. Many investors, including some of my clients, have used this technique successfully, but you need to play the Starker very carefully. All the cautions your lawyer or CPA might give you are well founded. This does not mean you should completely avoid using the Starker, as in its right moment it can save you many potential tax payments.

Delay the Closing So That the Time Clock Does Not Start

It may be possible that the buyer of your property may be happy not to have to close on your property right away. When that situation presents itself, you may want to allow yourself periods of time that you can extend the closing of your property. Remember the 45 days/180 days time slots do not start until you have sold and closed on your property. To accomplish this all you need to do is have a provision in the purchase agreement that gives you that option. You might even have a provision that you can wait to close until you have found a replacement property. Most buyers (of your property) may insist on an outside date by which time you must close.

Elect Not to Use the Starker Rules

However, a safer route to follow is the simultaneous multiple exchange. This is an exchange that just does not happen unless you get what you want. In this situation, there is more than one party in the game. You might end up giving your property to A and ending up with property from D. Players B and C are in there somewhere, and each ends up with someone else's property. When multiple exchanges are taking place, play it safe, and close all at once.

Be very careful of being pulled into a Starker when the Starker should not have been used at all. Recently, a friend of mine recounted such a situation that happened to him. A prospective buyer for half interest in a property he owned came along. His lawyer, and just about every other advisor he spoke to, told him that he needed to do a Starker Exchange, and that is exactly what happened. Only, of all the properties he picked out in that critical 45 days after transfer of half interest, none worked out. Zap, the IRS nailed him quick for a lot of money. There was no need for the deal to have ever been classified as a Starker. All he had to do was tell the prospective buyer (after all, he was only buying half interest, and the two of them were going to develop the property later) to wait until he found the right property to buy. This could only have benefited the buyer, who would have had a free ride during that wait.

A QUICK REVIEW OF WHAT EXCHANGES DO

Because of the nature of exchanges, there will be at least two property owners who are involved. Keep in mind too that as exchanges are generally transacted through brokers there may also be two or more brokers in the transaction.

It is important that you pay close attention to the four key benefits that are the mainstays of exchanges. I will expand on these benefits and get into the fine points, as well as some creative twists to this fine tool later in this chapter.

Exchanges usually occur from the interaction of three or four parties. These parties are: the owners of at least two properties and the broker(s) (although there are rare instances in which two owners exchange properties without broker involvement). Therefore, the results of the exchange itself can be seen from at least two points of view. It is important that both points of view be analyzed briefly, as this will help establish the proper attitude toward the exchanges attempted.

Any exchange situation should be approached with a simple question: "Will the exchange solve or move you closer to a solution of the problem at hand?"

To answer this question, you must have a clear understanding of the problem. It is crucial to know where you want to go when it comes to exchanges. If the answer to the question stated above is "No, it does not solve my problem or move me closer to a solution," then, obviously, the exchange should not be attempted. There is an exception to this rule and you might be surprised how often it arises. If in the answer to the above question you answered it exactly as was shown but then added, "but what the hell, it is something to do and who knows where it might lead," then go for it, because if you are stagnating with the property you have, and can switch it for something else, what is the down side of the deal? If you do not see any, then a change, no matter where it takes you, might be good tonic after all.

KEY BENEFITS EXCHANGES BRING TO PROPERTY OWNERS

1. Tax-free benefit increased.
2. Increased depreciation.
3. Expansion of the market.
4. Cash out.

Tax-Free Benefit Increased

Under the tax changes of 1986, capital gains tax calculations that existed before the change were eliminated. As of 1987, the previous exclusions, which were allowed to reduce the taxable portion of a "capital gain," were removed, and all gain is to be reported as "earned" income. The 1031 provision allows, under circumstances I will outline in detail later on in this chapter, for the tax basis of the old property to be transferred to the new property. When there is a taxable gain, the actual gain is moved to the new property and is not taxable at the time of the exchange of the old property. It is possible that this gain will never be subject to a gains tax at all. The present tax laws of IRC 1031 allow exchanges of like kind property to avoid the payment of income tax at the time the transfer takes place. This has been referred to as "tax-free benefit," but this is really a misnomer. The tax is merely deferred until ultimate sale of the received property. Should the device of exchange be utilized time after time, the tax on the gain continues to be put off until a final sale.

Upon death, of course, other taxes come into play because the capital gain tax does not carry forward after the death of the property owner. Heirs or joint tenants with survivorship take on their new interest in the property at its present value. If the estate inherited has no "death tax" due, then the capital gains tax is gone forever. Nonetheless, the tax-law benefit has many applications and is one of the major reasons for exchanges. The law provides for the transfer of basis from the old property to the new property. Some tax may be due at the time of the transfer, but this will depend on a number of factors and will be covered later in this chapter in the discussion on the method of transferring the basis.

An exchange will be considered to be tax-free (IRC 1031) when two or more properties are exchanged that are like property. The term "like kind property" has caused much consternation in real estate circles. Like property is the intent of use more than the physical characteristic. So, to be specific, like kind property is any real interest that is held for use in a trade or business or held as an investment and was not acquired for a resale.

To simplify this definition, any property, which is owned by a nondealer, can be exchanged for any other kind of property to be used in the same category as the old property, as long as either property is not a residence, and qualifies otherwise for a 1031 like kind property. For example, Roland owns several vacant lots, which he used for outdoor storage of his equipment. There is no question that an exchange of one of these lots for another lot (to be used for storage) in another town would meet the like for like portions of the law.

Another lot, however, also owned by Roland, has not been used for several years. He did not sell it because he decided it would be a good investment and would increase in value in the future. He exchanges this lot for an apartment building. Because the apartment building can be construed as an investment, the exchange will meet the like kind property test.

There have been countless combinations of exchange in realty. In every instance, the like kind property test must be met for the exchange to have the deferment of tax at the time of the transfer. It is important for you to realize that both parties need not meet this test, nor does it have to be met at all for exchange to be beneficial. The advantage to the exchange, from a tax angle, will depend greatly on the situation and the individuals.

Increase Depreciation

Because investment and business property can be depreciated, there are times when exchanging is used with the primary reason being to increase the amount of depreciation the owner is currently obtaining. This advantage is available because of the tax deferment ability, but has special significance to many transactions. The value of the depreciation itself may be taken into consideration if the client needs a tax loss. Depreciation, by the way, is the old term for the declining value of an asset. For typical IRS illogical reasoning, the term was changed to MACRS, which is the acronym for Modified Accelerated Cost

Recovery System. This system is designed to bring all depreciation calculation to a standard format. This system thus establishes the term of years for which certain assets can be written off, or cost recovered.

The system provides for two separate lists of years, the shortest being the General Depreciation System (GDS), and the Alternative Depreciation System (ADS). Understand that this book is not a tax guide, and that although I touch on many different aspects of real estate tax, mostly as these aspects affect different financing techniques, the information I provide in that context may or may not apply to your specific situation. All IRS tax codes can be, and often are, very complex. There are many possible cracks in the rules that might be modified, or changed by some other rule or code. What I am telling you now, and frequently throughout this book, is to get a good tax advisor who knows real estate tax rules, and hope they guide you down the right path.

Take a look at the basic MACRS as it applies to rental and investment real estate (Table 12.9).

Depreciation is calculated against the portions of the investment that meets the above category. There are rules that cover items not mentioned above, which this book will not deal with. Table 12.9 covers the majority of depreciation for rentals.

Land is not a depreciable item, so must be excluded from the tax basis (book value) of the property you are dealing with. Every year that you deduct the calculated depreciation from your preadjusted taxable income, you reduce your tax basis in that property by the amount of that depreciation.

What this means is this. If you have an income of $25,000 before depreciation, and a tax basis from the previous year of $400,000, and your depreciation is $15,000, then your taxable income (assuming no other additions or deductions) would be $10,000. Your tax basis at the start of the next year would be reduced by the $12,000 so your new tax basis would be $388,000. The significance of this is, if you sold the property and netted

Table 12.9
Modified Accelerated Cost Recovery System for Residential Rentals

Item Covered	GDS (Years)	ADS (Years)
Appliances	7	12
Carpets	7	12
Furniture	7	12
Roads and driveways	15	20
Shrubbery	15	20
Residential rental buildings or their structures and components	27.5	40

after cost of sale $400,000, the IRS would be able to tax you on that $12,000 deduction because your gain (whatever it is) has increased by $12,000.

This is the entire essence of tax shelter. Take the deduction now if it works for you. Get the interest-free loan from the IRS, and pay it back when you are ready. However, do this only if this is the right thing for your overall master plan. You don't have a master plan? Then go back to the Chapter 1 that deals with setting your goals and work on it.

Let's take a look at what happens in an exchange versus a sale and purchase with respect to this depreciation matter. If you have not gotten the overall picture yet, don't worry; if this concept was easy, more people would be doing it.

EXAMPLE: EXCHANGE VERSUS SALE AND PURCHASE FOR EFFECT ON DEPRECIATION. Keaster owns 100 acres of land and an old farm building, which he has been leasing out along with the land. His base in the entire property is $45,000, since he paid $60,000 nearly 10 years earlier and depreciated the building to nearly zero. However, because the land has increased in value, this old farm and land has a present market value of $250,000. Against this value he has a small $15,000 mortgage balance leaving him with an equity of $235,000. If Keaster exchanges his equity ($235,000) for a large apartment house worth $900,000 with a first mortgage of $650,000 he will owe that owner $15,000 to balance the equities because the owner of the apartment house has $250,000 equity in that property. Keaster's new tax base following this exchange would be his old basis plus the net increase of debt. This would be $45,000 plus ($650,000 less $15,000) or a total of $680,000. The subsequent depreciation will then be calculated on that base, less an allocation for the land.

What would have happened if Keaster had sold the farm and then a year later bought the apartment house? Look at the two examples of this case study: (1) the exchange as it actually took place, and (2) the results from a sale and later purchase of the apartment house.

The amounts shown are net sums, and brokers' fees are not shown at this time. In comparing the two situations, you will see several important tax consequences. From the depreciation point of view, the exchange produces the new annual depreciation of $20,218, which amounts to 134 percent of the new investment (the cash portion of the exchange) paid to the other party ($15,000).

The sale followed by the purchase of the apartment complex required $86,750 new investment cash to close, and generated $26,181 of new annual depreciation or 30 percent ratio depreciation to cash.

The result of these two different events is that Keaster is the owner of the apartment house in either case. However, if he sells, then purchases, he has to come up with $86,750 in cash, whereas in the exchange he only invests an additional $15,000. The difference between these two amounts, interestingly, is the amount of tax that has to be paid on the gain of the farm. From a depreciation point of view, the immediate result is not overwhelmingly in favor of the sale/purchase deal as Keaster only increases his annual depreciation (on a 27.5 year depreciation term), by around $6,000 per year.

Keaster is likely much better off, as you would be, to take that cash (which he would have to already have in the bank anyway to do the sale/purchase), and buy an additional property, or to use it to improve the apartments (Table 12.10).

Table 12.10
The Exchange of Keaster's Property

Farm

Current depreciation	$ 0
Current equity	235,000
Existing mortgages	+ 15,000
Net market value	$250,000

Exchange equity of $235,000 for

Apartment Building

Net market value	$900,000
Existing mortgages	−650,000
Equity (apartment building)	$250,000
Equity (farm)	−235,000
Cash due	$ 15,000

Adjustment for New Base

Old base in farm	$ 45,000
Mortgage amount on farm	− 15,000
New mortgage on apartment building	+650,000
Cash paid at closing	+ 15,000
New base	$695,000
Ratio of value: land versus building (20% land versus 80% building)	
New base	$695,000
Land	−139,000
Building	$556,000

Average Rate (Estimated) Depreciation

Straight line 27.5 years	$ 20,218
Cash paid in transaction	15,000
Equity in apartment building	250,000

A Sale and Then a Purchase

Current depreciation	$ 0
Current equity	235,000
Existing mortgages	+ 15,000
Net market value	$250,000

Assume a Sale at This Price

Calculate tax due at the close of the transaction

Sales price	$250,000
Base	− 45,000
Gain	$205,000
Tax (estimated gains tax based on a 35 percent maximum rate)	$ 71,750

Total Proceeds from Closing

Cash received by seller	$235,000
Capital gains tax	− 71,750
Net cash to seller	$163,250

Sellers Now Want to Buy the Apartment Building

Price of apartment building	$ 900,000
Total mortgage	−650,000
Cash required	$ 250,000
Cash from sale of farm	− 163,250
Additional cash needed	$ 86,750

New Base

Depreciation base	$900,000
$900,000 × 80% =	$720,000

Average Rate of Depreciation

Straight line 27.5 years	$ 26,181
Cash paid in transaction	86,750
Equity in apartment building	250,000

The cash required to end up with the same property differs greatly, the reason being the tax, which must be paid in the sale. Keaster had no tax to pay at the time of the exchange, so his adjustments in arriving at a new basis did not reflect the addition of taxable gain.

Expansion of the Market

If you have a property that is difficult to move for one reason or another, then exchanging may provide an increased market. The key to this is to determine what you plan to do with the proceeds of the sale. If you intend to reinvest the money, or a major portion of it, in more real estate, then the exchange will not only be the extension of the market, but a tax saver as well. There are many dealers in the exchange market who will take property in trade just to make a move. These people are generally brokers or associates that have taken property from previous exchanges as a part of their fee.

The expansion of a market is important. There are many investors locked into large capital gains who cannot sell their investments without having to pay the tax. These investors look for exchanges to move their equity or to increase depreciation. It is not important that you may not want what they have. Often, their property is highly marketable for cash; they just can't sell at a price that would give them a beneficial return after they pay the tax due. But you can make the trade and then you can sell their property.

This points to one of the major motivations of a property owner who truly needs to make an exchange. Look at this simple, but very common problem.

For example, Bob owns a property he purchased nearly 25 years ago. It is a vacant tract of land, which cost him $15,000. Bob has taken the annual taxes as an investment expense, and made no improvements to the lot. His tax basis is still $15,000. After all this time, the land is now worth $600,000. If his selling expenses were $50,000, he would have a potential taxable gain of $535,000. Unless he had some losses to offset that gain in a year of sale, he might have to pay $175,000 in tax. This would leave him with only $375,000 to reinvest. See the following calculations:

Sales price	$600,000
Selling fees and costs (estimated)	− 50,000
Estimated income tax	−175,000
Total to reinvest	$375,000

If Bob wanted to reinvest in a property that gives him a 10 percent return on that amount of cash he would be left with $37,500 cash flow.

On the other hand, if he could exchange into an investment without having to pay the tax, and could get a return of 10 percent on the full value of the property, he would have an investment of $600,000 and would have a cash return of $60,000 per year.

Which of these two circumstances would you choose?

Cash-Out

This occurs when the owner of a difficult-to-sell-or-finance property exchanges it for another property that is easy to sell or finance. Cash, not the property received in the exchange, is the motivation and the benefit. Ruth owns a vacant lot, the value of which is $100,000. Ruth needs cash, but cannot sell or finance the vacant property. So she exchanges it for a free and clear home. The home is easily financed, and once she has raised $70,000 on it, she puts it on the market at $85,000. The $15,000 down payment and reduced price is apt to produce a buyer, whereas the same reduction on the lot would not.

For a cash-out, the easiest property to exchange into is a free and clear home up to $350,000. Some markets may support a higher priced home as well so don't consider this price as the absolute upper limit. The key to the selection of value will be a home that is no more than 20 percent above the average price for the area. This home becomes prime cash-out potential for Exchangers.

Investing in real estate is best done with some sort of plan. The desire to start here and end there may require more than one step or move. Exchanging should be considered as a part of the steps in a dance. Or would you prefer to sit this one out?

Seven reasons that people avoid real estate exchanges are:

1. BECAUSE THEY DON'T UNDERSTAND THE BENEFITS OF EXCHANGES. It is human nature to avoid something you don't understand. But remember this about your "comfort zone"; it works both for you and against you. As a real estate investor, you must strive to expand all those areas that can increase your profit potential, and one such area is that of real estate exchanges. When you know the techniques of this kind of investing, you no longer can use this excuse. But in dealing with people ignorant of exchanges, you will have to go slowly to avoid giving the "sharpie" look to what you are doing.

2. BECAUSE THEY ARE ADVISED BY TRUSTED INDIVIDUALS NOT TO GET INVOLVED WITH AN EXCHANGE. There are people who do not understand exchanges, or the mechanics of dealing with them. Those people may include your lawyer, or accountant or real estate agent or broker. They may have had a bad experience themselves, and honestly believe they are helping you avoid the same mistake they made in the past. In fact, they may have had a truly horrible situation occur to them or a client of theirs. That may give you some insight as to how much credibility you can give to their ability to advise you. Nonetheless, it will not be the end of the world if you skip the exchange proposed to you. But don't miss something that may be good for you without seeking a second opinion.

3. BECAUSE THEY BELIEVE THAT ONE PARTY TO AN EXCHANGE GETS THE RAW END OF THE DEAL. I won't say this doesn't happen from time to time, but it can happen in anything you do. How many sellers feel they got the most they could? How many buyers feel they paid the lowest price possible? Any prospective buyer or exchanger who says that he or she will make one offer and it will be a take-it-or-leave-it offer is being very shortsighted. After all, if the seller said, "Okay, I'll take it," that buyer would forever wonder if he or she hadn't offered too much.

The more you know about exchanges, the more you will recognize that for some people an exchange is more beneficial than a sale. Some sellers will accept in an exchange a property they would not have purchased (given a wide selection and the cash to make the purchase), because the exchange was offered to them and the cash was not.

Your use of exchanges will show you that both sides of the exchange can and most often do come out smelling like a rose. The biggest proof of this is that many exchanges occur between members of the real estate profession, brokers and salespeople exchanging real estate in their own portfolios with other brokers and salespeople. These exchangers form clubs and networks where they deal with each other. The slipshod or shifty dealer is quickly recognized and is "dealt" out. Naturally, because of the Starker form of exchanges most people can have their cake and eat it too, so to speak, by selling their property then purchasing exactly what they want.

4. BECAUSE THEY BELIEVE THAT PEOPLE WHO EXCHANGE SET TWO PRICES: ONE FOR EXCHANGE AND A REAL ONE FOR CASH (WHICH IS MUCH LOWER). This is often true and is one of the drawbacks of the exchange side of investing, unless you know how to deal with it. The basic reason for setting prices this way is that most people don't understand that since exchanges can save you tax money, the exchange should be at a lower value than what the sale would have to be to end up at par after paying the tax. After all, I'd rather have a $40,000 lot in exchange (if I wanted the lot) than $45,000 in cash and a $12,000 tax to pay. Other people set higher prices on exchanges than on cash sales out of defense. Personally, I like to quote one price and then stick to it like glue to glue. However, you can easily counter the double standard of pricing by never asking someone the value of the exchange, but, instead, always asking what the price is for sale. Work from that evaluation every time.

5. BECAUSE THEY BELIEVE THAT IF YOU ARE GOING TO EXCHANGE, YOU MUST END UP WITH EXACTLY WHAT YOU WANT. This is a downright silly misconception about exchanges as a comparison to a sale. When you sell your property, it is unlikely that you will end up with the exact terms you had hoped for. If you truly understand your goals, you will have an easier time with this negative view of exchanges. A clear view of your end goal will enable you to see when the exchange is taking you closer to that goal. When it comes to real estate exchanges, you need to recognize the benefit in another property as it is compared to what you are trying to get rid of. Of course, often the first step to this process is to recognize that a property you own is not taking you closer to your goal in the first place. If the potential replacement property does not have any benefit for you, or in any way move you closer to your goal, then that is not an exchange you should consider. Remember: any exchange that moves you closer to your goal is a good exchange.

6. BECAUSE THEY CAN'T ACCEPT THE CONCEPT OF TAKING SOMETHING THEY DO NOT WANT AS AN INTERMEDIATE STEP TOWARD THEIR GOAL. The professional exchanger will frequently go through a multiple exchange to end up with a beneficial exchange. For example, if I want to acquire a duplex, I might offer the owner of the duplex some cash (which I'll get from refinancing the duplex) as the first part of the deal. To balance off the equity I could offer some vacant land out of my Armadillo Ranch near Naples, Florida. If the duplex owner doesn't want my vacant land, the deal could hit a snag right there. But it probably won't if I explain that he doesn't have to keep the vacant land, that we can exchange it for something he does want or is willing to take if he will allow me the time for the extra legwork. I tell him I will still put up the cash part of the deal, so now all he needs to do is take that cash, and the vacant land, and acquire what he wants.

If he agrees to allow the deal to be tied together (binding us both to the exchange if I can dispose of the vacant land for him by bringing in something he will take), then I can work out the rest of the deal. He might say he would take a vacant lot, but only if it was in the Florida Keys. I might find a lot he would take, but that owner doesn't want the vacant land in Naples, Florida. I keep going until I find someone who will fit the slot and make the whole jigsaw go together.

I'm not sure what the world record of legs to an exchange is, but I know of one that had more than 25 different steps before it was finally put together. Patience is an essential factor to successful exchanges.

7. BECAUSE PEOPLE BELIEVE YOU HAVE TO OWN SOMETHING TO MAKE AN EXCHANGE. The answer to this is simply that you can exchange property you don't even own. How? What you are going to do is this: find out if the seller of the property you want will take another property as part of his or her "sale." You get some specific information as to what that seller would take, even if it is only for a small part of the overall deal. Remember, if the seller will tell you that he or she would take something else for 10 percent of the deal, if all the other terms and conditions are okay, the seller might take 30 to 40 percent (or more) in this other kind of property. Now you locate something that is similar to or exactly meets that requirement and borrow it for a while until you make the deal.

Let's say you are interested in buying a small office building you have located in your town. The property is offered at $300,000 and has an existing first mortgage of $110,000 and second mortgage of $55,000. You know you can refinance the building, generating around $210,000 net after mortgage costs.

The seller started the negotiations saying he wanted all cash to the existing financing, but in the end game agreed to take a minimum of $100,000 cash and hold some paper. The seller confided to you (or your agent) that he needed the cash to buy some vacant land on which to build some apartment buildings.

Armed with this knowledge, you now see a possibility of finding some apartment land and making an exchange. You search around for a few days and find a tract of land that is zoned for business and commercial use, but can also be used for apartment sites. The property has not sold as a business site because it is a poor site for that kind of use, but it's ideal for apartment construction. The property owner will sell the land for $75,000 on easy terms.

The fact that the land is not labeled "apartment property" (it's zoned for business) causes many investors to forget that labels in real estate mean very little. It is what you can do with the land that is important, not the specific category of the zoning. Most zoning (get to know yours) comes in grades: business, industrial, commercial, residential, and so on, in varying orders of classification. In many parts of the world the building regulations permit a "down use": for example, the right to build apartments on a business-zoned property, but not the right to build a business on apartment land.

You have found an owner of some vacant business land who can't sell it, but wants to sell it. You then offer him a "soft deal" that ties up the land so you can make your exchange on the small office building you wanted in the first place.

For example, you set this exchange up by telling the owner of the land that you will buy the land giving him $5,000 down and a $70,000 second mortgage on the office building across town. You tell the owner that you are about to refinance the office building and it will have a new first mortgage of $215,000. You set the interest on the second mortgage lower than the market rate because the seller of the vacant land would rather have some cash coming in than keep the cash-eating land.

You now go back to the seller of the small office building and tell him that you will do the following:

1. Give him $25,000 cash.

2. Take over his existing financing, subject to your obtaining the new financing mentioned.

3. Give him the apartment land (which can also be used for commercial and business use as a bonus). The value of this land is $100,000.

4. Give him a personal note signed by you for $100,000.

If he accepts this, you will then apply for the loan you want of $215,000, which, less $5,000 in loan costs, will net you $210,000. You will use this to pay off the existing mortgages on the small office building, a total of $165,000 (a first of $110,000 and a second of $55,000). This will leave you with $45,000.

But wait, you have to pay the seller of the land $5,000, so that also comes out of the $45,000, leaving you with $40,000. You then take another $25,000 from that and give it to the office-building owner. You end up owning the small office building and have $15,000 left over for fix-up or for further negotiations if this deal didn't fly on the previously described offer. In short, you have another $15,000 to play with to make your cashless deal work.

Even if you had not been able to increase the value of that vacant land, you were putting yourself in a far better economic position than by trying to buy the office building with the usual financing. The landowner, after all, was willing to take soft paper, which enabled you to maximize your leverage of the office building with some mortgage at below-market value.

HOW TO FINESSE YOUR WAY INTO GREAT EXCHANGES

Every time you buy real estate, there are four things you should do to ascertain whether the seller can be enticed into this kind of transaction:

1. GET TO KNOW THE GOALS OF THE SELLER. In the previous example, knowing that the seller wanted to build apartments was what started you off on this tangent.

2. TAKE A QUICK LOOK AROUND THE MARKETPLACE TO SEE IF YOU CAN HELP THE SELLER MEET THE DESIRED GOAL. Sometimes the seller has picked out exactly what he or she wants to buy. If you can find out what it is and then talk to the owner of that property, you might find you can still do the "soft paper" deal shown in the previous example. You do not want to be hunting for pie in the sky, however. Some sellers set unrealistic goals, and since even they won't find them, why should I spend my time looking for them?

3. Tie up the "borrowed property" before making the offer to the seller of what you want. You must have control of a property before offering it in an exchange. If you have only a loose deal based on a handshake, it may not survive to the closing. Remember, good intentions are offset by many things, and greed is the number-one cause of death of real estate deals.

4. Understand that "ideal" doesn't exist, so don't overlook other alternatives. Perhaps the seller would build office buildings instead of apartments. If there aren't any apartment sites you can tie up to use in an exchange, try something else. Any property owner can and will take something in exchange. As long as you can "buy" a property on soft paper and move that paper onto the property you are going to buy, you have something to exchange. In this way you can generate a "cash" equivalent of property equity. You might tie up a North Carolina lot by agreeing to give the owner $20,000 (full price) in a soft mortgage on the $75,000 duplex you are buying. If you can give the seller of the office building the $20,000 lot as your total down payment, then you've just made another cashless deal.

PITFALLS OF THE BORROWED-PROPERTY EXCHANGE

Of the usual pitfalls, the most common is not having good control of the property you are dealing with. Another pitfall is that using a property you do not own is that by making a cashless deal you might end up taking on greater debt than the property will support. Becoming debt heavy is something you need to watch out for. Using a soft mortgage deal as a part of the total financing structure will aid you in the economics of the buy, but that may not be enough to give you breathing room in your financing. You must watch your pro forma carefully and not kid yourself about what you and the property can produce.

Real Estate Exchanges Are Prime Options for Buyers and Sellers

The fortunate thing about real estate exchanges is that you will have the opportunity to use them as both a buyer and a seller. Your ultimate benefit, of course, is not to be a buyer or seller when using exchanges but to be an exchanger.

PEOPLE WHO ARE LIKELY TO WANT TO EXCHANGE

Because you need to have at least two parties to make an exchange, it is helpful if you know where to get started. Understanding the motivations of why people will take your property as all or part of a deal is the first step in finding those people. Take a look at the seven primary motivations why people will accept an exchange:

1. Must sell, but no buyer has come forward.
2. Has a tax problem that can be softened or eliminated with an exchange.
3. Has a zero investment in the property that he or she does not want.

4. Wants out and is in over his or her head, either financially or emotionally.

5. Is an aggressive investor who understands the technique of exchanges.

6. Has nowhere to go, no place to turn, and wants to save face.

7. Can be motivated, or turned on to your property; in essence, sold on the idea of owning what you now own.

The best sources for people who meet the seven motivations are:

1. Local real estate brokers who specialize in exchanges.

2. Real estate lawyers.

3. Tax advisors who specialize in real estate tax law.

4. Sellers of property that have been on the market for a long time.

5. Anyone who might have offered you a deal you turned down.

6. Someone who is headed toward foreclosure.

7. Any owner of a property you want to own.

Using an Exchange as a Buying Tool

When you learn the motivation of the seller, you often realize that the exchange might be your way to do one or both of the following things:

1. Get rid of something you don't want to keep. If the seller of what you want is highly motivated, he or she is apt to be willing to take as part or all of this equity something you have in exchange.

2. Motivate the seller because of tax benefits. The seller hanging on the fence might be motivated by the tax savings you can show him or her through the exchange you are offering.

Using an Exchange as a Selling Tool

As a seller, there will be times when you have to dig deep down to the bottom of your soul and come up with some powerful tricks. After all, not all real estate will sell itself; sometimes you have to find a taker for your property, as that is often the start of a deal.

Offering your property, or part of your equity, for an exchange will broaden your market. There are buyers out there trying to find what you have, only they don't have money. Try to show them how to make a cashless deal that will solve your needs.

In finding "takers" for your property, you generate additional options for yourself: "Give me your property, take 80 percent of your value in cash, and all you have to do is take this lot for your remaining equity."

If I accept this deal, I now have cash and a piece of land, which I can keep, exchange, or offer out on the same basis. I could even hold a new first mortgage myself and take something for 20 percent of the lot's equity. I have gone from trying to get rid of 100 percent of a problem to end up with 80 percent cash, and a much smaller problem.

I've made million-dollar exchanges in which only a small portion of the transaction was property taken in exchange while the majority of the deal was cash and mortgage. One such exchange arose out of my need to sell a large tract of oceanfront land I controlled in the Vero Beach area. My marketing program simply didn't produce a buyer, no matter what I did. Then I decided to open the property up for exchange. The exchange was neither the most desirable nor the most practical thing to do because of my partners in the ownership of the property. Nonetheless, I knew finding a taker was essential.

Shortly after placing the land on exchange, the offers began to come in. A large villa in Spain, an orange grove in Ocala, Florida, and other proposals that didn't get to the writing stage were just a few of the properties discussed. I paid more attention to who was making the offer than what was offered. I was looking for someone who wanted the oceanfront, not someone who wanted to get rid of their villa in Spain or orange grove in Ocala.

Then an offer to take some vacant land as a major part of the exchange was presented. The land was free and clear of debt and the owner wanted us to hold a sizable first mortgage to balance the equity. After some negotiations I was able to entice the "buyer" to add some cash so that my partners and I could recover most of our original investment at the closing. This offer came from a highly qualified "buyer" who thought of himself as an exchanger. Through heavy and long negotiations for more than four months (nothing else was happening on the property anyway), the deal was concluded. The exchanger saved face by reducing the amount of vacant land he would give me, and increased the cash and mortgage portion of the deal. What started out as an exchange with no cash ended up as a lot of cash and very little exchange.

When you find a taker for your property, you have the choice of moving on your own property or moving off the exchange property. For example, if I offered you a small duplex as part of a deal to buy your motel, you might say: "I'll take the deal if I can find a buyer or other exchange for your duplex, as I don't want it."

If I'm motivated to take your motel, I'll sit still for a while and let you go in both directions at the same time. I can't stop you from making a deal without me if someone else comes along to buy or exchange for your property. I'm at the mercy of your intent to try to move off my duplex onto something else. I can, of course, try to find a buyer to take the duplex out of the picture and give you cash.

All sellers should investigate their opportunities and examine the value of an exchange. Even the seller who says "I can't exchange, because I need cash" might find that there are no buyers for what he or she has to sell and that the only way out is to exchange into something that is sellable.

THE MECHANICS OF MAKING EXCHANGES

There are several essential mechanical aspects of making exchanges. The first is the balance of equities. The others relate to presentation and the maximizing of gains.

Balancing Equities in Exchanges

All exchanges must have a balance of equities. There are three ways to achieve this balance:

1. THE CASH BALANCE: Assume that you own a duplex worth $75,000 and owe $50,000 in a first mortgage against it, so your equity is $25,000. You want to exchange for Peter's apartment building, worth (to you) $200,000. Peter has a first mortgage of $130,000 on the building, giving him an equity of $70,000. You want to make the exchange and will balance the equities with cash, as shown in Table 12.11.

In balancing equities with a mortgage, you add an additional mortgage to the property you are to take. In this case, you give Peter a $45,000 mortgage against the property you are taking from him, or some other property you already own.

2. THE MORTGAGE BALANCE: If you don't have enough cash to balance the equities, you might try a mortgage balance, as shown in Table 12.12.

3. THE COMBINATION BALANCE: In the combination, you might give Peter $10,000 in cash and $35,000 in the form of a mortgage. Or you would augment your equity by adding other properties. Nothing will keep you from offering Peter the duplex, a gold watch, and seven partridges in a pear tree in addition to some cash and a mortgage.

Table 12.11
Cash Balance of Equities

	You	*Peter*
Property given up	$75,000	$200,000
Outstanding mortgages	−50,000	−130,000
Equity	$25,000	70,000
Cash balance (who gives cash)	+45,000	+ 0
Balance of equities	$70,000	$ 70,000

Table 12.12
Mortgage Balance of Equity

	You	*Peter*
Property given up	$75,000	$200,000
Outstanding mortgages	−50,000	−130,000
Equity	$25,000	$ 70,000
New mortgage owed	− 0	− 45,000
Balance of equities	$25,000	$ 25,000

PRESENTATION: ALL THE MARBLES

The key to all exchanges is the presentation to the other party. Does this sound familiar? It should, because so much of your success in real estate investing depends on the tone set at the time the original offer is presented, and how well the pressure of the deal is both maintained and accepted.

If you are dealing with a real estate broker who has not dealt in exchanges, you are apt to have some problems from the very start. For the same reason, however, it is very difficult for you to make your own exchanges. So your first step is to acquaint yourself with someone knowledgeable in exchanges in your area. I'd suggest a call to the local board of realtors, or a look in a newspaper for a real estate exchange column, or just call several brokers and ask them whom they would recommend you talk to. Since having the best representation won't cost you any more commission than the worst, and the worst can be more expensive in the long run, try to find the best in your area. I stress this last part because finding a great buy 1,000 miles away won't do you a dime's worth of good.

Seven Things to Avoid in Any Exchange Presentation

1. Never ask the other party what the exchange value is of their property. You only want to know the sale value. As I've mentioned before some sellers believe that there should be two values—namely, a sales price that is more reasonable than the exchange price. This is shortsighted because if the exchange can actually save you money (by reduced taxes), and get you closer to your goal faster than waiting out the poor buyer's market, then the exchange is worth more to you. However, because it is normal for sellers not to understand this, expect there will be this double standard, and deal with it by not stressing actual values, but point out the benefits that the seller is gaining.

2. Never presume the other party will turn down anything. Only soothsayers are good at presumption, and even so, look where they are. The first person who is apt to lead you away from the potential of an exchange could be the seller's broker or salesperson. I can tell you from more than thirty hard-fought years as an educator to the real estate profession, most salesmen and -women are not versed in any form of creative financing. Some states, such as Florida and California (and others), have continuing education that touches on some of the current tax laws, and other financing techniques, but only a slight touch. The salesperson who tells you, "I know Mr. Seller would not take your lot in Hilton Head as a part of the deal," can only say this truthfully if that salesperson is actually the seller. You should take the position that no one knows exactly what anyone will do until faced with the opportunity to make an informed decision. It is easy for a seller to condition the salesperson by making statements like, "I want all cash, or nothing." Salespersons can believe this if they want, and if they do, they are likely to lose sales that could have come together otherwise.

It is much easier for you to make your offer the way you want to do it. Sellers may not want your lot in Hilton Head (or whatever the property), but might just see that the rest of the terms to your deal take them out of their darkness and into the light of their desired goals.

3. AVOID TOO MUCH TALK. Simply put in writing, in a professional offer format, the concept that: "I want to buy your property, Mr. Seller, and I'll give you five acres of pine woods and $10,000 as my deal." Sounds much better this way and won't upset a never-before exchanger. Far too many transactions fail because one or more of the parties talks too much. One of many good examples is what happened to a very good friend and major property owner who was very anxious to sell an oceanfront hotel he owned. He was a super guy who had made a lot of money in real estate. He knew everything about everything, and proceeded to let you know that every chance he got. He would simply talk people out of wanting to buy his property. What the prospective buyers did not recognize was that all this talk was his way of trying to cover up his anxiousness. Too bad he did not see the ultimate sale of the oceanfront hotel, but his estate did. Action speaks loudest.

4. NEVER PRESENT AN OFFER WITHOUT DOCUMENTATION FOR THE OTHER PROPERTY IN THE EXCHANGE. Have some back-up package on what you are offering, too. If you let your broker go off to present your offer without a package, you will lose the edge. When you are ready to start making offers for property that will involve an exchange of one of your own properties, make sure that you have a professionally drafted presentation on the property. If you have never done this before you may want to list the property for sale and/or exchange with a qualified real estate broker who knows about exchanging. Keep in mind that in the initial offer to exchange, the owner of the property you want may not know anything about your property other than a geographic location. Photos, descriptions of the area, examples of value from recent sales or other offered property in the area, and so on all help build your case.

5. DO NOT GIVE UP. Be persistent in your offers. Make them until you are blue in the face, but don't be too conciliatory too quickly. "Look, Mr. Seller, I'm very interested in your property and will keep coming back to you if I can think of something to make this deal work." No genuine seller will want to turn you down too flatly, as you are demonstrating that you are a taker for his or her property. Given the right set of circumstances you might end up a buyer.

There is a tricky balance between this item and number 3 above. You can be persistent, however, without lots of talk. The idea is that as long as the property is on the market, you can let the seller know that you have continued interest. If the seller did not react positively to your first offer, try to find out why. Often the seller only needs to be educated to the benefits of the exchange.

6. NEVER BE TOO SET ON WHAT YOU WILL DO. Exchanges are a new, wide-open game for many people. You might be turned on by an offer for an around-the-world cruise on the

QE 2 as part of a deal, and who in the world would have thought of that? Options that are opening up to you will be exciting. Live with them for a while. The exchange business is a two-way street. Today, you initiate the offer, whereas tomorrow someone else is offering you something. This will happen as the local real estate brokers who deal in exchanges find out that you are a potential player. You may have made an offer through a local exchanger-broker only to have his or her seller reject your offer. Suddenly that broker is bringing you other possible deals. Keep your eyes open. Several positive events happen. First of all, when you find another possible taker for your property that now gives you something else to exchange. This is the key to dealing in multiple exchanges. Assume you made an offer to the owner of a motel you want to buy, and he or she turned down your vacant commercial lot. Later a person with a nice home wants to exchange it to you for your vacant commercial lot. Instead of saying, "I don't want the darn house," think, "I wonder if the motel owner would take the home instead of my lot." The only way to find out might be to tie up the home by signing the exchange subject to your making another exchange (or sale) within a reasonable time.

7. NEVER CLOSE DOORS TOO HARD. It is all right to ease them closed: "I'll say no to this, as it doesn't solve my problem, but I do appreciate your interest and I hope we can work something out." The real estate community in any town can be very small. What you do gets around pretty quick, and how you treat others in the market will come back to you. Be courteous and respectful of sellers and their salespeople and you will find that keeping the door open, even if only a crack, pays off. The seller you deal with today may become a buyer of another property of yours in the future.

Getting into Exchanges

The only way to get into exchanges is to make exchange offers. You don't make exchanges by waiting for someone to come around and ask you if you want to exchange. The best way, I believe, is to find an exchange-minded salesperson and then go through a learning process with him or her. All investors who expect to make profits over a long haul, and to reduce or eliminate as much risk as possible, will be continually learning. I know that I feel slighted if I don't learn something every week I am in business. Fortunately, I never feel slighted because I usually learn something every day. All that learning doesn't always keep me out of trouble, but it sure keeps me from being bored.

THE PITFALLS OF EXCHANGES

Frustration is the enemy of the exchanger. There is a lot you can get frustrated about when it comes to exchanges. You will be dealing with people who think you are out to take them, or at best, will pretend they don't understand anything. You will have to deal with double-pricing situations, with hotshot salespeople who will tell you that a five-story building is a seven-story high-rise. You will get turned on only to find that what was described as a beautiful home by the sea just washed out at a high tide.

But, as Elbert Hubbard once said, "There is no failure except in no longer trying." When it comes to exchanges, you have to keep trying. Your day and the right deal will come along.

From an economic point of view, you need to watch your tax laws and your own tax situation when it comes to the exchange at hand. It is possible that you will be better off making a sale and then purchasing, accepting the tax liability in that year, rather than allowing your old basis to carry over to the new property. You see, if your old basis in that $200,000 investment property is only $25,000 you would have a $175,000 gain in that year. It is always worthwhile to use a strategy that will reduce or even eliminate your tax burden. However, if you also had a major loss in the same year, say $175,000 worth, you might prefer a sale in which your losses would offset the gain. You could then step up your basis in a new property, beginning fresh rather than passing along a $200,000 value with only $25,000 of basis.

ESTABLISHING EXISTING TAX BASIS AND CALCULATING NEW TAX BASIS

If you have owned a property for a long time, it is likely that you do not have an accurate calculation for the tax basis of that property. This is because most people do not record all the capital expenditures they make to a property. This is important because if you sell, and perhaps if you exchange that property, you can have a tax liability based on the gain you have. That gain, as I have already discussed, will be the adjusted sales price, less your current tax basis.

Table 12.13 will assist you in keeping track of your tax basis and help you calculate your new tax basis in the event of an exchange.

Note that in Table 12.13, there can be a fine line between what a capital improvement is, and what is a replacement or repair. Because you can deduct repair and maintenance cost from income for investment properties, you may want to discuss the potential of shifting from capital improvement to repair. Talk this over with your CPA or other tax advisor to see how this might apply to your specific property and situation. Your personal residence is treated differently by the IRS. You cannot use a loss on your personal residence against investment income. Because of this, you generally want to capitalize rather than expense. This means that when you add onto your home, that cost is added to the tax basis, and will reduce the amount of gain you may eventually have when you sell or otherwise dispose of the property. This goes for replacements too. If you replace all your kitchen appliances with new ones, what you have actually done is get rid of the old ones

Table 12.13
Annual Tax Basis Adjustments

Calculating Annual Tax Basis Adjustment	*Dollar Amounts*
1. Original price you paid for the property.	
2. Any capital improvements made this year.	
3. Less any allowed depreciation or loss.	
4. Less any partial sale (use adjusted sales price).	
5. Less any improvements you removed.	
6. Your new property tax basis at year-end.	

(sell off for nothing or get some small trade-in value), at the price you originally paid for them, and replaced them with newer more expensive ones. The net result is that you have increased your tax basis by the difference.

This points out the need to have a value for everything in the residence, which you may eventually replace. When you purchase an existing home or apartment or other residential property, you should establish a value for all the items in the house. You can easily accomplish this by having an inventory list with values that the seller agrees to, or have an independent evaluation of all of these items prior to closing. When you ultimately replace the items then the capital improvement works for you.

Depreciation is a tax break that is given to investment property and not your personal residence (as long as it is actually used as your residence). However, if you have a co-use of the residential property, you may have the right to depreciate some of the property. For example, if you have a business office in your home, or otherwise use part of your property for some business use, then you may be allowed to deduct not only a depreciation for that part of the property, but some of the expenses that go to the upkeep of that portion of the real estate or other residential category. For most people this is not as attractive as it might first appear. The depreciation portion may not be that much to worry about when you consider the potential for an IRS audit on that point. Also, the amount that you depreciate the value of the property will increase the gain tax if and when you sell or otherwise dispose of the property.

When you close on a 1031 exchange, you will want to establish your new tax basis. The calculations are easy if you use the following checklist. Please note, some of the amounts used in this checklist are found in Table 12.13. It will be necessary to calculate portions of that checklist first (Table 12.14).

My suggestion is that you don't try to be an expert on tax ramifications unless that is your business. Hire the services of a professional in tax law and taxes. It is important that you give your advisors as much factual information about yourself, your goals, and

Table 12.14
New Basis in the New Property Following an Exchange

The Calculations	Dollar Amounts
1. Sale price or value of the old property.	
2. Less allowable fix-up expenses.	
3. Less selling expenses.	
4. Adjusted sales price.	
5. Plus any cash you paid to the other party at closing.	
6. Plus mortgages you assume on new property.	
7. Plus gain recognized (see line 17 of the 1031 tax calculations shown earlier in this chapter).	
8. Subtotal.	
9. Less cash you received at the closing.	
10. Less other taxable boot you received at the closing.	
11. Less any loss, which might be recognized.	
12. Tax basis of all property you received at closing.	
13. Less value of boot you received at closing.	
14. This is the new tax basis of your 1031 property.	

any other property you might be considering. Make sure they understand what you want, and that they are experienced in all of the investment techniques covered in this book. Recognize that when your lawyer or CPA gives you quick negative advice about using a creative technique it might be because he or she are not well versed in the field. It has been my sad experience that many lawyers and accountant types are not as up-to-date on some of these creative strategies as they should be. It is a simple fact of life that when an advisor does not know or understand something, they are likely to advise against it. I can assure you that some very smart lawyers who were also owners of the property in question were giving themselves the wrong advice.

One of the basic reasons you should have as much knowledge about what works in this business is that you will find that you must help the other party along in the process of getting the deal done. Of course, you have to be careful about teaching the other party anything. This can be viewed wrongly, and after all, no one likes to deal with a smart-alecky investor.

When you find a seller who will approach an exchange as a beneficial move on his or her part, or a seller who will take an exchange as a part of the deal, you are on your way to building equity for yourself prior to the deal and making a cashless transaction. You can do this even if you don't own the property you are going to exchange. In fact, you can make more exchanges at greater profit if you don't own the property in the first place.

IMPROVING YOUR ABILITY TO MAKE MORE BENEFICIAL EXCHANGES

1. BE ON THE LOOKOUT FOR EXCHANGES WHEREVER YOU GO. Whenever you talk to owners or prospective buyers of real estate, ask them if they have anything they would like to exchange. Sometimes a buyer will suggest a piece of property you have not been talking about and the seller is always a prime candidate for the tool.

2. LEARN TO NEGOTIATE WITH OTHER EXCHANGERS. You will benefit from their experience, or at least will become comfortable in the language they use. It is a good idea to write up several hypothetical deals for practice before you sit down with your clients. If there aren't any advanced exchangers around to talk to, don't worry. See your attorney and have him or her go over one of the standard exchange forms with you so you will be able to use it properly. Tell your attorney that you are going to make some big deals (you will if you try), and that as your business improves your attorney's will, too.

3. DON'T GET HUNG UP ON THE MATH OF THE EXCHANGE. First of all, it is not hard. You only have to follow the sequence, as shown in this chapter, to get at the right answers. Much of the time you will have help. When it comes to calculating the tax on the gain, you will have to pass that task on to the client's accountant anyway. The tax examples shown here are only estimates. You will never be able to arrive at the exact tax unless you have considerable knowledge of the client's other income. Whenever you do show a tax consequence, be sure to point out the assumptions you made. Once you have the client's accountant working with you, he or she will do the rest of the calculations. Keep in mind that in math, there are different ways of arriving at the same solution. Don't be quick to tell the accountant that he or she has figured it out wrong, unless you see the calculations and know what assumptions were used.

4. USE EXCHANGES IN OTHER PARTS OF FINANCING. This is a tool to be used for finding solutions to your clients' problems. You can and will find ways to mix this form with others. For example, it is possible to take a property and break it up into land and buildings. Once values are set, you can sell part and exchange the other. Sale and leasebacks can be intermixed into exchanging. A property can be sold, leased back, and the leasehold later exchanged for some other property. The possibilities are many.

5. DON'T BECOME A PROFESSIONAL EXCHANGER. There are a few people who have made that transition successfully. I am of the opinion, however, that exchanging is just one way to skin the cat. If you rely on this format alone and are unwilling to consider the possibility that you or your client should not exchange, then you will not be objective in your service. Be flexible.

6. TAKE THE UPPER HAND. You can become experienced in exchanging in a very short time. Try to read more about the topic. Articles often appear in some of the major real estate publications. Look for these new ideas used by others. Watch for changes in the law that affect exchanges.

THE BOTTOM LINE: REMEMBER YOUR GOALS

Real estate exchanges, of any kind, are simply tools you can use. They work well in all kinds of markets and can help you move closer to your goal. Remember, any exchange that takes you closer to your goal can be a good exchange.

Chapter 13

HOW TO MAXIMIZE YOUR USE OF PYRAMID FINANCING

GOAL OF THIS CHAPTER

This chapter shows you an exciting technique that allows you to shift equities in such a way that it becomes possible to purchase a property and to obtain new financing that may exceed the actual cost of the property. Although you may never use the technique in that way, its flexibility can open doors to many opportunities that might otherwise evade you.

DEFINITION OF A PYRAMID MORTGAGE

In the world of creative financing, one of the best methods to quickly build wealth is with pyramid finance. This method is highly creative and, although not used widely, it can be combined with other techniques outlined in this book. *Pyramid financing* should not be confused with the old-time sales pyramids that are illegal. The finance pyramid is where you start small, and as you expand your equity, you use that equity as the security for a down payment or investment funds for more property. The finance pyramid works so well in many instances that the primary pitfall is the potential to over-leverage your investment.

Pyramid financing is present when you pledge the equity on a property you own or have under contract as collateral to a first or second mortgage that you acquire for another investment. The reasons for doing this vary. Next, we discuss several reasons for using this technique.

Primary Reasons for Using a Pyramid

1. *To create a "free and clear" purchase to allow new financing.* This can be a situation where the seller of the property you are to acquire is agreeable to hold a soft (low interest and/or easy repayment terms) second mortgage. However, you also want to refinance the entire purchase of the property to maximize leverage you will gain. Institutional financing generally restricts second financing. Therefore, by moving the seller's second mortgage to another property, the new first mortgage can be placed without worry of such restriction.

2. *To make another property more saleable.* This is one of the best uses of this technique. Anytime you acquire a property and the seller is open to hold financing on the property they are selling, look at your portfolio. Do you have something you would like to sell, and know that by having soft financing on that property it would sell quickly? If this is the case, then offer the seller (of the property you are acquiring) to hold a second mortgage on that property. Notice I said "second mortgage." Even if your "for sale" property was free and clear, a soft second mortgage, plus a low first mortgage that you may create (by a new mortgage) or one that you hold can greatly aid in attracting a buyer.

3. *To obtain cash from the transaction.* Cash might be needed to fix up the property, or to use for a second acquisition.

EXAMPLE 1.   You are acquiring an apartment building worth $230,000. There is an existing mortgage of $125,000 at reasonable terms from a local institutional lender. That would mean a seller's equity in the property of $105,000. However, the seller tells you he would like to hold a first mortgage in the amount of $100,000. This presents a problem, because the existing mortgage would have to be paid off, and you don't want to invest $130,000 in cash ($230,000 less the seller held first of $100,000). You look at what other assets you own that might help you make this deal. You own a vacant lot you purchased 10 years ago for $50,000. Based on recent sales of similar lots in the subdivision, you conservatively estimate its value to be $150,000. You could offer the seller of the apartments this property as security for the $100,000 first mortgage he wants to hold. So you offer the seller the following:

- You will assume the existing first mortgage of $125,000.
- You will give the seller $5,000 cash.
- You offer the seller the remaining balance of $100,000 as a first mortgage on the vacant lot.

Because the seller's primary goal is to get rid of the apartments and hold a long-term first mortgage, then this deal might work well. There are some very good tax benefits to a seller in this kind of situation if he has a sizable gain in the apartment complex. You save part of your cash to negotiate if it becomes necessary to improve your offer.

Here is the breakdown of the deal thus far:

Price of the apartment complex	$230,000
Existing first mortgage	125,000
Your cash down payment	5,000
The first mortgage on the building	100,000
Balance of equity in the deal	$230,000

You then arrange new financing from a local lender for the maximum amount possible, say $175,000. You pay off the existing $125,000 former mortgage and end up with $45,000 cash (after deducting the $5,000 down payment).

EXAMPLE 2.   In the same basic situation but the seller only has an existing first mortgage of $40,000 on the apartment building. This gives him greater equity than you can come up with unless he takes a second mortgage on the apartment complex or you refinance the apartment building. Let us try a new approach. You offer to pay the same price of $230,000 as follows:

The seller has $190,000 of present equity ($230,000 less the existing mortgage of $40,000 = $190,000).

Your initial offer looks like this:

1. You will get a new first mortgage in the amount of $175,000; pay off the existing $40,000.
2. You will pay him cash at closing of $90,000.
3. You will give him a first mortgage on your lot of $100,000.

In this deal, the seller gets a lot of cash and does not mind holding the first mortgage on your lot. What did this deal cost you? See the following:

Apartment building price	$	230,000
Existing mortgage	−	40,000
Seller's equity	$	190,000
You borrow $175,000 on the building		$175,000
You pay off the first mortgage on the apartment building	−	40,000
Balance from the loan	$	135,000
The seller gets the balance of the mortgage		$90,000
The seller holds a first mortgage on your lot	+	100,000
Balance of equities in this transaction	$	190,000

As the buyer, you had $135,000 net proceeds from the loan. The seller got $90,000 of that, and you were left with $45,000 cash in your pocket.

Assume that the amount borrowed is net of any closing cost. This is still a good deal for a lender.

NOT FOR THE TIMID INVESTOR

This advanced technique—pyramiding—is not for the faint of heart.

There is no investment strategy that requires a greater confidence in one's abilities than does pyramiding. If you have doubts about your ability to use this technique properly, do not use it until you have gained more knowledge of your abilities, your goals, and the marketplace in which you are about to invest.

Pyramiding has an element of risk that I will cover in detail. As was mentioned at the outset, the greatest risk is in getting too deep in debt too quickly. As a short-term loan, however, the pyramid is at its best. By short-term financing, consider that if either of the two examples (pages 322–323) follow a plan designed to reduce presumed equity to aid negotiation so that you can make a quick sale, the added financing may actually help you sell the property. In that instance then, the added debt could be worthwhile. Just be sure your plan is a sound one and you know what is going on in your marketplace. In this kind of situation the real risk in using the pyramid is that you will spend a lot of time to put the deal together only to have the seller reject it in the end. If you are a seller to another party using the pyramid, you must be overly cautious and follow my guidelines in this chapter to ensure that you are taking prudent care of your investments.

Works Best in a Rising Economy

Pyramid financing works best in a rising economy where property values are going up. This is, of course, the situation where virtually all financing will benefit the borrower. If you consider that property values go up generally because the income potential has increased, then the more you have locked into low interest rates for payback, the greater your return will be in succeeding years. All that is necessary is for the interest rate to be less than the demand you want on your investment. For example, if you can borrow at 10 percent, and the property is capable of paying a return of 14 percent of your initial investment, then you are in good shape because the income produced by that investment is increased. As you become confident in your knowledge of your comfort zone, you will begin to see properties where you can quickly and often inexpensively increase value in a very short time, when the added value can result in increased income, or profit can warrant the high leverage. You will use this method of financing when it produces the best repayment terms of all other alternatives available to you.

Pyramid financing also works well in situations where the seller is motivated and will hold secondary financing with a low loan-to-value ratio. The ability to move a seller into a first mortgage on another property you own (even if it costs you something to make it free and clear) may entice that seller to take your offer.

MECHANICS OF PYRAMID FINANCING

When you use the pyramid, you often maximize the amount of debt you owe. However, because you are mortgaging another property (separately or in addition to the purchased property), you should not reach the maximum loan-to-value ratio on the combined assets involved.

> EXAMPLE 3.   You purchase a $2 million office building with the following terms:

- You assume the existing debt of $500,000.
- You borrow from another lender $500,000 with a second mortgage on the office building, and pay this to the seller. The total loan-to-value ratio in the combination of the first and second mortgage is 50 percent. This is a favorable loan ratio and should produce favorable terms on the second mortgage.
- You give the seller a second mortgage of $1 million on a shopping center you own that is worth $3 million and the existing first mortgage is only $500,000. The seller of the office building takes this second position because the combined total of the existing first and the second is also a reasonable loan-to-value ratio of 50 percent.

Each of the loans in question represents a reasonable risk to the mortgagee (the lender), because the loan-to-value ratio as it relates to the specific security, is within the normal risk range. This presumes, of course, that the above values are accurate. However, many lenders insist that their mortgage documents contain provisions that limit the borrower to a first mortgage position, or a specific loan-to-value ratio. Some institutional lenders may also restrict or even prohibit any secondary financing on the same property, which is one of the big advantages of using a second property as security for the added debt.

A Pyramid Resembles a Blanket Mortgage

When a lender restricts or prohibits secondary financing, the pyramid may be the only way to obtain the secondary financing. Take note that the pyramid is much like a blanket mortgage, without the cross-collateralization effect that is essential in blanket mortgages.

> EXAMPLE 4.   I buy your free and clear home and give you $20,000 cash and a first mortgage on a vacant lot I own in Texas as the balance, and I have used a simple pyramid.

If that same transaction included the home I purchased from you as well as my Texas lot as security in a mortgage, the financing method would no longer be a pyramid but, rather, a straight blanket mortgage.

The Pyramid Can Be Used in Conjunction with a Blanket Mortgage

It is possible to use a pyramid that incorporates a blanket form as well. Therefore, remember that you can use the advantages of the blanket as a seller to secure the mortgage with additional security. In this situation, I might buy your home, give you $15,000 cash (less cash, but a more secure mortgage) and a first mortgage for the balance with a lot in Texas and a lot in North Carolina as security. The combined effect of more than one property makes the pyramid also a blanket. It would be helpful for you to review the advantages and disadvantages of the blanket mortgage in Chapter 9 to see how this additional twist might make the pyramid system work even better.

Sellers Prefer Pyramid Financing over Second Mortgages

There are several reasons why the pyramid works better for the investor than conventional financing and even better than normal seller-held financing. Let us look at a case study to examine these different attributes.

EXAMPLE 5.   Ryan is just getting started in real estate investing and does not have much cash to invest. He owns a small home he bought for $155,000 four years ago. At that time, he obtained a first mortgage for $125,000 and invested $30,000 cash. An estimate of the value of this home today is $245,000. Ryan has paid down his mortgage to the point where he now owes $42,000. This gives him an overall equity of $203,000 ($245,000 − $42,000 = 203,000). The most cash he can come up with at this time is around $35,000.

Ryan wants to buy an income property. He has found a nice four-unit apartment building that he can buy for $210,000. He is sure that with some minor fix-up he can increase the rents substantially. There is no mortgage on this apartment building, and the seller has indicated that he would hold some financing. The seller wants a sizable down payment though if she is going to hold that secondary financing.

Ryan offers the seller the following terms:

- A purchase price of $200,000.
- A cash down payment of $125,000. Ryan knows that he can borrow up to $175,000 on this purchase from a local lender.
- A second mortgage on Ryan's own home for the balance of $75,000.

This kind of offer will have a very strong chance of success for the following reasons:

- The amount of cash down is more than the seller thought he or she was going to get. That is in the seller's favor, and he or she may drop the price because of that.

- Because the seller will not have to hold the second mortgage on his or her own property, the seller will feel relief that he or she is not financing 100 percent of the transaction. Sellers like the idea of being out of the deal.

- This is where the greener grass concept comes into the picture. Because the second mortgage is not on the seller's property, the seller does not feel as though he or she is taking a big risk. After all, if she were to hold a second mortgage behind the existing financing, which she may believe is only going to be the $125,000 cash she will get, then Ryan would have purchased the property with zero cash down. That is a clear 100 percent loan-to-value ratio. In reality, as this has progressed, Ryan is in a position to acquire this property without any of his own cash. If he can borrow more than the $125,000 that it takes to do this deal as it stands, then he might have another $50,000 to invest along with his own cash.

Ryan sets the terms on the second mortgage on his home. Since this mortgage is private, there will be no lending institution involved. This means that for that $75,000, there will be no closing costs, points, or the like associated with the mortgage, only state stamps on mortgages, recording costs, and preparation fees will apply. Of course, Ryan will have all the normal cost to get the loan from the local lender.

In the presentation of his offer to the seller, the secondary financing that the seller is being asked to hold is introduced as though it is part of the package and not something separate to be negotiated. Ryan says, "In addition to the $125,000 cash, I will give you a $75,000 second mortgage against this home (showing a photo of the home), which is where I live." Ryan would continue to explain the terms of the $75,000 mortgage. "I know the $75,000 will be of interest to you, Mr. Seller, and this second mortgage will pay back to you $435.50 per month for the next 120 months and then balloon in full at $75,000. That would return to you a total of $127,500 over that term" (interest of $52,500 plus the balloon of the principal of $75,000).

THE GRASS ALWAYS LOOKS GREENER ON THE OTHER SIDE

This statement is true in all forms of investing and financing. People from New York City think prices in Florida are low, people in Florida think prices in South Carolina are low, and so on. The pyramid thrives because of the natural human trait that causes most people to look at something else and believe it is better than what they have. "Here, I'll give you this beautiful box. Now, I'll tell you what, if you give me the box back, plus $10, I'll give you this bigger box." This is real life drama that we can see almost any night watching TV. Because we often look at what other people have and wish it were ours, and often are glad to get rid of what we have to get theirs, this fuels the whole aspect of the pyramid. This very human syndrome also works wonders for the real estate exchanger.

Once Ryan has outlined the basics of the deal and the seller shows interest by agreeing (at least in principal) to accept the price of $200,000 and the amount of cash down, the rest of the deal is simply formality. The mortgage is presented almost as though it were already in place: "In addition, I'll give you a $75,000 mortgage against my own home." This positive approach should be applied in every kind of transaction where you are creating an exchange. The essence is, "I'll give you the mortgage instead of the cash." However, you would never say that. Never compare or offer an alternative that you are not offering. You, after all, are not giving the seller a choice. Do they want the cash, or the mortgage? So, be careful how you present it.

Some novice investors wrongly turn this into a negative statement. "You wouldn't take a second mortgage of $25,000 instead of cash, would you?"

"Heck no" is the answer that any seller would immediately give you.

Etch into your mind never to make a comparison between two events or circumstances when only one is available. Sellers fall into this trap by making a direct comparison with the actual terms of a contract, as they would compare to what the seller wants. Ryan offered a price that was acceptable, a lot of cash (from the bank of course), and a second mortgage. He did not give the seller the option of taking cash instead of the mortgage. Buyers fall into this trap too, and get hung up on what they want. Ryan wants to purchase this property for the above-stated terms. If there is no flexibility in his negotiations, he might have the property slip by. Likewise, if Ryan did not know about the pyramid he might try to get the seller to hold the second against the property being sold. Sometimes this works, but when the loan-to-value ratio is close to or at 100 percent, the normal secondary mortgage usually is not acceptable, and sellers know it.

Once the deal seems to be workable between the parties, the details should be discussed. Of course, the method of payment of the mortgage will not work in all situations. If the seller felt a need to cash out the mortgage more quickly, the 120-month payment (10 years) would be a bit long. On the other hand, if the seller had a seven-year-old child (or grandchild), the mortgage would provide a nice annuity to set up an education fund for the child. If the money was reinvested each time Ryan made a payment, over the 120 months at even a modest interest rate, there could be in excess of over $150,000 in the bank.

If the seller balked at the terms, Ryan might have to sweeten the deal. So far, he is still $10,000 under the original price, which he thought was a good deal. In addition, there is room to maneuver with the terms of the second mortgage on the house. If Ryan had done some homework on the seller, he might have had his own stockbroker show how these payments into a mutual fund or insurance annuity could turn out. The idea in all negotiations is to get the other party to focus on the parts of the deal in which you have room for modifications to the terms.

By the way, the concept of the "grass looking greener" is so real and so infectious many investors have gone astray because of it. Consider this a warning that there will be a day that you might feel a strange tingle (in your wallet) as you see a property that looks so good, and so cheap (in comparison to what you are used to) that you cannot possibly fail to purchase it. I have fallen victim to this illness, and let that be enough of your exposure so that you continually ask yourself these questions:

- Is that property within my comfort zone?
- Will my investment in that property move me closer to my goals?
- Can I afford to lose whatever capital I will put into that deal?

A no answer to any of these three should cause you to sit back and reconsider the situation. If you still feel compelled to move forward with the transaction, at least make sure that your purchase agreement allows you a substantial due diligence period in which to do as much research into the property as possible. Critical in this is that you also must have enough time, which you can devote to that due diligence.

This pyramid transaction is easy to follow:

- Assuming the deal is sound, Ryan could go to an institutional lender and borrow the $175,000 without any problem. As long as there is no second mortgage on the property, which in this case there is not as the second mortgage is against another property (Ryan's home), the lender will not be bound by any rules or limitations on lending with the presence of secondary financing. The advantage here is that Ryan will get a better loan than if he were trying to get the maximum loan on the property, or if he did want to get a maximum loan he could pocket some additional cash if he wanted to.

- By using the grass is greener approach, the second mortgage that is at a lower than market interest rate may be accepted. After all, the seller is out of the property, has pocketed a bundle of cash, and can go about his or her business collecting from Ryan on the second mortgage. All Ryan has to offer the seller is a better return than if the seller had invested the cash himself in triple A-rated bonds or a good money market. It is important to remember that the seller may have some additional benefits in this transaction. If the seller were to have a taxable gain from the sale, the portion of the sale proceeds that are deferred, that is, paid over a period of years, would fall under the tax break provisions of the installment sale.

The IRS allows any seller the opportunity to spread the tax on the gain over the period of time that the money is actually received by the seller. This is a very important IRS rule that has a major effect on a seller's reinvestment return. Because you can demonstrate the benefit to the seller by holding secondary financing of any kind, you should know how to calculate this benefit. Later in this chapter, I explain this and other benefits you can use in selling the seller on taking your offer. First, let us look at the benefits to the buyer:

- Can avoid existing mortgage limitations to secondary financing.
- Reduces debt service.
- Increases yield on cash invested.
- Gets a yes from the seller.
- Gives you flexibility.
- Can put cash in your pocket.
- Is a great cashless investing technique.
- You can purchase two properties at the same time.

Take a look at each of these buyer's benefits separately.

Can Avoid Existing Mortgage Limitations to Secondary Financing

When the existing financing on a property is being assumed by the buyer, you need to be careful of all the terms contained in both the mortgage and the mortgage note. Many lenders insist that the loan be limited to or prohibit the future existence of any secondary financing on the property that secures their loan. The idea behind this is that the lender does not want to have the property over-leveraged to the point that additional financing increases the total loan-to-value ratio above the initial percentage when the loan was made. This does not matter what position the loan is, as a second mortgage that you want to assume, may contain this same kind of provision, even if the first mortgage does not. When you encounter any kind of secondary loan prohibition this may affect any kind of secondary lien being created against that property. This would likely rule out wraparound mortgages, regular secondary financing, and blanket mortgages, as all of these forms generally cause a direct lien against the same property that secures the existing loan or loans in question.

The pyramid takes care of this situation because the security for the loan is another property. Keep in mind that it would be okay to use a blanket mortgage or wraparound mortgage as long as the combined security did not include the new investment.

Reduces Debt Service

This is a relative benefit of course, and while an ideal benefit, it may not always be available. Any time you can move some of the financing you need to obtain to a less expensive kind of financing then you will benefit in the long run.

EXAMPLE 6.   You need $125,000 in total financing, and the market rate from institutional lenders is 9 percent interest per annum. In addition to paying the annual interest on that $125,000, you would owe, at the closing of the loan, all the loan costs that would be applied against the $125,000. By getting the seller to take part of the deal in soft financing, in Ryan's case, $75,000 of the deal at 7 percent interest per annum, you improve your overall position to get a better new first mortgage. If Ryan could reduce the interest on a $125,000 new first (when he could borrow up to $175,000), he would likely drop his interest rate by a point or two, and could likely carry the loan out over more years. This alone could reduce his annual interest charged on the mortgage payment between the two mortgages. Consider that his option was to borrow the full $175,000 from a local lender at 9 percent interest per year. That would cost him $15,750 the first year just for interest. By dropping the rate to 7 percent for each loan, the interest charge is only $12,250 for that first year. A savings of $3,500 in interest alone goes directly to the bottom line. An increase of $3,500 in the NOI of the apartments would increase the value of that property to at least $35,000. While a 2 percent savings on the overall debt of $175,000 may not seem much, you also save on the loan origination cost. In real estate, every penny counts.

Increases Yield on Cash Invested

As you contemplate using the pyramid, you should take into consideration that this is one of the very best cashless investing techniques available to the smart buyer. Because you are introducing soft terms to a transaction while at the same time reducing your cash invested, your overall yield of cash on cash is increased. Clearly, in the Ryan case, he invested none of his own cash in the initial purchase. Any cash that he now spends can be directed 100 percent to the improvement of the property. Improvements, Ryan knows, will increase his cash flow.

Gets a Yes from the Seller

You begin every negotiation with the initial goal to tie up the property. The next step is getting the seller to agree to a price and terms that work for you. It is essential that the deal includes provisions that do not force you to close until you have accomplished necessary studies and have attained the desired comfort level to cause you to move forward. Keep in mind that the very initial price and terms that you both agree to may not be the final terms of the deal. You must first be in control of the property in such a way that the seller is bound, but you are not. In the purchase agreement you spell out the terms and conditions you want. You present the agreement and negotiate the fine points to a point where the seller will say yes. That is your goal at this point of the game. It is important that those terms and conditions are substantially the deal as you want it to end up. However, as you will have a due diligence period, whereby you can make inspections and investigate the property, its zoning, city rules and regulations, and so on, you will have the unilateral right to back out of the deal unless you find everything as presented, or as you expected it to be. That gives you a later opportunity to go to the seller to renegotiate the deal. This needs to be done carefully because you must stay in control all the time. If you let the deal expire then the seller has an out, and he or she may take it. Getting the yes then is critical, and the pyramid goes a long way when secondary financing is needed.

You will discover as you negotiate your future acquisitions that one of the hardest things to do is to get a seller to agree to all the factors that must fall into place and meet your approval before you ultimately close on the property. Some investments may require approvals so that you can actually utilize the purchased property, or to build the kind of buildings you want to own. These approvals may take months, if not years to obtain, and in the end you may never get those approvals despite having spent considerable funds to reach that point. Because of this, you need to get over the shock of this potential eventual time period with the seller. If they are a novice, or out of date in the reality of these things ("Why, it only took me 10 minutes to know I wanted to buy this property." This approach was fine 50 years ago when that farmer purchased his tobacco farm for $100 per acre, but not today when you are offering $200,000 per acre so that you can build a high-rise office building.), some sellers will never understand these realities so move on to those who do.

Can Put Cash in Your Pocket

The prospect of buying a property and ending up with cash in your pocket is very possible when you use the pyramid. That is the good; the bad is you will end up with more than 100 percent of the purchase price being debt. A quick example of how easily this can be accomplished follows.

EXAMPLE 7. In the Ryan purchase, suppose that he offered the seller $200,000, with a cash payment of $125,000 and a second mortgage on his house of $75,000. Only, instead of borrowing just $125,000 from the local lender, he borrows $175,000. After paying the closing costs on the loan he will still end up with around $40,000 cash in his pocket. This cash can be used to benefit the new purchase, or can go to work in another transaction.

Is a Great Cashless Investing Technique

As long as you have real equity in one property, you can use that equity as a source for pyramid mortgages for other transactions. The biggest advantage in using this technique is that it allows you to keep the property you own, rather than having to sell it or use it as a direct exchange. This is important to the greener grass syndrome that works. By keeping the property you demonstrate that you feel it has value. "Take this second mortgage on my home" has a very sincere feeling about it. Sellers would rather take the mortgage than the property.

You Can Purchase Two Properties at the Same Time

This is a technique I do not recommend a novice real estate investor attempt, yet it works in many situations and can be exactly the tool you need to close the right transaction.

This kind of transaction requires that you identify two or more properties you want to purchase. You are sure of the market and what you can do with these properties. They are in your comfort zone and you are ready to pick them up. The only problem is you want to maximize your investment cash to the fix-up and not the actual purchase of the properties. What you do is get control over one of the properties, then springboard into another.

EXAMPLE 8.   Suppose you do not own any property at the moment, but you do have $50,000 cash, and a lot of talent in being able to fix up a property. You have spent a lot of time looking for properties and have found two you think will work well for you. In fact, because they are very near each other, you can maximize your time by working on both of them at the same time.

Property A is a three-bedroom home with a separate detached garage that has an apartment over the parking area. Selling price will be $225,000, and there is an existing mortgage of $50,000 that is due now.

Property B is a five-bedroom home that needs a lot of cosmetic and landscape work. Selling price will be $205,000. There is an existing mortgage of $70,000 that can be assumed.

You offer seller A the following terms:

- You will pay off the existing first mortgage that is due.
- You will give seller A $100,000 cash at closing.
- You will give the seller a $75,000 second mortgage on property B.

You offer seller B the following terms:

- You will assume the existing mortgage.
- You will give seller B $35,000 in cash.
- You will give seller B a $100,000 second mortgage on property A.

To accomplish this double transaction, you would go to a local lender and show how you were going to improve property A. Your plans show how you will convert this home and garage into a five-unit apartment complex that would be easily worth $350,000. All you want to borrow is $175,000. Why, that is a 50 percent loan-to-value ratio for the finished product. You agree to let the lender hold back $25,000, which you will use for fix-up. Out of the $150,000 left, you will be able to pay off the existing first mortgage and give the seller $100,000 cash at closing. You will balance the deal with seller A by showing him or her your plans for property B that you are going to turn into a beautiful executive law office.

Now let us look at deal B. Because the bank is holding the funds needed to fix up property A, you do not need all your cash for that. Therefore, you take $35,000 of your $50,000 in cash and give it to seller B, and give him or her a second position on property A in the amount of $100,000. You show how that property will be worth $350,000, and that you have allocated the funds to do that work. You are off and running, and still have a bit of cash left over.

HAVE YOUR CAKE AND EAT IT TOO: THE REAL BENEFIT OF THE PYRAMID

The strategy of pyramiding is to use equities from other properties as acquisition capital for new investments. This allows you to move into new real estate transactions with a minimum cash payment. Because you use equity as a basis for the transaction, you retain ownership of the previous property and at the same time gain another.

Any property owner with equity can go into the marketplace and find someone who will take that equity as security for the property being sold. Generally speaking, there will always be properties available, because there are always owners who are highly motivated. These sellers will do anything that gives them an opportunity to relieve themselves of what they own. While many of these situations would fall into the category of distressed properties, sometimes it is the owner who is distressed and not the property. Many investors make a lot of money looking for prime properties of distressed owners. This strategy works for virtually any kind of investing, and is not restricted to real estate.

Pyramiding Is a Risk That Can Be Worthwhile

You should not get the impression that pyramiding is to be avoided because there are many situations that are acceptable for all parties. It is only necessary for you and other participants in a pyramid to be aware of the risks involved. Without a doubt, pyramiding is one of the highest leverage forms of financing available to the broker or his client. There will be times when the risk is well worth the possible gain.

Because every real estate property is unique, it is very difficult to establish exact value terms. Comparative values can give you a good guide, but unless a lot of research and study is made, two exact buildings situated across the street from each other can vary in value depending on very subtle differences. When you purchase a property that is distressed, it is likely that through cosmetic improvements the apparent equity can be increased in a very short time. This new equity, or surplus over what you have invested, becomes the power behind the pyramid. In a rising market, this value may have the promise of rising further, adding to the security of the potential junior mortgage to be used in the pyramid.

HOW TO BUILD A FORTUNE IN A HURRY BY PYRAMIDING EQUITY

The amount of risk you take when using the pyramid depends on the amount of equity you have. If you purchase a property with $5,000 down, and spend another $5,000 in cosmetic fix up, your invested equity is $10,000. If you have no contingent liability to the debt on the property, that is to say, if you defaulted on the existing debt you would only lose the property, then this $10,000 is the total possible capital risk you have. If you establish an apparent equity in this property of $20,000, that does not increase your risk any as you still have invested only $10,000. Keep in mind that if you are personally obligated to the existing debt and you get into economic difficulties, your risk is greater than the capital invested.

The best way to explain pyramiding is to go through a detailed example. I have chosen an extreme example because it points out the many aspects and benefits of this exciting tool.

EXAMPLE 9: HOW ONE INVESTOR STARTED HIS PYRAMID WITH $30,000 AND ENDED UP WITH $510,000.   Blackburn owned a building worth $90,000. Against this value there was a first mortgage of $60,000 and he had a real equity of $30,000. His desire was to buy more properties, but he was limited by the capital he had to invest which was only $30,000. While he could live without the income from his investments, he could not invest more cash than the $30,000. Blackburn's long-range plan was to build as much equity as possible, sell out, and retire to a ranch in Montana. Everything he had was dedicated to this goal.

Within Blackburn's comfort zone, he located several interesting apartment houses of varying sizes. Each needed some improvements to increase the income, but Blackburn believed that these repairs would substantially increase the value. The first property was a duplex for sale at $100,000. The property had a recent first mortgage of $70,000.

Blackburn offered to buy the duplex for the full price of $100,000. However, he did not want to invest cash. He offered to assume the first mortgage and give the seller a second mortgage of $30,000 secured by Blackburn's original building. This increased his total debt to $90,000 on his original building. This offer was accepted and closed. Now in ownership, Blackburn added $8,000 in cash from his bank account to improve the property.

With the improvements made, the rental income from the duplex was quickly improved and the fair market value increased to $140,000. It took Blackburn six months to accomplish this build up of value, and at the end of this period the first building had also increased in value by $15,000 due to an overall improvement of the market. Blackburn now owned in his real estate portfolio:

- A building ($105,000 value, against the total mortgages of $90,000 leaving an equity of $15,000).

- A duplex worth $140,000 with mortgages of $70,000. This left him with equity of $70,000.

- He still had $22,000 of cash left in his bank account.

The next step: moving into another transaction. Next Blackburn found a six-unit apartment house also in need of repair. The estimated cost for repairs was $15,000.

Although the seller was asking more, Blackburn believed he could buy the property for $180,000. There was a mortgage of $100,000 on the property so the seller's equity was $80,000.

Blackburn went to his banker and told him he would like to borrow a net of $140,000 on the six-unit complex. (An additional $4,000 was needed for closing costs to cover the lending expense, and so on; so the total loan required was $144,000.) Blackburn explained to the banker that he would spend $15,000 on the property after the closing, and with this improvement the property should be worth over $220,000. He showed the banker a pro forma he and his accountant had worked out, indicating the rental potential after the minor improvements and repairs. All he was asking for was a loan at a loan-to-value ratio of around 65 percent of the proposed value.

The banker agreed. Blackburn then offered the seller:

- $25,000 cash.
- A second mortgage on the duplex he owned of $55,000 to equal the seller's $80,000 equity.
- $100,000 to pay off the existing financing.

The total cash needed in this transaction was: $25,000 to the seller, $100,000 to pay off the existing mortgage, $4,000 for closing costs, and $15,000 for improvements ($25,000 + $100,000 + $4,000 + $15,000 = $144,000).

Blackburn had made the transaction totally out of the new loan proceeds, and therefore did not have to touch his remaining cash in the bank.

At the end of 12 months, the three properties were worth more and the picture looked like this (The reduced mortgage amount is due to principal payments made.):

Property	Present Value	Total Mortgages	Equity
First building	$112,000	$ 86,000	$ 14,000
Duplex	150,000	125,000	5,000
Six-unit complex	220,000	144,000	76,000
Totals	$482,000	$355,000	$127,000
Plus $22,000 in cash			

In each of these transactions, Blackburn had to be sure that the income from each property would cover the debt service being placed on it. Because the second mortgages are always from the previous purchase, Blackburn did not attempt additional pyramid transactions until there was income to support the new second to be used as part of his subsequent acquisitions.

Blackburn did not stop here, however, but continued to do the same thing on a larger scale.

Blackburn found an old industrial building, which would convert nicely into a miniwarehouse and storage facility. He knew he would have to put all his remaining cash into the renovations, but the deal looked promising. He outlined the plan to his accountant who confirmed that the numbers were correct. Blackburn moved forward. Here is what happened.

Blackburn offered the owner of the warehouse complex the following: a second mortgage of $75,000 secured by the six-unit apartment house to assume the existing mortgage on the industrial building of $325,000.

He then went to the bank holding the mortgage on the building. He got them to extend the loan by the amount of interest for one year and at the same time put a one-year moratorium on principal payments. He told the bank he was going to put another $22,000 into the property and presented them with a detailed pro forma prepared by his accountant showing how he expected to double the present revenue within 12 months. Since the bank was concerned about the future of the present loan, they liked Blackburn's idea and decided to work with him.

At the end of another year, Blackburn had increased the value of the warehouse to $550,000, with the promise that in a few years it would exceed $600,000.

If you succeed once, why not try again? Because of his luck in the last venture, Blackburn did the same thing across town. He bought an even larger industrial complex, which had been vacant for over two years and put $100,000 into remodeling the buildings.

How did he get the $100,000? The complex was on the market at a rock-bottom price of $1,025,000. Blackburn knew his bankers would lend up to $750,000 since the existing loans on the property were only $225,000. Blackburn was able to show the bankers his success rate in turning property around. This success impressed the bankers.

Blackburn went to the owners and explained what he wanted to do. He offered them a deal, which, after much negotiation, ended up as follows:

Cash paid to the owners	$370,000
Payoff of existing mortgage	255,000
Second mortgage secured by the mini-warehouse	150,000
Total thus far	$775,000

Blackburn then offered the owners the following terms: Annual payments of $20,000 on a land lease under the complex's property to be held by the sellers. The land lease was to be subordinated to a first mortgage not to exceed $750,000. The land could be purchased by Blackburn at any time within the next 20 years for a fixed price of $275,000, or the lease would continue for a total of 40 years. As an additional kicker for Blackburn, the rent did not start until 12 months after closing. The transaction went as follows:

Cash paid to the owners	$ 370,000
Payoff of existing mortgage	255,000
Improvements	100,000
Paid as loan cost	15,000
Legal and other closing costs	10,000
Amount borrowed from Blackburn's bank	$ 750,000
Value of land Blackburn leased	275,000
Full asking price	$1,025,000

Remember, the $275,000 value of land is not actually paid, unless Blackburn exercises his option to purchase. In the meantime, he owns the buildings as a leasehold asset. His obligation to pay the rent is much like a second mortgage that has interest-only payments. However as he refinanced the buildings, the lease was more desirable to the new first mortgage lender because the land lease was fully subordinated to their position.

At the end of 12 months, with the new complex fully rented and doing well, Blackburn's overall financial picture, due to increases in value and principal reductions, looked like this:

Property	Market Value	Mortgages	Equity
First building	$ 120,000	$ 83,000	$ 22,000
Duplex	155,000	122,000	13,000
Six-unit complex	235,000	215,000	15,000
Miniwarehouse	575,000	475,000	100,000
Industrial complex	1,110,000	750,000	360,000*
Totals	$2,195,000	$1,645,000	$550,000

*Buildings only.

In very few years, Blackburn had built his net worth from $60,000 to $550,000, with only equity and $30,000 in cash to work with. Within a few more years, he estimated that he could refinance his total debt to pay off some of the higher interest loans and recapture the land under the industrial complex. At this point, he should be generating a cash flow of about $85,000 per year. At this stage in Blackburn's plan, he could retire to Montana to live out his life punching cows, or stay in the pyramiding game a bit longer.

HOW TO SET UP THE MOST PROFITABLE PYRAMID

There are two major factors to keep in mind when you approach pyramiding:

1. Pyramiding is highly risky.
2. The property taken in the pyramid should have the potential to substantiate the risk.

Once these cautions are clear in your mind, you are ready to go to work to make use of this high-leverage financing tool.

Six Key Steps in Building a Strong Pyramid

In keeping with the step-by-step procedure, follow these six steps to pyramiding:

1. Review your goals. Then work toward these ends.
2. Outline your risk equity and/or cash.
3. Substantiate your equity by appraisals or pro forma.
4. Look for property that has not reached peak income potential.
5. Make an offer.
6. Do not move on until the new property will support new pyramiding by carrying a secondary loan.

Suppose you want to build an estate, and you determine that to build this estate quickly you can risk going into the pyramid program. The next step is to establish the value of the equity on which you plan to build. In Blackburn's case, he started with $30,000 equity plus $30,000 cash. (Cash is not always a requirement, but some may be needed following the closing to improve the properties being acquired.)

An appraisal made by a qualified source that local lending institutions would accept would be helpful to show the real equity in the property with which you plan to start. Appraisals generally work to the owner's advantage since it is rare for a property to sell for a price over the appraisal, and market value often is somewhat below market comparison value. Most appraisals made to market comparisons, therefore, will give a value above the actual marketable sales price in the majority of cases. If you know that the market will support a higher price than that given by the appraiser, then be ready to support that price with hard facts. If you do not want to spend the time and money to hire a qualified appraiser, you have a couple of options to follow. The easiest is to check the tax appraisal on the property as it is, and then compare that appraisal with other similar, but already fixed up properties. Both of these comparative appraisals will go a long way to substantiate your value. You can also make your own appraisal by following the techniques that professional appraisers follow. Although this kind of appraisal would not be accepted by an institutional lender, you may use this technique to learn more about the values in your comfort zone. You may also discover you were way off base with your initial assessment and move on to other properties prior to spending the money for a professional appraisal.

The quickest way to do your own appraisal is to visit every similar property that is listed by real estate brokers until you find one or more that have recent professional appraisals used to substantiate the offered price. Get a copy of all such appraisals you can, and use them as a guide to make your own. In both of these situations you will find that a visit to the Property Records department of your county will be helpful in finding out new information. Remember, all public data on property is available. You can find out what every similar property has sold for, often going back several years. Your real estate broker can be helpful in working out this information, and in fact may print out the information for you in a matter of a few minutes if the data is available online or through one of several data sources used by lawyers and realtors alike.

Armed with an appraisal, the equity for the pyramid will be apparent. This equity will determine the amount of a second mortgage to be secured by it.

One of the best sources for properties that may be available for pyramid buying will be the local exchange group. In essence, the pyramid buyer is exchanging a mortgage in one property for equity in another. If you do not have an exchange group in your area you may find your job more difficult, but not impossible.

In either case, start with what you would like to buy. Make sure that you are capable of managing or developing it into a winner. It may be possible to work out a transaction that blends the pyramid into a normal transaction. We saw how Blackburn was able to use the pyramid and give the seller cash by refinancing the existing mortgages. Look to the combination of as many forms of financing as possible to meet the goals you have set.

Getting Ready to Present the Pyramid Offer to the Seller

Once you have located one or more properties that seem to be worth considering, make an offer on each one. Follow these tips in the presentation of the offer.

But first, do not do the following.

"Mr. Owner, I notice you have an apartment house on 2nd Street that has a 'For Sale' sign in the yard."

"That's right."

"I was wondering, you wouldn't be interested in taking a mortgage back on another property instead of cash down, would you?"

"Are you nuts?"

It is obvious that this type of approach is not professional or effective. However, because this is the approach that many buyers do take, a brief analysis is needed. First, very few sellers know what kind of transaction they will accept until they actually accept one. Second, a negative approach (you would not be interested, would you?) invites a negative reply. Enough said.

FIVE STEPS OF HOW TO EFFECTIVELY PRESENT THE OFFER

1. HAVE ALL THE DATA ABOUT THE SECURITY ON THE PROPERTY BEING USED TO LEVERAGE UP IN THE PYRAMID. A survey, appraisal, income statements (if the property is an income

producer), comparable sales values, and photographs are helpful. Be ready to take the seller over to the property if he or she wants to see it.

2. BEGIN THE PRESENTATION IN A POSITIVE MOOD. If you know you are going to make the deal, you will begin with an edge.

3. DON'T BECOME DEFENSIVE WHEN THE SELLER REJECTS THE IDEA. It is normal for a seller to be skeptical and even negative about something he or she does not understand. It is a natural reaction to what the seller wants, and most times you will get a first reaction that is negative.

4. RESTATE BACK TO THE OTHER PARTY (EITHER BUYER OR SELLER) ANYTHING THEY HAVE SAID TO YOU IN THE NEGOTIATION PROCESS THAT YOU EITHER DO NOT QUITE UNDERSTAND, OR WANT TO MODIFY. This is an effective negotiating process and one that can work to make minor, but important changes in the agreement. You begin by agreeing with the seller (e.g., that the offer does not satisfy his or her desire to receive cash instead of the mortgages). Then restate the objection in a softer tone. "Mr. Seller, I understand that you want more than I am able to offer, but there are some aspects that deserve careful consideration." At this point, you should talk about the property, which the seller will have as security for their mortgage (actually your mortgage but refer to it as theirs). Go over some of the material you have brought for this purpose. From time to time, mention what you plan to do with the new property. If you already plan to spend cash to upgrade it, say: "And I will be investing additional cash, too." This may show your sincerity and close the deal.

5. CALL ON YOUR VERY BEST CLOSING TECHNIQUES; THE REST IS UP TO YOU. When it gets down to this stage, there are no guidelines to follow. You must play it by ear the rest of the way. Some sellers will have to sleep on the offer. Do not get pushy here, since pyramiding may be a very new concept to them. Other sellers may go to the dotted line right away.

USING PYRAMIDING AS A SALES TOOL

There are times when a property is difficult to sell because of the low mortgages it carries. A free and clear property may be extremely difficult to sell unless there is some form of financing available, either from the seller or from other sources. When a combination of the following factors is present, the pyramid is used to benefit the seller:

SELLER'S CHECKLIST TO SEE IF PYRAMIDING CAN AID A SALE

✓ The seller's equity presents a problem in the sale. This will occur in many situations where a high equity and minimal existing financing require a high capital investment on the part of the buyer.

✓ The seller cannot or will not hold purchase money financing to facilitate the ultimate sale.

✓ The conventional financing market does not offer effective refinancing of existing financing. This may be the major stumbling block in the sale of the property in the first place. If the property is an income producer, a high interest rate and a high constant rate may not be absorbed in the net operating income to offer a respectable yield to the investor.

✓ The seller wants to reinvest in more real estate. This factor makes the seller a buyer, and the pyramid program can be examined in detail to see how it can be used to satisfy all four of these criteria.

✓ In a situation that involves a seller and where all four of these criteria can be met, you can then move into a pyramid.

The objectives of the pyramid for the seller are to help make the property more salable, and at the same time reinvest the equity into more real estate. The example that follows shows a step-by-step application of these principles for the seller.

EXAMPLE 10.   Bristow was the owner of a retail complex that consisted of seven shops. He is one of many investors that like to build and own with a high-equity position. In this case, he had built the complex with his own cash and had no mortgage at all.

Over the years, he realized that his attitude toward real estate investing was not giving him the desired leverage on his capital. Thus, he wanted to sell the retail complex and build a larger one by using the capital from the first.

He discussed this with his accountant and then with me. When I examined his property and his situation, I realized that his conservative approach would make the sale difficult. First, he needed to realize most of his equity to move ahead with his plan. Second, he therefore could not hold much paper, if any, at all. To test the third item on the checklist, calls to the local lenders were made. These indicated that while there was money available for mortgages on the present complex, they would be costly and could hurt the ultimate value since the constant rate was high.

The fourth item on the checklist was already met, as the seller was indeed ready to reinvest. There were numerous options to follow in a marketing plan. The property could be put on the market with new financing, but I felt that the loss of value, due to the cost of the money alone, would make this choice secondary if we could come up with another solution. To be specific, the value of the property was determined to be $250,000, based on the fact that the NOI was $25,000 and a 10 percent capitalization rate was felt to be warranted in this situation.

Commercial money was available at 9¾ percent per annum, over 17 years. This created a constant rate of 12.07 percent, or $22,631 per year (P&I) on the maximum loan of $187,500 (75 percent of the value). On top of this, the loan cost would be approximately $8,000.

With an NOI of $25,000 and a deduction of the annual debt of $22,631, a cash flow of only $2,369 would remain. If the investor wanted a 10 percent return, the total capital payment would have to be $23,690. However, as $8,000 of that would go to the cost of the loan, the seller would receive the $187,500 plus $15,690, or $203,190. Thus, with conventional financing the seller would get only $203,190 for a $250,000 value. A loss of over $46,000 was too much to take without further study.

How the Pyramid Got the Seller the Full $250,000 Value. I knew if financing could be put on the property that would provide a 10 percent constant, at no cost to the ultimate buyer or seller, the overall value of the complex could be sustained.

In counseling with the seller, I ascertained that he wanted to buy a vacant tract of land where he could build another, larger complex. He did, in fact, have several locations in mind, even though he had not negotiated on any of them. His conservative nature had kept him from buying until he sold. One site was a three-acre tract that was well suited for his needs. It was on the market for $210,000, a very fair price, and was free and clear of any debt.

My first approach was to see if the owner would consider an exchange for the shops. An offer was presented in the normal exchange procedure. He would not exchange. Yet, I learned that he only wanted a secure return and would sell with a very low down payment and hold paper for the balance. However, this would not solve my investor's problem, as he needed the land free and clear to obtain a development loan and had to sell his property.

A pyramid was structured. We presented the seller of the three acres with a contract that would allow Bristow to meet his needs, if all went well.

The offer was structured as follows:

- The owner of the three acres was to receive $10,000 cash.
- In addition he would receive a first mortgage in the amount of $190,000 on Bristow's shops as the full price for the land. The mortgage was set up on these terms: 8 percent per year, interest only for the first three years, then an amortized payout over the remaining 25 years with a balloon on the fifteenth anniversary of the closing. The closing was to occur upon the sale of the retail complex, providing this sale could be accomplished within 60 days.

How the Pyramid Helped Sell the Retail Complex. In an instant, the retail property now had a $190,000 first mortgage that offered an investor who would ultimately purchase the shops, a mortgage with excellent terms and potential for return. That the interest rate on the mortgage was 8 percent for the first three years meant that the annual debt service on the $190,000 would be $15,200. This would leave a cash flow of $9,800. If the property were to sell for $250,000, the down payment of $60,000 would show a 16.33 percent yield. This provided excellent positive leverage for those three years.

At the end of the interest only period, the annual debt service would go to a 9.27 percent constant, or $17,613. If there were no improvement in the NOI (which was projected to go up), the cash flow would be $7,387 or a 12.3 percent yield on the original investment of $60,000. The balloon did not hamper the sale of the property, as the time period allowed ample opportunity for future refinancing of the loan prior to its balloon payment coming due. On this basis, the sale of the units was rather easy and was accomplished well within the 60-day period.

The investor who ultimately did purchase the shops did well, and so did Bristow, who sold the retail complex for its full value of $250,000. He took $10,000 of the $60,000 he received on the sale and paid that over to the seller of the three acres. Then, the $190,000 mortgage was established to the benefit of all the parties involved. Bristow now proceeded to develop a larger complex on the three acres that he owned free and clear.

Fine Points in Finalizing the Pyramid

The pyramid can be used in many different ways to allow you a foot in the door, as well as "the final close" to a purchase or sale you are trying to accomplish. Some highly creative aspects of the pyramid come into play when you begin to use it in connection with other techniques that either have been discussed thus far or are covered in the book later on. To give you an overview of some of these combinations and a preview of things to come, take a look at the following four examples of very creative uses of the pyramid.

Remember that the pyramid uses value in another property as a security for debt you will place on a property you are trying to buy. This is the natural grass is greener on the other side of the fence aspect that occurs in this technique that makes it so powerful and effective.

EXAMPLE 11: THE DISTANT PYRAMID. The distant pyramid is where you double up on the use of the pyramid concept to the extent that two sellers are involved, each taking the other property as security for a second mortgage on the purchase of their property. In this creative look at the pyramid, you will actually buy two properties more easily than one. Earlier in this chapter, I gave an example of how this would work. Here is a more detailed example of a distant pyramid.

Alex wanted to buy a 10-unit apartment building. He had approached the seller with several different techniques, each using a low down payment offer, and each offer was turned down with the same reply from the seller: "Look, son, I'm not going to finance any buyer that doesn't have equity to back up his offer." The seller you are dealing with may not put it that bluntly, but the end result might be the same. The fact of the matter is that many sellers balk at the very idea of holding financing on their own property simply because they remember how much they paid for that property. After all, if they paid $20,000, how can they justify holding $80,000 in secondary financing on that same property, even if they are selling for $300,000?

While Alex was fooling around with this apartment building, he found a strip store complex that he liked and felt would be a good investment. He made several offers on that property and found the same kind of response from that seller.

Alex decided to offer the apartment seller a second mortgage on the strip store as security for that part of the contract. At the same time, he offered the strip store seller a second mortgage on the apartment building as a part of that purchase offer.

Each owner would be taking a mortgage position against the other property. In each situation, Alex was careful to word the contract so as not to be misleading. He made sure that each seller knew that the second mortgage was to be on a property "that I am in the process of buying," and Alex covered himself with an "out" provision that both transactions were to close at the same time or the deal would be cancelled at Alex's option. Another example of a distant pyramid is shown in the following example.

EXAMPLE 12: WHAT WORKS WELL TWICE MIGHT BE BETTER THRICE.   It would stand to reason, thought Brad, that if you could buy two properties with a pyramid without using any of your own cash, then three properties would be even easier. He tied up three separate properties using the pyramid.

1. Property A was a vacant lot on which he was going to build. It was offered at $50,000, and Brad offered:

   $5,000 cash

   A $45,000 second mortgage on property B

2. Property B was a small strip store that Brad wanted to fix up and remodel. He was going to turn it into a medical complex to complement the demand for such services in the area. The price was $470,000. He felt that he would need another $35,000 for remodeling of the center. His offer was as follows:

   A new first mortgage of $350,000

   A third on property C for $50,000

   A land-lease set at a value of $70,000, which Brad could buy any time over the next 12 years at that same amount. The annual rent was to be $6,300.

3. Property C was an apartment building that consisted of 15 units near the beach. The owner was operating it as an annual apartment building, but Brad knew that if he converted it to seasonal units, putting into the building a hotshot young couple he knew could take care of the property, he could increase the income substantially. The price was $400,000, and he offered the sellers the following deal:

   A $300,000 wraparound mortgage to wrap the existing financing of a first mortgage of $265,000.

   A second mortgage of $35,000

   A first mortgage on property A of $30,000

   Plus $65,000 cash

To accomplish this, $105,000 cash was required to close on all three properties. If Brad could show that property B would be worth $575,000 due to the new income projection, he might be able to borrow up to 80 percent of that amount, or $460,000 (an increase of $110,000 over his original mortgage on that property of $350,000). Even with some added expenses for that mortgage, Brad could buy these three properties without using any of his own cash.

Brad could have extended this concept even further by bringing in another property and so on, but the more properties you have in any transaction, the greater the difficulty in closing the whole transaction. Therefore, even though it might be tempting to bring in additional properties in pyramid transactions, it is best to keep the new deals to a minimum. However, it would not matter how many second or third mortgages you offered on properties you already owned as part of the package.

PYRAMID TRANSACTIONS OFFERING LAND LEASES

Several examples shown thus far have included land leases as a part of the financing package. In the previous example, Brad owned several different properties, all of which were producing more income than was needed to support the expenses and current debt service that was on the property. This gave Brad a positive cash flow that increased the value of the property substantially over his original cost. He wanted to remove some of this equity, but wanted to keep the cost of the new debt at a minimum.

One of the best ways to keep the cost of debt at a minimum is to use the land lease format. However, the major problem to overcome in using a land lease is how you deal with the question of subordination of title. If the property you want to buy already has existing financing on it, that lender would require that the land be subordinated to the lease. This is essential for the lender because lenders want to protect their position in the event of a default. As you are buying the property improvements and leasing the land, the landowner remains the previous mortgagor. The lender would have to agree to an unsubordinated situation, which is unlikely, or to get the landowner to subordinate his or her interest to the lender. This puts the landowner in a position that can be risky, depending on the amount of the debt to which he or she is subordinating their position. Because of this, many property owners balk at giving a subordinated land lease.

The pyramid land lease is a potential answer to this problem. Remember, when sellers have a potential large gains tax to pay in a sale, the land lease can be a very motivating factor. Therefore, on one hand the seller wants to take a land lease, and on the other is frightened of the risk.

To solve this problem, you give the seller land under another property and lease that back. If you can demonstrate that the loan-to-value ratio is reasonable, then the land lease you offer can be more attractive to the owner than the land under his or her own property you are buying.

Under Everything Is Land

There are many people who believe that ownership of the land is the best, and better than holding a mortgage is holding actual title to the land. There is no argument from me about that, and as long as the lease is favorable to my needs I will take a land lease just as I would cash, in fact, sometimes quicker, for reasons that I will explain.

Brad got to a point in a negotiation on a small office building where he needed to move some of the seller-held debt to another property so he could obtain higher (excess?) leverage on the property he wanted to buy to generate the cash to make the transaction. He looked over his inventory of real estate and discovered that in several situations he could create extra debt without hurting himself or the property.

EXAMPLE 13: BRAD CREATES A LAND LEASE.   Brad had a 12-unit apartment building. It was throwing off a net operating income of $46,000. From this, he had existing debt service of $31,000 (which represented annual payments on $305,000 of mortgages). The office building he was trying to buy was offered at $275,000 and was free and clear. The seller demanded a minimum of $150,000 cash down and said he would hold a first mortgage for the balance. That would not work for Brad, so he "created" a land lease on his apartment building. He sat down with his lawyer and had a simple, but effective lease drawn up. It had provisions that I will show you later on in this chapter, and an annual rent of $11,250 per year. In addition, it had an option to buy the underlying land for $125,000 any time within the first 12 years of the lease, which was a 40-year lease.

Brad then offered the seller the $175,000 cash he wanted and the land under his twelve-unit apartment building subject to lease. In essence, Brad was offering to give the seller of the office building the twelve units at the end of the 40-year lease if Brad had not bought out the land prior to that time. In the meantime, the seller would have full ownership of the land. Brad put in several other provisions that we discuss next.

LAND LEASE CHECKLIST

✓ Do provide for an option to buy back the land. Try to keep it at the same set price you have established as the value of the land at the start.

✓ Do have the land lease extend more than 35 years, or at least 10 years plus the option term past the longest term of an existing mortgage. Assume that the longest mortgage was 15 years, and your option to buy back was 12 years. You would then have a total of 10 + 15 + 12, or 37 years. The reason for this is you may want to refinance the mortgages that are on the property prior to the termination of your option to buy. You would need a minimum of 10 years beyond that new mortgage term to have a lease in effect for most lenders to approve the loan. As you might wait until the end of the first option to buy the land back to decide if you want to keep the land lease instead of buying it back (12 years), you would need that term plus a similar term for a new mortgage, or an additional 12 + 15 years. Longer would be good, but you anticipate buying back the land within your first refinance term or letting someone else worry about that as you may sell the property within a short time. Keep in mind that some lenders would not lend on this kind of a deal without full subordination from the owner of the fee in a land lease situation. Other lenders may have different criteria as to the term of a lease beyond the payoff date of their mortgage.

✓ Do allow for a refinance during the term. If your land lease is subordinated to the existing financing only, you would not be in a position to refinance the property once the existing financing has been paid off. So provide for additional refinancing, but be ready to limit the amount to some percentage of the value of the land and buildings, say, 80 percent of the lender's appraisal of the land and improvements.

✓ Do make sure the document is a land lease and not a mortgage. Your lawyer should make sure that this is the case. If you are using this technique to take advantage of the tax laws that fit your circumstance, and the document that says "land lease" is deemed by the IRS to be a mortgage, it could be a costly mistake.

✓ Do not have a required payback agreement, where you must buy back the land. That is one of the first IRS red marks that suggest that the land lease is really a mortgage.

✓ Do not have your rent payment increases tied to a cost-of-living index, or any other index that has no known future value. You will not establish any index adjustment unless you can do the following: (a) can time the increases to come into effect following a date on which you believe you could exercise an option to buy the property; (b) can limit the effect of any future index by obtaining credit for payments of rent against the purchase price, or by having only a percentage of the increase of the index apply; or (c) have no other choice and are ready to take the risk that the cost-of-living increases will not decrease the lease's benefit to you.

✓ Do not make your offer with the idea that the land lease is something that will be established or negotiated. You might flex a bit on its ultimate value, but never on the terms of the lease. The idea is you do not want to open the door for negotiations unless absolutely necessary.

✓ Implement, if at all possible, the opportunity to slide the asset that is being leased to another property of similar or greater value. This may be more difficult than when sliding a mortgage, but can be very useful. The following is an example of this technique.

Sliding Land Leases and Mortgages

Let us start with the mortgage first because it is often easier to accomplish and to understand. When you establish a mortgage of any rank (first, second, so on) there is a property that is pledged as security to that mortgage. If you fail to make the payments on the mortgage you are in jeopardy of losing control of the situation. You may, in the best-case scenario, have to renegotiate the terms of the debt, or at the worst end of this story, you may face foreclosure and the loss of the property. However, assume that all goes well and at the time you made the loan you included in its terms a provision that would allow you to substitute the collateral that is the security to that loan from the existing property in question to another. The provision would allow you to keep the debt but to move it to another property without having to satisfy the debt (in full or in part). Say for example that you purchased an investment property (or whatever) and you gave the seller a second mortgage for $50,000. Its terms called for 10 years of annual interest payments at 6 percent interest with a balloon at the end of that time. Two years later, after you had fixed up the property, you wanted to refinance the existing first mortgage to pull out tax-free cash. Unless you had a subordination agreement with the holder of the second mortgage that would allow you to place new financing ahead of his or her second, you would have to satisfy that mortgage. However, you do not want to do that for any number of reasons. One of the best would be the fact that interest-only payments at 6 percent might be below the market, and you wanted to keep the use of that $50,000 as long as possible. Knowing of this possibility, you had a sliding provision in the mortgage that said something like this:

> Anytime during the term of this mortgage the mortgagor may elect to substitute the collateral from the property located at (address) mortgaged property to any other real estate that has a value and an equity greater than that of this mortgaged property.

The mortgagee will likely insist on further wording to clear up any potential misunderstanding, such as a clause that spells out what kind of evaluation are we talking about, and how is equity determined. There may even be a clause that says the mortgagee must approve the substitute property, but cannot unreasonably withhold that approval.

Once your (and their) lawyers have worked out the final wording of this provision you then, at that future date, seek to slide that debt to another property.

Now, apply this same technique to a land lease. You, just as Brad is doing in the example we are looking at, have a debt structured as a land lease. Much like a mortgage it has a satisfaction date (the option to buy removes the lease completely), and a set of payments in a schedule (the lease payments). However, actual title is not in Brad's name as the property is still owned by the other party or a third party. So, attempt to negotiate a substitution provision which would allow you to "exchange" the leased property for another property you own, or purchase keeping the schedule of payments and the option (if possible without renegotiation) in place.

Brad had created a lease that had an annual payment of 9 percent, which at the time was better than he could do with a second mortgage or in any institutional first-mortgage situations. The seller took the land lease because he would rather retain title to the property, and as he was not selling the land part of the deal he would not trigger any capital gains tax on that portion of the deal at that time. Of course, if and when Brad exercised an option to purchase there could be the potential for a gains tax. If the seller had passed away and the property is now in the hands of heirs, then their stepped up tax basis may eliminate any gain at that time.

Pitfalls with Land Leases

Land leases can generate problems for both sides of a deal. Generally, the problems come from three major areas:

1. THE CARELESSNESS OF ONE OR MORE OF THE PARTIES TO LEAVE SOMETHING IMPORTANT OUT OF THE LEASE: Remember that memories are meaningless when it comes to what was intended to be included in a contract that looks bad to one side later on. If the contract is not absolutely clear, you will absolutely have problems.

2. THE SUBORDINATION DILEMMA: If you are on the receiving side of this deal, you should know that for this to work for the investor the land lease would have to be subordinated to the existing and possibly future financing. This means that the "position of lien" has been subordinated (given up) to allow the mortgages to come ahead of the actual ownership of the land in the event of a default on the mortgages. Should such a default occur later on, the owner of the land may find him or herself having to take over a mortgage to get his or her own property. If the investor has run the property into the ground, there may not be income available to support the mortgage, and value may have eroded as well. Keep in mind that this problem would be similar to that of a junior mortgage holder.

3. THE TIME PROBLEM: I have seen investors actually let a land-lease option to buy slip past and expire because they "forgot" when it was coming up. You cannot rely on your lawyer, your banker, or your accountant either.

Despite these kinds of problems, there remains a world of flexibility in land leases and pyramids.

GENERAL SUMMARY

In a general summary of the pros and cons of pyramids, there are a number of elements that I have covered that should be repeated and remembered:

- Pyramids work on the greener grass theory.
- It is critical to have control of one property prior to moving on to the second one.
- Pyramids can be the box behind the silver curtain.
- Sellers will hold something they "see" as valuable that is not theirs. Let your superior knowledge of your "comfort zone" lead you to the right properties.

- Look for win/win situations where you close transactions that help the other side of the deal (as well as you) move closer to your respective goals.
- You can pyramid off real estate you own or do not own.

In going into a pyramid program, you should review some of the general advantages and disadvantages.

Two Factors That Create a Risk in Pyramids Bring a Swift End to Pyramids

1. The ability to pay the increased debt service.
2. The danger of having greater debt than value.

As you can see, both of these factors are related. If the buyer extends his or her value-to-equity ratio to the point where there is no real equity at all, the excessive leverage may cause all of the cards to come tumbling down. We have seen this effect in other improperly used techniques.

What are the advantages and disadvantages? First, remember that there are two different parties involved. The buyer's goals and motivations will generally be greatly different from those of the seller. Each party should look at the end result of the transaction from his or her own position and needs.

	Advantages	*Disadvantages*
The buyer: The person who generally instigates the pyramid	Expands holdings A low-cost financing tool for reinvestment Establishes good *selling* terms Fantastic estate builder Interest on debt may be tax deductible	Possibility of excessive leverage One failure and the whole pyramid can fall Buyer limited to fewer sellers
The seller: The person who feeds the pyramid	Creates a sale Tax advantages, due to spread of gain on the sale to the terms of the mortgage taken Provides long-term income Secured by other property with visible results	Sale generates paper, not cash Paper may not be secure Another remote transaction could have a great effect on this security Paper is flexible in terms

The seller in the pyramid is generally a person highly motivated to sell. He or she considers and later accepts the offer for paper because it is the best deal offered. If you were to compare the pyramid offer to an all-cash offer of the same value, there could be no question as to the better, less risky transaction. However, this is not a proper comparison.

The seller wants to sell and has a plausible offer. Hence, it may be worthy of acceptance and better than holding onto the property.

How to Make the Transaction Work

The pyramid can be a very safe and profitable way to finance new acquisitions if used conservatively. This means the amount of real equity transferred via a mortgage should be kept at a low to moderate amount. In most cases, the total debt service on the property should not exceed 80 percent of the net operating income of that property. In very stable income properties this percentage may be extended to 90 percent. There should be a 10 percent or greater buffer between income and expenses. In taking over a new property, the buyer should consider out-of-pocket expenses to bring the income up, and this out-of-pocket must be taken into account before the transaction is completed. It should be figured into the total price or at least accounted for in later expenditures. If the buyer is able to generate this needed out-of-pocket cash from additional financing on the acquired property, then the total debt should be reasonable and not excessively leveraged.

The market conditions themselves will provide some limitation to the amount of leverage, as it will be difficult for the buyer to obtain excessive financing on marginal properties. However, the domino effect of the total pyramid can build up quickly if you are not careful. When one property fails (goes into foreclosure, for example), events tend to accelerate and it may be very difficult to restructure other debt to save the pyramid from total destruction.

The seller should exercise caution in any transaction that does not involve cash. However, that caution should not mean a pyramid transaction is not worth considering. To the contrary, the property being sold may not be saleable by any other method.

THE INSTALLMENT SALE: ANOTHER IRS BENEFIT

Earlier in this chapter, I mentioned that the IRS allows a seller to delay or in some instances to avoid tax payment on gains. Two methods mentioned earlier are the IRC Section 1031, which is the tax-free exchange that works well for investors who are able to plan ahead and work toward a major investment goal. The other method outlined is the installment sale whereby the seller does not receive all the payments due under the sale at the time of closing. In essence, the installment sale form of reporting capital gains on the sale of real estate is available to most sellers who will receive at least one payment of the purchase price at anytime following the year of the closing of the sale. This provision may not be applied to a loss, nor is it available to every type of real estate transaction. As with any Internal Revenue Code, it is important to discuss this kind of sale with your tax advisor. You can checkout the current rules, however, by going online at irs.gov and when their home page opens, go to the search box in the upper right-hand corner and write in "installment sale provisions"; follow the prompt to get to "general rules."

The following description of the installment sale will give you a basic understanding of how it works.

Definition of an Installment Sale

An installment sale is any sale where you are not paid all the proceeds of the sale in any given tax period. If there is a taxable gain as a result of the sale, you are allowed (not required) to spread the gains received in a prorata basis over the terms of the installment sale. Simply put, if your gain equaled 50 percent of the total contract price, then one-half of each dollar that is applied toward the principal amount of the price you get would be gain, and taxable as such. Money you receive that is interest on the debt is earned income and not treated as a capital gain.

EXAMPLE 14. In 1985, you purchased a property for $100,000. You put $20,000 down on the property, and the seller held a purchase money mortgage for the balance of $80,000. In 2010, you sold the property for $190,000. At that time your loan balance was $40,000. While you owned the property your depreciation on the property totaled $15,000 and you made no improvements.

The terms on your sale are:

- Zero down payment.
- Three installments of $50,000 due over three annual payments.

Calculate an installment sale on the transaction as follows:

1. Find gross profit:

Selling price	$190,000	
Less adjusted tax basis (original purchase price less depreciation)	− 85,000	
Gross profit	$105,000	Amount of taxable gain

2. Find contract price:

Sales price	$190,000	
Mortgage relieved of	− 40,000	
Contract price	$150,000	Amount of sales proceeds

3. Establish ratio/gain to proceeds

Divide gross profit by contract price: $105,000 ÷ $150,000 = 70 percent

In this example, 70 percent of the total amount of sales proceeds equals taxable gains. Every time you would get a payment of $50,000, 70 percent of that or $35,000 would be taxable gain; the rest, $15,000, would be return of part of your original invested capital or mortgage amortization. Any interest that would also accompany the annual payments would be taxable as return on investment and may be treated separately as a return on a long-term capital investment.

There is some fine-tuning you need to know about when calculating the installment sale. The most critical aspect to watch out for is the situation that occurs when you are relieved of a mortgage that exceeds your basis. This frequently happens when people own property for a very long time and depreciate the asset down to a low level, then somewhere along the time of ownership obtain new financing. If in the previous example, you had a loan outstanding of $90,000, or greater, you would have a mortgage in excess of tax basis. The IRS calculates that this excess mortgage is capital you have already pulled out of the property. While that was not taxable at that moment, it will be taxable at the time of the sale, even though you may not get cash at closing.

Sellers can benefit using the installment sale, by spreading a large taxable gain over several years. Because this is very positive tax planning, buyers should point this out to a seller every time the buyer is trying to use secondary-seller-held financing as a part of the purchase price and terms.

Sellers should be aware that if the mortgage allows full repayment by the mortgagor at any time, those payments could trigger receipt of capital gains during a year when other capital gain receipts may also come in. This might elevate the mortgagee's tax in that year. If you anticipate this in advance, provide a clause in the mortgage that requires the mortgagor to give advance notice (a year ahead) of any such prepayment or full payment. If the mortgage contains a substantial amount of capital gain you have yet to receive, and will result in a substantial tax, it may be wise to include a penalty to the mortgagor to cover those tax payments. It is not unusual for mortgages to have penalties for advance payments for a number of reasons. Another important reason would be that the lender wants to protect the yield they are receiving on the interest rate charged on that loan.

Chapter 14

THE DISCOUNT SALE AND LEASEBACK AND BUYBACK

GOAL OF THIS CHAPTER

This chapter continues to give you investment alternatives. Often a property owner becomes a seller simply because of the failure to recognize that the need for capital does not mean that a sale is the only way to obtain that capital. When the real estate market becomes a buyers market and the buyers control the purse strings, sellers generally are forced to lower their price, or accept terms that are not as attractive as they would like. In this instance, it might be that your goals are served more effectively by keeping the use of the property, by converting your ownership from fee simple to a leasehold. In this way, you sell outright ownership of the real estate but retain the use by becoming a tenant.

As a buyer, you also find that the sale-leaseback works nicely where you acquire property that comes with a good income stream directly from the former owner. Everyone likes to find a bargain. One of the best ways to find them in real estate is to look for people who need capital but want to keep their property (use or right to recapture). Offer them a discount sale.

DEFINITION OF A DISCOUNT SALE AND LEASEBACK

A discount sale, as it applies to real estate, is a sale at a drastically reduced price in relation to the supposed value. The principal ingredient in this technique is that the seller has an option to repurchase the property at a future date (buyback). This technique is often used when there is no reasonable financing available for the property, and the seller has a use for the property. When financing is hard to find at reasonable terms, the property owner may find that a sound economic strategy is to sell the property and retain a buyback at a later date. The seller will generally combine this technique with a leaseback as well, but not always, as you will see.

Advantage of Using This Technique

The advantage of the discount sale-buyback or leaseback is the seller can generate capital while retaining interest in the property. If the property sold is vacant land, the seller has the added advantage of getting capital out of the property without having the obligation of meeting debt service.

EXAMPLE 1: DISCOUNT SALE.   You own a vacant tract of land that you believe is in the path of progress, only progress is taking longer than you had anticipated. You estimate the value is around $400,000, but there are no takers at that price. Even if there were, you want to hold out for the big bucks that will come when the new highway this property will front is completed. Your immediate problem is you could use some cash now for other purposes.

Your initial choice is to borrow money against the property to generate the needed cash. However, you quickly discover that no one wants to loan anything on the vacant land at rates that are even close to being reasonable. Therefore, you decide to offer the land at a bargain sale price of $250,000 to generate the needed cash. To give yourself protection on the up side, part of this transaction includes your option to buy the land back within six years at a substantial increase. In essence, you agree to sell the land for the tax appraisal value, which is $250,000, and have an option to buy it back within the next six years at $443,000. A simple check of compound interest tables and you will realize that the actual cost to you to buy the property back is as if you were accruing interest at 10 percent compounded annually. If the property value skyrockets, as you hope it will, the actual value six years from now could be much more. If not, you had the use of the $250,000 for that same period and do not have to exercise your option.

To state this in other terms: You go to a private lender to borrow the money. You show him your backup comps on the value of similar property in the area, what other tracts have sold for recently, and attempt to justify that the land is worth $400,000. In addition, you are sure that the land is going to go up in a very short time. He cannot lose, and the only reason you will pay him 10 percent interest is that you need to borrow money *now.*

The lender looks over your material and smiles. He might just have you over the barrel. So, he says, "If you are right, and I think you are, then I'll give you $250,000 tomorrow, and you don't have to pay me any interest or anything for four years. At the end of that time or sooner if you would rather, you can write me a check for $443,000 and we part friends. You with your property, and me with $443,000 in the bank. Deal?"

He has cut you short on the time, so your actual cost now, if you chose to pay it, is a greater interest than you wanted to pay. However, there are some advantages to you. You have four years to hope and pray that the road is completed (or has it even started yet?), and if something pops sooner, you can simply pay this lender off and cash in on the gold mine you know is going to come in.

The lender knows you are getting desperate, so has proposed a deal that you just might take. He is sure that $250,000 is a good deal, and he is also pretty sure that when the end of the fourth year rolls around, you will not be in a position to recapture the land. He has given you money, and better than a mortgage, now is holding title to the real estate.

Why would you do this? As a seller, it is not the best way to generate capital, but remember we are not looking at too many options. In fact, there may be no other option except let the land go to the highest bidder. If you wonder about that option, let me tell you that in an absolute auction you might end up with much less than the $250,000 and would have no option to recapture.

BE CAREFUL OF THE INTERNAL REVENUE SERVICE

The Internal Revenue Service (IRS) may look closely at a discount sale to see if it has been contrived as a method of reducing possible tax on a gain. Of course, the sale may never come to its attention, but do not count on that because the IRS may very easily examine such a transaction at some time in the future. The three-year statute of limitations on audits of past income tax returns will not hold if there is reason to believe that fraud was committed. If the discount sale was accomplished to evade tax, fraud may be claimed. Be sure that you properly document any possible discount sale, or for that matter, any sale where you have a buyback or leaseback as a part of the transaction. To help you ascertain if there is any danger of having an IRS audit, follow the checklist that I provide for you in the following paragraph. If you can answer no to all of the questions, then you should be able to justify the use of a discount sale. In using this checklist, however, it is wise to check with your tax advisor to see whether he or she thinks that the discount sale may create a future tax liability.

Checklist to Determine Whether a Discount Sale Can Be Used

All questions must be answered no. Even one yes answer may raise doubt as to the acceptability of using a discount sale as a method of selling a property.

✓ Is the buyer a relative of the seller?

✓ Is the buyer a close business partner or associate of the seller?

✓ Does the seller owe the buyer money or any special favors?

✓ Is the sale price below the assessed value of the property?

✓ Is the sale tied to other terms or conditions involving other property?

✓ In the event of a leaseback by the seller, are the terms of the lease unreasonable for either party based on the market area?

✓ Is there a mandatory recapture provision where the seller must become a buyer at a future date?

✓ Is there reason to believe that the seller does not need immediate cash or other financial relief?

✓ Are there buyers at a higher price, with reasonable terms?

✓ Have similar properties been sold above the sale price within a reasonable time-span?

✓ Has the seller taken a large long-term capital gain in the same tax period?

✓ Is the seller's lawyer, accountant, real estate broker, salesperson, or listing agent the buyer or part of the deal in any way other than in your professional capacity?

Assuming you have answered no to all these questions, you can now proceed with the discount sale as a method of helping your seller accomplish his or her goals. If you have answered yes to any of these questions, then you need to look at the situation surrounding that question. A yes to questions 5, 6, and 7 will almost automatically cause the IRS to sharpen its pencils. For example, if you sold the $400,000 property for $200,000 and leased it back for $20,000 per year, with a mandatory buyback in 10 years at $400,000, then IRS will likely call this transaction a mortgage and not a sale. This may not affect you at all, but could create problems for the buyer who will be treated as a lender. The overall return might be usurious in your state if this were treated as a loan. Of course, the IRS could consider that the low lease terms allowed you to escape a capital gains tax, and attack the sale by giving a value to the leasehold interest as well as the cash portion of the sale.

The discount sale has a real function. It can often be the only solution, short of financial disaster, for some clients and some properties.

A Discount Sale Generally Means Cash

A sale at half the value may, after all, be the only cash price you can get due to market conditions. Because the reason for a discount sale is usually the need to produce immediate cash, it is generally associated with the cash sale.

If you are in need of immediate cash, and are not in a position to or are unwilling to borrow the required sum of money, then the sale of a real property becomes the only suitable solution. You may find yourself looking to the discount sale to satisfy your needs. Raising cash in a tight mortgage market may automatically direct you to the discount sale. Keep in mind that the value of any property is relative to time and place. If you own property at the wrong place at the wrong time, options available to you diminish quickly.

From the buyer's point of view, a purchase at a bargain price is more appealing than buying at a market price. Of course, the all-cash requirement may limit the quantity of buyers who would offer on the property. However, you might be surprised to discover the number of possible buyers who come out of the woodwork when a "steal" is offered.

If you are the seller, the viability of the transaction depends on what problems you are trying to solve. If your most critical need is for cash, then you can raise cash with more ease by utilizing the discount sale. Often, the need for cash is overshadowed by the necessity to get out or to be released from financial burdens of existing financing, which you are unable to support.

EXAMPLE 2: A DISCOUNT SALE CAN GENERATE IMMEDIATE CASH. Roscoe owns an apartment lot suitable for 10 rental apartments or condominium units. In a good rental market, the lot might bring $225,000. In fact, a few years ago, this price may have been attainable. However, times are now tough and rental properties are overbuilt and have high vacancy factors. Roscoe has been hurt by the decline in the economy and needs some ready cash. Roscoe realizes the property cannot be sold at its past value. However, some prospective buyers have indicated a willingness to pay $125,000, but only with a very low down payment and a long low interest seller-held mortgage. Since Roscoe needs cash immediately he turns to the discount sale as a method of solving his problem.

Roscoe sells the lot for $100,000 cash. Because of the obvious "steal" at this price, a buyer was found almost overnight. However, the discount sale has a buyback option, so Roscoe retains the right to repurchase the lot within the next 48 months for $125,000. If he fails to do so, the option is lost forever.

The discount sale solved the immediate cash need Roscoe had, and at the same time offered him an opportunity to buy back the property in the near future if the market reversed itself. Should the value return to the lot within the 48 months, or increased values make the lot worth more than the supposed $125,000, then Roscoe will have the opportunity for a profit.

The buyer of the lot will have a limited gain should Roscoe recapture the lot within the 48 months. Yet, his gain could be respectable and above the interest yield available to him or her from a savings deposit. For this reason, the bottom line for the buyer is the recapture. He may gain much more if Roscoe cannot or will not recapture within the time period allotted. There are several ways that Roscoe could sweeten this deal, if it was necessary. I will touch on several techniques that can be used to close the deal later in the chapter.

LEASEBACK, BUYBACK, RECAPTURE, OR OPTION BECOME A NECESSARY PART OF THE DISCOUNT SALE

Leaseback, buyback, recapture, or option: one of these methods is almost always used in conjunction with the discount sale to provide for future gain to the seller. It is this trade-off of values that allows the seller to give the buyer a secure position in the property. This secure position is what attracts money to this kind of deal.

How can these methods be useful? First, accept the fact that the discount sale offers the most potential when the market for the type of property being offered is not at a peak, or when you need to retain the use of the property. After all, when there is a demand for what you are offering, you need not offer a discount. When the sale of apartment lots is down and not many buyers are around, it may be necessary to seek drastic measures in order to sell. Of course, the poorer the market the greater the discount required to buy a "steal." If you need to retain the use of the property, or anticipate a strong increase in the value of the property over the next few years, then the right to retain use or future buyback rights is important. Without one of these future values in your hand, the only reason for a discount sale is if there is absolutely no other remedy to your problem other than letting the property go at whatever the market will bring.

At times, the discount by itself is still not enough to entice a buyer. You may have a floor price under which you cannot go. As the seller you may have financial obligations to pay off or may simply be unwilling to sell below a fixed price. Many sellers have lost all their equity in a property rather than drop the price to a level at which the property would sell. It is a hard fact of real estate investing that market price often has very little to do with actual value. Keep in mind that what you paid for a property and have invested in it is your value. Market value is what someone else is willing to pay for that property.

In the discounted sale, the seller generally wants to retain either existing use, or a future benefit, or both. A discounted sale combined with a leaseback of the property (with or without a later option to recapture the property) is not uncommon. In such a situation, the seller arranges to lease the property from the new buyer for a period of time. This is the same as a sale and leaseback, but with a discount on the sale. The basic difference would be that the terms of the leaseback would reflect the reduced price on the sale.

If the seller has a use for the property and can produce income to pay the lease, the reasons to lease back the property may be sound. With the discount off the sales price and additional income (in the form of rent), the transaction may entice a buyer, and the transaction proceeds to close. The amount of the lease payments can usually be lower than an economic return on the price, as the buyer is looking at the discount as the major incentive for buying. This is another flexible aspect of this form of financing. You can negotiate different time periods of the lease, amount of the lease, and discounted prices. The variance on any one could be advantageous to one party and not the other. A balance of these variations may be necessary in the negotiations on this kind of transaction.

Recapture Allows the Seller to Recoup Value

With a recapture clause in the lease, the seller may, at a later date, buy back the land at a price fixed in the contract or at a price adjusted by other agreements.

The most common extra provision used with the discount sale is the option to buy back. Because the seller is taking a reduced price, he or she may want to buy back at a future date. This future price may be considerably higher than the price the property was sold for in the first transaction. Consider the following example.

EXAMPLE 3: RECAPTURE TO RECOUP.   Aston owns 200 acres of farmland outside the city in a growing area. Land nearby has sold for $1,500 per acre. Based on this information, the current value of the land should be $300,000. The tax assessment on the property is $100,000. Aston wants to get some cash to buy a yacht and spend a year or two at leisure. He paid $50 per acre 20 years ago and presently has no use for the farm site. The current market conditions indicate that there are not many buyers ready, willing, or able to buy this land today or, for that matter, in the very near future. Aston had a loss on the sale of a business property that year of around $80,000 and could take a gain without creating a taxable situation that year. His accountant advised him that if he could take advantage of the loss he would be ahead of the game.

At what price then does the property become a steal? When you can answer that question to the highest dollar amount, you have the probable discount price. In this case, it was $500 per acre. Remember, the discount sale may require all cash to suit the client's needs. If the $100,000, which can be generated by the discount sale, is less than Aston needs, then he may back off, sell only a portion of the property at a discount, and hold on to the rest. However, because Aston needed the $100,000, he proceeded to market the property.

In the future, Aston's 200 acres may skyrocket in value due to a new subdivision nearby or for some other reason. If the value should go to $3,000 per acre, some of the new value of $600,000 could be recouped if Aston had taken an option to buy back the land at the time he sold it. What if the land value went to $30,000 per acre? This price might be cheap in many market areas.

The Option Is the Carrot—What If You Don't Take Advantage of It. An option to recapture the property may hold out some hope to the buyer. Hope that you will not recapture the property so that if there is a profit to be had, they will benefit. For this reason, an option to buy back, is normally not granted for a long period of time, except in a long-term leaseback that may have more than one option period during which the property can be recaptured. The reason is simply that the option is one-sided, and the new owner may not want to be locked into the property for a lengthy period of time without being able to sell it or, as is the situation with a leaseback, have a return on his or her invested capital. Because Aston felt the land would appreciate greatly within a few years, he negotiated for a short option at a lower recapture price rather than a long option at a high price.

Aston settled for a five-year option to recapture the land at $150,000. This would give the new owner a $50,000 profit, less his carrying cost if Aston buys the land back at the end of that time. If the land went to $600,000, Aston could buy it back at $150,000 and have a nice profit, plus the original $100,000 he received from the first sale. Had Aston made the decision to sell the property for its top value of $300,000, that would have been the maximum top dollar he would have received and, even taking advantage of his $80,000 loss to offset the gains tax, there still would have been a tax to pay.

Recap of the Transaction. Aston had land similar to that, which had sold for $300,000. To get a quick sale, he took a discount and sold it for $100,000, but with an option to buy back within five years at $150,000.

Three years later, Aston realized that a new subdivision nearby had opened up this farmland and that it could be sold for as high as $500,000. Therefore, with time on his side (he had 24 months before the option came due), he put the land on the market. He knew that he could exercise his option to recapture the land if he got a buyer.

A month later, a buyer came along, and Aston sold his option to him for $260,000. This meant that Aston ended up getting a total of $360,000 for his property. The new buyer ultimately exercised the option for $150,000. Aston had sold the option rather than exercise it because the buyer wanted the extra time—another 24 months before he had to pay off the $200,000 to recapture the land.

ADVANTAGES OF A DISCOUNT SALE

There are four basic advantages of the discount sale:

1. Cash in a hurry.
2. Fast closing.
3. Action in a bad market.
4. Very flexible.

The discount sale can be used effectively in these situations:

- Seller needs cash.
- Market is difficult.
- Property is difficult to sell.
- Seller needs a fast transaction.
- Seller needs a cash-out for an exchange.
- Can be a catalyst for a joint venture.

Although the discount sale is a seller's and a broker's tool, it can be used by an astute buyer as well. The buyer can go into a transaction offering a reduced price. The later buy-back can become a negotiating point. It can follow many avenues and can be very flexible.

The discount sale and buyback option offer the seller more possibilities for return when the property has the promise of fast appreciation. In the event of a property valuation decline, the seller simply does not use the option and walks away from the property.

DISADVANTAGES OF A DISCOUNT SALE

Many things can go awry in planning a discount sale. It may be that the price is reduced too low, or the terms of the buyback are too high or for too short a period of time. The value in appreciation may not warrant the buyback and the seller may have missed part of the gain. Many things can and do go wrong, but this is more often a fault of the planners and not of events. You cannot fit the discount sale format into all situations. In those cases where there is a three-fold increase in the value of the property the year after the option is dropped, the planning was obviously wrong.

Just because the discount sale is highly effective, the buyer should not rush out to use this tool until he or she has looked at all other possible options. An overzealous broker can sell a lot of property with the discount method, but not always to the benefit of the seller.

A discount sale holds considerable risk for the seller if the market value of the property does not appreciate to cover the pick-up cost, or if his or her situation changes and he or she cannot exercise the option when the time comes. The amount of risk the seller is taking depends on the amount of the discount and the probability of appreciation.

When it appears probable that the value of the property will go up, any price below the current market value reduces the risk of the investment to the buyer. It is normally the seller who is telling the buyer how great the value of this property will be in a few years. In essence, the buyer turns that around and says, "I'll give you part of your price now, and if you are right about the future, you can buy the property back at a reasonable price and make a lot more later." The seller has been saying how the $100,000 lot was going to jump to $300,000 as soon as the new bridge was finished, so the buyer offers to pay $60,000 for the lot now and give the seller a piece of the action if the property later sells above a floor amount the two negotiate. In this instance, the buyer pays $60,000 now and gives the seller the right to recapture the property at $110,000, but if the lot is resold (by the former owner) within three years, then 50 percent of the sales price that exceeds $120,000 must be split with the discount buyer. Naturally, all the terms of such a transaction are negotiable. One element to consider is that the original owner may recapture with the idea of using the property and not selling it. To cover such an event, a simple provision is used whereby he could recapture without any further obligation (to give the discount buyer a percentage of a future sale); he could have an absolute recapture at a higher amount, say $150,000.

Just the very offer of a property at a discount can attract a would-be buyer who might also believe the value is destined to jump to a much higher price.

REVIEW THE DISCOUNT SALE FROM THE SELLER'S POINT OF VIEW

The following guide will be helpful in reviewing the discount sale from the seller's point of view. Keep in mind that the discount sale is effective when:

1. Fast cash is needed.

2. The seller has no other acceptable way to get the cash.

3. A fast closing is needed.

4. The property is very difficult to sell.

5. A cash-out for an exchange is needed.

6. The seller knows the value will increase substantially.

If one or more of the six preceding factors is not present, the discount sale will probably not be the best form to use.

Fine Points in the Discount Sale

Because the seller is in a give-and-take situation by virtue of the discount on the price, he is able to negotiate terms not normally possible on the later buy-back, or leaseback and recapture. However, the buyer knows that the longer the time period of the option, the less value the discount has, unless there is another counterbalance. It is possible to structure these counterbalances to provide some protection to the seller for a longer time, without unduly burdening the buyer.

EXAMPLE 4.   You have offered the seller $50,000 as a discount price for a lot and are now attempting to negotiate the terms of the buyback option. The seller wants a seven-year option to buy back, which you feel is a very long time for the discount sale in question. However, a number of factors can be brought into play to make it feasible. Review the following elements as suggestions of how to provide recapture terms:

• THE FUTURE PRICE TO BE SET AT A PREDETERMINED BASE PRICE, WITH AN APPRAISAL TO BE MADE AT THE SEVENTH YEAR. If the appraisal price is lower than the predetermined price then no further adjustment is taken and the seller can either recapture or not. If the appraisal is higher than the predetermined price, then an adjustment to the predetermined price could apply. The amount of the adjustment would be a negotiating point. For example, you set a price that would be good any time during the seven years for the recapture to be no less than $100,000. At the end of seven years, the appraisal suggests the value is $150,000. If you and the seller have agreed to a 20 percent increase of the overage, then the seller's recapture price would be $110,000 (the base recapture price of $100,000 + 20 percent of the $50,000 overage or $100,000 + $10,000 = $110,000).

• GIVE THE BUYER THE RIGHT TO "BUY OUT" THE OPTION WITH A PAYMENT TO THE SELLER. This provision will allow the buyer, for a sum of money, to null and void the option. It is possible that the buyer may want to sell or even develop the property, and with the option over his head that may not be practical. The sum of the buy-out is normally at least the balance to the discount plus some profit. If the value was $100,000 and the discount sale was at $50,000, the buy-out may be at $45,000. However, this is a highly negotiable point, and could be set on an annual scale, or a formula. For example, in addition to the seller's right to recapture the property any time during seven years for $100,000 you have the right to buy back the recapture during the first three years (or any other time that suits you), for $45,000. If you take a good look at this, you will see that this is much like buying the property for $95,000 with a deferred payment at zero interest over three years. This term may not affect you, but the seller might have to impute interest in that payment. As long as you have run the details of any such transaction past your tax advisor, you should be okay.

• FIRST RIGHT OF REFUSAL. This may be all the seller can get, or may run with the property for a period of time after the option to buy back has expired. For example, you give the seller a very short buyback recapture option, say for one or two years. Then the seller can have a first right of refusal for another five or so years. Be cautious about giving anyone a first right of refusal, as unless you are very clear in the terms of how the right is to be exercised, your hands can be substantially tied in trying to sell the property. For example, if the seller had a two-year option to buy, then a five-year first right, you would spell out clearly the terms of that first right. Such terms might be as follows:

• After the second anniversary of the closing, the seller shall retain the right of first refusal to meet any terms of a sale of the subject property.

• Should the owner of the property elect to sell the property and receive a bona fide offer, the owner would provide a copy of said offer to the seller who would then have a period of five working days to match the exact terms of said offer.

• The seller, after matching the exact terms of the bona fide offer, would have a period of 30 days of inspection time of the subject property. At the end of the 30 days, the seller could elect to proceed to close under the exact terms and conditions of the bona fide offer, or elect to withdraw.

Terms such as the above would clearly tie your hands if you were the owner of the property, for a period of at least 35 days. A prospective buyer offering you a bona fide transaction may not want to wait that period. Worse than that, if the seller did not elect to meet the terms of the offer, and the buyer proceeded with his or her own due-diligence period, only to come back and want changes in the agreement, you might be forced to go back to the original seller to give him or her another shot at the first right of refusal.

Another hazard of first right of refusal is what happens if the bona fide offer is an exchange. This can truly complicate events, and to anticipate this, it would be a good idea to include wording that covered that potential problem.

Should the bona fide offer contain an exchange of property or boot, the offer will also contain a purchase price, which would allow the original seller to match under the provisions of the first right of refusal. Because the owner of the property has accepted the property or boot as a part of the bona fide offer, nothing shall prevent the seller from negotiating the price of said property or boot with the party making the bona fide offer.

ESCALATING OPTION OR LEASE PRICE.   The seller may agree to a series of higher prices in future options to buy back. The same may occur in the lease payments. This and other long-term options or provisions are used in vacant and other nonincome-producing properties more often than in income-producing property. Buyers should remember that if they make the buyback terms too difficult, there may be no incentive for the seller to want to recapture the property. This is important if the property includes buildings that need to be maintained. An excessive buyback may encourage poor maintenance of the infrastructure of the property.

REVIEW OF THE DISCOUNT SALE

The discount sale is viable when viewed as a technique to raise quick money, at reasonable interest rates, for relatively short periods of time. There are many problems that the seller must understand and check out before using this kind of technique. The following are some of the pitfalls that await the user of the discount sale:

PITFALLS FOR THE BUYER

- Is the price truly a discounted price, or have the values been manipulated to appear to be a discount?
- Has the leaseback term been contrived to entice the buyer into "too good of a deal"?
- Are there sufficient future benefits to encourage the seller to recapture the property at the increased price contained in the terms of the transaction?

PITFALLS FOR THE SELLER

- Will the seller's capital gains tax be excessive? If so, then the IRS may red flag this transaction and proceed to a full IRS audit.
- If the market is headed down, there may not be a future benefit in the option to recapture.
- Is there sufficient time to plan for the recapture of the property?

Are There Alternatives Swimming around in Your Mind?

By now every time you see an example in this book, you should let your mind conjure up different scenarios. There are many different ways to make these deals work, and until you propose a way you will never know what might have sweetened the deal.

What would you have to offer that one of the buyers or sellers in these examples did not have? How could you have balanced equities or sweetened the deal that was presented?

Chapter 15

HOW TO PROFIT WITH DISCOUNTED MORTGAGES

GOAL OF THIS CHAPTER

This chapter brings a new dimension to the structure of mortgages. There can be substantial profit made by purchasing mortgages at a discount. Many seller-held mortgages can be acquired by investors seeking this kind of investment. Knowing this, a seller may use this as a method to cash-out of a sale, while at the same time offering a buyer easy financing.

Anyone who enters the world of real estate investing, either as an actual investor or in one of the many different professions that deal with buyers and sellers of real estate, will come across an opportunity to profit from acquiring mortgages at a discount. The more you understand about the effect of interest and time on debt, the better you will be able to profit from the manipulation of that debt. This is the world of the true insiders.

LEARN HOW TO USE DISCOUNTED MORTGAGES

The ability to increase the yield on a mortgage by buying it below face value is a great way to make money quickly and safely. The concept of mortgage discounting is widely used in the world of finance from institutional banking to government loan programs as well as in the private sector. This chapter shows you why a discounted mortgage will give its new holder a greater yield, and the specific techniques of how and when to discount the mortgage to get the highest possible yield.

DEFINITION OF A DISCOUNTED MORTGAGE

The discounting of a mortgage occurs when the holder of the mortgage sells the note to either the maker or the third party at an amount less than the current amount owed. This current amount would be the combined total of outstanding principal plus unpaid interest. The result is that the buyer would, upon satisfaction of the note at its contract rate and terms, receive a greater yield than the original mortgage would.

EXAMPLE 1.   Frank sold his home four years ago and took back a second mortgage for $50,000. The mortgage called for monthly payments of $416.66 that consisted of interest only payments at 10 percent payable for 10 years, with a single balloon payment of the outstanding principal due at the end of the tenth year. The loan has six years remaining and Frank needs some cash to make another investment. Bob comes along and says he will give Frank $40,000 cash for the outstanding loan. In taking this offer, Frank has discounted the second mortgage to Bob. Bob gets $5,000 per year (the interest only payments of 10 percent on the face amount of the loan) paid to him in monthly installments of $416.66 each month. Because Bob has paid only $40,000 for this mortgage, his return is a 12.5 percent yield. To calculate this, you simply divide the annual interest collected, which is $5,000 by the total amount paid for the mortgage. Therefore, $5,000 divided by $40,000 equals the annual percent of interest earned.

Remember, when the loan is paid off in six years or sooner, there will be another $10,000 bonus because the pay-off is based on the original face amount of the loan, which was $50,000. Because Bob only paid $40,000 for the mortgage, that bonus jumps the average yield up. The actual yield in this example would be the 12.5 percent he received in cash each year, plus the interest on the $40,000 that will, over those six years, total $10,000 at pay-off time.

MATHEMATICAL ASPECTS OF A DISCOUNTED MORTGAGE

There is no easy way to become truly comfortable with some of the mathematical aspects of finance except to read the material first without trying to grasp what is truly happening. In doing that, you will get the feel for what happens. If you are happy with that part of things and are not curious about "how in the devil did he get that answer," then slide on through this chapter and save it for another day. The moment you see the opportunity to get involved with a potential profit situation dealing with a mortgage, however, rush back to the comfort of this book, reread this chapter, and let it carry you through the details of your present situation.

If you are a student or a professional in any field that deals with real estate, which would include lawyers, mortgage brokers, realtors, and lenders of any kind just to name a few, then you should concentrate on these inner workings of the techniques and mechanics contained in this chapter. You cannot rely on searching the web for the answers.

Finding the Yield Rate in a Discounted Mortgage

In the Frank and Bob example, we have a mortgage that is repaid with interest-only annual payments and then a balloon of the full amount at pay-off time. The pay-off time must be before the end of the sixth year, but in reality, the mortgagor can repay the loan at anytime, provided there is no provision in the mortgage or mortgage note that would prevent that. For Frank the only interest rate of importance is the interest-only annual payment he would get which is calculated at 10 percent interest per annum. That rate is based on the purchase money mortgage that Frank held that replaced $50,000 that the buyer of his property (at that earlier sale) did not pay, and therefore still owes him. However, Bob's interest that he will earn is computed not on the original $50,000 but the $40,000 he paid for the note. That was the discounted price. Therefore, he receives the same "interest-only" payments as did Frank because no principal is being paid to reduce that. His interest then, as we saw earlier, amounts to 12.5 percent of the $40,000 investment, which he expects to get back at pay-off time. So far, that is easy to follow. However, at pay-off time Bob will also get a bonus of $10,000. Since that bonus can come at any time, we can first look at what would the equivalent interest rate be that would turn $40,000 into $50,000 if it was paid back at the end of the mortgage term. Then we can also look at what would that return be if it was paid back earlier than the deadline (due date).

The interest rate of any bonus that has no principal reduction during the term will be found using Table C in the Appendix of this book. Table C can also give you the number of years or periods of time that will pass, the actual amount of the bonus if you did not know that. However, for the moment, we are only concerned with current yield. Unless we can compute the total yield Bob will get, he will not know just how good (or not so good) the deal can be. The missing interest rate is calculated by the compound interest table (Table C).

In this example, we know the amount and the number of years (periods), the initial payment ($40,000), and the total amount, that will ultimately be paid ($50,000). Keep in mind, because the $50,000 amount is fixed, and can come at anytime, it should be clear to you that the amount of interest it will take to let $40,000 grow to $50,000 will be greater the shorter the number of periods to the pay-off date. To start with, the only pay-off date we know is fixed in stone is the six years to arrive at the pay-off date. In essence, the question is: at what interest rate will $40,000 grow with annual compounding of interest (but no additional payment of principal) to $50,000 in six years? That growth is the built-in bonus that Bob has the moment he purchased the mortgage. Clearly, you should see that if the loan was repaid at the end of one year, the bonus would result in a yield of 25 percent on top of the 12.5 percent interest that the borrower pays each year. Take a look at the actual mathematical formula of this problem:

$$(1+ i)^N \times Pv = Ca$$

Where $(1 + i)^N$ = the interest rate and the period of time and
i = interest at which the present value will be compounded (this is the unknown amount).
N = the period of time at which the interest is calculated.
Ca = the ultimate compounded amount, which will be $50,000 in this example.
Pv = the present value at the start of the process, which is the amount Bob paid for the discounted mortgage.

Thus, a quotient that is $(1 + i)^N$ is a combination of 1 plus interest raised to a power of N. By using this formula, we can see that if you want to know how much $500 will be over five years at 7 percent interest per year, the formula would be:

$$(1 + .07)^5 \times \$500 = Ca$$

This could also be written as:

$$(1 + .07) \times (1 + .07) \times (1 + .07) \times (1 + .07) \times (1 + .07) \times \$500 = Ca$$

To find the value for $(1 + .07)^5$ you would look in Table C in the Appendix for a one time per year compounding at 7 percent over 5 periods. Or you can do that simple math with any inexpensive calculator once you are sure the machine is not rounding off to less than 8 positions to the right of the decimal point. Therefore:

$$(1.40255173) \times \$500 = \$701.27586 \text{ rounded up to } \$701.28$$

The result of the math to arrive at $(1 + .07)^5 = 1.40255$ is what Table C in the Appendix will provide. It will be stated depending on the interest rate it takes to compound for a period of periods. Take note here that the key word is periods. The N factor will relate to the number of times a year that the compounding takes place. In this instance, we will use one single period to equal a full year. However, if there were to be a prepayment early, we may have to break the periods down to smaller amounts of time, therefore more periods per year. If you did that, you would expand the problem at hand to the full periods from start (of the acquisition of the mortgage) to its pay-off.

Be careful of the number of periods in your calculation. Think of periods of time and not number of years when calculating mortgage amortization or compounding of principal.

The following chart illustrates this relationship, as it would be shown if the annual interest rate were to be 12 percent:

Calendar Period	N per Year	Interest Rate of N (%)	In Math
Annual	1	12 (12)	.12
Semiannual	2	6 (1/2)	.06
Quarterly	4	3 (1/4)	.03
Monthly	12	1 (1/12)	.010

The result of $(1 + i)^N$ then gives us a number (shown in Table C of the Appendix) that can easily create an error if the relationship between i and N is not properly understood. If there are 2N per year, then the interest rate that will be discovered will be half of the annual rate. If 4N then it will result in a rate that is one quarter of the ultimate rate, and so on. This magic number to be found in Table C of the Appendix when multiplied by the present value ($40,000 in this example) it will give us the combined total of an original sum that, without any additional principal payments, will grow to the ultimate compounded amount (which is $50,000 in this example). It is, in essence, just like a savings account where you had made one deposit (the Pv) and the bank added interest each year. At the end of any series of years (N), you decided to withdraw the total compounded amount (Ca). The relationship of N and i is critical because we have to adjust i to how many times the interest is applied each year. As in this example there are no actual payments made which will affect the final answer, we need to ascertain what interest earned each year would result in the Ca (which in this case we know as the bonus).

Therefore, in review, if N was calculated more than once a year, for example semiannually, for the period of six years, there would be there would be 12N and the answer we would ultimately ascertain would be interest for half of the year. If it were to be calculated each month, N would be 12 per year multiplied by 6 years, or a total of 72N and the interest rate per n would be ½ the annual rate.

As Table C of the Appendix shows a range of interest rates, beginning at 2 percent to 15 percent, you can easily calculate many payment schedules. If you had a compounding event that occurred in quarterly increments, at an annual interest rate of 8 percent, such as a zero coupon mortgage that would balloon in 10 years, there would be 40 such events during that 10-year period. Therefore, you would use the 2 percent row for 40 increments. $(1.02)^{40}$ would equal 1.47987. If the amount of the principal owed was $30,000, at the end of the 10 years the pay-off would be $30,000 multiplied by 1.47987 or a total of $44,396.10.

However, as mentioned earlier, there is no actual compounding taking place for Bob in this deal thus far, with 1N equals one year. All we are attempting to do is to arrive at an accurate interest rate that he would earn. The bonus of $10,000 will be paid no matter when it is paid off because that is the real amount borrowed and which must be repaid. Yet, from Bob's point of view he only lent (paid for the mortgage) $40,000. For Frank, the mortgage was $50,000 from day one, and he was paid interest with no principal paid during the life of the mortgage. However, because Bob acquired this mortgage for $40,000 he would receive the bonus whenever the mortgage paid off. If it was paid off early, say one year after Bob purchased the mortgage, the bonus would still be $10,000 and his yield would be 25 percent for that one-year wait. The only element we do not know to satisfy the formula is the interest being applied. The N part of the equation is established the day the mortgage is satisfied. However, going back to the problem at hand, assume that the mortgage goes its full six years remaining at the time Bob purchased it:

$$(1 + i)^N \times Pv = Ca$$

Substitute what we know and we have:

$$(1 + i)^6 \times 40{,}000 = 50{,}000$$

Divide 50,000 by 40,000 and the result is $(1 + i)^6 = 1.25$, therefore:

$(1 + i)^6 = 1.2500$ (make sure you have at least 4 numbers to the right of the decimal point)

Go to Table C in the Appendix and run your finger down the column for six years. Do not confuse this with the monthly interest payments the mortgagor pays, as that has nothing to do with the bonus amount of the discounted mortgage. Therefore, six periods if the mortgage is paid off at that time would be the number 1.2500. In the row for 3.75 percent interest, you will see the number 1.24718 and under the 4 percent interest the number 1.26532. This tells you that your missing interest rate is between 3.75 percent and 4 percent.

Eyeball your potential solution to move one of these two numbers closer to your target of 1.2500. It is clear that the end result will be slightly closer to 3.75 percent and no one will argue the points if you simply say, "Okay, call this 3.8 percent."

Now, add that to the annual return we saw earlier of 12.5 percent and we can estimate relatively accurately that Bob will earn 16.3 percent (12.5 + 3.8 = 16.3 percent) on his investment. That is, unless the mortgage is paid off early.

The Effect of an Early Pay-Off When the Bonus Is Fixed

The ultimate annual return on any investment, where the total repayment comes over a period of years (two or more), will depend on when the payments are made and what percentage of the total are those payments. This is particularly important when you acquire a mortgage by paying less than what the face amount of the total principal payment would be. If the mortgage that Bob is now holding is paid off at the end of four years, instead of six, what would his total return be? To calculate this, return to Table C in the Appendix. Along the 4 period line (N = four years this time) look for the same 1.2500 number as before. This number relates to the bonus and in this example is $10,000 no matter when the mortgage is paid off. The only element to change is the period of years, which will change the interest rate. Shorter term to pay-off and the yield goes up, a longer term will reduce the interest as it relates to the bonus. Under 5.75 percent along the 4n column, you will find 1.25061 and under 5.5 percent you find 1.23882. The actual percent will be just slightly less than 5.75 percent, so call it 5.70 percent

Add that to the increased yield from the interest payments made monthly of 12.5 percent, and the overall yield is now 18.2 percent (12.5 percent + 5.7 percent = 18.2 percent). This is a substantial jump from the former rate, and shows how dramatic an early repayment of a discounted mortgage can be.

Review Mortgage Situations

Let us review the different elements of any mortgage. In the previous mortgage situation where Frank sold, at a discount, a mortgage he held to Bob, we saw how Bob benefited substantially in two ways. First, from the yield on the interest that jumped from 10 percent to 12.5 percent. Then he would benefit again with the pay-off bonus when the principal amount was paid as he received the principal spread of the discount (which was $10,000). But then, there was the prepayment situation when he got the bonus two years early. That had an additional increase to the bonus. All a matter of time, and it had no effect on the amount of interest paid by the mortgagor.

Results of Different Payment Schedules

ALL INTEREST AND PRINCIPAL REPAID IN ONE PERIOD.   I lend you $50,000 at 10 percent interest per annum. You pay me $55,000 at the end of the year. I have received my original principal, plus $5,000 in interest. My return is 10 percent per annum.

EQUAL PRINCIPAL PAYMENTS PER PERIOD PLUS INTEREST.   I lend you $100,000 at 10 percent interest per annum and you pay me $60,000 at the end of the first year, and $55,000 at the end of the second year. In this example, the payments were spread over two years, at equal principal payments each year plus 10 percent interest on the outstanding balance. I still have a return of 10 percent per annum. But your first payment is larger than the second.

What if I lend you $500,000 at 10 percent interest and you want to spread your debt service payments out over five years? At equal principal repaid each year, the first payment would be $150,000 the first year ($100,000 is the principal repaid each year, and as the loan is for $500,000 at 10 percent there will be $50,000 in interest added to the principal for the first payment but only $40,000 the second year). The third year would be $100,000 plus $30,000 or $130,000 for that year. I still have a 10 percent return on what I lent you, but if you had purchased an income property you may have a hard time having any positive cash flow for a few years (if ever) with that kind of a repayment schedule.

NO PAYMENTS UNTIL THE END OF THE TERM.   However, thus far each annual installment of interest has come at the end of each year. What if I lent you $500,000 at 10 percent and you made no payments at all for three years? At the end of that time, you paid me $650,000. That amount could be made up of $500,000 plus 10 percent of the $500,000 times three. Okay, so I get my $150,000 interest plus the entire principal. What is my yield? Is it 10 percent? What if you did not make any payments for 10 years (this is sometimes called a Zero Coupon Mortgage)? At the end of that period, you paid me $1,000,000. After all, that is the original $500,000 plus $50,000 of interest times 10.

INTRODUCING PERIODS OF TIME TO THE EQUATION. This is where the time factor comes to play. If you are calculating a 10-year return, a $1,000,000 repayment of $500,000 that was borrowed at 10 percent interest would yield me an average of 10 percent. But what would that actually cost you? In other words, to pay $500,000 of interest 10 years from now, how much money would you have to invest each year at a compound interest rate that would equal $500,000 at the end of 10 years? You will see that the amount you need to invest will show that by waiting until the end of 10 years to collect my $1,000,000, I have earned less than 10 percent.

DISCOUNTING THE VALUE OF MONEY PAID LATER. Assume you could invest the money at 6 percent per year, and wanted to build up to the $500,000 you would need at the end of the tenth year. How much would you have to pay in each year over those 10 years into a savings account (or investment account) that earned 6 percent per year to compound all the way to $500,000? The answer to this question will require a different formula than that used in the Frank and Bob case because now we are simply making a value comparison between what the lender gets versus what the borrower actually pays. The borrower still pays only $36,933.50 per year. If I valued my money at no less than 6 percent, and I was really getting the equivalent of $36,933.50 per year, instead of getting 10 percent, I am really getting 7.59 percent return. Have you ever seen such a thing? The note and mortgage says the 10 percent and calculated at a fixed $50,000 times 10 years, but the real payment is considerably less. Clearly, the sooner I get my money the better it is for me. But wait, look at this from another point of view.

Look back at the earlier example that called for interest-only payments at the end of each year. If you paid me $50,000 per year, at the end of each year for 10 years in a row, that would amount to $500,000. Add the principal payment in one single balloon payment and you have paid $1,000,000. That is the same total of payments that I would have received from the previous example. But if I would do nothing but deposit that $50,000 each year into an account that earned 6 percent per year, how much money would I have at the end of 10 years in that account? The answer is $659,039. That plus my original principal that you repay on the last day of the tenth year gives me $1,259,039 in the bank. What is my yield now? In average terms, the 10 percent paid in one lump at the end of 10 years will be $659,039 of interest. This is 131.807 percent of the amount lent ($500,000), so on the average I would have received $\frac{1}{10}$ of that amount each year, which is 13.18 percent (divide the total interest by $500,000 to get 131.807, then divide that by 10 years to get the average rate per year). This kind of math is what some stock market funds use, by the way, to describe the increase in value of a stock over 10 years and does not take into account any compounding of values.

RETURN RATE IS TIED TO WHEN THE RETURN IS RECEIVED. What is my real return? You can see that the real dollar value of what I get (above the principal amount I loaned to you) depends on when I get it, and what I can do with it in the meantime. Because of this, it is important that you understand that what the mortgage document says is not necessarily what, in real annual yield terms, you get.

MODERN MORTGAGES USE CONSTANT PAYMENT MORTGAGES.   Consider now that the conventional type of mortgage that is used in the United States is amortized over long terms with fixed payments of variable interest and principal. This is a magical form of mathematics that allows a borrower to repay the loan over a long period of time with the same monthly payment. Unlike several of the earlier examples that required lump payments or large early payments, the form used enables an investor to better manage their income and expenses and to easier relate their investment to a yield term. By this I mean, if you want to earn 10 percent on your invested capital from your real estate purchase, and there were no such thing as a lender or for that matter a mortgage, then for every $100,000 in return you have to invest $1,000,000 in cash. But with an easy to repay loan, where you can get some positive leverage in your loan-to-value ratio, all you need to do is keep your debt service under 10 percent of what you borrow to increase your yield. For example, you want to invest $250,000 and generate 10 percent cash return on that. Assume you can borrow money at a constant rate of 9 percent of the amount owed (your debt service of principal and interest payment combined), and can borrow up to 75 percent of the purchase price of the property. If the maximum cash you have is $250,000, that would dictate that at a 75 percent loan-to-value ratio that the $250,000 would represent 25 percent of the total value of the investment. That would allow you to invest up to $1,000,000 in purchase price (25 percent of $1,000,000 is $250,000). Assume you found a property whose seller was asking $1,150,000 that had a Net Operating Income (NOI) of $95,000. Under the criteria I just mentioned, the most you could pay would be $950,000 to get a 10 percent return if you had to pay all cash. But, as you only have $250,000 cash, you may have to bring some creative juices to the table. Is there a way to do this deal if you could purchase the property for $1,000,000? Even the full asking price.

CONSTANT RATE OF DEBT SERVICE IS A COMBINATION OF PRINCIPAL AND INTEREST.   In the previous paragraph when discussing the total annual debt, service of 9 percent that the actual interest rate and term of years was not important at that time. This is because when you use this kind of math, there is considerable flexibility in this combination of interest and principal that make up that fixed payment. If only the term of years is increased but the interest stays the same, the payment will go down; if the interest is the only element decreased and the years remain the same the payment goes down. Move one up slightly, and the other down just a bit, and the payment may still go down. With this in mind, you offer $1,000,000 on the property. In the terms of the offer spell out the following: your down payment will be $250,000. The balance of the purchase price will be made up of new financing and seller held financing. The combination debt service of this total debt, which will not exceed $750,000, and the total annual debt service will not exceed $65,000. Based on the NOI of $95,000 you would actually have $70,000 left to meet debt service. (deduct your 10 percent return on your own invested capital from the NOI—$95,000 less $25,000 = $70,000).

However, you feel you need (rightfully so) even a small buffer between success and foreclosure. To meet your desired cash flow return you need $25,000 per year. This is after all expenses, including management that you have added in early in the process because while you do not mind working for yourself, you want to be paid for the effort. By now, you have seen a number of creative ways to close this minor gap. Look at the easiest of all, if the seller is in the slightest way motivated. You borrow $600,000 from the local lender, at a total debt service rate of 9 percent (remember this is the combined interest and principal totals of each payment). This has obligated you to $54,000 a year in mortgage payments. The interest rate and the term of years will have to be hammered out, but as long as you can keep this rate, and have positive amortization along the way, you will take that loan. Positive amortization is simply reducing principal every time you make a payment.

Okay, but what about the remaining $150,000 to total the balance owed? Offer the seller two choices to see what happens. The first choice might be a second mortgage on your home in the amount of $150,000 at 5 percent interest for three years, then 5.5 percent for the next three years, then 6 percent for four years. You then balloon the mortgage and pay off the unpaid principal of $150,000. Your second choice might be: You give him a lot you own in Sedona, Arizona, that is worth $150,000 and if he does not want it for any reason after five years, you will buy it back at that same price.

CREATIVITY MAY STIMULATE A TRANSACTION'S SUCCESS. The seller may not know how to deal with this offer. He knew his price was a bit high, so the price you offered might work, he tells you. He may take a while to consider if either of your two options is acceptable or even worth fine-tuning into an acceptable deal. The seller may not know how to massage either of them. I honestly cannot tell you which one I would think a seller would take because like that game show with the boxes, you can never tell. The lot in Sedona? Well, if you have ever been to Sedona you might say that would be a shoo-in. The key to maneuvering one party or the other to a mutual meeting of the mind can be greatly facilitated by an astute broker or other advisor. Sometimes it is up to the buyer or seller to make suggestions that move the deal along. That is why a two-pronged attack, such as take this or take that, has merit and may be worthwhile. However, make sure that whenever you offer anything that is not cash, that you are specifically clear on all aspects of the proposal. If a mortgage or other element is introduced, be sure to include a package of information so that the other side knows exactly what they will get, and why it is worth what you say it is.

LOOKING AT THE MATHEMATICAL CALCULATION OF MORTGAGE LOANS. Virtually all real estate mortgage loans follow a mathematical sequence that arrives at a payment (monthly or otherwise) that remains the same over the life of the mortgage (or until it balloons), which does not change each month. However, as we have seen, the combination of principal and interest that make up that payment does change.

Assume you need a mortgage for $500,000. A local lender offers you that amount with a payment schedule that spreads the repayment over 25 years at 8 percent interest. The example that follows shows only the first five years of that mortgage's life and looks only at the annual totals that are the combined total of 12 months' rent. Follow these steps to arrive at the answers shown.

How to Calculate an Amortization Table

1. In the Appendix of this book, in Table A, look for the constant interest rate for 8 percent interest for 25-year term. The constant shown is 9.262.

2. Multiply 0.09262 by $500,000 to arrive at the total of the 12 months of every year. This math results in $46,310. This is the annual payment each year for the total of 25 years, which will pay off that mortgage. See this in column IV on page 379.

3. For the remaining calculations, I have lifted a part of Table A and show it just above the amortization illustration. We now want to find what total principal has been paid off by the end of those first 12 months. In essence, we really want to know how much principal will be paid off using the same annual total of 12 monthly payments over 24 years. Therefore, look at Table A at the constant rate for 24 years (to go) at 8 percent. You will see 9.385.

4. Divide the total annual payments you discovered in step 2 by 0.09385 ($46,310 ÷ 0.09385 = $493,446). Round off the cents. This amount, $493,446 is the amount owed at the end of the first year (of a 25-year term), so it is also the beginning amount of a 24-year term.

5. To find out how much principal was paid off over the first 12 months, we need to deduct $493,446 from the amount of principal at the start of those 12 months ($500,000 − $493,446 = $6,554 [column V, page 379]). Remember, each successive year you must deduct the amount at the end of the year from the amount at the start of that same year. This will change each year.

6. Find the amount of interest paid over those first 12 months by subtracting the amount of principal from the total amount of the payment ($46,310 − $6,554 = $39,756 [VI]).

7. Calculate each successive year the same way. Continue to move backward in Table A. The next column in the illustration below to calculate will be for 23 years to go. Look in Table A under 23 years at 8 percent and you will see 9.521. Continue as indicated above.

Tip: Calculate the ending balances for each year first. Use the items taken from Table A (partially reproduced here). All you do is divide the annual payment $46,310 by the mathematical equivalent of the constants. Then calculate the total amount of principal for each year.

Interest	20 years	21 years	22 years	23 years	24 years*
8%	10.037	9.845	9.674	9.521	9.385

Amortization Table Example

I	II	III	IV	V	VI	VII
Year Ending	Years to go	Amount owed— start of year ($)	Payment Amount ($)	Principal Amount ($)	Interest Amount ($)	Balance ($)
1	24	500,000	46,310	6,554	39,756	493,446
2	23	493,446	46,310	7,048	39,262	486,398
3	22	486,396	46,310	7,692	38,618	478,705
4	21	478,705	46,310	8,314	37,996	470,391
5	20	461,392	46,310	8,999	37,311	461,392

Source: Taken from Table A in the Appendix.

Study this illustration and check back to see how each amount was calculated. This will help you become familiar with the use of Table A in the Appendix and will allow you to compute many different mortgage calculations.

WHAT IF YOUR CALCULATORS DO NOT AGREE.   As you can see, we are dealing with a typical mortgage amortization table. Do not worry if your financial calculator has not come up with these exact amounts as some calculators round off differently. The important element I want you to become aware of is how the interest and principal amounts change each month. Also, I suggest you make your own chart using the same beginning principal, $500,000, but apply 9 percent interest on a schedule of 30 years to see the amount of the initial payments and what would represent interest and principal.

When Should a Mortgage Be Discounted for Cash?

A mortgage should be discounted whenever the need for cash, or the yield which can be obtained with the cash, exceeds the return on the mortgage. Naturally, there are other alternatives, such as obtaining a loan against the mortgage or seeking the funds elsewhere. These alternatives, which may be highly desirable solutions in normal circumstances, may not work quickly enough or produce the desired results as effectively as a discounting of the mortgage.

The cash discount is a sale of the paper (note or note and mortgage) at a reduced price to enable the buyer to have an overall yield greater than the contract rate on the mortgage. This cash sale of the paper can occur at any time after the mortgage has originated.

In many instances, there is a big market for *underperforming mortgages*, which are mortgages that have not met all their payments and have either been called into default, or are at that point when they can be. Some specialty lenders, particularly mortgage REITs, have made millions of dollars picking up such loans, often from other lenders who would rather sell them at a fraction of their face amount and take the accounting write-off than maintain them on their books. Some of these loans are to developing countries. The ultimate salvage of an underproducing loan is to help the borrower to get back on his feet so that the loan can be repaid.

A mortgage that has some maturity and has a good or relatively good repayment record would not fall into the category of an underproducing loan because they are considered to have a performance record, and hence may have a lower discount than if it had no record of payment. Mortgages discounted in the early years will generally have an additional penalty for this lack of seasoning. This will depend on the type of mortgage and the position in rank and the overall total loans to value. For example, if the property was worth $200,000 and there were three mortgages against the property totaling $180,000, this establishes a 90 percent loan-to-value ratio. If the mortgage to be discounted was a third, mortgage for the $40,000 risk in buying this loan is much greater than buying a first mortgage of $40,000. In either event, however, the total loan-to-value ratio is such that the property owner may be over-leveraged and the absolute creditworthiness of the mortgagor needs to be carefully reviewed.

It should be obvious that a second mortgage will not be as saleable as a first mortgage on the same property. Therefore, it may require a greater discount. Yet, a third mortgage on one property may be more marketable than a first mortgage on another property. The loan-to-value ratio is important throughout this ranking process. If a property is valued at $100,000 and there is a first mortgage of $40,000, the loan ratio is 40 percent and the equity is 60 percent. That same property with an additional loan (second) of $20,000 would have a loan ratio of 60 percent to value and the equity ratio of 40 percent. Therefore, the loan-to-value ratio is crucial and the remaining equity as a percent of the total value is essential to determine the risk factor when purchasing the mortgage.

Use Creativity to Move a Difficult-to-Sell Mortgage

Some mortgages are difficult to sell unless they are heavily discounted. However, they still have value, and if you can combine them with other benefits they can be passed onto another party for a greater value than you would get in a direct sale.

Example 2.   Castile had taken back a third mortgage when he sold his office building nearly two years earlier. The mortgage now has 10 years to go and the unpaid balance is $105,000. The contract rate is 8 percent and the monthly payment to amortize the balance is $1,528.88. Castile wants to sell the mortgage at a price that will give an investor 10 percent on the invested capital. This means that the investor could pay no more than

$96,390 to have that yield. The first potential investor looked at the discounted price and was interested. He asked Castile what the loan percentages and equity percentage ratios were. Castile was not sure what the investor meant, so they figured them out together. The estimated value on the property was $600,000. The mortgage represented 17.5 percent of the total value, and the superior financing totaled $425,000 or 70.8 percent of the value. This meant there was a total of 88.3 percent financing and 11.7 percent equity. The investor decided that with only 11.7 percent equity between the mortgage and foreclosure, he needed a minimum of a 12 percent return for such a risky mortgage. The mortgage would have to sell for $69,930 to show a 12 percent yield. Castile decided to keep the mortgage, since his need for cash would not generate a 12 percent return.

However, later in the same year Castile found a small apartment building he could buy if he could pay cash to the existing mortgages. The apartment building should throw off nearly 13 percent cash. He tried to get the owner of the building to take the mortgage as part of the transaction. Failing that, he went back to the cash investor and discounted the mortgage to come up with the cash to buy the apartments. Castile now had a greater use for the cash than the present return generated from the yield on paper.

But Castile may have missed the opportunity to close a deal when he failed at his attempt to exchange the mortgage rather than discount it. He was on the right track in opening new doors to solve his problem but somehow was unable to convince the seller to accept the mortgage as part of the purchase price. It might have been something as simple as the seller's fear of holding a third position on the property Castile had sold. If that was the situation, either a broker in the transaction or Castile himself should have discussed the situation. Castle could have offered to give his own personal guarantee to back up the repayment of the note. If Castile had done this, the seller may have taken a harder look at the proposal, and Castile may not have had to discount the value at all.

Using mortgage paper you hold as a result of a sale you had completed in the past or by way of purchasing debt from other people (at a discount, I hope) can be a good way to profit by shifting your asset to a property you want to purchase. Remember, usually the most motivated party in a transaction is the seller. Because this is such a good way to move off mortgages, let's look at several other ways that Castile could have sweetened the deal for the seller of the apartment building he wanted to buy. The first step in this process is to have some idea about what goals most motivate the seller. What does the seller need: cash, relief of debt, sick of property management, want to move to a far and distant place? Is his reluctance to hold debt because of any of those factors or simply because a friend has said, "Don't be stupid and hold a third mortgage"?

How could Castile sweeten the deal? One way would have been to offer additional collateral to improve the security on the loan. He could do that by giving the new holder of the mortgage a second or third position on the apartments he was buying, or his lot in Sedona, or some other property he owns. If Castile discovers that the seller really wants to purchase a sailboat and go around the world on it, then he should jump for joy.

Many sailboat sellers will take a second or third mortgage on dry land to sell their boat. Castile could show the seller how to take the newly created mortgage and use it as a part of his purchase of the sailboat.

Take a look at the following to gain a better insight into using discounted mortgages in exchange.

When Should a Mortgage Be Discounted in Exchange?

Castile attempted to get the owner of a property he wanted to buy to take paper he held. This was a step to exchange the paper at its face amount. Later in the negotiations Castile tries to make the paper more attractive by discounting the face amount, but the apartment owner's need for cash overshadowed the yield any reasonable discount could generate. While Castile failed in the exchange of the paper, he was at least on the right track in trying to better the buying power of the paper by using it as a part of a transaction rather than discounting it.

When an investor attempts to buy a property, it is wise to offer as a part of the total transaction any paper that investor holds, especially if the paper has a yield less than the expected return on the property being purchased.

EXAMPLE 3: REDDING'S TRANSACTION.   Redding, an investor, offered to buy a strip store from Shelly. Redding has up to $250,000 in cash and a $150,000 first mortgage he was holding on a vacant piece of land he had sold the year before. This gives Redding a total of $400,000 in equity (cash plus mortgage) to be used to acquire the strip store. Shelly was asking $1,650,000 for the property that had a first mortgage of $1,200,000 and an annual debt service of $120,000. The NOI of the store was $145,500, and a cash flow of $25,500 ($145,500 less $120,000 = $25,500). Her equity (at the price offered) was $450,000, and if Redding paid $450,000 (in cash or combination of cash and other benefits), his "cash flow" would be 5.67 percent return. (What return is $25,500 on $450,000 invested? Divide $25,500 by $450,000 to get 0.0567, which is 5.67 percent.)

Redding made the following offer to test the water:

Price	$1,500,000
Assume the existing first mortgage	$1,200,000
Pay Shelly cash at closing	100,000
Shelly will hold a second mortgage	+ 200,000
Redding's first offer	$1,500,000

Shelly rejects the offer and counters with an increased price of $1,550,000 and a down payment at closing of $250,000 and agrees to hold a second mortgage of $50,000:

Price	$1,550,000
Redding assumes the first mortgage	$1,200,000
Redding pays cash at closing	200,000
Shelly holds a second mortgage for	+ 150,000
Total offer	$1,550,000

The $150,000 mortgage Redding wanted to give, paid would give him $18,000 a year in interest only installments of $1,500 per month. This mortgage was to balloon no later than 10 years, but the mortgagor would have to pay off the debt if he wanted to build on the property or decided to sell it to another party. Redding is planning on making his counter offer and to give Shelly the mortgage at its face value and to close the deal in that way. But instead, he does the following:

Price	$1,550,000
Redding assumes the first mortgage	$1,200,000
Redding pays cash at closing	200,000
Shelly holds a second mortgage for	+ 130,000
Total offer	$1,530,000

The second mortgage, Redding explains, will have monthly installments of $1,500 per month that are made up of 8 percent interest per year on the outstanding balance owed, and the rest of the payment goes toward principal each year.

Review what we know about the second mortgage Shelly will hold. The face amount is $130,000, payment is $1,500 per month, and interest rate on the outstanding balance is 8 percent. We do not know the number of years that will take to amortize the loan, or what the balloon will be at the end of 10 years. So, what is the constant payment rate at day one? Dividing $18,000 (total of 12 monthly payments) by $130,000 equals 13.846 percent constant. Look along the 8 percent line for the number of years, which have an 13.846 percent constant. The closest constant you will find will be 8 percent interest for 11 years, which is 13.699 percent. To double check how close you are, find what the monthly payment would be at that constant for 11 years. To do this, multiply the constant by $130,000 to get $17,808.70 per year, divide that by 12 to get $1,484.00 per month. In essence, the payment Redding makes will easily retire the loan in full at 11 years; so without any further calculation he could either make it an 11-year loan or leave the amount of the balloon unstated. "I'll pay you the balance due at the end of 10 years," will suffice.

If Shelly accepts this deal as presented, look at how Redding benefits. He gets to keep his first mortgage on the vacant land, and simply takes the payments from that mortgage to pay off the Shelly second mortgage in full in 11 years. At the end of the tenth year, the vacant land loan will be paid off in full, putting 100 percent of the principal due on that of $150,000 into Redding's pocket.

If Shelly accepts this proposal, is there any doubt that she would have jumped at the chance to accept the full $150,000 value of Redding's first mortgage? Or even the first $130,000 of the principal payout? But if she accepts the monthly payments and full amortization (almost) in 10 years at 8 percent, the result meets her expectations and the deal takes her closer to her goals.

Analyzing the Market for a Discounted Mortgage

To some degree, it is the old story of how long must your legs be? The answer is, of course, long enough to reach the floor. In the discounting of mortgages, the amount of the discount must be sufficient to market the paper. Investors dealing with mortgage paper look to a demand rate that is generally greater than the yields on the property securing the paper. If the mortgage is a first mortgage and there is a low loan-to-value ratio, the discount will be reduced as the risk is lessened. On the other hand, if the mortgage is a second or third mortgage and the total loan-to-value ratio is high, equity is therefore low and the discount must be increased.

The motivation of the seller of the paper must be considered as the most important factor. If the seller must have cash, then he has little choice but to increase the discount until the paper sells. But if his need for cash is limited to a portion of the mortgage, he may be able to borrow the needed funds by placing the mortgage up as security for the loan. The interest paid on such a loan can be greater than the yield offered in the discount, and yet the total cost is less than if the mortgage were discounted.

This seller may actually take a bit less than you would have, just to have the cash. When you make your offer, you can say, "This $150,000 mortgage will pay out at a fair interest rate, but if you want to convert it to immediate cash, here is a possible buyer at $13,000. However, I'd recommend you keep it as it is a good investment at $150,000." This strategy allows you to maximize your paper when using it as a part of another transaction.

Finding the Discount Amount

There is a direct relationship between all mortgages that have a constant periodic payment that will fully amortize the mortgage over a set period of time. As we saw with the use of Table C in the Appendix where the variables in the equation were the period of time and the interest rate, same situation applies, but because we are using a fully amortizing mortgage, where principal payments are being made along with interest payments, the problem is considerably different. In the following problem, we will use the constant annual percent tables provided in this book as Table A in the Appendix, which have been used earlier. These tables have many uses, one of which is an easy way to arrive at the discount amounts for mortgages. The method of finding the discount of a self-amortizing mortgage is explained in the example that follows.

EXAMPLE 4: DISCOUNTING A FULLY SELF-AMORTIZING MORTGAGE.   Look at a simple discount situation. You have a mortgage that amortizes fully over 15 years. It is at 10 percent interest per annum.

In the table of constant annual percentages, you would look in the 10 percent interest column for the 15 years. The answer would be 12.895, representing the constant amount of annual payments (which consist of 12 monthly installments) to pay off any mortgage in full within 15 years. As the example we will use has a face amount of $150,000, that amount times the constant of 12.895 will require a total annual debt service of $19,345 from 12 monthly installments of $1,611.87.

Assume that a buyer is found who will buy that mortgage from you, but they want to earn 14 percent interest on that mortgage. What is the constant rate at a demand rate of 14 percent for this same term of 15 years? Look along the 15-year line at 14 percent interest rate and you will find: 16.326 is the constant for the demand rate.

If the mortgage had a present face value of $150,000, what price would the buyer pay? There are two ways to ascertain the answer. One way is to find the discounted percentage. That is, what percent of the original face value will represent the discounted price that will give the desired 14 percent yield to the buyer?

The formula to find the amount of discounted percentage is:

Constant annual percent ÷ Demand rate constant = Discounted percentage

That percentage, when multiplied by the face amount of the mortgage, will give the purchase price that would give the desired return.

Constant (12.895) divided by 16.326 equals 0.78984, which is stated as 78.984 percent. The discounted percentage then is 78.984 percent. (When used in math it becomes 0.78984.)

To apply these results, multiply the face amount of the mortgage by the discounted percentage ($150,000 × 0.78984 = $118,476).

Use the chart that follows to quickly calculate the answer to the question. I have provided a blank version of this same chart at the end of this chapter so that you can make photocopies for later use.

MORTGAGE DISCOUNTED VALUE TO GIVE A DESIRED YIELD

1. Face amount of mortgage (present balance owed)	$ 150,000.00
2. Contract rate	10%
3. Total annual payments of (monthly ___x___, quarterly _____, semiannually _____, annually _____; check one)	$ 19,342.50
4. Constant annual percent adjustment (line 3 ÷ by line 1)	12.895%
5. Demand rate	14%
6. Mortgage term	15 years
7. Constant at demand rate (find by looking in demand rate column for number of years, in this example 14%)	16.326%
8. Discounted value (line 4 ÷ by line 7)	78.984%
9. Discounted price (line 1 × line 8)	$ 118,476.00

If a mortgage repayment schedule is other than monthly payments, use the total annual payment of all the periods within the year. You can still use Table A in the Appendix for your calculations, and while you may not be exactly on the mark, the error will be slightly less than the proper amount.

Finding the Interest Yield on a Mortgage That Is Discounted

It will be necessary from time to time to know how to calculate the yield on a mortgage that is offered at a discount.

EXAMPLE 5.   Sterling has a $50,000 mortgage with 15 years remaining at 8 percent. The payment is $478 per month. Sterling offers this mortgage for sale at a 20 percent discount. The purchase price of the mortgage is therefore 80 percent of the face amount ($50,000 × 80 percent = $40,000). What is the yield to an investor?

The following chart will assist in this calculation. Note that it is very similar to the previous discount chart but with one important difference: We do not know the demand rate.

The formula in this computation is:

Constant annual percent ÷ Discounted value percent = Constant at yield rate

YIELD ON A DISCOUNTED MORTGAGE

1. Face amount of mortgage (present balance owed)	$ 50,000
2. Discounted sale price	$ 40,000
3. Contract rate	8%
4. Total annual payments of (monthly __x__, quarterly _____, semiannually _____, annually _____; check one)	$ 5,736
5. Constant annual percent adjustment (line 4 ÷ by line 1)	11.472%
6. Discounted value amount ratio (line 2 ÷ by line 1)	80%
7. Constant annual percent of discounted mortgage (line 4 ÷ by line 6)	4.33%
8. Find yield from Table A in the Appendix	

Locate closest constant rate at 15 years:

Constant Rate Found	Corresponding Yield
14.210%	11.75%
14.402%	12.00%
Estimate yield at approximately 11.87%.	

How Sellers Can Use Discounted Mortgages to Help Them Sell Their Property

Given a standard set of circumstances, any buyer will pay more for a property on terms than he or she will pay if investing 100 percent of the price in cash. This will be a given factor if the buyer does not have 100 percent cash available for the purchase as well as two major assumptions that the investment will provide one or more added benefits to the buyer by using terms. These two assumptions are: (1) the buyer can earn a greater yield on his capital from the income of the property than the cost of the financing. In essence, positive leverage through financing and (2) there is this alternative available either through the market or from the seller, and the buyer will qualify for such financing.

If the buyer wants to pay cash, there is no problem and the discounted mortgage aspect does not enter into the picture. However, to broaden the market, or to create a market for a property that is difficult to sell, the seller may offer reasonable financing.

EXAMPLE 6.   Robinson owns a 50-acre tract of land. It has been on the market for $20,000 per acre ($1,000,000) for 18 months. His broker suggests that the terms he wants (50 percent down and short payout) are the major drawbacks. Robinson, however, needs at least $400,000 cash to acquire a 300-acre farm 30 miles away and agrees to reduce the price to $18,000 per acre to move the property ($900,000), but he still needs 50 percent down. His broker examines the situation and proposes that Robinson keep the price at $20,000 per acre since it is reasonable for the market, but that he be willing to accept only 10 percent down. The 90 percent balance will be broken into two mortgages: a first mortgage in the amount of $500,000 and a second for $400,000.

The terms are 15 years at 8 percent on the first mortgage with full amortization at monthly payments of $4,778.33. The second mortgage of $400,000 will be at 10 percent interest with interest only payments of $40,000 made at the end of each year with a balloon payment due at the end of 15 years. There would also be a provision in the second mortgage that required the mortgagor to pay off the loan if the property was sold, or in any way subdivided.

The broker then suggests that Robinson look to a discount of the first mortgage to generate the cash required. Even if he discounted the mortgage by $50,000, it would show a nice return of approximately 9.75 percent. Because it was a first mortgage, with a low loan to value ratio, the broker was sure he could get a buyer for the mortgage.

He did exactly that too, only the buyer wanted a yield of 10.25 percent. What would Sterling have to sell that mortgage for so that the buyer would earn 10.25 percent on his investment?

This is easy and quick to find. In Table A of the Appendix go to the 10.25 percent line. Slide across to year 15. You will find this constant: 13.079.

We know the monthly payments are $4,778.33; so the full year debt is $4,778.33 multiplied by 12, which equals $57,339.96. Now divide the debt service ($57,339.96) by the constant of 0.13079; the result is $438,613.63.

Sterling jumped at that price, and that, plus the down payment of $100,000 allowed him to acquire the 300-acre farm, and still have positive cash flow from the second mortgage.

Can you think of other alternatives that Sterling might have used to reach his goal (the 300-acre farm)?

Had Robinson offered the property at $900,000, it is unlikely that it would have sold. Instead, the broker used creative financing to convert a difficult property into a more easily marketable one. The buyer needed only $100,000 down, and had a low-interest first mortgage and an interest-only second mortgage, both highly acceptable forms of financing for a buyer. Also, since the seller was offering the property with 90 percent financing, little room was left for negotiations by the buyer to reduce the price.

The buyer of the mortgage obtained a good yield at a safe risk. In Robinson's case, the land was at a fair value so the risk was slight. Robinson came out better than he had thought in that the package produced a sale. The tradeoff of a discounted mortgage, instead of lowering the price, will work in many areas of real estate. A free and clear property where the seller can use a first mortgage for the discount, as did Robinson, is best for such a transaction, but the secondary mortgages can be discounted as well.

FINDING INVESTORS WHO WILL BUY DISCOUNTED MORTGAGES

There are several markets for mortgages. The most organized is that consisting of mortgage brokers. These professional people make their living by placing and making mortgages. They deal with private investors as well as institutional funds and will act on their own behalf or as broker agents. Because they have daily contact with this field, they are a prime source for discounted mortgages.

Locating these sources is relatively easy. Most will be listed in your phone book. You can also obtain the names of others who are outside your area from your banking sources. The contact you make with them is important.

Not all the mortgage brokers you may contact will be viable. Some do not have the contacts that others may have, or may find dealing with you uncomfortable.

Mortgage brokers are but one source. Trust departments and pension funds that may be located in your area are also candidates for good mortgages, and they like the idea of leveraging up on a discounted mortgage. These sources are found in your local commercial banks and insurance companies. The commercial bank is a great place to start, and you might as well go right to the top: the secretary of the president. This astute person will direct you to all the right people. Often, a recommendation from the secretary to the person you want to deal with is more important than if the president himself called the trust officer and said you were on your way. How so? Follow this suggestion: Meet and establish good rapport with the bank's president. This is essential to other dealings you will have in the community anyway. Go over some of the services that the bank offers. Does it have a trust department? If so, what type of trust services does it provide? Once you have had at least two meetings with this bank president, you will have made contact with his secretary. Be sure he or she knows who you are and that you are on friendly terms with the boss.

The day you want to sit down with the trust officer, give the president's secretary a call and ask the name of the trust officer in charge: "Is it a Mr. Rankin?" you might ask. Then ask if he or she would mind giving Mr. Rankin a call as an introduction for your appointment that day. The secretary usually will also have something nice to say about you.

Once you are with the trust officer, ask about services. He or she will become a sales-person, giving you data about the department. Do not rush in to a trust officer you have never seen and confront him or her with a discounted mortgage you must sell by that afternoon or else risk blowing a big deal.

Ask about the mortgage brokers the officer deals with in buying private mortgages for the trust account or pension fund the company represents. If he or she gives you some names remember them, but the important thing you have learned is that the bank does buy such mortgages. Ask the trust officer who approves such private mortgage purchases how you would go about presenting a package.

Private investors are numerous, although very difficult to cultivate. Earlier chapters have dealt with this private investor in mortgages. But to summarize, remember the private investor in mortgages is like the investor in real estate. They both recognize the advantage of realty as a security. However, the mortgage investor is usually willing to take a lower yield at a reduced risk than the real estate investor.

Don't Forget the Mortgagor

The mortgagor may be a prime buyer for a discounted mortgage. After all, they are making the payments on that mortgage. It is possible that they actually have cash or the ability to raise the cash. They might actually jump at the opportunity to pay off a debt that would allow them to reduce their monthly outlay of cash. So, before you run off and seek out other investors, offer the discount to the person who makes the monthly payment.

Sources That Will Buy Discounted Mortgages

- **Mortgage brokers:** For the broker who will not deal frequently with discounted mortgages, this source can be consistent and easy to approach.

- **Trust funds and pension funds:** A little harder to approach, but one of the prime sources used by the mortgage broker. These sources are found at your commercial banks and insurance companies.

- Private investors: Look first at your own realty investors. Some of these clients may like a good discounted mortgage. Other private investors will advertise in local papers or can be found through your bank or savings and loan.

- Real estate brokers: Many brokers and salespeople will take a discounted mortgage as part of their commission. All you have to do is ask.

- The mortgagor: Never overlook the person who writes out the monthly check that pays off the loan.

When to Offer a Partial Discount to the Mortgagor

It may be possible to raise some quick cash by going to the mortgagor and suggesting a discount on the future payments if he or she will prepay some of the outstanding principal. I was involved in such a case some time ago.

Example 7.   Emory was holding a $45,000 second mortgage on a business he had sold several years earlier. The mortgage had fifteen years remaining at 8.5 percent interest per annum. The annual payment was based on monthly payments of $443.25. The constant annual percentage on this mortgage is 11.82 (found in constant table under 8.5 percent at 15 years). Emory needed a quick $15,000 and found that if he were to discount the mortgage the yield necessary would be 12 percent. This meant the sale price would be $36,936 (11.82 ÷ 14.40 × 45,000). Emory felt this was too great a discount to take in order to obtain the $15,000 needed.

He approached one of the local mortgage brokers to see whether he could borrow against the mortgage, but that did not produce any positive results. By the time Emory called me, he was at his wits end. "I need the cash by the end of the week," he said, "and it seems that the more I need it, the tougher it becomes to get it." Sounds very familiar, I know.

After counseling with Emory, I suggested we make the following proposal to the mortgagor. The mortgagor would prepay $15,000 on the outstanding mortgage. This would bring the unpaid principal balance down to $30,000. Based on this balance, the monthly amortization would be reduced to $295.50. As an inducement or bonus to the mortgagor, Emory agreed to reduce the interest rate on the mortgage to 6½ percent rather than the 8½ percent for its remaining term. This gave a new constant of 10.45 and a monthly payment of $261.25 instead of the $295.50. What this meant was that the mortgagor was obtaining a discount for the remaining balance by the prepayment of the $15,000. Over the balance of the term, the mortgagor would save $6,165. The cost to Emory was not really the $6,165, however, as the reduction of the interest lowered his pretax income and converted future payback (the mortgage) into ready cash. A discounting of the mortgage would have caused a greater reduction of total earnings, and hence all parties benefited.

There were many other ways to approach the benefit Emory had given the mortgagor, but this solution seemed to be the best for Emory. The mortgage, as it turned out, was paid off four years later when the property was sold by the mortgagor. No doubt, the low interest on the second was somewhat instrumental in attracting a buyer, even though the property was refinanced anyway. The gamble Emory took in reducing the interest rate was well calculated. Had he reduced the principal amount in the discount, that sum would have been a lost item regardless of when the mortgage was paid back. The reduced interest was an expense to Emory only as long as the mortgage was in force. Emory knew that most mortgages had a maximum life span of 7 to 10 years in the type of business he had. The life span of mortgages is important in discounting. The early retirement of a mortgage will boost the yield to the holder when the face amount is discounted.

Assume that Emory had sold his $45,000 mortgage at a discount that would have yielded 12 percent. As we saw in the example, the price would have been $36,936. Remember, the face amount on the mortgage is $45,000. If the loan were paid off at the end of the first year, the new mortgagee (the investor who bought the mortgage from Emory) would have been paid approximately $48,800.

As the investor paid only $36,936 for the paper, his return on his investment for one year would be $11,864 or a yield of 32.12 percent. Each year this bonus will decline, and by the fifteenth year, the yield is down to the 12 percent discounted yield. The incredible bonus interest that comes with this early prepayment is one of the real advantages of the discounted mortgage and should never be taken lightly.

Examination of the total financing on the property may disclose a potential necessity for refinancing in which a mandatory prepayment of a mortgage may be imminent. For example, a first mortgage is offered for discount. It is a 20-year mortgage at a moderate interest rate. Because of the term of years, the discount will be rather high. The mortgage broker examines the underlying mortgages and finds a large second mortgage that is interest only for three years with a balloon payment. The combined financing is less than 60 percent of the value and the second mortgage is nearly half that total. The mortgage broker concludes that the owner of the property will refinance all of the mortgages into one new first mortgage before the end of the three years when the second mortgage balloons. Not only is such a mortgage a good risk, but the discount and probable bonus will give an exceedingly high yield. It is relatively easy to check what mortgages have been recorded against a property. It is possible that there could be a mortgage that was not recorded due to error, neglect, or that it was simply taken out an hour ago and has not been taken to the county for recording as yet. For that reason, it is wise to check the title prior to lending or buying existing debt. Let your lawyer handling the transaction do that for you. As for checking the title yourself, clerks at the county property records office generally are helpful in teaching you how to do that. Some counties' record offices are even available on the Internet and the data nearly instantly available.

Another situation of a diamond deal just waiting for you could be a discounted mortgage that is a second mortgage behind a low-interest-rate first mortgage that is nearly paid off. Such mortgages have a high constant rate and become prime candidates for refinancing even though the new interest rate would be higher. The constant rate for income property is often more important than the interest rate. Once the mortgage is refinanced, the second mortgage would automatically be paid off.

The combinations are endless. The motivation of the mortgagor is also important. Some mortgagors have a history of early prepayment. If you have this information, it is worth its weight in discounted mortgages.

MORTGAGE DISCOUNTED VALUE TO GIVE A DESIRED YIELD (BLANK FORM)

1. Face amount of mortgage (present balance owed)	$
2. Contract rate % (interest on mortgage note)	%
3. Total annual payment (monthly _____, quarterly _____, semiannually _____, annually _____; check one)	$
4. Constant annual percent adjustment (line 3 ÷ by line 1)	%
5. Demand rate	%
6. Mortgage term	years
7. Constant at demand rate (find by looking in demand rate column for number of years, the demand rate shown in line 5)	%
8. Discounted value (line 4 ÷ line 7)	%
9. Discounted price (line 1 × line 8)	$

Chapter 16

TWO PRIME INSIDER TECHNIQUES

Preferred Income Sweeteners and Options

GOAL OF THIS CHAPTER

This chapter introduces two highly effective negotiation strategies that can help you close transactions whether you are the buyer or seller. Each of these two techniques, preferred income sweeteners and options, has a different approach to several problems an investor can face if negotiations fail to produce a satisfactory purchase agreement. First we look at some of those problems.

SELLER'S STATEMENTS SOUND TOO GOOD TO BE TRUE

Few buyers will take, as gospel truth, everything the seller says or illustrates about the property offered for sale (or lease). This is clearly a natural reaction and it is often very hard to overcome a seller's reluctance to accept an offer or terms that do not measure up to the value of the property that is fixed in the seller's mind. Dealing with this situation can be extremely difficult for several reasons. The obvious reason is that indeed the seller has stretched the truth well past reality. Income, for example, is far less than the pro forma indicates, and expenses overlook many costs that either came directly out of the seller's pocket, or never went there in the first place. Management and other tasks that a seller may do and then not get paid for is a good example of how expenses can be understated.

However, there are honest mistakes that can cause income and expenses to be misrepresented. This might simply be that the seller is uninformed about some of these realities. Accounting procedures and terminology can be different from what the buyer is accustomed, and can cloud the bottom line, when in reality, the seller has presented a truthful accounting of the facts.

Often, the problem is in asking one question and getting the answer to another one. For example, the buyer asks the seller, "Are there any code violations with this property?" The seller might reply, "I can honestly say that in the 30 years that I have owned this property, I have never received a notice of violation by the City of Fort Lauderdale. No sir, not once." Now, that's a good answer, but does not take into account that the reason there has never been a notice of violation is because there has never been a city inspection of the property. So, all the obvious fairly recent remodeling that has been done the last few years may not have permits. No permit, no inspection, but lots of violations.

The two strategies, sweeteners and options, can help bring negotiations to a close when there is not a meeting of the minds on the true status of the situation. Keep in mind, however, there will be times when all the strategies in the world cannot put that broken deal back together.

BUYERS WHO DOUBT HOW GOOD IT REALLY IS

This is the other side of the coin just covered. The seller can genuinely be telling the truth, but the buyers just don't meet the price and terms needed to close the transaction, or worse, they simply stay away. In this situation, the seller must be proactive to not only be as truthful as possible, but to be willing to entice a buyer to take a hard look at the property. Often, once the buyer has taken time to see, firsthand, just how good the deal can be, the mental objection that kept them away can be overcome.

MORE TIME IS NEEDED

Time is the great equalizer in any real estate transaction. That does not mean that time alone can solve or breach every objection, but it can go a long way to close transactions. The principal reason for importance of time in most real estate transactions is this: Time is a function of value. This is because time is expensive, but the failure to properly do one's due diligence of a property before committing to buy it can be even more expensive. When a buyer is forced to make a decision to buy without obtaining permits or approvals to do what is needed for that buyer to receive benefits from the acquisition then the proper decision would be to back off, or just walk away from the deal. From a buyer's point of view, it is better to feel regret to have walked away when someone else makes a fortune from the same deal than to have moved forward and ended up in an economic lion's cage.

Sellers need to understand the reality of time from the buyer's point of view and to use the offer of time as an incentive to attract buyers. Buyers need to understand, too, that there is a natural reluctance from most buyers to "give away" anything. While time may not be an economic factor to some sellers, those who are motivated to act because their time is short will have to accept the reality that to short circuit the process will cost them dearly.

GUIDE TO MAXIMUM BENEFITS WHEN USING SWEETENERS AND OPTIONS

Like most financing tools, both sweeteners and options can be used together, or in combination with many other techniques discussed in this book. Each of these two techniques functions at a different level of the transaction. However, both will work when they address the motivation of other parties to the deal. This will become evident as you progress through this chapter. So, let's start with the first of these two techniques.

PREFERRED INCOME SWEETENERS

Preferred income forms of financing are often found in joint ventures or partnerships. Here an equity partner puts up all or most of the initial capital investment with a working partner or syndicator who has put the deal together. However, the technique works well in sweetening secondary financing, therefore can be applied to any transaction where the seller is to hold any form of purchase money debt, such as a second mortgage, or provide a long-term land lease under the building being sold. Income sweeteners also are a way to overcome the first two factors mentioned earlier where the deal looks too good to be true, or the real benefits of the transaction are not clear in the buyer's mind.

Definition of a Preferred Sweetener

When you bring in a partner or borrow money (from the seller or anyone else), you can offer the party a piece of the income as an incentive to use a portion of his or her capital in the acquisition process. One of the most effective methods to accomplish this is to offer a preference of income. This income comes off the top of net revenue, prior to any splits for the balance of the equity. A sweetener can be anything you can offer another party to close the deal; in this instance we are dealing with actual money that is based on the income the property produces. Ideally, you look for sweeteners that do not take away from your required benefits. In the preferred income form of a sweetener, if the seller's income pro forma is correct, then offering a partner or lender (including the seller) preference on their return does not diminish your return.

The beauty of this strategy is that when the seller has touted the great cash flow this property will throw off, you may take him or her to accept their own statement by offering (as a last resort) a piece of the action that is above the income level presented in their income and expense statement.

EXAMPLE 1: PREFERRED INCOME USED IN A JOINT VENTURE.   You invite a fellow investor to put $500,000 of his money in a project of yours. Together, you borrow, in the form of a purchase money mortgage, another $2,400,000 to acquire an apartment building you are going to manage. Assume that this $2,400,000 mortgage has an annual debt service of $220,000 per year. You and the investor are 50/50 in ownership, even though the investor has put up all the capital to get the deal started. You know that this property has a great potential, and that your management abilities can reduce the seller's stated expenses, and that in a year or two you can increase the cash flow. To entice this investor you agreed to give him 12 percent return on his Invested $500,000. This investor insists that the 12 percent return be preferred. This means that he expects to get $60,000 of the income from the project before you get anything. The numbers are as follows.

Assume the project is a 100-unit rental apartment complex. Note income and expenses:

Gross rents collected	$600,000
Other income	+ 50,000
Total income collected	$650,000

So far, this looks like a normal kind of partnership split. However, assume that this property was a turn-around property and that the income for the first couple of years was not projected as high as that indicated above. You can see what would happen if the NOI for the first year was only $280,000:

Net operating income	$280,000
Less debt service	−220,000
Cash flow	$ 60,000
Less preference income to partner	− 60,000
Balance	$ 0
You take your share	− 0
Balance to be divided equally	$ 0

The investor insisted on the preference income because he wanted to be sure that if there was any income at all, he would have first shot at it. As the originator of this deal, you might be more inclined to divide some income first, then offer a preference on any overage.

In this kind of situation, you might set the terms of the preference so that the cash investor and you will split the first $40,000 of cash flow, giving each of you $20,000. Overage would be divided on a different scale, either by preference of yield on the investor's $500,000, or by division of the percent, say the cash investor gets 60 percent and you get 40 percent of the next $100,000 of cash flow revenue before going back to the 50/50 split mentioned earlier.

These yield or split divisions are totally negotiable and can be tied to other provisions to modify the effect in a long-term relationship. You might even introduce an option to "take the investor out of the deal" at some future date by paying him or her back for the capital invested at a mutually agreed formula.

Keep in mind, however, that this "take out" or "buy back" may have the effect of creating a mortgage situation from day one. That could have a negative effect to one or both of the parties in the transactions. Clearly, unless the "take out" scenario took into effect any appreciated value in the property, then the party being taken out of the deal would not have those benefits from day one. Appraisals can be vague, and may not satisfactorily solve the potential problem of arriving at such a formula.

EXAMPLE 2: PREFERRED INCOME AS A SWEETENER TO ENTICE THE SELLER TO HOLD A MORTGAGE.   In this example, assume you want to buy a strip store and keep the existing financing in place. However, to do this you must get the seller to hold some form of secondary financing. The price for the center is $1,500,000. The existing first mortgage is $900,000 and you have $300,000 cash to invest. You ask the seller to hold a second mortgage for the difference of $300,000, and you offer interest only at 8 percent per annum. He balks at this and asks for 10 percent per annum. In your own mind, you are ready to go to 9 percent anyway, but why not give yourself some edge in the deal? After all, the seller has been telling you how good the income is in the center and how rents are scheduled to go up in a few months. You tell him that you will offer him 9 percent interest on the mortgage for every year that the net operating income of the center equals the revenue the seller promises it will do.

If the seller balks at that proposal, you might then offer a sweetener of an extra return of up to 2 percent of the outstanding mortgage the seller is holding (8 percent + 2 percent = 10 percent) every year that the NOI exceeds the present NOI as stated by the seller. If the mortgage balance is $280,000 and the NOI was only $2,800 above the pro forma NOI (as given to you by the seller), then the bonus would only be an extra 1 percent that year (1 percent × $280,000 = $2,800). To get a full 2 percent add on bonus (another word for preferential income) for that year, the amount over the pro forma NOI would have to be $5,600.00.

Use a Sweetener as a Way to Reduce Risk

One of the primary rules of smart investing is: Reduce your risk. I have referred to this idea often, and thus far, you have seen many different techniques that allow you to accomplish exactly that. If you were the investor in the above example, you would have substantially reduced your risk in this transaction by taking a preferred position against the income. In the case of the seller holding the mortgage, his increase in interest was dependent on how confident he or she was in the ability of the property to do well. At the same time, the buyer of the property has buffered his or her risk by the fact that they were ready to go to 9 percent anyway. Any year that the NOI only meets or falls behind the pro forma NOI the seller will save that extra 1 percent (from 8 to 9 percent).

Remember, you can reduce your risk in a variety of ways, and risk is relative to your knowledge and ability. While one man's risk might be another man's fun, investment capital leans to the safer side of any transaction. As the investor, this chapter gives you the real insider techniques on how to get the maximum benefits from preferred income transactions. As the entrepreneur to a deal, looking for added capital, this chapter helps you obtain needed funds to complete the transaction.

EXAMPLE 3: TRADEOFFS: REDUCE THE RISK BY REDUCING THE YIELD.

"I will pay your price if you accept my terms." This works for any savvy buyer since the buyer knows the alternatives available to make the terms fit the price he or she is willing to pay. What happens is this: You find a property you want to buy. You then approach the seller with the news that you are interested in buying and will pay a reasonable price. The seller views reasonable price in different terms than you do, but let us not argue at this stage of the game. You look the seller in the eye and say, "Tell me your price, Mr. or Ms. Seller. If I can work it out, I am interested in buying." Everything that happens from that moment on is a series of tradeoffs. The first place you generally look to make tradeoffs is with the seller. Remember, the seller has a goal in sight and might be willing to settle for something less than full attainment of the goal. If by selling the property most of the goal is reached, then the seller's motivations make him or her the initial candidate for a preferred deal.

EXAMPLE 4: PREFERRED PURCHASE: A SWEETENER TO THE SELLER.

One of my early clients taught me about this kind of transaction. It is a magnificent way to get down to the nitty-gritty in any deal, especially where the seller is telling you, "I would love to keep this property but I need some cash." Mind you, this kind of transaction is based on a sizable amount of cash going to the seller. Remember that the cash invested may not be your money. Frequently the cash can be obtained from other sources, but from the seller's point of view, cash is what is going to talk.

Assume you are looking at an office building that is offered for sale at $6,000,000. The property has a 10 percent vacancy factor, and yet is throwing off an NOI of $540,000. You know you can borrow $4,800,000 at a constant annual debt service of 8.29 percent, which will cost you $397,920 per year (this relates to an interest charge of 6.75 percent over a 25-year amortization). If you could purchase the building for $5,500,000 by investing the difference of $700,000, your cash flow is $142,080. This is an excess of 20 percent yield on your invested capital. You make that offer, but the seller tells you they are absolutely firm on the price of $6,000,000. However, by now you have learned that they only owe $2,000,000 on the property. Armed with this information, you make the following counteroffer.

You offer $6,000,000 with your ability to finance $4,500,000 from your local banking source. You want them to hold a second mortgage in the amount of $900,000. At this point your total debt is $5,400,000 and your invested cash is down to $600,000. The second mortgage would be subordinated to your modest $4,500,000 first mortgage. (If the first mortgage lender balks at this, be prepared to offer some other collateral to the seller of the office building.)

You have reduced your requirement for the first mortgage because you can now borrow at a constant of 7.92 percent, which relates to 6.25 percent interest over 25 years. You offer the seller an interest only payment schedule of the same 6.25 percent on the mortgage. That would mean that your overall debt service would be:

First mortgage payment of principal and interest:	$355,500
Second mortgage interest only payment	+ 56,250
Total annual debt service	$411,750

At an NOI of $540,000, your cash flow would be $128,250. Based on your cash investment of $600,000, your cash flow yield is now 21.375 percent.

This gives you some room to negotiate the fine points of this transaction if need be. As the sellers will get a substantial amount of cash at the closing table, their motivation to sell and the arrival of their asking price may clench the deal.

EXAMPLE 5: PREFERRED INCOME TO REDUCE BUYER'S RISK.   Charles owns a beautiful office building in downtown San Francisco. It is fully rented, or nearly so, and Charles has a nice suite of offices in the building. He has a pro forma showing the income and expenses, and projects that within a year or so, when he can increase the rents in the building, the investment will provide a very good return to a prospective buyer. But Charles has some other opportunities and tells his broker that he needs some cash.

Now, buying an office building is one thing, but assume that you aren't in the business of managing office buildings. You like the idea of the rent and the income and the tax shelter, but the idea of management isn't to your liking. Besides, you live in Chicago.

In this deal, Charles reports the following:

Price	$4,500,000
Mortgages	−3,050,000
Cash to buy	$1,450,000

The debt service on the existing $3,050,000 mortgage is $320,000 per year. Charles reports that the operating expenses and taxes and the like total another $380,000 per year. Gross revenue at the moment is $850,000.

If these figures were correct and you paid $1,450,000 cash for this deal, and all the numbers Charles gave you were correct, you would be making the cash flow shown:

Gross revenue	$850,000
Operating expenses	−380,000
Net operating income	$470,000
Debt service	−320,000
Cash flow	$150,000

This $150,000 is 10.3448 percent on your invested capital ($150,000 ÷ $1,450,000 = .103448, which converts to 10.3448 percent). This is an excellent return and you have other benefits with this deal. There is ample tax shelter and future equity build-up. If the rents can be increased and costs held down, there is even appreciation. Not a bad deal at all.

Except that Charles has overestimated on the pro forma a little. The expenses are probably low by $30,000 to $40,000, and there is no vacancy factor accounted for. There is a maximum of around $60,000 in income at risk here, although that's being conservative from the buyer's point of view. But the property is a very nice building and you would like to own it.

You offer to buy 50 percent of the building and will pay $800,000 cash for that opportunity. This represents approximately 55 percent of the $1,450,000 down payment to buy 100 percent of the building. This is a premium to Charles, and all you want is the following:

- To be preferred (to receive from the top of the cash flow), 12 percent on your cash invested. Based on a cash investment of $800,000 your preference income would amount to $96,000. The seller takes the next equal amount, and everything else is split 50/50.

- All or most of the depreciation. This is a negotiating point; depending on the deal and the motivation of the seller, you might end up with the building and the seller with the land (land is not depreciable).

- When you sell or refinance the property, you will share in the proceeds on a 50/50 basis only on the assumption that your share is at least $800,000.

- There are other points you could have asked for, such as the right to buy out the seller's interest. This could be at a time in the future with a formula you present now. Or you might be satisfied with an agreement of a first right of refusal. You might find that out as the loan is paid off, and the value increases. This may enable you to be able to buy out the partner through funds obtained in refinancing the property.

EXAMPLE 6: CREATIVE BUILD-UP OF INVESTMENT. In Example 5, you could also have asked for the deficit (if any) of your preferred interest to build up and add to your investment. For example, say there is a bad year and the total cash flow is only

$100,000. As you would get the first $96,000 you would get nearly the entire $100,000, and Charles would only get $4,000. If the income fell to a cash flow of only $86,000 then you would be $10,000 short of the amount you needed. If the agreement contained a provision to allow you to have a build-up on a deficit, then your invested capital for next year's calculations is now $810,000. You could even provide that any deficit would apply as purchase price paid in a buyout of Charles' interest. Or, you could have it set up so that Charles' actual interest in the property is reduced by a set percentage. This would go on until some defined point where the partner would see his share eaten up and would drop out of the picture.

Why would a seller accept a deal like this? Well, look at it from his point of view. He is getting $400,000 in cash and still has 50 percent of the deal. He might insist on having the management contract for the property. That would give him income, and as a nonpreferred owner, this gives him incentive to properly manage the property.

If Charles has confidence in the deal, he will quickly see that within a few years he is going to profit far more than if he had sold the property and taken the $1,450,000 cash to the mortgage. But, note one very important aspect here: Charles isn't being given the choice of $1,450,000 or the preferred deal. He must choose between this preferred deal or his best offer (if any) from another buyer.

The buyer's advantage is easy to see. As the investor in this deal, you have purchased sound management and given it motivation to stay in place and do a good job. If you were concerned about Charles' ability to manage the property, then you had best stay away from the deal unless it was so good that outside management could be found, easily and quickly.

In making this kind of deal, you might well find the seller suddenly changing his or her tune about how good the project is. "Well, I don't think the income will be that good" is the aftermath of some preferred presentations.

Smart investors use the preferred deal to nail down solid projects with good management and a motivated seller who needs some cash. In the development business there are often good managers and developers who get cash-short on a new project and for construction overages or whatever. These deals make for the mainstay of the preferred deals, but they aren't necessarily limited to that kind of project.

You can buy a business or any small venture on this preferred plan. Whatever, you buy that is income producing has the potential of being financed in this way. If you are looking at a business, don't buy 100 percent of the investment, but instead keep the current owner in at a percentage of the deal. That way you can move into many varied deals without losing your flexibility.

Using the Preferred Income Technique as a Sweetener to Debt

Later on in another chapter, I discuss a technique called percent of income. That technique frequently is tied to leasehold interests, or joint ventures and can work somewhat like the preferred income. However, there are some differences you will find when you get to that chapter.

Using a preferred income technique as a sweetener to secondary financing works like this.

EXAMPLE 7: BONUS PAYMENTS ON A SECOND MORTGAGE TO SELLER.

You want to buy an income property that the owner tells you has a solid NOI of $50,000. As part of the deal, you offer the seller a second mortgage in the amount of $150,000 over 15 years at 7 percent interest per year. The seller balks and cries on your shoulder that 7 percent is too low. You tell him or her that any year that the NOI exceeds $55,000 you will pay an additional 2 percent interest on the unpaid balance of the mortgage. You can see that there are several elements that can be negotiated at this point; why not 3 percent, why not a floor of only $50,000, and so on. The idea is that you have moved the seller into negotiating for the sale, rather than deciding if he or she wants to take the deal.

HOW TO MAXIMIZE YOUR RETURN WHILE REDUCING YOUR RISK AS THE MONEY MAN

Whenever you are the source of funds in a preferred deal, you will find it helpful to review this chapter.

Set the Stage

A friend of yours comes to you with the proposition to invest in a strip store he is considering purchasing. The deal would require you to come up with $800,000 and as your benefit in the deal you would have a 50 percent ownership in the property, and receive 12 percent preferred on your invested cash. In short, your annual return would be $96,000. Your friend would pocket the next $96,000 of the cash flow and all other benefits you would split 50/50. What are some of the negotiation points to this deal that would allow you to reduce your risk?

ELEMENTS IN NEGOTIATION THAT CAN HELP YOU REDUCE YOUR RISK

1. LOWER THE DOWN PAYMENT. Once the deal is pretty well set, work on reducing the down payment. In general, negotiation follows a standard pattern. You make an offer that is usually lower than you will ultimately go, and the other side makes a counter that is usually higher than they will expect to end up. Once you have gone through a couple of offers and counteroffers you should have a pretty good understanding of where you expect the other side wants to end up. If you understand the techniques of negotiation as have been offered in this book, you know the importance of letting the other side of the deal win. This concept of winning is even more important in a preferred income deal because if the party you are dealing with is going to manage the property you don't want to start out with a partner who thinks you shouldn't deserve what the contract says you

should get. However, having said this, as a final tradeoff you may offer to let the other side win a point or two, to give in, if he or she will reduce the up-front cash you were to invest. If, for example, instead of putting $800,000 up front, you invested that amount with $600,000 at closing, and two payments of $100,000 plus interest at 10 percent, you will have increased your yield (you get 12 percent on $800,000 remember), while at the same time you decrease your risk.

2. SPLIT THE DOWN PAYMENT INTO EQUITY AND DEBT. The above example is a division of payments of equity over a period of time, but why not divide the $800,000 into a down payment of $500,000 and a straight second mortgage of $300,000? This second mortgage might be negotiated into a first mortgage on another property, if you had something else. The key here is that your return is still based on $800,000, and the yield of 12 percent (as in the previous example) remains at $96,000 even after you have paid off the $300,000 second mortgage.

3. TRADE THE DOWN PAYMENT: ALL OR PART. Keep in mind that the seller might benefit from an IRC 1031 exchange. If this is the case, then a partial or full exchange of the needed equity of $800,000 might work to both your benefits. Never overlook the opportunity to get rid of a property that does nothing for you. Even if it is only a small part of a deal, this is your chance to have it be absorbed into the transaction. One of the brokers might end up with it as a part of a commission.

4. TIE THE YIELD TO A COST-OF-LIVING INDEX. Nothing says that your yield has to remain fixed to any predetermined amount. If you can tie down 12 percent in earlier negotiations, and the seller wants something that you might be able to give up, ask to have your yield indexed to the All Items Cost-of-Living Index. This is a standard index that is published by the United States Department of Labor and Statistics, and has been mentioned many times in this book. Your lawyer or real estate broker should know how to incorporate that into the transaction. The end result of this would be that if the cost of living went up 10 percent over a couple of years, your yield would also go up. Remember, no matter what income you get out of the transaction, it is only your share in preference. If there is sufficient income left over for the other partner or partners to get their equal share, then everyone ends up fine. You can remind the seller or partner of this when they balk at why your preferred income should go up.

5. GET OTHER COLLATERAL FROM THE SELLER OR PARTNER. Even though a preferred income might be good, there are other things that can make the deal even better and increase your return while lowering your risk. A motivated partner who doesn't have the extra capital it takes to do the deal, or the motivated seller, may be willing to give you extra security to bring you into the deal. Look to the transaction first to see if there are ways to get additional security from the other side. Will they stay on the debt? If you don't have to sign personally, that is a benefit to you. Will they assign rents from other projects or put up other property as security? All are important ways to reduce your risk. In tradeoff, you

may allow this additional security to drop off the deal at a future date, or when the income reaches a much higher level of safety than it currently has been projected.

6. GET A BUYOUT PROVISION. This is usually the most important, and often the most difficult provision of the deal to negotiate. Because of this, I suggest you do not even bring it up until the very end of the negotiations. Why? Because it is likely that they will bring it up first. Generally, it is better to be working to an agreement than working against someone who doesn't want to even approach the subject. Buyout provisions do not have to be equally fair. In fact, because it is your money that is making the deal work in the first place, you should get the advantage of the buyout provision. Some of the elements that can be negotiated have been shown earlier in this chapter. For example, if there is any deficit in income off your preferred amount, that can apply against a buyout or build up in your equity side of the deal. You might have a set buyout amount for a period of years, say, and the right to buy the other side out of the deal based on fixed amounts at the end of certain years. Another method is to have a formula that follows an increase of a certain set percentage every year until the buyout is accomplished. Avoid getting into a situation where one side has the right to match the other's offer. This kind of a buyout works as follows: If I want to buy you out, I can offer you an amount. If you decide to buy me out, you can follow the same formula that I offered you. This is a bad deal for you as the money person.

Before You Go for the Money, Review These Six Key Factors

1. HAVE CONTROL OVER THE TRANSACTION. This is the same advice I give to syndications or anyone else looking to generate a joint venture or raise money from potential partners. If you don't have the deal locked up, then you might as well go out on the street with a cardboard sign that reads "Might have deal, need money." Real estate is all about control. Brokers need exclusive listings or they cannot spend the time and money to sell the property, and if you are looking for partners of any kind, it is critical that you get the property tied up 100 percent before you go out looking for money.

2. REMEMBER, UNTIL THE DEAL CLOSES, THERE IS STILL ROOM TO NEGOTIATE. This means that even though you have the deal tied up, you still have room to negotiate. As long as you have a reasonable due diligence period to make inspections and review different aspects of the transaction, you can still get out of the deal. If you cannot, then you have not tied up the deal correctly. This "out" clause can be a simple right to approve the final inspection to your satisfaction. Sellers may not like your coming back to the bargaining table at the last minute, but if you discover something that makes you believe you need to renegotiate some of the terms, including the price, then do so. Later is often better than sooner, from your point of view. Sellers start to mentally spend the money and make other plans. In addition, while you are doing your due diligence, you may be negotiating several other aspects of the deal. This could be a refinance of a mortgage, the purchase of secondary financing at a discount or establishing new leases; any of these items may generate a reason to reopen negotiations.

3. KNOW HOW FAR YOU CAN GO WITH THE DEAL. This is very important because when it comes down to the nitty-gritty, many investors may be more astute at the fine-tuning of the deal than you. The more you know about how far the income will meet its projections, the better off you will be. If you are out looking for money, you have already set yourself into the ranks of the lesser astute. The more astute already have the money, so learn from your mistakes and learn how they do deals. If you can find a good real estate broker who understands what it takes to make deals, rather than follow instructions, then you will be ahead of the game.

4. BE FLEXIBLE. As with any real estate negotiations, the more flexible you are, the more likely you are to make deals. Keep in mind that the majority of people buying and selling real estate are not professionals, nor are they loan sharks. They are likely to be just like you and anxious to do a deal. Be as honest as you know how, and that honesty will go a long way to help keep you out of trouble.

5. OFFER THE OTHER PARTY AN OPPORTUNITY. Any time you have something good to offer someone, make sure he or she understands that you are doing a favor. You are not asking for a loan, you are giving the chance to be a part of something good, and you have so much confidence in the deal you are willing to back that confidence up by giving preference of the income.

6. HAVE EVERYTHING READY FOR THEIR SIGNATURE. The professional approach is to make sure that all bases are covered, and that the documentation of the presentation is clear and backs up what you have said about the deal. Then have the proper documents that would allow you to get a commitment from the money source. The better your preparation, the easier your task will be. A well-documented presentation shows that you are serious, and that if you get a no, you are ready to move on to another property.

Five Pitfalls in Preferred-Income Transactions

As with anything you can do, there are pitfalls that await you. Take a look at the most critical pitfalls from the point of view of the money source:

1. INACCURATE OR OVERLY OPTIMISTIC INCOME AND EXPENSE FIGURES: Income and expense figures are rarely correct, even when every item is properly accounted for. There are many reasons for this. Property owners let the business rent their car, pay their health insurance, pick up the tab for travel, and so on, all on the up-and-up, but not the way you might do it. Then, there are property owners who have been known to actually lie about what they take in, or spend. Many syndicators get so enthusiastic about what they are doing that they puff up the income numbers and downplay the expenses. If you are the seller who is given the opportunity to make a couple of extra interest points if the income comes in as you promised, be sure to ask yourself if the numbers you gave the buyer were correct.

2. Narrow-minded approach to competition: Some income properties look good, but if you are going to invest your capital, make sure that the competition is not about to overwhelm you. This is especially the case with people properties, such as motels, hotels, restaurants, apartment rentals, and so on. Lenders have been burned by not taking special care to see what else is in the marketplace now that will compete with this property, and what is on the drawing board for the near future. All of this can be checked, and is essential.

3. Overvalued property: Clearly, if you put up $500,000 as a down payment to existing financing of $2,000,000 to get a 50 percent interest, and the property is worth only $2,400,000, then you have overpaid, even if you get 18 percent preferred income. Whenever you are offered anything that looks good, be sure to find out just how good or bad it really is.

4. Excessive debt—High loan-to-value ratio: Overleveraged transactions bring with them greater risk. This risk may be worthwhile, and you might find ways to help cover your exposure to that risk. But all real estate transactions need to have some breathing room. If all the cash goes into a deal that is running on the edge of the bankbook every month just to make mortgage payments, then more capital needs to be put into the deal. When you are asked to come up with the initial capital, and the other parties tell you they will supply additional funds, if and when needed, you may discover that, if and when the funds are needed the other parties don't have any funds. The greatest failure of any business is lack of proper capitalization.

5. Incomplete due diligence: One of the most common errors that investors make is to cut short, or overlook some aspect of due diligence that must be effectively made. There are many hidden defects that can lurk within any real estate that can cause the expenses to suddenly hit new highs. They may or may not be known defects, but simply your failure to hire competent inspections of the property. Failure to check factors such as code violations, new code ordinances, and other governmental rules are the usual elements that may not be completed in a comprehensive way. Even factors that may be grandfathered in for the building's existing use or the existing tenants may limit the use of the property or even make it off limits to many prospective tenants—even tenants that fit the zoning code, but due to some grandfathered violation they cannot use that building. Fire violations, distance from a prohibited other use (a block away even), size and quality of storm shutters, new setback rules, encroachments on neighboring properties, or your property encroaching on neighboring properties can present serious problems and expense and reduce revenue.

Options

There are many different forms and uses of the option. It is found in almost every real estate transaction to a certain degree and has a use by itself that can put you into control, buy you time, and reduce your overall cost in any real estate deal. Because the option is a great tool to "buy time," that aspect alone can allow you to solve all the other problems that would otherwise hold you back from moving forward. The option buy only 50 acres now, and have the option to buy the other 50 acres of that 100-acre tract of land in two years hence (where you want to build homes) can save you a bundle in carrying cost, while giving you time to harvest the benefits of the first 50 acres first.

DEFINITION OF AN OPTION. An option is defined as a choice. In real estate terms, it is the right to buy, sell, or otherwise dispose of an interest in property at a specific or defined time, at specific or defined terms. The person who has the option controls the situation.

EXAMPLE 8: AN OPTION TO BUY. You agree to give the seller $5,000 to allow you 12 months time to have your architect design a home for a lot. During that time, you have the option to buy the property for $50,000, and apply the $5,000 against the purchase price. If you do not exercise your option to buy within that time, you lose the $5,000. A seller who is in no rush might see the option payment of $5,000 as found money. I am sure, however, that you can quickly see several elements that might become negotiable. For example, why not $7,000 as the option fee? Or why get credit for any or all of it when the property is purchased? Can you think of others? As the buyer, you could have asked for a two-year option, and if the seller was pushing for the right to keep the option fee and not give you any credit at closing time, you might say, "Okay, if I take the full two years, you get to keep the option fee of $5,000. But if I close at the end of the first year, I get full credit." The seller laughs, and extends his right hand, "You got a deal, bud." At least, that is what you hope he would say.

EXAMPLE 9: AN OPTION TO LEASE. You sign up for a 12-month lease, and ask the owner to give you the right (option) to lease for another 12 months at the same terms. At the end of the first year's lease, you have to notify the owner that you exercise your right to renew at the option price. Remember, the option only is binding on one party. If at renewal time you believe the option price is too high, and you think the owner will reduce it, then before you take a pass on the option, see if you can renegotiate the lease terms. If not, you move out or bite the bullet and pay the price.

Lease terms can have many different option opportunities; the one just mentioned is the most simple and direct of all. What about an option for three extensions, at two years a pop? Or an option to purchase the property sometime during the lease? Or a first right to purchase the property if someone else negotiates to buy the property, thereby giving you the first opportunity? And so on.

EXAMPLE 10: DUE-DILIGENCE APPROVAL. In your contract to purchase an oceanfront hotel, you have a period of 60 days to make a series of inspections. These include review of employment contracts, current reservations, future reservations, maintenance records, and so on. At the end of the 60 days, you have the option to close on the property or to cancel the deal. Due diligence is, as I have and will continue to repeat, an essential part of every real estate transaction. I don't care if the property is brand new (even more dangerous perhaps because no one knows how bad the plumbing, electrical, and mechanical aspects creak, groan, and drip green stuff), every property needs to be inspected. Sellers who will not represent the condition of a property give you a warning that there might be a problem. Mind you, my recommendation to you is *not* to represent the condition of property you sell, simply because there might be a problem that you are not aware of Much better for you, as a seller, to say to the buyer, "Look Mr. Buyer, I just don't want you get mad at me if I honestly tell you I don't know the answers to this list of 50 questions you have handed me. I would much rather let you get one or two inspection companies to satisfy you that you should buy, or tell you that you should not buy."

Options Put Time on Your Side

Buying with an option is an ideal way to put time on your side. The option contract gives you the opportunity to put up some money that can build into a sizable equity in a hurry if you are right about the trends. If you are wrong, then you have kept your risk at a minimum. As you will discover in this chapter, you can use options that will absolutely reduce your risk to zero.

TWO BASIC KINDS OF OPTIONS

There are several kinds of option agreements, but for the most part they fall into two categories: the straight option, and the conditioned option.

The Straight Option

The straight option is, as the name would suggest, a standard type of agreement that simply gives one party a right to buy or lease a property at a set date in the future at a price agreed to. The time periods and the actual terms can be specific, set to a formula, tied to appraisals, based on income, or any other method of calculating price. The optionee (the person who has the option and is in control) may or may not have paid money for the option. Keep in mind that all options should have some kind of consideration, but the actual consideration does not have to be money. Note the following examples in which something other than money is the consideration to the option:

1. Buyer to undertake inspections; then gives the owner copies of the inspections.
2. Buyer to verify zoning; essential to ascertain if the property can be used to fit the Buyer's needs.

3. Buyer leases with option to buy; the consideration is the lease.

4. Buyer promises to have lawyer draw up contract; the consideration is that the buyer spends money to create a future benefit to the property owner.

5. Buyer promises to make zoning change request; to suit the buyer's needs, and as an improvement to the property if the buyer does not exercise option to buy.

Each of these five items should spark your own imagination to think of other similar examples where you, as a buyer, can obtain control over a property, even if for a short period of time.

All aspects of a contract are flexible and open to negotiation up until the contract is closed. The key to any negotiation is to be in control for as long as possible. Control means you have the right to buy (or lease or whatever), and the other side must go along with what the terms of the deal call for. However, because the optionee is in control with a choice, the optionee can elect not to exercise the option. This is critical because it reopens the door for more negotiation to fine-tune the deal.

EXAMPLE 11: USING THE OPTION TO RENEGOTIATE THE DEAL.   You have a two-year lease on a home. The lease contains a provision that gives you the right to renew the lease for another two years at the same terms, or, at your option, you can buy the home for $150,000 any time during either term of lease. As with all options, this puts you in control of this property to the extent that as long as you do not default on the lease, you know you can buy this property for $150,000. Keep in mind that the seller can sell the property subject to your lease and option, for whatever price the seller can get. But aside from that, the fact that your option is for $150,000 does not preclude you from coming back to the table and attempting to negotiate for a reduced price. After all, you have lived in the house for a year and some months now, and know exactly what needs to be fixed. You can negotiate from a very strong position.

Opening the door to negotiations is what the option is all about. By gaining control over a property you generally shut down the seller's efforts to try to sell or lease the property to someone else. As long as you play your cards right, that is, pick the right time to negotiate for an improvement in the deal, you might be successful.

WHEN TO GO BACK TO THE NEGOTIATION TABLE.   The timing on opening up negotiations again depends on the transaction and the time you have to work with. The most important factor is not to wait until time works against you. The key to this is to make sure you really want to buy the property. Once that decision has been made, then you can begin to make overtures to the seller that all is not as you would like it to be. Care must be taken that you do not relinquish control in the deal. The following is an example that occurred the same week that I was writing this chapter. Take a look at how one prospective buyer stuffed his foot in his mouth by accidentally giving up control.

EXAMPLE 12: LOSING CONTROL OF THE OPTION.   Mick and Jake were partners who tied up a 100-unit oceanfront hotel in Fort Lauderdale for just under $5 million (subject to a cheap land lease). They had a long due-diligence period, which they insisted on because they lived nearly 2,000 miles away from the property. During the due-diligence period, they came back to the negotiation table several times. Each time they would have their local lawyer send a letter to the seller with a statement that unless certain redress to the price and terms could be agreed to between the parties by a specific date, they may be forced to exercise their right to withdraw from the agreement. The letter looked like a very strong demand that they were going to withdraw, but each time the date the letter specified approached, the seller caved in to the demands and reduced the price, gave in to interest terms, and so on, setting a pattern that only made Mick and Jake want to test some more.

Deposits eventually went hard (the point when they should be nonrefundable), and suddenly another letter comes in from the lawyer. This time the letter cited several problems that had come up and claimed the sellers had grossly misrepresented the deal, and demanded a refund of the deposits, and canceled the agreement. Somehow, the lawyer made a mistake. What he meant to say was, "If you do not clear up this matter by a certain date, they may be forced to rescind the contract." Suddenly the seller had an out. Back in control, the buyer had to scramble. If he truly wanted out of the deal, he was now going to have to fight for his deposit. If he wanted back into the deal, he was going to have to fight for that position. This was a prime example of going back to the well once too often, and at that, doing it incorrectly.

THE OPTION IS NO GUARANTEE OF A SUCCESSFUL CONCLUSION TO THE CONTRACT.   In any option, there is no guarantee the optionee will follow through and close. If the seller has been compensated by the option money for the time the property is taken off the market that might be okay, but usually the option money is not enough to make up for the lost time. Or worse, it might be that the time the seller gives up is a period when things happen that make the property less valuable. The buyer skips town, and no other buyers are around to take up the slack.

NEGOTIATING THE BEST OPTION TERMS WHEN YOU ARE THE SELLER.

Start with a Free Option—It May Entice a Buyer to Want Your Property. Sellers can use the option as a tool to entice a prospective buyer or tenant. If you own a commercial tract of land and think it would be a great spot for a fast-food restaurant, you might be willing, or even excited, should a major fast-food restaurant come to you and ask for a 90-day free option to allow it to ascertain if your site was the best one. If you can understand this concept, take it one step further. Why not go out and find all the fast-food restaurants that are not in the immediate area and offer them a 90-day free look at your site? All you want is to make sure that they actually spend the time and effort to make a decision.

When Do You Get Paid for the Option. There is a time when you should not be expected to give the prospective buyer any more of a free look. At this time, which generally follows a reasonable due-diligence period, the contract should call for a deposit to go hard, and a timetable established that winds down to the actual closing. The following is a provision I have used, and as with all examples in this book, it is shown as an example only. Any phrases or paragraphs you use in any legal document should be reviewed and approved by your lawyer. There are many reasons for this caution because the laws of different states can vary.

> . . . and further, at the end of the 90-day period of due diligence, the buyer shall either give notice of intentions to close, under the provisions of closing as covered elsewhere in this agreement, or buyer may elect to continue the due-diligence period another 90 days, thereby retaining the option to purchase the subject property at the terms and price contained herein, by payment to the seller of $50,000. This $50,000 will be payment in full for this additional 90-day option and will not be refunded to the buyer should the buyer fail to close on this contract for any reason. Seller, however, will give the buyer credit for said $50,000 against the purchase price provided that the buyer close on this property no later than 30 days following the termination of the additional 90-day due diligence.

You can see that there are many different ways to negotiate a transaction. It is important to both parties that there be a very clear understanding of the terms and conditions surrounding the option. Does the option money get to be applied as part of the purchase price? When is the buyer in default? Is there any other term in the agreement that might extend time periods, and cause dates to conflict? Very careful reading of a contract is essential. If it is not in plain language, as some lawyers seem to pride themselves in avoiding, then get the darn thing redrafted so that it is clear.

Conditioned Option

Here the optionee has included in the contract some conditions that can cancel or change the contract. These conditions might be such that the price will change, or the time to buy will be increased or decreased; most importantly, the conditions may call for a full return of the option money if something doesn't occur (or does occur, as the case may be).

From the buyer's point of view, the conditioned option is the least risky of deals. If you have an option agreement and can tie up a tract of land for a period of time, and because of some condition in the agreement (which you may control) you can get your option money back, you haven't risked anything.

POSSIBLE CONDITIONS IN A CONDITIONAL OPTION

1. *Soil test:* Your right to test and approve the subsoil conditions.
2. *Survey certification:* Your approval of the exact dimensions, and so on.
3. *Test holes:* A more detailed subsoil examination.
4. *Site plan approval:* Appropriate agency approval of your planned development.
5. *Issuance of building permit:* Actual and final stage before building.
6. *Partner's approval:* A clear out if your partner nixes the deal.
7. *Corporate ratification:* Similar to the above.
8. *Obtaining satisfactory financing:* Necessary in many deals.
9. *Government approval:* This covers a wide range of conditions.
10. *Prior sale of a third property:* When you need to sell something else.
11. *Prior development of a section 1031 exchange:* You have to develop an exchange before you can close.
12. *Preleasing of to-be-developed space:* Many lenders will demand this before calculating a loan.
13. *Environmental inspections:* Many lenders insist on this.
14. *Code and city ordinance review:* Make sure everything is clear and above board.

Of these 14 items, you can see that some can be simply accomplished and would not normally take a long time, while others can take months or in some cases, such as government approval, years. In all cases, you (the buyer) have control over these items and can make sure the condition fails to be met.

The seller in the conditioned option contract will naturally object to tying up his land with the buyer having a full right to a refund of option money in situations where the buyer can back out of the deal. In essence, what has been created is a free option, with the money being not much more than good-faith deposit. Yet, despite the fact that many sellers will object to such contractual agreements, many conditional agreements are made each day. Sellers try to limit the time for these conditions, realizing that the option is free, and to provide for other safeguards to counterbalance the lack of security in the refundable deposit. Such counterbalances are in strict timetables, elements of past performance being a main criterion in the decision to go along with the condition if it is time consuming. In essence, if the optionee is genuine and can give the impression he or she is going to buy, his or her chances are improved in using a conditioned option agreement.

All the previous items used in the option contract can be conditions in the actual sales agreement as well, and when they are used in that form of purchase they convert the buy-and-sell agreement into a conditional option agreement.

USING OPTION AGREEMENTS

The scenario is as follows: A tight money market, increasing interest rates, and unrest in the real estate market. It is a growing buyer's market, and while the trends indicate that there is a turnaround somewhere down the road, you aren't sure when that is going to be. You have found a property that you want to buy. You know that the more you reduce your risk, the more profit potential you have in the future.

The price you feel you can get for the property is $300,000. The seller has been asking more, but that's what you want to pay. You find that current interest rates are around 9 percent in the prime market, around 9.75 percent in land sales.

Your first offer is a conditioned option agreement. You offer $10,000 option money for the right to buy the property for $280,000. You agree to give the seller $10,000 right away. As a condition of the deal, you call for your unqualified approval of a subsoil test. You want to make sure that there are no subterranean conditions that will make building on this site very expensive. You allow 120 days for this test to be made. If you disapprove of the results, you get your money back and the deal is off.

If you approve the test, you have nine months in which to exercise the option to buy. You agree to put up another $20,000 at the time you must say yes or no. That means at the end of 13 months you now have a total of $30,000 at risk. All you have to do to exercise the deal is to sign the buy-and-sell agreement attached to the option and return it to the seller. You have 60 days to close on the deal after that. When you close on the property, the option money you paid is to be applied to the sales price. If the seller accepts this deal you are sitting pretty. Even so, you still have another $20,000 to counter and still be into the property for your price.

The soil test condition gives you four months to examine the property to decide if you want to go through with the deal. If you go ahead, you have another nine months before you exercise the option to buy. At that point, you are committed. After that you have another 60 days to close on the purchase. In all, you have one year and three months to close the deal. You paid $10,000 at the beginning, which is counted as a part of the purchase price. Even if the seller had insisted that the $10,000 not be counted at closing, you would have tied up the property for about 3.5 percent interest for those first 13 months ($10,000 is 3.5 percent of the price at $280,000).

When You Know You Are Going to Buy, Use the Option

You can see that when you aren't sure about buying, the option gives you some time to make the final decision. It locks up the price and terms so that you know exactly what to base the decision on. But when you know you are going to buy, the option gives you added appreciation and reduces your carrying cost for the first year or so.

In the deal described above, you would have tied up a property you were willing to offer $300,000 to purchase, for 15 months at no real cost in the long run. You would have a total of those 15 months during which time you didn't have to pay the real estate taxes, carry insurance on it, or pay interest on a mortgage. Best of all, you would get all the appreciation of value if any occurred. As long as you don't need immediate title to the property, the option-to-buy deal is a great way to get a head start on appreciation.

Use the Option to Finance Your Way to a Fortune

As you have discovered thus far, there are many ways to use the option in real estate investing and financing. The creative ways in which you use this tool will depend only on your full understanding of four elements of the option:

1. The option is a one-sided event that gives one party control over some future event that the owner of the property does not have.

2. The option has a psychological effect on sellers and buyers alike depending on the circumstance and use of the tool.

3. Options can be used successfully by both the buyer and the seller.

4. Options are a promise of a future event, a box behind the curtain that holds a lure to the other party that can be more attractive than the desire to have a specific offer that never shows up.

Using the option to your best benefit will depend on its placement in the right situation. Look at several examples of how you might use the option and win.

THE PRIMARY OPTION: A STUDY IN THE EFFECT OF GREED

The primary option transaction is a basic study in greed. In this technique, the buyer uses the option to keep the cost of the total financing at a minimum, while tying up the property for a period of time in which the buyer can back out of the deal without excess cost. As in all option transactions, the buyer holds the cards and all the aces.

The significance of this specific kind of option is the buyer knows ahead of the game that he or she is absolutely going to buy. The advantage of the option in this case is purely as a delaying tactic to the usual costs of a closing: down payment, interest, costs, and so on.

The transaction follows this scenario: A seller is asking, say, $1,800,000 for the tract of land on which you want to build a shopping center. You know that you will buy the land and are attempting to lessen the interest cost between now and the exact date you have to fund the construction project, and reduce your immediate cash outlay. To accomplish these ends, you make the following offer. You will get a "free" period of time, say, 90 days to make certain studies of the property, check out the market, and the like. If at the end of those 90 days you are interested enough to start spending money to see if you can obtain the necessary governmental approvals to construct what you want to build on the site, then you will pay an additional $50,000 as option money to allow you to make a feasibility study of the specific site for commercial use. For this payment, you will be allowed 240 days in which to complete the study. If you are satisfied with the study, you can proceed to a closing. If you need more time you can purchase up to three extensions for $50,000 that will give you 180 additional days each extension. If you determine at the end of that time that the commercial venture is not feasible for any reason, the seller keeps the option money paid and you are released from any further obligation to that party. On the other hand, the contract indicates that if you determine that you want to purchase the property, you can proceed with the closing. At the closing, you will receive full credit against the purchase price for any and all option money thus far paid to the seller.

The end result of this transaction is ideal for the buyer, who has tied up the property for 870 days for only $200,000 and half of that comes after the first 510 days.

Option to Buy in a Lease Transaction

In a sale leaseback, one of the most critical elements to the transaction is the option to buy the property, and if possible all sale leasebacks should contain the option to buy back.

Remember, options are absolutely one-sided. The best time to establish them is when you have control in the transaction. If you are leasing, insert a simple option provision in the lease if you can. If you are selling your own property and leasing it back, even the most hard-hearted buyer is apt to grant an option for you to buy back your own property at a more than generous profit to the buyer down the road. Keep in mind, this option may end up having no value to you if you overestimate the future growth of the area or that specific property. On the other hand, if things go as they have in the past, you might find that the sale of your option in the future is far more profitable than the sale of the property the first time.

Whenever you have a sale leaseback, the option to recapture the property is a benefit that you should attempt to negotiate into the deal. You may have no interest at the moment of ever owning the property, but times change and property values can skyrocket when future events create demands not deemed possible at present.

WRITING THE PURCHASE OPTION

"The lessee herein has the option to purchase the subject property any time during the lease or its extensions for $1,000,000." It might be as simple as that, but most likely it will be far more complex. As in all contracts, it is important that you get it right, and that means get it done with a good real estate lawyer.

The following list should be reviewed by you and your lawyer when it comes time to draft the option agreement into the lease or sale-leaseback portions of the contract. Many of these items are business decisions on which you and the other party will have a mutual agreement. Since you should know more about the property and what you can do with it, than your lawyer, that decision should be solely yours.

The five key elements to include in the option contract:

1. THINK BEYOND WHAT YOU THINK YOU NEED. This is where most people overlook the option in the first place. "I never thought about asking for an option." Well, now you will, right? You should attempt to put the options in every agreement you can whenever you buy or lease real estate. Remember, the worst that can happen is that the other party will want to remove it, giving you the opportunity to counteract by putting in another benefit to you. If you are leasing, ask for an option to renew the lease at the same terms, or to buy the property, or to have the first right of refusal if someone else wants to buy it. The option puts you in control. If you can get one for free, then jump at it.

2. USE THE OPTION AS A NEGOTIATING TOOL. Assume that you are trying to lease a home. The property owner agrees that you can have a two-year lease at $1,500 per month. The price is okay, but you want to push for additional leverage or benefits in the deal. You say something like this: "Mr. Property Owner, my wife and I plan to improve this property while living here. To show the extent of those improvements, here is a list of what we will do the first year. Notice the new Italian ceramic tile we would like to install in the ground floor area in addition to a complete painting of the interior and exterior of the house. Because we truly love this home, we would like to have the option to buy the home at the end of the lease. If we can establish a fair price to you at this time, we will write that amount in the lease. That will give us incentive to improve the property. Naturally, if I get transferred to California and we are unable to take advantage of the option, you will keep the improvements we do to the home."

There are several subtle elements here to help the property owner make up his mind to give you the option: you will have improved the property, you agree to the price, you will create an incentive for the lessee to improve (and stay) and pay rent on time, and best of all, the lessee might be transferred to California and lessor keeps all those improvements.

If you are leasing an office within an office building, ask for an option to buy the building. "Mr. Office Building Owner, as we may have to expand over the years, it is possible that we may need the whole building sometime in the future. If that were to occur, I think it would be the time for us to own the building. We will sign your lease right now if you could give us an option to buy the building within the first 10 years of our lease."

3. WATCH OUT FOR SELLERS OR PROPERTY OWNERS WHO TRY TO ENTICE YOU WITH THE OPTION. There is a program called Shared Equity Transactions. This is a wealth-building plan that works on buyers' or tenants' motivation to own their own property.

The plan works this way: A real estate investor will buy a property for $340,000 and then advertise that he will sell 50 percent of the equity for nothing down. When someone comes along, the deal is described as follows: The prospective buyer, who has nothing to put down, will move into the home (or apartment) and pay all actual costs. These costs might include (1) payments on a $255,000 mortgage; and (2) taxes, insurance, and upkeep of the house. The deal is that if the prospective buyer will stay in the house for five years, the house will then be sold, and the prospective buyer will get 50 percent of the net proceeds of the sale that exceed $120,000 above the amount of the mortgage that is still outstanding. In essence, the buyer has $85,000 tied up in the property ($340,000 − $255,000 = $85,000). He has no income coming in during those five years, but neither does he have any expenses to pay out. Say the house is sold at the end of the five years for $500,000. At that time, assume the mortgage balance outstanding is $240,000. That means there is a net from the sale of $260,000 ($500,000 − $240,000 = $260,000 no other costs or expenses calculated). The first $140,000 goes back to the investor, which he would calculate as: Return of his $85,000 cash invested and $55,000 of unpaid interest over those five years. This is a simple average of 12.94 percent per year on the $85,000, but he had to wait five years to get it—a reasonable return from his point of view. So, the remaining funds to be split would be $120,000 ($260,000 − $140,000 = $120,000). The investor gets $60,000 of that, and you get the other 50 percent.

The actual numbers may differ, but the plan works by enticing the prospective buyer to believe there is equity in the home and that entering into a lease with this kind of option has value. It may have, but you should always know values prior to making that kind of contract. The people who teach the courses that instruct the real estate investor how to use the shared equity plans stress the profit that comes upfront in the deal through increased value from the day the property was bought to the day it is leased under the kind of option explained (even if that was day two of the transaction). In some situations, you may find that the mortgage on the home is really a combination of two mortgages. Say the investor really paid $300,000 for the property and the $255,000 in debt is a combination of a first mortgage of $225,000 (which would mean he has $75,000 tied up), and a second mortgage in his wife's name for another $30,000. In the end, that investor will have made a very handsome return, and that, my friends, is the side of the fence to be on.

Options offered to tenants that have unrealistic prices or formulas to arrive at a price have no value to the deal and should be viewed as the bait to the deal. Of course, you can keep the option in, but be sure you recognize what might be nothing more than an attempt to get you in the property. Make sure that you are not making the lease for that reason alone.

4. KNOW YOUR OPTIONS IN THE NEGOTIATIONS. Many people ask for an option, and when the sharp property owner puts in a paragraph that looks like an option they are satisfied. Here are some elements you can ask for in option provisions:

- *Option to extend your lease.* If your lease was for one year, ask for options to extend for additional years by doing something each year on the eleventh month. That something might be a notice to the owner, or payment of $50 or whatever you can put into the lease.

- *Option to buy during the lease.* You can ask for, and some owners will agree to give you, credit for some or even all of the rent paid. This will be determined by the need of that property owner to get the place rented in the first place. Your option to buy during the term of the lease should also include extensions of the lease, so that your option to buy would not terminate simply because you extended the term of the lease.

- *Options should have a specific price, or clear formula of establishing prices for new rent or purchase prices.* There are many different ways to approach this. A percentage of the cost of living, or the entire increase of a cost-of-living index can be used. However, there are several different indexes, so ask your lawyer about this format. I recommend that you remember the term "All Items Index" as that averages out the specific items index that can rise quicker than the average.

- *If all else fails, get a first right of refusal.* This is an option triggered only when the owner has a bona fide contract from another party, which is acceptable to that owner. You would have a period of time to accept the same terms. This is the weakest of all options, but gives you some control over the property.

Remember, when it comes time to take advantage of the option to renew your rent or buy the building, you don't have to do it as the contract says. The option only binds the other party to those terms. "Mr. Property Owner, my option to buy is at $150,000. However, as conditions are not as attractive now as I had thought they might be, I don't feel the property is worth more than $125,000. I'll pay that now, or wait a couple of more years to see if I could afford the full price covered in my option."

5. USE OPTIONS AS AN ASSET WHEN BUYING OTHER PROPERTY. As a part of the deal, you can offer the seller of a property the same option you have with the office building owner. If you own property, you can use the option as a future benefit bonus in any transaction you want to move forward.

REVIEW THE CONCEPT OF GREED

I have never met a seller that didn't want to get the most he or she could out of the deal. Even the most practical thinker of the bunch truly wants to come out on top of the deal. This competitive nature of doing business in real estate can and frequently does place the money ahead of just about everything else. This is not the right way to look at the transaction, and can most certainly get in the way of the deal coming together when both parties feel the same way about who is going to come out on top of the deal. The fact of the matter is that you can either go with the flow, or you can get caught in the riptide and drown.

Using greed as a tool to the transaction is what both the preferred income and the option do. Here, take this now, and it is yours; see how you came out ahead of me. The reality is that in a truly sound real estate transaction, where the numbers work for the buyer, the preferred income is protection, not extra money. Protection is good, of course, and being able to give up something that does not actually take money from your pocket is even better.

The best use of the option is, as has been stated, when you know you are going to buy. This is the time when you get the full benefits of gaining time without having the expense to carry the property. Later techniques, such as sweat equity, and other barter strategies where time (yours) and effort (also yours) are what is at risk, can also incorporate the option into the overall plan. Continue to open your mind to the concept that what you are really doing is moving assets, and that time and effort are but two of those commodities you have when you play the real estate game.

Chapter 17

FIVE POWERFUL SECONDARY FINANCING TECHNIQUES THAT EFFECTIVELY CLOSE DEALS

GOAL OF THIS CHAPTER

This chapter introduces five powerful closing techniques that are effective. Every real estate investor would like a magical technique that could be pulled out of the hat at the right moment. For some, that technique is there, just when needed. For others, they make the wrong gesture, say the wrong words, and, instead of a closed deal, they end up with a dead rabbit. This chapter expands on five unique forms of financing mentioned earlier. They are as follows:

1. Leasehold financing.
2. Land leases.
3. Percent of income.
4. Joint ventures.
5. Syndications.

All five techniques are very important and they offer the user a wide range of flexibility to best suit the situation. Each has a special benefit to offer the buyer as well as the seller. When you are coming down the home stretch of closing your deal, no matter if you are buyer or seller or broker, knowing how and when to pull one of these magic rabbits out of the hat can often mean the difference between making or not making a deal. The purpose of this chapter is to cover these methods of financing. This will enable you to see how they are used, what they do to help you make more transactions, and when you can bring them into play.

LEASEHOLD FINANCING

Leasehold is the ownership of a right to use a specific property for a term of years for which the lessee pays rent. The tenant has a leasehold interest in the property or space. If he or she meets the terms of the lease that interest is real and can be pledged as security on loans.

Real estate consists of various rights that are divisible; any of those rights can be leased, sold, exchanged, optioned, or gifted to other party or entity. The method of such disposition could also be subject to a wide range of terms and conditions. Because this section deals with leasehold interests, we should consider that a property owner could lease any such interest or combinations of interest. The list of these interests include land, mineral rights, air space, building occupancy (all or part), and so on, for any term of years (or part of), with any possible limitation of use, for any sum of exchange, or any other term which is legal, and mutually agreeable between tenant and lessor.

When dealing with any property interest, to maximize the ultimate benefits, the property owner must keep in mind that when entering into any disposition of any single right, there should be a specific understanding as to the status of the other rights. For example, if you enter into a land lease with a farmer so that the farmer may utilize the land for growing crops, unless specified, that farmer may also have control over all the other rights owned by the property owner, that go with the land during the term of the lease.

Let's start with one of the more common situations that might occur with respect to a land lease (also called a ground lease). For example, Ronnie has 89 years remaining of an original 99-year lease on the land under his hotel. This lease was created when he acquired a 30-year-old oceanfront hotel from its original owner. At that, time the seller wanted to split his asset value into two portions: (1) the land itself, and (2) the improvements or buildings on that land. The total value of the land plus the building had been calculated to be $2 million. Instead of taking the $2 million, the seller wanted to establish an income stream for the land portion of the value, which was pegged at $1 million. Ronnie then agreed to pay rent on this for a period of time as long as he had an option to purchase the land back. This scenario was attractive to the seller because the majority of the value was in the appreciation of the land and the seller did not want to trigger a large capital gain tax at that time. This splitting of the asset value also appealed to Ronnie because his ultimate goal was to remove the buildings and build a condominium apartment building on the site at some future date. However, he knew that the property would generate a high level of cash flow for at least 10 years, which was just about the life expectancy of much of the assets of the building. By splitting the asset into land versus buildings, he could also avoid having to pay a much larger price. By paying rent, instead of interest, the actual land value would not likely have a major jump in value from the tax appraiser.

The rent for the land portion of that transaction was to be calculated at 2 points above the highest jumbo certificate of deposit from a list of 10 different (and nationally recognized) commercial banks at the date of the closing of the transaction. At the time of the transaction, the highest of those rates was 5.4 percent per year. Ronnie's annualized rent (based on the total of 12 monthly installments) was $74,000 a year. The lease format was a 99-year term, and the option to purchase was any time after the tenth anniversary of the closing of the deal.

The purchase of the buildings was a separate transaction and was in essence the purchase of the business of the hotel for $1 million, with the seller holding 70 percent of that as a first mortgage that would fully amortize within those 10 years. Ronnie's down payment of $300,000 clenched the deal.

At that time, Ronnie acquired a property on which he fully expected to exercise the option to purchase that the lease provided. Because of that, he did not negotiate a provision that would require the seller to subordinate the land to new development financing. If the landowner were to subordinate his or her interest to a lender, then a lender would have a lien against the land ahead of the owner's rights. Without the subordination, the lender could only lien Ronnie's rights, which are those rights granted to him by virtue of the lease. Those rights are his "leasehold rights." Generally, lenders shy away from lending on unsubordinated land leases, but under some circumstances, this is possible.

However, as often happens, financing for the condominium proved more difficult because of the present lack of demand and overbuilt condition of the condominium market. Nonetheless, the hotel business was booming and there was a lot of interest from several lenders to finance a new hotel at that location. Before he knew it, Ronnie had such a lender, who understood leasehold interest, liked the property, and was satisfied that due to the nature and terms of the lease, the life remaining of 89 years was more than adequate for a 30-year term of a loan. Because the rent had been set at $74,000 a year, without any escalation for the full term of the lease, the value of the lease far exceeded the value of the land.

Let's backtrack a moment to see how this happened. When Ronnie purchased the property, its value was set at $1 million. This might have been slightly above the maximum anyone would have paid for a vacant tract of land at that time. Therefore, for the seller to get that value, pay the capital gains tax on that amount, and put it in a long-term certificate of deposit would never have provided him with a $74,000-a-year income stream. From the seller's point of view, his sale was both a sale and a lease, both of which spread out the return over a long period of time to the result that he only had to pay a gains tax on that portion of the buildings that were the sale part of the deal. The seller was pleased with the end results of the deal, knowing that it was likely that he would get the $1 million (face amount of that virtual Certificate of Deposit) at the end of 10 years. The seller knew that because he did not provide subordination in the lease, his position was very secure. Perhaps like gold in his pocket.

As it turned out, as 10 years passed, the value of the land skyrocketed. Even a very conservative appraisal would now value the land and buildings at close to $5 million with all of that value assigned to the land only.

Ronnie's acquisition of the property had turned into a gold mine for him as well. His $74,000-a-year lease payment had the negative value of not more than $740,000. This is a value easy to estimate as the present day value of which $74,000 would pay off in 40 years, the 40 years factor being a period of time longer than any leasehold loan which Ronnie might obtain. At the present lending rates, a constant rate of 10 percent would be very conservative in this approach. Because the present value of the land by itself would be $5 million, Ronnie's leasehold value could then be seen at that value less the negative value of the lease. Therefore,

$$\$5,000,000 - \$750,000 = \$4,250,000$$

In essence, a buyer who had an appropriate and viable use of the property that could be fully capitalized within the remaining term of the lease, which is 89 years, could justify that value. The caveat to that is the words "had an appropriate and viable use." This means a *use* that the terms of the lease will permit *and* the *conditions,* which must be met to make that use viable.

Because the land lease does not commit the owner of the land (the "fee simple") to subordinate his or her interests to a mortgagee, that lender can only look to the borrower him or herself, the value of the improvements either there now or to be built, and the value of the leasehold as security of the loan.

Seven Elements That Establish the Value of a Leasehold Interest

Type of Property Leased.   Different properties will obviously have different values. Is the lease for land only, buildings only, or the combination of land and buildings? If it is land only, then either there are no improvements on the land, or the improvements are separate from the land. For example, in Ronnie's case, the lease is applicable to the land only; he separately purchased the improvements as a combined lease plus purchase. However, because the hotel purchased sat on all of the land his leasehold interest would, unless prohibited by lease terms, have the same merit and value as if he owned that land. His lease payments would have no long-term effect once the negative value was subtracted from the overall value any more than his annual payment of taxes and or insurance. In reality, in Ronnie's case, even less effect as his rent is fixed at $74,000 for the life of the lease. However, if the land lease were under a 100-unit cooperative apartment building, the leasehold interest owned by an individual apartment owner would have a value that would have to take into consideration the value of the property as a 100-unit apartment structure. Some merit might be given to the unlikely event that all 100 of the apartment units could be purchased. However, in the case of the multiple ownership of separate lease-hold interests on the same property, there is no possibility of using the land as "fee simple" unless all such interests were controlled by the same entity. That entity would presently be the ownership association of the cooperative apartment building.

ANNUAL RENT OF THE LEASE.   The rent payments on lease will govern the actual value. The leasehold equity will become the primary security for the unsubordinated loan. Appraising the space or property finds property value. This value may vary within similar leased space. After you deduct the capitalized value of the rent from the value, the remaining amount is the leasehold equity. For example, F.P.A. Corp. has a 60-unit hotel on the beach. It is located on leased land. F.P.A. Corp. owns the right to use the property, for which it pays an annual rent of $26,500. Assume it had no financing and built the hotel with cash. The finished value of the building was $1,050,000 and the land, according to comparable values in the area, was $875,000. Therefore, the total combined value is $1,925,000. As F.P.A. Corp. pays $26,500 in rent, this amount can be said to represent a cost of a capital investment for a period of time (the lease term). Setting a Demand Yield Rate of 10 percent on this cost would relate to an investment of $265,000. An 8 percent yield rate would increase the comparative investment to $331,250. Similar value could also be justified as what Present Value the $26,500 would amortize a mortgage of that PV over the term of the lease.

Keep in mind that leasehold financing will ultimately be based on the terms of years of the lease and generally, the lease should be at least 10 years longer than the mortgage amortization. In this case, however, I have used the Demand Yield Rate. As this is an existing hotel, this would be a logical and appropriate method to use. See the computations that follow to determine the leasehold equity at 10 percent and 8 percent yield rates with a leasehold mortgage of $800,000. It should be clear that the cost of the lease, in terms of annual rent, must be capitalized to give an adjustment in the equity. The rate used may vary

Yield Rate (or Constant Rate of Debt Repaid over 40 Years)	10%	8%[a]
1. Annual rent on the lease of land	$ 26,500	$ 26,500
2. Capital investment at a demand rate	265,000	331,250[b]
3. Combined value of land and buildings[b]	$1,925,000	$1,925,000
4. Less existing financing	− 800,000	− 800,000
5. Gross equity before adjustment for a land lease	$1,125,000	$1,125,000
6. Less amount from line 2	− 265,000	− 331,250
7. Total leasehold equity	$ 860,000	$ 793,750
8. Less capital investment	− 100,000	− 100,000
9. Leasehold equity appreciation	$ 760,000	$ 693,750

[a]This amount should either be the yield shown or the present value amount, which a mortgage payment at line 1 will retire over 40 years. See the Ronnie example mentioned earlier.
[b]Line 3 should be an acceptable value for combined land and buildings either by using the tax appraised value, or more accurately, by using a value adjusted to recent sales of similar compatible properties in the area.

from property to property and from lender to lender. It is a good idea to show the leasehold equity at two different rates and then take the lower rate in your loan package. In any event, the fact that F.P.A. Corp. is leasing the land at $26,500 per year, and the land has a current value of $875,000, is some indication that there will be excellent leasehold appreciation and equity. Yet, the leasehold equity must consider the improvements and their existing financing.

PERIOD OF TIME REMAINING ON THE LEASE.   If the lease expires in one year, the leasehold equity will be that equity which can be substantiated economically over the remaining term of the lease. The hotel owned by F.P.A. Corp. on leased land will continue to have value, as will the land. F.P.A.'s leasehold value, however, will begin to decline at a point in time when the remaining term of the lease does not allow return of capital at a reasonable rate of return for that remaining period.

For example, the hotel has a value based on the economic return. In most income producing properties, the value established by the economic approach is proper and should be close to or below the replacement cost evaluation. If the replacement value were lower than the economic value, it might be more prudent to build a new hotel. Nonetheless, this economic return may continue for 20 years in a reasonable projection. However, F.P.A. Corp. may have only 10 years in which to enjoy the benefit of the leasehold if the lease expires at the end of that time. An investor interested in purchasing the leasehold from F.P.A. Corp. would analyze the yield only for the remaining term, giving little credit to the actual value of the property, unless the lease could be extended. A lender would look at the leasehold equity in the same way.

The owner of the fee simple must also consider the impact of a lease term on the value of the underlying property.

TERMS, OBLIGATIONS, RESTRICTIONS, AND PROVISIONS OF THE LEASE.   Each lease is a new ball game. There are many provisions or conditions, which can make it desirable or undesirable. Rights to sublet, diversity of use, high maintenance costs, lack of subordination, outright limitation of use, and the like will be examined carefully by any lender prior to a loan. Because these terms are so important in possible financing, a lessee should make every effort to create a lease that will offer a good basis for leasehold financing. To do this will require a careful study as to what can and cannot be done at that location. Remember, Location, Location, Location are not the most important words in real estate. They are, Location, Use, and Approval. Therefore, it is important to look beyond the lease itself and examine what other governing elements can restrict or cause new obligations over and above the lease itself.

USE OF THE PROPERTY.   One of the important trio just mentioned is use. By this, I do not mean the use as is presently evident. Instead, I mean the uses is allowed by any governing element. The lease may have such restrictions, as do many leases for office space, shopping center locations, and so on. There the owner of the property, either the fee simple ownership or the building ownership frequently has provisions within the lease that restrict the use of the space. The tenant who leases space for a barbershop in a shopping center is likely to be restricted to that single use. Any time there is a restriction that had that effect, the value of that space may be adversely impacted. On the other hand, certain uses can be so valuable that to be in a prime location where all the other tenants are restricted against competition with that single use can have a positive impact on the leasehold value.

When the building is a single-purpose structure and can not be converted easily or economically to another use (if allowed by the lease or city ordinances) this will lessen the intrinsic value of the leasehold. These are important factors to the lender, not only because he or she may end up with the building, but for the tenant to survive and the leasehold equity to be maintained, opportunity to build into the lease flexibility in the tenant's use will enhance the value of any leasehold.

THE TENANT.   Of course, the lender always will take a good long look at the tenant. After all, it is the tenant that wants to borrow the money. All lenders are very interested in the person and/or entity they lend money to. Your credit history will play a big role in your success in obtaining any loan, no matter if it is for a leasehold interest, or fee simple ownership.

OPTIONS AVAILABLE TO THE LESSEE.   Of all the items in a lease that can have effect on the leasehold value, the most critical are options that give the lessee rights to future benefits. These benefits can vary, and can include any of the following: Option to buy, option to extend the lease, option to remove buildings without replacing them, option to recast debt to old levels or greater, option to obtain full or partial subordination at a future date or dates. When you negotiate a lease of any kind, the best time to ask for and get options is at the beginning. In some situations, the lessor may not grant certain options because the option would not be practical. If you were leasing an office or space in a building, to have an option to buy the building may not be an advantage to you. However, being able to renew the lease for long terms at past rent levels could be a great advantage to you in establishing a leasehold equity.

These seven factors will be the main criteria, which will create leasehold financing. Each factor is important on its own, but it is the combined effect of all seven that will provide a package that is financeable.

How Lenders Deal with Security from Leasehold Equities

Leasehold financing is secured in two different methods: subordinated fee and unsubordinated fee. There is a considerable amount of money lent with the security established by either of these two forms of security. In general, however, the majority of the larger loans are on leasehold interests with subordinated fee. The situation of F.P.A. Corp. with its hotel on leased land is a good example. The land lease had a provision, which enabled F.P.A. to obtain a first mortgage that would be secured by the improvements as well as the land. The owners of the land subordinated their interest to the lender on the first mortgage and took a second position. The lender could foreclose on both the improvements and the land if F.P.A. Corp. defaulted on the mortgage and the landowners did not step in to take it over.

Giving the lessee the right to give a mortgage right to a lender, by virtue of having the land owner subordinate that right to the lender, increases the land owner's risk. The tradeoff to this is that just about anything in a lease that increases the owner's risk will increase the leasehold equity of the tenant. In certain situations for certain leases, this aspect can help make for a good lease. After all, if the property owner wants to establish a steady long-term tenant, giving that tenant flexibility to grow and expand can be important. So important in fact, that the offer of subordination may actually entice a better tenant than would be available otherwise.

Many owners do not want to subordinate their land or other interests so that the leasehold owner can use their equity to obtain a loan. After all, when the land is subordinated, the lender will look to the real value of land and buildings without deducting the capitalized rent cost to arrive at a leasehold equity. If the owner does not subordinate the fee to the lender, then the financing must be made with unsubordinated fee.

The terms of the lease become most important here, if the lease is for a very long term; usually the term of the loan plus a sufficient remaining term allow the investor to benefit from a build-up of equity, say 150 percent of the mortgage life. In addition, if the lease payments are not onerous, then the lender will look to these leasehold interests as though the tenant actually owns the property. This fee simple or ownership of the land is seen as a clear use of the land, and if all other factors work out, a loan can be made without the subordination.

There are some areas in the world where almost all the land is leased and most all real estate financing is leasehold. Hong Kong and Hawaii are good examples of places where leasehold financing is rather prominent. In England, it is not uncommon for whole towns to be situated on leased land. The rights of the tenants may filter back to the original owner through many different subtenants. One property that I know well in downtown London has over fifteen subtenants. The building's owner pays a very high land lease to the most recent subtenant, who pays a lesser amount to the person, from whom he or she leases the property. That person, the second subtenant in line pays a lessor rent to their lessor (also a subtenant) and so on, all the way back to a member of the Royal Family, whose original lease may go back several hundred years ago.

LEASEHOLD FINANCING CAN BE A DEAL MAKER. The ability to pull apart a property to a fee simple equity and a leasehold equity can be a useful form of financing that can provide moneymaking benefits to both the property owner and the tenant.

I have discussed how a sale and leaseback can be one method for a property owner to raise capital while at the same time keeping the use of a property. This type of lease is generally the sale of a property tied to a leaseback by the seller, but may also be a sale with a lease that is obtained by the seller prior to or shortly after the closing of the sale. Because every property has different rights that can be sold or leased, it is possible to separate each of them so that some of these rights are sold, while others are leased or retained. Take a look at some of the rights that you may own when you own a vacant tract of land.

LAND LEASES

There are a number of important aspects of land ownership to be aware of including:

- *Mineral rights:* Just because there is oil or gold under your land doesn't mean you own it. Often mineral rights were retained by some previous owner, or sold or leased to a third party long before you came along. However, if your deed gave you these rights, then they are yours to keep, sell, lease, trade, or otherwise dispose of them, even if there is nothing down there worth anything. Remember, what might be there may not be valuable simply because no one has figured out a use for it yet.

- *Subterranean rights:* These are not exactly the same as mineral rights. Subterranean rights can allow you to dispose of space under your land for a tunnel, parking garage, wine cellar, or whatever.

- *Surface rights:* Generally surface and some subterranean and some air rights go together in one package; however, if what you own is an antenna that sticks up into the sky, and don't need the surface or subterranean part of the land, then those rights can be disposed of separately.

- *Air rights:* The acquisition or lease of air rights is big business. If you have a large parking area for your business, you are free to sell, lease, or otherwise dispose of these rights as long as the use of them does not diminish your needed parking area. The construction of an office building or hotel over city parking, for example, is not uncommon in major cities.

- *Riparian rights:* When a property fronts on a body of water, there may be riparian rights that go with the land. These rights allow the owner of them to use the water or bottom to certain distances from shore. Local laws may govern that use, so the value of the riparian right will vary.

- *Water rights:* These may coincide with riparian rights, but generally are more extensive. If the land fronts on a large body of water, the landowner may have the right to lease areas of this water for certain uses. These uses may include mooring facilities for boats, docks, fishing piers, and so on. Generally, these areas are public waterways, and the rights can be leased but not purchased.

- *Subdivision rights:* The right to subdivide the property is a very important right. This is a function of local rules and regulations more than a right that runs with the land. When you can subdivide a property this means you can divide it in such a way that you can dispose of each division separately. Some properties are zoned in such a way that the minimum size that a property can be will not permit further subdivision of the land. When this occurs, unless the zoning is changed, or the property rezoned, there could be more division of the property.

Any of these rights can be leased, sold, or otherwise disposed. It may be feasible to sell the land, keep the mineral rights, and lease back the land and build on the land. You could sell the land, with or without the mineral rights with a leaseback on the land, then sell the building subject to a new subtenant lease. You could lease the riparian rights, lease the mineral rights, sell the land, lease back the land and build a building on it, which you keep.

Using a Lease as a Financing Tool to Close Deals

If you remember that financing is a shift of equity from one party to another, you can see that a lease can do that much in the same way as does a mortgage. There are, however, some very important differences between selling a property and leasing it. The important part of this is to take into consideration what is the best way for you to attain your goals. If you are a seller, you might find that you will attract more buyers if you package your property into two separate elements. You can, for example, sell the improvements subject to a land lease. Later in this chapter, I illustrate some of the benefits to both parties in such an example. By comparison, of the benefits that come from selling or leasing you will be able to establish a method of the disposition that maximizes your benefits of the deal. As a buyer, you should know what advantages and benefits you can gain by leasing or by only buying. There can be substantial benefits depending on which method you use. Review the following section to see how you could choose which method works best for you.

Advantages and Disadvantages of Selling a Property

YOU MAY CREATE A TAXABLE GAIN. If your adjusted basis is lower than the contract price of the property then you may have a tax to pay. It is important to know if you have any losses or other tax credits that can offset the taxable gain. If you do, you may want to take advantage of those losses while you can, and the sale, even with a potential taxable gain, might be the best way to go. If you have a taxable gain, and no losses to offset the gain, you might want to look to other options that could help reduce or eliminate the gain.

You sell a property for $750,000. Your adjusted tax basis (what you paid for the property adjusted for any improvements and depreciation) is $395,000. This means you will have a taxable gain of $355,000. Your tax is likely to be based on at least a 33 percent bracket, or a total of $117,150, or more.

YOU ESTABLISH A CAPITAL LOSS.   Selling a property at a loss is rarely a benefit, but there are times that cutting your losses by getting rid of a property is a smart move. Not all losses can be used to offset gains. At present, the tax laws do not allow you to apply a loss on the sale of your residence against other capital gains. This is likely to change in the future, so before you sell your own home or apartment, double check all the current tax codes to see if there has been such a change. It is useful to prepare a worksheet such as this:

You bought a home five years ago for	$500,000
You added a pool, closed in the garage at a cost of	+100,000
Your tax basis in this property is	$600,000
You sell for	−540,000
Your loss is	$ 60,000

Keep in mind that the above method does not take into account the potential that other elements need to be included, such as a home office that has been depreciated or other costs and expenses that may change the actual tax basis of the home. As this property is a home, you get no benefit from the loss. However, if prior to the sale you have acquired (via purchase or lease) a new residence, and have converted your home into (for IRS purposes) an investment income property by renting it out, you may have the right to deduct any loss from other capital gains during that period of time. It is possible that by simply going through the steps to rent the home out, such as turning it over to a real estate agent or hiring a property manager, you may establish your intention. Naturally, check with your accountant and lawyer prior to making any such commitment.

YOU HAVE A TAXABLE GAIN BUT NO PROCEEDS TO COVER IT.   This is not a nice situation to be in, and happens when your tax exceeds the amount of cash you are left with after the closing. Usually this occurs when there is a low down payment, and the seller has mortgaged over his or her tax basis. Because the IRS allows you to borrow money on property without having to pay any tax on that money, the extent to which that borrowed money exceeds your book value (adjusted tax basis) in the property will then be taxed. The fact that you spent that money five years ago is no consolation, as you may have to dig into your pocket to pay the tax.

For example, you have an income property that cost you $500,000. The present value is $750,000. You have depreciated it 29 years and your adjusted tax basis is now $100,000. (This means you likely had paid around $100,000 for the land and $400,000 for the building, which has now been fully depreciated.) While the buildings may have no value, the combination of land and buildings (whatever their respective worth) has appreciated to $750,000. From your point of view (as well as the IRS), you likely (in this situation) will have a capital gain of $650,000. $750,000, less your tax base of $100,000=$650,000.

Two years ago, you borrowed $550,000 and have spent all of it.

You sell the property for $750,000 at $200,000 cash to your mortgage. Your gain is $650,000 and at a 28 percent tax bracket (your bracket could vary up or down depending on other gains or losses for that year), your tax would be $182,000. Because you have already spent the $200,000 you got as a down payment, you now may have a problem. The lesson here is you should know what your tax obligation will be before you sign the contract to sell the property. Plan ahead.

Advantages and Disadvantages of Leasing Land and Purchasing the Improvements

As the lessor, you still own it; you have not created a gain or a loss. There is, however, an income tax to be paid on the rent you earn from the transaction. Because you do not have a taxable gain in the disposition of the property when you lease it, it is possible that you will save considerably in the reinvestment potential by leasing the portion of the property that has the gain, and selling or leasing the nongain portion of the property. For example, you own a 10,000-square-foot office building that you constructed five years ago on a lot you have owned for more than 20 years. When you purchased the lot it cost you $15,000 and for most of the 15 years prior to constructing the office building you leased the lot to a nearby new car dealer as a place to store cars. A buyer who want your office building who offers you $750,000 net of any costs you might have in the sale and transfer, to buy the building and lot combined.

You review your records and discover that your depreciated tax basis on the office building is $380,000. If you add your cost of the lot to that, your book value (adjusted tax basis) in the property is $395,000. You have a first mortgage, which you took out to build the building and still owe $350,000. Review your potential tax liability based on this information:

You sell the building and lot for	$750,000
Subtract your adjusted tax basis	−395,000
Your taxable gain	$355,000
Your tax bracket (assumption)	× 33%
Your estimated tax	$117,150

If you had gotten all cash in the sale, you would be left with $282,850 after you have deducted the mortgage and the tax ($750,000 − $350,000 = $400,000 − $117,150 = $282,850).

You invest your cash at 10 percent, and your return is $28,285 per year. This $28,285 is a comparable return from the reinvested cash left over after the sale.

You offer the office building for sale subject to a land lease.

Instead of taking this offer, you decide to sell the building for $400,000 and give the buyer a ground lease on the lot at $35,000 per year. Here is how this deal turns out:

Sale of the Building

Sale price	$400,000
Less adjusted basis in building	−380,000
Taxable gain	$ 20,000
Tax bracket (yours may vary)	× 25%
Estimated tax	$ 5,000
Cash you get at closing[a]	$ 50,000
Less the tax you pay	− 5,000
Cash left over	$ 45,000
You reinvest this at	× 10%
Interest you earn on the cash	$ 4,500
On the Lease of the Land	
Annual rent	$ 35,000
Add interest earned and rent[b]	$ 39,500

[a]Remember, you owe $350,000.
[b]This is your total annual benefit.

You can see that by using the land lease as a part of the financing package, you have increased your reinvestment potential from $28,285 to $39,500. The reason for this is the result of two factors. First, you do not have to pay the gains tax, and second the tax you do pay is at a lower tax rate (assuming that the sudden gain of the sale would increase you to a higher tax bracket).

How the Buyer/Tenant Benefits

Buyers benefit in several ways. First of all, in the above example, the land lease functions much like an interest-only mortgage. Because the buyer cannot depreciate the land, and as the rent paid is an allowable deduction against income, the amount of invested capital, which is the lease payment, is a 100 percent tax deduction. The fact that the buyer does not have to come up with the cash to buy the land means that he or she buys the property with less invested cash.

Because the overall cash invested in the acquisition is generally less using a split lease/purchase transaction, the cash flow yield should be increased. If this does not happen, then a review of the situation should be taken to see if there is an imbalance in the values. It could be that given the opportunity to purchase both land and improvements in one shot that the overall down payment may not be much more than the split deal, and if there were, ample leverage through financing the land lease may have no advantage to the buyer/would-be tenant.

For example, Roy has been negotiating to acquire a large warehouse. The seller and he came to a meeting of the minds at an overall price for everything at $2 million. Roy anticipated that at the price he would need to put at least $500,000 of his own cash into the deal and he could borrow the balance at a constant rate (P&I annually) of 9 percent. The seller suggested that he wouldn't mind splitting the equity into a land lease and a sale of the buildings. If he did that, he would want to set the value at $1 million for the buildings and $1 million for the land. He would hold a 50-year lease with an option to purchase anytime after the first five years. The initial rent would be $80,000 per year, paid in monthly installments. The lease would have a cost of living index to be adjusted every five years, tied to the cost of living "all items" index (check the U.S. Bureau of Labor and Statistics on the Internet for this and other such cost of living indexes). The option to buy would require Roy to notify the landowner 90 days in advance of the purchase, and the purchase price would be adjusted at that time to be applied at the closing date. Because this would coincide with the first opportunity to buy (end of the first five years), Roy would have an incentive to purchase at that time, otherwise the price would surely be adjusted upward as the cost of living was (at that time) averaging around 3 percent per year. That would mean an increase of at least $150,000 in the price. If he leased and purchased the buildings, he discovered he could borrow $700,000 of the improvement side of the deal, provided the land was subordinated to the lender. Here is a summary:

	Roy Buys Everything	Roy Buys Building and Leases Land
Value of Purchase	$2,000,000	$1,000,000
1. Cash to close	− 500,000	− 300,000
2. To be financed by management	1,500,000	700,000
3. Mortgage payment	135,000	63,000
4. Rent per year (first 5)	0	80,000
5. Mortgage/Rent total	− 135,000	− 140,000
6. Assume NOI of	200,000	200,000
7. Cash flow	65,000	60,000
8. Cash flow yield (line 7 ÷ by line 1)	13%	20%

Note: Mortgage/Rent total equals the mortgage at 9% constant rent as shown in the lease.

In this case, the results suggest that even if Roy has no problem coming up with the cash to close, he might be better off with the outright purchase. After all, the lease scenario produces only $5,000 a year after cash flow than the purchase. With a $200,000 less down payment, his cash flow yield would be substantially greater, so, if his goal was to maximize his cash flow, the land lease would attain that goal. However, there is the risk that at 90 days prior to the end of the fifth year he would not be able to refinance the loan. The uncertainty of his tenant situation, vacancy factor, and overall NOI at that time may cause him to stick with the straight purchase. Roy's ability to know the market, anticipate what upside to the property he could promote and benefit from would be the determining factor in making a sound call on this. Keep in mind, the seller has several decisions to make as well. Should he subordinate to such a loan? If he didn't, then it would be likely that Roy may not get the loan at the same constant, or that his down payment for the building portion of that side of the deal could increase to the point where the unforeseen risk five years from now was too much to take. Equally, the seller could end that speculation by saying that he would not sell the package deal and the only way to go would be with the land lease. If the seller was so adamant and truly wanted the income stream of the land lease, then he may have to be more flexible in the terms of the lease. As it is, a subordinated lease, with five-year adjustments in price and lease terms is fairly loose. It is not uncommon for adjustments to be made annually on both the rent amount as well as any option to purchase price. Personally, if I were the seller in this situation, I would want the purchase price within the option terms to be increased by a formula, say 10 times the annual rent based on 12 months of the last month's rent prior to the closing. In essence, if the last month's rent (prior to the closing of the option to purchase) was $9,000 the option to purchase the annualized rent (as to this formula) would be $108,000. Multiply that times 10 and the purchase price, at that time, would be $1,080,000. I would establish it this way because adjustments in rent may contain items that take into consideration other factors besides those contained in the Cost of Living Index. In any event, whatever formula is used is obtained through negotiation, with some possible trade-offs to other terms and conditions.

Using Land Leases to Buy Property Otherwise Not for Sale

There are many property owners who are reluctant to sell because of the large tax liability they will have in a sale. By the time they pay the tax due, the remaining cash cannot be reinvested at a high enough rate to give them a reasonable benefit. If you were dealing with a seller who owned such a property, that seller may be unwilling to sell, or have an unreasonable price to cover tax liability. If you approach the transaction by offering a land lease, you may turn around a difficult purchase into one that benefits both of you. In many cases, you will have to educate the seller to see where the benefits come from. Remember, this seller has priced the property at $900,000 to cover a $150,000 tax payment. The real value in benefits to the seller is only $750,000. If that is a more reasonable price, then you need to make an offer that gives the seller benefits worth the $750,000 without you having to pay that much for the property. The ability to obtain new financing on leased land or on leasehold space in other buildings will depend on your contacts in the money market. It will also depend on the total combined effect of the seven factors shown in the earlier part of this section. The rise and decline of the leasehold equity is, of course, the most important aspect of leasehold financing. The security offered by this equity, along with other risk reducers such as personal signature and guarantee on the note and pledge of other collateral or security, makes the leasehold mortgage a most interesting form of financing. Your ability to use this kind of financing in a future deal will depend on your clear focus on your goals. Everything you do in investing should be directed toward this end. Your ultimate success, as I continue to reiterate, will be enhanced by your pursuit of your goals.

PERCENT OF INCOME

In real estate financing, the sweetener percent of income is one of the most sought-after bonuses that institutional lenders look for. It is a simple giving by the borrower to the lender of a percentage of the income derived from the investment. In application, there are many different ways to express this sweetener, and many different terms and conditions that can be dealt with. This portion of the chapter is devoted to showing you how to use this aspect to your benefit, either as buyer, seller, or lender.

EXAMPLE 1: YOU ARE THE BUYER.   You want to buy Charlie's apartment complex. You have offered him nearly the amount he has been asking, $1,200,000, only he has turned down the offer because he will not hold a wraparound mortgage for $1,195,000 so that you can purchase the property with $5,000 down. Therefore, back to the drawing board you go. Which you do and you come up with a new plan. You offer him $1,200,000 with 20 percent cash down. That is, with you coming up with $240,000 as a down payment and he then holds a wraparound mortgage for $960,000.

The wraparound mortgage is for a reasonable interest rate and terms, each designed to be good for you, and to provide benefits for Charlie. The closing item is that you offer Charlie a bonus to the transaction of 5 percent of all revenue that exceeds his pro forma NOI for the first three years following the closing. If he does not accept this deal as offered, at least you are now dealing in negotiations that will not cost you anything.

If he had artificially puffed up the NOI, he will want to back off this kind of negotiations. This can be a clue to you that this project is not what it was presented to be. If he wants to fine-tune this kind of deal, he is showing confidence in his pro forma.

EXAMPLE 2: YOU ARE THE SELLER.   The buyer is balking at the deal, and you are grasping for something to close the deal. His last offer, which was well below your counter, was $900,000 cash down, with you holding a second mortgage of $2,000,000 at 9 percent interest per annum, over the existing financing of $45,000,000. You countered that you needed a minimum of $2,000,000 down. So there you are, $1,100,000 apart.

You counter again, this time pulling out all the stops in hopes of showing your confidence in the deal. You will accept $1,300,000 cash down, and will hold secondary financing of $1,600,000 at 6 percent interest per annum provided that for the term of the second mortgage you also receive a bonus of 15 percent of all income in excess of the NOI projected during the terms of the mortgage. In following counteroffers, you may deal with both the time period and the actual interest bonus, but you are now back on track. Whatever the bonus you get, over and above the interest rate of the mortgage, is not out of the buyer's pocket. The project is paying that cost.

EXAMPLE 3: YOU ARE THE LENDER.   You are Mr. Big Bucks and are used to getting high interest rates for your money. I come along and tempt you with a very interesting project and ask for your seed money of $500,000. You want 14 percent interest for your money. I offer you 7 percent interest on the loan plus 15 percent of all revenue over the projected NOI, after debt service has been deducted. We set the term for the overage at 10 years, even though the loan will be paid off in 15.

This form of percent taking is far more frequent than the sharing of actual ownership. Here the lender will receive normal payment of interest and principal to pay back the loaned amount. In addition to those payments, the lender will also receive a bonus of all or part of the income above a set standard.

EXAMPLE 4: INSTITUTIONAL LENDERS.   Insurance Company A loans all the money needed to build a major shopping center. The loan provisions indicate that they will receive a bonus of 20 percent of all income above a gross revenue of $2,500,000. Another lender, REIT B, has just financed a 10-story office building. The loan states they get a bonus of 3 percent of the gross income above $200,000.

Both these situations required the borrower to pay a percentage of the income on the project to the lender. These types of loans are very similar to rents under leases that require the tenant to pay a bonus or percent of the gross income. Sometimes the lender will look to these leases as a source of the bonus on the mortgage. If the tenants in a center average 3 percent overages on their leases (that is to say, the leases are set at 3 percent of gross income against a minimum rent), then once the base rent is reached by the calculation of the 3 percent of gross income, all income above that will earn the bonus of 3 percent to the landlord. If the lender is participating in the income with the developer, then one method may be to split or in some way divide the over-ride of gross income on the leases.

Lenders usually have a cutoff on this revenue to assure that they do not exceed the usury for the area. For example, if the maximum interest, which could be charged, was 12 percent, then the total interest earned by the lender for that year could not exceed 12 percent. In most areas, there is a difference in usury between private parties and corporations, with the corporation having the highest chargeable interest. Because of this, most lenders wishing to participate in ownership or percentage of income will require the borrower to be a corporation. This will give them a higher amount of interest that they can receive and an additional buffer between earning and potential earning.

Offering a percent of the income on a property as an incentive to the lender to give good terms has its merit. If the base income passes through without any bonus to the lender, then only that income that may come because of improvement or appreciation in the property will go to him. In addition, since the investment and cash flow are improved for the buyer, he or she also benefits from the transaction.

Using this same principle, it is possible to entice a seller to hold a good second mortgage on the sale of an income property.

EXAMPLE 5: SHOPPING CENTER PURCHASE. Wilton wants to buy a small shopping center that Miles owns. Miles is asking $650,000 with $225,000 cash to his existing $425,000 mortgage. The existing cash flow based on the current debt service is $24,000. However, Miles is sure that the income will increase, as there are several vacant stores and rents will undoubtedly go up with new tenants. Wilton, however, demands at least a 12 percent return on his invested cash and can't quite see how to get it out of this center.

I looked at the situation nearly four weeks after Wilton had given up on the Miles center. Wilton had come to me to see if I had anything else he might like to buy. During the several visits we made to other centers, he kept talking about Miles' center. I asked him why he was unable to put it together. "Miles won't take paper" was the reply. I spoke with the broker that had shown Wilton the Miles center, and we agreed that if I could get Wilton back there and show Miles how a deal could be made, we would split the fee.

The first step was to go visit Miles with the other broker. I wanted to see how strongly Miles felt about the future of the center, and what his motivation was to sell. It turned out that Miles was motivated to sell because of an inability to cope with the problems of the center. He was not management oriented, and the tenants had quickly found that they could get what they wanted by bugging Miles to death. Yet, he did feel strongly about the future of the center and knew that if someone had the knowledge to manage it properly it would show a greater return than it presently did.

Based on this information, Wilton and I went over the income statement of the center. Wilton agreed that the income could be increased, but he had to be sure of a 12 percent return.

Here is what Wilton did: He offered the full price of $650,000, since it was a fair price. He was to pay $150,000 cash at closing and give Miles a $75,000 second mortgage to make up the balance. The payout of the second mortgage was as follows: 10-year interest only at 7 percent per annum. At the end of the 10 years the total outstanding balance would be paid (Wilton would refinance the first mortgage at that time). As an inducement, Wilton added the provision that Miles would receive an additional bonus of 25 percent of all cash flow above $24,000.

Aside from some minor changes added by Miles to clarify the term "cash flow," we were able to sell him on the contract. Wilton could not prepay the second mortgage without a stiff penalty so Miles is still collecting on it. The income is over the original estimate and the property is throwing off better than a $33,500 cash flow. Miles is receiving an annual bonus of $2,375 along with his interest-only payment of $5,250, giving him a total yield of 10.17 percent. In addition, the income is apt to increase before the mortgage is paid off.

The use of percent ownership or percent of income as negotiating points will depend on their introduction at the right time. At times, the adversary in the negotiations brings these factors into the picture when you don't want them. A lender, for example, may want a piece of the action, but your client has not anticipated this possibility and has not allowed for such an eventuality. Many brokers do not know how to handle this type of situation and become confused by the lender's suggestion. Many lenders will look you right in the eye and tell you that they all want this kind of action. That may be true, of course. They may want it, but not all lenders demand it. Stick to your guns when you are unwilling to give up a piece of the action, but don't close the door. See what the lender is willing to do to get it.

JOINT VENTURES AND SYNDICATIONS

These two forms of financing will be discussed together because they both involve some similar techniques. To some degree, they can be the same thing, depending on your point of view. A joint venture is a joint effort by two or more people who combine abilities or capabilities. The joint venture can take many forms. It may be a landowner who joins up with a developer. The landowner puts up the land and the builder his or her knowledge of building, and together they develop the land. Alternatively, it could be two doctors who join forces to buy a lot to build a medical complex. In a joint venture, each party generally has a specific and unique role to play. One party is the developer, another manages the property later, while another may provide the financing.

A syndication, on the other hand, is generally thought of as a group of people who combine their monetary ability to buy land or other property for a mutually profitable end result. As you can see, the syndication is a form of joint venture, even though not all joint ventures take the syndication route. In most syndications, there is one person or entity that is the founder of the group. A syndicator, for example, would be that person or entity that puts the deal together and then offers the opportunity to other people or entities to invest in that development or acquisition.

There are numerous legal forms of ownership for both types of investing and financing. Limited partnerships have been used for both joint ventures and syndications and have special tax privileges that, to some degree, still hold up under the new tax laws. Investment trusts, corporations, professional associations, and partnerships all are legal forms of ownership, which can be used in both of these creative forms of financing.

The purpose of this section of this chapter is not to make you an expert in joint venture enterprises or syndications. This takes considerable study and knowledge. Instead, the brief passages on these topics are meant to spark your interest in these exciting fields and to acquaint you with their potential methods of use in your own investment strategies.

What Joint Ventures and Syndications Can Do for You

There will be times when the price or size of a property you represent is beyond the capability of the average investor. When this situation presents itself, the solution may be to divide the ownership interest among several buyers. This division of ownership could take the form of a syndication and you would become the syndicator.

Remember, no matter which form of financing you use, your goals are the first factor to consider. If all parties are suited for a joint venture, then this tool can be used satisfactorily. However, the joint venture transaction will keep the seller in (if the seller is a joint venture partner, of course) and this fact may not provide the desired results; and remember, any form of financing which will give reasonable results should be attempted.

Where Do You Find Partners for Joint Ventures?

They are almost everywhere. The first step is to determine the probable use of the property. Once you know, or at least have some idea of, the use, which would be economically feasible, you will know where to go to find a partner for the transaction. For example, if you represent the owner of a tract of land that is suitable for construction of a shopping center, you would look to developers of shopping centers as possible partners.

Your build-up of contracts in other areas will help. Mortgage bankers, mortgage brokers, architects, and general contractors all have leads that can direct you to someone actively looking for such a transaction.

What You Can Do to Make the Transaction More Appealing to the Possible Joint Venture Partner

This is the most important part of the process. Once you have a property and feel that the joint venture is best suited for your seller, the move you make to entice the developer into the transaction may mean the difference between a deal that will work and one that will not. There are many ways to structure a joint venture deal, and the actual transaction itself can vary from the original plan with just minor changes. Most sellers are not aware of the special clauses that are often inserted in such transactions. Many make the deal workable while others just complicate it. All are important, however. Some of the more important fine points are discussed in the following section.

Five Important Features in Joint Ventures

PREFERRED RETURN.   Often, one of the partners will demand a preferred return on the investment. Either the seller or the other partners can request this, but it is generally the money partner who will prevail. The seller may offer this as an inducement to get big money investors. The preferred return, in essence, is a condition that allows the first percent of the income to go to this investor. The percent can be a set percentage, such as 12 percent, or some other percentage based on income gross. For example, Reynolds invests $100,000 into a joint venture deal and is preferred 12 percent on his investment. This means he will get the first $12,000 of income. The other partners then get the next $12,000, and the overage is split based on other provisions of the agreement.

GUARANTEED RETURN.   This is much stronger than the preferred return and is not used too often. The same occurs as in the above situation, except that Reynolds will be guaranteed the return of 12 percent. What happens if the income did not total enough to pay his return would depend on the balance of the terms of the agreement. However, a guaranteed return may constitute a security and should be used only in situations where the sellers can sell securities under the laws of the state in which they act and meet federal security laws as well. It is best to seek the advice of a lawyer on this matter. This type of agreement is widely used outside the United States, and is seen in international real estate transactions frequently.

ACCRUAL OF UNPAID BUT EARNED RETURN.   This can be used with both the preferred return and the guaranteed return. Here, the investor will not be paid the amount of the preference or guarantee, either because of a lack of income from the project or desire not to receive the funds until a later date. The amount of his or her investment is then increased by the amount not paid, thus increasing later return.

For example, Reynolds was not paid $12,000 this year because the income and expenses broke even. His total investment is now calculated at $112,000 and his preference or guaranteed income will be based on that amount, instead of the original investment of $100,000.

SUBORDINATE INTEREST.   While either party can subordinate its interest, it is generally the seller who is called on to do this. The seller puts up all or a part of his or her equity in the transaction behind financing to be obtained. This will allow the joint venture to benefit from the full equity and obtain the maximum mortgage available. This requires the party giving the subordination to accept higher risk, but may be warranted if the transaction is economically feasible.

LAND BANK.   At times, the owner of a tract of land may be willing to carry the cost of the land while the joint venture partner gets the development ready. In essence, the cost of carrying the land will become an additional expense for the owner, but land banking is sometimes essential for obtaining the other partner. It is usually used when the time needed to bring the property to development cannot be determined, or is already known to be such that immediate development will not be possible, and when the joint venture partner does not want to hold land.

Your ability to use these features to make the joint venture attractive for developers or investors will depend on your understanding of the area's and the investors' needs. For example, it would not be productive to look for a developer for a hotel if hotels cannot be financed or are in disfavor in your area for some reason. In addition, the use of the property must be almost immediate. However, remember that the time it takes to develop a shopping center is much longer than the time it takes to build a strip store. Because of this, the time needed to begin construction will vary. A major center will take at least two years from the word "go" to the word "open."

What You Can Do to Become Involved with Syndications and Joint Venture Deals

The first step may be this book. It contains most of the tools used by both the syndicator and the broker to put together joint ventures. Study these tools and see how they can be used in these forms of financing. The application of all the aspects of financing will be no more difficult when dealing with a group of buyers for a syndication or a builder for a joint venture than when dealing one-to-one with a buyer. The only difference may be the size of the commission, which might be greater in the syndication or joint venture.

Ask your lawyer to help you with the syndication or to give you some information about the joint venture deals he or she has put together. If you can read over some actual joint venture and syndication prospectuses, you will learn a great deal.

Be careful of the legal requirements in syndication. There are many laws that control the sale of securities, and most syndications will fall within one or more of these laws. These laws may be vaguely drafted, which makes them difficult to understand. If you are a professional syndicator, the IRS is likely to more frequently audit you, and you may not qualify to take the usual capital gain treatment as your gain may be treated (by the IRS or state revenue collectors) as regular earned income. Seek legal opinion from a qualified person in this respect prior to attempting to form a syndication or joint venture.

Chapter 18

ELEVEN CREATIVE FINANCING TECHNIQUES THAT MAKE YOUR TRANSACTIONS FLY

GOAL OF THIS CHAPTER

This chapter continues to expand your "out of the box" thinking when it comes to real estate investing. It is essential to remember the real estate you look at is not always what it appears to be. It might not even be close to what you want it to be. The beauty of real estate investing is that people who have a good imagination are able to see hidden value that they are able to cultivate by making a change in the use, or in the physical aspects of the property. This kind of thought process needs to be supported by a treasure chest of creative methods to make it all happen. Not all real estate transactions need to follow the common formula that consists of a down payment and purchase money mortgage. Be creative to attain your goals.

CREATIVE THINKING EXPANDS YOUR OPPORTUNITIES TO CLOSE DEALS

There are few people who know more than a handful of methods to structure a real estate transaction. Unfortunately, on the top of that very long list of such people, you will find the names of many real estate salesmen and women. This is especially true following a boom sellers' market. In those times, such as the one that peaked in 2006, agents became order takers and not salespeople. Buyers were in such a hurry to acquire property before

442

someone beat them to the punch that thousands of new agents flocked into the real estate industry. Few were experienced, and they did not learn how to be creative.

To survive the vicissitudes of the market, well-informed investors know that investors who know how to solve problems and help the other side of the deal get closer to their goals will capture the best deals when the market slows down.

USE TECHNIQUES THAT CLOSE THE GAP TO CREATE WIN/WIN SITUATIONS

Creative financing is the art of developing a financing package that solves the problems that have been blocking the way to the desired goal. It is important that you remember that aspect because it applies to all financing techniques. The only difference, then, between creative financing and normal financing is the application of the tool. Much of creative financing occurs in secondary mortgages or when the property owner or the seller (not always the same people) participates in the structure of the debt. This happens when any of the elements in the previous two chapters are applied, so this may also include the use of leasehold interest, joint ventures, options, and a black hat full of such magic tricks.

CREATIVE FINANCING GIVES YOU FLEXIBILITY

If you go to a bank or other lender to borrow money to buy a house, they will approach that loan in one singular and usually uniformly designed format. There is almost no deviation in how you will get the loan, and how its payback will be set up. You can negotiate little except the interest, the number of years of amortization, if there will be a balloon or not, and when will it come. Sometimes there is a penalty for early repayment that might be negotiable, but once the penalty is there, it rarely is removed completely. There is nothing creative about this, nor is there much room for you to tailor this kind of loan package to fit something specific that is important to you.

On the other hand, when you and the seller are focused on a single result (even though you may likely see that result from different perspectives), you both are anxious to see you purchase or otherwise acquire the property. You must never underestimate the importance of that statement. Buyers want to purchase, and sellers want them to. Because this single factor is uniquely the same for both parties, you might wonder why so many people forget that often buyers and sellers each believe they are really in an adversary relationship with each other.

YOUR GOAL COMES FIRST

As you undoubtedly have noticed, I continually reference your goals as being the most important element of the equation if you expect to maximize your results. Without even the weakest of goals, you will never know if you have reached a point in your life when you need to raise them, or start in another direction altogether. The beauty of having clear goals is that if you do not reach the goals on schedule, you can adjust the schedule, and that is not so bad. What is bad is not to have any goals in place. Goal activity in making real estate deals is like target practice. You can't hit the bulls-eye unless there is a target. Both buyer and seller are motivated by their respective goals. However, both buyer and seller share one single goal. Both sides of the transaction want the buyer to buy. Each party, therefore, has an opportunity to help the other party reach their individual goals. The seller can help the buyer by making the transaction possible, and the buyer can equally respond to help the seller move closer to his or her goals. There are, of course, roadblocks in the way that cannot always be overcome or circumvented.

However, far too many transactions fail to occur because the parties missed out on some opportunity. Usually this happens because they failed to understand just how flexible they could be to reach those goals.

I have already given you many financing techniques that are highly creative, and that serve different aspects of putting deals together. In this and other chapters to follow, I open up more doors to some very unique concepts in mortgage financing or techniques and strategies that can help bring a transaction together, even when it looked like it was going down the tube.

This chapter covers the following list of financing techniques:

1. Sliding mortgage.
2. Double finance.
3. Glue transaction.
4. Discounted paper.
5. Other people's property.
6. Shared equity.
7. Zero-coupon bonds financing.
8. Split funding.
9. Future rent.
10. Management interest.
11. Three-party blanket.

Each of these techniques has its own niche in real estate financing, as well as its own specific kind of problems. While I don't intend to spend as much time on these techniques as I have on other forms of financing in this book, by now you should have a good understanding of how to take a creative concept and apply it to your own specific problem, using, as a model, some of the other techniques thus far discussed.

I follow the same pattern in each of the 11 financing methods in this chapter as well as the four techniques in the following chapter to make it easier for you to assimilate the form of the technique and its problems. This form will:

1. Give a brief definition of the technique.
2. Give an example.
3. Show several fine points to the method.
4. Show the pitfalls to the technique.

The Sliding Mortgage

The sliding mortgage technique is when you slide a mortgage from one property to another. In essence, you replace the security to the debt with another asset. By moving that specific debt from one property, you are substituting collateral. The new collateral may be other real estate or some other asset or element that has value. This technique is a very good tool to use in several different kinds of transactions. One situation would be when you want to assume a favorable existing mortgage because of its term, interest rate, or other provisions but at the same time, you want to take out new financing. If you can move the existing mortgage over to another property or asset, you can accomplish that task, and often buy a property without having to invest any of your own capital. If you have purchased a property and the seller is to hold a purchase money mortgage, ask for the right to slide that mortgage to another property that was of equal or greater value. By obtaining this right you have more flexibility with the purchased property. This technique is often best set up when you purchase a property and the seller holds a first or secondary mortgage. A simply written provision in the mortgage document can establish this flexibility. If your own lawyer is drafting the mortgage document for the seller's review, have him include a provision that will allow you to accomplish this. As most sellers have never heard of this potential, be ready to carefully explain it with an example or two.

EXAMPLE 1: PAVING THE WAY FOR THE FUTURE.   Christie purchased a small block of apartments from Roger. The property had an older interest-only first mortgage that had only four years to go before it ballooned. To help make the deal, Roger had agreed to hold a second mortgage in the amount of $300,000 so that Christie would not have to come up with more than 15 percent cash at the closing. Christie had her lawyer draw up the second mortgage document with a provision that said something like this:

> This mortgage will allow the mortgagor or assigns to substitute the collateral of this loan with any other property or asset that meets the criteria of this paragraph. Those factors are listed below:
>
> • Notice of the mortgagor's intention to make a substitution of collateral must be given to the mortgagee in writing mailed or sent by Federal Express or the U.S. Mail with notice of delivery.

- There is no outstanding late payment or other charges due to lessor.
- If the substitute collateral is real property, then there must be clear evidence that there is equity in the property that is three times the outstanding unpaid balance of this mortgage. There may be a first mortgage on that substitute collateral, but it must not exceed 30 percent of the appraised value of the property. Appraisals that will be accepted will be the county tax appraisal and no other. If there is an existing mortgage on the substitute collateral, it cannot have an interest rate of more than 7 percent, and a debt service that exceeds 12 percent of the outstanding balance of that mortgage in any given year.
- Any other asset may also be used as a substitute provided that the mortgagee approves that asset. Said nonreal property asset will be placed in safekeeping at a mutually agreed to place, until the debt to which it is now a substitute collateral has been satisfied.

Naturally, there are many different scenarios that you could include or exclude in such a document. The seller may insist that any substituted collateral move the second mortgage to a first position. That might allow the value to only be twice the amount of the outstanding debt. The idea of substituting collateral works well for the seller too. Any time the seller's position can be improved that would be a positive direction in which to move. Changing a second mortgage that is behind a large first mortgage for a first mortgage in a verifiably acceptable property is an okay thing in my book.

EXAMPLE 2: A CASHLESS TRANSACTION.

Donald has contracted to buy a small home for $303,000. The seller has agreed to the following: A down payment of $55,000, and Donald to assume the existing debt, which consisted of a first mortgage of $128,000 payable over four remaining years at 8 percent interest, and a second mortgage of $120,000 payable over 10 years interest at 6 percent. This second mortgage is held by the previous seller and was initially a 15-year mortgage.

Donald's plans are to tie up the property, give himself an out in case his plan fails, then go to the former owner of the property who is now holding this below-market second mortgage and offer to slide it to another property. If he is successful, Donald would then anticipate some minor fix-up of the home. He would refinance the transaction at closing by putting a new first mortgage on the home at the maximum percent loan to value. This would allow him to pay off the existing first mortgage and give the seller his $55,000 cash, cover the cost of the transaction, and if all goes well pocket some cash at the same time.

The Deal Progresses. The small home appraises out at $310,500. Donald gets 70 percent financing on the $303,000 purchase price, or a total of $212,100. The former owner of the home agrees to slide the mortgage over to a free and clear lot Donald owns, which he will sell or build on, and which has a real, fair value of $160,500. To give the mortgagee a bonus, Donald will prepay him $5,000 principal against the amount owed on that loan. The former owner is no longer in a second position, has gotten some cash, and has strong value behind his loan so he has improved his situation. Because he has moved $120,000 of the total purchase price to his vacant lot, the total remaining is $183,000 ($303,000 less the $120,000). He closes on the new mortgage and the house and divides up the proceeds of the new first mortgage.

The cash from the loan goes:

To the seller	$ 55,000
To pay off the first mortgage	128,000
To the former owner, now mortgagee on the lot	5,000
Loan and closing costs	3,800
To Donald's pocket (tax-free, too)	$ 20,300
	$212,100

Donald has improved his position in several ways. He took a good mortgage with good terms and put it on a vacant lot that will help him sell the lot if he so desires. He has pulled out some of his equity from the lot without having to go to a lender and take out a mortgage. Many lenders don't like to make vacant lot loans either, so the deal worked several benefits other than getting Donald the home and cash in his pocket.

The lender came into the deal and made a usual 70 percent loan. From the lender's point of view, it was a good deal. The former owner also benefits by moving to a first position and putting $5,000 in his pocket. Everyone is happy.

Fine-Tune the Sliding Mortgage Transaction. To fine-tune this deal might be tough. However, other deals might not be as clear as this and need some finesse. Getting the mortgagee to want to move to another security is not always easy. If they think they can block the deal by staying put and require you to pay them off, they sometimes will do exactly that.

Setting up a purchase to allow your mortgages to be slid to another security is one way of helping a prospective buyer to come along and take you out of a property when it is time for you to sell. After all, the seller in this example got what he wanted: cash.

EXAMPLE 3: A FUTURE SUBSTITUTION OF COLLATERAL.   You have made an offer to buy a vacant lot on which you think you may build a small office building in a few years. The seller has agreed to hold an $80,000 first mortgage for a period of 15 years payable interest only for five years then interest plus a small principal payment so that at the end of the term there is a balloon of $50,000. The interest rate is only 7 percent, which was part of the seller's plan. You didn't negotiate too hard on the price because you got great terms. In this seller's situation, as will happen with sellers who are looking to set up an income stream for a period of years, it would not be difficult to include a sliding mortgage provision in the contract. To give you a second version of how this can be drafted, here is how one client drafted the purchase offer:

> . . . and furthermore, the mortgage will contain a provision that allows the mortgagor to slide the mortgage to a substitute collateral at any time during the term of the mortgage, provided that the mortgagor is current and not in default in this mortgage and that other provisions of this paragraph are met. The substitute collateral shall be the replacement security of this mortgage, providing that the substitute collateral meets the following criteria: (1) the collateral is real property located within the State of Florida, (2) has an appraised value equal to 150 percent of the outstanding principal of the mortgage, (3) has no secondary debt against the property, and borrower agrees not to place any secondary debt against the property.

If there is a dispute by the holder of the mortgage as to the value of the substitute collateral, the mortgagor will present an appraisal made by a MAI registered appraiser. This would show the current market value of the property; if the holder of the mortgage continues to dispute the value, the mortgagee will have a period of 60 days to present his or her own appraisal made by another MAI registered appraiser. If the mortgagee's appraiser shall be the deciding appraisal, and if the value shown by said appraisal does not equal 150 percent of the loan balance, the mortgagor may, at his option, slide the mortgage to the new collateral by reducing the outstanding debt to such a level as to not exceed the 150 percent of loan balance.

To establish mortgages that can be slid to other collateral is not too difficult if you have the mortgage drafted to allow it. The difficult part of this is to get the mortgagee of an existing mortgage to allow this to occur.

The mortgagee needs the control of the future collateral by having a qualified appraiser show him or her real value of the property. At the same time, as mortgagor, you have the right to pay down the mortgage if the appraisal did not clearly show the value of the new property was sufficient to meet the criteria of the contract. It should be clear that if the mortgage principal outstanding was $50,000 that the value of the property needs only to be $75,000. If the appraisal presented by the mortgagee showed the property to be worth $60,000 then the maximum amount that the mortgage could be would be $40,000. Being able to slide a $40,000 mortgage at great terms to this other property may still be worthwhile to you.

BENEFITS TO THE MORTGAGEE TO SLIDING A MORTGAGE IN THIS EXAMPLE

- If he or she holds a junior mortgage, it becomes a first mortgage.
- Will have a more favorable value-to-loan ratio.
- May have a chance to renegotiate the terms of the loan.
- Might be the term that entices the buyer to take the property.

PITFALLS IN SLIDING MORTGAGES.   There are not too many pitfalls for the investor other than the risk that he or she has if they have overextended the capability of the property to carry the new debt. If Donald is able to unload his lot quickly, however, now that he has some attractive financing to assist that purchase, he will have made a very satisfactory transaction.

The big risk comes to the mortgagee that is allowing his or her mortgage security to be shifted from something he or she knows to something he or she doesn't know. Yet, by being careful in this matter, that problem can be safely covered. Donald, by the way, as will you, knows of many other ways to entice the mortgagee to slide. Both sides of a transaction can use the sliding mortgage technique, and both sides need to make sure that the mortgage document takes into consideration every likely problem that might come up—another very good reason to have a good real estate lawyer on your team.

Double Finance

Double finance is simply the application of two or more techniques of finance to allow the buyer to maximize the financing and minimize the capital invested. In many situations, like Donald by using the Sliding Mortgage technique, he also refinanced with a conventional lender, obtaining more than 100 percent financing. The surplus went into his pocket, or to be used as a down payment for another property.

EXAMPLE 4: TWO OR MORE TECHNIQUES COMBINED.   Frank needed $800,000 to purchase a strip store complex that consisted of 25,000 square feet of shops. He wanted to upgrade the center at an estimated cost of $100,000 and hoped to be able to buy the property and do the fix-up with no more than a total cash outlay of $75,000.

Several Creative Tools Frank Used to Meet His Objectives. Frank knew that, as in all financing techniques, he had to have control of the property, so he went to contract with the seller, which gave him a period of 90 days in which to obtain all the financing required to close on the transaction.

Have a clear understanding with the seller on the terms. In this instance, those terms were the following:

1. Price of $800,000.
2. With the price broken into two segments:
   - The improvements (at $600,000)
   - The land (at $200,000)
3. The land would be optioned at $200,000.
4. Frank would lease the land for $18,500 per year with increases in the rent as per a cost-of-living index every three years. The land lease would be subordinated to

a new first mortgage not to exceed 80 percent of the appraised value of land and improvements. The improvements would be paid: $425,000 cash at closing and the remainder of $175,000 in an exchange for some land Frank owns in a growing area west of town.

Make all the estimates of work needed to make the needed improvements prior to talking to any lenders about new financing.

Present the total package to the lenders. Frank knew that if he showed the improvements and how that would allow him to increase the rents substantially and thereby increase the value, the loan to Frank should be more than enough to take care of the cash requirements.

Frank was sure he would be able to show an appraised value of $1 million based on the improvements he plans. Based on this, he would be able to obtain a new loan of $800,000.

A quick review of Frank's cash flow showed that he would need $425,000 to pay off the seller and $100,000 to fix up the property. This would leave Frank with $275,000 cash in his pocket. Even after the loan costs, he would have sufficient money to buy the land if he wanted. On the other hand, if the property could support the debt service, Frank might be better off taking the cash and buying more real estate.

PITFALLS IN DOUBLE FINANCING.   The pitfalls of double financing are the same as any overleveraged property. Frank might be correct in his assessment that once the center is fixed up he can get more rent and afford a greater debt service. However, if he was cutting things short, and there was a delay in construction, or some unforeseen problem came up that caused the plan to go awry, then Frank might need to dig into his own pocket and meet the heavy debt payments. If he had already spent his bankroll then his house of cards may be on the way down.

FOUR STEPS TO AVOID THE PITFALLS OF DOUBLE FINANCING

1. Know and understand your own goals and where you are in your path toward them. How much risk can you absorb?

2. Fully understand the nature of the property and its projected cash based on projections that may require events to happen over which you may have no control.

3. Have a long-range plan that fits your goals. Are you keeping to that plan? Does the plan have safeguards?

4. Learn money management. Start by watching each dollar spent and don't let your income drop below your cash outlay without knowing full well the reasons for it, and have some plan to reverse that situation.

The Glue Transaction

A glue transaction is any financial transaction that occurs where the *glue* person puts up his good name and/or credit to a transaction and other parties put up the initial cash, or bring the deal together for a piece of the transaction. This is the basis of many joint ventures where the money partners put up all the cash just to do a transaction with a glue person or glue entity. It is important to recognize that in the glue deal the money person or people come to the glue person and not the other way around.

EXAMPLE 5: GLUE MAKES THE MONEY STICK. Insurance companies often seek out top developers or investors in an area to join them as joint venture partners. The insurance company puts up the money, and the developer does what he or she has been doing for years, only this time has a built-in source for loans, plus a partner.

As you develop your knowledge of your comfort zone area, you will begin to recognize opportunities for investment. As you add to that knowledge, the techniques of investing and financing found in this book and in other sources such as seminars, books, tapes, college courses, or night adult courses, you will begin to demonstrate that you are confident in your abilities in real estate investing. Each time you find some area in which you are weak, act to improve in that area and remove that weakness. All of this can and will happen if you want it to, and if you understand that it is not an overnight process and there is no single source, no magic key that can unlock your future without your direct and continual growth and action. Success in anything is enhanced when you are proactive in seeking the path to your goals.

A recent transaction that I participated in as a broker was an assembly of an entire block of real estate in the downtown area of Fort Lauderdale, Florida. This assembly was the long-term effort of dealing with a relatively large number of property owners. As it is with this kind of case, the culmination of the deal is often dependent on getting the signature of the final person, or who we generally refer to as "the holdout."

EXAMPLE 6: EVEN LOCAL INVESTORS BENEFIT. Alex has done everything necessary to establish himself as an expert in the area. He has learned his comfort zone like the back of his hand, and has bought several properties in the area and turned them into cash cows (it just sits there cranking out cash like a cow does milk).

Alex's specialty and strength are in finding properties that are underused. He discovered early in his real estate investing that if he could buy a home that was on a lot that would permit multifamily living, he would be able to convert the home into apartments, increasing the income potential, and increase the value by a greater ratio.

Alex knows that each time he converts a property from one use to another he improves the income potential. As income increases so does the value of the property. He is making the best of his investments and is building profits along the way.

All of Alex's success was not going unnoticed by his friends and others in the neighborhood. Some of them had gone to some of those high-priced seminars that promised overnight success, but they ended up having to look in awe at Alex's success. One day one of them got a terrific idea. Why not let Alex help them make money?

This is the first step to a glue deal and for Alex to becoming a *glue person*. Someone recognizes your ability, and then comes to you. You don't go to him or her. If you do go to them first, it isn't a glue deal. It might be a syndication, or a joint venture, or whatever.

SEVEN RULES OF VALUE THAT ALL GLUE PEOPLE FOLLOW

1. All real estate value is related to the actual or potential income from a specific property.

2. Value goes up when the actual or potential income goes up; conversely, value goes down when the actual or potential income decreases.

3. If you can buy a property, when you know ahead of time that the actual or potential income can be increased or is bound to go up, you ensure that there will be increases of value.

4. Value of income property is based on a capitalization rate of a realistically sustained income. That is, if the anticipated yield is of an investor or buyer is 10 percent on actual cash invested and the net operating income is $10,000, the value would be $100,000.

5. Every dollar of increase in net operating income will increase value by the multiple of the capitalization rate. If the cap rate was 10 percent and income went up $2,000, value would go up $20,000.

6. Profit is the increase of equity above your cash investment. If you put $25,000 down on a property worth $125,000 that had a net operating income of $12,500 and you increased that income to $14,500, your value increases to $145,000 ($125,000 plus the $20,000 value increase as described in rule 5). In the beginning, your equity was $25,000. You increased income by 16 percent (16 percent of $12,500 equals $2,000). Your value went up the same percentage. However, your equity increased from $25,000 to $45,000. That is an increase of 80 percent.

7. Learn this kind of math. It works wonders for the pocketbook.

THE GLUE CONTRACT.   When this person contacts you, you will want to enter into an agreement; that is, of course, if you plan to go ahead with the deal. There are some specific elements that you will want to know and understand about the other people involved and the property in question. Most importantly, you have to decide who is going to be in control of the deal. You or them? Each answer will have different specifics to consider, and you will have to examine the total deal to make that judgment. To help you in coming to this decision and to set up the contract between you and the other people, follow this checklist:

Do's and Don'ts of the Glue Person

✓ Do get to know all the other people involved, including wives and husbands alike. When you are in a joint venture of any kind, it can be the hidden partners (the spouses you didn't meet) who can make your life miserable.

✓ Do try to get a feel for their objectives and goals. Keep in mind that one single property may not fill each person's objectives or goals the same, if at all. Will that cause infighting later on? Alternatively, will everyone be happy no matter what?

✓ Do let it be known the moment you feel you want to do the deal that you expect to be compensated handsomely. Keep in mind that they are going to be more demanding later on than now, so if you don't get your piece of the action tied down up front, you may find it slipping away into that dark abyss called poor memory.

✓ Do have the option to buy them out. Set a fair formula so they will always have a profit, and then never take advantage of that agreement unless there is an absolute break-up of the group. Even then, you may want to pass any additional profits (if any) on to them.

✓ Don't let people use your name in some deal over which you have no control. They will ruin your name far more easily than their own.

✓ Don't stick with a sinking ship. If the deal is going sour and they won't get out, make sure you have had the foresight to build in an escape provision for yourself.

✓ Don't help people obtain objectives or goals that are against your own principles. You don't need that kind of money, those headaches, and those sleepless nights.

✓ Don't sign your name to a mortgage unless you have a majority control and interest in the property, and have absolute confidence in your abilities, and the full understanding and potential of the property.

✓ Do insist on terms and conditions that deal with any shortfall in the income to meet the debt service. This is critical and you need to be strict (and swift) to enforce the penalty to investors who do not meet their obligation. One such penalty is that if they falter at that critical moment and don't pay their share of a shortfall, you can take their interest and sell it to cover that shortfall. In hard times, if you are the only one with money in your pocket you may have a hard time getting your partners on the phone.

✓ Don't hesitate to enforce any penalties on your partners. That is only sound business, and if you try to struggle through it may put the whole project in trouble and your future as well.

✓ Don't let this keep you from doing a glue transaction. They can be great, and if you approach each deal with the knowledge that you can make a profit doing something you know and love to do, and help others too, then why not? You will find that by taking on some partners you may be able to buy a larger property than you would have by yourself. This can allow you to grow in confidence and ability and take you to more and greater opportunities.

PITFALLS IN GLUE TRANSACTIONS.   Pitfalls in glue transactions occur mostly when you don't know much about your partners and/or their goals. As long as you follow the checklist and avoid overextending your own abilities or failing to get compensated properly for your time and effort, you should be okay.

Discounted Paper

Discounted paper is notes or mortgages that you buy or create and use in a transaction at a discount. Generally, this transaction is done to improve the sales potential of the property, which is security for the to-be-discounted paper, or as a way to get the seller to reduce your down payment.

EXAMPLE 7: BUYERS USE DISCOUNTED PAPER TO CLOSE TRANSACTIONS.   You want to buy a home but do not have the cash down the seller wants. You do own a small apartment building that is presently financed with a low (loan-to-value) first mortgage. You go to the seller and offer to give her a second mortgage on the apartment building you have been thinking of selling in the near future and you create such a mortgage in the offer, but it does not exist. In your offer, you make reference to this second mortgage as follows:

> . . . said second mortgage having, at the closing of this transaction a principal balance outstanding of $150,000 and is payable at a term of 120 months remaining and is payable at 5 percent interest only, to balloon at the end of the term.

You offer the seller $50,000 cash and this second mortgage. This looks like you have offered a value of $200,000. However, the seller of the house does some calculations on the math of that mortgage and tells you that the interest rate is so low that she cannot value the mortgage at $150,000.

You ask her if she would take the mortgage anyway if you increased your cash down by $20,000. In essence, discount the mortgage by $20,000. This would increase the return on the mortgage to 6.33 percent. The seller agrees and you close on the deal.

The benefit to you is double. First, you need only invest $70,000 of your own money in the new house, and you have put a great second loan on the apartment building, which may now help entice a buyer. Within these same amounts of money, is there something else you could have offered? What if instead of increasing your cash at closing, you had offered to pay a bonus to the second mortgage of $2,000 a year? This is still a form of discounting the mortgage, but now, as you are planning to sell the apartment building you can benefit even more. Once the building is sold, the new owner will be making the payments at 6.33 percent instead of you.

EXAMPLE 8: GOOD FINANCING ON WHAT YOU BUY AND WHAT YOU WANT TO SELL.

Lou is interested in buying a condo so that he and his wife, and their little dog, can live close to his business a few blocks away. At the same time, Lou has decided he would like to sell a motel he owns on the beach. The motel is already financed with both a first and second mortgage. If Lou were to use the discounted paper as a technique in this deal, he would need to create a third mortgage on the motel at reasonable interest and pay-back terms, and then offer the mortgage to the seller of the condo as part of the contract. To make the mortgage more attractive, Lou would be quick to discount the mortgage so that it would give a better yield to the seller.

Lou would want to keep the terms and payback of the mortgage as light as possible because he has to make the payments until he sells the motel. If the terms are attractive, the mortgage may make the motel more saleable, and at a higher price, too.

Since debt payments distract from the ultimate cash return of any investor, whoever buys the motel will want to keep the debt payments as low as possible, thereby increasing the cash return. If Lou creates a $75,000 mortgage that is payable over 15 years at 9 percent interest, the mortgage payment would be $750.69 per month, or $9,008.28 per year.

Lou makes his deal on the condo using this mortgage as part of that transaction, as though it were cash, but had to offer the seller of the condo an improved yield of 10 percent. In this case, the actual face value of the mortgage would be $75,000, but, because of the discount, Lou would only get credit for $70,788.75. You may want to review the chapter on mortgage discounts to learn the math to use in obtaining this discount. A quick review of what happened follows.

The mortgage Lou creates is for $75,000, 15 years, with monthly payments of $750.69 (see the mortgage rate Table A: under 9 percent for 15 years: 12.171; multiply this times $75,000 to get the annual total of the 12 monthly payments or $9,128.25; divide by 12 to get the monthly payment of $750.69).

The condo seller wants a 10 percent yield. To find the discount, you take the constant rate at the face amount (12.171 from the foregoing calculations), and divide it by the constant rate for the yield wanted. To find the constant at 10 percent, look at Table A in the Appendix under 10 percent for 15 years to find 12.895. Divide 12.171 by 12.895 to get the discount of 0.94385, which means that 94.385 percent of the face amount of the mortgage will be the discount needed to give a yield of 10 percent. Multiply the original mortgage of $75,000 by 0.94385 to get $70,788.75, which is the discount amount that Lou would get credit for at the closing on the condo.

Why would Lou do this? One reason is to make the deal without having to add that much cash to the condo deal. It might also have been that Lou was using this technique to be able to take cash out of the condo through new financing. However, one additional benefit occurs with the financing on the motel.

Lou might find that in the mortgage market, a third mortgage on the motel would not be available through normal sources. If Lou leaves the mortgage off the motel, all that does is increase his equity and gives a prospective buyer additional areas to negotiate. In the end, it might reduce Lou's ultimate profit or price in the transaction. In addition, to make the deal Lou might have to end up holding a mortgage like that himself, and that would put him back into the position of having to pay cash for the condo now. After all, the condo seller wants to satisfy his primary goal, the sale of the condo. If he is willing to take the paper at a discount, then let him.

Lou knows that a realistic third mortgage on the motel might be at a rate closer to 12.5 percent or higher. A $75,000 mortgage for 15 years at 12.5 percent would have an annual payment of $11,092.50, which is $1,964.25 more than the payment on the mortgage Lou has set up. Let's go back to the value rules for a second. Remember, if the cap rate the buyer wants when he buys the motel is (say) 10 percent, the added cash in the investor's pocket due to Lou's smart move with the condo seller would be $1,964.25, which is worth $19,642.50 in value. Lou traded the mortgage at a discount for less than $4,300 and gets back an extra $19,642.50 or so from the motel sale. He has accomplished this with no expense to himself in the end. Since the seller of the condo is happy and Lou is happy, so would the buyer of the motel be who now has to invest less cash to make the motel profitable.

These are just a few examples of mortgage discounts as transaction makers. You will have to examine all other potentials that may present them. By rereading the chapter on mortgage discounting and by applying these concepts to other techniques, you will come up with many different methods of using this highly creative tool. You should always remember that the tradeoff (Lou's first discount to the condo owner) between the discount and the benefit of the good terms (the sale of the motel) should be designed to work in your favor.

PITFALLS IN DISCOUNTED MORTGAGES.   Remember the baker who thought a dozen was 13? Well, when it comes to the mathematics of finance, you have to be sure you are using proper math. When you calculate yields in mortgages, you will find that due to the multiples of cap rates or the kind of amortization schedule you are using, a small error in the formula is exaggerated with the end result you may get. I discovered just recently that a calculator I had been using was rounding off its built-in formula on amortization schedules to the point that in a sizable mortgage discount the end result could be substantially off. For that reason, I suggest that you use the following step to check your calculator's built-in finance programs to see if you are getting correct answers to your math problems.

Solve this following problem using your calculator.

1. Calculate the monthly payment on a $150,000 mortgage payable over 30 years (360 months) at 12 percent per annum (1 percent per month). Write down the monthly payment your calculator shows you.

2. Now, go to Table A in the Appendix. Look for the constant rate that corresponds to 12 percent interest for 30 years. That constant rate is 12.343. Convert the constant percentage to a mathematical number by moving the decimal left so that you now have 0.12343.

3. Multiply that times the mortgage amount ($150,000 × 0.12343 = $18,514.50). The result, $18,514.50, is the annual total of the 12 monthly payments.

4. Now divide the annual total by 12 to get $1,542.87 as the monthly payment.

5. Compare this last answer with the answer on your calculator. If your calculator gave you anything more than a couple of dollars less than $1,542.87, then it is rounding off decimals to the extent that you are obtaining improper and potentially damaging information.

Take the calculator back to the shop where you bought it and get your money back. Alternatively, use it just to add, multiply, divide, and subtract. You can use the tables in this book to obtain more accurate information. Keep in mind that if you get an answer that is very close to the $1,542.87 it could be that you have a calculator that is carrying the problem to more decimal places than the table, in which case you are in good shape.

You can find out by taking the monthly payment you get and working back to the constant rate. Assume you got $1,543.13 as your monthly payment from your calculator. Multiply that by 12 to get the annual amount, which is $18,517.56. Divide that by the amount of the mortgage ($150,000) to get your constant rate in a mathematical form, which would be 0.1234504 more or less. If your calculator shows 0.1234 or 0.12345, you have a good financial calculator and can work with it to obtain accurate calculations.

Using discounts properly will depend on your use of this kind of math. Do not rely on a banker or mortgage broker to come up with these calculations, for you may be getting wrong information if they have an old calculator that is rounding everything off.

Other People's Property

Some people say that the way to true riches is to invest as little of your own cash as possible and as much of other people's money (OPM) as available. Buying real estate using other people's property, and not their cash, is a technique where you use an asset that isn't yours as security to acquire something of your own.

Using other people's property (OPP) would mean buying, exchanging, or leasing property where you give as all or part of the equity in the transaction a property you do not currently own. This can be accomplished through mortgages, exchange, or barter. Unlike the concept of buying with OPM, you can use other people's property as a method of acquiring the real estate you want to own. This works if you keep in mind that it is benefits that count, and any benefit can have the same importance to a transaction as its money equivalency. In fact, sometimes the benefit is more acceptable because it pushes the hot button.

EXAMPLE 9: PART CASH, PART EXCHANGE.   Dominic wanted to buy a vacant lot on which he planned to build a small apartment building. The price of the lot was $55,000. Dominic offered to pay $20,000 cash out of the apartment building's final draw on the construction loan. For the balance of $35,000 he agreed to give the seller a vacant lot in the Florida Keys. This was okay, only the Florida Keys lot was not owned by Dominic. Dominic had made a side deal with that owner to exchange for the lot, giving the lot owner one of the condo apartments to be built on the lot.

EXAMPLE 10: PART CASH, PART MORTGAGE.   Jane wanted to buy a home in Charleston. As a part of her deal, she offered the seller a second mortgage on a mountain home in the Beech Mountain area of North Carolina. Jane didn't own that home, her mother did. She had made a deal with her mother to take a piece of the action on the Charleston home when it was sold.

EXAMPLE 11: PART CASH, PART BARTER.   Roger, a good handyman kind of investor, offered a two-week holiday every year for the next five years as part of an OPP transaction. The resort was actually a timeshare facility in the Bahamas. The owner of the property Roger wanted to buy would be getting a solid $15,000 to $30,000 value depending on how many people actually traveled. Of course, Roger didn't own the resort, but he had made a side deal with a friend who owned a large block of timeshare weeks at the resort. Roger's barter to this person was $20,000 worth of carpenter time.

In each of these examples, the buyer knew of someone who had something that could be offered as a part of another transaction. It is likely that you will have no problem finding someone whom you could use, if the opportunity came up, as an OPP part of the deal.

You can go out and find a few people right now who have property they would sell to you under the kind of terms that would work. These terms could range anywhere from their taking a second position in the property you buy, holding some other security, or just becoming a partner with you in the deal. Line some of these people up and have them ready and willing when the time comes.

Parents and relatives may not be the best place to go to get them to "lend you" one of their properties, unless you are ready to give up a piece of the action on the property.

For example, meet some rental apartment owners in your area that own and operate tourist types of rentals. They will have units that are vacant during specific times of the year as a natural course to their business. Those people will make deals with you. The best way to make an enemy out of a relative is to use that person or their assets to the point where you profit at their expense. If you deal with a relative, give him or her some added benefit. It might be the depreciation available from the income property you own or end up purchasing, or it might be a percent of the ultimate sale in the future.

PITFALLS IN USING OTHER PEOPLE'S PROPERTY TRANSACTIONS. The biggest pitfall is not having the deal with the other property already worked out in advance. Have it up front, and have it in writing. Working on good faith, you are apt to go out and cut a deal with a seller only to find that your brother in-law now says, "Hey now, Charlie, I don't remember saying you could have that lot of mine up in Maine to use in buying that run-down fish cannery."

Make sure that the plus and downsides are covered. Never make an OPP deal without the other property owner understanding his or her risk. If it is slight or limited to temporary use of the other property, be sure you spell it out.

Shared Equity

Throughout the history of real estate, people have shared property. Several dozen families live in this cave, half a dozen in another. Families rent houses together, cohabit in apartments, and in general have become comfortable with the idea of sharing property. Using this as a basis for a form of financing, can become a good closing tool in certain deals.

In a shared equity transaction, you "sell" your property to a tenant, who will get a percentage of the equity at the time of a future sale. Alternatively, you can be the tenant who goes to the owner to set up the deal whereby you improve the property for a future profit. In turn, the owner gives you a reduced rent and you both profit in the future.

EXAMPLE 12: LOCK IN A TENANT. You own a couple of rental homes that are just too far away for you to bother with them. You go to the tenants in each and offer them the same deal. If they will buy the property they are now leasing, you will let them close with zero cash down, and reduce their monthly payments at the same time. The real bonus is, that at the end of five years, or sooner if you both agree, the property will be put on the market and sold. The tenant will get 50 percent (this is open for negotiation by both sides) of the profit. Profit to be determined as all cash left over after the deduction of closing costs, the purchase money mortgage you established at the time of the sale. As one further condition to the transaction, each tenant must agree to fix up the property according to a very detailed list of improvements.

You agree to pay for any items needed for the fix-up (to be added to the balance of the purchase money mortgage), and the tenant is to do all the work. Each tenant accepts the deal and you draw up the papers and close.

If this property is in a state that has a Homestead exemption for the purpose of real estate taxes, the fact that the owner of the property now lives in the home will reduce the annual tax bill. As either you or the tenant was paying the bill before, this is a benefit from the deal.

EXAMPLE 13: LOCK UP THE LANDLORD.   You have been living in a condominium apartment owned by Craig. It is an okay apartment but needs work. You are a salesman for a home decorating firm and have access to just about everything it would take to fix up this apartment. You go to Craig and show him a very detailed list of improvements, and the retail cost of the improvements plus labor to accomplish the fix-up. You also show Craig the potential sales profit a year or two from now when the apartment will be finished. You tell Craig that you will do all the work, and pay for all the materials if you are allowed to take the cost of the materials out of your rent. The labor part will give you a 50 percent interest in any profit that is above a price the two of you agree is the present value of the apartment. Your actual cost of the materials is about half of what the retail cost is, so you benefit there. Craig gets a good deal too, if you do a good job. His downside is some loss of rent, but if the apartment doesn't sell, and you move out, then he is left with a fixed-up apartment.

EXAMPLE 14: BUY, FIX UP, AND SELL TRANSACTIONS.   Saul is going out and tying up properties that he wants to buy. He has been doing his homework and has found properties owned by motivated sellers on which he has negotiated excellent prices. One such property is a home that he can buy for $245,000. It needs a little work, and Saul plans to spend $5,000 on the property.

Thus far, the deal is that Saul is buying the property. Assume that he is able to spend the $5,000 to paint and fix up the property and the seller agrees to hold an unsecured note for $30,000 as part of the $245,000 and get cash for the balance. The note calls for interest only payments of 7 percent annually for six years with a balloon at the end of that term or whenever Saul sells the house, whichever comes first. Saul knows that once the property has been fixed up, it will be worth at least $325,000. He talks to his friendly loan officer at a local savings bank and shows what he is planning to do. The bank approves a loan of $250,000 net of any mortgage and closing costs. The loan will be at 6.75 percent interest for a term of 30 years. However, they will hold back $25,000 (which Saul anticipates his labor and materials in the paint and fix up would be worth if he had to hire other people to do the work). When the work is done the bank will give Saul the held back funds. Here is how things end:

Cash in Saul's pocket	0
Purchase price of the house	$245,000
Less the unsecured note the seller holds	− 35,000
Cash Saul needs to close on the house	$210,000
Amount Saul borrows	$250,000
Amount the bank holds back	− 25,000
Amount the bank pays at the closing of the mortgage	$225,000
Saul pays the seller cash	−210,000
Cash in Saul's pocket as he leaves the closing office	$ 15,000
Cash spent for materials for the fix up of the house	− 5,000
Cash left in Saul's pocket	$ 10,000
Check from bank now that fix-up work is completed	+ 25,000
Cash in Saul's pocket now (Equals what he still owes)	$ 35,000

Remember that Saul still owes the original seller $35,000.

He advertises that the home can be purchased for only 10 percent down at the low price of $350,000. Along comes a prospective buyer, Bill, who has only $30,000 cash, so Saul says he can work it out with that amount but Bill will have to add the extra $5,000 to the purchase price—$30,000 down and the balance of $325,000 in the form of the first mortgage of $250,000 and a second mortgage of $75,000 which will be paid to Saul over 15 years. Here is how the transaction looks:

The deal is signed and the buyer gives Saul	$ 30,000
Assumes the total debt which is made up of the 2 mortgages	+325,000
Total Transaction	$ 355,000

Here is what Saul made from this deal once he pays off the $35,000 note to the seller of the house he fixed up and resold:

Price of the house (which includes the $35,000 note)	$245,000
Cost of materials	+ 5,000
Total cost	$250,000
Total profit is ($75,000 mortgage + $30,000 down)	$105,000

How Saul's Deal Might Have Been Structured. How would the deal look if Saul had made up the mortgage in a different way? Instead of letting the buyer assume the existing $250,000 mortgage and adding on the balance due to Saul of $75,000, what if he made the $325,000 by using the following scenario:

Existing first mortgage	$250,000
Note to original seller	35,000
A second mortgage	+ 40,000
Total debt	$325,000

Now Saul doesn't have to pay back the $35,000 note to the original seller; he can let the new buyer do that at the end of six years. That puts an extra $35,000 in Saul's pocket at the closing as he now holds a $40K mortgage instead of $75K.

EXAMPLE 15: PULL OUT EQUITY, LOCK IN TENANT.   Francisco owned a small condo for a couple of years and learned of the shared-equity kind of transaction. He put a maximum mortgage on the property to pull out tax-free cash. Francisco had placed a $125,000 new mortgage on the property, and as the "shared equity" was based on the value of $160,000, the "partner" in the deal with Francisco would benefit only above the equity of $35,000 ($160,000 value less the $125,000 mortgage equals $35,000 equity). In essence, Francisco would be paid the first $35,000 above the mortgage at the time of the sale and then both Francisco and the "partner" would split the balance as would be agreed. All the tenant had to do was live in the apartment and maintain it in like-new condition. Francisco had a list of simple repairs and some fix up that could be done on weekends. The tenant would pay "rent" that was equal to the mortgage payments, taxes, and insurance, which totaled about half of what a comparable rent would be for that apartment. The worst-case scenario would be that the property would not sell and the tenant would have to move out after the initial lease of three years.

What Makes Shared Equity Deals Work. The motivation in these transactions seems to be the ability to entice "buyers" through the nothing-down concept. Property owners feel that a tenant who thinks she is building up equity will be a better tenant and that the long-range profit will be greater for both parties than if the comparison is to "rent only."

In Francisco's deal, he has already taken out the majority of the equity tax-free, and he likes the thought of keeping the tax shelter for a couple of years longer. In addition, and the real plus factor for Francisco, it would be unlikely that he could sell this condo for $160,000 in the current marketplace anyway.

PITFALLS IN SHARED EQUITY TRANSACTIONS.   Whenever you approach a technique with the idea of pulling the wool over someone's eyes, you are apt to have problems. While the shared-equity format can work nicely for both parties, most of the transactions I have seen have been based on the dumber than dumb concept. In this type of transaction, the temptation to "boost" the current values to above the current marketplace is great or there are gullible buyers who are used to renting because they never have enough cash for a down payment, or their credit is below 200. It is possible to entice these people to the deal. What sounds like lower rent really is not because the property owner is getting repairs at a cheap price. In addition, because the tenant-come-carpenter feels he is building up equity the rent becomes steadier.

Once the tenant moves in and begins to realize that he is paying more rent than everyone else in the building, or if there is a decline in the market and he sees values dropping or people offering to sell similar apartments at lower prices than his "base equity for participation," this "buyer" becomes very disgruntled. Disgruntled tenants have been known to move to Texas in the middle of the night, taking with them refrigerators, carpets, drapes, sinks, ranges, and light fixtures, nailed down or not, some even dump a bag or two of concrete down the toilet.

Of course, you and Saul and the rest of the people doing shared equity deals might be giving your "buyers" the best deal in town. In addition, if that is the case, your problems will be small ones.

Zero-Coupon Financing

Zero coupons are a function that stockbrokers and bond dealers use. The essence of this kind of financial transaction on the stock or bond market is that the instrument sold is a note, bond, or debt obligation that has an original face value, and that no payments are made against the debt for a period of years, then the debt balloons.

EXAMPLE 16: BASIC ZERO-COUPON BOND.   Ace Corporation sells $5,000,000 worth of zero-coupon-debt obligations that are divided into certificates or debt instruments of $100,000 each. This means there are 50 of these separate obligations being sold. The obligation carries an interest rate of 10 percent per year, but Ace makes no payments until the final balloon payment when all debt and interest comes due at the same time, five years later. This payment would be the accumulation of all interest compounded for the five years and would total $1,611,051.00 in interest plus the original $5 million.

In the marketplace, these kinds of investments either sell at a price that would give the holder the actual yield stated (10 percent in the above example), or a yield over or under that yield, depending on the quality of the debt and the interest rate demanded by the market.

ZERO-COUPON FINANCING IN REAL ESTATE.   When this zero payment of interest or principal formula is applied to real estate, it can have some very interesting results.

Example 17: Two Zero Coupons Put Cash in Buyer's Pocket.   Brad had negotiated with Frances to buy her home, and they were very close to making a deal. Frances didn't need any cash, but didn't want to do a deal that wasn't secure for her. The price was agreeable to both parties: $300,000.

The property had a first mortgage that Brad could assume in the amount of $150,000. What was in question was the balance. Brad offered to give Frances a note that had a single payment at the end of 15 years of $150,000. In addition, he would give her right now a zero-coupon bond that would pay another $150,000 at the end of 15 years. Frances didn't need the cash, so she took the deal by putting the note and the bond in the names of her three grandchildren for their college fund.

Brad closed on the deal by putting a new first mortgage on the home for $189,000. He paid off the existing $150,000, bought a 15-year zero-coupon bond that would pay off at $150,000 for $35,000, and paid for the mortgage with the balance. Brad had no thought of keeping the house for 15 years, so wasn't concerned about the other payment of $150,000 down the road 15 years from now. He expected that appreciation in the property would ultimately give him a profit, and pay off the amount owed Frances.

Frances didn't do all that badly. The total amount owed to her of $150,000 would turn into $300,000 at the end of the 15 years. If she did not have a taxable gain in the property she would not have to worry about having cash out of the deal to pay off Uncle Sam. The income would not come in for 15 years, so unless she sold the debt to someone else, the interest would simply accumulate. Her actual yield on the $150,000 would be slightly less than 5 percent. While not high, she might not do better in savings, and the fact that the deal solved her problem had a certain value. She might have been ready to drop her price to a point that the outstanding would only be $100,000 so the $300,000 return was really a yield of 7.6 percent.

Fine Points in Using Zero-Coupon Financing.   The first step is to learn everything you can about what the bond is and how it increases in value. To do this, you need to understand compound interest. This is interest that is added to the principal. The two factors that govern compound interest are time and interest rate. Time falls into two segments. How often does the interest get added to the principal, so that the principal becomes larger and more interest can be added? If it is annual, the interest is added at the end of each year and the next year would earn interest on the original principal plus interest on the previous interest added. Obviously, monthly is better than annual, and daily is better than monthly. The other time factor to consider is the total duration of the bond. If it is a 10-year bond, it doesn't get paid off until that time; a 30-year bond pays off 30 years down the road, and so on. However, you can sell these bonds prior to that time and take the price someone is willing to pay at that time.

To sell or discount a zero-payment real estate debt is possible. The prices would fluctuate due to market demands as to the yield that investors would expect to earn based on the remaining time on the debt. If there are other higher paying forms of investments than the yield on the debt you want to sell, you may find that you have to take a big discount. If it is a long-term bond that you haven't held for too long, it is possible to lose money selling these forms of debt. On the other hand, if the yield is better than other investments, the face value owed may support a bonus if you sell the debt on the open market.

Some real estate debt is financed by institutional or municipal bonds. Some of these bonds are given tax-free status to entice investors to buy them, despite the low yield interest. These bonds are generally secured by a first mortgage or pool of first mortgages.

PITFALLS IN DEALING WITH ZERO-COUPON DEBT. The biggest pitfall is ending up taking a zero-coupon bond as part of a sale without realizing what its actual "cash out" value is at any future date. Don't fool yourself by taking a 30-year bond that will pay $200,000 30 years from now and think it is currently worth that. If you had to sell it right now, you would be shocked at what you would receive.

On the other hand, if you view the bond as additional security and don't mind sitting back and not getting any return for a while, there are situations in which this form of financing can be attractive.

You may discover that you will have a tax disadvantage taking back a seller a second-party zero-coupon bond. Review your tax circumstance with an accountant prior to accepting any zero-coupon mortgage when you sell a property. You may discover you have a tax to pay that is greater than your cash down.

The buyer has little to worry about as long as he or she understands what is going on. Too many people get caught up in the use of a technique without really understanding what is going on. Don't let that happen to you by using zero-coupons incorrectly.

Split Funding

Split funding is a psychological approach to payment. It gives the buyer the opportunity to say, "I'll pay you what you want as a down payment; only, I'll pay it when I'm good and ready to." Sometimes this works, sometimes it is good for the seller, not only the buyer.

Split funding occurs when the buyer splits the down payment or purchase price into more than one payment, but where the total of all the payments never add up to more than the original amount. In essence, a payment over a period of time without any interest added in. Simply, a payment split into two or more increments.

EXAMPLE 18: BASIC SPLIT FUNDING. The seller is asking $500,000 with $200,000 down. You start your negotiations by saying, "I'm okay with the $200,000 down. Will you hold a $300,000 first mortgage over 30 years at 8 percent interest with equal payments for the full term?"

The strategy is to move the seller's focus to the terms for the moment. As the seller believes you have agreed to the down payment part of the deal, the seller might soften on the balance. In any event, the negotiations will center around whether or not you pay on a $300,000 mortgage or a $250,000 mortgage. The terms will eventually sort themselves out.

Once you and the seller have a mutual agreement on that, you have the final draft of the agreement made. It contains a provision that now spells out the split funding of the down payment, something like the following:

> . . . and as has been agreed, the buyer will pay a down payment of $200,000 as follows: at closing there will be an initial payment of $100,000, and each year thereafter for a term of four years, an additional payment of $25,000 until the entire down payment of $200,000 has been met.

Will you have more negotiations over this kind of payment? You might, and you might not. The cost to the seller at this point, if money is worth 8 percent, would be a loss of interest of $20,000 before taxes. If the seller is in a 30 percent tax bracket, the cost to the seller is only $14,000 in total. Of course, cost is not the only criteria, as the buyer has now bought the property with only $100,000 down. If this is an income-producing property, much of the annual $25,000 of split-funded down payments can be met by income. That is very good for the buyer.

EXAMPLE 19: GIVE THE SELLER WHAT HE WANTS.

You have offered Bob, a seller of a small office building you want to buy, a purchase price of $250,000. The terms of your offer consist of $25,000 down with your assumption of the existing first mortgage of $150,000. Bob will hold a second mortgage for the balance of $75,000 for seven years at 8 percent interest.

He objects, as would many sellers, to the low down payment and the high second mortgage. He insists on a $50,000 down payment.

Using the split funding method, you would meet his objection with a positive statement: "Okay, Bob, I'll pay the $250,000 price; I'll give you a $50,000 second mortgage for nine years at 9½ percent. Now, instead of the $75,000 second mortgage it will only be $50,000. Okay?"

While he is beaming, you go on to explain the full details of your counteroffer. "Here's how we'll handle the down payment. We will 'split fund' the payment as follows: At closing, I'll give you $25,000 and at the end of 18 months the second $25,000. Naturally I will be making payments on the second mortgage each month in addition to this split funding of the down payment."

What you did, of course, was agree to the $50,000 down payment, only you won't pay it all at once. The net effect of this split fund is it will give you an opportunity to obtain some other financing during that 18-month period, or at least collect some income on the building to help make the payment. For Bob, it took an additional $25,000 from the mortgage and got it into his pocket earlier which results in a benefit to both parties.

How to Fine-Tune the Split-Funded Payment. There are several fine points to this example that you should look at now. First, you show no interest on the second $25,000 payment. This is a matter subject to negotiation between you and Bob. If you can get away with no interest, great. There is no law that says you have to show or provide interest on this kind of payment. From Bob's point of view, the IRS will assume that he received interest in that second payment and that the principal amount was less than $25,000 and the difference was an interest imputed into the deal.

Another factor that generally comes to play whenever you "give in" to the other side's demands is a counteroffer to even out the deal. In your split-fund counter, you have reduced the second mortgage to $50,000 but at the same time have extended the term to nine years and reduced the interest to 9½ percent. This tactic may do nothing but move Bob's attention to that factor and cause him to say, "Okay, but the mortgage has to be the same term and interest rate as before." On the other hand, you might end up with some compromise that is more in your favor.

Advantages in Split Funding on Closings at the End of the Seller's Tax Year.

Split funding often works to the seller's advantage when it allows him or her to divide taxable funds over two separate tax years. If you discover that it is likely that you will close near the end of the seller's tax year, you can use this to your advantage. Keep in mind that the IRS allows you to establish tax year-ends other than December 31. If you were going to close around August 31 and you discover that the seller's year-end is October 31, you might be able to show the seller the advantage of splitting the money into two or more taxable years. Under the IRS provisions for reporting capital gains or earned income on an installment sale basis, it is possible to spread that income over more than one taxable year, which may reduce the overall tax by holding your tax rate at lower levels. This is particularly important if you have multiple sales in the same year or tax period. One word of caution: If you plan to use the installment provisions of the tax code to spread gains out over multiple years, remember, if the mortgage you are holding allows prepayment of the debt, the mortgagor may pay you off in an a year that bumps you into a higher bracket. If this were to be a burden you may wish to impose a penalty for prepayment, or have a period of years that the mortgage cannot be prepaid. In any event, it is always a good idea to discuss tax planning with your accountant as the IRS tends to change rules, or have new interpretations on older rules.

Mixing the Split Fund with Other Creative Techniques.

If the assumption is that you will meet the obligation of this split-funded down payment from the property itself, you need to plan the purchase accordingly.

The following are two methods of getting cash out of a property you just bought. Each of these methods is described in more detail in other chapters in the book and is shown here only to illustrate the need for you to be as creative as possible in combining techniques.

EXAMPLE 20: SPLIT-FUND SPLIT-DEAL. You have just contracted to buy a 100-acre tract of land. The purchase price is $250,000. The down payment is $50,000 split into two payments. A payment of $20,000 is due at closing, and the balance of $30,000 is due in 18 months. The balance is a first $200,000 mortgage held by the seller for 15 years at 7 percent per annum.

Your plan is to sell off some of the 100 acres so that you can generate sufficient cash to cover the balance owed on the down payment. You know from your homework that by breaking this 100 acres into smaller tracts you can increase the value of the sites on a per-acre basis and profit greatly.

INTRODUCE MORTGAGE RELEASES TO ALLOW PARTIAL SALE OF THE COLLATERAL. However, you must be sure that you have set up the purchase money mortgage to allow you to obtain releases from the first mortgage to permit you to sell off some property. Keep in mind that when you have a mortgage secured by property you now own, that mortgage creates a lien on all of the property. When you anticipate or want the right to sell off some of the property you buy, you must make sure that you obtain an agreement from the seller in the very beginning that will allow you to release land from the mortgage. The following is an example of the kind of language you can use. Be sure that your lawyer drafts language that fits the exact transaction and tries to take into account your potential future intentions with respect to a sale of some of the land. The following is more of a catchall that can cover most eventualities; it is taken from a contract that I used in the acquisition of a 300-acre tract of land in Palm Beach County some time ago:

> . . . and furthermore, as long as the mortgagor is current and not in default on any of the payments of this mortgage, the mortgagor will have the right to obtain partial releases of the security to the mortgage. These releases will be in increments of the land of no less than one acre, and will follow the following pattern:
>
> The pattern of releases will be that the land will be divided into blocks of land consisting of no less than one acre. (Draw such a sketch that blocks out the land as you anticipate it might be developed or need to be released.) If in the future this pattern proves to be impractical for reasons beyond the control of either party, then the mortgagee will not unreasonably object to a revised pattern provided that the intent of this formula is followed, giving the benefit of any change to the mortgagee.
>
> Releases of the land will be based on an accelerated price of 125 percent of the pro/rata per acre loan ratio. The per acre loan ratio is found by dividing the amount of principal plus unpaid interest outstanding by the remaining number of acres secured by the mortgage prior to a release. For example, if the total loan (principal plus outstanding interest) were $200,000 and 100 acres remained as security to the mortgage, then the per acre loan ratio is $2,000 per acre. As the release price is 125 percent of

that amount, the next release price would be $2,500 per acre. The mortgagor may make principal payments against the amount owned without taking the release those payments may provide. If the mortgagor has made payments without asking for a release from the date of closing or the date of a previous release, the mortgagor may accumulate all principal payments made and apply them to a release at a future date. If this occurs, the calculation as to release price would be made as though none of the principal payments had been made. All expenses to accomplish the release will be paid by the Mortgagor, and these expenses shall include but not be limited to: Recent survey of the actual property to be released, all cost to record, pay documentary and other transfer taxes as may be applicable and mortgagee's legal cost.

Be sure to have your lawyer draft the actual mortgage document, and don't just try to insert this previously shown paragraph into a standard mortgage. There may be conflicting wording in a standard mortgage that will complicate your ultimate plan. It is important to remember all the different aspects of a purchase money mortgage that can be inserted, such as right of substitution of collateral for sliding mortgages, subordination, and assumption of the mortgage by a future buyer, and so on.

FINE-TUNING PARTIAL RELEASE FROM MORTGAGE STATEMENT.   There are many other provisions that could be put into a mortgage release statement, and many different forms of releases could be devised. The $2,500 payment in the foregoing example is what would be termed above par payment (125 percent) and would pay off the mortgage faster than the original schedule as you released land. The mortgage of $200,000 relates to $2,000 per acre in the beginning. If you made a prepayment to release 20 acres at the initial per acre price of $2,500 you would have to pay $50,000. This would reduce the amount of the mortgage to $150,000 and there would be 80 acres remaining as security to the mortgage. The loan to acre has dropped to $1,875 ($150,000 mortgage ÷ 80 acres = $1,875). The next release price is going to be 125 percent of that amount or a total of $2,343.75 per acre.

If the seller called for a 150 percent release, the release price would be 150 percent of the allocated value per acre of the face amount of the mortgage. Keep in mind that some lawyers would draft a release to say 150 percent of the per acre purchase price. This is not what you wanted so this becomes a negotiating point.

Armed with the release provision, you could then anticipate that to meet your split fund and pay the release you would have to sell sufficient land to pay the $30,000 balance on the down payment, and (at 125 percent) a release of $2,500 per acre for the initial release.

How much would you need to sell? The total you need to meet the balance of the down payment is $30,000, plus the amount to release the land, which at this point is $2,500 per acre.

If you can sell small tracts at $5,000 per acre, then you will have $2,500 left over from each full acre to pay the release. Because you have to release in full acre increments, you will have to sell 12 acres:

Proceeds from 12 acres at $5,000 per acre	$ 60,000
To release from the mortgage 12 acres	−30,000
To pay the balance of the split funded down payment	$ 30,000

By using the split fund with the split deal, you would have the flexibility to spin off some of the land to meet your other obligations as well. It is important to remember that whenever you buy a property that can be divided, you should attempt to allow for releases within the mortgages. If financing already exists on the property, you may not have the opportunity to change those mortgages, but you can ask for that as a condition to the transaction. Previous mortgages can be altered by mutual agreement between the mortgagee and the mortgagor, and the prospect of an early payment or advance payment through releases may be attractive to mortgagees of mature mortgages.

THREE PROVISIONS THAT ARE CRITICAL IN LAND RELEASES

1. THE RELEASE PATTERN: You must allow flexibility to suit your needs or development plans. Sellers or mortgagees will want to ensure that the remaining property more than secures the mortgage balance owed. For this reason, sellers or mortgagees will want to keep the prime portions of the property under the mortgage umbrella.

2. WHERE ADVANCE PAYMENTS APPLY: If you stated "any advance payment of principal will apply toward releases as well as the next scheduled payment" you will have an ideal method of payment for a buyer. In this format, you may take care of three years of scheduled payments with one release, and not have a principal payment for three years in so doing. The other side of this coin is the statement "and any advance payment in excess of the normal scheduled principal payments will be applied to the last payments due on the mortgage." This statement is the usual provision in mortgages, which simply means that if you make an advance payment you don't affect the mortgagee's schedule for regular payments except by accelerating the ultimate payoff of the mortgage.

3. PENALTY IF THE MORTGAGEE DOESN'T GIVE THE RELEASE: You might have a sale and not be able to deliver because the mortgagee decides that he or she isn't going to give you the release no matter what the mortgage says. A paragraph added by your lawyer could give you some protection in this event by allowing you to provide some incentive for the mortgagee to act according to the original agreement.

Future Rent

Future rent is simply the obligation or the benefit (depending on which side of the payment you are) of rent for one or more periods that will take place sometime in the future. Because this is both a benefit and an obligation, it is an ideal financing tool that can be used in many different ways. If you are a buyer, you can use this benefit as a part of the cash down, a benefit of prepaid rent at another location, and as a "free" option to entice you into the transaction in the first place. As a seller, you can hold out "free" future rent for other concessions, accept trade or barter in lieu of the future rent, and guarantee all or part of the projected future rent available to be passed on to the buyer.

EXAMPLE 21: PART OF CASH DOWN.   The seller is insisting on $150,000 cash down for the office building you want to buy. The total price is $700,000 and there is a first mortgage of $200,000. The seller says she will hold the balance in secondary financing.

You split the deal into building and land lease, so that there is a $20,000 annual land lease payment. Assume you cap the land lease at 8 percent, so the $20,000 represents a value of the land at $250,000. At this point there is a total of $450,000 in financing arranged: the existing mortgage of $200,000 and a $250,000 (value) land lease. You now ask the seller to hold a second mortgage of $250,000 at 7.5 percent interest for the balance of the financing. This gives you a total of $600,000 in financing. Of the $150,000 down payment, you categorize $50,000 of this as prepaid rent.

You offer the prepaid rent when you get a tax break by calling part of the deal "prepaid rent." There would be no other advantage, but when it works for you, it can allow you to offset current income against future obligations you pay now. Please note this is a deal by deal situation and may not apply to your circumstances. Be sure you have a need for the extra expense, and that you are able to take advantage of it.

EXAMPLE 22: AS PREPAID RENT IN ANOTHER LOCATION.   You are buying a home from Jake and discover that he is looking for a place to store equipment he uses in his construction business. You just happen to own a warehouse that has some vacant space, so you offer Jake three years prepaid rent, worth $40,000 as your down payment on the home.

EXAMPLE 23: PREPAID IN THE SAME PROPERTY.   This occurs if you pledge two years' free rent to the seller's son in one of the apartments in the building you are going to buy and get credit for it off the closing statement.

EXAMPLE 24: AS A SELLER, YOU AGREE TO TAKE PART RENT.   If you have a live buyer, to get him to close, you agree to reduce his down payment by taking two years prepaid rent for your own office space in the building you are selling.

EXAMPLE 25: YOU EXCHANGE RENT.   You have several vacancies in a strip store you own, so you exchange the space for other benefits. To one tenant you take all of one year's rent for roof repair work on that and several other buildings you own. Another tenant gives you barter dollars for part of the rent. Another offers you merchandise for part of the rent, and so on.

There are many ways to use future rent as part of a real estate transaction. It might be to pledge the rent of another property as security for a note or mortgage on the property you want to buy. Alternatively, you might offer the seller the right to stay on for a period of time as a tenant without paying any rent. It is important for you to think again in the area of benefits and not money. If you have something you have not been able to rent, or even thought about renting, why not offer that on your next deal? If one of those things you own is a mountain cabin, you could offer free holiday rent in that cabin facility for some period of time.

Nonetheless, the usual method of using this technique is to take rent you are getting as a security against a note or loan you want to obtain or offer to another party. In this way the seller of the property you want to buy doesn't have to have a need for the property for rent, only recognize that its rent is a value that can secure another note or mortgage.

EXAMPLE 26: THE BROWNIE DEAL.   Brownie got right down to the last straw in trying to make a deal with Roco. The only thing that was holding them apart was that Roco wouldn't take Brownie's unsecured note for $50,000 due in full at the end of two years as part of the down payment. Brownie countered with the same $50,000 note, but added as a security all rents above the first $1,800 Brownie would collect as total revenue each month from a four-unit apartment building Brownie owned. Each apartment rented for $650 and so had a gross monthly rent of $2,600. The building also had no debt against it. Roco saw that his note would be secured providing that Brownie agreed not to put any additional financing on the apartment until the note was paid off. Brownie countered that he would agree not to put any debt against the building. Roco felt that was reasonable and a deal was made.

EXAMPLE 27: ANOTHER FUTURE RENT.   In another future rent deal, Oscar offered the owner of a small home the right to stay in the home until Oscar's building plans were completed for the rental apartment building he wanted to build. Then, as the total price for the transaction, Oscar offered the sellers a lifetime right to rent one of the new apartments for $1 per month.

Oscar knew what he was doing because he had calculated his yield on the amount of money it would have taken to buy the house just to get the lot. He also knew from the ages of the participants that it was a good investment to offer the life estate for $1 per month because on the actuarial calculation the apartment would be vacant within

10 years. Oscar calculated that even if he had to give up the use of that apartment for 20 years, he was making a good decision.

The seller loved the idea, and told Oscar, "What a wonderful incentive to live another 100 years."

Pitfalls in Future Rent Deals.

• The deal is not properly documented. If you are going to offer or take prepaid rent as a part of any transaction, make sure that there is a properly drawn lease that meets all the criteria that both parties understand to be the situation and have it agreed upon prior to the final closing of the deal. If there is no such lease predetermined and executed at the closing, then you are bound to have problems in the future.

• Do not let the future rent benefit or obligation go too far in the future without indexing the value. By this I mean that if you are giving up five years of future rent, make sure that a value is put on that future amount. If the lease has a cost-of-living index increase, and the increase bumps the annual rent above the amount, which you have given (or gotten) credit for, then the overage is due in cash. Remember, if you are getting a future value today, without having to wait for it, then that is worth more now than in the future.

On the other side, if you pay for the future benefit (because you gave it up now), then you should have some benefit of that added value. For example, I sell you my home, but stay in the home for two years rent-free as a part of the deal. If two years rent is worth $4,000 per month, then that is a total of $96,000 over 24 months. If I prepay that by allowing you a reduction in the price of the home, then I have given you a value greater than $4,000 per month if you had to wait month after month for 24 months to get it.

Management Interest

Obtaining real estate through a management interest is where you agree to manage a property on the basis that you will receive an ownership interest in the property as part of the remuneration for your efforts.

Mike knew a couple of real estate investors who needed a tax shelter. He found a small 10-unit apartment building and tied it up on a contract. He then told these investors that if they took over his contract he would manage the building and take for that effort a 20 percent ownership in the building.

They went along with the deal, and for a while it worked out for all until some problems set in. Before we look at Mike's problems, let's look at another example.

EXAMPLE 28: MANAGEMENT FOR AN INTEREST IN OWNERSHIP.   David was an expert at hotel management. He was asked to manage a property in the Bahamas Islands by some offshore investors. He said he would if they gave him a 10 percent ownership in the property with an additional 5 percent for every year that he increases the net operating income by 5 percent or more. David also added that when and if his interest reached 50 percent he would have the right to buy out the other partners on a formula based on the income average for the past three years.

The owners calculated that for David to reach 50 percent ownership he would have to have eight years of growth and that the new operating income would have to increase by 80 percent or more. Based on that, they could afford to sell at the formula offered.

The key to this scenario was that David was an expert in hotel management. He knew that the property was currently poorly managed and that he could slowly build the business so that by the time he reached the end of eight years the place would just be ready for even bigger things.

Some property owners try to find good employees by offering this same kind of incentive. The same basic idea works here.

EIGHT ESSENTIAL CONDITIONS TO A MANAGEMENT INTEREST AGREEMENT

1. HOW TERMINATED: Specific terms as to the duration of the agreement and how it can be terminated. This is the toughest part of any such agreement. How does the current owner lock in the "employee" but not to the extent that if it is a bad relationship it can't be ended? On the other hand, the "employee" doesn't want to do everything according to the agreement, succeeding to the terms of the management interest payouts, only to find that the owners want to eliminate him or her now that the property is running smoothly.

2. "GOLDEN PARACHUTE" PROVISIONS: What happens if the company or property is sold? The new owner is not going to honor any such agreement that gives away interest to some other party. If you were that other party, you would want protection over and above your actual interest at that moment to the proceeds of the sale.

3. LIMITATION OF EMPLOYMENT OR COMPETITION TRADE AREAS: If you leave or are fired for reason, the owners will want some kind of protection that you won't take all the clientele and go into business for yourself down the street. This is difficult to establish, but it is apt to come up.

4. CALCULATIONS OF INTEREST, PROFITS, AND DIVIDENDS: If you don't have control and have a formula on which all your interest, share of profits, or dividends are calculated, make sure that you have a clear understanding of the accounting. Normal business expenses can also include salary to key people, and the other partners could legally be entitled to salaries that could eat up any profit and take away any bonus you thought you were going to get. Also, to arrive at a net operating income requires deductions from the gross income of all such operating expenses. You might find that unless you had set up things very clearly that gross goes way up, but net drops each year.

5. ALL PARTIES MUST AGREE TO THE PRO FORMA OR ESTIMATED INCOME AND EXPENSES AND A TARGET FOR THE FUTURE: To do this, make sure you get copies of past years' income and expense statements. Base your future growth and formulas on known factors. Take into account that things are going to go up, that rent won't be the same, and that the phone bill will increase five years down the road. However, establish those patterns and follow them if you are on a formula percentage basis.

6. KNOW THE GOALS OF YOUR PARTNERS: If your partners are happy with a small operation, they might be frightened when you turn it into a big operation. Scared partners do things you can't anticipate.

7. BUILD A PERIODIC REVIEW INTO YOUR AGREEMENT: This allows you to stop any problems you might have with your partners before they get out of hand. It is good for them, too, but a series of constantly positive reports makes it difficult for anyone to claim that he or she suspected that you were taking petty cash for the past six years.

8. DON'T PLAY AROUND WITH WHAT YOU ARE DUE: If you meet the objectives of the contract, demand what you have coming. When it comes time to exercise your option to buy, remember that you can offer less. The option is one-sided for you, and you can take it or leave it or offer less.

PITFALLS IN MANAGEMENT INTEREST TRANSACTIONS. There are five important pitfalls in management interest transactions:

1. Getting in over your head with a project you can't handle.
2. Not having everything in writing.
3. Not living up to the spirit of the agreement.
4. Giving cause to be fired when you are really doing a good job.
5. Getting tied down to a job you hate and people you don't like.

Each of these five pitfalls has its obvious counterpart. Use caution and obtain good legal advice prior to entering into the agreement, and do your homework as to the people, the plan, and the future potential.

Three-Party Blankets

A three-party blanket occurs when you add additional property to a mortgage that you don't own. This provides additional security to the lender, who is usually the seller of a property you are buying. Remember, a blanket mortgage is any mortgage that has one document (the mortgage and mortgage note combined) that is secured by two or more properties.

EXAMPLE 29: PART OF THE BLANKET IS BORROWED. Ruth wanted to buy an apartment in Tulsa. She offered the seller $168,000, which was slightly less than the $175,000 she was asking. The terms offered were: $25,000 cash down, $110,000 to assume the existing mortgage, and $33,000 second mortgage on a duplex that Ruth owned in San Francisco.

The seller agreed to the price, but balked at the second mortgage on the duplex. "Not enough equity," he said.

Ruth tried several other tacks, but nothing worked. Then she asked her father if she could "borrow" some land that the family owned for a couple of years. What Ruth wanted to do was to add the land to the security of the second mortgage. Ruth offered her father a kicker of a percentage of the ultimate sale, and pledged her own equity in the house to her father should anything go wrong.

Ruth's plan was to move into the house and fix it up, refinancing the improved home and selling it for about $230,000. If all worked out as she hoped, there would be room for the kicker percentage that she offered her father, and little risk for everyone.

BRING IN A PARTNER.   The three-party blanket is a method of bringing in a partner who gets a small part of the deal, or some other kicker because he or she doesn't have to invest any cash. The advantage is to the seller as he or she is being appeased with additional equity in any paper he or she may hold.

Since the value or quality of the paper has been improved, other terms in the deal often can be counterbalanced to offset the kickers that Ruth and you may have to pay to get the "use" of the other property.

Notice that the end result is similar to what might happen with the OPP techniques discussed earlier. The technique here is the use of the blanket mortgage in this method. You may wish to review the chapter on blanket mortgages in this book.

This technique often is used with first-time buyers who need additional security to make their transactions work. Sellers being asked to hold paper are naturally reluctant to extend credit to "fresh" investors who are still wet behind the ears. In those situations, the buyer has to dig deep into a bag of tricks to find a technique that is acceptable to both the seller and to any third party he or she is going to find to help.

PITFALLS IN THREE-PARTY BLANKETS.   If you were the third party and you allowed Ruth to use your land as additional security on her mortgage, and Ruth defaulted on her mortgage, you could be at risk for the mortgage in a foreclosure or risk action against your land to recover the amount owed on the mortgage.

Be very careful if you are the third party. Obviously, the solution is to weigh the risk against the kicker being offered. If you are to become a partner in the deal, have not put up any cash, have little risk in losing your security, and the gain potential is good, the whole transaction is sound.

This stresses the prime benefit of using the third-party blanket as an investment tool. The person who generally benefits the most often is, in fact, the person who put up the security in the transaction.

Like cosigners, which will be covered in another chapter, the one who helps someone else put a deal together often is the one who profits the most. Keeping this in mind, as the investor you have to make sure that bringing in a partner, even in the form of a third-party blanket, is worth the effort. Ask yourself this question: "Have I tried everything I could to buy that property without a partner, or do I need someone to share my lack of confidence in that property?" The answer to that question might surprise you if you are honest with yourself.

Chapter 19

FOUR TECHNIQUES
Where You Keep Part and Dispose of Part

GOAL OF THIS CHAPTER

This chapter illustrates that it is not essential to sell, lease, or otherwise dispose of 100 percent of your real estate to reach your desired goals. Sometimes, in fact, by selling only a part, and keeping the balance, you accelerate your journey to your goals.

In this chapter, I cover four creative techniques that give you effective methods to conclude transactions you might miss otherwise. In each of these techniques, you keep part of the deal, at least for the time being, and sell part:

1. Landscape transaction.
2. Keep the plus, sell the negative.
3. Private timeshares.
4. Subdivide and sell or exchange.

Each of these techniques allows you to obtain the maximum benefit through 100 percent or more financing. Each technique is easy to use, and each has built-in flexibility to allow you to combine the technique with other methods of financing.

The Landscape Transaction

Of all the creative transactions you will read about, this is one of the best, when the situation fits. Naturally, several criteria have to fit the deal to make any economic sense, but when the parts fit, you can benefit nicely.

A landscape transaction is when the prospective buyer can sell off landscaping from the property being purchased.

EXAMPLE 1: FINDING A LANDSCAPE DEAL. You have been looking for fixer-upper properties that are found in pleasant areas of town, but that have been overly run down. You know that this kind of property usually is owned by a owner who may be experiencing difficulties with finances, health issues, age related problems, unable to deal with the required management, or a combination of all of these circumstances. These properties often stand out like sore thumbs because of the overgrown landscaping, which hides the buildings and creates an overall distressed look to the property. A lot of plants and trees can actually do a property harm. The leaves clog gutter drains, accumulate on roof areas and rot. Roots crack foundations and the dark damp conditions create mold; algae can turn pools into penicillin ponds, stain drives, walks, and patios, and so on. All this becomes a nasty situation when you see it. Yet, it is also an opportunity.

You find such a house, and you take steps to get control. Remember, get control, then spend the time, effort, and money to analyze the situation and plan the next step. You enter into negotiations and after a couple of offers and counteroffers, you arrive at a point in the process where you feel you have reached the best deal you can. At this stage of the game, the deal looks good. You have won points and the seller is satisfied with the transaction. You actually want the seller to be satisfied. When a seller begins to believe he or she has sold and made a good deal doing it, he or she begins psychologically to spend the money.

You start down your checklist of things to do, and one of them is to find out if there is any green in all that green. In short, can you sell the landscaping for enough money to make it worthwhile?

Savvy real estate investors rarely try to keep up on what plants or trees are worth at any specific time because that depends on the market. When you are dealing with mature plants and trees, the prices you can get can be very attractive. You might be surprised to find that some moderately sized trees can bring several thousand dollars from the right buyer. The key, of course, is to know who the right buyer is.

You make a few phone calls, and within a few days have gotten some offers for all the mature landscaping around the house. You have your own landscaper give you an estimate of what plants you might want to keep to enhance the property. Then you cut the best deal you can to sell or trade the unwanted landscape. Naturally, you cannot deliver the landscape to a buyer until you close on the property. However, with careful planning you can make it a simultaneous deal separated by only a few minutes if your lawyer can schedule it that tightly.

EXAMPLE 2: FINDING THE RIGHT BUYER. You have just bought five acres of land, which you plan to hold for a couple of years. The idea is to build a fast-food restaurant on part of it, and resell or hold the balance. The land is full of trees, which the broker who has it listed tells you, "Should not cost more than $5,000 to clear off." You smile, and a fleeting thought runs through your mind, "Little does that agent know."

You get control of the property by negotiating until you have a binding agreement. You do not play too hard nose at this stage, and get through the negotiations rather quickly. I like to follow the pattern that if I think it is worth my time as an investor, there might be someone else who will come to the same conclusion. I need to beat those investors to the punch. So do you.

At this point, you are in control. You have negotiated a 45-day due-diligence period to walk the property through your predevelopment checklist. This checklist will be very extensive and will include everything from checking environmental rules and regulations, to finding out the history of the property. If it were once a site for storage of waste oil products, you can just about stop there and move on. One obvious step you will want to check out well is the potential value of the landscape. You or someone you hire will make an inventory of what is potentially saleable. You list the type, size, and condition of every potentially saleable plant on the property. If there are one or more really valuable trees on the site, take photos of them. Be sure to have a person standing next to it to give perspective to the size.

You make up the inventory list, without prices, and send it to a dozen developers in town who are building new properties. These might be homes, apartment buildings, or commercial projects. All these need new plant material, and they are used to paying top dollar for quality stuff.

If that does not produce some quick phone calls, then you can call around to some better landscapers to discover if there is a potential market for the material. Quality material will sell. You can be sure of that.

BE CREATIVE: SPLIT FUND-PLANT TRANSACTION.   Remember the split-fund technique we discussed in Chapter 18? Tie this into the plant landscape transaction for some very creative financing. The plan is to sell crops, timber, or plants on the property for sufficient cash to meet the obligations of the down payment owed.

This idea works well in farm or timberlands as you might visualize, but also in areas where the property may have an overgrowth of "landscape quality" plants. The deal is simple to set up provided you do your homework in advance. If the investment is farmland, you have to have a good understanding of the marketing of that type of produce. Buying farms that have groves or crops in the field is a very special kind of investing and generally not for the novice. Nonetheless, it is possible that you are buying the land for another reason and that the land just happens to be an old farm or grove. Why not capitalize on its potential to spin off some additional income one last time before you turn it into a subdivision?

Selling standing timber is easy to set up if there is a market in the area. There should be timber brokers, mills, and the like who could give you some help in this area. The state agricultural agent is a good source of information. You can find the agent by calling your state's Department of Agriculture.

A landscape deal requires a bit more finesse, since you might have a gold mine under your nose and not recognize it. Landscapers will pay a lot of money for the right kind of plants. If many "large style" developments are going on in your area, such as clubhouses, banks, shopping plazas, airports, hospitals, and so on, mature plants will be in demand.

SEVEN TIPS ON SETTING UP THE LANDSCAPE TRANSACTION

1. GET TO KNOW TWO OR MORE LANDSCAPERS IN YOUR AREA AS PART OF DEVELOPING YOUR COMFORT ZONE. It is important that you obtain some basic information early about the cost in landscaping. You will find that maintaining shrubs and plants is one of the best ways to improve the value of a property. However, the larger and more mature the plant, the more costly it is. You can buy a small plant for $2.50 that will be worth $150 in a few years. Many landscapers have price lists that they provide to real estate developers and contractors.

2. BECOME A LANDSCAPE WHOLESALER. It is easy for you to become a "qualified" buyer of wholesale products by incorporating or taking out a city occupational license as a "decorator" or "home repairer." Usually nothing more than a municipal fee of $50 or so is required for that title. Then if your state has a sales tax, contact the local sales tax office and get the forms and a tax identification number. This is usually required for businesses that will buy wholesale and sell retail. That tax number is the key to the wholesaler that you have done the required steps to be able to buy at the below-retail price. It will also be needed for possible reports you may have to periodically file with the state tax offices.

3. BUY A BOOK ON LANDSCAPING. Get one that has photographs or illustrations of plants that are available in your area. Check the values of those plants by visiting retail outlets to give yourself a general idea what kind of profit the wholesaler can actually make. Always use the wholesale price since that is the maximum price you will get from a landscaper.

4. WHEN YOU FIND A PROPERTY LOADED WITH VALUABLE PLANTS, DO A THOROUGH EXAMINATION AND LIST THE PLANTS ALONG WITH THEIR SIZES. Go to a couple of landscapers to see if they are interested and at what price. It is possible that information alone could entice you to buy the property.

5. NEVER CLOSE ON A PROPERTY BASED ON THE VERBAL PROMISE FROM THE LANDSCAPER. If you are counting on the sale of the landscape material on the property you are acquiring, make sure you tie up the property first, then give yourself an out or two in the contract. Once that is accomplished get firm quotations from two or more landscapers as to what they are interested in purchasing and how much they will pay. You may ultimately deal with more than one buyer as not all landscapers will have ready-to-go buyers for what you are offering. Make sure the prices are "in-the-ground" prices and that when they remove the plants they will fill any holes left.

6. IF YOU NEED DIFFERENT PLANTS FOR THAT OR OTHER JOBS, CONSIDER ARRANGING AN EXCHANGE WITH THE LANDSCAPER FOR THE TYPES AND SIZES OF PLANTS YOU MAY NEED.

7. DO NOT OVERLOOK THE FACT THAT MANY OLDER HOMES LOOK BETTER ONCE THE LANDSCAPE HAS BEEN CLEANED OUT AND NEW SMALLER PLANTS HAVE BEEN PUT IN PLACE. It could be that a complete change in the landscape around an older property can give it such an uplifting look that values can be increased overnight. By using your contacts with the landscapers, you will find that you can buy and also sell plants profitably.

Dealing successfully in landscape does not mean only tropical items or crops. Keep in mind that beautiful green grass can be turned into green cash too. The sod may be expensive, but if that five acres of yard is just sitting there waiting for the right person to sell it, why shouldn't you be that person?

Keep the Positive and Sell the Negative or Vice Versa

By now you should be thinking about benefits you get or give up and not just the money part of the transaction. Every property you own or will ever own will have its problems and its benefits. As a real estate investor you need continually to review your investments to ascertain if the benefits are worth putting up with the problems. The moment the problems win the argument it is time to consider making a change. As I have shown in previous situations, making a change does not automatically mean getting rid of the property. Oddly enough, as you will discover, you can obtain benefits by keeping the negative and selling the positive.

This section deals with dividing the positive and the negative of a property. You need to ascertain if there can be a division between the two. If this is possible you can sell one and keep the other. If you discover that you can make the division, then the next decision to make is which to sell and which to keep. The answer is not as obvious as you might think.

This form of financing is a shift of equity to another person. This equity, or value, is a divisible part of a property. As you can sell it, lease it, or exchange it, it is open game for you to use this in your real estate investment plan.

EXAMPLE 3: FINDING THE POSITIVE AND THE NEGATIVE BENEFITS.

Remember: Every property has both a positive benefit and a negative problem. Review the following chart that shows some usual benefits and negatives. Keep in mind that you may have benefits that are not shown, and experience none of the negatives showed.

Type of Property	Positive Benefits	Negative Benefits
Vacant lot	Appreciation, some income if it can be rented as a parking lot, storage field, u-pick it farm, and so on	Government and environmental problems, little income potential, taxes to pay, cleaning up after trash is dumped, and so on
Strip stores	Income, appreciation, jobs, tax shelter	Vacancies, maintenance, expenses, and management

Office building	Income, appreciation, jobs, tax shelter	Vacancies, maintenance, expenses, and management
Rental apartments	Income, appreciation, jobs, tax shelter, place to live	Vacancies, maintenance, expenses, and management
Your home	Place to live, appreciation	Maintenance, taxes, no income
Rental house	Income, appreciation, tax shelter	Maintenance, vacancies, taxes, and management
Hotel or motel	Income, appreciation, jobs, paid, tax shelter, place to live	Management, maintenance, vacancies, expenses
Second home	Possible income, slight tax shelter	Maintenance, taxes, little tax shelter, little income, loss of value

Explanation of Benefits

- **Income:** Suggests that there would be rental income greater than the expenses it takes to own the property. These expenses would include real estate taxes, interest on any mortgage, maintenance, management, and a modest cap rate on your investment. (If you have invested $100,000 and money is worth 5 percent, then 5 percent of your investment should be considered a part of the expenses.)

- **Appreciation:** The potential amount your property is going to increase in value. If this is not happening, or you cannot see an improvement in value, then the lack of appreciation will become a problem and not a benefit.

- **Tax shelter:** Tax shelter is the benefit you get from buildings and other assets that are a part of those buildings when you deduct the allowed depreciation of those assets from income. As this reduces income tax, it is called a tax shelter. This benefit can come back to bite you if you do not plan for it properly. However, even if it becomes nothing more than an interest-free loan from the government that is worthwhile.

- **Jobs:** Some real estate is a very good investment because it can give a whole family jobs and wage income. Some of the best examples of this are hotels and motels, restaurants, large apartment rental complexes, farms and other similar agricultural ventures, office buildings, and other commercial buildings. This benefit is very real if you have a large family of hard workers.

- **Expenses:** Think of a whole family that owns and works at a restaurant—wages, food, insurance, even cars to drive. Families that own and operate hotels and rental apartments even can get a place to live on the house. Another very good benefit when it fits your needs or goals.

Explanation of Problems

- **Maintenance:** Some properties have greater maintenance requirements than you may anticipate. Look carefully at this aspect of any property. This includes everything from fixing up, to plumbing, electrical, pool, yard, and so on.

• MANAGEMENT: The number-one problem. Taking care of the tenants is only part of it; taking care of the employees another.

• VACANCIES: This is the major source of reduced income. Vacancies then relate to loss of income. The inability to get good tenants who will pay good rents puts the property into a downward trend. Lack of sufficient rents means reduced maintenance, which translates to reduced value. The biggest problem with vacancies is that it is very difficult for most income properties to operate at 100 percent occupancy. Because of this, the key to overcoming most of the other problems is to reduce the vacancy factor while at the same time bringing a better-than-average level of tenant into the property. This is the major problem to attack.

SIX CHOICES OF HOW TO DEAL WITH THE NEGATIVES

1. Dispose of 100 percent of the property.
2. Dispose of only a part of the property.
3. Net lease 100 percent of the property.
4. Sell and leaseback 100 percent of the property.
5. Sell and leaseback a part of the property.
6. Sell or lease part of the property and keep part of the property.

GENERATE INCOME FROM A LOST BENEFIT.   Often we own property that has benefits that do not appeal to us. These benefits were not the principal reason we purchased the property, or we no longer need or have use for those benefits. The problem with this is that those benefits usually attribute to the cost of ownership of the property and now become a negative to the ownership of that property.

EXAMPLE 4: LEASE THE LOST BENEFIT.   One example of this is abundant in my hometown, Fort Lauderdale. Many people want to live on deep water (any waterway, canal, river, bay, or ocean inlet in Fort Lauderdale that has access to the ocean). Some of the general reasons for ownership on this kind of property are to enable you to tie your boat or yacht right next to your home. If this was the reason to buy such a property, you might find, as do thousands of people in Fort Lauderdale every few years, that owning a boat or yacht is not what they really thought it would be. They sell the boat and are content to have the waterway behind the house. However, they are paying for that waterway in the form of higher taxes. To purchase a deep-water lot in a good area of Fort Lauderdale can start at around $550,000 and go up from there. A dry lot in the same area (if you could find one) would be well under half that. This added value could then cost the homeowner anywhere from $2,000 to $5,000 every year in added taxes.

One way to get rid of this negative is to rent out the dock. In a city where dock space for large yachts is going at a premium, a dock capable of taking a boat over 45 feet in length would easily command an annual rent that would offset almost all taxes. An added benefit to this is the beauty of having a valuable yacht behind your home, and to be invited out on it from time to time by your tenant.

LEASE, SELL, OR EXCHANGE PART OF THE LOST BENEFIT. If you own a second home, it is likely that you had a very good reason for buying it. Whatever that reason was at the time, it is likely that the ownership has many gaps of use. These are all lost benefits, which you can transfer into other benefits somehow. The mechanics of doing this can come through a lease, outright sale, or an exchange of those lost benefits for something else that will be useful to you. When you cannot lease the unused time, you might join a local barter club or organization. Look in the Yellow Pages of your local telephone guide and you will discover several such organizations. I have found it easy to barter time my second homes this way, gaining a wide range of other benefits that include scrip in local restaurants, Italian ceramic tile, and carpets, professional services that include dentistry to plastic surgery, and on and on.

SELLING THE NEGATIVE CAN BE THE ANSWER. "For Sale: 50 percent interest in a Mountain Cabin." This is not a bad idea, and if you have a nice property there shouldn't be a problem in making this kind of sale. In fact, you might want to sell 25 percent to three people so that you keep the remaining 25 percent. This percentage can be divided into specific times during the year, much like a timeshare apartment or resort, only with one major difference: the facility will get less use than the timeshare and will provide much more flexibility to the investor.

SELL THEM THEIR POSITIVE AND KEEP YOUR POSITIVE. Some investors have discovered that they can add to their wealth quickly by looking for a property that is all positive to someone. When the investor locates this kind of property, he or she can then divide up the positives, keeping the benefit wanted in the first place and selling off the other positives. One of the best ways to sell them the positives while you keep your positive is by creating your own private timeshare.

Private Timeshare Properties

By constantly looking for the positive property, the investor will discover that if he or she sets up the transaction properly he or she can establish many such timeshare facilities. These do not have to be limited to real estate either; boats and airplanes can do nicely in this kind of transaction.

Setting up your own private timeshare property can be easy, fun, and profitable. It may be the very best way to increase your real estate benefits without having to spend any of your own cash. The method I shall describe is one of the best uses of other people's money I know of. If you try it, you will find that there are many potential problems you can avoid using the following tips:

1. LOOK FOR POSITIVE PROPERTIES. As I mentioned earlier, these are properties that have benefits that are extended throughout the year. These benefits might not appeal to everyone, but you will only sell that segmental benefit to the person who wants that specific use, so there will be little or no negative time for sale.

2. ANTICIPATE THE KIND OF MARKET YOU WILL BE SELLING IN BEFORE YOU TIE UP THE PROPERTY. If the property is in the mountains and one of the benefits to sell is ski time, you will want a property that is well located relative to ski areas. Even though you want the place for the cool summer nights and don't care about the proximity to the ski lifts, you need to consider the needs and benefits for the other owners.

3. MAKE OFFERS THAT TIE UP THE PROPERTY BUT GIVE YOU AN OUT. When buying a property for a syndication or private timeshare ownership, you will want to make sure that you don't get locked into a deal that you can't handle by yourself. One of the best ways to give yourself this out would be to make your offer subject to the full 100 percent subscription to the joint venture you are forming. Give yourself 90 days or more, which begin after you have approved the inspection of the property. Don't forget to also allow yourself time to make the inspections without being rushed. Nothing beats honesty in this kind of transaction, and if the seller is anxious to make a deal he or she is apt to go along with you. After all, you are trying to buy his or her property.

4. HAVE ALL YOUR BASES COVERED. This means anticipate every possible question that will be asked and have the right answer. The most important questions to deal with will center on the following: who is in control, upkeep, time periods, income potential, how to sell, and form of ownership. In the beginning you are in control. After that the group votes in a new person every year or so. You make the rules up front, so make sure you have a printed list of exactly how all this is going to work, and what penalties there are for those who don't come up with their share of expenses, and so on. The tougher the penalties are the better everyone will like it (because everyone thinks someone else will be the one to default). The same goes for upkeep; have it all down pat. Have a local company who will do the cleaning after every visit (to be paid for by the person who used the facility last).

Let people shift their time around, but have a clear understanding of how that will work. As to income, it is important that you have a local company who will rent out the facility, but also line up a couple of barter organizations in your home town who will trade you and the other owners services and goods for time at the facility. How to sell and the form of ownership is something you need to discuss with your lawyer. The logical way is not to restrict the sale of time, but to require the owner to offer it first to the existing members. A first right of refusal generally works well.

5. HAVE A GOOD JOINT OWNERSHIP AGREEMENT DRAFTED BY A LAWYER. Explain to the lawyer that you are going to do a joint venture form of private timeshare. Have the lawyer go over the specific forms of ownership you can use and make sure you're aware of the laws of the state where the property is located. In setting up the documentation, there are several important factors that you must attend to, as follows:

KEY ELEMENTS TO PUT INTO YOUR PRIVATE TIMESHARE AGREEMENT

1. A COPY OF THE PURCHASE AGREEMENT. Don't try to hide any of these details of your deal with the seller from the other investors you will invite to join you in co-ownership of the property. They'll find out anyway.

2. PROVIDE DETAILED INFORMATION ON THE OBLIGATIONS OF ALL PARTIES WITH RESPECT TO THE MORTGAGE (IF ANY), AND ALL COSTS THAT RELATE TO THE UPKEEP OF THE PROPERTY.

3. HAVE VERY STRICT PENALTIES FOR THOSE MEMBERS WHO DO NOT MEET THEIR OBLIGATIONS. One way is to prohibit their use. Another would be to rent their time to help cover any unpaid bills. The ultimate penalty would be the sale of their interest to cover the payments or money that is past-due. I have found that strict and quick-to-be-enforced rules actually appeal to investors as they too will worry what will happen if the other investors turn out to be the ones to shirk their obligations.

4. MAKE SURE YOU ARE IN THE DRIVER'S SEAT. This is your deal, your property, your contract. You are "allowing" other investors to buy a part of your deal. One form of ownership you might consider would be a general partnership. Here you would be the general partner and all other investors would be limited partners. Another form available in some states would be a land or investment trust. Here you are the trustee and the other investors are beneficiaries of the trust.

5. GET PAID FOR YOUR WORK. This means that you are in charge for the control over the property, and that you should get paid for your time. Don't try to be magnanimous about this because there will be things to do and times you don't want to do it. If you provide for payment you can hire others to help, but get paid and have it as a part of the deal from the very start.

6. PROVIDE FOR A FUND FOR THE REPLACEMENT OF FURNITURE AND FURNISHINGS. This might be a small sum per person deposited into a money market account, but have it because you will need it sooner or later. On this same subject, be sure that all members know that if they break something they have to replace it. On the other hand, if something mechanical stops working, then that is the responsibility of the whole group. Anticipate what your refurbishment expense will be over a period of ten years. Carpet will be replaced twice. Soft goods like towels, sheets, pillows, and so on will be replaced every three years or more. AC units and small appliances will be replaced at least once. Major appliances might

last 15 years or longer. Add 25 percent to the original cost for the replacement, then figure out how much needs to go into the fund each year. I recommend you have at least two payments into the fund for replacements to spread the expense out and to find out sooner rather than later who might balk at the payment.

7. HAVE A RESERVE FUND IN THE CHECKBOOK. A good idea is to keep three to six months ahead of any anticipated expenses. This gives you a better night's sleep.

8. HAVE AN OPTION TO BUY BACK THE OTHERS' INTEREST. This keeps you in control, and if they want to sell at any given time you could either buy then, or let them sell to someone else and retain that option. However, be flexible enough to let the option rise in value or to revert to a first right to buy so that the investor can participate in the appreciation of the property.

9. MAKE SURE YOU HAVE FULL AND AMPLE INSURANCE TO COVER ANY POTENTIAL CASUALTY OR LIABILITY.

10. HAVE A DO'S AND DON'TS LIST THAT SERVES AS THE RULES AND REGULATIONS FOR ALL THE OWNERS TO ABIDE BY. The list should include the responsibility for non-owners who may use the facility.

11. DO YOUR HOMEWORK ON THE PROPERTY, THE AREA, AND BENEFITS OF OWNERSHIP FOR ALL TIMES OF THE YEAR.

12. DO NOT HAVE A TELEPHONE INSTALLED IN THE FACILITY. We live in a world of mobile phones, and there is no reason to submit to monumental phone bills when the teenagers of one of the co-owners runs up a bill to their friends in Australia.

PITFALLS TO TIMESHARES.   Timeshares are filled with traps that can attract even the smartest of all developers and will then cause them to lose their investment capital promptly.

The reason for this is the fantastic profit potential that the winner can take home if he or she hits the timeshare market right. The kind of timeshare I am talking about is the one you see that advertises itself as the "best resort in the Rockies," or "Orlando's Finest Timeshare Resort." It is the "hotel-minded" kind of place that caters to you during your week. These places are hard-sell, expensive properties that the developer sells for one week or more at a price of from $3,000 up to $20,000 per week depending on the place and the week.

In Orlando, Florida, the most "populated-by-timeshares" place in the world, a two-bedroom timeshare apartment could easily cost $15,000 or more per week during prime summer months. In addition to that initial cost, the upkeep and taxes for that same week could cost the owner as much as $595 or more each year (just for that one week).

If the developer sells his week 52 times, and the average price is around $12,000 per week, the gross price for the apartment is $624,000. I can assure you that the apartment would not have that resale value if you owned all 52 weeks. This fantastic price is buffered by the incredible cost to market. Timeshare developers will admit to as much as a 55 percent marketing cost and more in many cases. When you consider that the developer may start with a 100-unit project (or much larger), which would mean to 5,200 actual weeks to be sold, it's understandable that the developer may want to "blow out" inventory when he or she gets down to the last 100 weeks. With so little time to close with such a small inventory, the actual cost to market those last weeks could be as high as 70 percent on an average project. However, that still leaves lots of room for unbelievable profits.

This is where the pitfalls begin. Those profits are all in the minds of the projectionist, and in reality the cost to develop and the cost to "create prospects," "carry the line," and "buy back bad paper" can eat up the best project and the developer with the deepest pockets.

The former president of the Florida Timeshare Council once said, "No one ever woke up and looked in a mirror and said to themselves that today was the day they were going to buy a timeshare." He was so very right. To counteract this problem and to provide the salespeople (the "line" all prospects must "run") with fresh minds they can sell, the developers have to spend a lot of money in upfront advertising, direct mail, and prizes that get the prospects in the door. The cost to "carry the line" is very high. A good "line" will close one out of six prospects that walk in the door no matter what.

Most developers have lenders that finance these overpriced products so that the average buyer can get his or her holiday week for as little as $500 down (which the salesperson might lend him or her) and with payments as low as $99 per month. The problem for some of the smaller timeshare developers is that most lenders require the developer to guarantee the paper they are holding. This insurance takes the form of a "buy back of bad paper" agreement. Here, the developer promises to take back any units that the buyer defaults on, and then repays the lender for the balance of the mortgage. Sometimes this buyback is only for the first few years of the total mortgage term, while other lenders force the developer to hang onto the deal until the final payments are made.

Developers often take this risk because they feel they are making sufficient profit to warrant some buyback. However, this most precarious domino will topple the soonest. If a project goes sour, sales fall off, salespeople leave, sales get worse, those who have bought stop making payments, bad paper comes back to the developer, and the whole house of cards comes tumbling down.

THE RESORT TIMESHARE CAN BE THE BEST OF TWO WORLDS. The timeshare concept is best when the project is designed to provide the best possible comfort, benefits, and accommodations for the least possible cost. No one minds reasonable profit going to the developer or to the general partner, but when greed enters into the picture, watch out.

The best way to avoid this pitfall is to examine the benefits you are looking for when you commit to a private timeshare. If your goal is to add to your real estate ownership, to provide yourself with second-home benefits, to have added equity build up, and to do that through the private timeshare program, you will succeed.

If you want to profit by selling units in private timeshares and don't care about the other aspects of the deal, then you may succeed; most likely you will fall into the same pit that seduces half of the developers, who think timeshares are gold mines.

Subdivide and Sell or Exchange

When you can tie up a property for a substantial period of time, it may be possible for you to spin off some of the property you have under contract in such a way that you close simultaneously on both contracts. This double-dealing can generate the capital or benefits you need to close on the property you are acquiring. As this is a technique to generate new capital, the end result is a neat way to finance a deal.

Subdivision is the act of subdividing a larger property into smaller properties; it is the essence of real estate development. Whenever you take one property and break it into smaller parts, this is the act of dividing the property into separate legal descriptions. These separate legal descriptions allow the property to be properly described as independent tracts or lots. The end result creates a subdivision, which in general real estate jargon is an area of specific geographic entity that has been divided by a uniform or common method. In most communities the actual procedure of making a subdivision requires that very specific parameters be followed. West Lake subdivision, as an example of a name the developer may select, would be a tract of land. The developer would, in most communities, be required to have a surveyor and land-planning architect draw detailed maps showing the lots, or tracts with all streets, utility easements (if any exist or are required by the community), and other criteria that local ordinances demand.

Generally, the subdivision is broken up by lots and blocks, that is to say that each individual lot or parcel would be identified by being a specific lot number within a specific block. This description becomes what is known as the legal (description), such as, Lot 5 of Block 10 of West Lake subdivision. Where the local community requires that the subdivision be recorded in the public records, the legal description would include the plat book and page number where the subdivision was first recorded. Such subdivisions can be described by tracts, such as Tract 1, 2, 3, and so on, or Tract A, B, C, and so on.

EXAMPLE 5: SELL OFF SOME.   You contract to buy a 100-acre tract of land with a 180-day time period for due diligence. Your overall purchase price is $500,000 with $50,000 down, and the balance over a 10-year payout. The proposed mortgage will allow releases of land from the mortgage at $6,500 per acre. You anticipate that your land development costs will be $4,000 per lot.

While you are going through your studies, you have your surveyor draw up a subdivision of the tract into 200 half-acre lots. You contact a couple of builders and give two of them the opportunity to pick up 20 lots each at a bargain price of $12,000 per lot. This would be $240,000 from each builder, or $480,000 in total. The 40 lots you are preselling will cost you $160,000 to develop. Your release price for these lots is $6,500 for each lot, or a total of $260,000. You need $50,000 to close on the deal. You will take in $480,000 from the developers, and pay out $470,000 and be left with $10,000 to cover the surveyor's bill.

Of the original 100 acres, you are left with 60, and because you have paid off $50,000, the original down payment, plus the release payment of $160,000, you only owe $290,000.

EXAMPLE 6: EXCHANGE SOME.   What if the whole idea of getting this subdivision was so that you could have lots that you could exchange to Bobby, who owns a shopping center you would like to acquire? This center is free and clear of any debt, and is worth $1,000,000. Bobby needs some cash, but really wants to get back into the single-home-building business where he had made a lot of money once. You have offered him 60 single-family lots in West Lake subdivision worth only $18,000 per lot. You show him the plans from the two other builders who have 20 lots each, and are getting ready to put up model homes. These 60 lots have a value of $1,080,000 and a first mortgage of $290,000, and require $240,000 of development cost to finish. Your equity is $550,000.

You will give Bobby the equity in the 60 lots, $250,000 cash, and a second mortgage of $200,000 on the center, subject to your obtaining new first mortgage-financing equal to 75 percent of the value.

You borrow $750,000 on the center, give Bobby $250,000 of that amount, and put aside $250,000 for some future venture elsewhere, and save the balance of $250,000 to cover your costs and fix-up money.

FOUR KEY POINTS TO REMEMBER ABOUT SUBDIVIDING AND SELLING OR EXCHANGING.   Many of the different techniques covered in this book use exchanges from one person to another. You should remember that I stress the single element: benefit. This includes all exchanges, money, and scrip, barter, sweat equity, paper, subdivided property, or whatever works best when the investor remembers and follows these four key points:

1. PEOPLE WANT TO FEEL THAT THEY HAVE MADE A PROFIT IN THEIR TRANSACTION. No one wants to be told "You sold that too cheap" or "You idiot, that property was worth twice what you got." Yet that kind of talk comes easy from the very person who would not have offered you even that much. When you offer something of value to a person who can't sell a property, no matter how much that item might have cost you, no matter if it is your spare time waxing his or her cars or being his or her CPA for a year or doing five gold inlays, the element you offer has value. Best of all, that value allows the seller to say, "Boy, did I get my price" or "I got every penny I asked for."

Sellers will do almost anything to avoid loss of face. Therefore, when you come along and don't knock the price, but instead examine the benefits you are willing to give up for the benefits you will get, people will take bags of gems or envelopes full of stamps.

2. ALWAYS STRIVE TO BE HONEST. At the same time, remember that memories are short and people will believe what they want, think what they find convenient, and want more than they have. You will sleep better at night if you know you did your best to present anything you offer in an exchange at a realistic value. Now that doesn't mean you have to offer a bargain or give away any secrets, but it does mean that you must allow the other side time to check values, to seek legal advice, to back out of the deal if they feel wronged.

3. MAKE SURE YOU HAVE GOT THE PROPERTY TIED UP FOR A LONG ENOUGH TIME TO WORK OUT THE DETAILS OF THE OTHER TRANSACTIONS. If you think you need 90 days, ask for 120 or 160. You never want to be in a rush (even if you need to hurry), because that is apt to tip your hand and a savvy buyer or exchanger may wait you out and pick up your project when you fall flat on your face.

4. BE SURE YOU HAVE THE TERMS IN YOUR ORIGINAL TRANSACTION THAT GIVE YOU THE RIGHT TO SUBDIVIDE, AND TO HAVE RELEASES TO MAKE IT WORK. If this is your first deal like this, make sure your lawyer knows exactly what you want to be able to do. The purchase money mortgage on the original deal must provide releases in such a way that you are not tied up in where or how the property is released. One very good technique at this point is to have a condition in your purchase money mortgage (to the seller of the initial property) where any prepayment of principal counts against the next principal payments due. This simple phrase will do wonders to your payment schedule of a 10-year payout.

For example, if your mortgage was $450,000 over 10 years, at principal payments of $45,000 per year plus interest at 8 percent on the outstanding principal, your payment schedule would look like the following:

Payment Period	Principal ($)	Interest ($)	Total ($)	Remaining ($)
1	45,000	36,000	81,000	405,000
2	45,000	32,400	77,400	360,000
3	45,000	28,800	73,800	315,000
4	45,000	25,200	70, 200	270,000
5	45,000	21,600	66,600	225,000
6	45,000	18,000	63,000	180,000
7	45,000	14,400	59,400	135,000
8	45,000	10,800	55,800	90,000
9	45,000	7,200	52,200	45,000
10	45,000	3,600	48,600	0

If the mortgage allowed that any prepayment of principal counted against the next in line principal payments, if you released 40 acres with a payment of $260,000, your payment schedule would now look like the following:

Payment Period	Principal ($)	Interest ($)	Total ($)	Remaining ($)
1	260,000	36,000	296,000	190,000
2	0	15,200	15,200	190,000
3	0	15,200	15,200	190,000
4	0	15,200	15,200	190,000
5	0	15,200	15,200	190,000
6	10,000	15,200	25,200	180,000
7	45,000	14,400	59,400	135,000
8	45,000	10,800	55,800	90,000
9	45,000	7,200	52,200	45,000
10	45,000	3,600	48,600	0

If the mortgage terms had not allowed the prepayment of principal to apply toward the next principal payment due, the above schedule would not appear this way. The normal way a mortgage is amortized is if you prepay principal, then the remaining balance is adjusted to account for the new amortization schedule.

PITFALLS OF SUBDIVIDING AND SELLING OR EXCHANGING.   What happens if you are counting on getting rid of the property through a sale or exchange and the market goes to pot? Alternately, you overestimate your ability and underestimate the cost to subdivide? Alternately, the city or the county imposes moratoriums on such things as subdividing? These are some of the pitfalls that lie in the darkness for the developer.

Be careful of the laws in your state with respect to land sales. Florida and other states have very specific ideas of what a subdivision should consist of and what you have to do in order to meet the requirements of the state. These often can be very expensive requirements if you fall under the control of those government bodies.

Fortunately, even the strictest state will have a cut-off point at which you would not fall into their full or even partial control. Know exactly what that is before you get started.

KEEP IT SIMPLE

The best way to do anything that involves other people is to consider their benefits as your own. Buy the property because you want the property. Let them in because they too can benefit from the property. No one will ever correctly say you asked too much or took too much and gave too little if you approach things that way.

Chapter 20

USING YOUR TALENT AND HIDDEN BENEFITS TO BARTER YOUR WAY INTO REAL ESTATE

GOAL OF THIS CHAPTER

This chapter reinforces your use of your own natural or learned talents and abilities as well as the hidden benefits of properties you own or will acquire as a method to help solve problems, yours and the other party to your negotiations, by the use of barter.

There are several key words in this stated goal. Let us discuss them before moving into the chapter. They are:

- Natural or learned talents.
- Abilities.
- Hidden benefits.
- Properties you own or will acquire.
- Solve problems.

Natural or Learned Talents

When you look to what you can contribute to the overall improvement of a property you may acquire, or offer to its seller as a value to the transaction, you will examine your own talents, as well as those of any partner in the venture into real estate. Good decorating skills, ability to paint and get 99 percent or more of the paint on the wall and not you, good at choosing colors, a love for gardening with proof that you don't kill whatever you plant are some of the elements of which I am speaking. However, there is more that you may not directly relate to the fixing-up or remodeling of a home or apartment building. Management skills are also a good and often more natural skill than one learned. Without the ability to manage your tenants, or deal with other workers you will hire from time to time, you may have difficulty in owning and operating income property. Are you a good cook? How can that relate to fix-up of real estate? What if you thought about opening a breakfast-lunch diner, or wanted to throw a catered party for the seller of a property you wanted to buy and offered that service as a part of the down payment? Can you or your partner sew? Make drapes, hang them, fix broken ones, and so on. All little things that make up a great team for acquisition of real estate that needs some tender loving care to bring out the real (and often really big) profit that lay hidden under lack of care.

Abilities

By this, I mean what you do as a living. Is your skill valuable to you in the quest to find properties? For example, are you a computer whiz, and can surf the tax rolls and other databases that are so very helpful in getting the facts you can use in making sound and well-informed decisions about what property to purchase? Or do you have a service that is connected to the building or construction industry that will not only help you in the actual work to fix up and maintain your own property, but which is a value item that can be offered to the seller instead of money? Even if your profession may not be related to any of these, you may still be able to offer a service or product that the seller can use and will take as a part of the value of the down payment when they sell you their property. Often overlooked is the ability to acquire items or services that the seller would take that you cannot directly provide because of your own abilities. By the time you finish a chapter, you will have a bank of lights switched on in that cartoon cloud above you.

Hidden Benefits

Most real estate has benefits that may go unused or even undetected because of many different reasons. This book is dedicated to helping you ascertain what those are and if you cannot obtain direct benefit yourself, then perhaps you can sell them, barter them, or otherwise get benefit from them in one way or the other. Some of them are obvious, but still not used. The boat dock behind your house or the property you are going to acquire can be rented out, and that is the benefit of an income stream that you or the seller can keep for a period of time. The timeshare of a mountain cabin you own but hardly use or the timeshare you get by exchanging some part-time labor (yours or your partner's) on a couple of weekends, and so on. The possibility of this sort of thing is nearly endless once you dig down and really look at the possibilities.

Properties You Own or Will Acquire

The boat dock is one such benefit that comes with either your own dock or the one at the property you are going to buy. However, the idea here is to look at what other benefits perhaps you have not thought about. Is there room to plant fruit trees or plant a garden? If so, a small investment in certain types of fruit trees or a garden can have several important benefits in a few years. Fruit to serve to your friends and families, make up into gift baskets, exchange to local restaurants for cash or even scrip to dine in their restaurant, (which can provide a great value that extends well beyond your growing season). Of course, the fruit and veggies you grow can be sold, but you will quickly find that the scrip aspect might have a far greater value to you. Try offering the owner of that duplex you want to buy $5,000 worth of tomatoes and see how far you get. Not very far unless that owner has a way to deal with that much produce. However, a local chain of restaurants might be very glad to pay you top dollar for those vine ripe tomatoes or corn or eggplant, or whatever if they can pay you in scrip redeemable at their own restaurants. You will see how the landscape at the property you want to buy also has value that the owner didn't think of. Let that value work for you in helping you purchase his or her property.

Solve Problems

The way to a win/win situation is to be able to solve your problem as well as that of the other party. You will do this by understanding the nature of real estate transactions. The vast majority of sellers have an agenda that they feel compelled or are compelled to satisfy. That is their problem. It comes from such a long list of scenarios that I am sure you can think of many such situations. Often, what the seller sees as the solution to their problem is not the only solution. It may not even be the best one. Sell? That is generally what sellers see as their way out. However, what are the steps to that end? Rent? That is where many opportunities are found because to rent a property that is slipping into a status of poor management and upkeep can be a declining potential. Yet, that is what many people who cannot sell do, because of the bad market at the time or because the really poor condition of the property has dictated it. I have stressed that the way you succeed in anything that involves another person is to help that person reach or at least get closer to his or her goals. If you can show them that path, and at the same time are offering them one of these values or hidden benefits of which all this has been directed, you can solve their problem, and help yourself gain your goal as well as move the other party closer to their own.

Real estate investing is a simple matter of transferring benefits from one pocket to another. Yet, most people who buy and sell real estate are rarely able to relate to this concept. One reason for this is that there is nothing more personal or valuable than the benefit that you obtain from what you own. You have probably heard someone who just had his offer rejected say, "They think they own gold?" Well, that's exactly what many people think about what they own. The unfortunate aspect of this is that they often have this opinion without considering what the actual value of those "benefits" is. If you accept my constant and perhaps nerve-racking obsession that the key to success in real estate investing is to have a good grasp and a strong focus on your goals, then you can see where I am heading with this premise. Because most people do not have clear-cut goals, or for that matter, any definable and measurable goals at all, you can see how difficult it is to place a value on these benefits. Worse still, they may not really know what benefits they need to maximize to best attain their desired goals.

BARTER: THE ANCIENT WAY OF THE NEW MILLENNIUM

Equating a benefit value to everything you own is possible. Your car gives you certain benefits that may include transportation to and from work. Your television set provides entertainment or keeps the kids occupied while you do something else. Real estate also provides benefits, and these benefits vary from property to property and from person to person.

For example, take a person who owns a home. As long as the person lives in that home, the benefit derived from the investment is the basic use of the facility and the long-range appreciation the asset may be limited to: the benefit of living space and the ultimate appreciation of the asset.

Both benefits are real, yet it is the anticipation of appreciation that makes ownership desirable. The homeowner who sells his or her house transfers his or her benefit to another person. This new property owner may view the benefits differently, depending on the goals of the original owner. The seller takes his or her new benefit and moves into another position.

You must think of everything in terms of benefits. The connection of the success to your investing in real estate to your goals is a tight circle. If you overlook proper orientation to your goals, then you kiss a real success goodbye. If you know what you want and strive to get it, you succeed. However, knowing what you want is not a dollar goal, but a benefit-oriented goal.

We all seek to obtain a "package" of benefits. We may not have a clear focus, but we can think of it as success, or financial independence, or to be rich. Therefore, those are targets to be sure, but difficult to measure, hard to keep in focus, and have no specific interim goals established to take us toward that desired point.

Once there is a clear focus and we can establish what benefits are more important and which will transport us to our desired goal, it becomes relatively easy to make decisions of what assets do not provide either the benefits we want or need. To this end, it is critical to recognize the benefits that are lost or not maximized. A lost benefit is like putting all your money in a box and hiding it under the bed, instead of depositing it in the bank and earning interest, or investing it in materials to fix up your home.

With this idea in mind, we can relate to our ultimate goals. We can learn far more quickly with much greater dedication and focus on the steps that must be taken to succeed in the quest to build our real estate portfolio. In making this determination, we can then decide to get rid of a particular property in exchange for another property that provides the desired benefits and sought-after goals.

Barter Things You Own That You Do Not Need

Bartering is neither new nor unique; it is one of the oldest forms of commercial enterprise, and has been mentioned in several chapters thus far. The exchange of goods, products, services, and promises for similar items has been going on for thousands of years and will continue if you realize that others want what you have.

Barter includes just about everything and every service of which you can think. From services as a bartender, CPA, lawyer, doctor, or gardener, any item you have around the house, office, or backyard is available for barter. Keep in mind that the chapter on real estate exchanges goes into the 1031 type of exchange and, to get a full understanding of barter and exchanges, that chapter would be worth rereading.

EXAMPLE 1: FINDING WHAT YOU HAVE TO BARTER.   Phillip wants to buy a condominium from Ocean Development Company in Miami Beach, Florida. The drawback is that he doesn't have sufficient cash to make the down payment. However, he does have something to barter, if he'll only make a proper inventory of what he does in fact own.

Assume for a moment that Phillip is a CPA. That ability has value, and that value is an item he could consider to exchange or barter to Ocean Development Company. If he had to offer his time, off hours, for a year or two, as the down payment on the condominium of his dreams, and it was acceptable to the seller, another barter transaction will have succeeded.

On the other hand, Phillip may be a mechanic working for the local gas station. It could be that his hobby is gardening and that the backyard of his father-in-law's house, where he and his wife live, is filled with rare and unique plants, the kind of plants that developers look for when they decorate their condominiums. If Phillip is lucky, he might find that his plants were more than enough to be his down payment. Chalk up a second barter deal that just succeeded.

Barter Your Way to Your Goal

As you head down the pathway to wealth and fame as a real estate investor, keeping your goals firmly in sight, you might have a very common hurdle to overcome. Bad credit. One of the hardest things for some investors to overcome is bad credit. Without good credit, getting loans can be absolutely out of the question. That is, getting loans from a bank. Getting a mortgage from a motivated seller who is more willing to get rid of a property that he or she cannot handle might be more important to them than your credit rating.

However, you still have to have something to put down to clench the deal. Okay, here is your predicament. Like many investors, you have discovered that the biggest problem in buying is to come up with either super triple credit or to have a sound and valuable down payment. You can almost always make a deal if you can give a down payment. Owning property starts the ball rolling. Once you own something solid, like real estate, you have equity. The more equity you have, the simpler your task is of getting a mortgage, or other needed financing. Therefore, one of the foundations of creative financing is the transfer of equity. Barter can help you create equity and make deals. Look at the following example.

EXAMPLE 2: REALIZING YOU NEED TO GET CLOSER TO YOUR GOAL.

I own a vacant lot, free and clear of all debt, which is worth $150,000. My intrinsic benefit is a banking of $150,000, yet this benefit is not the same as a realized benefit. The lot does little for me unless I look at it either as an investment that I hope will increase in value or as a future building site where I want to build a new home, or office building, something that will produce and grow rather than sit there costing me money just to hold onto.

On one hand, if the area was booming and property values were going up each week, I would look to appreciation as the benefit. However, it is important for me to make some judgment on this lot. Why do I own it? What do I want to get out of it? What are the benefits I hope to obtain from owning this lot? Can I swap it for that immediate benefit or another benefit closer to my goal?

Charlie offers me $110,000 cash. This now creates a scale against which I must weigh the benefit of the lot. Would $110,000 cash provide more benefit than the vacant lot? Alternatively, should I hold out for a greater payment, or something else? Whatever the answer is, I should review my goals once again.

Then, Alex enters the picture. In exchange for the lot, he offers me a 48-foot sailboat that has a mortgage of $60,000 against it. This presents another dilemma, another opportunity to examine the benefits I want versus the benefits offered.

Barter as a Pathway to Your Goals

You need to look at your assets as a route to your goals. Through barter and exchange, you can frequently go directly to GO and collect that desired benefit. That three-year-old car sitting in your driveway might be the down payment to get you into that duplex across town that in turn will help you attain a part of your desired goals.

Real estate investors need to open their eyes to the potential of barter. It may be that barter will only be a decisive factor to a deal and not the total transaction itself. Professional dealmakers know the value of some final benefit to lock up a hard-to-close transaction.

An example of this is what I often call the "vacation on me" barter transaction. The goal of this type of closing technique is to be in a position to offer the seller something that guarantees your deal. The item here would be a vacation for the seller and his wife.

Example 3: Offer a Benefit.   "Mrs. Seller, you will notice that I have adjusted your counteroffer only slightly, giving in to the majority of your needs. To compromise those areas that were not possible, I want to offer you and your husband accommodations for seven nights, space available of course, in any resort in the world affiliated with the RCI organization. I have a catalog of the several thousand such resorts located around the world from which you can select the area and specific resorts you might like to visit."

RCI is the primary timeshare exchange network in the world. Timeshare properties are usually a condominium form of ownership that is divided into "week" segments. For example, the 23rd week of the year at Orlando International Resort Club would relate to my actual ownership and fixed use during my ownership of that week at that location. However, through RCI I'm able to "bank" my week's use and swap it to another location at another time with other timeshare owners banking their weeks in the same manner. If I owned only one timeshare that was approved by RCI and I was a member of the organization, I could select to exchange my week for any other location for any time of the year and I could give you or another person that week's vacation. This simple act might be enough to close the deal. In addition, if you are like me and own more than one timeshare property, it becomes an ideal way to get life and benefits out of a timeshare you forgot to put into the rental pool or its exchange potential will shortly expire.

But what about those thousands of you who don't own a timeshare week that you could so simply offer as a deal maker? Don't worry, you can either obtain your own timeshare week, or at least obtain use of a week through barter. The key here is to know someone who has a timeshare week that you can borrow for a year.

Assume that you know me and that you feel that if you offered the seller a week's vacation somewhere you could tie down the deal. You could come to me and say, "Jack,

   a. I'll paint your car, or
   b. Supply carpets for your rental units, or
   c. Do your income tax calculations for two years, or
   d. Reupholster your living room sofas, or
   e. Give you 10 hours of tennis lessons."

And so on, so that you could obtain the use of one of my timeshare weeks to use it as a decisive factor to one of your deals. I might find that one of (a) through (e) was more of a benefit to me than the timeshare week. If so, I would make the deal with you, and you in turn could use that week as a dealmaker. This naturally is just a hint of the hundreds of such potential transactions you could do for yourself with other kinds of benefits. It might be that the "deal-maker" for your transaction would be a seven-day cruise to Jamaica, a mink coat, or a sapphire and diamond ring. Each of these "things" can be obtained through barter.

What Is a Barter Club, and Should You Join One?

In most cities, there exists what are called "barter clubs." They have names such as Barter Center, Exchange Club, or Interchange. These organizations act as clearinghouses for barter of all kinds by giving their members "credits" or barter dollars for the exchange made between members. In this way, I could get from you barter dollars for an item or service I trade to you. Later on, I could "pay" to someone else those barter dollars for an item or service I was to get in exchange.

The concept is very sound and works out great on paper. In fact, in some real situations barter clubs serve a good purpose and actually give their members a fair value for the cost, which usually is a cash payment to the club based on a percent of the trade dollars you spend or receive (or both). The benefit to owning barter dollars is the freedom to make one deal and to spend the credits in several places.

One such barter club that I belong to has members that offer every kind of service you can think of from acupuncture to zebra rides. There are doctors, dentists, accountants, massage clinics, schools, auto repair, advertising, professional consultations of different needs, carpet sales, restaurants, vacations of various kinds and location, and so on. Each business barters their service or product for the barter dollars they will get, which they can then spend on other services or products available.

If you accumulated a bankroll of barter dollars, which you could very easily do by offering a service to the barter club members in your part time, you could use these "dollars" as part or all of a down payment on real estate you want to buy.

Join one of the local barter clubs that you find listed in your Yellow Pages under Barter, or Exchanges, or Trades. Whether you have a professional service or hobby you could offer, or just some hard work, such as cleaning offices or waxing cars, put a top price on the service.

As you collect barter dollars, you are on your way to accumulating equity that you may be able to use in your real estate investing. However, there is a drawback to these barter clubs. The people who offer their services often have double standards. I'll wax your car or do your books or paint your car for this cash price, but for barter-dollars, you have to pay more. While this might be realistic, in the end it cheapens the value of the barter-dollar. In addition, some people in the barter clubs get barter dollar heavy from one or two large transactions and then "dump" their dollars by buying anything they can get their hands on. This, too, cheapens the value of the barter dollar.

How to Tell If a Barter Club Is Okay

1. If it has been in business for more than five years, that is a plus.
2. Will it give you a list of members prior to joining? If not, forget about that organization.
3. Talk to some of the members. What do they tell you? Are they happy with the barter exchanges? If not, avoid the club.

4. Will the owner of the club give you references? If not, forget the club. If he or she does, check them out by calling the person directly. Ask questions such as, "How do you know this person?" "Have you dealt with the barter club?" "How so?" "Do you think my joining the club is a good idea?" Keep the person on the phone for a while. Even the best reference will start to tell you the nitty-gritty after a while. Improvise, but if you are not comfortable with what you hear, then forget that club.

5. Ask the Better Business Bureau if it knows anything about the club. If it does, it is apt to be through complaints. Get as much information on that aspect as possible.

Barter the Use of Your Home

One of the truly interesting things to do is take a long holiday in some far-off land. Sure, this kind of trip might be very expensive, but it will not be if you swap the use of your home for the holiday. This is easier than you might think. There are a number of sources for such swaps, and most come with a record of accomplishment of success. However, with everything as important as giving up your home for another person's home for a month or two, be sure to check out references from satisfied customers. Search the Internet (or get a teenager to do it for you), and simply look for these key words, "holiday home swaps," "House exchanges," or "swap my home for yours."

SWEAT EQUITY AS A BARTER CONCEPT

Your own sweat can be one of the very best of the barter elements. Since this form of barter is actually a separate technique, I will treat it as such.

Make Deals with Your Promise to Perform as a Valued Service

The first-time investor can look to the sweat equity kind of transaction as one of the very best to enable that first transaction to be made with a minimum amount of cash passing hands.

In essence, sweat equity is your own work or labor that will be used to transform a property or provide value to the seller, or both. You will use this future or promised value as the down payment (all or part) in the transaction.

Why Sweat-Equity Transactions Work

Sweat-equity deals sometimes work because the seller is enticed to believe that if the intended work is not completed on time, or if the buyer cannot then get the financing needed to complete the transaction, the seller will end up keeping the property that has now been improved.

Other sweat equity transactions work when the sellers are willing to sell on easy terms and need only be convinced that the transaction proposed by the buyer is "safe."

The equity the buyer brings to the transaction is in fact real. It is work, time, and effort, all of which are expensive and have value. Of course, the key is to find the right transaction.

Look at the guides on the following pages that outline the steps in looking for a property that will fit the profile for a sweat-equity deal.

Property Profiles for Sweat-Equity Deals

You will want to look for properties that fit one or more of the following criteria as possible. While it is possible to find properties outside of this list, as this may be your first sweat-equity investment stick to the guide if possible.

- Look for properties that are:
  - not more than a one-hour drive from where you now live.
  - in need of repairs or fix up.
  - in an area that has properties of greater value.
  - the kind of properties you would want to own.
  - properties that you feel you can handle.
- The first property you buy should be:
  - an income-producing property.
  - at least three separate rental units, or be convertible into three such units or more.
  - well constructed.
  - without any serious defects.
- For you to get the best deal, find an owner who is:
  - a successful and busy professional person (doctors make ideal sellers).
  - unable to manage his or her own property.
  - owner of other real estate.
  - local or not, but lives some distance from the property.
  - does not need immediate cash.
- Make sure you know what your sweat-equity abilities are by:
  - being honest with yourself as to what you can do.
  - trying to learn sweat-equity abilities if you have none.
  - assessing the amount of time you can devote to the work.
- You will find this property by:
  - developing your comfort zone.
  - looking for "For Rent" signs on neglected property.
  - finding a real estate broker you can relate to.
  - making offers.
- Before you buy you should:
  - visit the property during morning, afternoon, and evening hours.

- get a good understanding of the rental market in the area. Know what is for rent, what is not rented, and the prices and comparisons of rentals.
- know and understand the zoning restrictions.
- know and understand the subdivision restrictions if any.
- make sure that you can deliver your sweat equity offered.
- have a good real estate lawyer.

EXAMPLE 4: THE JOHNSON SWEAT-EQUITY CASE.   Robert Johnson worked as a manager of a supermarket. His wife was a secretary for a real estate office. They lived in a small one-bedroom apartment that was about 20 minutes from both their jobs. They had a little cash saved. Mr. Johnson could work different shifts at the supermarket and was more flexible with his free time. They took stock of their sweat-equity abilities.

ROBERT'S SWEAT-EQUITY ABILITIES

- Good at painting.
- A green thumb, so good at gardening.
- Good with light carpentry.
- Physically strong.
- Flexible with his time by working night or weekend shifts at the supermarket.
- Willing to learn other tasks that will help own real estate.

HELEN'S SWEAT-EQUITY ABILITIES

- Good at color selections.
- Can sew.
- Also good at gardening.
- Knows where and how to buy things right.
- Willing to learn other jobs.
- Free weekends and evenings.
- Very supportive of her husband's ideals.

You can see that the Johnsons are moderately equipped in the sweat-equity department. If it isn't on their list, we will assume that they are going to have to seek outside help. Therefore, if it requires plumbing or electrical or anything beyond simple carpentry, extra help will be needed. That means added expense, so when the Johnsons look for a property, they want to avoid properties that require work outside their major advantages. If you are an expert in electrical wiring of homes and other kinds of real estate improvements or are a plumber, you would look for those properties that could be improved with those specific talents.

Working Their Comfort Zone: The Search for a Property. The Johnsons had been studying a geographic zone that was near where they lived. It was a nice residential area that had a mix of different kinds of real estate. They were looking for a small apartment building or a large, older home that was in an area that was properly zoned to allow multifamily residences that they could convert to apartments.

They searched the area by using two methods. They had taken up riding bicycles as a form of exercise, so whenever they could they would ride their bikes through this area. They didn't just ride their bikes in a haphazard route, however; it was always carefully planned out, and a small map of the area and note pad accompanied them on their nearly daily trips in the area.

What they wanted to do was to become so familiar with this section of town that they would have a mental picture of each property, street, and opportunity when it came up. This process took time. As they would ride through the area and locate for-sale signs or any change in the status quo, they would make note of it.

If the for-sale sign were by a broker, they would have Phyllis, a real estate sales clerk they had met and liked, check it out. Phyllis was their second method of searching for their future investment. They had met Phyllis after talking to several salespeople at several different offices and felt comfortable that she understood their needs.

They soon began to know everything possible about the area. They started to get a feel for the streets and the neighborhood. They began to make value assessments based on elements that often are missed by the people who live in the area. Why is this street nicer to live on than another? Alternatively, what makes this building a better investment because of what is going to happen in the near future?

That last bit of news was the result of going to the monthly city council meetings where they learned that two blocks away a new government center was to be built that would employ nearly 300 people. The impact to the area would include demand for rentals and increased traffic. The opportunity might not last too long as sooner or later the information would sift down to all property owners. They also discovered that very few people ever showed up at these meetings. Once they looked around the room, they saw that the majority of the people there were lawyers, a few interested neighbors of the areas being discussed at the meetings. There were also a few real insider real estate investors, just like the Johnsons were becoming.

They Found the Ideal Property. The sign said, "For rent." It was on a property that they had noticed was going downhill for several months. An old beat-up pickup truck had been left in the front yard, the lawn was in bad shape, and in general the house was showing a lot of wear and little loving care.

When they called the number, they were told they had reached "Doctor Funt's office."

As it turned out, Dr. Funt had owned this property for nearly five years, renting it out for most of that time. The last tenant had turned out to be a deadbeat, however, and left in the middle of the night, literally taking with him the kitchen sink as well as anything of value that wasn't nailed down. The Johnsons said they simply wanted to see the inside of the home and did not get into any negotiations with the doctor at this time. They didn't even ask if the property was for sale.

After spending about an hour looking through the home, Robert and his wife realized that all that was needed was cleaning, paint, new carpets, new drapes, a new lawn, and attendance to the shrubs. The home would be well worth their effort if they could buy the property on terms that worked for them. The real ace for them was the separate garage, which, due to the zoning, could be converted into an apartment and rented out.

Sweat-Equity Plan. The Johnsons did their homework. They made a long list of all the items that needed repair, cleaning, paint, and so on. The list was very complete, and alongside each item was an estimate of the time needed to repair, clean, paint, and so on.

Next, there was a separate list of material needed. This list was equally as complete, and the prices for the material were estimated with the help of a sales clerk at one of the local builder supply stores in the area.

Offer to the Owner. Armed with this proposal, the Johnsons met with Dr. Funt and proposed that he sell the home to them on the following terms:

1. A purchase price that was reasonable. Johnson suggested $270,000. This was nearly $25,000 more than Dr. Funt had paid for the property five years earlier according to the records down at the county records office.

2. The Johnsons would repair, clean, paint, and fix up the house according to the detailed proposal that Robert Johnson had prepared.

3. All Dr. Funt had to pay for were the materials, which would cost around $8,000. It was agreed that this $8,000 was to be included in the purchase price.

4. At the end of the fix-up period, the Johnson's would have 160 days to obtain a new first mortgage on the property of at least $250,000.

5. Dr. Funt would hold a personal note for $20,000. The note would be interest only for seven years at 7 percent interest per annum, payable annually with a balloon at the end of that time.

Dr. Funt thought about this for a while and then rejected the proposal. The Johnsons let it rest for a few days and then got back in touch with Dr. Funt, asking him to meet them at the house. There they went over each repair that they would make to the property. They stressed the condition of the home, and the time needed to put it into shape.

Robert Johnson reminded Dr. Funt that in the proposal to buy the home the transaction was conditioned on the Johnsons finishing all of the work. If they didn't do so within 90 days, Funt could keep the house with the work done thus far. To show additional good faith, Johnson also agreed to move in by the 90th day and start paying $1,500 a month in rent up until the day they closed on the property. The rental agreement would be month by month so that if they did not close for any reason (such as they could not get the mortgage), they would move out.

Johnson also reminded Dr. Funt that the property would need most of the work done anyway just to get it rented again, so the doctor couldn't lose. He would get a fair value for the home, or he would get a lot of work done at little or no cost to him.

A couple of days later, the doctor signed the deal that was drafted by the Johnsons' lawyer. The Johnsons went to work, and by the time they had finished the home looked like a million dollars.

A savings bank appraised the restored home for $350,000 and agreed to lend up to $260,000 net of any loan costs. To soften the terms of the loan, Robert Johnson took only $255,000. He gave the proceeds of $255,000 to Dr. Funt, paid $1,200 to his lawyer for his efforts, and put $3,250 in his savings. The Johnsons had succeeded; their equity was because of their sweat . . . and their brains.

FIVE CRITICAL ELEMENTS OF A SWEAT-EQUITY PROPOSAL

1. Put everything down in the contract: exactly what you are expected to do and what you will get because of it.

2. The option for you to buy the property must be very specific.

3. Be sure to give yourself ample time to complete the work and to get the financing. Check with your local lenders to know how long the financing may take. Double that time.

4. Start looking to improve your position right away with your new property. Can you sell it or exchange it prior to having to close on it, making a profit along the way? Keep your options open.

5. Perform on the deal. A thousand things can come up that you didn't count on. However, do everything you can to fulfill your deal. Future deals will count on it.

There Are Many Forms of Sweat Equity

Sweat equity has many faces and can be used in many different kinds of transactions. Your sweat equity can come via a three-way deal. You might barter your future work to me for something I'll give you. Then you exchange that with some other party. Also, as in all kinds of exchanges and barter, you can swap your sweat equity for a note or mortgage. In this way, you can then exchange or swap the mortgage to the seller instead of your sweat equity. This technique would be useful if your specific ability was not needed for the property, but you still needed to create equity from some source other than money.

Of course, you might just as well learn how to print your own money, called *scrip*. In fact, this method of adding to the deal is used all the time and can be very helpful to you in closing many kinds of transactions.

CREATING YOUR OWN LEGAL CURRENCY SCRIP.

Scrip comes in whatever shape, color, and form you print it. It can look like Monopoly money or play cash or it might resemble the currency from some foreign government—just as long as it doesn't look like U.S. currency. Scrip can be for specific values as you decide, and it is good for whatever specific item or service you can provide.

EXAMPLE 5: RESTAURANT SCRIP.

If you own a fried-chicken restaurant, you could print up a couple of thousand dollars' worth of your own money in $10 increments and use this cash as part of your down payment on your next real estate investment.

EXAMPLE 6: FISHING SCRIP.

If you own a fishing boat, you could print up scrip in $200 increments to be applied to fishing trips. Or, if you could borrow your father's Cadillac from time to time (paying for gas, oil, and a small rental, of course), you could print up scrip in $100 increments to be applied against your nightly limo service.

The opportunities to create your own scrip are endless, as you will discover. In each instance, the concept of dealing with scrip is a deal closer and not necessarily as the total deal. Nonetheless, there will be transactions that can be made with your using scrip as your total payment to the seller.

EXAMPLE 7: FRIED-CHICKEN SCRIP.

The owner of the fried-chicken restaurant, Charles, printed up $5,000 of his own scrip in $10 bills. He indicates on the scrip that it must be redeemed by a specific date and that it cannot be used to pay tips or tax and that no change will be given against the scrip. To ward against counterfeiting, Charles signs each bill with his fountain pen and marks each bill with an invisible pen (visible only under ultraviolet light).

Charles did all of this because he had seen a small duplex that he wanted to buy. He had made an offer several weeks earlier, but was turned down because he didn't have enough cash to put down. The seller of the duplex was asking $115,000 for the property. He had a small mortgage of $65,000 and wanted $30,000 cash above the mortgage.

Armed with his scrip, Charles went back and offered to buy the duplex for $95,000 with assumption of the existing mortgage, pay Charles $18,000 cash and $10,000 in scrip at his restaurant. The seller countered: Total price of $100,000, assume the mortgage of $65,000, and pay $25,000 cash and $10,000 in scrip. Charles knew that he could swing this deal now by putting up the $10,000 in scrip and borrow the balance from a local savings bank.

EXAMPLE 8: KITCHEN APPLIANCE SCRIP. Ellis owned a kitchen appliance store. He too wanted to use scrip to buy real estate. Therefore, he printed up scrip in $250 denominations and indicated on the scrip that it had to be redeemed within 12 months, and that it was not good on any red-tagged sales items during that time.

Ellis had found a property he wanted to buy. It turned out to be owned by a local real estate investor who owned many different kinds of properties. Some of these properties included rental apartments. Ellis knew that this seller would have use of kitchen appliances sooner or later, so this seller fit nicely into Ellis' plans.

This points out the advantage of knowing something about the seller prior to making the offer. Once you know the seller can use the kind of scrip you have, you have the edge in making this type of transaction. Ellis' offer would be a simple $10,000 in kitchen appliance scrip as the down payment on the desired property. The deal may require other techniques to be used in addition, such as outside financing or additional seller-held financing, or some other highly creative technique provided for you in this book.

WHAT IF YOU DON'T OWN A RESTAURANT OR APPLIANCE STORE? There are several ways to create scrip. Having your own business helps, but it is not the only way to use this very effective tool. In essence, there are two basic methods of generating your own scrip from outside sources. In my book *Real Estate Investing with Other People's Money*, I discuss these two methods as "Watered Scrip" and "Commissioned Scrip."

Watered Scrip That Comes from Others at a Discount. The basic element to understand here is that you will acquire from other people credits against their services or products. You will print up the scrip that they agree to honor, and you will buy it from them, either at a discount or by using paper you create against things you now own or are about to buy.

The people who own the businesses must be shown that the scrip you are going to create will bring them business they don't already have, which in turn will generate more business that will be on a cash basis. Scrip business then has an advertising value that accounts for the discount to you. In addition, by offering to buy future business now you can frequently get a substantial discount for that alone. Couple these factors with the idea that you aren't going to pay money for the scrip, and the idea becomes very attractive for you. Best of all, since you are going to tailor the scrip to the transaction, you will have a higher success rate in real estate transactions. You can go out and get the kind of scrip that will fit the deal.

Buying Scrip on Your Terms. You say to Mr. Furniture Store Owner, "I'll give you a $10,000 second mortgage against a five-unit apartment building I'm buying if you will sell me $12,000 in scrip good only in your store." Alternatively, "Mr. Schultz, I'll give you an option to buy my five-unit apartment building, good for one year, for $5,000 worth of hotel scrip in New York City." Alternatively, "Mr. Marks, I'll give you a two-year lease in the garage apartment for you or one of your clients if you will give me $12,000 in scrip good for meals in your chain of restaurants." Alternatively, "Mr. Hennington, I'll give you $12,000 in scrip for meals in Mark's restaurant chain if you'll give me $14,000 in scrip good for cars on your used car lots."

In each case, you want to offer something of value for scrip at a greater face value. The difference between the two is your profit for doing the transaction, but it comes to you at no real cost to the other side of the scrip transaction. The furniture storeowner has a markup of products and may want to move some furniture. The owner would want to make sure the scrip didn't apply to sale merchandise, so the $2,000 profit you make in the scrip versus second mortgage trade is warranted. By the way, it is possible that the owner would take your second mortgage and use it as a down payment on something if he or she was unable to swap furniture for the property he or she wanted to buy.

Commissioned Scrip. Unlike the watered scrip that you "buy" at a discount, the commissioned scrip is scrip that you establish through some third party and then redeem as cash, less your commission.

This kind of scrip doesn't have the benefit of allowing you to exchange a long-term payback as you can if obtaining watered scrip by giving a three-year mortgage on the five-unit property you are going to buy. However, it does have a very strong impact on a transaction and can help you close transactions that need this kind of kicker. You will get a discount nonetheless and frequently get up to a year or so to pay for the scrip.

EXAMPLE 9: COMMISSIONED SCRIP TRANSACTION.   Assume for a moment that you are attempting to buy a vacant tract on which you will build a small strip store. The owner of the site is asking $200,000 for the site and you have offered $175,000.

The negotiations have gone on for a week or so, and the seller is agreeing to the following terms in his most recent counteroffer to you:

- *Price:* $185,000
- *Cash down payment:* $50,000
- *Terms on the balance:* Cash within 18 months with interest at 12 percent per annum. If you want to build right away, the mortgage would have to be paid off at the time you took out a construction loan.

Most of this is acceptable to you because you are going to build right away, only you hate to put up the $50,000 now as you are going to mortgage 100 percent on the project.

In dealing with the seller, you discover that the seller likes to travel, so you come back with this following proposal:

- *Price:* $185,000

- *Down payment:* $70,000, made up of $20,000 cash and a ticket on a *QE 2* around-the-world cruise that leaves in 14 months with a double, deluxe outside cabin for two that has a value of $50,000. The balance is as the seller wants.

If the seller takes this transaction, you will have made a good deal as you have met the seller's terms but you only have to put up $20,000 cash plus a deposit on the cruise of around $1,500. In around 10 months, when the cruise has to be paid off in full, you will not have to pay the full $50,000 price because you will have made an arrangement with a travel agent to become one of their salespeople. In essence, you get a commission on the cruise.

Back up a moment. There are certain things you can buy that you wouldn't get until sometime in the future. Cruises and other vacations of almost any kind are prime examples of closing kickers that you can offer any seller. If the seller likes to travel, he or she is apt to bite at that offer, even though they may not have spent that much money on themselves.

You can see that you didn't have to own the travel agency to make the deal work. Whenever you acquire scrip that you will redeem in the future, you will have a discount built in through the commission. However, if you follow the tips in this chapter, there are other discounts you have to take into account that add to your profit in the transaction. All of these profits require that you set up the scrip transaction properly, so look at the checklist that will aid you in commission scrip deals.

CHECKLIST ON HOW TO MAKE PROFITABLE COMMISSION SCRIP DEALS

- ✓ Never enter into a commission scrip deal until you know exactly how much scrip you will need and for what specific product.
- ✓ Do, however, look for the kinds of products that will generally be useful and begin to make contacts in those areas. Meet the owners of these prime scrip products and services:
  - Travel agencies.
  - Kitchen and other building and home appliances and products dealers.
  - Lumber yards.
  - Jewelry stores.
  - Restaurants, and all other food vendors.
  - Resorts (include timeshare resorts).
  - Legal services.
  - Accounting services.

- Used car lots.
- New car agencies.
- Auto repair shops.

✓ Have a firm agreement with the owners of the businesses that you are doing business with. Make sure the agreement covers these following items:

- The name and address of the business or businesses honoring the scrip.
- The term for which the scrip shall be good (ample time).
- What the scrip includes and excludes.
- A statement that if the business is sold the liability of the scrip shall continue, or the scrip will be bought back for cash.
- A penalty if the scrip is not honored. If you have to redeem the scrip for cash yourself, you won't get the commission, so you should be owed that commission from the original party.
- How and when you are to redeem the scrip and for what price, less what commission.

✓ Check on the transaction from time to time to see if any scrip you may have traded is being turned down.

No matter what you do, there is apt to be a problem or two if you try to cut your deals too tight. Remember, the dealer in the product or service has to see a benefit. They are dealing in business for a profit and if you hit them for too much commission or don't redeem the scrip on time, the rest of your deal can fall apart. Also, remember that scrip and barter transactions work best when they are offered later on in the transaction and not right up front. They are kickers that close deals that you are getting close to, but just can't seem to nail down. You will find sellers who are willing to take scrip as the total down payment or outright purchase, but those transactions are far more difficult to find and make.

Hidden Benefits You Need to Do Homework to Find

Other kinds of kickers that you can use as deal makers often are overlooked because you don't spend the time or homework needed to find out what might turn the seller on.

Take a look at your potential kickers, keeping in mind that a kicker is any form of benefit that you can give or lend to the seller as part of the deal or as a bonus to entice him or her to make your deal.

The following is a list of your assets:

- You have your home.
- You own a cabin in North Carolina.
- You are an excellent tennis player.

Just looking at those assets it is clear that, as a starter you could offer a prospective seller some or all of the following:

- A holiday in North Carolina for two weeks.
- A holiday in North Carolina for two weeks for the next three years.
- A quantity of tennis lessons.

Each of these assets has a flexibility, and each has value that doesn't cost you anything other than some time or some inconvenience. Keep in mind that as you could offer the holiday in North Carolina to the owner of the sailboat, who could in turn provide sailing lessons to the seller you are dealing with, the opportunities are endless.

KICKERS USING THE TAX LAWS

There frequently are kickers that are of little or no benefit to you, but are cash in the pocket of the other party. For example, take the tax laws that you can work to your profit.

If you want to buy a property and are very close to making the deal, but no matter how much you try to close the transaction you are still a few thousand dollars apart, the depreciation kicker often works wonders. Let me set the stage of a transaction that is already filled with several different creative tools but still hasn't closed.

EXAMPLE 10: LOOKS LIKE A TAX BREAK.   Frank is the seller, and the property is a free and clear duplex that you want to buy. The price you and Frank have finally agreed on is $275,000. The terms that are agreeable to both parties are:

Price: $275,000 cash to Frank from a mortgage to be obtained by the buyer: $220,000.

Plus, as a part of the deal: $5,000 in scrip at Mark's restaurant chain.

In addition, as a part of the deal: $35,000 in the form of a second mortgage on a property you are buying down the street.

Plus, as part of the deal: $5,000 cabin on a two-week cruise for two to Alaska.

We are still $10,000 short. Frank wants that in cash, and you want to give him a second mortgage on the duplex in that same amount. You settle with $2,000 cash now, and the balance in three years plus 7 percent interest. Because Frank is getting cash at closing ($220,000 plus $2,000), he is satisfied.

SUMMARY OF BARTER, SWEAT EQUITY, SCRIP, AND KICKERS

In general, all these techniques are sound financing tools that can be used from time to time in making deals work for you. As I've mentioned several times, do your homework to try to fit the transaction to the seller, but don't worry if you make a cold offer when time or circumstances don't allow any homework. The worst anyone can ever do is turn you down. In addition, one thing all real estate investors know if they are ever to succeed in the game is if you aren't turned down from time to time you aren't making enough offers.

Beware of the Pitfalls of Barter Deals

The biggest pitfalls in barter, sweat equity, scrip, or kickers is knowing who you are dealing with, and then being sure to back up everything with good sound contracts. This means that you will have to have good legal representation in this area.

People get into trouble in barter by not checking values carefully, or, if the barter is through a barter club, by getting in too deep and building up too large a bank account. Barter dollars can be difficult to spend, and if the club folds they are impossible to get rid of.

Sweat equity is most likely the best single tool for the investor who has a strong back, good business mind, but little cash. It is hard to make too many errors if you are careful with your fix-up expenses. The worst area that gets investors using sweat equity into trouble is not having enough time to do the work promised. They start out thinking that they can do everything in days, only they get the flu or get transferred or a million other things come up. Be very careful of these kinds of problems.

Scrip has a mountain of problems if you are careless or don't document the deal properly. If you are dealing with a restaurant that is sold or goes out of business, your scrip is like bad checks. The people you gave scrip to will come back looking to you for redemption (some might even look for vengeance).

Kickers have few problems as long as you can deliver and as long as you don't tie yourself up with a commitment that you don't want to have to honor later on. For this reason, it is a good idea to have a "cash" value on all kickers that you can pay off if you want to or have to.

Chapter 21

NINE IMPORTANT STAGES OF SUCCESSFUL REAL ESTATE TRANSACTIONS

GOAL OF THIS CHAPTER

This chapter provides you with a fine-tuned checklist of critical stages that are important to the process that begins with finding a property to buy and successfully closing on it.

Many elements come to play in every real estate transaction that may be unique to that specific deal—things that happen that you may never experience again in the same way. There are nine stages of every real estate transaction that you should embrace as fundamental to every real estate transaction you initiate. These stages begin with the idea that you want to invest in or sell real estate and conclude with the actual closing of the deal. These stages occur for every buyer, and each side of the deal will have a different opinion and point of view of everything that happens. This chapter discusses each of these steps and attempts to give you a good idea what to expect, from either side of the fence, giving you tips on how to deal with some common problems and pitfalls that occur.

NINE STAGES OF A REAL ESTATE TRANSACTION

1. Laying the foundation to buy.

2. Getting the maximum benefit from the real estate profession.

3. Selecting a property to buy.

4. Negotiating to win.

5. Offering/contracting to buy to maximize your future gain.

6. Conducting detailed due diligence.

7. Getting the approvals needed with time to implement them.

8. Restructuring or fine-tuning the deal.

9. The closing.

Each of these stages has its own start and finish. While some stages may appear to overlap, what is really happening is that you may have moved too quickly into the next stage, without having completed the earlier one. This creates a gap that often appears as indecision or "purchase-itus" on the part of the buyer or "sellers-itus" that most sellers experience. This is when doubt creeps in and the parties to the transaction have to move back a step or two to decide to end the process, and move on to another property or buyer, or move forward to work out the reasons for this indecision. These periods can occur unexpectedly and can quickly kill months of what appeared to be friendly negotiations between the buyer and seller. I can assure you, as a broker caught in the middle of many such moments, what is often needed is a person or several persons who can act as an intermediary/referee/arbitrator to smooth out the feathers that were ruffled. Sometimes all that is necessary is that. Smooth the water, calm the nerves of one or both parties, make sure that everything is understood, and the parties are returned to their previous friendly mood.

Not all transactions are smooth events. There is the potential for considerable human drama. After all, the purchase or sale of real estate can be the most expensive transaction the parties will ever engage in—except getting married, or being divorced. Everything may be moving along smoothly. Then the storm can come crashing in and, in a second, the whole thing seems to fall apart. It is in those moments dreams disappear.

Each of the nine stages covered in this chapter has people involved: the buyer, of course, the real estate broker and/or sales agent, the other party to the contract, the respective lawyers, the closing agent, and the escrow agent, to name the usual subjects. Each takes time and adds to the complexity of the transaction.

Buying and selling real estate for a profit is not a one-person job. No highly successful investor has ever done it all alone. There simply is not enough time. Once your wealth begins to build up, the time it would take for some simpler tasks will best be left to others you can hire. It becomes a matter of priority, as your wealth grows, not a matter of your not being able to do the job yourself. Wealth does have its rewards.

Review each of these nine stages in detail.

LAYING THE FOUNDATION TO BUY

For the vast majority of real estate investors, the most important element to start with is an awareness that you do not have a clear understanding of your goals. Without the proper foundation, you will have, at best, a random chance at success. Granted, there are people who do have success at things they do and they have no foundation at all. You may have read about them or you may have known people like that. What did you say when you learned about the person down the street who sold his house for twice its value because he was the key piece to a redevelopment of that block? "That lucky son of a gun."

That's right, he or she was lucky, and many other investors will be just as lucky due to no specific act of their own. They just happened to make a buy that turned into a small pot of gold. Unfortunately, for every one of these "lucky" investments, there are dozens of not-so-lucky ones. Buying real estate is *not* a guaranteed route to wealth. Not everything you buy is going to go up in value fast enough (if at all) to cover the cost of holding on to it. Not every property will produce a profit; not every apartment building will be fully occupied and become a money machine. Losing your shirt investing in real estate is possible no matter how much you know.

In fact, some very smart investors lose their shirts. Not every investment I have made has turned out the way I wanted it to. I have taken a few high flyers that could have turned out like a diamond mine, but instead developed into a latrine. Other investments I have made where every bit of "insider" information suggested that the value jump would take place in a short period, say two to three years at the most, turned into a wait of more than a decade before the big strike would come. Yet, come it did, but only because I could hold onto the property in the meantime. Keep in mind that I did not have the advantage of this book when I started out in the process of building wealth in real estate. I made mistakes because everything I read about investing, and I read a lot, made it look so easy. I used to go to seminars and listen to people tout their systems of making fortunes without risking any of their own money; people who, if you met them in a party or outside the seminar circuit would appear to be of the most-unlikely-to-fail category. Few of those people are around today. I have attempted to learn from as many mistakes that have been made by others as possible. Unfortunately, I had to learn from some of my own mistakes as well. However, that is your gain.

The great healer of making a bad real estate investment is time. Time will make all things well, unless the investor has really screwed up. Time is so important that in your initial approach to buying any real estate you need to research this aspect more than another element. It should be the number-one item on your preliminary due diligence list. The preliminary list is the cursory things you do in determining if you even want to make an offer. Your detailed due diligence is what you do once, as a buyer; you control the situation. The time I am talking about is a combination of these factors. The amount of time you need to learn everything about the area where you plan to invest, the time it will take you to turn the investment into a profit, and what possible roadblocks can come between your anticipated timetable and reality. Never move into any time-oriented situation where you are being rushed or pushed to make a definitive decision.

In my case, the investments that turned sour for me were directly the result of miscalculations dealing with time. As it turned out, in the end, I had been right about everything that was going to cause the property to jump in value. Only, the time it took from pulling of the trigger of the "starter's gun" to finishing the race as a winner was a lot longer than anyone anticipated. However, the indications of a win on the way were still there. What had gotten in the way, what had unplugged the clock, so to speak, was the second element that should be in the preliminary due diligence list—people. Generally, when time suddenly slows down, it is due to people getting in the way. It might even be a member of your limited partnership who thinks he should be in control, or a lender who promised to loan the needed funds or, as is a growing case in many communities, local bureaucratic infighting. For me, these have now become the elements that I pay a lot of attention to. If I am to have a partner (which is a very rare situation these days), I want to know everything about that partner first. That may not ensure that there will be no problems, but it can weed out potential problems. As for politics and political infighting, it is not always possible to predetermine how it can affect your plans. What is a developer-friendly political environment can change by the morning following an election. But it is critical to examine, weigh, and make a decision about whether there are people and politics involved that will take a lot of time to make the transaction work. Any investor approaching any real estate acquisition should anticipate what he or she would need for it to be a reasonable success. If you need approvals from anyone for anything to succeed, the time to reach the successful culmination of that stage must be carefully analyzed—the time, as well as the money to sustain it.

So, the occasional high flyer (risky deal) should be left to the big player who can anticipate and afford the potential loss. Building your wealth in real estate will not always be a downhill ride. There will be times in even the most conservative investment when you may have to pull in the belt a notch or two to counteract temporary setbacks. Setbacks, such as high unemployment in your area (which does nasty things to rental projects), or city projects such as new roads that will have a future benefit, but meanwhile can cause you to lose tenants in your strip store because of the repaving of the road that is the only access to the property has been held up for 12 months.

Being able to bend with these elements of the game is all part of the road to success. If it were easy, it would not be so rewarding when you got there. Success is simply attained. Not easily, just simply. It requires only focus on your goals, dedication and persistence.

The development of your foundation is, of course, up to you. Some of you will get it in the school of hard knocks. That is, you will experience a bit more failure early in your learning, and if you hang in, the success will come later. Hard knocks, by the way, are really a misnomer. If you succeed, you will look back on all your failures as important stages in your success. You cannot simply have success without failure. This is the most important part of your total journey toward success.

People who are failures in life find a reason why each failure was not their fault. However, people who succeed in one project after another generally do so because they make an effort to find out what they did to cause any of the failures they had along the way, and have learned how not to do it again. The successful embrace failure because it is essential to advancement and success. Into every real estate investor's life a little rain must fall.

I have given you all the basics you need to know to get ready. Applying them is up to you. The six elements of success—knowledge, enthusiasm, motivation, perseverance, clear goals, and no fear of failure—are within you if you pull it together and make them work for you. You can be a small success or a big success. It will depend on how you have established your goals. You will find the balance, or you will simply find that real estate is not your thing.

GETTING THE MAXIMUM BENEFIT FROM THE REAL ESTATE PROFESSIONAL'S ASSISTANCE

One of the important short cuts you can make as a real estate investor is to build a great relationship with the local real estate profession. Realtors and other brokers in your area can help you in many ways. It is not essential for you to do this, but it is the smart way to become a real estate insider. I say this because as a realtor for over 40 years, I have known many real estate investors who go out of their way not to deal with realtors or brokers. Their rationale is that they save on having to pay a commission. In so doing, I have seen these same investors struggle to make deals, spin their wheels dealing with sellers who also avoid the real estate profession (with the same rationale that they are saving having to pay a commission). Accept the fact that you will become both a buyer and a seller. As such, you will streamline your success by finding and working with the real estate professional who is best suited to help you identify your goals, and then to help you quickly attain them.

Finding a Knowledgeable and Effective Real Estate Professional

There are two categories of real estate brokers and salespeople. There are realtors, and brokers who are not realtors. Let me explain it this way. The National Association of Realtors (NAR) is a nationwide professional organization, the largest of its kind. To join the NAR, agents must agree to be bound by a series of rules that govern their activities in many ways. They have their own internal professional standard code, and a strict self-policing of that code and its enforcement. Realtors make up the majority of the brokers dealing in real estate. Yet, not all brokers are in fact realtors. No state law requires the holder of a real estate license to be a realtor.

The major benefit to an investor in dealing with a realtor is the wider access to product than he would have with the nonrealtor. There may be other reasons to choose realtors. The National Association of Realtors would be quick to point out that realtors stick to a more strict code of ethics, but while that may be true, I have known many fine and qualified brokers and salespeople who did not become realtors for reasons of their own. It might be that their primary goal is to use the "insider" advantage of being licensed as a broker or salesperson to serve their own investment needs, or that the kind of real estate they deal in does not need the added advantages of belonging to a Board of Realtors.

Yet, because your interest is in finding the best selection of property for your invested capital, or as a seller looking to get the maximum profit, look first among the realtors in your neighborhood who are used to dealing with that specific type of real estate. Try to find a sales agent with whom you can develop rapport, someone who will put his or her total knowledge at your disposal that you will profit from. You want your interests to be at the top of his or her list.

The only way to find this ideal sales agent is to look for him or her. Ask around in your own circle of friends to see if they will recommend someone. The good sales agent usually has a wide range of satisfied clients who are that salesperson's best source of new clients. Let your friends know you are looking for a good real estate sales agent, and very soon you will have several names from which to choose.

Of course, that may not produce a person you feel you can work with. The importance of your having rapport with this person cannot be overestimated. He or she might be the best sales agent in town, but if you cannot get along with him or her, then seek out someone else.

Visit several real estate offices and ask to speak with a broker. Tell the broker that you are planning to invest in real estate and you feel you need to meet several sales agents. Say you want to find one you can work with over the years. If the broker is smart, he or she will discuss your needs with you and introduce you to one or two sales agents he or she feels would be right for you. If not, then try another office.

It is a good idea for you to explain to the salesperson that you want to find a sales agent you can work with and you do not want him or her to spend any time for you until you are ready. The sales agent will appreciate the fact that you want to find one sales agent to deal with and will respect that. There is nothing worse for a real estate sales agent than to be working with a client who has not told him or her about the other sales agent from a competitor's office with which he or she is currently working. A lot of time and effort is wasted in the real estate business because of this.

Ask questions, expect answers that show you that the sales agent is knowledgeable about the area and can be of help to you. If you do not get a good feel for the person, then do not waste your time or the salesperson's; move on. The time you spend in searching out a sales agent to work with will pay off in benefits later, and you will be glad you were cautious.

THE KIND OF REAL ESTATE SALESPERSON YOU DO NOT WANT

- THE SALESPERSON WHO DOES NOT ASK YOU QUESTIONS. This shows this salesperson does not know enough to find out what your goals, needs, and time requirements are. If the salesperson does ask questions but they are disjointed and unrelated to your goals, the time you have spent was for nothing. Move on.

- THE SALESPERSON WHO TALKS AND DOES NOT LISTEN. (The worst thing any salesperson can do!) Some do it because they feel they must impress you. Giving you a brief history of him or herself is okay for the salesperson, but you are there to have your problems solved—your goals met. He or she has to listen to do it effectively.

- THE SALESPERSON WHO IS IN A RUSH TO MAKE A SALE. The first sign of this is when he or she wants to take you out to see a property before he or she has found out sufficient data about your needs. This is a common trait with real estate salespeople and may be a sign of lack of confidence. Understanding your needs is important, so he or she will save time by showing you property that is closer to your needs.

- THE SALESPERSON YOU ARE UNCOMFORTABLE WITH. It does not matter why: she smokes and you cannot stand smoke, or the accent of his voice, or his hairstyle, or the funny mole on the side of her nose. If you are uncomfortable and cannot get rapport, move on.

EIGHT TRAITS OF TOP REAL ESTATE SALESPEOPLE

1. They listen.
2. They are prompt.
3. They ask pointed and direct questions aimed to help you shape your goals so that they will understand what they are.
4. They are constantly learning. Real estate is a profession that demands constant update and learning.
5. They are enthusiastic about their ability to solve your problem.
6. They display self-confidence.
7. They look successful.
8. They know the techniques of the trade that will enable you to make more deals.

Great real estate salespeople and their brokers know the value of being able to absorb the heat that can be generated between the buyer and the seller (or any other party to the deal). This is a critical and deal-saving attribute when it is properly implemented. You might ask the salesperson if he ever had a deal blow up in the midst of what looked like a smooth process toward closing. If he tells you he never has, he is either too new to have had that experience, or never realized he might have been able to diffuse it.

Once you have a real estate salesperson on your side and you have been candid with him or her about your financial position, you are ready to move onto the second stage of the transaction.

SELECTING A PROPERTY TO BUY

I have said much already about this stage. You know that the selection of real estate is very important because it sets the theme of the kind of real estate investing you are going to do. If this is to be your first buy, then you will seek a living investment; that is, one you can live in yourself. That might be a single-family property or an apartment complex. Whatever it is, you will make the proper selection by following the many suggestions I have given you in this book.

ELEVEN KEY FACTORS IN FINDING THE PROPERTY YOU WILL ULTIMATELY BUY

1. Constantly review your goals. Know exactly where you are with your interim goals, and are you still on your original or modified timetable? If adjustments need to be made, make them and revamp your plan if need be.

2. Stick close to your backyard. Your gold mine is close to where you are and is generally easy for you to reach.

3. Do not get beyond the scope of your ability, but know what that ability is.

4. Be willing to stretch yourself to the maximum limit of your economic capability.

5. Remember that risk is relative, and you can ease, reduce, or even remove risk by knowing as much as possible about the area, the market, and the property.

6. In building wealth, you must look for property you can improve. The top of the heap has no place to go but down.

7. Have property inspected for problems by qualified people. The cost is nothing in comparison to the benefit of knowing the real condition of the property.

8. Recognize that if you like, it and can afford it, this is one of the most important parts of buying real estate.

9. Do not overanalyze a deal. If it is good, by the time you have decided to buy it, someone else will have bought it. Besides, the likelihood is that your long-range projections will not be accurate anyway.

10. Trends are generally clearly visible if you know where to look for them.

11. History repeats itself in real estate; so to know what is going on, look back to the past.

In reality, you do not select the property you are going to buy, but instead you select property you would like to own. The time between wanting to own it and actually owning it has yet to come. It is highly possible that once you begin negotiating to buy, you will change your mind about the property in the first place. Price and terms the seller is willing to take can be the deciding factors. Or, as you continue to progress in the selection process you might start negotiating on one parcel of land or one building only to find another which suits your goals better than the first. In that event, simply break off negotiations and go on to the second property.

Sellers should recognize that a savvy buyer would not be bound to a deal until the contract is fully executed on all sides. The highly motivated seller, then, should keep in mind that a bird in the hand is worth a whole flock in the bush (in real estate that is the way it goes).

Naturally, it depends on the status of the real estate marketplace. If it is a seller's market, that is, if the demand to buy is greater than the supply to meet that demand, then the sellers sit in a good position. They will usually have several potential buyers out there, so the prices are firm and terms not as easy as in other markets. There is a danger here, however. If you are a seller and it may be a seller's market, it could well be that your property is not in that market at all. Real estate is not one marketplace; it is many. There is the single-family homes market, but even that is divided into different strata. Then there are vacant lots, acreage, office buildings, hotels, and so on. Not all markets are up at the same time, and fortunately, not all are down at the same time either.

When you enter the market to buy, the condition of that market will affect the method in which you negotiate. If it is a seller's market for the kind of property you want to buy, you cannot be too standoffish in your attempts to bring the price down or to get better terms in the negotiations. If you do, you are apt to lose the deal to a less finicky buyer.

In a buyer's market, the conditions are such that there are more sellers than there are ready and willing buyers. This is more often the case in vacant land and acreage because there is a lot of that kind of property. However, even this can become a hot item in a local area and then switch overnight from a buyer's market to a seller's market.

A buyer's market might be the ideal time to buy a property, but this is not always the case. You have to look to your own reason for buying and decide based on your own goal. If you want to use the property right away, or you anticipate the need for immediate income, a seller's market could be your best market. The buyers' market might have been created because of a recession or a slowdown in the growth of the area. These conditions might work against your goals, and buying at this time might not suit your needs. Price is a function of the use of a property, so as the need for the use (in the marketplace) goes down, so will the price.

Hotel sites in an area that is overbuilt with more hotels than the market can support will be a buyers' market. However, unless the buyer can find another use for the site or wait out the overbuilt condition, the purchase of that site at this time may not be prudent. Waiting until the time is right to build might be wiser even though the buyer would likely pay more for the site at that time. Builders and developers have long since recognized the fact that in a developmental program the cost of the land is only a fraction of the total picture anyway. It makes no economic sense to buy cheap and have the risks of holding for a long time when only an increased price (when compared with the total picture) will produce a ready and set property. You should remember this as well.

Now it is time to move into the fourth stage of the deal.

NEGOTIATING TO WIN

The key factors in negotiating and winning are discussed in this section.

Review Your Goals

You should always review your goals before making the offer to be sure the property fits in the scheme of things. There is no sense in starting on a negotiation that will end with a property not suited for your goals. A simple review of those goals will put you back on the right track. You will find on occasion that what has happened is that emotion has become an insider to the deal and has, at least temporarily, replaced your goals or at best clouded those goals from clear sight. Watch for that, because once you get away from the goals and let emotion run wild with the deal, you will find yourself rationalizing away the best part of your plan.

Avoid Personal Confrontation

Avoid personal confrontation during the actual offer. This is essential to successful negotiating. The buyer will do far better if he has a mediator, a broker or sales agent, between him and the seller, at least when the offer is presented. Every professional arbitrator, negotiator, politician, salesperson, broker, lawyer, and judge knows that placing the two parties (buyer and seller) face-to-face is not in the best interest of the best deal. Here is why. A buyer attempting to make the best deal for him is going to press the transaction. If that pressure is direct and face-to-face, the seller can and generally will react in a defensive way:

Buyer: "Mr. Seller, I realize you want $150,000 for this property, but the most I am prepared to offer is $95,000, and that is a good price."

Seller: "Well, you can take that $95,000 offer and stick it."

As you can see, negotiations have broken down. Or try this:

Buyer: "Mr. Seller, if it weren't for the blue-and-pink drapes in this house, which I'll have to replace, I would be offering more, but whoever picked those colors out had to be nuts."

Seller: "My wife picked them out, and if you don't like those colors then you don't have to buy this house. In fact, I don't think I want to sell to you."

And so on. I could continue giving you examples of what can happen. Now, granted, there are those rare people who can sit down and make a deal face-to-face with the seller. However, it is too risky, I think. Saying the wrong thing in such an encounter and ending up with a seller who doesn't like you is far too easy; that seller will not be reasonable from that moment on.

Good salespeople who know the art of negotiation can deal with a difficult seller (or when we turn things around with a difficult buyer) without compromising your interest in the deal. The salesperson can absorb (as he or she should) the heat of the negotiations so the other side of the deal can vent his or her frustrations at the broker and not at you.

Learn Something about the Other Party

Try to learn something about the other party and his or her goals. If you know what the seller (or buyer) is really attempting to accomplish, then you might have a better way to help him or her reach a goal. One example that comes to mind involved a client of mine interested in selling a lot he owned in a subdivision west of Fort Lauderdale. A prospective buyer made an offer through another office.

My client rejected the offer and countered $25,000 higher. The would-be buyer balked and said he would think about it. As he and the other broker were about to leave my office, he asked me what the seller was going to do with the money.

"He wants to get a summer home in North Carolina," I said.

"Well now," the buyer said. "I am a builder in Asheville. I have several homes I will trade."

The story did not end there. The owner of the lot never ended with a home this client had, but an exchange was made in which the builder from North Carolina did participate, and he did get the lot he wanted. The seller of the lot got what he wanted because of the North Carolina builder. Learning the true reasons for a sale or the real use to which the money is going to be put can be next to impossible sometimes. Your broker or salesperson will have to dig a little to find out what he or she can, and sometimes you are well into the negotiations before you find even anything that resembles the truth. Yet it should be clear to you that the more you know about the other party to the deal the better you can come out on top of the negotiation.

In fact, knowing more about the buyer is more important for the seller than the other way around. Best of all, the seller can find out information about the buyer once the negotiations start. Sellers being asked to hold secondary financing, for example, can rationally and logically ask for and usually receive financial information on the buyer.

References are a good source of data on the buyer, and most buyers attempting to buy hard will be forced to give up some of this information. You should be careful about relying on such references, however, because a buyer would not give you the name of someone who would badmouth him or her. However, you can get leads from a reference on where else to go to get more information about a person, so they are highly useful in that sense.

Be Flexible in Negotiations

Be flexible in the negotiations, but firm at the same time. Does this sound like a contradiction? It is not. The idea is to decide where you want to be flexible and where you want to be firm. If the deal is all cash, then you are closing the options you are giving the other party and the only place where there is any flex left is in the price. This is, in my opinion, a bad stand for a seller, as it places him or her in the tightest of all boxes to make a deal. Naturally, this stand must be taken at times when cash is the only way out, and there is no way to generate that cash from some outside source. But, the fact of the matter is there are so many options open to buyers to give sellers cash and yet keep their own out-of-pocket cash investment at a minimum that it is folly to assume that all cash to one party means all cash paid by the other.

Financing from a third party can usually be found in one form or other to help the deal along. Remember, "I'll pay your price if you accept my terms." Or, said another way,

"I can't budge on the cash down, but I can work out the terms," or "I know I can get the best terms to suit my deal if I'm flexible in the price."

You will see a clearer path in the decision on where you want or need to be firm by having a good understanding of your goals, of course, but it is more than just that. The property and its ability to sustain a profit while it produces income are very important. You don't want to overburden the transaction with heavy debt that can't be sustained unless a miracle happens, just because you are getting the price you were willing to pay.

There Are Other Fish in the Sea

Remember, that there are other fish in the sea. I've seen buyers go into deep depression because they lost out on a property they wanted to buy. Losing deals will happen to you if you plan to buy and sell real estate. There will be other investors who have snookered you out of a great deal, and other times it will be turned around. Yet, crying over spilled milk won't get you anything. Move on to the next deal. Be careful, however; you might act a little quicker the next time out of fear of losing the next deal, so watch out for this overreaction. However, you need to reflect back on why you lost the deal. Were you too hardnosed in your negotiations? Did you or the seller become offended at something done or said or what was believed to be happening? Perhaps the broker said or did something that upset the apple cart. Find out and make changes, if you can, to avoid that situation in the future.

Remember the Alamo

You see where it got Davy Crockett don't you? Like Davy and Daniel Boone, sellers should be careful about holding out too long. There is a time and place for holding out for a better offer. With typical 20/20 hindsight, I'll tell you that the time and place is only when you get a higher offer. Unfortunately, many sellers turn down offers that are never bettered. It might be possible that the seller will get a higher price sometime in the future by holding out longer, but you must consider the time element. If you are a tough seller and yet you really want to sell, keep in mind that as you hold on to a property you are losing the potential from the reinvestment of that capital. Not selling at $500,000 because you are sure you will get $520,000 is okay if you get an offer for $510,000 within a reasonable time. If you had to hold on to the property for even a few months more, the chances are you have lost ground rather than come out ahead. This depends somewhat on your motivation, of course, and what you might have done with the money from a sale.

Time Is the Key Factor to Profit

As you seek to find that ideal property, you should expect to be surprised. The thing that will surprise you the most is how fast things change when you have not been diligent in your physical presence in your investment area. It is like watching that tiny puppy grow up into a 90-pound guard dog. If you see the process from afar, say, one peek every month or so, the change is rapid. Watch the puppy on a daily basis and it is less so. To some degree, this is how it is with real estate. If you don't drive your investment area on a regular basis you suddenly are shocked to see that the vacant field where you used to play tag football in what seems like only a few years ago is now a field of affordable multifamily apartments and mixed use commercial space.

Yet, because there is only so much time you can devote to driving around, you need to get the maximum effective benefit from all the other sources available to you. Why wait until the affordable apartments are built? Why not be in on the scoop when it comes up before the Planning and Zoning Board? All it takes is for you to be on the mailing or e-mailing list from the different governmental departments. You can pick and choose which meeting you attend. Or even ask your favorite realtor to attend if you plan to be out of town at that time.

These seven factors will help give you some edge in the negotiation of the contract. You win, however, in every transaction that takes you closer to your goal. Naturally, the real win is viewed from the nineteenth hole. The fifth-quarter viewpoint of the game is always the easiest, and most investors look back at every transaction to decide if they have won or lost. While this might give the investor a more satisfactory view of his or her analysis of winning or losing, it does provide the investor with the rationalization of that win or loss. This is natural, however, even though it will distort the true win or loss.

The seller says, "You should have negotiated a little harder, because I would have taken much less than you paid."

In retort the buyer says, "That's okay, because if you would have held out for more I was ready to give you more than you got."

Your viewpoint on winning should be tied to what it is you want to accomplish. Your flexibility in the negotiations will be very important to keep alive all possibilities to achieve what you wanted in the first instance. Try to keep personalities out of the picture by avoiding direct confrontation with the other party. If you have a broker or salesperson, let him or her become the buffer in nailing down the best deal for you.

Remember, of course, that this salesperson or broker will have to see the transaction from three vantage points: yours, the other party's, and his or her own. As long as you keep track of your own interest and help point the salesperson in that same direction, you won't have to press the deal; the enthusiastic and knowledgeable salesperson will do that for you.

You have progressed well along in the buying or selling process if you have a contract. As a buyer, you haven't made up your mind sufficiently unless you are at that stage, and as a seller, nothing happens until there is an offer that can generate a contract. On to the next stage.

OFFERING/CONTRACTING TO BUY TO MAXIMIZE YOUR FUTURE GAIN

How you present your offers is an essential part of the negotiation process. There are four basic forms of offers: verbal, letter of intent, standard form agreement, and lawyer-drafted agreement. Not all are effective for each situation. Some may not be useful at all.

Verbal Offers

It should be noted that in the transfer of real estate the contract must be executed in writing to be legally enforceable. This doesn't negate the use of the verbal offer, however. With some people, their word is as good as their bond. I've seen many deals hammered out in verbal terms with nothing written down until everything had been agreed to. This is not unusual or uncommon. However, for each deal worked out through such methods, I've seen a hundred fall into one hassle or other as one of the parties lapses into forgetfulness as to what was exactly said, and the more formal agreement is never executed and the closing never occurs.

Frequently a buyer will instruct his salesperson, "See what the seller will take." This is generally followed by the salesperson asking the seller what is the lowest price the seller will take. These tactics generally don't produce any beneficial results and the salesperson won't find out the real facts in this maneuver. Most sellers don't know what they will take until a plan is presented to them that suits their goals (at that moment).

For the buyer to tell the seller (directly or through the salesperson) that he or she would like to buy the property and would the seller take, say, $400,000 is equally unproductive. If the seller was foolish enough to answer the question "Yes," the likelihood is that the offer will be $90,000 or more below that $400,000 target.

Thus, while there is a time and place for verbal offers, most sellers won't respond as effectively to a verbal offer as they would to a cash deposit and written contract. "Here's my offer, Mr. Seller, and here's a big check to show I'm real."

Letter of Intent: A Written Verbal Offer

The letter of intent is a quick process to ascertain if a meeting of the minds on the basic terms of a transaction can be obtained between the parties. These terms may be as simple as the price and method of payment, or more complex to include detailed elements of what would go into a formal purchase contract. The letter of intent may be a letter that the broker or the buyer himself will write to the seller. This letter states that the client (buyer) is interested in buying the seller's property on the basis of terms outlined in detail or in some loose form in the letter. The basics are discussed, yet the buyer often leaves out much of the detail that would constitute a contract. However, some buyers want to fill the letter of intent with as much of the elements that are absolutely critical to them, to make sure that if they proceed it is with clear understanding between the parties where each side stands on those terms. One such letter of intent begins on page 529.

Mr. Bradford J. Williams
President
Westmoreland National Insurance Companies
New York, New York

Re: Letter of Intent to Acquire Ocean Side Apartments

Dear Mr. Williams:

This letter is to indicate to you the intent of our client, Alex Baldbreeze from Aruba, Netherlands Antilles, to enter into an agreement for the purchase of the apartment complex your company owns known as OCEAN SIDE APARTMENTS, which is located in Hollywood, Florida. We have been informed by Mr. Baldbreeze that their legal representatives in Miami will draft the purchase offer and have it in your offices within five days from the date of your acceptance of this Letter of Intent. They are prepared to place $200,000 deposit with the offer.

The terms, which would, as of this time, be acceptable to Mr. Baldbreeze, are as follows:

1. A purchase price of: $5,750,000.

2. A cash down payment (of which the deposit is a part) of $2,000,000.

3. The balance of the purchase price would be held by the sellers as a first mortgage over 27 years term at a variable interest rate to be 2 points below prime as of the first of each month. (As a point of reference, as of this writing, Prime as published by the Wall Street Journal is 8.25 percent.)

4. Closing to occur within 45 days of approval of the various inspections to be made. These inspections will include:

   Structural of the buildings.
   Electrical of the buildings.
   Mechanical of the buildings.
   Plumbing of the buildings.
   Examination of the leases.
   Examination of payment records.
   Inspection of the maintenance records of the buildings.

5. In the event there is no approval given of these inspection items within 15 days from the date the last inspection report has been submitted to the buyer, the sales agreement will be null and void and each party released from further obligations to the other.

6. Each party understands and agrees that there will be other terms and conditions in the final purchase agreement, but the first five terms outlined herein are the basic terms being agreed herein.

It is understood that the prospective purchasers will proceed immediately with the legal document if you agree to the basic terms in this Letter of Intent. It is understood also that this letter is not to be construed as a contract and only in the approval and execution of the final document of sale, will there be a bona fide contract.

(continued)

Your approval of this letter in the proper place indicated below will demonstrate your interest to proceed on this matter and your approval in principle of the price and sale terms indicated herein. Furthermore, your approval will acknowledge that as seller your firm would be obliged to pay our fee at closing of title; said fee is Three Hundred and Fifty Thousand Dollars.

I have enclosed a packet of information on Mr. Baldbreeze, which I'm sure you will find highly informative. You will find ample references to check on, and I'm confident you will be impressed with the credentials of these prospective buyers.

Very truly yours,

Jack Cummings,
Cummings Realty, Inc.
Real Estate Consultants

Approval

I HAVE READ THE LETTER OF INTENT AND DO HEREBY ACCEPT THE TERMS OF THE SALE AS OUTLINED. THIS ACCEPTANCE SHALL NOT CONSTITUTE A CONTRACT, BUT MERELY AN AGREEMENT TO ACCEPT THE PRICE AND TERMS BASED ON THE SATISFACTORY APPROVAL OF A FULL AND BONA FIDE CONTRACT CONTAINING THOSE TERMS. OTHERWISE, THIS APPROVAL SHALL AUTOMATICALLY BE WITHDRAWN WITHIN _____ DAYS FROM THE DATE BELOW.

Date: _____

_____

Bradford J. Williams

There are many items in this letter of intent that could be altered or made less specific, and each letter of intent will be different. The idea is to indicate what you want to do and to proceed from there. These letters of intent aren't much more than verbal offers, but they do start things rolling. A more impressive way is to present a letter of intent and at the same time make sure you have the attention of the seller is to put a deposit with the broker and have him mention that deposit in the letter:

> " . . . and the prospective buyer has placed a deposit of $10,000 in an escrow account as a statement of good faith. This deposit will become a part of the total cash down at closing."

Many large transactions begin with the letter of intent format to get things moving as quickly and as timely as possible. This format enables the buyer and seller to negotiate without having the considerable cost of having their lawyers draw full contracts. However, this shortcut works only in some instances, usually in cases where the broker has a good standing with the seller.

As a realtor, I never hesitate to use the letter of intent if I know the buyer is sincere. In fact, I recommend using the letter of intent in many situations. But, when I know the seller will react more positively to the more formalized and customary form of offer, I shy away from the letter of intent.

Standard Form of Agreement

There are many forms of "standard" deposit receipt contracts or buy and sell agreements used by the real estate profession. These agreements are easy to spot, as they will have a notice of who the printer is and in many cases a statement showing the forms are approved by the local lawyers' association and/or were formulated by local realtors' associations. These forms will differ slightly around the country and may vary with the kind of real estate being bought and sold.

Condominiums, for example, generally require some different terminology to take care of the special items of interest in that kind of real estate. There will be the usual attention to the condo association application and approvals required, the recreation lease (if any), and the percentages of ownership of the common area. Vacant land also differs in the contractual needs as compared to improved real estate. A contract dealing with vacant land often can be far simpler than one dealing with the sale of a residence.

To see how the standard form works to your advantage, you need to understand some of the selling philosophy that surrounds its use. The form is simple and covers nearly every aspect of the transaction in common, easy-to-understand verbiage. If you are dealing with a Board-of-Realtors-approved standard form, you will have a form, which is up-to date on the needs of the area. It should have conditions which protect both the buyer and the seller, and spell out in detail the important aspects of the deposits and defaults and the like. The magic that works for you as buyer or seller is the simplicity of the form. Nothing will frighten a buyer or seller faster than a 20-page lawyer-prepared contract, even though the lawyer's agreement might be exactly the same, only spread out over more pages and in a different kind of type.

As a buyer, you want the salesperson presenting your offer to be able to concentrate on the deal and not on the form of the agreement. As a seller, you want your salesperson to be able to get the buyer in the heat of the moment to make the offer that might solve your problem and generate a sale.

To give you an idea of what one of these standard forms looks like, I've provided a copy of a contract form I have used in the past (pp. 532–539). This form can be used for any sale, although it does have some provisions that are superfluous to transactions involving vacant land. There is ample room for the buyer or seller to add additional terms or provisions, and you can, of course, alter any of the standard provisions. Having just said that, I caution you against using any "standard form" that may lack certain provisions that are required to be included in your state. These might be provisions that deal with environmental problems, homeowner associations, condominium associations or procedures, just to name a few items that might vary from state to state.

The form has been filled out as though I were buying a $1,800,000 waterfront home. Text that is in italics denotes sections of the standard form that have been filled in by me. The property has existing financing of $500,000, and I am asking the seller to hold some additional paper. See what other "buyer" techniques you can spot.

DEPOSIT RECEIPT AND CONTRACT FOR SALE AND PURCHASE

Jack Cummings et al., of 3015 North Ocean Blvd., Fort Lauderdale, Florida 33308 (954-561-0687), hereinafter called the Buyer, and *Hank Bigdeal of Boca Raton, Florida (PH n/p)* hereinafter called the Seller, hereby agree that the Seller shall sell and the Buyer shall buy the following described property.

UPON THE TERMS AND CONDITIONS HEREAFTER SET FORTH AND CONTINUED ON REVERSE SIDE OF THIS CONTRACT.

1. LEGAL DESCRIPTION *of real estate located in Broward County, Florida.*

   Tax Folio No. 14-869-2770
   Lot 11 plus East 1/2 Lot 12, Block H, Rio Mar Sub. Plat Book 1, page 105, Broward County.
   STREET ADDRESS: 1235 South East 15 Street
   PERSONAL PROPERTY INCLUDED: Carpets, drapes, kitchen appliances. The built-in
      bar. The pool table in den. Master bedroom furniture.
   Seller represents that the property can be used for the following purposes:
   Single-family residence.

2. PURCHASE PRICE IS:..$1,800,000.00

   METHOD OF PAYMENT:
   Deposit herewith ....$ 50,000.00
   Additional deposit to be paid upon acceptance of Contract by
      both parties on or before _____ 20 _____ $ 50,000.00
   All deposits to be held in trust by Cummings Realty Inc.
   Time is of the essence as to additional deposit.
   Principal balance of first mortgage, which Buyer shall take subject to $ 500,000.00
   Interest 6½ percent; Method of payment *monthly*
   Other: *Seller to hold a Second Mortgage in the amount of* $1,100,000.00
         for a term of 10 years. Payments to be interest
         only for the first five years, annual payments
         beginning the fourth year, monthly amortization.
         Interest to be 7 percent.
   U.S. Currency, certified or cashier's check on closing and
   delivery of deed (or such greater or lesser amount as may be
   necessary to complete payment of purchase price after credits,
   adjustments, and prorations). Said funds to be held in escrow
   pursuant to provisions of Paragraph R on reverse side of this
   contract ....$ 100,000.00
   TOTAL..$1,800,000.00
                                                              (includes the second deposit)

3. SPECIAL CLAUSES: (See page 4 or addendum attached, if any) *This offer is subject to the Buyer's unqualified approval of a Subsoil Test to be completed at his expense. Said test to be*

made within 30 days of acceptance of this offer and approval made (or not) within 10 days after that. If not approved for any reason this contract shall be null and void.

4. This offer shall be null and void unless accepted, in writing, on or before *March 4, 2010*

5. CLOSING DATE: This Contract shall be closed and the deed and possession shall be or before the 1st day of June 2011 unless extended by other provisions of this Contract or separate agreement.

WITNESS: Executed by Buyer on *March 1, 2010* Time: n/a

X *Jack Cummings* (SEAL)

Buyer

ACCEPTANCE OF CONTRACT AND PROFESSIONAL SERVICE FEE: *The Seller hereby approves and accepts the offer contained herein and recognizes Cummings Realty, Inc. as Broker(s) in this transaction, and agrees to pay, as a fee 7 percent of the purchase price, of the sum of one hundred twenty six thousand Dollars ($126,000) or one half of the deposit in case same is forfeited by the Buyer through failure to perform, as a compensation for service rendered, provided the same does not exceed the full amount of the agreed fee.*

WITNESS: Executed by Seller on Time:

X (SEAL)

(SEAL)

Deposit received on *March 1, 2010* to be held subject to this Contract; if check, subject to clearance.

By: *Cummings Realty, Inc* By:

Broker or Attorney

BE ADVISED: When this agreement has been completely executed, it becomes a legally binding instrument. The form of this "Deposit Receipt and Contract for Sale and Purchase" has been approved by the Broward County Bar Association and the Fort Lauderdale Area Board of Realtors, Inc.

Standards for Real Estate Transactions

A. Evidence of Title: The Seller shall, within _____ days (17 banking days if this blank is not filled in), order for Buyer a complete abstract of title prepared by a reputable abstract firm purporting to be an accurate synopsis of the instruments affecting the title to the real property recorded in the Public Records of that county to the date of this Contract, showing in the Seller a marketable title in accordance with title standards adopted from time to time by the Florida Bar subject only to liens, encumbrances, exceptions or qualifications set forth in this contract and those which shall be discharged by Seller at or before closing. The abstract shall be delivered at least 15 days prior to closing. Buyer shall have fifteen (15) days from the date of receiving said abstract of title to examine same. If title is found to be defective, Buyer shall, within said period, notify the Seller in writing, specifying the defects. If the said

(continued)

defects render the title unmarketable, the Seller shall have ninety (90) days from receipt of such notice to cure the defects, and if after said period Seller shall not have cured the defects, Buyer shall have the option of (1) accepting title as it then is, or (2) demanding a refund of all monies paid hereunder which shall forthwith be returned to the Buyer, and thereupon the Buyer and Seller shall be released of all further obligations to each other under this Contract.

B. Conveyance: Seller shall convey title to the subject property to Buyer by Statutory Warranty Deed subject to: (1) zoning and/or restrictions and prohibitions imposed by governmental authority; (2) restrictions, easements and other matters appearing on the plat and/or common to the subdivision; (3) taxes for the year of closing; (4) other matter specified in this Contract, if any.

C. Existing Mortgages: The Seller shall obtain and furnish a statement from the mortgagee setting forth the principal balance, method of payment, interest rate, and whether the mortgage is in good standing. If there is a charge for the change of ownership records by the mortgagee, it shall be borne equally by the parties to the transaction. In the event mortgagee does not permit the Buyer to assume the existing mortgage without a change in the interest rate, terms of payment or other material change, the Buyer at his or her option may cancel the Contract and all monies paid on the purchase price shall be refunded to him or her and the parties shall be released from all further obligations. Any variance in the amount of a mortgage to be assumed from the amount stated in the Contract shall be added to or deducted from the cash payment or the purchase money mortgage, as the Buyer may elect. In the event such mortgage balance is more than three percent (3 percent) less than the amount indicated in the Contract, the Seller shall be deemed to be in default under the Contract. Buyer shall execute all documents required by mortgagee for the assumption of said mortgage.

D. New Mortgages: Any purchase money note and mortgage shall follow the forms generally accepted and used in the county where the land is located. A purchase money mortgage shall provide for insurance against loss by fire with extended coverage in an amount not less than the full insurable value of the improvements. In a first mortgage, the note and mortgage shall provide for acceleration, at the option of the holder, after thirty (30) days default and in a junior mortgage after ten (10) days default. Junior mortgages shall require the owner of the property encumbered by said mortgage to keep all prior liens and encumbrances in good standing and forbid the owner of the property from accepting modifications, or future advances, under a prior mortgage. Buyer shall have the right to prepay all or any part of the principal at any time or times with interest to date of payment without penalty and said payments shall apply against the principal amounts next maturing. In the event Buyer executes a mortgage to one other than the Seller, all costs and charges incidental thereto shall be paid by the Buyer. If this Contract provides for Buyer to obtain a new mortgage, then Buyer's performance under this Contract shall be contingent upon Buyer's obtaining said mortgage financing upon the terms stated, or if none are stated, then upon the terms generally prevailing at such time in the county where the property is located. Buyer agrees diligently to pursue said mortgage financing, but if a commitment for said financing is not obtained within days (15 banking days if this blank is not filled in) from the date of this Contract, and the Buyer does not waive this contingency, then either

Buyer or Seller may terminate this Contract, in which event all deposits made by Buyer pursuant hereto shall be returned to him or her and all parties relieved of all obligations hereunder.

E. Survey: The Buyer, within the time allowed for delivery of evidence of title and examination thereof, may have said property surveyed at his or her expense. If the survey shows any encroachment on said property or that the improvements located on the subject property in fact encroach on the lands of others, or violate any of the covenants herein, the same shall be treated as a title defect.

F. Inspections:

1. Buyer shall have the right to make the following inspections at Buyer's expense, subject to the provisions of paragraph 4 below:

    a) Termite: The Buyer shall have the right to have the property inspected by a licensed exterminating company to determine whether there is any active termite or wood-destroying organism present in any improvements on said property, or any damage from prior termite or wood-destroying organism to said improvements. If there is any such infestation or damage, the Seller shall pay all costs of treatment and repairing and/or replacing all portions of said improvements, which are infested or have been damaged.

    b) General: The Buyer shall have the right to have a roof, seawall, pool, electric and plumbing inspection made by persons or companies qualified and licensed to perform such services. If such inspection reveals functional defects (as differentiated from aesthetic defects), Seller shall pay all costs of repairing said defects.

    c) Personal Property: The Seller represents and warrants that all appliances and machinery included in the sale shall be in working order as of the date of closing. Buyer may, at his or her sole expense and on reasonable notice, inspect or cause an inspection to be made of the appliances and equipment involved prior to closing. Any necessary repairs shall be made at the cost of the Seller and, unless otherwise agreed by the parties, the Buyer shall by closing be deemed to have accepted the property as is.

2. Escrow for Repairs: If treatment, replacement or repair called for in subparagraphs a, b, and c hereof is not completed prior to closing, sufficient funds shall be escrowed at time of closing to effect same.

3. Re-inspection: In the event the Seller disagrees with Buyer's inspection reports, Seller shall have the right to have inspections made at his or her cost. In the event Buyer and Seller's inspection reports do not agree, the parties shall agree on a third inspector, whose report shall be binding upon the parties. The cost of the third inspector shall be borne equally between the Buyer and Seller.

4. Limitation and Option Clause: Seller shall be responsible for all costs of the above treatment, replacement or repairs up to 4 percent (or 3 percent if this blank is not filled in) of the purchase price. In the event the total costs of items to be accomplished under

(continued)

subparagraphs a, b, and c exceed this amount, then either party shall have the option of paying any amount in excess and this Contract shall then remain in full force and effect. However, if neither party agrees to pay the additional amount above the applicable percentage of the purchase price, then, at the Seller's or Buyer's option, this Contract may be canceled by delivery of written notice to the other party or his or her agent, and the deposit shall be returned to the Buyer.

5. Time for Inspections: All inspections described in Paragraphs 1 (a) and (b) above shall be completed on or before five days prior to closing.

G. Insurance: The premium on any hazard insurance policy in force covering improvements on the subject property, shall be prorated between the parties, or the policy may be canceled as the Buyer may elect. If insurance is to be prorated, the Seller shall, on or before the closing date, furnish to the Buyer all insurance policies or copies thereof.

H. Leases: The Seller shall, prior to closing, furnish to Buyer copies of all written leases and estoppel letters from each tenant specifying the nature and duration of said tenant's occupancy, rental rate, advance rents or security deposits paid by tenant. In the event Seller is unable to obtain said estoppel letters from tenants, the same information may be furnished by Seller to Buyer in the form of a Seller's Affidavit.

I. Mechanics Liens: Seller shall furnish to the Buyer at time of closing an Affidavit attesting to the absence of any claims or liens or potential lienors known to the Seller and further attesting that there have been no improvements to the subject property for _____ days immediately preceding the date of closing. If the property has been improved within said time, the Seller shall deliver releases or waiver of all mechanics liens, executed by general contractors, subcontractors, or suppliers and in addition a Seller's mechanics lien Affidavit setting forth the names of all such general contractors, subcontractors, and suppliers and further reciting that in fact all bills for work to the subject property which could serve as the basis for a mechanic's lien have been paid.

J. Place of Closing: Closing shall be held at the office of the Buyer's attorney or closing agent, if located within Broward County; if not, then at the office of Seller's attorney, if located within Broward County.

K. Documents for Closing: Seller's attorney shall prepare deed, mortgage, mortgage note, bill of sale, affidavit regarding liens, and any corrective instruments that may be required in connection with perfecting the title. Buyer's attorney or closing agent will prepare closing statement.

L. Expenses: Abstracting prior to closing, State documentary stamps which are required to be affixed to the instrument of conveyance, the cost of recording any corrective instruments, intangible personal property taxes and the cost of recording the purchase money mortgage, if any, shall be paid by the Seller. Documentary stamps to be affixed to the note or notes secured by the purchase money mortgage, if any, or required on any mortgage modification and the cost of recording the deed shall be paid by the Buyer.

M. Proration of Taxes (Real and Personal): Taxes shall be prorated based on the current year's tax, if known. If the closing occurs at a date when the current year's taxes are not fixed, and the current year's assessment is available, taxes will be prorated based upon such assessment and the prior year's millage. If the current year's assessment is not available, then taxes will be prorated on the prior year's tax; provided, however, if there are completed improvements on the subject premises by January 1st of the year of closing, which improvements were not in existence on January 1st of the prior year, then the taxes shall be prorated to the date of closing based upon the prior year's millage and at an equitable assessment to be agreed upon between the parties, failing which, requests will be made to the county tax assessor for an informal assessment taking into consideration homestead exemption, if any. However, any tax proration based on an estimate may, at the request of either party to the transaction, be subsequently readjusted upon receipt of tax bill and a statement to that effect is to be set forth in the closing statement. All such prorations whether based on actual tax or estimated tax will make appropriate allowance for the maximum allowable discount and for homestead or other exemptions if allowed for the current year.

N. Prorations and Escrow Balance: Taxes, hazard insurance, interest, utilities, rents, and other expenses and revenue of said property shall be prorated as of date of closing. Seller shall receive as credit at closing an amount equal to the escrow funds held by the mortgagee, which funds shall thereupon be transferred to the Buyer.

O. Special Assessment Liens: Certified, confirmed and ratified special assessment liens as of the date of closing (and not as of the date of this Contract) are to be paid by the Seller. Pending liens as of the date of closing shall be assumed by the Buyer.

P. Risk of Loss: If the improvements are damaged by fire or other casualty before delivery of the deed and can be restored to substantially the same condition as now existing within a period of sixty (60) days thereafter, Seller may restore the improvements and the closing date and date of delivery of possession herein under provided shall be extended accordingly. If Seller fails to do so, the Buyer shall have the option of (1) taking the property as is together with insurance proceeds, if any, or (2) canceling the Contract and all deposits will be forthwith returned to the Buyer and the parties released of any further liability hereunder.

Q. Maintenance: Between the date of the Contract and the date of closing, the property, including lawn, shrubbery and pool, if any, shall be maintained by the Seller in the condition as it existed as of the date of the Contract, ordinary wear and tear excepted.

R. Escrow of Proceeds of Sale and Closing Procedure: The deed shall be recorded and evidence of the title continued at Buyer's expense, to show title in Buyer, without any encumbrances or changes which would render Seller's title unmarketable, from the date of the last evidence and the cash proceeds of sale shall be held in escrow by Seller's attorney or by such other escrow

(continued)

agent as may be mutually agreed upon for a period of not longer than ten (10) days. If Seller's title is rendered unmarketable, Buyer's attorney shall, within said ten (10) day period, notify Seller or Seller's attorney in writing of the defect, and Seller shall have thirty (30) days from date of receipt of such notice to cure such defect. In the event Seller fails to timely cure said defect, all monies paid hereunder by Buyer shall, upon written demand therefore, and within five (5) days thereafter, be returned to Buyer and, simultaneously with such repayment, Buyer shall vacate the premises and reconvey the property in question to the Seller by Special Warranty Deed. In the event Buyer fails to make timely demand for refund, he or she shall take title as is, waiving all rights against Seller as to such intervening defect except such rights as may be available to Buyer by virtue of warranties contained in deed. In the event the transaction is not consummated because of an uncorrected or unwaived defect in title, the Seller will be deemed to have defaulted under this Contract. Possession and occupancy will be delivered to Buyer at time of closing.

If Seller provided Escrow Disbursement insurance or if Buyer executes a Disclosure and Consent Statement, then disbursement of closing proceeds shall be made to Seller immediately upon closing. The broker's professional service fee shall be disbursed simultaneously with disbursement of Seller's closing proceeds. Payment shall be made in the form of U.S. currency, cashier's check, certified check, unless in the event a portion of the purchase price is to be derived from institutional financing or refinancing, the requirements of the lending institution as to place, time, and procedures for closing and for disbursement of mortgage proceeds shall control, anything in this Contract to the contrary notwithstanding.

S. Escrow: The party receiving the deposit agrees by the acceptance thereof to hold same in escrow and to disburse it in accordance with the terms and conditions of this Contract. Provided, however, that in the event that a dispute shall arise between any of the parties to this Contract as to the proper disbursement of the deposit, the party holding the deposit may at his option: (1) take no action and hold all funds (and documents, if any) until agreement is reached between the disputing parties, or until a judgment has been entered by a court of competent jurisdiction and the appeal period has expired thereon, or if appealed then until the matter has been finally concluded, and then to act in accordance with such final judgment; or (2) institute an action for declaratory judgment, interpleader or otherwise joining all affected parties and thereafter complying with the ultimate judgment of the court with regard to the disbursement of the deposit and disposition of documents, if any. In the event of any suit between Buyer and Seller wherein the escrow agent is made a party by virtue of acting as such escrow agent hereunder, or in the event of any suit wherein escrow agent interpleads the subject matter of this escrow, the escrow agent shall be entitled to recover a reasonable attorney's fee and costs incurred, including costs and attorney's fees for appellate proceedings, if any, said fees and costs to be charged and assessed as court costs in favor of the prevailing party.

T. Attorney Fees and Costs: In connection with any litigation arising out of this Contract, the prevailing party whether Buyer, Seller or Broker, shall be entitled to recover all costs incurred including reasonable attorney's fees for services rendered in connection with such litigation, including appellate proceedings and post judgment proceedings.

U. Default: In the event of default of either party, the rights of the nondefaulting party and the Broker shall be as provided herein and such rights shall be deemed to be the sole and exclusive rights in such event; (a) If Buyer fails to perform any of the covenants of this Contract, all money paid or deposited pursuant to this Contract by the Buyer shall be retained by or for the account of the Seller as consideration for the execution of this Contract as agreed and liquidated damages and in full settlement of any claims for damages by the Seller against the Buyer. (b) If Seller fails to perform any of the covenants of this Contract, all money paid or deposited pursuant to this Contract by the Buyer shall be returned to the Buyer upon demand, or the Buyer shall have the right of specific performance. In addition, Seller shall pay forthwith to Broker the full professional service fee provided for on the reverse side of this Contract.

V. Persons Bound: The benefits and obligations of the covenants herein shall inure to and bind the respective heirs, personal representatives, successors, and assigns (where assignment is permitted) of the parties hereto. Whenever used, the singular number shall include the plural, the plural the singular, and the use of any gender shall include all genders.

W. Survival of Covenants and Special Covenants: Seller covenants and warrants that there is ingress and egress to subject property over public or private roads or easements, which covenants shall survive delivery of deed. No other provision, covenant, or warranty of this Contract shall survive the delivery of the deed except as expressly provided herein.

X. Final Agreement: This Contract represents the final agreement of the parties and no agreements or representations, unless incorporated into this Contract, shall be binding on any of the parties. Typewritten provisions shall supersede printed provisions and handwritten provisions shall supersede typewritten and/or printed provisions. Such handwritten or typewritten provisions as are appropriate may be inserted on the face of this form or attached hereto as an addendum. The date of this Contract shall be the day upon which it becomes fully executed by all parties.

Notice:

Jack Cummings is a Registered Real Estate Broker and is dealing as a principal, and any profit or loss from a subsequent disposition of the Real Estate in this agreement is of no consequence to the Seller herein. This does not waive the rights of Cummings Realty Inc. to collect a commission herein.

This agreement shown above is simply a sample of what has been used in my part of the country. Not all brokers here use this kind of agreement; some opt for simpler agreements. Personally, I find this standard form to be adequate for almost all improved-property deals, although I prefer to see sellers use a form that which has the real estate being sold in an "as is" condition rather than have repair conditions for damage and the like. However, to a buyer, the provision for repairs is attractive.

If you are the seller in the transaction, you must take a very special look at any contract that has a condition that you repair items not working or any damage. I've seen many arguments over this result in the filing of legal actions. The buyer wants anything and everything that might be determined to be in need of repair fixed by the seller, while the seller will have a different point of view. Inspections are important, but often there is a narrow line on many items. Sure, the roof isn't new, but just because it is old doesn't mean it needs to be replaced, or even repaired, for that matter.

My suggestion to sellers is to either remove the repair-or-replacement part of the agreement, or count on having to spend up to the total maximum percentage of the price for that repair or replacement and take that into consideration on the counteroffer. Buyers should realize, too, that sellers will look at the offer this way and should anticipate the removal of these provisions; see the sample agreement provisions:

F: INSPECTIONS (a–d). A good way to counteract this is to anticipate the removal of this section.

When you make an offer to buy a property you should anticipate the seller making a counter to you. It is rare that sellers accept the first offer. This will, of course, depend a great deal on the market and your salesperson, but in the majority of instances anticipate a counter. To focus the attention of the seller on one item that you are flexible about (but he or she doesn't know that), then, will be wise. You do this by anticipating what factors of the deal are crucial to him or her or difficult in his or her situation. The inspections might be one area that you might be willing to bend on. If the total maximum exposure the seller would have in the deal due to the percent of price applicable to repairs was $35,000, then you might reduce your offer by that amount and be ready to drop that entire section as long as you had the right to make the inspections and approve of them. In that way, you could firm up a deal and if you found the suspected problem was nonexistent then you won. If the needed repairs were extensive, then you could opt to negate the deal and renegotiate for better terms, or walk away from the deal.

You win by letting the other side win, too. A smart buyer will put in some term or other that can be taken out of the offer as a face-saver for the seller. One good way to accomplish this is in the terms. The buyer offers a deal, which calls for the seller to hold a second mortgage at 5 percent for 18 years. The salesperson presents the offer that way and the seller balks at the terms. A counter, which the salesperson feels would be acceptable, is returned to you. The price is the same, the interest rate the same, only now the second mortgage has a 10-year balloon. You win because you anticipate paying off the mortgage within that time anyway, through a refinance of the total mortgage structure.

Sometimes it can be simple things like asking the seller to include some furniture, or to close within three months, when you didn't want the furniture or were ready to close much sooner.

As a seller, you don't want to play around with the offers and counteroffers that much. That is the advantage of being a buyer. However, because you might be the seller, keep in mind that the way in which you offer the property for sale is in essence your first offer. It is here that you can provide your "room to play," and can anticipate the first offer to be less than your offer for sale.

You will keep your negotiations as a seller to a minimum by offering good terms that have some flexibility for that buyer who wants to argue with you to win a point.

LAWYER-DRAFTED AGREEMENT.   Commercial or complicated residential transactions might require this agreement, but there's a good argument against its use. I've successfully sold to happy sellers and buyers properties in the million-dollar price range with the simplest of standard forms. On the other hand, I've had 20-page lawyer-drafted documents on some of the simplest deals that caused nothing but problems. Why? If you are a seller and a buyer comes with his or her high-priced lawyer and he or she presents you with 20 pages of legal language, what are you going to do? Go to your lawyer, if you see any merit, or throw the thing into the wastebasket.

Let's assume you go to your lawyer. What happens now? Your lawyer firm has to spend time reading each and every word, looking for deviations from the standard form they are familiar with. Also, to show that they are looking out for your interests and earning their fee, they will want to change a word or two, or a page or two, or rewrite the agreement.

Now you have a situation that can get out of hand. The two lawyers start to tear apart each other's agreement, and it seems to go on and on, with the heat of the moment cooling down and the deal lost.

Real estate salespeople know and understand well the emotions of the buy-and-sell situation. As a buyer or seller, I want my salesperson to have everything going for the deal. I know enough about what I want to look out for my interest as long as the legal aspect is taken care of. So in those events when I feel I need a lawyer's advice, or a client of mine wants to have her lawyer draft an agreement, I suggest the use of the standard form with changes or additions to protect where needed.

Most lawyers will go along with that when the contract can accommodate the deal. This will be the majority of the transactions, if the lawyer will acquiesce in allowing the standard form to be used. Some lawyers, however, wouldn't use a standard form under any circumstances. My advice from the realtor's point of view and as a buyer and seller of real estate is to keep it as simple as you can, but also listen to your legal advisor. If you have confidence in your lawyer, then you should listen to his or her advice and act based on that. It is rare, however, to find a lawyer ready and willing to come out in the middle of the night to draft an agreement and then stand by to work on the counter, as your sales-person is doing, to nail down the deal.

Every buyer or seller should have the opportunity to seek out legal counsel if the deal warrants it or he or she feels it is needed. The buyer has more time to do that before the negotiations get to the point of the offer; the seller should know where he or she is going once the property is offered on the market, before the first offer rolls in.

One way to keep everyone more or less happy is to use the standard form to speed up the process. But insert into that contract a provision that your attorney must approve the legal format prior to it becoming binding on your part. Once executed by the seller or the buyer, depending on who put that provision in the agreement, the lawyers can come into the picture. This is a salesperson's touch to nail down the deal even though there is an out. It is important to keep the emotions hot. You are the buyer and you make an offer the seller might be inclined to go along with. "I'll go along," he tells the salesperson. "But while the price and terms seem okay, I don't know how this part in the offer about my holding a wraparound mortgage will affect me. I want my attorney to review this before I sign."

The salesperson, knowing that you, the buyer, might have a change of heart the next day or the seller might have a different point of view after taking the unaccepted offer to his lawyer (as well he might), will opt to get an acceptance subject to the approval of the lawyer the following day.

Two things take place in this kind of situation that are important. First, the seller relaxes in the deal. He does want to sell, and so far, everything seems okay. He only wants the lawyer to check it over to see if it is a proper and correct deal. So he accepts the deal subject to the lawyer's review of the contract and approval thereof. The second and most important aspect is the mental release of the property. Sellers frequently hold on to property in their minds, not wanting to let go. If a salesperson can get this mental release to take place, then the problems seem to melt away. Both of these events benefit the buyer, and now there is a contract that has been approved by both the buyer and the seller. All that must occur is the approval by the lawyer. Of course, the lawyer can still nix the deal, and sometimes that is exactly what happens. However, it won't occur often, and when it does, usually it is for good reasons.

Keep in mind as a buyer or seller that there are times when you will need a lawyer-drafted contract. It is always a good idea for you to have a lawyer you can relate to who understands your goals to use as a sounding board and advisor for any transaction. Keep in mind the psychology of the deal and try to keep it simple. Smart lawyers know this and will often use the simplest form possible to get across the most complicated transaction.

A WORD ABOUT CONTRACTS.   Throughout this book, I've mentioned several items about contracts that I want to repeat as a general caution:

1. WATCH OUT FOR VERBAL OFFERS. Talk is cheap, and memories are as convenient as the other party wants them to be.

2. BEWARE OF RETURNED DRAFTS OF OFFERS. Sometimes they will have been fully retyped except for a slight change that zings you hard; a neat technique whereby your offer appears to be accepted, but what has happened is that the offer was changed.

3. SHY AWAY FROM THE STANDARD FORM THAT ISN'T STANDARD AT ALL. Some brokers, lawyers, and investors have developed their own contracts. They look exactly like the standard form I've included in this book except they are not. Also, they might have some standard-looking phrases that are very one-sided and don't work to your benefit. A protection to you is to deal with a broker or salesperson who will give you a copy of his or her standard form, which you can have your lawyer check over in advance of a deal. If the form is approved, you don't have to worry about the little things and can concentrate on the importance of the sale.

4. NEVER BE INSULTED BY AN OFFER OR A COUNTEROFFER. Too many deals are lost by sellers who are insulted by low offers. As a salesman, I tell my sellers that buyers often want to test the market. Making low offers isn't an insult; it is simply a buyer, interested in the property, looking to be educated. Don't feel that as a seller you have to counter on an offer that is very low. The best counter to a very low offer is often no counter at all other than a "Thank you, Mr. Buyer, but you had best check around. You'll find the price we are offering is a good price." Or simply say nothing.

CONDUCTING DETAILED DUE DILIGENCE

Comprehensive due diligence may be nothing more than a home or condominium inspection by a qualified company that does that sort of thing. In that instance the whole matter is relatively simple, and not too costly. In a larger transaction, it can be a long and expensive process. Add to that the need for approvals from wherever, where the decision can go against you no matter what you do, the cost can be a mountain of time, and many thousands of dollars down the drain.

Because the scope of my brokerage business has centered on land tracts for future development or redevelopment of one property into another use, I have seen a lot of qualified buyers, ready and willing to pay the top price, forced to abandon the project because the vote on the city council went against their proposed project.

Sometimes the vote is appropriate, and the developer, who was trying to overdo the development, scales back to a more manageable (from the city's point of view) operation and development. Other times, it is a pure battle of local politics and the vote goes the way it does to buy more votes or to appease existing enterprises, or out of lack of experience in making informed decisions.

Because of this, the later stages of your due diligence must be directed toward any such potential. As long as you are properly informed as to the local political situation, and can live with what you learn about that situation, at least you are working toward success as best you can.

To ensure that you do so, review the following checklist and make sure your team has included these elements in its due diligence process. Keep in mind that this list is not the final or definitive one for your project because there may be some factors that I have not included because of your unique situation. But at least include these:

- City and county code violations for any existing improvements.
- Full environmental inspections to check for oil or gasoline or other petroleum products on or in the property.
- Zoning and other building codes and restrictions as they pertain to existing buildings and more certainly anything you want to build.
- What are the steps that you have to follow (worst case scenario) to obtain all necessary approvals?
- Who can turn you down and where in this process can that occur?
- What is your plan B if you are turned down?
- Is it possible to survive a turn down by making changes that you could anticipate prior to entering into the process? For example, an application for a building permit is almost never turned down as long as you follow the building codes and established ordinances, which you can see in advance. However, if there is a city-imposed moratorium on building permits, you will not be technically turned down, just postponed until the moratorium is lifted at some yet to be determined date.
- When do the parties meet that have this power of approval or turn down?
- Can they postpone you to later meetings (months away)?
- What does your contract say about these "not within your control" events? Can you get the seller to ride along on those delays that hold you up?
- Are there state laws that protect you and the property owner from governmental legislation that can effectively take away property owners' rights?
- What would it cost you, in time and money, to fight the city even if you are right?
- Learn what the "gotcha" provisions are that lurk deep inside many building codes and city ordinances. These may not show up in the actual zoning that the property has at this time, but exist in a different section such as: development within 1000 feet of a school, or development within a certain distance of a 4:COP Liquor license (a bar/lounge license—COP means "consumed on premises"). These rules may not even occur within city ordinances, but may be equally governing county or state laws.

GETTING THE APPROVALS NEEDED WITH THE TIME NEEDED TO IMPLEMENT THEM

The previous section touches on many of the important due diligence elements that can cause you to run over time and budget and to cause a buyer to walk away from a project. As a seller of the property, not only are your future development rights at stake, you may have represented that the land you are selling can be approved for 20 floors height, and a density of 500 condominium apartments because you rightfully thought that was what the zoning allowed. And guess what, you might be right that the zoning says that is what can go on the site, but the project proposed by a buyer can still be turned down for multiple other reasons.

Will that buyer who has lost 18 months of his time and several hundred thousand dollars of money that has been paid to lawyers, architects, and engineers now take you to court for misrepresentation? What about your real estate salesman who may have given that impression for the same reason? Are you all going to be in court?

The answers to these questions involve both the buyer and the seller being aware of what is going on in the city. If the seller suspects that this might happen and wants to avoid a year or two delay (I've seen these battles rage on for many years), then they might consider selling the property to a farmer who only wants to make a strawberry u-pick-it farm or some other buyer with less grandiose ideas.

Once the buyer and the seller are entering into negotiations, it is critical for the seller to know what the planned development will be. Too often this is not fully explained, or is explained in a way that is in itself misleading. If the seller understands the project, then spell it out in the contract. This will at least keep an aggressive developer from trying to push through a development that allows far more development than the property will truly support. Such excessive development may be the developer's attempt to rezone or replatt the property which then fails and results in a reduction of real value to this site.

Restructuring or Fine-Tuning the Deal

When you have completed the detailed due diligence and all inspection reports have been reviewed, the buyer generally has a period of days to make his or her final decision to close or pass on the deal. In reality, there is another decision that the buyer has, which can be the most important one of all. That is the decision to attempt to renegotiate the transaction.

There are several elements that may cause that to happen. It might be that the time element has gotten in the way of your being able to make an informed decision to go forward or walk away. This happens frequently because it is getting more difficult to estimate how much time it will take to obtain inspections, get approvals, and secure the needed financing to bring a project to the "ready to go" position necessary to close. Sellers do not always respect or understand this aspect of the transaction. They don't appreciate this problem because most sellers remember how quickly they made up their mind and how smooth things were when they purchased the property, perhaps 40 years ago, when it was vacant pasture for $500 per acre. Now at $2 million per acre as a site for a mixed-use project of condominiums, hotels, and shopping centers, they suddenly don't understand why Simon and Debartolo didn't jump at the chance to own this great site.

Environmental studies, traffic studies, subterranean soil condition studies take time, and if the local building and zoning department turns you down because your studies did not take into consideration some factor that no one ever thought of, well, your clock might as well be stepped on.

But there are other elements that suddenly raise the go-forward or walk-away decision. Perhaps there has been a sudden shift in your ability to get financing, or bank rates have jumped and are still going up, or an airline strike has shut down growth to the area? These and more can cause you to want to either walk away, or fine-tune the deal so that it is a bit more to your liking.

Sellers, this is likely to happen, so be prepared. Never spend the proceeds of the closing until it is in your hands. There is one way that you can mitigate this situation, however, to at least ensure that if the final decision of the buyer is to walk away from the deal that you have not had your property tied up too long for no compensation.

You would want the contract to have a "hard" date when the deposit or deposits are final and would be lost no matter what happens at or beyond a certain date. The buyer is locked in, to a small degree perhaps, but for something.

Other than that, if the buyer can present a good case to you why he or she needs more time or even a drop in the price of the property, make sure you understand why. It is entirely possible that the plan the buyer has before the city or county for approval is great, only there is a new movement within the city or county that is against new development. That plan, that the buyer says he needs to push through now, because if he loses out, there is likely to be a change in the upcoming elections where two developer-friendly commissioners will be defeated. That would mean four years or more of developer-unfriendly government in the city or county where this site is located. I have seen this happen often enough to know that when that happens, property values can drop considerably because the would-be development that might be approved would be half of what the present one is planned to be.

A property should never be taken off the market either. This is especially the case when the current buyer has a long time in the contract to do his or her due diligence and to obtain their desired approvals.

THE CLOSING

In real estate terms, the closing is the stage where buyer and seller perform under the terms and conditions of the contract. The buyers put up the money and execute all documents required of them, and the sellers sign the deed(s), execute all the documents required of them, and transfer title in return for the buyer's money or other consideration.

However, there is a period of time between stage 4 and the successful conclusion of stage 5 that is often the most precarious period of all. It will be after the execution of the contract when the buyers begin their due diligence, that the sellers are in the limbo of not knowing for sure that they have a sale. Emotions can run wild during this period, and sellers get "back-out-itis," and buyers get "paid-too-much-itis." Deals can crumble because of the smallest issue that has, at its foundation, a much larger issue.

I have broken down this period of time that starts on the execution of the agreement to sell (lease, or exchange) to illustrate some of the tips and traps that will help you get to the closing in one piece:

FOUR DIVISIONS OF THE CLOSING STAGE

1. Due-diligence period.
2. Preclosing period.
3. Transfer of title.
4. Postclosing.

Due-Diligence Period

In most real estate transactions, the buyer has a period of time to conduct inspections and studies to ascertain the condition of the property and, depending on the type of property being acquired, a multitude of other determinations. Listed here are some of the different aspects of a property that a buyer may want to check out prior to closing and taking title. While the following list appears to be very comprehensive, there will be items that are unique to a property you want to buy that are not shown in this list; equally, there are many items on the list that will not apply to your specific deal:

ITEMS TO CHECK PRIOR TO CLOSING

- *Advance deposits:* Any property or business that takes in advance deposits will require a detailed check of these deposits. Buyer will get a credit for the amount taken in by the seller.

- *Advance reservations:* It is possible that there are advance reservations without deposits. If the buyer wants to honor these reservations, or if the contract requires the buyer to honor them, then a detailed list must be shown.

- *Asbestos:* One of the most important items to check for, and is generally part of an overall environmental check. If you are planning any remodeling, this can be one of the most critical aspects to look out for. Having to remove asbestos can be very expensive, if possible at all.

- *Bar licenses:* Any business or property that has a bar will have a bar or liquor license. Know exactly what the rules and cost are in making a transfer, in operation with the new license. If the old one has past violations there may be fees the seller should pay to allow the buyer to operate. The sale of alcoholic beverages generally will require a special license that may have a lengthy application and approval process. Check with the state department that deals with such issues to ascertain the procedure to follow.

- *Bill of sale:* When there are personal property items being transferred in the sale, it is customary and highly recommended to have a bill of sale signed by the seller. Values should be put in the bill of sale if the buyer anticipates future depreciation of these items.

- *Boilers:* Heating systems and hot water systems are expensive to repair so you want to make sure that everything is working prior to taking title.

- *Building codes:* Does the property meet all the current building codes? How does it stand up when you apply new building codes that have been approved but have not gone into effect yet, or building codes about to be approved? Check with the appropriate governmental departments that may have jurisdiction over the various codes that can affect your ownership of the property. These may extend beyond the actual city involved and may include county and state factors.

- *Business records:* Sellers want to limit your review of their business records, particularly if you are presently a competitor. The reason is clear: What if you opt not to close, and you have seen all their secrets? Buyers want to see the records for obvious reasons, to check up on what the seller said about how wonderful the business is. Somewhere there is a middle ground.

- *Catch basins:* Water catch basins are important when the heavy weather comes around. If you are buying during the dry season, you may want to have a tanker of water dumped in the area to check things out.

- *Code violations:* A city, county, state, or federal building code violation can be a minor event, or a very expensive major catastrophe and might be the reason the property is for sale. Check for possible future violations that are going to occur as soon as the new law (passed last week) goes into effect.

- *Computer apparatus:* Computers as a part of the personal property should undergo careful computer analysis. Are they outdated, old, or not working properly? Are all the software disks available? This can be critical because a failure of a component in the computer system may require reinstallation of the software or hardware drivers.

- *Condition of title:* There are many factors that contribute to a bad title. Some can be cleared up quickly; others can take years to sort out. You do not want to take bad title to any property.

- *Dedicated easements:* Often you cannot see the easement that runs across the property. If there are some, and you can get them released, then that is great. If you cannot, and the easement is for a potential gas line to run down the middle of your property, you may find your use greatly restricted.

- *Deed restrictions:* A previous owner or developer may have imposed a restriction in the deed. This may or may not be clearly evident by looking at the actual deed. Often a deed will have a phrase something like this:

. . . and further restricted by those deed covenants that are recorded in the Plat Notes of West Lake Subdivision, Page 7 or Plat book 1084 of the Property Records of Clay County, Georgia.

If you look up those covenants (another name for conditions or possibly restrictions), you might discover that they are very restrictive—so much so that you would not want to own the property.

- *Drainage:* Good or bad, drainage may not affect the property in its present use, but unless you know how it is, you may not know if you can build the office building you want to construct without major land work.

- *Dry wood rot:* In many areas of the country, this can be a problem. You want to make sure the problem is not extensive or expensive.

- *Easements:* A survey should indicate any easements that exist that may traverse or are contained on the property. These can include utilities of all kinds, as well as emergency vehicle passage, or inspection access to some other location that may adjoin your intended purchase or be distant from it. Sometime these easements are not in use and may never be. Check to see if they can be legally vacated. If so, this is often not a difficult process and will forever remove future problems when you go to sell the property.

- *Electrical appliances:* Do they work? Are they properly installed as per code?

- *Electrical wiring:* Is it up to code, proper for the present codes, not the past codes? Do you require greater amperage? Three phase? Is there sufficient power to the building?

- *Elevators:* All elevators must be inspected prior to your closing. Is there a maintenance log? Review it carefully. You may discover that the entire system has chronic problems that have required constant maintenance.

- *Emergency alarms:* Do they meet code? Do they work as they are supposed to?

- *Employment contracts:* Are you locked into keeping employees? Can you fire them? Should the seller be obliged to pay severance cost? How much sick or vacation time has been built up that you might get stuck paying for?

- *Encroachments:* Does anything on or under the property you are buying wrongly cross over the setback line or property line of a neighbor? Are there any on property violations of setbacks? Does your septic tank sit in the neighbor's backyard? These are all possible hidden events unless you have them checked out.

- *Environmental inspections:* Only qualified companies or individuals should be hired to do this. You will want to know if there are any problems. An old fuel oil tank for a boiler no longer present could have been leaking into the ground for the past 30 years. If so, and you close on the property, you might be in for a horrible surprise and expense.

- *Escalators:* Just like elevators, must be inspected prior to closing.

- *Estoppels to leases:* The lessee will sign the letter indicating that he or she knows the terms of the lease and that the termination date (contained in the letter) is correct. Will also attest to any violations or late charges or penalties due. Lessor will give you an estoppel of leases showing all leases, start dates, termination dates, rent charged, and penalties that can be imposed and other important data.

- *Estoppels to mortgages:* The mortgagee will let you know in this estoppel letter that the mortgage payments are current and there is no violation or default at present.

- *Fire alarms:* Do they meet the code? Do they work?

- *Fire inspection:* A good idea to have this included in any inspection to make sure that all is as it should be. If there are past violations, you will discover this in the final report on the inspection.

- *Fire retardation equipment:* Does it meet the code? Has it been properly inspected and refilled or serviced? Does it work?

- *Gas appliances:* Do they meet the code? Do they work?

- *Gas lines:* Are they properly installed? Do they meet the code? Do they work?

- *Grease traps:* Used in restaurants and other facilities that generate a grease residue (usually when cooking items or dishes are washed). Are they properly installed? When was the last cleanout? Do they meet code? Do they work well?

- *Gutters:* Often an essential part of keeping water out of certain areas (as per drainage). Do they work? Are they in need of repair?

- *Health Code Inspections:* If your intended use requires an inspection by an appropriate health department official, be sure you have that accomplished prior to closing. The needed approval may not be issued until after you close (and the property is properly recorded to your name) but at least you know the property has passed the requirements. If not, you may need to renegotiate the contract or better yet, make sure you have a provision that indicates that any deficiency in obtaining approvals be rectified by the seller at the seller's expense.

- *Incinerator:* Do they meet code? Are they properly installed and ventilated? Do they work?

- *Inside lights:* Do they all work? Are they adequate for your needs?

- *Inventory:* Detailed lists of inventory can be an essential part of buying a business or a property where the inventory is critical. A hotel or motel, restaurant, or bar are obvious examples. But in some properties, such as rental apartments, having a clear understanding what belongs to the property and what might belong to tenants is very important. Inventory needs to be visually checked, once with the list, and later just prior to closing to make sure things are as they were several weeks earlier during the due diligence period. Often the first inspection can be accomplished with a video camera. Instead of listing each item in a 300-room hotel, one very slow scan of a typical room, followed by 299 faster scans is an ideal way to keep everyone honest.

- *Kitchen appliances:* Important items in homes and restaurants. Do they stay? Do they work? Are they still within warranty?

- *Landscape material:* When landscaping is important, make sure that it is included in the contract. I have seen people remove some beautiful plants just prior to closing.

- *Lease contracts:* If you are buying a property where there are potential lease contracts of any kind, make sure you are given the current copies to review. Leases can be to tenants, or leases of items that the landlord pays for such things as ice machines, television sets, furniture, and so on.

- *Legal description:* This is very important. Is the property you think you are buying the property that is described in the contract? Sellers need to make very sure that they are not selling more than they want to, just as much as buyers want to be sure they are not paying too much for too little.

- *Liens:* There are many different kinds of liens that can be placed against the property, or against the seller of the property. You want to make sure that none of these liens that can jeopardize your ownership will survive the closing. If they cannot be cleared up right away, make sure that sufficient funds are withheld from the seller to take care of the lien.

- *Liquor licenses:* Just because there is a liquor license at the property now does not mean that you automatically get one at closing. Each area of the country has different laws about this so make sure you have this covered in the contract. If you are buying a bar or a restaurant with a bar, or a hotel with a restaurant and bar, then this is a very important item.

- *Maintenance records:* Things might look fine, but how well has the property been cared for? If the seller had a crash fix-up to sell the property is one thing, but if the property has detailed records on how everything has been meticulously maintained, that is better.

- *Mechanical:* Does everything that is not electric or gas work as it should?

- *Mortgages of record:* Just because the seller says he or she only owes $100,000 on a first mortgage does not mean there are not other mortgages recorded against the property. You will want to know all you can about the title, and this includes mortgages and other lien possibilities.

- *Operational licenses:* When buying a property that includes a business, make sure that you are clear on what is necessary to get the operational license. Often the city must make an inspection of the property prior to issuance of the operational license. If there are code violations or the zoning is not proper you may not get an operational license even though the seller's use was grandfathered in. Grandfathered use is dangerous. This occurs when there has been a change in zoning or some other rule or regulation (city code or ordinance) that no longer permits certain uses or businesses in the area. However, existing uses may be allowed to stay, as long as there is not a change of ownership or some other change. Along you come and you want to double the size of the building to expand the daycare center. Sorry, grandfather use, and you cannot do that.

- *Outside lights:* Do they work? Are they sufficient for your needs? Do they meet code?

- *Parking garages:* Are they sufficient for your needs? Do they meet code?

- *Parking pavement:* Is it in need of repair? Does it meet code? Are parking spaces properly spaced? Is the landscape adequate for the current code?

- *Pending assessment:* Cities often assess properties to cover the cost of city improvements. Just because there is no actual assessment charged to the property, is it common knowledge to everyone but you that next year the city will zap all the property owners in an area, including you after you have closed on a property there, with a hundred thousand dollars? Check it out.

- *Pending condemnation:* A new roadway has been approved, but the road right-of-way team has not gotten to your area yet. But everyone knows it is coming, everyone but you. Check with all road departments (city, county, and state) to make sure that there are no such pending events (roads, bridges, special right-of-way widening, tunnels, municipal expansion, down-town authority, and so on).

- *Personal property:* All items that are not considered realty should be listed or lumped into a common description and there should be a bill of sale at closing giving you title to those items.

- *Plumbing:* Checking the plumbing is a usual part of any property inspection, and should be especially important when the building is over 10 years old. Sometimes the older properties will have copper plumbing, which is a real bonus.

- *Pool:* Swimming pools or decorative ponds should be inspected from pumps to diving platforms.

- *Pool equipment:* Do they work? Do they meet code?

- *Property boundaries:* This is a very important item no matter how large or small the property. A visual check with a survey is good, but unless you know what to look for you might make a mistake. Always check the boundaries to be sure the distances match what the survey says they should be. Look for benchmarks or surveyor marks nailed into the street, or along retaining walls. A good idea is to ask for a recent survey.

- *Radon:* A gas you cannot see or smell and which is radioactive. Easy to test for. If it is present, you need to find out why, and if it can be eliminated and prevented from returning. If not, then move on.

- *Rails and banisters:* Many areas have specific heights and spaces between posts and rails of such elements. These codes may have been updated since the building was built, so the statement, "Yes, this building was built exactly to code" might mean to the code at the time, but not to the present code. Always check changes in codes to see if anything that once met code does not presently comply.

- *Restaurant licenses:* The same situation as liquor licenses. Check out what you need to do to transfer or get a new one. Make sure you know the cost, and if there are any seller violations you may get stuck with fixing prior to issuance of your new license.

- *Road right-of-ways:* Just because the road is there does not mean that it is not planned to triple in width in a year or two. Make sure you know what the immediate plans are. Road plans generally extend 5 to 10 years into the future so you can check out that far, at least.

- *Roof:* Part of the usual inspections. Is the roof in good repair, does it leak, is it up to code? All are simple items to check. If there are any problems, make sure you have this covered in the contract.

- *Sea-wall:* When the property abuts a waterway of any kind there may be a sea wall or other kind of retaining wall to hold back the land to keep the water from washing it away. How sound is the wall? Does it meet code? Is there washing out going on under the wall? These are expensive items to fix.

- *Security alarms:* Does the alarm work? Is it up to code? When was it last inspected?

- *Security devices:* Do they meet your requirements? Do they meet code? Do they work?

- *Septic tanks:* When was it pumped out last? Does it work? Does it meet code? Does the drain field encroach on other property? Where is the drain field anyway?

- *Soil-bearing tests:* If you are going to build on a property, you may want to know how stable the subsoil really is. Local code may require you to have a subsoil test. Did you ask if the seller had a recent one? He or she might have done one and that is why the property is for sale. If not, you might want to pay for one yourself.

- *Squatters' rights:* Not much of a problem anymore, but worth checking out. If the property is remote, or large and remote, this can be critical. A squatter can take your property legally if they live on it, or otherwise demonstrate that they are acting as though it is theirs, pay taxes on it, and have it for a period of years (see your state's laws on this).

- *Structural:* Part of the normal property inspection. This will let you know that everything seems to be correctly built, and that the building meets code.

- *Subsoil conditions:* What is under the ground could be important to you—muck, a sink hole, oil (tank), minerals that you can get title to. Be sure to question your agreement if there are any problems in this area.

- *Survey:* A recent survey should show encroachments, all easements, right-of-ways, and other potential boundary problems. If the seller gives you one, and you discover that the survey was not accurate, then you may have a case against the seller. Most title insurance will not insure against any claim that would have been revealed (either the claim or the reason for the claim) with a recent survey.

- *Tax assessment:* Every year the property will be assessed for ad valorem taxes. These taxes are collected by the county tax collector and are generally a total of various community and state charges against the property. Every now and then a special assessment is levied in addition to the annual ad valorem tax. Past due and unpaid taxes are the seller's responsibility unless the contract says otherwise.

- *Tax liens:* If the seller has not paid taxes, there could be a tax lien against the property. If any exists it can be paid off at the closing. However, the seller may contest the claim, as the seller could for any claim. If that is the case, then your lawyer can discuss with you options you might have to set aside funds from the seller's portion of the deal to cover that, or for the seller to buy a bond to cover the lien while he or she takes the case to court.

- *Telephone:* Are there any? Does it work?

- *Telephone equipment:* Is it sufficient for your needs? Does it work? Is it owned or leased? If leased, review the contract. Can you cancel the lease?

- *Tenant history:* Helpful but not always provided. Ask for it in the contract.

- *Termites:* Inspect for this pest and damage from them. Sellers can have a pre-inspection and obtain an insurance policy against infestation and damage.

- *Utility easements:* What kinds are there? Where do they go? Can you remove them?

- *Wall siding:* Condition and code compliance matters are most important.

- *Water leaks:* Often you will see stains from water leaks. Are they current leaks? Always check the stain to determine the possible cause. If the roof is the problem, then check the roof.

- *Yard setbacks:* Virtually every building code will have a prescribed setback for buildings and yards. If the building does not meet those codes it could be because a previous modification was allowed by the city. If that is the case then you may not have a problem.

- *Zoning:* Does it allow you to do what you want to do on the property? What are the restrictions in this zoning?

Preclosing Period

This period comes toward the end of the due-diligence period. This is the time that the buyer is discovering what is wrong with the property. This is the time that the buyer may want to renegotiate the contract to take into consideration the problems that have been discovered.

The current approach to selling real estate is to sell it "as is." This means that whatever the problems, the buyer will close on the property taking title to it without warranty to any condition of the real estate or personal property covered by the contract. This covers the seller from potential liability later on if a warranty fails to meet a future test.

The "as is" situation is not always good, however, because it almost insists that the buyer have a long period of "free time" to check out the property to be able to make a learned opinion of the condition of the property.

Residential properties, such as homes and apartments, often have a more practical approach to this situation. The buyer can make inspections, and if there are any problems, the seller is obliged to pay for the repair or correction of the problem up to a certain percentage of the purchase price. This percentage is a matter of negotiation (often 3 to 4 percent shown in the agreement). If the actual cost of the repair or correction exceeds that, then the seller can spend the additional money, or if not, the buyer can get out of the deal. This kind of transaction is safer for the seller than the buyer because the buyer knows that as long as the seller is willing to pay the required amount to fix or correct the problem, the buyer will have no option except to close, or lose his or her deposit (if any).

If the deal is an "as is" or the cost to fix or correct a problem is greater than the amount the seller is willing to pay to fix, then the buyer is almost guaranteed to attempt to renegotiate the deal. Sellers had best be ready.

Transfer of Title

This is the actual closing date. This is usually scheduled to take place at a lawyer's office, but can be anywhere the parties agree to. Usually the buyer picks the place, but that is a matter of convenience, and should be stated in the contract to keep from having a problem with this later on. What is important is to understand that it is not necessary for the two parties to come together for this process to work. In fact, it is usually better that the buyer and seller go to the closing separately. Let the lawyers or closing agents deal with the paperwork, and as long as everything has been properly attended to ahead of time, closings can be smooth events.

There are times, however, when closings are far from smooth events, and the following tips will help you avoid the rough waters of turbulent closings:

FOUR STEPS TO A SMOOTH CLOSING

1. Insist on the closing agents having a preclosing meeting to make sure all the paperwork is properly drawn.

2. Ensure that each party knows exactly what is going to be expected of them. Who is to sign, who is to bring the check or cash, and so on.

3. Plan to close early in the week rather than later in the week. If there is a last minute hitch and the scheduled closing was a Friday, then everything is on hold until Monday. Start on a Monday or Tuesday.

4. Make sure you understand the contract from top to bottom.

Postclosing

When you have closed, there is still a relationship between you and the seller. There may be tax bills that will have to be adjusted in the near future, and a smooth transition of ownership might be added if you and the other side stay friendly.

When the seller has taken back secondary financing, your relationship to the seller may be rather long standing. It is a good idea to be as prudent as you can with any payment to a former seller because sellers are quicker to call you in default and actually foreclose than a third-party lender.

The best thing about the postclosing period is that you can sit back and smile to yourself. You started out with an idea to buy, and persisted all the way from that moment until present. Now it is time to turn back to your goals and to make the most of this new investment.

Chapter 22

THE SIX MOST-ASKED QUESTIONS ABOUT REAL ESTATE FINANCING

GOAL OF THIS CHAPTER

This chapter gives you the answers to six of the most-asked questions about real estate financing. By providing you with these answers, you will see how easy it is for a would-be real estate investor to be confused with the steps they need to take to break through their own mental barrier to success in this field.

Over the past 30 years, I have appeared on hundreds of radio and television talk shows. This exposure along with the lecture and speaking engagements I have conducted has allowed me the opportunity to keep track of hundreds of questions dealing with just about every possible aspect of real estate investing. In my book, *The Real Estate Investor's Answer Book* (New York: McGraw-Hill, 1993), I have provided over 200 such questions along with answers drawn from my years of experience as a realtor and as an investor. This chapter will give you six of the most important questions asked of me during this 30-year period that pertain to the subject of real estate finance.

The following questions and their answers should help you maneuver around some of the most common problems you may face in building a successful and effective real estate portfolio:

1. If I have poor credit, how can I acquire real estate?
2. I know there are different kinds of mortgage payment schedules, what are they, and how do they affect my repayment of a mortgage?
3. Is there something special I can do to obtain a mortgage?
4. What should I do if I plan to hold secondary financing when I sell?

557

5. What is the very best category of real estate to buy before any other?

6. What is the number-one problem I should be ready to solve when I own property that has tenants?

IF I HAVE POOR CREDIT, HOW CAN I ACQUIRE REAL ESTATE?

The answer to this question will depend on the reason your credit is not good, and your ability to meet the financial obligations of the debt. First, are you sure about the status of your credit? Many people have better credit than they might think. Just because you were turned down for a credit card, or have had a problem in the past over a delinquent bill, does not automatically mean your credit has gone down the tubes.

Check Your Credit

Everyone has the right to check his or her own credit report. In most states, you can do this relatively easily, and if you have just been turned down for something due to a bad credit report, you will be able to get a copy of that report free. The first step in this process is to ascertain if a credit report was actually obtained, and which company issued the report.

You may be turned down for something without knowing that a credit report has been obtained. If you have applied for a job, a credit card, to buy something on time, to rent a car, apartment, furniture, a television set, or just about anything that will require you to meet some financial obligation, a credit report may have been obtained on you.

If you are told you cannot get the job, card, or rent something, ask why you are being turned down. If the answer is because we checked your credit, that may or may not be true. It is easy to say, "Your credit is bad." In any event, ask which company issued the report because it is your right to know, then call that company and discuss the situation.

Generally, you are entitled to a free copy of your report and can do so easily over the Internet by searching "free credit reports."

When you get the report, the first thing you will want to check is whether the report is actually about you. It is possible that an error has been made in the request for the report. If your social security numbers and birthdates are the ones on the report, then check the items that are shown. If there is something wrong, such as a history of late payments, or outstanding bills going back several months or longer, or judgments, or whatever, make sure those are charges made by you. It could be that your ex-spouse ran up all those bills on your credit card without you knowing it, and because the bills go to the house where you no longer live, you have been in the dark about this. Alternatively, one of your kids may have signed your name as co-guarantor to an account at the local video store and there is an outstanding balance of $4,000 owed them for back charges on adult video rentals. Alternately, the name on the account is yours, but the charges the report says you owe could not possibly be yours.

You can challenge any item in the report directly with the report company; however, the best method is to contact the store or source of the obligation such as the store or business or property owner that says you are a deadbeat and find out what the problem is. It could be something old that you took care of some time ago, but has never been recorded as having been paid or satisfied. Try to get the problem resolved as best you can.

When all fails in getting the credit agency to report your credit, then you can resort to an agency that deals with fixing your credit. Naturally, they cannot remove or fix valid problems that are showing up, but when there is a mistake or some other wrongly reported credit item, one of these credit doctors can be a big help. They will charge you for this service, of course, so you might want to shop around to find the best deal in town.

The credit agency and the company specializing in fixing these problems can be found in the local yellow pages of your phone book, under credit, or by searching the Internet. By the way, the three major national agencies that issue credit reports are TRW, Merchants, and Equifax. You will find 800 phone numbers that serve your area, and if you call, you are likely to get a voice-mail type of system with recorded messages that can walk you through some of the steps I have just mentioned.

Find Property Where Your Credit Is Not in Question

If you have followed this procedure and the result is that you really do have bad credit for valid reasons, all is not lost. The next part of the equation is to answer the question: Can you meet the obligations to pay on a mortgage? Your credit might be in the toilet because you refuse to pay on something you do not owe or feel you do not owe. However, until you remove the problem and get a proper resolution of the situation, your credit report is going to show that you have not met your financial obligations. Assume, then, that you are working on that problem, and in the meantime want to proceed to attempt to purchase real estate.

The first step is to find a property where good credit is not the criteria you will have to meet. Where do you find this kind of property? Just about everywhere. It is not the property that is going to check your credit; it will be the seller or an existing mortgagee that would do that. Some sellers are so anxious to get rid of the property that the question of your credit may never come up. This would be the case as long as the seller has not been asked to hold secondary financing. Some mortgagees are anxious to get rid of a property, perhaps because they have not made a payment on the mortgage for several months. The thought of a new person taking over the payments sounds good, no matter what. Even if the lender does get into the act, replacing a known and existing credit risk with a potential credit risk may be the better of the two choices.

Assume Existing Debt

Often you can take over existing debt without having to fill out an application of assumption. This may be a mortgage from a previous seller, or some other kind of private loan that is on the property. It might even be possible to get the seller of the property to agree to stay on the existing mortgage because you know you would not pass the credit report. Of course, there are creative ways that you can acquire property without having to ever deal with your credit. Remember, you can acquire property without having to own it, at least for the moment.

Creative Financing Can Provide an Answer

One such way is to lease with an option to buy. This can work well in situations where the property needs some fix-up and you have a good plan, and the time to accomplish the labor. If, at the end of one or two years, you have completed that plan and now can show "leasehold equity," you can convert that equity into real value to a prospective lender. You then exercise your option to buy and finance the previously agreed-on price.

During those couple of years, you work hard to also cure your credit problems so that when you do apply for a mortgage you will have smooth sailing. On the other hand, if the problems continue to exist, be sure to have an option to renew your lease so that you can continue to improve both your property and your credit. It could well be that the existing owner is so impressed with your work in the property that he or she will step in and allow you to assume the existing debt, while holding some additional paper (either secured or not) so that you can purchase, no matter what is your credit score. Some sellers might balk at this kind of arrangement, but if you are genuine and are prepared to pay something down then most sellers will come around. A lot has to do with the motivation and the market.

Get a Cosigner

This is an easy answer if you have someone who has good credit who is willing to lend that to you. Many investors have found that a good way to buy single-family fixer-upper homes is to find a partner who is a good handy person, who will live in the property as a "tenant" while paying "rent." That person becomes a part of the investment team. The tenant might be you, bad credit and all, and the investor a person with good credit, but no time or willingness to fix up the property for resale.

The deal is this: You pay just as you would if you rented the property; only you get a small break (a negotiable item) and a piece of the action when the property is put on the market a year or so later after you have fixed it up. You move in and use your sweat equity to fix the property up. Later, it is sold, and after the money person has gotten back the original investment, which may not be much, you then split the profits with him. There is no hard and fast rule on how these profits are split. You should not jump into a frying pan to discover that the "little fix up" becomes a full-time job for a year. You might even get free rent, and even a payment for labor that exceeds a certain number of hours you both agree to in the beginning.

Do Not Let Bad Credit Be an Anchor around Your Neck

There is nothing worse than living with bad credit. If you have it now, make yourself a promise that you will solve that problem as soon as you can. The quicker you can go from a negative to a positive, the better your chances for a future as a real estate investor. If you are truly up to your neck in debt, the best solution may be to talk to a good bankruptcy lawyer. This can help get you back on the positive side of your finances, and there is no negative stigma to bankruptcy. Some of the most wealthy real estate investors in America have found out that bankruptcy was their road to success.

I KNOW THERE ARE DIFFERENT KINDS OF MORTGAGE PAYMENT SCHEDULES. WHAT ARE THEY, AND HOW DO THEY AFFECT MY REPAYMENT OF A MORTGAGE?

Repayment schedules vary and each has a unique benefit that may be advantageous to you, or it may not be. The key is for you to know what each payment will require you to do, and what options you might have to choose another form of payback. This can be very important depending on other provisions in the mortgage. I will explain as we go through the different schedules.

NINE BASIC REPAYMENT SCHEDULES THAT ARE USED IN MORTGAGES

1. EQUAL CONSTANT PAYMENTS OF INTEREST AND PRINCIPAL COMBINED: The entire amount of the debt will be fully paid off at a future date, without any additional sums being added to the scheduled monthly payments. This may also be called a "self-amortizing loan" by many lenders, but that phrase may also be applied to other schedules so you need to dig deeper into the specific meaning as used by that lender. In this instance, each month the payment remains the same. However, it is made up of two main elements. The first is the interest the lender is charging you on the amount borrowed, and the second is the portion of that payment reducing the total amount that is still owed following that payment. In some mortgages, there are other items that are also collected by the lender, and these items can change either by increasing or decreasing amounts over the years. These can include, but are not be limited to, insurance, escrow for real estate taxes, and homeowner or association fees. As far as the actual amount of money that was borrowed is concerned, the interest and principal remain fixed for the full term of the loan. This is the usual format a commercial bank or savings bank would use, and this loan is called a *fixed payment self-amortizing loan.*

Here is an example of a fixed payment self-amortizing loan. You buy a new home and borrow $100,000 from your local bank, giving them a first mortgage as security. The payment schedule is set to amortize over a period of 20 years in 240 equal monthly installments at 9 percent interest per annum. This would be calculated by looking in the Appendix under interest Table A at 20 years and 9 percent interest. This would give you a constant payment indicator of 10.797, which represents the annual constant rate that would be the total of 12 equal monthly installments. You then find the monthly payment by dividing that number by 12.

To find the monthly mortgage payment, multiply the beginning mortgage amount of $100,000 by the constant rate of 10.797 ($100,000 × 0.10797 = $10,797). Remember, when you multiply by an interest rate you move the decimal two places to the left. This gives you the total annual payment. Divide this annual total by 12 and you end up with $899.75, which is the monthly payment that will, over 20 years, pay both the principal and interest due on this mortgage.

The constant rate is very important as this is often a number bankers and lenders will talk about. The Appendix of this book covers the use of these tables. With them, you can find a great deal about the mortgage payments and amounts due.

2. FIXED EQUAL PAYMENTS OF INTEREST AND PRINCIPAL COMBINED, WITH ONE OR MORE BALLOON PAYMENTS IN THE FUTURE: The balloon payment can be all or partial payment of principal in one or more lump sums. Generally, a balloon payment is one that requires the full payment of principal outstanding to be paid off earlier than the payment schedule would completely amortize. Monthly payments are always the same (fixed) until the balloon. This mortgage starts out exactly the same as the first payment schedule in the previous mortgage, except that instead of going the full course to amortize the entire outstanding principal, the mortgage will have one or more balloon payments of principal due at a date in the future. For example, if the $100,000 mortgage starts out with a 20-year amortization schedule at 9 percent the lender may insist that the full payoff take place at the end of 10 years. This sudden payoff is the balloon payment. You can calculate the amount of a balloon by looking at the constant payment rate if you know the interest being charged and the number of years remaining. If this time the mortgage had to be paid off at the end of the 10th year, to ascertain the amount of the principal due, you need to find the amount which the payment of $10,797 (the annual total of 12 payments) would pay off in 10 years (the remaining term of the 20-year mortgage).

Look in the Appendix under Table A and you will find the constant rate is 15.201 (10 years at 9 percent). Divide the total annual payment by that amount. $10,797 divided by 0.15201 and you will get $71,028.22, which represents the balance of principal that would still be owed after the end of the tenth year. If you were to pay off the loan at this date, that would be the principal amount of balloon payment. To that, add one month's interest for the total payment.

3. EQUAL FIXED PAYMENTS OF PRINCIPAL, PLUS A SEPARATE CALCULATION OF INTEREST ON THE OUTSTANDING BALANCE: Each month the amount of the payment due will change because the interest will be declining each month. This mortgage is different from the

first two payment schedules and is rarely used in institutional mortgages, but can be common in privately held loans, or foreign-generated loans. In this payment schedule, there are equal principal payments with interest added. For example, say the amount of the loan was $120,000 to be repaid over 120 monthly installments of equal principal plus interest on the outstanding balance at 9 percent per annum. First, you would divide the loan amount of $120,000 by the number of payments, which in this example are 120 payments. The monthly principal payment would be $1,000. To that amount, you would then add interest, which would change every month. See the following schedule for the first five monthly payments so you can see how this works:

Principal ($)	Interest ($)	Total ($)	Amount Still Owed after Payment ($)
1,000	900.00	1,900.00	119,000
1,000	892.50	1,892.50	118,000
1,000	885.00	1,885.00	117,000
1,000	877.50	1,877.50	116,000
1,000	870.00	1,870.00	115,000

4. PAYMENTS OF INTEREST ONLY: No principal payments until one or more future dates when principal payments are made. As long as the payment is sufficient to meet the annual interest due, each month would be the same. If the amount of the loan was $120,000 and the interest rate was 9 percent per annum, an annual payment of interest would be $10,800. Normally interest-only payments are made on a schedule throughout the year; these can be monthly at $900 per month or quarterly (three months at a time) at $2,700 per quarter or to any other schedule. As only interest is being paid, there would be no reduction of the principal amount during the term of this loan. At a specified date, the schedule would change to either some other payment schedule or the principal amount would be due and payable.

5. PAYMENTS OF ONLY PART OF THE INTEREST DUE, SO THE UNPAID INTEREST IS ADDED TO THE PRINCIPAL: This type of mortgage may also be called "a deficit payment mortgage." Here the amount owed grows until paid or another form of payback starts to take effect. Each month can be the same, or adjust to a formula. This is a deficit payment plan, only, unlike the Zero Coupon mortgage, where no principal or interest is paid until a future date; in this mortgage, a portion of the interest is actually being paid. As will happen with a Zero Coupon, the unpaid interest is added to the principal each month. This causes the amount of the outstanding principal owed to continue to grow as the unpaid interest is added to the principal amount. This mortgage is much like the interest-only schedule, except that not all the interest

due is actually paid. This creates a deficit that is added back to the principal amount, and the calculation of interest will be made on the larger amount each period. The following schedule illustrates how this works. Assume the mortgage amount at the start is $100,000, and interest is calculated at 12 percent per annum. The actual payment to be made is $500 per month. As you can see, the fixed $500 payment is short more interest each month:

Interest Due ($)	Actual Payment ($)	Deficit ($)	New Principal Owed ($)
1,000.00	500.00	500.00	100,500.00
1,005.00	500.00	505.00	101,005.00
1,010.05	500.00	510.05	101,515.05

This kind of payment schedule is rarely used as a full schedule. However, it could function this way with a balloon payment due in the future. This kind of payment schedule can be very useful at the start of a repayment program to give the buyer some relief in meeting debt obligations and is better for the lender than a complete moratorium of payments as will be shown in the zero payment shown below.

6. Zero coupon mortgage: In this schedule, there is no payment of principal or interest during a specified period of time. Principal owed grows quickly as interest that was due is added to the previous amount. This is a compounding effect on the debt owed. In this schedule, there is no payment made at all and all interest would add to the principal owed. Each month's interest would then be calculated on the growing principal amount owed. Remember, when you calculate interest, you must move the decimal two places to the left, then divide the result by the period of the year you are calculating. If the amount of the principal is $100,000 and the interest rate is to be calculated at 9 percent, you would multiply $100,000 by 0.09 and would get the total interest due on that amount for one year, which would be $9,000. If you were calculating a quarterly payment, you would divide that by four to get $2,250. Interest due for a monthly payment would be found by dividing the annual amount by 12 ($9,000 ÷ 12 = $750.00).

This method of repayment has an interesting use in mortgages on seasonal properties. Assume you were selling a mountain lodge you owned. It had two distinct seasons, the first is a four-month winter period, and the second is a four-month summer period. It would be possible for you to help the buyer by establishing a zero-coupon period in between these two times of year. No matter what method of amortization that was in place, it would be a simple matter to "suspend" actual payment of two months each side of the one or the other season periods. After two months of nonpayment, the usual schedule would return, based on the increased principal outstanding. Another effective use of this, as well as a partial deferred payment or even interest-only payments, is where you, as a buyer, negotiate one of these methods into a purchase money mortgage with the goal to increase your cash flow (or reduce your losses during your initial start up period).

7. ADJUSTABLE RATE MORTGAGE: This is the ARM you see advertised all the time. The interest rate charged changes on a periodic basis. Any of the methods described above can be used, and the only difference is that as the interest is changed, a new principal/interest schedule would be established. The method of "how does the interest change" is a negotiated factor in this kind of mortgage. Generally, however, institutional lenders attempt to make that a policy decision rather than a negotiated one. However, in large mortgages everything is negotiable. Usually each period between changes in the rate has the same monthly payment. This kind of mortgage is very popular with lenders as it gives them protection against a rising market rate. In this schedule, the interest changes from time to time, both up and down. The usual adjustments occur once a year and are tied to an easy-to-ascertain rate, such as the quoted rate (or average over the past three months) for U.S. Treasury 90-day notes, or some other clearly identifiable rates. Keep in mind that any such rate can be used, including setting the price of gold at an amount; then any increase or decrease in the quoted price of gold will cause the interest rate to adjust by the same percentage of rise or fall in the price of gold. While this kind of rate adjustment is not usual, I mention it to show you that almost anything could be used. Borrowers must be very cautious when giving a mortgage on adjustable rate terms. Insist on annual adjustments, with a cap on the maximum rate increase in any given adjustment period, a total cap on the highest rate that can be charged no matter what, and that they use the same formula for both rise and decrease in the adjustment index.

The adjustable rate mortgage has had a lot of bad press due to the link with the subprime lending market. The problem promulgating this bad press has been the surge in foreclosures that began in 2007. This rise in the foreclosure rate has been blamed on the misuse of the adjustable rate mortgage format. What occurred was a result of one or more various practices in the lending profession. These practices consisted of: overselling of debt to individuals who did not truly qualify for a loan in the amount provided, a lack of proper disclosure as to what could and likely would occur if and when the interest rate on the mortgages was adjusted upward, and the outright use of fraud in filling out mortgage applications in combination with a sudden and simultaneous jump in the cost of living (attributed first to the high cost of oil, ergo, transportation), and layoffs. The fact of the matter is that adjustable rate mortgages are simply a method to enable the borrower to have a breather for the first period of a mortgage payback. Borrowers are cautioned, however, to educate themselves about what penalty comes from the free lunch. Remember, in finance there really is no free lunch.

8. GRADUATED RATE MORTGAGES: The interest rate charged starts at one rate and graduates up or down as the payment progresses. Generally, this kind of mortgage (a GRM) starts with low interest rates and moves to higher interest rates. Each period between adjustments generally has the same monthly payment.

9. REVERSE MORTGAGE PAYMENT: Here the lender makes payments to the mortgagor until the total amount together with compounding interest needs to be repaid. At that time, the repayment schedule can be one of the earlier schedules. The initial payments made to the mortgagor are usually a set equal monthly payment, but can allow for some extraordinary lump payments to cover emergencies. This kind of mortgage is often advertised as a "Seniors Loan" where a retired person lives off the "income" generated by the lender. In my opinion, this is really a mortgage of "last resort," and if this is being considered, any borrower should pay very close attention to the terms of repayment. Ask many questions and make sure you understand every answer.

IS THERE SOMETHING SPECIAL I CAN DO TO GET A MORTGAGE?

There is a saying that if you do not need the money they will gladly lend it to you. Bankers are notoriously stingy about lending money. However, they are in that business, and unless they make loans, they soon go out of business. Once you understand several things about lenders, you will discover that there is a right way and a wrong way to deal with them. If you follow all the tips I am about to give you, your chance at getting a loan will be greatly improved.

First of all, let us take a look at the loan officer or other person who is attending to your request for a mortgage. This individual and others like him or her are responsible for keeping their employer in business. This means that the loans that are made should be good loans that will not go into default. Every time a loan officer brings in a loan that goes sour, that loan officer gets a big red X next to his name. Too many big red X's next to your name and loan officers go looking for another job. With this in mind, it is essential that everything the borrower does attempts to alleviate the loan officer's natural caution to avoid getting another big red X.

This means then, that from day one, the borrower must give the best impression possible that the loan will be repaid and never go into default. How do you do that? Take a look at the following checklist of what to do and what not to do:

FOUR PROACTIVE STEPS TO TAKE WHEN DEALING WITH A LENDER

1. BEGIN BY GETTING TO KNOW THE LENDER. When you have already established some rapport with a lender you will find that everything goes much smoother than if you walk in one day and ask for a million-dollar loan. Because this is so important, look at the following five items that will help you establish the right pattern to obtain a loan:

- Introduce yourself to the president of the bank (or other lender) or a senior officer.
- Explain that you are a real estate investor who is planning to make several investments in the area and would like to know about their lending policy.

- Let the president spend some time selling you on his bank and their services.

- Meet the president's secretary.

- Make sure he or she will remember you when you meet her or him by talking about something of interest. This is easy to do if you are observant. A photograph or some other clue on the desk can be the entry. This might be a clue that will allow you to give a compliment.

- Call the secretary a few days later and ask a question. Be thankful for the attention you got when you visited the president a few days earlier.

- Drop the secretary a note. Mention you will call in a few days and would like to know which loan officer would be proper for you to deal with for the kind of loan you need.

- Call and ask the secretary to introduce you to the loan officer. This is the key. When the president's secretary takes the time to introduce you to a loan officer, it is as though the president has actually done the introduction. A very good start with this loan officer.

2. Have a loan request presentation that looks highly professional. Look at the Outline for a Loan Request in Chapter 5. Follow this outline as closely as you can, making sure that all the supporting material is typed, and those photos, drawings, and other graphics used are neat and accurate. Go to a good quick print facility, and make several copies and have them bound with a title page behind a clear cover.

3. Whenever you meet with the loan officer be sure to dress the part of a successful businessperson. No matter what your business or job, you are asking this person to stick his neck out for you, and he wants to be sure that he is not going to get a big red X in his job satisfaction chart. If you bring your spouse along, make sure he or she dresses the part as well.

4. Always be a few minutes early to every meeting.

WHAT SHOULD I DO IF I WANT TO HOLD SECONDARY FINANCING ON A PROPERTY I SELL?

There are eight steps you should take prior to entering into any agreement where you hold secondary financing when selling a property:

1. Ascertain if the first mortgages (either existing or new) allow for secondary financing. Many new mortgages contain limiting conditions to additional financing on a property. It is possible that the existing financing, if from an institutional lender, or from a private party using an institutional mortgage form, also limits possible secondary financing. If this is the circumstance, any additional loans will have to be secured by other property.

2. Do you agree that the sale takes you closer to your goal(s)? This is always one of the most important aspects of a transaction. Are you accomplishing all or at least part of what you started out to do? The real answer to this must be found. Mind you, the truth might hurt, but it is better that you do not start rationalizing to yourself when it comes to your goals. It is at moments like this, right before you sign the sales agreement, that will require you to hold financing that you might discover the real truth that the goal you were aiming for was not the right goal. Be sure to check the bottom line math of the deal too. Have you calculated all the cost that will be generated as a result of this transaction? Will you have sufficient cash left over after you pay all those expenses? Will you end up selling the property and have to dig down deep to pay off things like closing costs, recording fees, stamps on deeds and/or mortgages, and your lawyer's fee, commissions, and do not forget your gains tax to Uncle Sam? As I have mentioned in this book several times before, it is possible to walk away from the closing owing more money than you get.

3. Check out the buyer. After all, you are going to rely on this person to make payments to you. You should run a credit check on the person, any related corporations, and have a detailed information sheet filled out that gives you names of references, the buyer's addresses, phone numbers, social security number, a driver's license number, as well as a recent balance sheet of assets and liabilities. Why do you want all of this? Just in case you have to go to court, the more past information you get, the easier it will be to collect. To run a credit check, look in the Yellow Pages of your local telephone book under the heading "Credit"; you will find several companies that can, for a modest fee, run a credit check on your prospective buyer.

4. Can you improve the security to the debt? One of the best ways to do this is to lower the amount of the mortgage. This is, of course, a negotiation factor at the time you are entering into the agreement. There are several approaches to this. One good way is to cut as hard a deal; you can on getting the maximum price possible. Don't be hard-nosed about the amount of the secondary financing at this point. If the buyer wants you to hold $50,000 and you don't mind, then let that issue alone for the moment. However, do provide a condition in the agreement that you have the right to run a credit check, including checking references, and subject to your approval, without qualification, of this check, you will agree to the secondary financing. The buyer will insist on a time limitation, so on the last day of that time period you tell the buyer that you will approve the second mortgage terms, but only if the amount is reduced to, say, $100 (or something more agreeable).

The following list suggests other possibilities of improving your security to the secondary financing you are being asked to hold that generally do not show up in most mortgage forms. Remember, a mortgage is a contract, and like any contract, you can have terms and conditions that are unique. The only limitation is that everything contained in the contract must be legal:

- *A personal guarantee:* Buyers like to let the properties be the sole liquidated damages in the event of a default. Hold out for personal signature and guarantee.

- *Get a cosigner:* If the buyer has dubious credit, then get additional guarantees on the note.

- *Get additional security:* Does the buyer own other property or stock or something valuable? Then get the buyer to pledge all or part to the security of your loan.

- *Make sure you do not subordinate without compensation.* Whenever you allow the buyer to add additional debt to the property that would come ahead of your secondary financing, you add substantial risk to the potential of a default on your loan. Get paid for that added risk or don't do it. Safest bet is never to allow subordination to additional financing unless you fully understand the added risk you put yourself into.

- *Have a much defined default clause in the mortgage.* Unless your lawyer is well versed in real estate law, you might find a commonplace general generic mortgage document that might be more suited for the buyer than the seller.

- *Have the right to inspections of the property.* This will allow you to make sure that your asset is being well cared for.

- *Insist on notice of payment of every other debt obligation, including real estate taxes.* You do not want to discover that every debt except yours is in default.

- *Have penalties for past due payments built into the mortgage and allow it to be your option to accept the penalty or to accelerate the payments and call the mortgage due.*

- *Be sure that the mortgage allows you to collect lawyers' fees and collection fees if you have to use legal means to collect on past due payments.*

- *Do not allow simple assumption of the mortgage by someone else.* This can happen when your buyer later on sells to someone else. That other person may not be as good a credit risk. You can protect yourself by having a provision that the mortgage is not assumable. Nothing is wrong with this. If the buyer wants to sell, there is always the opportunity to modify the agreement if a new buyer comes along that you would approve.

5. MAKE SURE YOU UNDERSTAND ALL THE TERMS OF THE NOTE AND MORTGAGE. Sounds simple enough, but this is absolutely critical. Have your lawyers read the documents to you aloud and slowly. Stop any moment there is anything you are unclear about and make sure you understand every word. You will be surprised how few people ever do this with documents they sign. In addition, you might be surprised to discover that your lawyer is going through a learning process too, and may find something disagreeable in what was just read.

6. REVIEW AND UNDERSTAND YOUR OPTIONS IF THERE IS A DEFAULT OF ANY KIND. Okay, what do you do if the monthly payment is late? Do you know? Most likely, you do not; in fact, most people do not know, so the time to learn this is prior to signing the contract

that will put you into a position of having to deal with this potential problem. In general, there is a procedure that will be covered by laws of your state. You can generally obtain a booklet on the rights of mortgagors and mortgagees from the state government printing office. To find this, call the general printing office in the state capital and ask. If there is nothing, then ask your top-notch real estate lawyer who is a part of your investment team. The procedure usually includes these following steps:

   a. When the mortgage payment is past the grace period, send a registered letter that calls attention to the fact that the payment is past due. This letter may state that if the payment, plus penalties (state what it is as provided for in the mortgage), is received by you no later than a reasonable date (usually no greater than 30 days), then you will not proceed legally to accelerate the mortgage or foreclose.

   b. Second notice can follow in seven days as a courtesy if there is no reply to the first letter.

   c. Now, you turn things over to your lawyer to start foreclosure.

   7. MAKE SURE THE NOTE AND MORTGAGE CLEARLY REFLECT THE DEAL. A standard form mortgage and note will not clearly reflect the deal, nor will a computer-driven note and mortgage from some other transaction. This should be cleared up when you and your lawyer read these documents together.

   8. MAKE SURE THE MORTGAGOR LIVES UP TO OBLIGATIONS 100 PERCENT. First of all, you must consider that you did not go into this deal willing to be lenient if the buyer is late on the payments to you, or stops making them. As long as you know what to do when the payment is late, then be ready to act. This is not a matter of being tough. It is a matter of being a good businessperson.

WHAT IS THE BEST CATEGORY OF REAL ESTATE TO BUY BEFORE ANY OTHER?

If you are about to become a first-time real estate owner, that must mean that you either live with someone, or you are a renter. Your first property should be one that leads you to a place to live. Naturally, this might be a place you can move into, such as a home or apartment. However, that makes the assumption that you can afford to carry the mortgage payments. If you were living with family members because you cannot afford rent, then your approach to this question would be different. For that reason, I will give you answers based on these two assumptions.

You Can Afford to Pay Rent

Okay, if you can afford to pay rent, it is likely that you can afford to own. In this case, I encourage renters to look for a small apartment complex of at least four units. Buildings with a greater number of units, up to say 15 units, would be fine as well, but they may be out of your budget for the time being. In my case, my wife and I lived with my parents for a short while after returning to the United States from Europe where I lived (as a renter). The first thing we did was look for a lot to build a four-unit apartment building. We found one, made an offer, and closed on the deal the day my contractor broke ground on the building. It consisted of three one-bedroom apartments and one "owner's" two-bedroom unit. We went the direction of building a new building because we could not find anything that was for sale that appealed to us. I also knew that the market was ripe for such a venture, and I knew that if I set everything up right we could finance the majority of the land and buildings.

We still own that building, and it is an example of just how good real estate is as an investment. My total out-of-pocket investment was less than $5,000 and today, I receive around $4,000 in rental income every month. Over the years, the three one-bedroom apartments carried the debt service and other expenses of the building, so during the time we lived in the owner's apartment it was a breakeven investment. Breakeven only as far as the cash flow went. Because the tenants paid off the debt for me (in 25 years) and as appreciation slowly but surely bumped up the value of the property, that $5,000 invest-ment is worth nearly $500,000 today. Benefits have piled up, too. Annual spendable cash flow has paid my taxes, utilities, and insurance of every home we have owned since mov-ing out of the owner's two-bedroom unit.

I mention all of this, because it is still, in my opinion, the best way for a renter to escape the clutches of their landlord. Become a landlord yourself.

To locate this category of real estate, you should look for an area of town that is established, and will present a good place to cultivate good tenants. As with all income-producing real estate, you rely on the caliber of your tenants to maintain the continued appreciation of the real estate. If you go to an area that is already a little run-down, with the idea that is where you will get a good deal, you are mistaken. Likewise, a new part of town may not be ideal for this scenario either, because the majority of "new" development is competition with your rental property.

Look for properties that have a vacancy, but are not offered for sale. The advantage of doing this is that you want to catch a property before the owner realizes they really want to sell it. This gives you the edge in finding something before others have picked over the spoils of the subdivision. Generally, this tactic also lets you get directly to the owner of the building without having to deal with an agent. This happens because most small buildings are managed by the owner. A small four- to eight-unit building generally does not support outside management.

The fact that the owner is dealing directly with you is very good news. This means that the owner is also dealing directly with all the problems of the building. The fact that there is a vacancy also means that the owner may not be making money from this investment, as compared with having the equity out of the building and investing in something else.

You might start your negotiations as though you want to rent the building. Discuss the rent, what the owner will do to fix the apartment to meet your standards, and ask, as if in an aside, if the owner would rent to you with your having an option to buy the property. If there is any sign or reaction from the owner that he or she would consider such a proposition, then proceed and make a direct offer. You can use any of the techniques that I have presented to you in this book. The likely best choice in this event would be exactly what you asked. Lease with an option to buy. Spell out the terms that work for you, but make sure you establish a purchase price before you sign the lease option deal. Once you have those terms, build into the transaction the right for you to begin to make improvements to the building—paint, landscape, and so on. Your tactic here is to improve the value of the building so that when you exercise the option to buy you will be purchasing a more valuable building than when you started out. In essence, you have built up leasehold equity that the lender will recognize. In addition, oh yes, ask (in the purchase agreement) that all or a portion of your rent be applied to the purchase price.

You Cannot Afford Rent and Live with a Family Member or Friend

This is not the end of the world for you. In fact, this actually may expand your options. If you and the people (family or whoever) get along, then use that "free" rent period of your life to invest your extra cash into real estate. In this case, as you don't need a place to live, you can look at any kind of property that needs tender loving care. I still recommend that you look for properties that can be rented out, and that will ultimately have multiple tenants as that aids your income stream.

One such property that may exist in your area would be older homes that are sitting on land that allows multiple use, or multifamily use. Many cities have subdivisions that consist of such zoning. So start with those areas.

You have seen what can be done, too. Haven't you seen a lawyer's office or doctor's office that is in a building that looks like an old home? Alternatively, a large home that is now apartments? Often you can find some properties that also have a separate garage building that may even have an upstairs apartment. I have participated in several conversions of this kind of real estate and it is relatively easy to do. The garage is converted to an apartment. The upstairs apartment becomes two apartments, and the home is subdivided into two or more apartments. Before you know it, you have a five-unit apartment complex.

WHAT IS THE NUMBER-ONE PROBLEM I SHOULD BE READY TO SOLVE WHEN I OWN PROPERTY THAT HAS RENT-PAYING TENANTS?

There is a simple mathematical equation that spells out this problem: Tenants + Real Estate = Problems. Learning how to deal with tenants will be your number-one "need to know" element of real estate ownership. Here is a list of things you must know about them and how to qualify them:

- WHAT IS YOUR FIRST IMPRESSION OF THE TENANT? This can be critical. How do they dress, speak, and behave? If you get a funny feeling about the tenant, you need to go to the application phase. This is when you say, "If you like, I'd be happy to take an application from you. There is a $50.00 deposit for the credit report of course. Also, I will need at least three references." You hand them an already prepared Tenant Application that requires them to give their name(s), addresses, their contact information such as phone numbers and fax numbers, social security numbers, drivers license numbers, place where employed, name of a contact there, past landlord (if any), auto license tag number, and copies of a credit card and their actual drivers license. Be sure to have them sign the bottom of the building rules and regulations showing that they have read them and agree to abide by them if their application is approved. As a part of this application, you will also have them sign a statement that gives you their permission to run a credit report, using their social security number to do so. If they ask about that $50.00 you can tell them (if you agree with this statement) that they will get credit for it off their last month's rent payment provided that they have not been in default on the rent during the lease. You go through this elaborate process because you may not have another tenant in the wings, and after checking their references and other data provided to you, you may discover that they are really good potential as a tenant after all.

- CHECK REFERENCES (SEE THE EXPLANATION OF NUMBER 1). Call everyone the tenant gives you. You can naturally expect that you will get a rosy picture of the tenant, but sometimes you are surprised to learn things that are not so great. The best reference of all to have will be the previous landlord. Ask specific questions such as, was their rent ever late, if so what reason did they give, did they leave the property in good condition? Why did this person not renew their lease?

- RUN A CREDIT REPORT. If you don't have the facilities to do so yourself, ask your insurance agent if they will do it for you. If they won't, change insurance agents.

- MAKE FREQUENT INSPECTIONS OF THE PROPERTY IF YOU DO RENT TO THEM. The first inspection should be within a couple of weeks after they move in. You can start to taper off after a while, but inspect once every several months anyway.

- CHECK YOUR LOCAL LIBRARY. Check the bookstore at your local Board of Realtors office for a publication that deals with tenant/landlord rights, so some title similar to that. You will find such a publication, and it will generally cover all the local laws that you will have to deal with. Although these laws may be similar all over the United States, there are bound to be some laws that are unique to your state. This publication will generally give you all the steps you will need to follow if you are faced with the next element to deal with: eviction.

- LEARN THE PROCESS OF EVICTION. It is not so difficult, but there are certain steps that you need to take. Visit your local county court house and enquire what the steps you need to take are. There will be a person at a desk or window somewhere there that can walk you through exactly what to do. These steps will include the following:

a. A notice of default that tells the tenant that they are in default of their lease and that unless rectified within 15 days you will be forced to seek to evict them from the apartment (office, store, whatever). Spell out exactly what the cause of default is. This could be late or nonpayment of rent, or a returned check marked NSF (nonsufficient funds), or a derelict car in the parking lot leaking gas or other liquids, or any violation of the lease and or the rules and regulations of the building. This notice should be sent by mail with certified return receipt, or by express delivery also with return receipt.

b. If you obtain no satisfaction from this notice, you go to that desk at the courthouse (the one you should have visited earlier), and follow their procedure to have a police officer or sheriff officer serve a notice of eviction. There is a cost in doing this, and it will come out of your pocket. That process may take a couple of days, and in the end, the tenant will either pay the required funds, or otherwise fix the problem or have to leave. The departure may be in the middle of the night, and may occur without you ever getting your money, but out they will go.

c. If they want to fight you in court, and that may happen, they will have to post the funds owed to you first. This will either happen and you may have to go to court, or that fact (the posting of the funds) generally prompts an earlier midnight departure.

d. If any tenant leaves still owing you money, and especially if they do so in a covert way, and usually leaving behind damages, trash, old beds, refrigerators full of food (electricity off for two weeks, too), you can seek to collect from them. There are lawyers in most areas of the world who will look at your case and determine if they want to help you (for their percentage of what they get you), or not.

Because of all these unpleasantness, it behooves you to spend the upfront time to check out those tenants before you let them into your property. Eviction is not an overnight process, so it is a good idea that you try to avoid that by starting out with nice people who have good references and a sterling credit score.

Chapter 23

KEEPING THE WOLF FROM THE DOOR

How to Deal with Foreclosure

GOAL OF THIS CHAPTER

This chapter quells any apprehension you may have about foreclosure. It also provides strategies to avoid foreclosure in the first place, and if it is too late to completely escape its clutches, I'll show you how to deal with it.

Foreclosure is what may happen if the lender is completely unsuccessful in collecting mortgage payments from the mortgagor. Generally, the lender will go a long way to avoid this situation because it disrupts their system, gives their investors a bad feeling about the competency of the bankers, and costs time and money. However, they will foreclose in the end.

There may not be any huffing or puffing to blow your door down, but when a lender turns nasty and the collection agencies start calling at all hours and you can even feel their hot breath over the phone line, you can feel the cold shivers of foreclosure creeping up to your front door. Well, take two aspirins and get a good night's sleep. Things are not as bad as you might think. Sure, you might be headed for bankruptcy, but there are far worse things that could happen.

Like bankruptcy, the word "foreclosure" has a ring of failure about it. In financing, foreclosure is the one thing that investors and borrowers alike seem to fear. The fact is, however, that neither foreclosure nor bankruptcies are the evil monsters that most borrowers believe them to be. Lenders, on the other hand, have good reason to be fearful of the consequences of foreclosure.

WHAT IS FORECLOSURE?

In essence, the act of foreclosure is the legal process that is begun by a mortgagee or lien creditor to gain title to property owned by the mortgagor. The foreclosure of the interest of the mortgagor is to defeat that interest or redemption of equity so that the mortgagee may have title to the property without any obligations to or interference from the mortgagor. The reasoning behind the law is usually to protect both the mortgagee and the mortgagor.

We all remember the stories of the banker calling on the widow who was two days behind in the monthly mortgage payment. The sinister banker would twirl his waxed mustache and then boot the widow out onto the dusty front steps. To many, this is foreclosure at its worst hour. Yet, this is not foreclosure at all. How about the widow? She pledged the equity in her ranch on a moderate percentage loan to value, and now just because she is behind in the payment is she to lose everything? I think not, and the courts would agree. Today, even with all the inequities and problems in the foreclosure laws, they are still much more protective of the mortgagor's rights than is generally believed.

No mortgagor, by right of most foreclosure laws, can be deprived of interest or equity redemption, which may exceed the amount of the debt (plus cost and outstanding unpaid interest, of course) without due process of law. The laws that deal with foreclosure, while different for many states, generally agree that the right of this possible redeemable equity should be retained by the mortgagor. In this chapter, we take a close look at foreclosure to see if it is such a terrible animal, and if so, who does it bite the hardest? We examine some ways to avoid foreclosure, and some sure-fire steps for moving from possible foreclosure to positive cash flow for income properties.

BEFORE FORECLOSURE, THERE MUST BE A DEFAULT IN THE MORTGAGE

The language used in mortgages to describe default and to pinpoint when default occurs varies. Some mortgages provide a grace period for payments. This grace period is a length of time that comes after the actual date the payment is due, and is generally a matter of 10 to 15 days. During this time, the mortgagee allows the mortgage to enter a period during which the payment is due but actual default has not occurred. These grace periods can be long or short, or there may be none at all. Even without a grace period, a mortgagee will generally allow a reasonable time for default since notice and legal actions that precede foreclosure would take time, and if the mortgage were brought current prior to a foreclosure being filed, the matter could be mute.

Everyone who seeks to borrow money should understand that the lender expects the funds to be repaid. Even if the mortgage does not require personal liability on the note or mortgage, this absence does not lessen the lender's desire to be repaid, even though it may reduce the obligation for repayment from a legal point of view. In a loan where security is pledged, and the borrower gives a mortgage to the lender to evidence the security, the lender will look to the loss of the security as the primary basis for the loan to be repaid. If the loan is not repaid, the security may or may not compensate the lender for the problems he or she must go through to collect the amounts due. This happens when the value of the property is no longer sufficient to cover the amount of the loan.

The lender's rights, or ability to collect beyond the security, are seriously hampered even when there are personal signatures guaranteeing the note. Lenders often find it difficult to collect beyond the property that has been pledged or "put up," because there are numerous ways a borrower can be insulated from action greater than a lender taking the security to the loan.

The recovery of an amount greater than the actual security occurs when values drop and the sale of the security generates an amount below the combination of principal, interest, and cost that is due. This fear of a potential deficiency is why most lenders want personal guarantees on the loan to cover them past the value of the security. Courts sometimes do not look favorably on deficiency judgments against borrowers on primary loans, and almost never on purchase money financing held by sellers. There are both pro and con arguments to this controversy, and the situation in your state will be different than in another state. It is a good idea to have a good understanding on how the courts in your state are likely to go prior to putting your name as a personal guarantor to a friend's loan.

When there has been a breach in the contract by the mortgagor, and that breach is not remedied, the mortgagee has the right to accelerate the payments. This means that the lender calls for a full and complete repayment of the amounts due. When the borrower does not comply, the next step is usually that the lender will seek foreclosure as a means of collecting funds. Alternatively, the lender can sue in a court of law on the debt (the note), attempt to attain a judgment against the mortgagor, and then execute the judgment on property owned by the mortgagor. With a judgment against the note, the lender is not limited as to what property to go against, and may look for property that has a much greater value than the amount of money owned.

Foreclosure is a process that must be preceded by a default. It is not the only process of remedy the mortgagee can seek to collect on the unpaid mortgage. Because default must come first, the simplest way to avoid a foreclosure is that you should never go into default. This may sound obvious; it is possible to obtain many concessions from the mortgagee for allowing the mortgage to slip into actual default under the terms of the contract (note and mortgage) without default being claimed. These concessions will be discussed in greater detail later on in this chapter. You should know that many mortgagees would do almost anything to stop a property from going into foreclosure. Highly institutionalized lenders will generally work with the average borrower. Private lenders, on the other hand, have a tendency of acting quicker to foreclose, as either they want to take over the property or to protect the possible advance of loss should the payments continue to go unpaid.

Once a default occurs, and the lender does not agree to an extension of the grace period, or to enter into a modification of the mortgage, the mortgagee is in a position to call on his or her rights to foreclose. Prior to the actual foreclosure, however, there is generally a period of foreclosure assertions. That is, the mortgagee threatens to foreclose unless the mortgage payment is made. This preforeclosure period is a maze of first, second, and final notices, then letters from the lawyer, and so on; all steps lenders take to avoid having to file foreclosure. Finally, there is the nice phone call from the executive vice president in charge of collections at the bank to ask if you are having problems.

It is during this time that deals can often be made that would curl your hair. However, never count on that last ditch transaction to save the whole ball of wax. Foreclosure proceedings tend to be drawn-out affairs that can be most unpleasant. Dealing with the respective parties during this period of actual foreclosure is often far more difficult than when the property was only on the verge of going into foreclosure. The preforeclosure period is when the mortgagee hopes or believes that the mortgagor will still make the payments. However, when the mortgagor does not make the payments, the mortgagee realizes he or she must now make good the threats to foreclose.

FORECLOSURE AS SEEN BY THE LENDER

The attitudes taken by lenders vary. The majority of all foreclosures are made by institutional lenders, so let us look at foreclosure from their point of view. Once the mortgagor knows how the lender looks at this final stage of the lending cycle, he or she will have some understanding of what to expect. Most institutional lenders (as well as many noninstitutional lenders) divide the foreclosure action into four periods:

1. The collection period.
2. The preforeclosure period.
3. The foreclosure.
4. The postforeclosure period.

Depending on the size of the lender and the staff available, a standard operating procedure is designed to take care of these four periods. Note that the institutionalized approach to this very critical event is impersonal. The people involved have very little actual knowledge of the person who borrowed the money or the property pledged as security.

THE COLLECTION PERIOD

1. Check calendar to see if payment arrived on time; if not, make note to follow-up within three days.
2. If follow-up indicates payment still overdue, then send out courtesy reminder that payment is due (first notice).

3. Continued late payments will be followed five to seven days after the first notice with another notice, indicating the date, which terminated the grace period (second notice).

4. Follow-up calls to ensure the borrower is aware the grace period has terminated (third notice).

5. If the payment is 30 days past due, an inspection is ordered to determine if the property has been vacated or if there are other problems.

6. If the property appears not to have been vacated, a registered letter is sent from the legal department advising the borrower that his or her loan is in jeopardy of being foreclosed (fourth notice).

7. No response to the registered letter within seven days will cause the matter to be placed in the preforeclosure period.

THE PREFORECLOSURE PERIOD

1. A notice is sent to the collection department to the effect that no payments on this loan will be processed without approval, since the loan has gone into default.

2. A second letter may be sent to the borrower asking for a conference to discuss the status of the loan and to see if anything can be done to avoid foreclosure (fifth notice).

3. The lender now prepares for the possible foreclosure:

   • Note and mortgage are reviewed and sent to legal department.
   • Records are examined; insurance and other matters pertaining to the maintenance of the file and the property are checked.
   • A field report is made showing the status of the property (occupied, maintenance of property, and so on).

4. A review of the situation is made by the proper authority and a decision is reached based on the alternatives given or proposed by the borrower. If none is offered or they are not plausible, then foreclosure is filed.

THE FORECLOSURE PERIOD

1. An appraisal of the property is made.

2. Accounting and collection departments prepare the status of the loan, total unpaid balance and other costs, indicating the bottom line needed by the association for their bid at auction, and the top line to cover their total cost bid by others.

3. The file and report are reviewed by the foreclosure panel and the top bid the association plans to make is decided; authorization is given to the officer or trustee of the association to make the bid as stated.

4. The sale takes place; the property is purchased either by the association or by another party who makes a higher bid.

THE POSTFORECLOSURE PERIOD

1. If the property were purchased by someone other than the lender, the funds received are processed. If less than the loan is collected, further legal action may occur.

2. If the lender purchased the property, then the appropriate departments process the property and files to account for the change in ownership.

3. The property is then turned over to the proper department for marketing.

These four periods vary from lender to lender. A foreclosure of a second or junior loan would require a slightly different procedure. If the first or superior mortgages are not joined in the foreclosure and the foreclosure was made subject to those loans, then the junior lender would make sure the superior loans were kept current during the entire process. Once the junior lender has made a successful bid on the property, he or she would take the necessary steps to assume the existing superior loans or give notice that he or she is the new owner.

If the property is an income producing property, the lender may ask the court to appoint a receiver to manage the property pending the outcome of the foreclosure. This may occur and the receiver is chosen by the court to look after the property for the sake of all creditors. Some property owners who are headed for foreclosure may seek protection of bankruptcy, which can turn this entire process into a long period of uncertainty that may end with the lender losing some or all of their equity in the security.

It has been stated earlier that the lender will generally do all possible to prevent the property from going into foreclosure. Of course, there is a limit to how far he or she will or can go. Nonetheless, if the borrower has shown good intentions in the past and has not been late in making payments, the lender will go a long way to keep the loan from foreclosure.

Why Lenders Avoid Foreclosure If at All Possible

In almost all states, the foreclosure process is often long and burdensome. The time element is the most costly of all, since much can happen to the value of the property while the foreclosure grinds to the eventual sale or redemption of equity. At best, it is not a simple event. At worst, years can pass before the final document is filed and title is granted to the winning bidder at the foreclosure sale. Many arguments have been made for changes in the law and a speeding up of the process. In addition, the law often seems to protect the less scrupulous mortgagor more than the one who attempts to do his or her best to pay back the monies owed.

If the property is an income producer, the mortgagor can slip behind in his payments, wait out the preforeclosure period, and prolong that by attempting to work out a settlement or payment plan. Then, in the end he or she will let the lender foreclose, knowing that without any debt service during this period of time he or she can milk the property until the lender can either foreclose or have a receiver or trustee appointed to operate it until the foreclosure is complete and settled.

Seasonal properties are most vulnerable to this type of "milking," and lenders are most cautious about lending in these areas when the equity is either vague or slight. Even then, the loan can be in jeopardy in a hurry since a milked hotel can drop 20 percent in value over the season. Goodwill can be destroyed and the property itself left in disrepair. Hotels and other volatile properties that depend on limited times of operation (e.g., amusement parks and recreational facilities) will generally have mortgages that have strong default provisions. These provisions, however, do not always provide sufficient security to prevent "milking."

The speed with which the mortgagee can remove the mortgagor's control of the property will vary. In some states, this removal can be accomplished in a relatively short time, while in others the time required will be longer. It may be possible for a mortgagor to claim that the mortgage interest is usurious or other aspects of the loan are onerous, and hence request the loan to be set aside. Such actions may cause the entire matter to go to court. Nevertheless, meanwhile, the mortgagor may be left in control of the property. Because the matter of foreclosure is a legal one, lawyers can often find many ways to delay the process. Lenders know this, of course, and while they may ultimately win the case, it may be only a paper victory.

It is often thought that the only type of property immune to the effect of mortgagor control is vacant land. Today, however, vacant land can become a victim of the timekeeper as well. In many communities, there are movements to change zoning. Usually, zoning changes have considerable effect on the value of property. Since most zoning changes affect vacant land, those changes can cause land to gain in value, or to drop in value. Some rezoning provisions allow for a period of adjustment, by allowing an owner to file for building permits under the old zoning by a cutoff date. However, if the land is in the midst of a foreclosure this may not be possible. In addition, once the foreclosure sale occurs the value of the land may be less than the amount of the mortgage.

In most office buildings and other income properties, where the gross income is gained from rents collected from tenants in the building, the mortgagee will have assignments of the leases. These assignments will permit him or her to step in and collect the rents in the event of a default. In this instance, the owner still has physical control of the building, but he or she no longer has control over the income from the property. The mortgagee will generally deduct the loan payments due and turn over the balance to the mortgagor while the foreclosure is proceeding. Keep in mind that once the mortgage has gone into default and a foreclosure has been filed, the only redemption may be for the mortgagor to pay off the entire loan and not just to bring the payments up-to-date.

OPTIONS AVAILABLE TO LENDERS AND BORROWERS WHEN A MORTGAGE DEFAULT OCCURS

1. THE LENDER AGREES TO WAIT FOR THE PAYMENT OR PAYMENTS. This is the usual first step option that lenders will hope works. The mortgagor can ensure that the lender will go along with this option by presenting a good case on his or her own behalf. However, if

this is the third or fourth time in the past six months that the borrower has fallen behind, promises to come forward may be ignored.

2. THE BORROWER BRINGS THE MORTGAGE CURRENT FOR INTEREST BUT HOLDS UP ON THE PRINCIPAL PORTION OF THE PAYMENT. This option occurs when the lender begins to flex some muscle, but the borrower does not have the ability to come up with the full amount of money to meet the principal and interest payments due.

3. A PARTIAL PAYMENT OF INTEREST IS MADE. This might be all interest or a combination of all the interest due plus some outstanding principal. The deeper you go in these options the stronger the lender is pressing the borrower.

4. A LUMP SUM OF INTEREST AND PRINCIPAL IS MADE AND THE MORTGAGE IS ADJUSTED TO CHANGE THE OVERALL TERMS TO PROVIDE RELIEF FOR LATER PAYMENTS. This option is taken when both parties agree that something needs to be done to stop a chronic situation of late payments. This can work to the benefit of the borrower, especially if interest rates have gone down. Borrowers can simply attempt to refinance the loan to a longer term at lower interest rate, pulling out sufficient cash to bring the past due payments current.

5. THE MORTGAGOR TURNS OVER ALL INCOME, LESS OPERATIONAL EXPENSES GAINED ON THE PROPERTY, FOR APPLICATION AGAINST THE DEBT SERVICE. This is the lender's option to get into control of the property without having to go through actual foreclosure. This is not a good move for the borrower, and if the lender is pushing this option, be sure to get a good real estate lawyer.

6. THE LENDER AGREES TO REFINANCE THE LOAN TO PROVIDE NEEDED CAPITAL TO BRING THE PROJECT BACK TO ITS FEET. This is the option, but what are missing here are the conditions on which the lender will insist. If options one through five have been approached, and now the lender is moving toward option six it is likely because the lender is not in as strong a position as they would like to be in the advent of a foreclosure. Perhaps they do not have personal guarantees and now want to see if they can get that by offering more money.

7. THE LENDER ADVANCES FUNDS ON A SECONDARY LOAN TO COVER THE DEBT SERVICE. This is a possibility that will follow the similar caveats as shown in option 6.

8. THE MORTGAGOR ADDS ADDITIONAL SECURITY, THE LOAN IS EXTENDED INTO A BLANKET MORTGAGE, AND ADDITIONAL CASH IS ADDED BY THE LENDER TO COVER THE DEBT SERVICE. The lender is looking to improve its position. This might be an okay situation for the mortgagor, but the mortgagor needs to be careful.

9. THE MORTGAGOR CAN GIVE UP PARTIAL OWNERSHIP IN FAVOR OF THE LENDER FOR A REDUCTION OF THE DEBT. This is not a likely option if the lender is a bank or savings and loan association, but private or large institutional loans might go this direction.

10. A PORTION OF THE PROPERTY CAN BE DEEDED OVER TO THE LENDER AS A PARTIAL OR FULL SATISFACTION OF THE DEBT. As with option nine, this is more of a potential with private or very large institutional loans.

11. THE MORTGAGEE ALLOWS YOU TIME TO TRY TO SELL YOUR INTEREST IN THE PROPERTY TO SOMEONE ELSE. This is another last ditch effort to keep from going to the foreclosure stage. The problem here is to what degree the lender will participate in this situation. Suppose you find a buyer and the lender will not let the loan be assumed by that buyer. This is not as viable an option for the mortgagor as it looks, unless the mortgagee is truly a nice person.

12. SEEK SECONDARY FINANCING FROM ANOTHER LENDER. This is more often than not the borrower's option to seek a source of funds to pay the amounts due.

13. A DEED IN LIEU OF FORECLOSURE (OFTEN CALLED VOLUNTARY DEED) IS EXECUTED BY THE MORTGAGOR TO THE LENDER AND THE DEBT IS SATISFIED. The next to last step has arrived. Failing in this, the lender is sure to move to the last stage.

14. FORECLOSURE. Not the end of the world, but the start of the legal action that might lead up to a sale of the security on the courthouse steps.

The first 12 of these options can occur alone or in combinations. The willingness of the lender or the mortgagor to enter into any of these options will depend on the nature of the property and the history of the mortgagor. If the property is not worth the mortgagor's efforts to pull it out of default or he has a history of going into default in the past, then the matter may be mute and the lender may look to only the last two options.

The deed in lieu of foreclosure is a most attractive way out for the lender in many situations. The borrower may also look to this as a way of saving face in the community or meeting his moral obligations if all else fails, especially if the impending foreclosure suit does not appear to offer the opportunity for the mortgagor to gain in overage at the sale. After all, by the time the property is about to go into foreclosure, most mortgagors have tried almost everything to sell it so the market has been tested to some degree. Of course, if the mortgagor is behind in the payments by a wide margin, the cost to bring the property current, just in past due interest alone, may make the sale preforeclosure difficult. More on this aspect later.

A deed in lieu of foreclosure is a way the mortgagor can get out from under the mess of foreclosure and allow the mortgagee to enter the property without a long battle. If the property has several mortgages, all in default, and the first mortgage holder takes the property back by deed in lieu, then that mortgagee is assuming the obligations of the junior mortgagees. In foreclosure and a forced sale, the junior mortgagees would have to either protect their interest by bidding in above the first mortgagee or hope other buyers bid in sufficiently to cover their position. Often, this will not happen. Hence, the first mortgagee must decide if the junior mortgagee will in fact protect his or her interest by bidding in or attempting to obtain a deed in lieu him- or herself, thereby assuming the existing mortgage or foreclosing subject to the superior mortgage and keeping that mortgage current. Frequently, the circumstances do not favor the first mortgagee allowing the property to foreclose if he or she can obtain a deed in lieu him- or herself, even if that means the mortgagee is assuming the junior mortgages.

If the property is seasonal in nature and the season is just around the corner, the mortgagee may pay the mortgagor to sell the deed in lieu of foreclosure. The fact that the mortgagor is behind in payments and owes the mortgagee money does not mean that the mortgagor has any equity in the property. To avoid the cost and time of foreclosure and the loss of seasonal income, the payment to the defaulting mortgagor can expedite the end result and perhaps allow him or her to receive some cash out of the mess.

WHAT IF THE FORECLOSURE SALE DOES NOT COVER THE TOTAL DEBT?

If the property sale on the courthouse steps, or wherever it occurs, does not return to the mortgagee the amount due (principal, unpaid interest, and penalties), the lender or lender's agent may sue to collect the deficient amount of funds owed. This may become a judgment call by a judge in the end. Some states and some judges in any state look more favorably toward the borrower in this situation and do not allow a deficiency judgment. However, it is a good idea to get your own lawyer's opinion on this prior to that final sale date. No matter what happens with respect to the deficiency judgment, such events are not pleasant and can have a negative effect on your credit for many years to come. It is far better to try to have a friendly deed in lieu of foreclosure if the bottom line means more court battles over a deficiency judgment.

WHAT A MORTGAGOR SHOULD DO TO HOLD OFF FORECLOSURE

When all good planning and hope fail, and the cash just is not there for the next mortgage payment, there are several things the mortgagor can do to hold off foreclosure:

• DEVELOP A GOOD PAYBACK RECORD. This means more than just paying on time. Whenever possible, get in the habit of paying early. Mortgages, credit card payments, and the like all fall into this category. If you have never borrowed large sums of money before, you have no real credit rating with the banks on your payback ability. One client of mine has never had to borrow money, but he has made it a practice to borrow up to $50,000 at once from one of the commercial banks in the area. He does this on his own signature and asks for the money for six months, but he pays it back in less than a month. The total cost to him is not much since he manages to get interest on the amount borrowed from another bank. He says he doubts the bank would ever turn him down now if he really needed money. I do not recommend that you follow this lead, but a loan every once in a while will establish a good credit rating if you pay the money back promptly or early.

- Do not attempt to overextend the loan-to-value ratio. Remember, the best way to keep from going into default is to be able to afford the debt service in the first place. Naturally, few investors would be able to carry all or at least a major portion of the debt service, so look to a prudent demand rate and safe mix of extension and leverage. When you buy, try to take into account the possibility of a reduced income, look at the break-even point, and be ready to risk some capital.

- Know your abilities. This means staying away from investments you know nothing about unless you are sure you can rely on your advisors and/or partners. Most bad real estate investments are really good investments, but are made by inexperienced investors. Do not look across the fence and think the grass is greener on the other side. Those investors who are experts in their field make their jobs look easy. In fact, however, some areas of real estate are very difficult and take years of training and experience to understand and master. In Florida, as I am sure it is elsewhere, bars, lounges, motels, and restaurants are the big thing. Investors often feel that anyone can run a bar, lounge, and so on. Wrong!

- Get to know the lenders you are dealing with. It is a good idea to be on speaking terms with them. Keep an account at all banks or savings and loans where you borrow. Drop in every now and then and talk to the officers about anything except foreclosure. If you are on friendly terms with them when you are making your payments, that rapport will carry over to a preforeclosure period if it should ever come along.

What to Do When Default Is on the Way but Has Not Yet Occurred

- If you know you will not be able to make the next payment on time, there are two things you can do. First, if the payments are over short periods, such as monthly or quarterly, it is a good idea to call the bank or savings and loan president and let him or her know you have a problem. This is just to inform him that you are concerned about your inability to pay on time. Second, if the payments are over long periods, such as semiannually or annually, you may not want to give prior notice that you may be late. Lenders who wait for long time periods between mortgage payments have a tendency to become very nervous when informed that a payment for which they have waited a whole year may not be in on time. These lenders will think the worst right away and may start planning what they will do the very moment the payment is not made.

- The rapport between the mortgagor and the mortgagee is very important. The record of past performance is likewise crucial, since a poor record will cause the lender to be most unsympathetic to tales of economic problems. Keep in mind that lenders have heard every story that exists, so keep the sob stories to a minimum, even if they are true. Remember, honesty usually works best when all else fails.

- If you think you will be delayed in making your next payment, send the lender a letter outlining very briefly your inability to make the payment on

TIME. If there is a good reason for the delay, state it. If not, then merely say that you will be unable to make the payment on time but that you hope to have the money before the grace period is up.

• REVIEW YOUR SITUATION AND LOOK AT ALL THE POSSIBLE ALTERNATIVES YOU MAY BE ABLE TO USE TO SOLVE YOUR PROBLEM. The fourteen options listed previously are open to you. Look at each one and play with the figures to see if any are plausible.

WHAT TO DO WHEN DEFAULT COMES AND YOU HAVE NO REAL PROSPECT OF PULLING OUT WITHOUT HELP

• This is the time for you to make the decision to hold onto the property or to attempt to make a settlement with the lender, which will allow you to back out. By now, you may have tried to sell your interest but to no avail. Many mortgagors hang on too long, even when the property is not worth the effort or aggravation. The time to settle on a deed in lieu will depend on the property of course, but you should make that decision early in the default rather than wait until foreclosure is already filled, since it may be too late by then. On a very large property, however, your lawyer may advise you that if you do hang on you may be able to pull the loose ends together.

• Assuming you decide to try to keep the property, this is a good time to sit down with the lender and work out a deal which will give you time or release you from the burden of the debt service, perhaps by some alteration of the mortgage. Sitting back and ignoring the lender's letters will not help your situation at all, and could show a lack of good faith on your part. If you are willing to cooperate, this probably will work to your advantage.

• Have a plausible program, which you feel will work. You may need help in putting this program together, so seek it. If you are representing a client in such a predicament, then you will do all you personally can to find a solution and will speak to those contacts you feel can help as well.

• If there is equity in the property, and you have a reasonable solution, which will solve the problem, but the lender refuses to go along, you may want to look to bankruptcy as another alternative. A Chapter 11 bankruptcy, for example, if acceptable in your situation, would hold off foreclosure and permit a settlement of the economic problems. This avenue is a good one to follow when there are a large number of unsecured creditors, because the bankruptcy court may tend to be lenient to protect the rights of these creditors. It is not uncommon for very large sums of debt to be settled by the courts for fractions of the actual amounts owed. This possibility should be considered. Do not feel that bankruptcy is something you should avoid, especially if it is your only chance to protect all the creditors. Remember, if the first mortgage forecloses and the market sale does not produce an overage above it, then those creditors may be wiped out. The bankruptcy, however, may allow a partial settlement for those creditors.

Chapter 24

HOW TO EFFECTIVELY DEVELOP AND IMPLEMENT YOUR COMFORT ZONE

GOAL OF THIS CHAPTER

This chapter illustrates the procedure to use to develop and then implement your investment comfort zone effectively with the maximum benefits.

By now you understand that there are two critical elements that will go together to ensure your success as a real estate investor: (1) your goals and (2) your comfort zone.

There are 11 principal steps that go into the building of your comfort zone. Consider this next list as the outline for this process. You may want to copy it and post it where you can see it every day, so for that reason I have included a separate list of these steps at the end of this chapter on a page by itself. It will be your guide, as well as a measuring stick that will show you exactly where you are in this important process.

ELEVEN STEPS TO EFFECTIVELY IMPLEMENT AND BUILD YOUR OWN COMFORT ZONE

1. Review your investment goals.
2. Understand the comfort zone strategies and goals.
3. Select the area where your zone begins.

4. Obtain the additional material to work the zone.

5. Lay the foundation to select property to acquire.

6. Begin to build your investment team.

7. Identify where you will meet the local "insiders."

8. Measure your own "insider information" potential.

9. Begin to make offers on properties in your area.

10. Slowly add to your comfort zone.

11. Continue to expand your experience in the world of real estate insiders.

Review the following complete outline that will cover the basics of building your comfort zone. Remember, as you proceed with this process, you will discover elements of the real estate market that are unique to your part of the world. There will be other governmental departments that may have a major impact on the approved use of certain properties. Local politics is always important, but never forget the long arm of a state or federal rule or regulation that can stop you in your tracks, or propel you to the top nearly as quickly as you can snap your fingers. Become alert to everything that goes on in those areas.

Review Your Investment Goals

Everything you do with respect to investing should be oriented toward the attainment of your goals. Failure to stay focused on those goals can set you back, and lost time means lost wealth, and perhaps an ultimate failure to attain those initial goals. The key is to keep your goals in focus, and to build effective interim goals that are your stepping-stones to that desired end. These interim goals should incorporate everything you need to do to be able to utilize the plan to establish an effective comfort zone to its maximum benefit. One of the hardest things you may have to do is restrain yourself from jumping into the investment fire without fully establishing your thorough knowledge of your zone.

Understand the Comfort Zone Strategies and Goals

People in the Old World of the Middle Ages, who lived in cluster cities that were designed as compact fortresses to be easily defended from attack, lived in communities where it was essential to know as much as they could about their neighbors. Political life was almost like family life and little happened without everyone knowing all the details of the event. Not so the life of more modern cities, such as those in the United States, where people can live in a building and not know the families on the floors above them or below them, perhaps not even those who live down the hall. I can attest to that in my Florida neighborhood. Even with only 135 homes in our homeowner's association area, I doubt I could tell you the names of more than a dozen of the families there, much less recognize anyone who did not live in the neighborhood.

The point here is simply this: People who own property in such circumstances know very little about what is going on, both within the neighborhood as well as politically in the city. Yet, the vast majority of what does go on is telegraphed (as would a boxer who twirls his fist just before throwing a right hook), and is available to any member of the public who will take the time and effort to find out about it. That process of finding out about it is what makes you an "insider." As an insider, you will soon discover that "that lucky son of a gun" scenario is not luck, but results from deliberately following a sound, effective, and proven plan. This plan is what I have mentioned earlier in this book as "developing your comfort zone." By implementing this plan you will learn more about the area where you want to acquire property than the owners. When you know more than the owner (seller or landlord) knows, you have the edge on where the market is going and an advantage in the negotiation process.

Your overall strategy is to learn the important elements of a comfort zone as quickly and as effectively as possible. In this book, I have touched on most of the steps that are not also contained in this chapter. Your success in achieving the desired success in the implementation of an effective comfort zone will be up to you; all I can do is give you the right map to that success. That success, by the way, will occur like a bright floodlight being turned on. You will suddenly see what it is that makes your backyard your investment gold mine, and investment opportunities will begin to pop out at you when in the past (say a few weeks earlier), you would have not given them a second look.

LEARN THE BASICS OF A COMMUNITY.   Begin by getting an overview of your entire community. At this point, you should not focus on any specific kind of property, but look at your area to get a feel for what is moving, both up and down, in value or in demand. Try to avoid being tricked into believing that because in San Francisco or Chicago, whichever city is the farthest from you, the single-family market is in the toilet that the same thing is happening in your neighborhood. It might even appear to be the case, at first. However, wait and see for yourself.

FIND THE AREA'S DEMOGRAPHICS.   One of the first things you want to examine is the demographics of the area. Where do the working people live? Where do the retired folks or young growing families live? Much of this information has already been compiled for you by local governmental departments. Go to the web pages of the cities in your area as well as the county web page. Search through the different services that are available to anyone with access to a computer. If you do not own a computer, they are available to you in most libraries free of charge, too. However, make it a goal to obtain one. It need not be an expensive one, and it will speed up your entire process.

Who lives there, what is their earning power, and the statistical data on ages and family profiles are all there waiting for you to seek it out.

A DIGITAL CAMERA.   This modern tool is indispensable to modern real estate investors. They are inexpensive to use, and you don't even have to print out the photos to see what pictures you have taken. You can purchase one for very little, and you will save hundreds of dollars over using film. You will have a record of things like for sale or for rent signs, the front of a house (that shows its address), and even the faces of local political big hitters or other important people.

GET A PORTABLE COMPUTER WITH INTERNET CONNECTION CAPABILITY.   If you do not have or know how to use a computer, it is time to make that step. We live in a fast-moving generation that will leave you behind unless you get on the train, even if it is the last coach in the line. Computers drive me nuts. It seems that every time I learn how to use a new software program, it is out of date. However, as frustrating as modern electronics can be, it is an essential tool for the real estate investor.

PLOT MARKET HISTORY AND PRESENT STATUS.   These are two areas that you will want to pay close attention to. Your realtor member of your investment team can be of great use to you here. Realtors will have access to statistical information that is compiled by the local listing services that they should belong to. Those services keep records on the number of sales, average prices, and other data that can help you plot trends in the unique area that is to become your investment zone.

LEARN THE LOCAL RENTAL MARKET STRUCTURE.   The rental market is one of the real estate buyer's best sources of important data, as well as being a source for potential properties to acquire. The market is critical because it can be a precursor to a number of events about to occur. High vacancy factors in moderate to low rental areas may suggest that the working class people, such as tradesmen and women, and service workers are leaving the area for more fruitful work areas of the city or state or even more distant. High vacancies of rental homes and apartments generally suggest a decline in overall sales demand, and that there are more properties for sale than buyers. We have seen this many times in the past. Just look back a year or so and you may have experienced that in your own neighborhood.

INVESTIGATE PROPERTIES FOR SALE.   There are times of the year for most neighborhoods when there are more properties for sale as a general rule. For South Florida, this would be the summer months, when there are fewer buyers in town, and many owners who have left for cooler climates for the hot (and hurricane prone) months have put their properties on the market. In addition, there are times of the year for some areas when housing starts and sales drop off, often the cold blistery months in the northern parts of the country when construction slows due to the weather. For those reasons, avoid applying statistics of those different areas to your own backyard but do learn what is going on and why different areas excel or fall below the standards of your comfort zone.

MAKE AN OVERALL ASSESSMENT OF THE MARKET. This will be your important guide. You will gain it as you follow this plan. You should be able to pinpoint a reason for whatever assessment you arrive at.

Become Familiar with Current and Future Infrastructure and Services in the Zone

When it comes to the overall quality of your comfort zone area, you need to be aware of the vast array of elements that make up your town and your comfort zone. The following is a list of some of the most important for most communities. There are certain attributes and drawbacks to each item on this list that you should identify. For example, some of these elements will be easily accessible to your area, others not. You need to weigh that aspect to ascertain whether or not being easily accessible is a plus factor or a negative one. This will be particularly important from a traffic point of view, and what pollution (noise, smell, smoke, etc . . .) that infrastructure can produce. As you go through this list, you will likely think of other such items that are particular to your area. The key here is to be aware of these items. They are what makes up the backbone of any community, or perhaps its Achilles' heel:

- Employment opportunities.
- Educational facilities.
- Parks and other recreational facilities.
- Roads, bridges, and other traffic items.
- Public transportation.
- Medical facilities.
- Police and fire protection.
- Religious facilities.
- Proximity to shopping.
- What is lacking.

Select the Area Where Your Zone Begins

The time has come to define what part of town is important to you. This will be the area that becomes your comfort zone. You will know it better than 90 percent of the people who live, work, or invest there. You will know its streets better than a cab driver; its schools better than their students; what makes the area good, bad, rising, falling; and what makes its real estate a good opportunity.

The following items and things to do will get you started off right. The idea here is to pick a sizable part of town. It might be a subdivision or more and does not have to be contained within one boundary. The important steps to follow are explained together with the items you need.

GET COMPREHENSIVE STREET MAPS OF YOUR AREA. This may be limited to a map or book of maps of the entire county. Later in the next section of this chapter, you will narrow down the zone to the initial and specific area where you will concentrate your efforts. It will be important to you, however, to have this larger overview of the area because things that happen outside of your comfort zone can be critical to events inside it. You will need this comprehensive overview for that purpose.

OBTAIN ACCESS TO LOCAL AERIAL MAPS. You don't need to purchase a large book of aerial maps. The key is to know where you can view or even purchase individual aerials. Many counties have aerials and other maps available on the Internet. These, in many instances, can also be purchased from the county at nominal prices. Realtors and surveyors (and other professionals) often subscribe to aerial services that maintain their portfolio of aerial maps to reflect new development. These aerials are generally renewed every few years.

Aerial maps are taken looking straight down and are often taken by satellites. These same photographs sometimes are made together with radar images of the ground that maps, in essence, contours, giving the viewer the ability to obtain not only an aerial view, but a topographical study as well.

When you are narrowing down on property you want to purchase, or already own, having this aerial view can be helpful in understanding the lay of the land, so to speak, and how buildings relate to each other. A view from ground level often is blocked to the point that many features (some good, some bad) cannot be seen. Only this straight down look may reveal them.

STAY WITHIN ONE GOVERNMENTAL JURISDICTION. You will want your initial zone to be confined to one governmental jurisdiction. By this, I mean that every governing body should be limited to within one city. If not a city, then to the county government. This will enable you to learn the ins and outs of the politics of the area without overlap of other city politics. This will also maximize your time of attending only one set of city council meetings, one set of city bureaucracy such as planning zoning departments, building departments, and so on. Once you start to experience what goes on in one city, you may at a later date, begin to expand into other city jurisdictions as well. However, always remember city ordinances and zoning rules and restrictions may vary between cities, even if the zoning actually goes by the same code name. Many investors have made major mistakes thinking that an R-4 zoning in one city that allowed 40 residential units per acre to be build was the same as an R-4 zoning in another city that might only allow four units per acre.

LEARN THE CHAIN OF COMMAND AND HOW TO COMMUNICATE WITHIN IT. Communication is very important. It is relatively easy to obtain a city hall and county courthouse list of personnel, together with titles and names, addresses, e-mail addresses, of virtually everyone of the important people and department heads you may want to reach. A call to general information at the city hall or country courthouse may be all you need to do to get on the track of that data. Be sure to get the web page address as well. Once you are armed with that data, you may be able to find all the other communication information you need.

Obtain the Additional Material to Work the Zone

Prior to obtaining any new material, make sure you have obtained all the items mentioned earlier. Become acquainted with them. Pay particular attention to the use of the local government web pages and surf through them to see what is and is not provided. Practice as much as you can at learning different facts. Of all the data that you will find, the most useful will be found in two areas. The first is the tax assessor's office or department. There is a wealth of information that is at your fingertips. It contains specific information that, if up to date (some older records that predate computerization may not be accurate even if available), will give you a wealth of information. For example, it will provide the property owners' names, transaction dates, buyer and sellers data, price paid, real estate tax appraisal values, amount of tax assessed, dates of major improvements that have valid building permits attached, value of those improvements (cost basis), and much more data. If you learn only one source of real estate investment (and free) information, let it be this one. Visit the tax assessor's office and someone there will walk you through the navigation of everything they have to offer.

The second source will be the City Hall building and zoning departments. Specifically, what you need to know is how to access the zoning ordinances, and all other building and zoning rules and regulations. Remember, Use is the second of the three most important words in real estate (*not* location, location, location!). By knowing what is permitted on a specific parcel of land (even if there is already a building there), you will build your fortune in real estate by realizing there is a more valuable use than that in existence at this time. Remember, economic conversion is buying something and changing its use. To orient yourself to your city of choice, follow these next items to build your comfort zone.

MAP OF THE CITY IN WHICH YOU WILL BUILD YOUR INITIAL ZONE. On this map, you will mark out your initial comfort zone. It should be relatively small, but to orient this to a number of properties, start with between 250 and 350 total properties. Be selective in this once you have completely scouted out the area.

When scouting an area, pay close attention to the zoning that exists there. By the time you actually choose an initial zone, you should have decided on which category of zoning (think of Use) you want to begin with as an investment. My suggestion would be to review the area with the city map in one hand and a zoning map in the other. Look at what you see. Is it the highest use according to the zoning? For example, you drive around the neighborhood and see many small, older homes. Yet, when you look at the zoning map, you see several different zoning actually exists under those small older homes. Many older neighborhoods are developed on land that has a higher (economic) value due to its prescribed zoning. If the zoning allows professional use or multifamily uses and yet all that is there are single-family homes, you may have stumbled into a virtue gold mine.

If, however, you see multifamily and business uses and the actual (current as it may have changed over the years) zoning does not allow those uses, you must be very careful. Those uses may be "grandfathered" and will be what is called "nonconforming" uses. What this means is that as long as nothing happens to require the owner to conform to the actual zoning, then the use can stay. Okay, that's true, but what can trigger the owner to be forced to convert the use to its actual zoning uses? Many things, and they may differ between local ordinances. In general, however, anytime a major part of the structure is to be altered, that may pull the trigger. This can happen because of a fire, flood, or a major remodeling of the property. "Bang," you now have to do what the law says you must, so kiss that gold mine of a doctor's office goodbye. Other factors can come to play here, too. Usually a fire code issue is paramount in bringing about the need to make major changes, and they are not grandfathered. Therefore, make the next item a priority.

ZONING ORDINANCES OF THAT CITY.   These are available in printed form, often rather bulky and expensive, as well as free on the Internet. My suggestion is you first visit the Building and Zoning Department of the city of choice, and have someone walk you through that process. Small cities may be more advanced than bigger cities (less to look for), but don't count on that.

WORD OF WARNING.   As mentioned earlier in various chapters, zoning is unique and its terminology is not uniform. The total complexity of a zoning requirement or, for that matter, the building codes rules and regulations may not be manifested in one single place within the respective codes. There can be other elements scattered throughout the code that can, when combined, have a negative or (but rarely) positive impact on the use and value of a property. For example, the code may allow a building to be constructed to a height of 200 feet. This would generally indicate that a building of around 16 to 20 stories high would be possible. However, elsewhere in that code there may be a "setback" rule that indicates that for every foot of height above a specific height, say 35 feet, the building must be set back an additional X number of feet on all sides. (X being a number set by that code). This setback is in addition to the minimum setback for that specific zoning. When this is applied, it is entirely possible that long before the building reaches even 80 feet in height, one or more of the setback distances will cross over the setback coming from the opposite side of the property. In essence, the top of the building has been reached or the building size reduced to the point of being uneconomical because of this single issue.

CODES FOR OFF-STREET PARKING IN YOUR AREA. While these codes may not show up in the specific zoning ordinances, they can also limit the total volume of saleable or rentable space you can build. So learn the maximum amount of square footage of realistically useable space that can be constructed when looking at land on which you wish to build.

CITY AND COUNTY BUILDING CODES. These codes are usually not in conflict, but it is possible that one will be a bit stricter than the other. If both have jurisdiction over the property then the stricter code will win. This becomes critical if the specific property must go through a process of platting, which may need to occur before a building permit can be issued. *Platting* is one of the planning zoning's greatest weapons against development. This process is one where the property owner (or prospective buyer) goes through a long and sometimes expensive bureaucratic dance to certify the land to have passed approval by every governing agency for a specific zoning use. Not all communities agree on the severity of this process, but most like to have their shot at the property owner to get for free what they might otherwise have to pay for in a condemnation or eminent domain proceeding. I suggest you discuss this issue with your head of the Planning and Zoning Office. He or she will be candid with you (usually), and if the political environment is pro development, it is possible to acquire a property that can be replatted to a higher use. This may also require a rezoning at the same time, but when the cards are in your favor, many nice things can happen for the developer who has a development plan that is good for the city and the people who live there.

DEPARTMENT OF TRANSPORTATION MASTER PLAN. The West was won by the land barons who knew where the railroad was going to be built. Alternatively, was it that they made sure the railroad was built? In any event, money talks, and often the building department imposes what they call "impact fees," which are really taxes to a builder who wants the right to build something. These fees can be expensive, so much so that sometimes they render a project no longer viable. These fees are usually directed toward the need for some needed infrastructure to support the added growth or drain on existing resources. If the builder balks at paying the fee, no permit is issued.

The office of the Department of Transportation (DOT) is found in the local arena (city, county or state). The state DOT controls state highways, many of which are also local streets within cities. Become friendly with someone at the state DOT because they have a wealth of information about the future of roadways in the whole state. They usually are fairly accurate up to the 10-year plan, although that doesn't mean what they want to have in operation will occur within that time. However, there is a strong likelihood that they will.

STATE LAWS THAT MAY PERTAIN TO YOUR COMFORT ZONE AREA. These might be laws that deal with things like mining, or forestry, or environmentally sensitive issues. However, they can also deal with anything that touches on state-controlled licenses and state

DOT rules and regulations. If you have a use that requires any state or federal license, it could become the Achilles heel in your plan if the license cannot be issued and you have already purchased the property.

SIGN UP FOR NOTICE OF MEETINGS AND THEIR AGENDA.   The following are the minimum list of frequent meetings that you should attend, obtaining the agendas in advance of the meeting:

- City and county commission meetings.
- DRC meetings within the building department.
- Planning and zoning meetings.
- Board of adjustment meetings.
- Homeowners' association meetings in your zone.

You need not attend every meeting, but unless you have the agenda in advance, you will not be able to make the determination as to what you should attend. You will obtain the advance notice of the dates, places, and subjects to be discussed by signing up for them. Go to the appropriate web page (with your new laptop), and you should be able to search for the agenda, or perhaps, advance notice of city (or county) meetings. If that doesn't give you the correct place to sign up then give the city hall and county Courthouse a call and ask whoever answers to put you through to the appropriate place.

Personally, when I am in a new town or part of the world, I like to start at the highest level I can easily reach. I call the mayor's office, get his secretary on the line, and ask her if she can give me the right person to talk to. I have, by the way, used this technique in many parts of the world—Madrid, Spain; Malaga, Spain; Paris, France; Bishkek, Kyrgyzstan; Kingston, Jamaica; Nassau, Bahamas; and Mexico City, Mexico, as well as many cities across the United States. I have saved myself a lot of running around, and have always obtained generally error-free information. Please, feel free to do the same.

These government meetings are where the action becomes reality. Some of these meetings will be very boring, so you need to skip meetings that do not pertain to anything important to you, your comfort zone area, or real estate for that matter. You will meet the real insiders at these meetings, too. More on that later. Take note of these meetings:

- CITY AND COUNTY COMMISSION meetings are where local laws (called ordinances) are approved or removed. Other business may include changes of zoning, review of new developments, and a slew of local business in the running of city and county operations.

- THE DEVELOPMENT REVIEW COMMITTEE is a part of the building and zoning department. This is part of the building permit process and is the preliminary step where the builder brings his initial plans to the table for comments as to any problems that the developer may face in obtaining approval and a building permit. Because this is the first step in this process, an investor can get a big jump on what is planned long before the rest of the world learns of it.

• PLANNING AND ZONING MEETINGS are the next step to approvals of a building project. Not every building or development will come before these meetings, but every project that will have a major impact on the neighborhood will.

• THE BOARD OF ADJUSTMENT is a body of local citizens (none of them are voted to this board, instead they are appointed, as are most of the board of the planning and zoning committee). They hear grievances from other citizens of the city or county where those people are attempting to obtain relief from some city ordinance, rule, or regulation. It might be a setback issue, or their neighbor's trees that overhang their lot line.

• HOMEOWNER ASSOCIATION MEETINGS can be a real drag and are full of insider fighting of a neighborhood. However, if you like reality TV shows, these meetings can beat *Survivor* any night. The ones to attend will be when there is a local developer going through the steps of building his political base and local approval for a project that might be controversial. This happens all the time, and when it comes to approval votes of these projects at the city or county commission meetings, local support for the project by the neighbors is very important for the developer.

Lay the Foundation to Select Property to Acquire

You are now properly equipped to begin in earnest. The following 10 steps will launch you on your way. There is no specific order to these steps, and you should make an effort to do some of everything in this list every week. Ready? Go.

START TO ATTEND GOVERNMENT MEETINGS. If you have not already signed up for the agenda, you can do so at the meeting. There will be someone in charge for that purpose. By the way, that same person may sign you up to speak (should you be there for a specific event on the meeting's agenda).

COLOR CODE YOUR CITY MAPS BY ZONING USES. Have a city map and several colors of highlighter pens available. Make sure the highlighter is translucent so it will let you read the names of streets and see lot lines clearly behind the color. Most cities have already colored the maps they use. Maps are rarely for sale already colored, but you can get a good idea where they put what colors by looking at the legend of zoning codes. If you can, follow as close to their system as possible.

LEARN THE SIGNIFICANCE OF ZONING. Study the different zoning classifications. You will note that the code is generally a pyramid of use. By this, I mean that if you start at the highest use and work back to the lowest use (within a specific category) you will find that the permitted use is usually more restrictive as you backtrack. For example, commercial zoning is often broken into C classifications, B classifications, and I classifications—C being a general commercial use, B a more business-oriented use, and I an industrial use. Going in the order of most restrictive to least restrictive, you might find something like this: C-1, C-2, C-3, B-1, B-2, B-3, I-1, I-2.

Now look at them in reverse:

I-2 Heavy Industrial, May include junkyards, heavy manufacturing, paint and body shops, outside storage and everything allowed in I-1.

I-1 Light Manufacturing, no outside storage, no paint and body shops, and everything allowed in B-3.

B-3 Auto sales and repair (no paint and body shops without a special exception approval). May also include wholesale sales and distribution facilities and everything allowed in B-2.

B-2 Shopping Centers and mixed-use facilities including residential apartments, and everything allowed in B-1.

This gives you an idea of how this can progress, all the way down to a single-family home. This is not to show you a specific zoning category because each city may differ greatly in this aspect of nomenclature. The point is to impress on you that what you see sitting on a property may not illustrate what can be put there. The older the neighborhood, the more likely that is the case.

HIGHLIGHT PROPERTIES THAT ARE UPGRADABLE.   Save a specific color or have a separate map of your comfort zone that you mark with that color any property that has a present use that is upgradable. By upgradable, I mean a use that can produce a greater economic benefit than the present one. That single-family home that is sitting on a lot that is really zoned for office buildings or multifamily properties or a used car lot would be an example of that. Equally, the fact that it is upgradable does not mean that is good for you as an investor. You may have no interest in putting in a used car lot, but you would certainly not want to buy a property that was adjacent to an old home that was on a property that would allow a junkyard; even if it is a pretty home with nice trees all around it, it may not stay that way. If there is any single element that can build your wealth faster than knowing the zoning and how to use it, I haven't found it.

TRAVEL THROUGH THE NEIGHBORHOODS.   Real estate investing is definitively hands on. If you don't see it, you certainly should not buy it. However, you need to take that one giant step forward. If you have not visited the site several times, then you have not done your due diligence properly. While it is possible to accomplish effective due diligence after you have tied up the property, you will be far more effective in your assessment of the value of the property if you first develop a comfort zone. One of the critical steps in this effort is to learn everything you can about the area where the property is. Later, when you have picked out a property to buy, you can then tie it up and do the due diligence.

PHOTOGRAPH PROSPECTIVE PROPERTIES.   This is where that digital camera comes in handy. I take photos of houses, buildings, vacant lots, For Sale or For Rent signs, anything important in my comfort zone. I file them on a CD and make notes along with the photos to remind me where the property is located. I know investors who are more advanced with their electronics than I am and they take the photo, immediately transfer it to a file, link that file to a map with a little dot on the map. All they have to do is open the map, touch the dot, and shazzam, the photo and a data page opens up. In the old days, I relied on photographs with the data handwritten on the back. That still works too, by the way.

VISIT OPEN HOUSES.   Any time you see an open house in or even near your comfort zone, stop and take a look at it. While this is likely to become a weekend event, you can also make note of properties that have For Sale signs in the yard and give the respective agent a call and make an appointment for a private viewing of that property.

These visits serve several very interesting purposes. First, it is a good idea to know what is going on in the area, even if you don't buy homes. Learning of their value can reflect back on the value of other properties in the area. If home prices are going up, generally so does other property in the same area. That may not, by the way, work in reverse. If high-rise office buildings are replacing the nice boutique shops that make the area more like Rodeo Drive than Broadway and Seventh Avenue, the immediate residential area might suffer.

Second, if you get to meet the owner at the open house or can learn something about that owner, you might find that they are moving away to be closer to their grandkids or some other valid reason. "Do they have any other property for sale?" you could ask. You might be in on the ground floor with the answer, even if it is out of your comfort zone. When a good tip falls your way, spend a little time to check it out.

Inquire about For Rent and For Sale properties. It should be obvious that you will want to know about For Sale properties, but never overlook the ones that have a For Rent or Vacancy sign out front. Rental property owners do sell their properties from time to time, and often sell before they thought about selling. If you like the property, you can always check out the ownership situation on the Internet by going into the tax assessor's tax roll. You will see when they purchased the property and how much they paid, together with enough information that you should be able to contact them, say, that same afternoon.

OBTAIN TAX ROLL DATA FOR THE INITIAL ZONE.   Now that you are in the tax roll checking out that for rent property, why not (if you haven't done it yet) download the data on the entire area? Usually you can do that by street or avenue, by bracketing the street numbers you want to pull: 220 to 500 would potentially give you 380 different addresses, and all the data that goes with it. However, you may also be able to pull down the entire subdivision at once.

OWNER'S NAME AND ADDRESS.   This is the address where the tax bill is sent. It may not be the property in question because the owners do not necessarily live there. Sometimes you also get the phone number at the same time.

PRICE THEY PAID FOR THE PROPERTY.   This is one of the most important bits of information you will collect. Since you have now downloaded the entire subdivision, perhaps your entire comfort zone, you can chart out each property you are interested in, and several properties nearby. By knowing what and when each owner paid for the property, you can get a pattern of values in the neighborhood. If the owner purchased the property several years or more ago, also chart the current tax assessment value. Be sure you relate that value to their original purchase price. This is important if the state where you are at the time has a cap on the value that the tax assessor can increase the assessment. Failure to take that into account can give you a false indication on what might look like a declining trend. Many states, Florida and California for two, have this type of provision. It protects a homeowner from having their real estate (ad valorem) tax sharply increase. A property owner who has owned his or her home for 30 years will likely have a much lower assessment of a similar home that was purchased last year, even if the two homes are side by side.

DATE OF ACQUISITION.   This information is helpful when it comes time to make an offer. If they had purchased within the past couple of years, and their asking price does not suggest they are making a killing selling way above what they paid (you know what they paid), then there is some other motivating factor working for you. *Do not ask what it is.* Keep it to yourself that you might be onto something good. A reason will likely be given anyway, and just like the one you would get if you had asked the question, it would likely not be the real one.

OTHER INTERESTING DATA.   Some tax roll data can be fairly accurate about improvements added. If the information shows this, it may also show the amount that the builder put on the permit application as to the cost of that addition or repair. If it is a repair, check it out as part of your due diligence once you have tied up the property.

Other information may also show up. Some tax roll data is linked with the Board of Realtor data. You may have to have your realtor run that for you if the tax roll database does not show it. That will have a host of information about the property and the buildings that you cannot see from the street or from your aerial photos.

KEEP A JOURNAL OF YOUR FINDINGS.   Keep a journal of your data. You never know when you will change your mind about property you looked at three years ago. A log that shows a change over even that short of time can be very helpful.

Begin to Build Your Investment Team

If you have a partner in life, I suggest you elicit that person as your number-one advisor and confidant. This is particularly important if he or she has a talent you can use and lay claim to part (half?) of the investment capital that will go into any investments. From that point on, the investment team is pretty easy to ascertain.

LINE UP A REALTOR YOU CAN RELATE TO.   I know many investors who flit around to many different realtors; then when they do buy, they do it through their sister-in-law's daughter. That is a good way to burn their bridges with all of those realtors they had working on their behalf. I believe, trying to be unbiased at the same time, that it is far better to have one or two realtors that you can work with. It is best not to pit them against each other because each may bring you the same property. Now what do you do?

Yet, not all realtors and their prospective clientele have a magic chemistry between them. If you feel uncomfortable with the person, skip the coffee after the lunch and move on.

HAVE A LAWYER YOU LIKE AND TRUST.   Developing a relationship with the lawyer you will undoubtedly need can be more difficult. Many lawyers take the position that if they do not understand something, it must be bad and will advise you to avoid something in your comfort zone that you really know more about than they do. Nonetheless, a lawyer will be needed, so shop around. Make sure they know real estate and have practiced it for more than a couple of years. One of the better ways to find such a person is to meet the lawyers that attend the different governmental meetings I have already listed. They may be there representing a client who is a developer, or at the board of adjustment defending their client's rights.

It is a good idea to meet as many people as possible when you are at these meetings.

HAVE A QUALIFIED CPA ON YOUR TEAM.   This will be a person who may already know a lot about you. Nevertheless, just like lawyers, not all CPAs know real estate as well as others do. Check around and make sure your CPA is qualified. Here, too, speaking with people at the different government meetings and asking one of the property owners there to recommend a good CPA may lead you to a great one.

DEVELOP RAPPORT WITH GOVERNMENT INSIDERS WITHIN CITY AND COUNTY GOVERNMENT.   This is surprisingly easy. All it takes is charm, a logical story, and follow up. First, here are the departments to evoke that magic:

- City and county hall.
- Building department.
- Planning and zoning.
- Department of transportation (city, county, and state).

Charm is worth its weight in smiles. So, if you don't have any, hope that your partner in life does. However, you can work on your charm. Here are some tips.

Charm is not what you think you are doing, it is the combination of things that cause other people to feel good about you. There are simple steps that should be followed. An easy friendly pace is critical to the first meeting with anyone. Compliments are not absolutely necessary, but, if the occasion allows one to flow naturally, include it in your introduction.

For example, the person you want to introduce yourself to is on the zoning staff, and they have made a sterling presentation on something before the city commissioners. Later, you approach that person and introduce yourself. You hand him your card, the one that simply has your name and e-mail address and the title of what you do (Real Estate Investor). You say nothing for a second, which helps him to look at your card. As he does, you repeat your name. Then you speak, "I just wanted to thank you for such a clear and concise report on the new bridge (or whatever he was talking about before the commissioners). I was hoping to stop by the zoning office one day next week and visit with you. When would be convenient?"

If the person is inclined to sustain the conversation, do not rush to explain what you want to discuss when you visit him. Instead, direct your interest to the person himself. How did he become the head of the zoning department, do you detect a southern accent? Where is that . . . Savannah? "Oh, I just love Savannah, don't you?"

The real clincher to charm is the follow-up. In your life as an "insider," you will do a lot of follow-up. In this instance, I would recommend a note, perhaps handwritten on special stationery and envelopes uniquely designed to support your profession as real estate investor. Short and sweet, "Dear Miss Zoning Person, It was delightful speaking with you the other night. To give you some time to think about why I want to visit with you, it is a matter of a property I am looking at purchasing in the Rio Mar section of town. It is an old house (address here) that seems to be on a lot more than double the others in the area. Do you think it would be possible to divide it into two lots? I am looking forward to seeing you next Thursday at 2:00 PM. Sincerely yours, . . ."

Identify Where You Will Meet the Local Insiders

First, let me give you my definition of a real estate insider. To me the term relates to a person who has dedicated a substantial part of his or her time learning about the process of real estate investing. He or she knows that knowing rules of any activity means it is essential to know as many of the good players as possible and to emulate those people's successful traits. The insider also knows that one does not have to make a mistake to learn from it, and when possible, he or she learns from the mistakes of others. Most certainly, he or she will also recognize his or her own mistakes and will stop and ascertain what went wrong, instead of blaming someone else for the mistake. It may not be essential to acknowledge to anyone (except the person blamed) that blame had been misdirected in error, as long as the lesson is learned and a sincere effort is made not to repeat it.

Real estate insiders exude confidence in their knowledge of a community and most of all in their comfort zone. There is little about that area of town that they do not know and understand. If they learn something new, they make note of it and tell themselves not to make the mistake of not knowing that fact again.

Real estate insiders are successful in their pursuit of investments that are oriented to their goals and which they purchase wisely, and sell timely. They also know that mistakes will befall them, and that minor failures might even creep up on them. However, all insiders know and understand that failure is the sweetener of success; so on the occasional parade rain will fall.

Real estate insiders make a habit of meeting and helping other insiders. So remember that every time you help a person you deal with move closer to his or her goals, you are moving up the ladder of this grand club of real estate insiders.

Real estate insiders are found in many places. Start in the following locations, which I have already discussed:

- City hall and county courthouse.
- Building and zoning departments.
- Local newspapers and legal publications.
- Government meetings.
- Mortgage brokers.
- Commercial and savings banks.

Measure Your Own Insider Information Potential

Answer with confidence these questions:

- Have you attended a minimum of four governmental meetings?
- What kinds of properties in your zone have the best market?
- Have you discussed investment potential with local bankers and mortgage companies?
- Would you say your selected zone is going up in value?
- Have you identified any opportunities you would like to own?
- Do you feel you are ready to test the market?

If you have answered any of these in the negative, you need to review why, and then spend some time building your confidence. If you have answered yes to all except the last question, I would suggest you stand in front of a mirror and directly to your face acknowledge your trepidation of moving forward. Then turn around and reface yourself and say out loud, "So go out there and make an offer anyway."

Begin to Make Offers on Properties in Your Area

- Make reasonable offers 10 to 15 percent below recent sales.
- Have provisions that allow you 45 days minimum for due diligence.
- Make sure you have an escape provision that lets you cancel the deal on or before the end of that due diligence period.
- Spend the time wisely to inspect the property.
- See what financing you can line up.
- Fine-tune the deal if need be.
- Walk away if things do not work out to your benefit.
- Avoid burning bridges.

Slowly Add to Your Comfort Zone

- Expand your zone within the same governmental area.
- Expand outside that governmental area.
- Continue to seek out other insiders.

Continue to Expand Your Experience in the World of Real Estate Insiders

The cliché—the more you learn, the more you realize you don't know—is true. The key to using the comfort zone plan is that you don't ever have to journey, investment wise, outside that zone. By staying focused on your zone and your area of expertise, you will excel at what you do. You will diminish risk to its best acceptable level. You will snub your nose at that greener grass that is just outside your comfort zone until you have expanded that zone to encompass it. By now you have been exposed to everything you need to start your exciting journey into building your wealth in real estate. The essence of this book will serve you well in any facet, endeavor, or profession of which real estate is a focal point.

This book can be your easy to use companion in the years to come (until the next updated edition, of course), and when that time comes I recommend that you reread the new book because my readers keep in touch with me and help me pass on newly experienced mistakes that they stumble into. Remember what I said about insiders helping insiders.

ELEVEN STEPS TO EFFECTIVELY IMPLEMENT AND BUILD YOUR OWN COMFORT ZONE

1. Review your investment goals.
2. Understand the comfort zone strategies and goals.
3. Select the area where your zone begins.
4. Obtain the additional material to work the zone.
5. Lay the foundation to select property to acquire.
6. Begin to build your investment team.
7. Identify where you will meet the local insiders.
8. Measure your own insider information potential.
9. Begin to make offers on properties in your area.
10. Slowly add to your comfort zone.
11. Continue to expand your experience in the world of real estate insiders.

Appendix

HOW TO USE THE CONSTANT TABLES

The purpose and goal of this Appendix is to give you three simple to use and easy to understand financial tables that will assist your problem solving when dealing with virtually any facet of mortgage financing. You will not have to deal with complicated to use and often highly inaccurate handheld calculators. Instead, these three tables and a simple calculator can do the job.

GETTING STARTED

First, look at the critical factors that go into problem solving for any mortgage. There are seven basic factors here:

1. Time allowed.

2. Contract rate.

3. Contract principal.

4. Constant payment percent.

5. Actual payment (as applied to the repayment of the debt).

6. Early repayment.

7. Mortgage holder's actual yield.

Review each of these seven factors. Remember that not all seven are needed to solve your problem. Generally, all problems will center on the first three factors. The remaining four are all functions of the events that occur within the structure of the debt.

Time Allowed

This is the period set for the repayment of the debt. The debt is the "Contract Principal," which is the amount of money borrowed at the creation of the loan. In general terms, most mortgages are established on a repayment schedule for a set number of years, during which time the borrower makes monthly payments to the lender or acts as the collection agency that services the loan. This time may be for a longer period than the actual payoff date of the mortgage; for example, the loan may be set for a repayment schedule based on 30 years (more or less because this is subject to negotiation between the borrower and the lender). However, the loan may have a call date (payoff date) that occurs much sooner, say in 10 years. This would cause a sudden repayment of the balance outstanding at that date. This type of mortgage is often called "a balloon payment mortgage." It is important for you to understand that mortgages are negotiable instruments, which means they can be bought and sold and the original bank or lender that made the loan may have sold a pool or package of such loans to another institution. The new owner is the recipient of the payments the borrower makes. Because the new owner of those mortgages may have paid more or less than the amount of money actually lent, the return or yield to the new owner will usually vary from that which was evident to the original lender.

The time factor becomes important because of the way the repayment schedule is established. At any given interest rate, a greater number of payments will cause a lower monthly payment. Clearly, if you borrowed $100,000 and had to pay it off in 10 years at 12 payments per year, the principal amount of each payment (if we overlooked interest for a moment) would be $833.33 per month ($100,000 ÷ 120 months).

However, if that were spread out over 20 years, you now have 240 payments (12 × 20 = 240) over which to spread the principal. This would (still overlooking interest) cut the monthly installment of principal down to $416.67 per month. However, lenders do not overlook the interest factor when they make loans. Because of this, the lending institutions have discovered a vast array of methods by which to calculate the repayment of the principal owned, together with the interest charged. The combination of these two factors can create horrendous repayment schedules, which would make your real estate investments less than desirable in many instances. To illustrate how this happens, consider a $250,000 loan that is made with a repayment schedule of 20 years. If we were to first divide the contracted principal amount of $250,000 by the 240 months provided you would see a monthly payment of principal only, of $1,041.67 per month. Now add interest to the picture. To do this, I will speed up the process by looking at a yearly total rather than a monthly installment. If the repayment were to be 20 annual installments, the annual amount due for principal at the end of the first year would be $12,500 ($250,000 ÷ 20 years). If we were to calculate interest at 6 percent per year, the total interest due at the time of the first annual payment would be 0.06 multiplied by $250,000 equals $15,000. The combination of principal and interest is now $27,500. If that were spread over 12 months, we would have a debt service of $2,291.67 per month. That is a hefty bite which would likely result in far fewer loans being made. To make this a bit more complicated, although this payment method has the same amount of principal repaid each month for the entire life of the loan, the interest is going to steadily decline each month. The very last payment, as an example, would be $1,041.67 plus interest on that amount (for only one month) which would be 0.06 multiplied by $1,041.67 divided by 12 equals $1,046.88. That is very different from the $2,291.67, which was the amount of the first payment. Therefore, to make financing more palatable to investors or homeowners, a new method of math was created that would spread out the payments at an even keel for the life of the mortgage—if not for the whole life of the loan, for as much time as possible, to enable the borrower to get the most out of that investment.

The new math takes into consideration both time and interest so that the monthly payment is a set amount for the time allotted. Because the amount of the payment does not change, this type of loan is called a *constant payment mortgage.* This payment will amortize the loan fully if allowed to run the full length of time. Each payment, however, will have a slightly growing principal portion and a slightly reducing interest portion. The actual payment amount is found by using a complex formula that considers three factors. Those factors are the time allowed, the original contract principal, and contract rate.

Contract Rate

Let's look ahead a moment to look at this interest rate scenario and to see how time and interest combine to even out that repayment schedule. The contract rate is the interest that is used to calculate the payment. Using the formula for amortizing mortgages, a calculator or fixed table will do the work for you. In essence, once you know two of the factors, the third is relatively simple to find. It is important for you to recognize that this formula takes into consideration certain factors that are arrived at by agreement rather than fact. For example, the element of time is simply 12 months a year. There is no distinction between the number of days per month or, for that matter, the number of days in a year, except when doing a midterm proration for a payoff or assumption of the debt. Also, most calculators will round off the results of their calculation at a fixed number of decimal points. These two factors can cause different results depending on the rounding off of the desired answer. Because of this, it is possible an answer you arrive at by using one of my tables will differ from the answer your calculator gives you. It is likely that the tables I have worked out for you will be more accurate when the time period and interest used is the same as the data programmed into the calculator. If you choose to use a calculator, be sure to practice several different types of problems before you absolutely need to get a quick answer. Not all financial calculators work the same (even though the keyboards may be similar), and it generally is possible to program even inexpensive handheld calculators to round off with more factors to the right of the decimal point. The biggest advantage of using one of the three tables I have programmed is that you get to see the answer to your problem, as well as the structure around it. By this I mean, when you find an annual constant rate (Table A) for a mortgage at 9 percent interest over 25 years, you instantly see the rate for all the other interest rates and different terms of years that surround the answer you just located. This is not easily possible using a hand calculator. I suggest you pay attention to this collateral information when using these tables; it will add to your overall knowledge of what is going on, as well as give you instant alternatives.

Generally, when the loan calls for a contract rate of 6 percent, this will be the annual interest rate that is calculated into the repayment schedule. If the actual payment is monthly, the rate charged to each payment of the loan is 6 percent divided by 12. This is ½ of a percent per month, which is shown in math as 0.005. If the contract rate were 12 percent per year, the monthly charge would be 1 percent or 0.01 per month. Because the lender may set the repayment schedule to some period other than monthly, say for example, quarterly or semi-annually, you need to be careful to apply the rate as it would apply to the actual payment. So, 6 percent over four quarterly payments would be 1.5 percent per period, a semi-annual payment would apply 3 percent (for the annual rate of 6 percent) per payment.

Some mortgages may provide for reduced payments during early years of the loan. It is not uncommon for a loan to have a contract rate at, say 6 percent, but the loan calculation would only identify the interest portion of each payment at 3 percent. This would be 0.0025 multiplied by the actual outstanding balance owed at the time of the payment if there were 12 installments a year. The lender is not forgetting about the real contract rate; he is adding the deficit amount to the balance owed. In this kind of mortgage, the principal owed increases each time this "unpaid interest" is added back to the balance owned. This kind of repayment schedule is a good tool to use when a property is difficult to sell, or the buyer needs to spend substantial sums to rehab or upgrade a property. Sellers that understand this technique can take advantage of this when negotiating the sale. The benefit to a buyer is that the first few years of such payment schedules provide a breather to the buyer. This can be critical in investment properties where time is needed to build up rental income.

However, any term of any mortgage that you do not fully understand can cause extreme hardships in later years when the interest rate changes, or balloon payments come due. Crisis in the lending sector generally will occur because of wholesale misunderstanding or even gross misuse of the lending practices. Buyers who are lulled into taking out mortgages simply because they believe they have cut their loan repayment in half may have a rude awakening when the actual terms kick in.

Loan documents are drafted much like rental car agreements. When was the last time you read every word of the one- or two-page document the rental car agent had you sign and initial before he ran your credit card through the machine? The only difference is, the mortgage has some tough penalties that can cost you far more than being charged for a fender bender you did not even cause. Read every word of every document that deals with real estate investing or financing. If you do not fully understand what you read, do not sign anything or commit to anything until you do understand. And this critical word of warning: *Do ask the lender (or the car agent either) to explain to you what that means.* But remember, they may not know or they may simply repeat something they were told to say which might not be the whole truth.

Contract Principal

This is the amount of the loan at the start of the process. As I just mentioned in the previous section, it is possible that the principal outstanding can increase when the unpaid interest is added back to the original contract principal. Also, the amount of money that the holder of the loan (not the original lender) has paid for that instrument may differ from the contract principal. A good example of this can occur if you take back a purchase money second mortgage when selling a property. In this example, the buyer might ask you to hold a $50,000 second mortgage that they can repay to you at the end of five years. During those five years, you may negotiate minimal payments, or even no payments at all for the period. If the loan simply had a one-time payment of both principal and unpaid interest (with interest calculated on the unpaid interest), the amount of the loan to be repaid would be a combination of the $50,000 and the interest compounded over the period. This type of problem is quickly solved by using Table C, which is a compound interest table based on annual compounding. You can arrive at any type of compounding by using the formula:

$$\text{Contract principal} \times (1 + \text{Contract rate})^n$$

Many inexpensive calculators will do this math quickly and easily because all you do is solve $(1 + \text{Contract rate})$ raised to the nth power. Assume you are using 12 percent annual interest with monthly compounding for that five-year period. To complete the formula you would have $(1.01)^{60}$. Remember, the n is the number of periods, so five years of compounding monthly would require 60 as the number. Also, because the interest used in each compound would be that interest for the specific period (which monthly is $\frac{1}{12}$ of the Contract rate), the formula is resolved as $(1.01)^{60}$. If the calculator has a key or function with the symbol Y^X, you would enter 1.01, then press the Y^X key and enter 60; and press the equal symbol to get the answer 1.82 that when multiplied by the original contract principal of $50,000 would give you the final payoff of $90,834.83 at the end of five years. You could, of course, simply go to Table C and find 12 percent interest at five years and get the answer 1.76234 which is a compounding of 12 percent once each period for five years. The difference between 12 percent over 5 periods (in this case, years) and 1 percent over 60 periods (months) is that, although the total time passed is the same, the more times the principal is compounded, the greater the end result. Once a year for five years results is $88,117.08 instead of $90,834.83. Review similar problems and their solutions found in Chapter 15.

Constant Payment Percent

This is a percentage of the principal remaining to be repaid that when multiplied by that principal would result in a number that is equal to the combined principal and interest portions of the repayment. Turn to Table A. In the 18-year column, slide your finger down to 12 percent (note the percentages in the far left column). The constant payment percent corresponding to 18 years (remaining payout) at 12 percent is 13.583 percent. This number is pure magic because when it is multiplied by the remaining balance of the loan (the current contract principal amount) it will solve the annual total of 12 monthly payments. Assume the principal amount is $50,000, you know the interest rate, 12 percent, and the exact number of years is 18.

$$\$50,000 \times 0.13583 = \$6,791.50$$

To solve for the monthly payment, simply divide the annual total by 12. This equals $565.96. Note that most amortization tables will give you a monthly amount, which is okay if you know that you are getting the monthly amount and not the annual constant. I choose to use the annual figure (rate) because there are other factors that relate directly to the annual elements of an investment. For example, positive leverage is a factor that every investor strives to attain when financing his or her real estate investments. Assume you wanted to earn a minimum of 10 percent of spendable cash on your cash invested in the acquisition of a rental property. In order to have positive leverage by obtaining part of the acquisition cost through financing, your total debt service would have to be less than 10 percent for that leverage to have a positive benefit to your cash flow. This one example of the benefit of getting used to thinking constant rate in your financing is worth the small effort to divide the annual amount by 12 to get the monthly installment.

Keep in mind, then, that Table A solves many different mortgage problems provided the mortgage is monthly payments. Table B is similar, except it is based on a single annual payment each year coming at the end of the year.

Stay with Table A for a moment. Let us go through several different kinds of problems and I will show you how quickly you can arrive at the solution using this table.

First look at the relationship of the constant rate and the two factors of principal and payment amount:

A. The Constant rate × Contract principal = Total annual payment
B. Total annual payment ÷ Constant rate = Contract principal
C. Total annual payment ÷ the Contract principal = Constant rate

Problem: Find the amount of principal still outstanding in a mortgage that pays out at $428.34 per month at a contract rate of 9 percent with 23 years remaining.

Step 1:   Convert the payment to an annual total by multiplying by 12:

$$\$428.34 \times 12 = \$5,140.03 \text{ (Total annual payment)}$$

Step 2:   Find the constant rate that corresponds to 18 years at 9 percent interest. Go to the 23-years column and slide down to 9 percent.

Answer: 10.311

Step 3:   Total annual payment divided by the Constant rate equals the Contract principal:

$$\$5,140.03 \div 0.10311 = \$49,849.97$$

Tip: Round up to the next even dollar if 50 cents or greater. $49.850.00.

Problem: Find the interest rate of a mortgage that has 30 years remaining with a monthly payment of $1,428.50 and $150,000 principal remaining.

Step 1:   Convert the payment to an annual total by multiplying by 12:

$$\$1,428.50 \times 12 = \$17,142.00$$

Step 2:   Annual amount divided by Contract principal equals the Constant rate:

$$\$17,142.00 \div \$150,000 = 11.428$$

Step 3:   Go to Table A and run your finger down the 30-years column until you find the 11.428 constant percentage, or the closest number to it. In this instance, it will be that exact constant rate of 11.428 percent and corresponds to an annual interest rate of 11 percent. Just for fun, scan Table A and, without looking in any specific column or interest row, find another constant that is close to the target constant of 11.428. The closest will be 10.5 percent interest over 24 years at a constant percent of 11.430. The ability to see other combinations will help you in designing payment schedules that fit the overall business or investment plan of the acquisition.

Tables A and B are constant payment percentages. Table A shows individual percentages that are based on a combined total of 12 monthly installments. Table B is based on one single annual payment at the end of the year for each year allotted.

Actual Payment (As It Is Applied to the Repayment of the Debt)

The actual payment is the installment. It can be monthly, quarterly, semiannually, or annually. There may not even be an interim payment and the mortgage could simply balloon with one single payment together with unpaid interest. Some mortgages split fund the mortgage to have several balloon payments during the repayment period. This book has discussed a number of such payment schedules, and they may play a big role in your investment strategies. Remember, the reduction of the debt service during early years may help the investor increase cash flow at the most vulnerable time of the investment.

Early Repayment

Early repayment occurs in the majority of all real estate mortgages. In single family financing, it is common that a buyer will refinance the existing mortgage on a property, or at least pay off any secondary financing that a prior seller held to assist in the closing of that earlier transaction. Secondary financing generally has a provision that may limit the assumption capability of that loan. The prospect of early repayment of debt opens many doors of opportunity to investors who seek to acquire existing debt. Often a little homework can suggest to such an investor the likelihood of a mortgage being repaid early and present a bonus to that investor.

This occurs when the holder of a mortgage, often but not limited to secondary mortgages, wants to generate immediate cash from a sale of his or her mortgage holdings. This seller could be a mortgage broker, bank, or private party who either made the original loan, or acquired the instrument through another acquisition. When the mortgage is sold at a discount from the outstanding contract principal, there is a future bonus that will come to the new holder. The amount of that bonus can be easily ascertained using Tables A or B, depending on the situation. However, because there is no guarantee as to when that loan will be repaid, the total yield amount that will come to the new holder cannot be ascertained until the repayment actually occurs.

EXAMPLE. Able sold his shopping center and took back a second mortgage of $500,000 to facilitate the buyer. It is a straight amortizing loan over 20 years at 8 percent interest per annum. By using Table A, we can quickly see the constant rate is 10.037 percent (20-years column at 8 percent). By multiplying $500,000 by 0.10037, we get an annual total of $50,185.00 which when divided by 12 equals $4,182.08 per month. Ten years later, Able needs some quick cash, so he offers the mortgage to you. You look back to Table A to ascertain how much principal is still outstanding. You would look under the 10-years column at 8 percent where you would find a constant rate of 14.559 percent.

In essence, 0.14559 times the remaining balance would equal the annual total of 12 payments. So construct the formula:

Constant rate × Contract amount = $50,185.00

Contract amount = $50,185.00 ÷ Constant rate

Contract amount = 50,185.00 ÷ 0.14559 = $344,700.87

Amount still outstanding = $344,700.87

Now the negotiation to acquire this mortgage comes into the picture. Remember, the contract rate is 8 percent. But Able needs cash and does not want to play games so he tells you he will sell the mortgage at a discount so that it will return you 11 percent on the amount you pay. What is that amount?

Here is what you know:

- The annual payment (of 12 monthly installments) is $50,185.00.

- Unless there is an early repayment, the mortgage has 10 years remaining.

Go to Table A and find the 10-years column and slide down to 11 percent interest. What is the constant rate? You will find it to be 16.530 percent.

Question: 16.530 percent of what amount equals $50,185.00?

Answer: Divide 50,185.00 by 0.16530. That equals $303,600.00.

If you paid $303,600 for the mortgage, your return would be 11 percent because you acquired the mortgage at a discount. But what if there is an early repayment? When this happens to a mortgage you purchased at a discount, you will receive a bonus over and above the interest you were being paid.

Assume, for the sake of argument, that the loan is paid off at the end of the first year you own it. The principal amount outstanding would be based on the contract rate of the original loan, which is 8 percent, so look at 9 years (end of your first year so the loan still has 9 years remaining if it were to continue to be repaid as per the schedule). The constant rate is 15.622 percent so the total annual payment is still $50,185.00. Divide that by 0.15622, and we see the payoff balance at the end of the first year will be $321,245.70. Let us see what you have in your pocket at the end of that first year:

1.	Payments received:	$ 50,185.00
2.	Payoff:	+321,245.70
3.	Total:	$ 371,430.70
4.	Your investment:	−303,600.00
5.	Profit:	$ 67,830.70

Yield (Line 5 ÷ Line 4)

Your Yield will be the combination of the interest paid and the bonus due to the early repayment of the discounted mortgage. The result is   22.34%

Mortgage Owner's Actual Yield

As you can see from the previous example, you leveraged your investment to a very nice return. There was some risk, of course; all financing has some risk attached to it. However, a matured mortgage with 10 years of payment history, and a first mortgage with a history that can be reviewed, lead to good investment opportunities.

Your yield was set at a minimum of 11 percent, so any early repayment of the debt would come with a bonus.

Naturally, if the loan you hold goes sour, and the borrower fails to meet his obligations, then the cost to recover anything may exceed what you actually earned. In those instances, the results are likely due to your own poor judgment or lack of due diligence, and your yield could slip into the negative.

All this points to your understanding what is going on with the mortgage, the borrower, and the condition of the property. You want to know what to expect, and then make your judgment call based on accurate, up-to-date information.

MOVING INTO THE WORLD OF FINANCE

We live in a world of computers and sophisticated calculators and often rely so much on their use that when it comes to relatively simple math, we have to stop and think twice or more before attempting to multiply $1,200.00 by 12. In an attempt to bring you back to the numbers, I have provided three comprehensive tables that will work wonders for you and your pencil and paper even if you do not happen to have a calculator handy. Armed with a less-than-10-dollar calculator, you and these tables will be able to calculate everything you need from discounts of mortgages, to finding balances owed, payment schedules, interest rates charged, and more.

The first step is to understand how to read the amortization tables. There are two such tables. Table A is to be used for the usual mortgage calculation where the mortgage calls for monthly payments. Table B is for mortgages which have but one annual payment. In each table, the mortgage must be amortizing of principal and interest, rather than a mortgage which may be interest only, or have set payments of principal each month plus interest on the balance. In the amortizing mortgage, the monthly payment will be the same throughout the life of the mortgage. Yet within that payment, the amount allocated to principal and the amount charged as interest will change each month. This occurs because in the early years of the mortgage the amount of interest charged against the amount owed is much greater than in the later years because the mortgage is continually reduced. Some of the following information restates material covered earlier.

REVIEW THE EARLIER EXAMPLES OF A MORTGAGE WITH EQUAL MONTHLY PAYMENTS OF PRINCIPAL AND INTEREST COMBINED WITH A CONSTANT ANNUAL PAYMENT

If a loan were $100,000 for a 25-year period at 12 percent, amortized then over a total of 300 payments, the monthly payment would be $1,053.25 per month. Of this payment the amount of interest for the first payment would be $1,000 and only the balance of

$53.25 would be principal. On the other hand, the last payment would also be a total of $1,053.25 but the allocation to interest would be only $10.43, and the amount of principal reduction to the mortgage would be $1,042.82. Sometime during this 25-year term, the amount charged against interest and the allocation to principal was equal.

In a mortgage of 25 years at 12 percent as indicated, where the amount borrowed is $100,000 the loan officer of the lending institution would ascertain the monthly payment you would have to pay by using a table such as Table A. By looking under the 25-year column and moving down the page to the interest rate of 12 percent, you would find the number 12.639, which would be the constant rate for that mortgage at the day it was to begin.

The interest is 12 percent as shown earlier, but the charges, which would reflect both interest and principal payback, would be this slightly higher amount of 12.639 percent. By multiplying the gross loan outstanding by the constant rate ($100,000 × 12.639 percent) we would end up with an annual amount of $12,639. To get the monthly payment, simply divide that amount ($12,639) by 12 to end up with $1,053.25 per month.

It is critical that you remember that these constant tables are an annual percentage figure. To get the monthly payment, you would use Table A only (as Table B is for single annual payments per year). When using Table A, always divide the annual payment by 12 to end up with the correct monthly payment of principal and interest.

TAKE NOTE OF WHERE TO PLACE THE DECIMAL POINT

When doing a math problem with a percentage amount, remember to move the decimal point two places to the left (the same as dividing by 100). For example, in the multiplication of $100,000 by the constant for 12 percent interest at 25 years, you found the constant rate to be 12.639 percent. In the actual multiplication, you would have used $100,000 times 0.12639 to end with $12,639.

If you have a calculator that will multiply by percentages, you would not have to move the decimal over to the left. If you are unsure about your calculator then do the following:

How to Check Your Calculator

1. Make sure your calculator is cleared.
2. Multiply $100,000 by 0.12639.
3. Check the results: It should be 12,639 (or 12,639.00), the annual amount.
4. Now divide $12,639 by 12. The answer should show as 1,053.25. This is the monthly amount of that mortgage. If the results you get in line 3 or 4 differ from what is shown here, your calculator is rounding off short of what you need to compute problems using these tables.

EXAMPLES

Finding the Constant Rate When Term and Interest Are Known

Find the constant rate for a mortgage that is 30 years long at 15 percent interest, with monthly payments.

1. Look for the 30-year column in Table A.
2. Go down the page for the 15 percent interest indication.
3. Make note of the constant rate: 15.173.

With this information you could multiply the math number of 0.15173 times any loan amount (for that rate and duration) and divide the annual amount by 12 to get the monthly rate. For example, $100,000 loan, times 0.15173 equals $15,173 divided by 12 equals $1,264.42.

Find the Interest Rate When Term and Payment Are Known

Find the interest rate for a mortgage of $80,000.00 over 22 years, with 12 payments per year with a payment of $805.80 per month. In this situation you will use the table to help you establish terms on a mortgage to suit a transaction you are working on. You might have discovered that there are existing mortgages on a property you want to buy that will be fully paid off in 22 years. You want the seller to hold a mortgage for the balance of the deal for that term. She wants $80,000 to make the deal. You can afford a monthly payment of $805.80. What's the interest rate?

Find the Interest Rate When You Know the Years and Amount Owed

1. Arrive at the annual payment by multiplying the monthly payment by 12 ($805.80 × 12 = $9,669.60).
2. Divide the annual payment by the loan amount owed that day ($9,669.60 ÷ $80,000 = 0.12087). Note: It is important here that you make sure your calculator will write at least three numbers to the right of the decimal point. If you round off at 12.01 then you will not have a very accurate number to work with. Either get a new calculator or divide by a smaller number, for example 800, and omit the next step.
3. Take the number you have ended up with (step 2) and move the decimal over two places to the right, 0.12087 will become 12.087.
4. Go to Table A and find the 22-year column.
5. Go down that column until you find the constant rate of 12.087 percent or the closest possible rate. You will notice that 12.087 percent is a constant rate for 11 percent interest.

Find the Mortgage Amount When Term, Interest, and Payment Are Known

This is a rather common problem that comes from different circumstances.

You may be working with a seller who doesn't know the amount he or she owes on a mortgage. The seller can tell you the payment (make sure it is principal and interest only and that it does not include taxes and insurance, and so on), knows how long it has to run, and even the interest rate. It has 20 years to go, the monthly payment is $805, and the interest rate is 10.5 percent. Here is what you do:

1. Get annual payment again ($805 × 12 = $9,660.00).

2. Go to the 20-year column at 10.5 percent interest and see the constant rate, which would be 11.670 percent.

3. Divide the annual payment by the constant ($9,660.00 ÷ 0.11670 = $82,776.35, rounded up from a slightly larger number).

Find Term of Years When You Know Amount Owed, Interest Rate, and Payment

When you are negotiating on a deal, you may find that the flexibility of a mortgage term might bring the payment into reach. In this situation you might be fixed at having to pay off a $90,000 mortgage at 12.5 percent interest, with only $970 per month available from the current income of the property to support the added debt service. You and the seller agree to set the mortgage so that the $970 will pay out the mortgage. But what is the term?

1. Get the annual payment again ($970 × 12 = $11,640).

2. Divide the annual payment by the amount of the loan owed that day ($11,640 ÷ $90,000 = 0.12933).

3. Move the decimal place over to the right two places (0.12933 then will become 12.933).

4. Go to Table A, and look at the interest rate charged in the mortgage (in this case, 12.5 percent). Move along the line until you find the same or closest rate to match the number you found in line three above. This is the rate you will try to match. (However, you will not find that rate exactly.) Under the 27.5-year column you will find 12.923 constant at the 12.5 interest rate, and at the 27th year 12.951 constant. The answer you need would fall between these two time periods. As a buyer you might try to settle for a 27-year payout at $970 per month or 27.5 years at the 12.923 constant rate. As a seller you'd opt for the $970 for 27.5 years, or the 12.951 percent constant for the 27 years.

Discount of Mortgage

When you are dealing with mortgages at a discount, you will find that almost any problem that you can think of dealing with mortgage discounts can be ascertained using the constants.

Look at this question: When I sell my property, if I take back a second mortgage that is for $50,000 payable over 10 years in equal monthly payments calculated at an amortization of principal and interest, with interest at 10 percent, and I want to sell the mortgage, what price will I get?

Now this is a very good question, here is the answer: A $50,000 second mortgage, 10 years in monthly payments at 10 percent. Buyers of mortgages usually want a discount to increase the yield of the mortgage for that buyer. For example, if the buyer of the above-mentioned mortgage wanted a 15 percent return rather than the 10 percent rate on the mortgage, he or she would have to buy the mortgage at a discount price that would accurately provide that yield.

To begin with, find the constant rate for the mortgage as it now stands. To do this, look in the 10-year column of Table A, and go down to the 10 percent interest rate line. You will find a constant rate of 15.858 percent. This indicates an annual payment (the total of 12 monthly payments) of $50,000 times 0.15858 or $7,929. This relates to a monthly payment of $660.75.

Now find the constant rate the buyer of the mortgage (at a discount) requires. The same number of years is in effect, so go to the 10-year column, and go down to the 15 percent line. The constant rate for this yield is 19.360 percent.

The relationship between these constants is as follows: If you take the constant of the existing contract rate (10 percent interest, and a constant of 15.858 percent) and divide that by the constant for the desired rate (15 percent interest desired, and a constant rate of 19.360 percent) and move the decimal two places to the right, you will end up with the percent of discount needed to discount the mortgage to permit the desired yield.

Existing constant (15.868) ÷ 19.360 = 0.8197 converted

Desired constant = 19.360

Discount = 81.97%

Multiply this percentage of discount by the face amount of the mortgage at the day of the discount, and you will have the amount the buyer would pay under these circumstances to obtain a yield of 15 percent on a mortgage that has a contract rate of only 10 percent interest.

Amount of the mortgage × Discount percentage = Price

$50,000 × 0.8197 = $40,985

This same mathematical sequence can be turned around to find any part of this type of problem as long as you have sufficient data to close the circle.

Find the New Yield of a Discounted Mortgage

Charles may own a mortgage with six years to go of $35,000 payable monthly at an interest rate of 11 percent interest per annum. He might offer it to you at a price of $25,000. Would it be a good deal? You would want to know your yield (as well as much more about the security, the mortgagor, and so on) before you said yes to his offer.

Here's how you find the solution:

1. Find the constant at the contract rate in Table A. Go to the 6-year column at 11 percent interest. You will find a constant rate of 22.841 percent.

2. Find the discount percentage. To find this, divide the price of the mortgage ($25,000) by the face amount owed at the day of the discount ($35,000).

$$\text{Price of mortgage} \div \text{Amount owed}$$
$$\$25,000 \div \$35,000 = 0.7143 \text{ or } 71.43\%$$

3. Now take the constant rate found in step 1 (22.841 percent) and divide that by the discount percentage (71.43 percent).

$$\text{Existing constant rate} \div \text{Discount percentage}$$
$$22.841 \div 71.43 = 0.3198 \text{ or } 31.98\%$$

4. This new percentage (31.98 percent) is the new constant rate for the discounted mortgage. If you then look down the 6-years column until you find a rate equal to or close to this new rate, it will correspond to the yield on that mortgage. In this case, you will find 31.958 percent under the 6-years column at 24.5 percent interest. In essence at $25,000 the purchase of this $35,000 mortgage would yield you over 24.5 percent interest should the mortgage go to its full term.

5. Mortgages rarely go the full term, however, and whenever you have purchased a mortgage at a discount, and that mortgage pays off sooner than the contracted term, a bonus will result.

Review of a Discounted Mortgage Transaction

If you paid $25,000 for that mortgage that has a face value of $35,000, and you held the mortgage for one year and the mortgagor then paid the mortgage off, you would get the following:

1. One year's payments of $7,994.35.

2. At the end of the year there is still an outstanding balance on the mortgage of $30,640.26. This is found by taking the constant rate for the mortgage for the remaining term (five years) at 11 percent interest (26.091 percent) and dividing that into the annual total payment ($7,994.35):

$$\$7,994.35 \div 0.26091 = \$30,640.25$$

This is the payoff amount at the end of year one. This little step can be most useful in other financing problems as well.

3. Add the total payments gained, and the payoff:

$$\$7,994.35 + \$30,640.25 = \$38,634.60$$

4. Subtract the amount paid to buy the mortgage: $25,000.00. Return of other than principal: $13,634.60.

5. Divide by the number of years you held this mortgage $13,634.60 : 1 = $13,634.60 (this mortgage might have been held longer). This amount is your average return of interest per year.

6. Divide the average return ($13,634.60) by the price you paid for the mortgage to get the average yield actually earned:

$$\$13,634.60 \div \$25,000.00 = 0.5454 \text{ or } 54.54\%$$

This indicates that you have actually averaged a 54.54 percent yield on this mortgage. Remember: The contract rate is still only 11 percent.

By playing around with the constants in these few problems, I've provided in this Appendix, you will find many new ways to use the constant formulas to solve your specific problems.

NOTES

1. Calculations will result in slight errors if mortgages calculated are less than annual payments. However, the error will not be sufficient to warrant not using the table.

2. A constant annual payment percentage is that percentage which when multiplied by the loan balance will give an amount representing the annual payment of principal including interest. The table given will allow the user to take the interest rate to be paid, locate the term of years, and determine the constant annual percentage. This percentage multiplied by the principal owed will give the total annual payment, which, in the case of Table A, is made up of 12 monthly installments. It is important to remember that the constant interest rate changes each year whereas the amount paid does not. This is due to the fact that the principal owed and years remaining diminish each successive year of the loan.

Table A Amortizing Mortgages with Equal Monthly Payments

Percent	Years							
	1	1.5	2	2.5	3	3.5	4	4.5
3	101.632	68.261	51.577	41.569	34.897	30.133	26.561	23.784
3.25	101.769	68.395	51.710	41.701	35.030	30.266	26.694	23.917
3.5	101.906	68.529	51.843	41.834	35.162	30.399	26.827	24.050
3.75	102.043	68.663	51.976	41.967	35.295	30.532	26.961	24.185
4	102.180	68.798	52.110	42.100	35.429	30.666	27.095	24.319
4.25	102.317	68.932	52.244	42.233	35.562	30.800	27.229	24.454
4.5	102.454	69.067	52.377	42.367	35.696	30.934	27.364	24.590
4.75	102.592	69.202	52.511	42.501	35.831	31.069	27.499	24.726
5	102.729	69.337	52.646	42.635	35.965	31.204	27.635	24.862
5.25	102.867	69.472	52.780	42.770	36.100	31.339	27.771	24.999
5.5	103.004	69.607	52.915	42.904	36.235	31.475	27.908	25.136
5.75	103.142	69.742	53.050	43.039	36.371	31.611	28.045	25.274
6	103.280	69.878	53.185	43.175	36.506	31.747	28.182	25.412
6.25	103.418	70.014	53.320	43.310	36.642	31.884	28.320	25.551
6.5	103.556	70.150	53.456	43.446	36.779	32.022	28.458	25.690
6.75	103.694	70.286	53.591	43.582	36.916	32.159	28.597	25.830
7	103.832	70.422	53.727	43.718	37.053	32.297	28.735	25.970
7.25	103.970	70.558	53.863	43.855	37.190	32.435	28.875	26.110
7.5	104.109	70.695	54.000	43.992	37.327	32.574	29.015	26.251
7.75	104.247	70.832	54.136	44.129	37.465	32.713	29.155	26.393
8	104.386	70.968	54.273	44.266	37.604	32.852	29.296	26.535
8.25	104.525	71.105	54.410	44.404	37.742	32.992	29.437	26.677
8.5	104.664	71.242	54.547	44.541	37.881	33.132	29.578	26.820
8.75	104.803	71.380	54.684	44.679	38.020	33.273	29.720	26.963
9	104.942	71.517	54.822	44.818	38.160	33.413	29.862	27.107
9.25	105.081	71.655	54.959	44.956	38.299	33.555	30.005	27.251
9.5	105.220	71.793	55.097	45.095	38.440	33.696	30.148	27.396
9.75	105.360	71.930	55.236	45.234	38.580	33.838	30.291	27.541
10	105.499	72.068	55.374	45.374	38.721	33.980	30.435	27.687
10.25	105.639	72.207	55.512	45.513	38.862	34.123	30.579	27.833
10.5	105.778	72.345	55.651	45.653	39.003	34.266	30.724	27.979
10.75	105.918	72.484	55.790	45.793	39.145	34.409	30.869	28.126
11	106.058	72.622	55.929	45.934	39.286	34.553	31.015	28.274
11.25	106.198	72.761	56.069	46.074	39.429	34.697	31.161	28.422
11.5	106.338	72.900	56.208	46.215	39.571	34.841	31.307	28.570
11.75	106.478	73.039	56.348	46.356	39.714	34.986	31.454	28.719
12	106.619	73.178	56.488	46.498	39.857	35.131	31.601	28.868
12.25	106.759	73.318	56.628	46.639	40.001	35.276	31.748	29.018
12.5	106.899	73.457	56.769	46.781	40.144	35.422	31.896	29.168
12.75	107.040	73.597	56.909	46.923	40.288	35.568	32.044	29.318
13	107.181	73.737	57.050	47.066	40.433	35.715	32.193	29.469
13.25	107.322	73.877	57.191	47.209	40.577	35.861	32.342	29.621
13.5	107.462	74.017	57.332	47.351	40.722	36.009	32.492	29.773
13.75	107.603	74.158	57.474	47.495	40.868	36.156	32.641	29.925
14	107.745	74.298	57.615	47.638	41.013	36.304	32.792	30.078
14.25	107.886	74.439	57.757	47.782	41.159	36.452	32.942	30.231
14.5	108.027	74.580	57.899	47.926	41.305	36.601	33.094	30.384
14.75	108.168	74.721	58.042	48.070	41.452	36.750	33.245	30.539
15	108.310	74.862	58.184	48.214	41.598	36.899	33.397	30.693
15.25	108.452	75.003	58.327	48.359	41.745	37.048	33.549	30.848
15.5	108.593	75.144	58.469	48.504	41.893	37.198	33.702	31.004
15.75	108.735	75.286	58.612	48.649	42.040	37.349	33.855	31.159
16	108.877	75.428	58.756	48.794	42.188	37.499	34.008	31.316
16.25	109.019	75.570	58.899	48.940	42.337	37.650	34.162	31.472
16.5	109.161	75.712	59.043	49.086	42.485	37.802	34.316	31.630
16.75	109.303	75.854	59.187	49.232	42.634	37.953	34.471	31.787
17	109.446	75.996	59.331	49.379	42.783	38.106	34.626	31.945
17.25	109.588	76.139	59.475	49.525	42.933	38.258	34.781	32.104
17.5	109.731	76.281	59.619	49.672	43.082	38.411	34.937	32.263
17.75	109.873	76.424	59.764	49.820	43.233	38.564	35.093	32.422
18	110.016	76.567	59.909	49.967	43.383	38.717	35.250	32.582

(continued)

Table A Amortizing Mortgages with Equal Monthly Payments

Percent	5	5.5	6	6.5	7	7.5	8	8.5
3	21.562	19.746	18.232	16.952	15.856	14.906	14.075	13.343
3.25	21.696	19.880	18.367	17.088	15.992	15.042	14.212	13.480
3.5	21.830	20.014	18.502	17.223	16.128	15.179	14.350	13.618
3.75	21.965	20.150	18.638	17.360	16.265	15.317	14.488	13.757
4	22.100	20.285	18.774	17.497	16.403	15.455	14.627	13.897
4.25	22.235	20.422	18.911	17.634	16.541	15.594	14.767	14.038
4.5	22.372	20.558	19.049	17.773	16.680	15.734	14.908	14.180
4.75	22.508	20.696	19.187	17.912	16.820	15.875	15.049	14.322
5	22.645	20.834	19.326	18.052	16.961	16.017	15.192	14.465
5.25	22.783	20.972	19.465	18.192	17.102	16.159	15.335	14.610
5.5	22.921	21.112	19.605	18.333	17.244	16.302	15.479	14.755
5.75	23.060	21.251	19.746	18.475	17.387	16.446	15.624	14.901
6	23.199	21.392	19.887	18.617	17.530	16.590	15.770	15.047
6.25	23.339	21.532	20.029	18.760	17.674	16.736	15.916	15.195
6.5	23.479	21.674	20.172	18.904	17.819	16.882	16.063	15.344
6.75	23.620	21.816	20.315	19.048	17.965	17.029	16.212	15.493
7	23.761	21.958	20.459	19.193	18.111	17.176	16.360	15.643
7.25	23.903	22.101	20.603	19.339	18.258	17.325	16.510	15.794
7.5	24.046	22.245	20.748	19.485	18.406	17.474	16.661	15.946
7.75	24.188	22.389	20.894	19.632	18.554	17.623	16.812	16.099
8	24.332	22.534	21.040	19.780	18.703	17.774	16.964	16.252
8.25	24.476	22.679	21.187	19.928	18.853	17.925	17.117	16.407
8.5	24.620	22.825	21.334	20.077	19.004	18.077	17.271	16.562
8.75	24.765	22.971	21.482	20.227	19.155	18.230	17.425	16.718
9	24.910	23.118	21.631	20.377	19.307	18.384	17.580	16.875
9.25	25.056	23.266	21.780	20.528	19.459	18.538	17.736	17.033
9.5	25.202	23.414	21.930	20.679	19.613	18.693	17.893	17.191
9.75	25.349	23.562	22.080	20.831	19.767	18.849	18.051	17.351
10	25.496	23.712	22.231	20.984	19.921	19.006	18.209	17.511
10.25	25.644	23.861	22.383	21.138	20.077	19.163	18.368	17.672
10.5	25.793	24.012	22.535	21.292	20.233	19.321	18.528	17.834
10.75	25.942	24.162	22.688	21.447	20.390	19.479	18.689	17.996
11	26.091	24.314	22.841	21.602	20.547	19.639	18.850	18.160
11.25	26.241	24.466	22.995	21.758	20.705	19.799	19.012	18.324
11.5	26.391	24.618	23.149	21.915	20.864	19.960	19.175	18.489
11.75	26.542	24.771	23.305	22.072	21.023	20.121	19.339	18.655
12	26.693	24.925	23.460	22.230	21.183	20.284	19.503	18.821
12.25	26.845	25.079	23.617	22.388	21.344	20.447	19.669	18.989
12.5	26.998	25.233	23.773	22.548	21.505	20.610	19.835	19.157
12.75	27.150	25.388	23.931	22.707	21.668	20.775	20.001	19.326
13	27.304	25.544	24.089	22.868	21.830	20.940	20.169	19.496
13.25	27.458	25.700	24.248	23.029	21.994	21.106	20.337	19.666
13.5	27.612	25.857	24.407	23.190	22.158	21.272	20.506	19.837
13.75	27.767	26.014	24.567	23.353	22.323	21.439	20.675	20.010
14	27.922	26.172	24.727	23.516	22.488	21.607	20.846	20.182
14.25	28.078	26.331	24.888	23.679	22.654	21.776	21.017	20.356
14.5	28.234	26.489	25.049	23.843	22.821	21.945	21.189	20.530
14.75	28.391	26.649	25.211	24.008	22.988	22.115	21.361	20.705
15	28.548	26.809	25.374	24.173	23.156	22.286	21.534	20.881
15.25	28.706	26.969	25.537	24.339	23.325	22.457	21.708	21.058
15.5	28.864	27.130	25.701	24.506	23.494	22.629	21.883	21.235
15.75	29.023	27.292	25.865	24.673	23.664	22.802	22.058	21.413
16	29.182	27.454	26.030	24.841	23.834	22.975	22.235	21.592
16.25	29.341	27.616	26.196	25.009	24.006	23.149	22.411	21.771
16.5	29.501	27.779	26.362	25.178	24.177	23.324	22.589	21.951
16.75	29.662	27.943	26.528	25.347	24.350	23.499	22.767	22.132
17	29.823	28.107	26.695	25.517	24.523	23.675	22.946	22.314
17.25	29.985	28.272	26.863	25.688	24.697	23.852	23.125	22.496
17.5	30.147	28.437	27.031	25.859	24.871	24.029	23.305	22.679
17.75	30.309	28.602	27.200	26.031	25.046	24.207	23.486	22.863
18	30.472	28.769	27.369	26.204	25.221	24.385	23.668	23.048

(continued)

Table A Amortizing Mortgages with Equal Monthly Payments

Percent	9	9.5	10	10.5	11	11.5	12	12.5
3	12.692	12.111	11.587	11.114	10.685	10.292	9.933	9.603
3.25	12.830	12.249	11.726	11.254	10.825	10.433	10.075	9.745
3.5	12.969	12.388	11.866	11.394	10.966	10.575	10.217	9.889
3.75	13.109	12.529	12.007	11.536	11.108	10.718	10.361	10.033
4	13.249	12.670	12.149	11.679	11.252	10.863	10.506	10.179
4.25	13.391	12.812	12.293	11.823	11.397	11.008	10.653	10.326
4.5	13.533	12.956	12.437	11.968	11.542	11.155	10.800	10.474
4.75	13.676	13.100	12.582	12.114	11.689	11.303	10.949	10.624
5	13.821	13.245	12.728	12.261	11.837	11.452	11.099	10.775
5.25	13.966	13.391	12.875	12.409	11.987	11.602	11.250	10.927
5.5	14.112	13.538	13.023	12.558	12.137	11.753	11.402	11.080
5.75	14.259	13.686	13.172	12.708	12.288	11.905	11.556	11.235
6	14.407	13.835	13.322	12.860	12.440	12.059	11.710	11.391
6.25	14.556	13.985	13.474	13.012	12.594	12.213	11.866	11.548
6.5	14.705	14.136	13.626	13.165	12.749	12.369	12.023	11.706
6.75	14.856	14.288	13.779	13.320	12.904	12.526	12.181	11.865
7	15.008	14.441	13.933	13.475	13.061	12.684	12.341	12.026
7.25	15.160	14.595	14.088	13.632	13.219	12.843	12.501	12.188
7.5	15.313	14.749	14.244	13.789	13.378	13.004	12.663	12.351
7.75	15.467	14.905	14.401	13.948	13.538	13.165	12.826	12.515
8	15.622	15.062	14.559	14.107	13.699	13.328	12.989	12.680
8.25	15.778	15.219	14.718	14.268	13.861	13.491	13.154	12.847
8.5	15.935	15.377	14.878	14.429	14.024	13.656	13.321	13.015
8.75	16.093	15.537	15.039	14.592	14.188	13.821	13.488	13.183
9	16.251	15.697	15.201	14.755	14.353	13.988	13.656	13.353
9.25	16.411	15.858	15.364	14.920	14.519	14.156	13.826	13.525
9.5	16.571	16.020	15.528	15.085	14.686	14.325	13.996	13.697
9.75	16.732	16.183	15.692	15.252	14.855	14.495	14.168	13.870
10	16.894	16.347	15.858	15.419	15.024	14.666	14.341	14.045
10.25	17.057	16.512	16.025	15.588	15.194	14.838	14.515	14.220
10.5	17.221	16.677	16.192	15.757	15.365	15.011	14.690	14.397
10.75	17.386	16.844	16.361	15.928	15.538	15.185	14.866	14.575
11	17.551	17.011	16.530	16.099	15.711	15.360	15.043	14.754
11.25	17.717	17.180	16.700	16.271	15.885	15.536	15.221	14.934
11.5	17.884	17.349	16.871	16.444	16.060	15.714	15.400	15.115
11.75	18.052	17.519	17.044	16.618	16.236	15.892	15.580	15.297
12	18.221	17.690	17.217	16.793	16.413	16.071	15.761	15.480
12.25	18.391	17.861	17.390	16.969	16.592	16.251	15.943	15.664
12.5	18.561	18.034	17.565	17.146	16.771	16.432	16.126	15.849
12.75	18.732	18.207	17.741	17.324	16.950	16.614	16.310	16.035
13	18.904	18.382	17.917	17.503	17.131	16.797	16.496	16.222
13.25	19.077	18.557	18.095	17.682	17.313	16.981	16.682	16.411
13.5	19.251	18.733	18.273	17.863	17.496	17.166	16.869	16.600
13.75	19.425	18.910	18.452	18.044	17.679	17.352	17.057	16.790
14	19.600	19.087	18.632	18.227	17.864	17.539	17.246	16.981
14.25	19.776	19.266	18.813	18.410	18.049	17.726	17.435	17.173
14.5	19.953	19.445	18.994	18.594	18.236	17.915	17.626	17.366
14.75	20.131	19.625	19.177	18.779	18.423	18.104	17.818	17.560
15	20.309	19.806	19.360	18.964	18.611	18.295	18.011	17.755
15.25	20.488	19.987	19.544	19.151	18.800	18.486	18.204	17.950
15.5	20.668	20.170	19.729	19.338	18.990	18.678	18.398	18.147
15.75	20.849	20.353	19.915	19.526	19.180	18.871	18.594	18.344
16	21.030	20.537	20.102	19.715	19.372	19.065	18.790	18.543
16.25	21.212	20.722	20.289	19.905	19.564	19.260	18.987	18.742
16.5	21.395	20.907	20.477	20.096	19.757	19.455	19.185	18.942
16.75	21.579	21.094	20.666	20.287	19.951	19.651	19.384	19.143
17	21.763	21.281	20.856	20.480	20.146	19.849	19.583	19.345
17.25	21.949	21.469	21.046	20.673	20.342	20.047	19.783	19.548
17.5	22.134	21.657	21.237	20.867	20.538	20.246	19.985	19.751
17.75	22.321	21.847	21.429	21.061	20.735	20.445	20.187	19.956
18	22.508	22.037	21.622	21.257	20.933	20.646	20.389	20.161

(continued)

Table A Amortizing Mortgages with Equal Monthly Payments

Percent	Years							
	13	13.5	14	14.5	15	15.5	16	16.5
3	9.299	9.018	8.756	8.513	8.287	8.075	7.877	7.691
3.25	9.442	9.161	8.900	8.658	8.432	8.221	8.023	7.838
3.5	9.586	9.305	9.045	8.804	8.579	8.368	8.171	7.987
3.75	9.731	9.451	9.192	8.951	8.727	8.517	8.321	8.137
4	9.877	9.599	9.340	9.100	8.876	8.667	8.472	8.289
4.25	10.025	9.747	9.490	9.250	9.027	8.819	8.625	8.442
4.5	10.174	9.897	9.641	9.402	9.180	8.973	8.779	8.597
4.75	10.325	10.049	9.793	9.555	9.334	9.128	8.935	8.754
5	10.477	10.201	9.946	9.710	9.490	9.284	9.092	8.912
5.25	10.630	10.355	10.101	9.866	9.647	9.442	9.251	9.072
5.5	10.784	10.511	10.258	10.023	9.805	9.602	9.412	9.234
5.75	10.940	10.668	10.416	10.182	9.965	9.763	9.574	9.397
6	11.097	10.826	10.575	10.342	10.126	9.925	9.737	9.562
6.25	11.255	10.985	10.735	10.504	10.289	10.089	9.902	9.728
6.5	11.414	11.146	10.897	10.667	10.453	10.254	10.069	9.896
6.75	11.575	11.307	11.060	10.831	10.619	10.421	10.237	10.065
7	11.737	11.471	11.225	10.997	10.786	10.590	10.406	10.236
7.25	11.900	11.635	11.391	11.164	10.954	10.759	10.577	10.408
7.5	12.064	11.801	11.558	11.333	11.124	10.930	10.750	10.582
7.75	12.230	11.968	11.726	11.503	11.295	11.103	10.924	10.757
8	12.397	12.136	11.896	11.674	11.468	11.277	11.099	10.934
8.25	12.565	12.306	12.067	11.846	11.642	11.452	11.276	11.112
8.5	12.734	12.476	12.239	12.020	11.817	11.629	11.454	11.291
8.75	12.905	12.648	12.413	12.195	11.993	11.807	11.633	11.472
9	13.076	12.822	12.587	12.371	12.171	11.986	11.814	11.654
9.25	13.249	12.996	12.763	12.549	12.350	12.167	11.996	11.838
9.5	13.423	13.172	12.940	12.727	12.531	12.349	12.180	12.023
9.75	13.598	13.348	13.119	12.907	12.712	12.532	12.365	12.210
10	13.774	13.526	13.298	13.089	12.895	12.716	12.551	12.397
10.25	13.952	13.705	13.479	13.271	13.079	12.902	12.738	12.586
10.5	14.130	13.886	13.661	13.455	13.265	13.089	12.927	12.777
10.75	14.310	14.067	13.844	13.640	13.451	13.278	13.117	12.968
11	14.490	14.249	14.029	13.826	13.639	13.467	13.308	13.161
11.25	14.672	14.433	14.214	14.013	13.828	13.658	13.500	13.355
11.5	14.855	14.618	14.401	14.201	14.018	13.850	13.694	13.550
11.75	15.039	14.804	14.588	14.391	14.210	14.043	13.889	13.747
12	15.224	14.991	14.777	14.582	14.402	14.237	14.085	13.944
12.25	15.410	15.179	14.967	14.773	14.596	14.432	14.282	14.143
12.5	15.597	15.368	15.158	14.966	14.790	14.629	14.480	14.343
12.75	15.785	15.558	15.350	15.160	14.986	14.826	14.679	14.544
13	15.975	15.749	15.543	15.355	15.183	15.025	14.880	14.746
13.25	16.165	15.941	15.737	15.551	15.381	15.225	15.081	14.950
13.5	16.356	16.134	15.932	15.748	15.580	15.426	15.284	15.154
13.75	16.548	16.329	16.129	15.946	15.780	15.627	15.488	15.359
14	16.741	16.524	16.326	16.146	15.981	15.830	15.692	15.566
14.25	16.935	16.720	16.524	16.346	16.183	16.034	15.898	15.773
14.5	17.130	16.917	16.723	16.547	16.386	16.239	16.105	15.982
14.75	17.326	17.115	16.923	16.749	16.590	16.445	16.313	16.191
15	17.523	17.314	17.124	16.952	16.795	16.652	16.521	16.402
15.25	17.721	17.514	17.327	17.156	17.001	16.860	16.731	16.613
15.5	17.920	17.715	17.529	17.361	17.208	17.068	16.941	16.825
15.75	18.120	17.917	17.733	17.567	17.416	17.278	17.153	17.039
16	18.320	18.120	17.938	17.774	17.624	17.489	17.365	17.253
16.25	18.522	18.323	18.144	17.981	17.834	17.700	17.579	17.468
16.5	18.724	18.528	18.350	18.190	18.045	17.913	17.793	17.684
16.75	18.927	18.733	18.558	18.399	18.256	18.126	18.008	17.900
17	19.132	18.939	18.766	18.610	18.468	18.340	18.224	18.118
17.25	19.336	19.146	18.975	18.821	18.681	18.555	18.440	18.336
17.5	19.542	19.354	19.185	19.033	18.895	18.770	18.658	18.556
17.75	19.749	19.563	19.396	19.245	19.110	18.987	18.876	18.776
18	19.956	19.772	19.607	19.459	19.325	19.204	19.095	18.996

(continued)

626

Table A Amortizing Mortgages with Equal Monthly Payments

Percent	17	17.5	18	18.5	19	19.5	20	20.5
					Years			
3	7.516	7.352	7.197	7.050	6.911	6.780	6.655	6.537
3.25	7.664	7.500	7.345	7.199	7.061	6.930	6.806	6.689
3.5	7.813	7.650	7.496	7.351	7.213	7.083	6.960	6.842
3.75	7.964	7.802	7.648	7.504	7.367	7.237	7.115	6.998
4	8.117	7.955	7.802	7.658	7.522	7.394	7.272	7.156
4.25	8.271	8.110	7.958	7.815	7.680	7.552	7.431	7.316
4.5	8.427	8.267	8.116	7.974	7.839	7.712	7.592	7.478
4.75	8.585	8.425	8.275	8.134	8.000	7.874	7.755	7.641
5	8.744	8.585	8.436	8.296	8.163	8.038	7.919	7.807
5.25	8.905	8.747	8.599	8.460	8.328	8.204	8.086	7.975
5.5	9.067	8.911	8.764	8.625	8.495	8.371	8.255	8.144
5.75	9.231	9.076	8.930	8.793	8.663	8.541	8.425	8.316
6	9.397	9.243	9.098	8.962	8.833	8.712	8.597	8.489
6.25	9.565	9.411	9.268	9.132	9.005	8.885	8.771	8.664
6.5	9.733	9.581	9.439	9.305	9.178	9.059	8.947	8.841
6.75	9.904	9.753	9.612	9.479	9.353	9.236	9.124	9.019
7	10.076	9.926	9.786	9.654	9.530	9.414	9.304	9.200
7.25	10.249	10.101	9.962	9.832	9.709	9.593	9.485	9.382
7.5	10.425	10.277	10.140	10.010	9.889	9.775	9.667	9.566
7.75	10.601	10.455	10.319	10.191	10.071	9.958	9.851	9.751
8	10.779	10.635	10.500	10.373	10.254	10.142	10.037	9.938
8.25	10.959	10.816	10.682	10.556	10.439	10.329	10.225	10.127
8.5	11.140	10.998	10.865	10.742	10.625	10.516	10.414	10.318
8.75	11.322	11.182	11.051	10.928	10.813	10.706	10.605	10.510
9	11.506	11.367	11.237	11.116	11.003	10.896	10.797	10.703
9.25	11.691	11.554	11.425	11.306	11.194	11.089	10.990	10.898
9.5	11.877	11.742	11.615	11.497	11.386	11.283	11.186	11.095
9.75	12.065	11.931	11.806	11.689	11.580	11.478	11.382	11.293
10	12.255	12.122	11.998	11.883	11.775	11.674	11.580	11.492
10.25	12.445	12.314	12.192	12.078	11.972	11.872	11.780	11.693
10.5	12.637	12.507	12.387	12.274	12.170	12.072	11.981	11.895
10.75	12.830	12.702	12.583	12.472	12.369	12.273	12.183	12.099
11	13.025	12.898	12.781	12.671	12.570	12.475	12.386	12.304
11.25	13.220	13.095	12.979	12.872	12.771	12.678	12.591	12.510
11.5	13.417	13.294	13.180	13.073	12.975	12.883	12.797	12.717
11.75	13.615	13.494	13.381	13.276	13.179	13.089	13.004	12.926
12	13.815	13.695	13.583	13.480	13.385	13.296	13.213	13.136
12.25	14.015	13.897	13.787	13.686	13.591	13.504	13.423	13.347
12.5	14.217	14.100	13.992	13.892	13.799	13.713	13.634	13.560
12.75	14.419	14.304	14.198	14.100	14.009	13.924	13.846	13.773
13	14.623	14.510	14.405	14.308	14.219	14.136	14.059	13.988
13.25	14.828	14.717	14.613	14.518	14.430	14.349	14.273	14.203
13.5	15.034	14.924	14.823	14.729	14.643	14.563	14.488	14.420
13.75	15.242	15.133	15.033	14.941	14.856	14.777	14.705	14.638
14	15.450	15.343	15.245	15.154	15.071	14.993	14.922	14.856
14.25	15.659	15.554	15.457	15.368	15.286	15.210	15.141	15.076
14.5	15.869	15.766	15.670	15.583	15.503	15.428	15.360	15.297
14.75	16.080	15.978	15.885	15.799	15.720	15.647	15.580	15.519
15	16.292	16.192	16.100	16.016	15.938	15.867	15.801	15.741
15.25	16.505	16.407	16.317	16.234	16.158	16.088	16.024	15.964
15.5	16.720	16.623	16.534	16.453	16.378	16.309	16.247	16.189
15.75	16.934	16.839	16.752	16.672	16.599	16.532	16.470	16.414
16	17.150	17.057	16.971	16.893	16.821	16.755	16.695	16.640
16.25	17.367	17.275	17.191	17.114	17.044	16.979	16.921	16.867
16.5	17.585	17.494	17.412	17.336	17.267	17.204	17.147	17.094
16.75	17.803	17.714	17.633	17.559	17.492	17.430	17.374	17.322
17	18.022	17.935	17.855	17.783	17.717	17.657	17.602	17.551
17.25	18.242	18.156	18.078	18.007	17.943	17.884	17.830	17.781
17.5	18.463	18.379	18.302	18.233	18.169	18.112	18.059	18.011
17.75	18.685	18.602	18.527	18.459	18.397	18.340	18.289	18.242
18	18.907	18.826	18.752	18.686	18.625	18.570	18.520	18.474

(continued)

Table A   Amortizing Mortgages with Equal Monthly Payments

Percent	Years 21	21.5	22	22.5	23	23.5	24	24.5
3	6.424	6.317	6.215	6.117	6.024	5.935	5.850	5.769
3.25	6.577	6.470	6.368	6.272	6.179	6.091	6.006	5.925
3.5	6.731	6.625	6.524	6.428	6.336	6.248	6.165	6.084
3.75	6.888	6.782	6.682	6.587	6.495	6.408	6.325	6.246
4	7.046	6.942	6.842	6.747	6.657	6.571	6.488	6.409
4.25	7.207	7.103	7.004	6.910	6.821	6.735	6.654	6.576
4.5	7.369	7.267	7.169	7.075	6.987	6.902	6.821	6.744
4.75	7.534	7.432	7.335	7.243	7.155	7.071	6.991	6.914
5	7.701	7.599	7.503	7.412	7.325	7.242	7.163	7.087
5.25	7.869	7.769	7.674	7.583	7.497	7.415	7.337	7.262
5.5	8.040	7.940	7.846	7.757	7.671	7.590	7.513	7.439
5.75	8.212	8.114	8.021	7.932	7.848	7.768	7.691	7.619
6	8.386	8.289	8.197	8.109	8.026	7.947	7.872	7.800
6.25	8.562	8.466	8.375	8.289	8.206	8.128	8.054	7.983
6.5	8.740	8.645	8.555	8.470	8.389	8.312	8.239	8.169
6.75	8.920	8.826	8.737	8.653	8.573	8.497	8.425	8.356
7	9.102	9.009	8.921	8.838	8.759	8.684	8.613	8.546
7.25	9.285	9.193	9.107	9.025	8.947	8.873	8.803	8.737
7.5	9.470	9.380	9.294	9.213	9.137	9.064	8.995	8.930
7.75	9.657	9.568	9.483	9.404	9.328	9.257	9.189	9.125
8	9.845	9.757	9.674	9.596	9.521	9.451	9.385	9.322
8.25	10.035	9.948	9.867	9.789	9.716	9.647	9.582	9.520
8.5	10.227	10.141	10.061	9.985	9.913	9.845	9.781	9.720
8.75	10.420	10.336	10.257	10.182	10.111	10.045	9.982	9.922
9	10.615	10.532	10.454	10.381	10.311	10.246	10.184	10.126
9.25	10.811	10.730	10.653	10.581	10.513	10.448	10.388	10.331
9.5	11.009	10.929	10.854	10.783	10.716	10.653	10.593	10.537
9.75	11.209	11.130	11.056	10.986	10.920	10.858	10.800	10.745
10	11.409	11.332	11.259	11.191	11.126	11.066	11.009	10.955
10.25	11.612	11.535	11.464	11.397	11.334	11.274	11.219	11.166
10.5	11.815	11.740	11.670	11.604	11.542	11.484	11.430	11.378
10.75	12.020	11.947	11.878	11.813	11.753	11.696	11.642	11.592
11	12.226	12.154	12.087	12.023	11.964	11.908	11.856	11.807
11.25	12.434	12.363	12.297	12.235	12.177	12.123	12.072	12.024
11.5	12.643	12.573	12.508	12.448	12.391	12.338	12.288	12.241
11.75	12.853	12.785	12.721	12.662	12.606	12.554	12.506	12.460
12	13.064	12.998	12.935	12.877	12.823	12.772	12.725	12.680
12.25	13.277	13.211	13.150	13.094	13.040	12.991	12.945	12.901
12.5	13.491	13.426	13.367	13.311	13.259	13.211	13.166	13.124
12.75	13.705	13.643	13.584	13.530	13.479	13.432	13.388	13.347
13	13.921	13.860	13.803	13.750	13.700	13.654	13.611	13.571
13.25	14.138	14.078	14.022	13.970	13.922	13.877	13.835	13.797
13.5	14.356	14.298	14.243	14.192	14.145	14.101	14.061	14.023
13.75	14.576	14.518	14.465	14.415	14.369	14.327	14.287	14.250
14	14.796	14.739	14.687	14.639	14.594	14.553	14.514	14.478
14.25	15.017	14.962	14.911	14.864	14.820	14.780	14.742	14.707
14.5	15.239	15.185	15.135	15.089	15.047	15.007	14.971	14.937
14.75	15.462	15.409	15.361	15.316	15.274	15.236	15.201	15.168
15	15.685	15.634	15.587	15.543	15.503	15.466	15.431	15.399
15.25	15.910	15.860	15.814	15.771	15.732	15.696	15.662	15.632
15.5	16.136	16.087	16.042	16.000	15.962	15.927	15.894	15.865
15.75	16.362	16.314	16.270	16.230	16.193	16.159	16.127	16.098
16	16.589	16.543	16.500	16.461	16.424	16.391	16.361	16.333
16.25	16.817	16.772	16.730	16.692	16.657	16.624	16.595	16.568
16.5	17.046	17.002	16.961	16.924	16.890	16.858	16.830	16.803
16.75	17.275	17.232	17.193	17.156	17.123	17.093	17.065	17.039
17	17.505	17.463	17.425	17.390	17.358	17.328	17.301	17.276
17.25	17.736	17.695	17.658	17.624	17.592	17.564	17.538	17.514
17.5	17.968	17.928	17.891	17.858	17.828	17.800	17.775	17.752
17.75	18.200	18.161	18.126	18.093	18.064	18.037	18.012	17.990
18	18.433	18.395	18.360	18.329	18.300	18.274	18.251	18.229

(continued)

Table A Amortizing Mortgages with Equal Monthly Payments

Percent	Years							
	25	25.5	26	26.5	27	27.5	28	28.5
3	5.691	5.616	5.544	5.475	5.408	5.345	5.283	5.224
3.25	5.848	5.774	5.702	5.634	5.568	5.505	5.444	5.386
3.5	6.007	5.934	5.863	5.795	5.730	5.668	5.608	5.550
3.75	6.170	6.097	6.027	5.960	5.895	5.833	5.774	5.717
4	6.334	6.262	6.193	6.126	6.062	6.001	5.943	5.886
4.25	6.501	6.429	6.361	6.295	6.232	6.172	6.114	6.058
4.5	6.670	6.599	6.532	6.467	6.405	6.345	6.288	6.233
4.75	6.841	6.772	6.705	6.641	6.579	6.521	6.464	6.410
5	7.015	6.946	6.880	6.817	6.756	6.698	6.643	6.590
5.25	7.191	7.123	7.058	6.996	6.936	6.879	6.824	6.772
5.5	7.369	7.302	7.238	7.176	7.118	7.061	7.008	6.956
5.75	7.549	7.483	7.420	7.359	7.302	7.246	7.193	7.143
6	7.732	7.666	7.604	7.545	7.488	7.433	7.381	7.332
6.25	7.916	7.852	7.791	7.732	7.676	7.623	7.572	7.523
6.5	8.102	8.039	7.979	7.922	7.867	7.814	7.764	7.716
6.75	8.291	8.229	8.170	8.113	8.059	8.008	7.959	7.912
7	8.481	8.420	8.362	8.307	8.254	8.203	8.155	8.109
7.25	8.674	8.614	8.557	8.502	8.450	8.401	8.354	8.309
7.5	8.868	8.809	8.753	8.700	8.649	8.600	8.554	8.511
7.75	9.064	9.006	8.951	8.899	8.849	8.802	8.757	8.714
8	9.262	9.205	9.151	9.100	9.051	9.005	8.961	8.919
8.25	9.461	9.406	9.353	9.303	9.255	9.210	9.167	9.126
8.5	9.663	9.608	9.557	9.508	9.461	9.417	9.375	9.335
8.75	9.866	9.812	9.762	9.714	9.668	9.625	9.584	9.546
9	10.070	10.018	9.969	9.922	9.878	9.835	9.796	9.758
9.25	10.277	10.225	10.177	10.131	10.088	10.047	10.008	9.972
9.5	10.484	10.434	10.387	10.343	10.300	10.260	10.223	10.187
9.75	10.694	10.645	10.599	10.555	10.514	10.475	10.438	10.404
10	10.904	10.857	10.812	10.769	10.729	10.691	10.656	10.622
10.25	11.117	11.070	11.026	10.985	10.946	10.909	10.874	10.841
10.5	11.330	11.285	11.242	11.202	11.164	11.128	11.094	11.062
10.75	11.545	11.501	11.459	11.420	11.383	11.348	11.315	11.284
11	11.761	11.718	11.678	11.639	11.603	11.570	11.538	11.508
11.25	11.979	11.937	11.897	11.860	11.825	11.792	11.761	11.732
11.5	12.198	12.157	12.118	12.082	12.048	12.016	11.986	11.958
11.75	12.418	12.378	12.340	12.305	12.272	12.241	12.212	12.185
12	12.639	12.600	12.563	12.529	12.497	12.467	12.439	12.413
12.25	12.861	12.823	12.788	12.755	12.724	12.695	12.667	12.642
12.5	13.084	13.047	13.013	12.981	12.951	12.923	12.897	12.872
12.75	13.309	13.273	13.240	13.208	13.179	13.152	13.127	13.103
13	13.534	13.499	13.467	13.437	13.409	13.382	13.358	13.335
13.25	13.760	13.727	13.695	13.666	13.639	13.613	13.589	13.567
13.5	13.988	13.955	13.925	13.896	13.870	13.845	13.822	13.801
13.75	14.216	14.184	14.155	14.127	14.102	14.078	14.056	14.035
14	14.445	14.414	14.386	14.359	14.334	14.311	14.290	14.270
14.25	14.675	14.645	14.618	14.592	14.568	14.546	14.525	14.506
14.5	14.906	14.877	14.850	14.825	14.802	14.781	14.761	14.742
14.75	15.138	15.110	15.084	15.059	15.037	15.017	14.997	14.980
15	15.370	15.343	15.318	15.294	15.273	15.253	15.234	15.217
15.25	15.603	15.577	15.552	15.530	15.509	15.490	15.472	15.456
15.5	15.837	15.811	15.788	15.766	15.746	15.728	15.711	15.695
15.75	16.071	16.047	16.024	16.003	15.984	15.966	15.950	15.934
16	16.307	16.283	16.261	16.241	16.222	16.205	16.189	16.174
16.25	16.542	16.519	16.498	16.479	16.461	16.444	16.429	16.415
16.5	16.779	16.757	16.736	16.717	16.700	16.684	16.669	16.656
16.75	17.016	16.994	16.975	16.957	16.940	16.925	16.910	16.898
17	17.254	17.233	17.214	17.196	17.180	17.165	17.152	17.140
17.25	17.492	17.472	17.453	17.436	17.421	17.407	17.394	17.382
17.5	17.730	17.711	17.693	17.677	17.662	17.649	17.636	17.625
17.75	17.970	17.951	17.934	17.918	17.904	17.891	17.879	17.868
18	18.209	18.191	18.175	18.160	18.146	18.133	18.122	18.111

(continued)

Table A   Amortizing Mortgages with Equal Monthly Payments

Percent	29	29.5	30	30.5	31	31.5	32	32.5
3	5.167	5.112	5.059	5.008	4.959	4.911	4.865	4.820
3.25	5.329	5.275	5.222	5.172	5.123	5.076	5.031	4.987
3.5	5.494	5.440	5.389	5.339	5.290	5.244	5.199	5.156
3.75	5.661	5.608	5.557	5.508	5.461	5.415	5.371	5.328
4	5.832	5.779	5.729	5.680	5.634	5.589	5.545	5.503
4.25	6.005	5.953	5.903	5.855	5.809	5.765	5.722	5.681
4.5	6.180	6.129	6.080	6.033	5.988	5.944	5.902	5.862
4.75	6.358	6.308	6.260	6.214	6.169	6.126	6.085	6.045
5	6.538	6.489	6.442	6.396	6.353	6.311	6.270	6.231
5.25	6.721	6.673	6.626	6.582	6.539	6.498	6.458	6.420
5.5	6.907	6.859	6.813	6.770	6.728	6.687	6.648	6.611
5.75	7.094	7.048	7.003	6.960	6.919	6.879	6.841	6.805
6	7.284	7.238	7.195	7.153	7.112	7.074	7.037	7.001
6.25	7.476	7.431	7.389	7.348	7.308	7.270	7.234	7.199
6.5	7.671	7.627	7.585	7.545	7.506	7.469	7.434	7.400
6.75	7.867	7.824	7.783	7.744	7.706	7.670	7.636	7.603
7	8.066	8.024	7.984	7.945	7.909	7.874	7.840	7.808
7.25	8.266	8.225	8.186	8.149	8.113	8.079	8.046	8.015
7.5	8.469	8.429	8.391	8.354	8.319	8.286	8.254	8.224
7.75	8.673	8.634	8.597	8.561	8.528	8.495	8.465	8.435
8	8.879	8.841	8.805	8.771	8.738	8.706	8.676	8.648
8.25	9.087	9.050	9.015	8.982	8.950	8.919	8.890	8.862
8.5	9.297	9.261	9.227	9.194	9.163	9.134	9.106	9.079
8.75	9.509	9.474	9.440	9.409	9.379	9.350	9.323	9.297
9	9.722	9.688	9.655	9.625	9.596	9.568	9.541	9.516
9.25	9.937	9.904	9.872	9.842	9.814	9.787	9.762	9.737
9.5	10.153	10.121	10.090	10.061	10.034	10.008	9.983	9.960
9.75	10.371	10.339	10.310	10.282	10.255	10.230	10.206	10.184
10	10.590	10.559	10.531	10.504	10.478	10.454	10.431	10.409
10.25	10.810	10.781	10.753	10.727	10.702	10.679	10.657	10.636
10.5	11.032	11.004	10.977	10.952	10.928	10.905	10.884	10.863
10.75	11.255	11.228	11.202	11.177	11.154	11.132	11.112	11.092
11	11.480	11.453	11.428	11.404	11.382	11.361	11.341	11.322
11.25	11.705	11.679	11.655	11.632	11.611	11.591	11.572	11.554
11.5	11.932	11.907	11.883	11.861	11.841	11.821	11.803	11.786
11.75	12.160	12.135	12.113	12.092	12.072	12.053	12.035	12.019
12	12.388	12.365	12.343	12.323	12.304	12.286	12.269	12.253
12.25	12.618	12.596	12.575	12.555	12.537	12.519	12.503	12.488
12.5	12.849	12.827	12.807	12.788	12.770	12.754	12.738	12.724
12.75	13.081	13.060	13.040	13.022	13.005	12.989	12.974	12.960
13	13.313	13.293	13.274	13.257	13.240	13.225	13.211	13.197
13.25	13.547	13.527	13.509	13.492	13.477	13.462	13.448	13.435
13.5	13.781	13.762	13.745	13.729	13.714	13.700	13.686	13.674
13.75	14.016	13.998	13.981	13.966	13.951	13.938	13.925	13.914
14	14.252	14.234	14.218	14.204	14.190	14.177	14.165	14.154
14.25	14.488	14.472	14.456	14.442	14.429	14.416	14.405	14.394
14.5	14.725	14.709	14.695	14.681	14.668	14.656	14.645	14.635
14.75	14.963	14.948	14.934	14.921	14.908	14.897	14.887	14.877
15	15.202	15.187	15.173	15.161	15.149	15.138	15.128	15.119
15.25	15.441	15.427	15.414	15.401	15.390	15.380	15.370	15.362
15.5	15.680	15.667	15.654	15.643	15.632	15.622	15.613	15.605
15.75	15.920	15.907	15.895	15.884	15.874	15.865	15.856	15.848
16	16.161	16.149	16.137	16.127	16.117	16.108	16.100	16.092
16.25	16.402	16.390	16.379	16.369	16.360	16.351	16.343	16.336
16.5	16.644	16.632	16.622	16.612	16.603	16.595	16.588	16.581
16.75	16.886	16.875	16.865	16.856	16.847	16.839	16.832	16.826
17	17.128	17.118	17.108	17.099	17.091	17.084	17.077	17.071
17.25	17.371	17.361	17.352	17.343	17.336	17.329	17.322	17.316
17.5	17.614	17.605	17.596	17.588	17.581	17.574	17.568	17.562
17.75	17.858	17.849	17.840	17.833	17.826	17.819	17.813	17.808
18	18.102	18.093	18.085	18.078	18.071	18.065	18.059	18.054

(continued)

Table A   Amortizing Mortgages with Equal Monthly Payments

Percent	33	33.5	34	34.5	35	35.5	36	36.5
3	4.777	4.736	4.695	4.656	4.618	4.581	4.546	4.511
3.25	4.944	4.903	4.863	4.825	4.787	4.751	4.716	4.682
3.5	5.114	5.073	5.034	4.996	4.959	4.924	4.889	4.856
3.75	5.287	5.247	5.208	5.171	5.135	5.100	5.066	5.033
4	5.462	5.423	5.385	5.349	5.313	5.279	5.246	5.214
4.25	5.641	5.603	5.565	5.529	5.495	5.461	5.429	5.397
4.5	5.822	5.785	5.748	5.713	5.679	5.646	5.614	5.584
4.75	6.007	5.970	5.934	5.900	5.866	5.834	5.803	5.773
5	6.194	6.157	6.122	6.089	6.056	6.025	5.995	5.965
5.25	6.383	6.348	6.314	6.281	6.249	6.218	6.189	6.160
5.5	6.575	6.541	6.507	6.475	6.444	6.414	6.386	6.358
5.75	6.770	6.736	6.703	6.672	6.642	6.613	6.585	6.558
6	6.967	6.934	6.902	6.872	6.842	6.814	6.787	6.761
6.25	7.166	7.134	7.103	7.073	7.045	7.018	6.991	6.966
6.5	7.368	7.336	7.306	7.278	7.250	7.223	7.198	7.173
6.75	7.571	7.541	7.512	7.484	7.457	7.431	7.406	7.383
7	7.777	7.748	7.719	7.692	7.666	7.641	7.617	7.594
7.25	7.985	7.956	7.929	7.903	7.878	7.853	7.830	7.808
7.5	8.195	8.167	8.141	8.115	8.091	8.068	8.045	8.024
7.75	8.407	8.380	8.354	8.330	8.306	8.284	8.262	8.241
8	8.621	8.595	8.570	8.546	8.523	8.501	8.481	8.461
8.25	8.836	8.811	8.787	8.764	8.742	8.721	8.701	8.682
8.5	9.053	9.029	9.006	8.983	8.962	8.942	8.923	8.905
8.75	9.272	9.248	9.226	9.205	9.184	9.165	9.146	9.129
9	9.492	9.470	9.448	9.428	9.408	9.389	9.371	9.355
9.25	9.714	9.692	9.672	9.652	9.633	9.615	9.598	9.582
9.5	9.938	9.917	9.896	9.877	9.859	9.842	9.826	9.810
9.75	10.162	10.142	10.123	10.104	10.087	10.071	10.055	10.040
10	10.388	10.369	10.350	10.333	10.316	10.300	10.285	10.271
10.25	10.616	10.597	10.579	10.562	10.546	10.531	10.517	10.503
10.5	10.844	10.826	10.809	10.793	10.778	10.763	10.749	10.736
10.75	11.074	11.057	11.040	11.025	11.010	10.996	10.983	10.971
11	11.305	11.288	11.272	11.258	11.243	11.230	11.218	11.206
11.25	11.537	11.521	11.506	11.491	11.478	11.465	11.453	11.442
11.5	11.769	11.754	11.740	11.726	11.713	11.701	11.690	11.679
11.75	12.003	11.989	11.975	11.962	11.950	11.938	11.927	11.917
12	12.238	12.224	12.211	12.198	12.187	12.176	12.165	12.156
12.25	12.473	12.460	12.447	12.436	12.424	12.414	12.404	12.395
12.5	12.710	12.697	12.685	12.674	12.663	12.653	12.644	12.635
12.75	12.947	12.935	12.923	12.912	12.902	12.893	12.884	12.876
13	13.185	13.173	13.162	13.152	13.142	13.133	13.125	13.117
13.25	13.424	13.412	13.402	13.392	13.383	13.374	13.366	13.359
13.5	13.663	13.652	13.642	13.633	13.624	13.616	13.608	13.601
13.75	13.903	13.892	13.883	13.874	13.866	13.858	13.851	13.844
14	14.143	14.133	14.124	14.116	14.108	14.101	14.094	14.088
14.25	14.384	14.375	14.366	14.358	14.351	14.344	14.337	14.331
14.5	14.626	14.617	14.609	14.601	14.594	14.587	14.581	14.576
14.75	14.868	14.859	14.852	14.844	14.838	14.831	14.826	14.820
15	15.110	15.102	15.095	15.088	15.082	15.076	15.070	15.065
15.25	15.353	15.346	15.339	15.332	15.326	15.321	15.315	15.311
15.5	15.597	15.590	15.583	15.577	15.571	15.566	15.561	15.556
15.75	15.841	15.834	15.827	15.822	15.816	15.811	15.807	15.802
16	16.085	16.078	16.072	16.067	16.062	16.057	16.053	16.049
16.25	16.329	16.323	16.317	16.312	16.307	16.303	16.299	16.295
16.5	16.574	16.568	16.563	16.558	16.553	16.549	16.545	16.542
16.75	16.819	16.814	16.809	16.804	16.800	16.796	16.792	16.789
17	17.065	17.060	17.055	17.050	17.046	17.043	17.039	17.036
17.25	17.311	17.306	17.301	17.297	17.293	17.290	17.286	17.283
17.5	17.557	17.552	17.548	17.544	17.540	17.537	17.534	17.531
17.75	17.803	17.799	17.795	17.791	17.787	17.784	17.781	17.779
18	18.050	18.045	18.042	18.038	18.035	18.032	18.029	18.027

(continued)

Table A Amortizing Mortgages with Equal Monthly Payments

Percent	37	37.5	38	38.5	39	39.5	40
3	4.478	4.445	4.414	4.383	4.353	4.324	4.296
3.25	4.649	4.617	4.586	4.556	4.527	4.498	4.470
3.5	4.824	4.792	4.762	4.732	4.704	4.676	4.649
3.75	5.002	4.971	4.941	4.912	4.884	4.857	4.830
4	5.183	5.153	5.123	5.095	5.068	5.041	5.015
4.25	5.367	5.337	5.309	5.281	5.255	5.229	5.203
4.5	5.554	5.525	5.497	5.471	5.444	5.419	5.395
4.75	5.744	5.716	5.689	5.663	5.637	5.613	5.589
5	5.937	5.910	5.883	5.858	5.833	5.809	5.786
5.25	6.133	6.106	6.081	6.056	6.032	6.009	5.986
5.5	6.331	6.305	6.281	6.257	6.233	6.211	6.189
5.75	6.532	6.507	6.483	6.460	6.437	6.416	6.395
6	6.736	6.711	6.688	6.665	6.644	6.623	6.603
6.25	6.941	6.918	6.895	6.874	6.853	6.832	6.813
6.5	7.150	7.127	7.105	7.084	7.064	7.044	7.025
6.75	7.360	7.338	7.317	7.297	7.277	7.258	7.240
7	7.572	7.551	7.531	7.511	7.493	7.475	7.457
7.25	7.787	7.766	7.747	7.728	7.710	7.693	7.676
7.5	8.003	7.984	7.965	7.947	7.929	7.913	7.897
7.75	8.222	8.203	8.185	8.167	8.151	8.135	8.119
8	8.442	8.424	8.406	8.390	8.374	8.358	8.344
8.25	8.664	8.646	8.629	8.613	8.598	8.584	8.570
8.5	8.887	8.870	8.854	8.839	8.824	8.810	8.797
8.75	9.112	9.096	9.081	9.066	9.052	9.039	9.026
9	9.338	9.323	9.308	9.294	9.281	9.268	9.256
9.25	9.566	9.552	9.538	9.524	9.512	9.499	9.488
9.5	9.795	9.781	9.768	9.755	9.743	9.732	9.721
9.75	10.026	10.012	10.000	9.988	9.976	9.965	9.955
10	10.258	10.245	10.233	10.221	10.210	10.200	10.190
10.25	10.490	10.478	10.466	10.455	10.445	10.435	10.426
10.5	10.724	10.712	10.701	10.691	10.681	10.672	10.663
10.75	10.959	10.948	10.937	10.927	10.918	10.909	10.901
11	11.195	11.184	11.174	11.165	11.156	11.147	11.140
11.25	11.431	11.421	11.412	11.403	11.395	11.387	11.379
11.5	11.669	11.659	11.650	11.642	11.634	11.626	11.619
11.75	11.907	11.898	11.890	11.882	11.874	11.867	11.860
12	12.146	12.138	12.130	12.122	12.115	12.108	12.102
12.25	12.386	12.378	12.371	12.363	12.357	12.350	12.344
12.5	12.627	12.619	12.612	12.605	12.599	12.593	12.587
12.75	12.868	12.861	12.854	12.847	12.841	12.836	12.830
13	13.110	13.103	13.096	13.090	13.084	13.079	13.074
13.25	13.352	13.345	13.339	13.333	13.328	13.323	13.318
13.5	13.595	13.588	13.583	13.577	13.572	13.568	13.563
13.75	13.838	13.832	13.827	13.822	13.817	13.812	13.808
14	14.082	14.076	14.071	14.066	14.062	14.058	14.054
14.25	14.326	14.321	14.316	14.311	14.307	14.303	14.299
14.5	14.570	14.565	14.561	14.557	14.553	14.549	14.546
14.75	14.815	14.811	14.806	14.802	14.799	14.795	14.792
15	15.061	15.056	15.052	15.048	15.045	15.042	15.039
15.25	15.306	15.302	15.298	15.295	15.291	15.288	15.286
15.5	15.552	15.548	15.545	15.541	15.538	15.535	15.533
15.75	15.798	15.795	15.791	15.788	15.785	15.783	15.780
16	16.045	16.041	16.038	16.035	16.033	16.030	16.028
16.25	16.292	16.288	16.285	16.283	16.280	16.278	16.276
16.5	16.538	16.535	16.533	16.530	16.528	16.526	16.524
16.75	16.786	16.783	16.780	16.778	16.776	16.774	16.772
17	17.033	17.030	17.028	17.026	17.024	17.022	17.020
17.25	17.281	17.278	17.276	17.274	17.272	17.270	17.268
17.5	17.528	17.526	17.524	17.522	17.520	17.518	17.517
17.75	17.776	17.774	17.772	17.770	17.768	17.767	17.765
18	18.024	18.022	18.020	18.019	18.017	18.016	18.014

Table B Amortizing Mortgages with One Equal Annual Payment

Percent	Years							
	1	1.5	2	2.5	3	3.5	4	4.5
5	105.000	70.850	53.780	43.543	36.721	31.851	28.201	25.365
5.25	105.250	71.060	53.971	43.722	36.893	32.018	28.365	25.526
5.5	105.500	71.270	54.162	43.902	37.065	32.186	28.529	25.688
5.75	105.750	71.481	54.353	44.081	37.238	32.354	28.694	25.851
6	106.000	71.691	54.544	44.261	37.411	32.522	28.859	26.013
6.25	106.250	71.901	54.735	44.441	37.584	32.691	29.025	26.177
6.5	106.500	72.112	54.926	44.622	37.758	32.860	29.190	26.340
6.75	106.750	72.322	55.118	44.802	37.931	33.029	29.356	26.504
7	107.000	72.533	55.309	44.983	38.105	33.198	29.523	26.669
7.25	107.250	72.744	55.501	45.164	38.279	33.368	29.690	26.833
7.5	107.500	72.954	55.693	45.345	38.454	33.538	29.857	26.999
7.75	107.750	73.165	55.885	45.526	38.628	33.708	30.024	27.164
8	108.000	73.376	56.077	45.708	38.803	33.879	30.192	27.330
8.25	108.250	73.587	56.269	45.889	38.979	34.050	30.360	27.497
8.5	108.500	73.798	56.462	46.071	39.154	34.221	30.529	27.663
8.75	108.750	74.009	56.654	46.253	39.330	34.393	30.698	27.830
9	109.000	74.221	56.847	46.436	39.505	34.565	30.867	27.998
9.25	109.250	74.432	57.040	46.618	39.682	34.737	31.036	28.166
9.5	109.500	74.643	57.233	46.801	39.858	34.909	31.206	28.334
9.75	109.750	74.855	57.426	46.984	40.035	35.082	31.377	28.503
10	110.000	75.066	57.619	47.167	40.211	35.255	31.547	28.672
10.25	110.250	75.278	57.812	47.350	40.389	35.428	31.718	28.841
10.5	110.500	75.489	58.006	47.533	40.566	35.602	31.889	29.011
10.75	110.750	75.701	58.200	47.717	40.743	35.775	32.061	29.182
11	111.000	75.913	58.393	47.901	40.921	35.950	32.233	29.352
11.25	111.250	76.125	58.587	48.085	41.099	36.124	32.405	29.523
11.5	111.500	76.337	58.781	48.269	41.278	36.299	32.577	29.694
11.75	111.750	76.549	58.976	48.453	41.456	36.474	32.750	29.866
12	112.000	76.761	59.170	48.638	41.635	36.649	32.923	30.038
12.25	112.250	76.973	59.364	48.822	41.814	36.824	33.097	30.211
12.5	112.500	77.185	59.559	49.007	41.993	37.000	33.271	30.383
12.75	112.750	77.398	59.754	49.192	42.173	37.176	33.445	30.557
13	113.000	77.610	59.948	49.378	42.352	37.353	33.619	30.730
13.25	113.250	77.823	60.143	49.563	42.532	37.529	33.794	30.904
13.5	113.500	78.035	60.338	49.749	42.712	37.706	33.969	31.078
13.75	113.750	78.248	60.534	49.934	42.893	37.883	34.145	31.253
14	114.000	78.461	60.729	50.120	43.073	38.061	34.320	31.428
14.25	114.250	78.673	60.924	50.307	43.254	38.239	34.497	31.603
14.5	114.500	78.886	61.120	50.493	43.435	38.417	34.673	31.779
14.75	114.750	79.099	61.316	50.679	43.616	38.595	34.850	31.955
15	115.000	79.312	61.512	50.866	43.798	38.773	35.027	32.131
15.25	115.250	79.525	61.708	51.053	43.979	38.952	35.204	32.308
15.5	115.500	79.738	61.904	51.240	44.161	39.131	35.381	32.485
15.75	115.750	79.951	62.100	51.427	44.343	39.311	35.559	32.662
16	116.000	80.165	62.296	51.614	44.526	39.490	35.738	32.840
16.25	116.250	80.378	62.493	51.802	44.708	39.670	35.916	33.018
16.5	116.500	80.591	62.689	51.990	44.891	39.850	36.095	33.197
16.75	116.750	80.805	62.886	52.178	45.074	40.030	36.274	33.375
17	117.000	81.018	63.083	52.366	45.257	40.211	36.453	33.554
17.25	117.250	81.232	63.280	52.554	45.441	40.392	36.633	33.734
17.5	117.500	81.446	63.477	52.742	45.624	40.573	36.813	33.914
17.75	117.750	81.659	63.674	52.931	45.808	40.754	36.993	34.094
18	118.000	81.873	63.872	53.120	45.992	40.936	37.174	34.274
18.25	118.250	82.087	64.069	53.309	46.177	41.118	37.355	34.455
18.5	118.500	82.301	64.267	53.498	46.361	41.300	37.536	34.636
18.75	118.750	82.515	64.464	53.687	46.546	41.483	37.717	34.817
19	119.000	82.729	64.662	53.876	46.731	41.665	37.899	34.999
19.25	119.250	82.943	64.860	54.066	46.916	41.848	38.081	35.181
19.5	119.500	83.157	65.058	54.256	47.101	42.031	38.263	35.364
19.75	119.750	83.372	65.256	54.446	47.287	42.215	38.446	35.546
20	120.000	83.586	65.455	54.636	47.473	42.398	38.629	35.729

(continued)

Table B Amortizing Mortgages with One Equal Annual Payment

	Years							
Percent	5	5.5	6	6.5	7	7.5	8	8.5
5	23.097	21.244	19.702	18.398	17.282	16.316	15.472	14.729
5.25	23.257	21.403	19.860	18.555	17.439	16.473	15.629	14.886
5.5	23.418	21.562	20.018	18.713	17.596	16.630	15.786	15.043
5.75	23.578	21.722	20.177	18.872	17.755	16.788	15.945	15.202
6	23.740	21.882	20.336	19.031	17.914	16.947	16.104	15.361
6.25	23.901	22.043	20.496	19.190	18.073	17.107	16.263	15.521
6.5	24.063	22.204	20.657	19.350	18.233	17.267	16.424	15.682
6.75	24.226	22.365	20.818	19.511	18.394	17.428	16.585	15.843
7	24.389	22.528	20.980	19.673	18.555	17.589	16.747	16.005
7.25	24.553	22.690	21.142	19.835	18.717	17.752	16.909	16.169
7.5	24.716	22.853	21.304	19.997	18.880	17.915	17.073	16.332
7.75	24.881	23.017	21.468	20.160	19.043	18.078	17.237	16.497
8	25.046	23.181	21.632	20.324	19.207	18.243	17.401	16.662
8.25	25.211	23.346	21.796	20.489	19.372	18.407	17.567	16.828
8.5	25.377	23.511	21.961	20.653	19.537	18.573	17.733	16.995
8.75	25.543	23.676	22.126	20.819	19.703	18.739	17.900	17.163
9	25.709	23.842	22.292	20.985	19.869	18.906	18.067	17.331
9.25	25.876	24.009	22.458	21.152	20.036	19.074	18.236	17.500
9.5	26.044	24.176	22.625	21.319	20.204	19.242	18.405	17.670
9.75	26.211	24.343	22.793	21.486	20.372	19.411	18.574	17.840
10	26.380	24.511	22.961	21.655	20.541	19.580	18.744	18.011
10.25	26.548	24.680	23.129	21.823	20.710	19.750	18.915	18.183
10.5	26.718	24.849	23.298	21.993	20.880	19.921	19.087	18.356
10.75	26.887	25.018	23.468	22.163	21.050	20.092	19.259	18.529
11	27.057	25.188	23.638	22.333	21.222	20.264	19.432	18.703
11.25	27.227	25.358	23.808	22.504	21.393	20.437	19.606	18.878
11.5	27.398	25.529	23.979	22.676	21.566	20.610	19.780	19.053
11.75	27.569	25.700	24.151	22.848	21.738	20.784	19.955	19.229
12	27.741	25.871	24.323	23.020	21.912	20.958	20.130	19.406
12.25	27.913	26.043	24.495	23.193	22.086	21.133	20.306	19.583
12.5	28.085	26.216	24.668	23.367	22.260	21.309	20.483	19.761
12.75	28.258	26.389	24.841	23.541	22.435	21.485	20.661	19.940
13	28.431	26.562	25.015	23.716	22.611	21.662	20.839	20.120
13.25	28.605	26.736	25.190	23.891	22.787	21.839	21.017	20.300
13.5	28.779	26.910	25.365	24.067	22.964	22.017	21.197	20.480
13.75	28.954	27.085	25.540	24.243	23.141	22.196	21.377	20.662
14	29.128	27.260	25.716	24.420	23.319	22.375	21.557	20.844
14.25	29.304	27.436	25.892	24.597	23.498	22.554	21.738	21.026
14.5	29.479	27.612	26.069	24.775	23.677	22.735	21.920	21.209
14.75	29.655	27.788	26.246	24.953	23.856	22.916	22.102	21.393
15	29.832	27.965	26.424	25.132	24.036	23.097	22.285	21.578
15.25	30.008	28.143	26.602	25.311	24.217	23.279	22.468	21.763
15.5	30.185	28.320	26.780	25.491	24.398	23.461	22.653	21.948
15.75	30.363	28.498	26.959	25.671	24.579	23.644	22.837	22.135
16	30.541	28.677	27.139	25.852	24.761	23.828	23.022	22.322
16.25	30.719	28.856	27.319	26.033	24.944	24.012	23.208	22.509
16.5	30.898	29.035	27.499	26.215	25.127	24.197	23.395	22.697
16.75	31.077	29.215	27.680	26.397	25.311	24.382	23.582	22.886
17	31.256	29.395	27.861	26.579	25.495	24.568	23.769	23.075
17.25	31.436	29.576	28.043	26.762	25.679	24.754	23.957	23.265
17.5	31.616	29.757	28.225	26.946	25.864	24.941	24.146	23.456
17.75	31.797	29.938	28.408	27.130	26.050	25.128	24.335	23.647
18	31.978	30.120	28.591	27.315	26.236	25.316	24.524	23.838
18.25	32.159	30.302	28.774	27.499	26.423	25.505	24.715	24.030
18.5	32.341	30.485	28.958	27.685	26.610	25.693	24.905	24.223
18.75	32.523	30.668	29.143	27.871	26.797	25.883	25.097	24.416
19	32.705	30.851	29.327	28.057	26.985	26.073	25.289	24.610
19.25	32.888	31.035	29.513	28.244	27.174	26.263	25.481	24.804
19.5	33.071	31.219	29.698	28.431	27.363	26.454	25.674	24.999
19.75	33.254	31.404	29.884	28.619	27.552	26.645	25.867	25.195
20	33.438	31.589	30.071	28.807	27.742	26.837	26.061	25.391

(continued)

Table B Amortizing Mortgages with One Equal Annual Payment

Percent	9	9.5	10	10.5	11	11.5	12	12.5
5	14.069	13.480	12.950	12.472	12.039	11.644	11.283	10.951
5.25	14.226	13.637	13.108	12.631	12.197	11.803	11.442	11.111
5.5	14.384	13.795	13.267	12.790	12.357	11.963	11.603	11.273
5.75	14.543	13.954	13.426	12.950	12.518	12.124	11.765	11.435
6	14.702	14.114	13.587	13.111	12.679	12.287	11.928	11.599
6.25	14.863	14.275	13.748	13.273	12.842	12.450	12.092	11.763
6.5	15.024	14.437	13.910	13.436	13.006	12.614	12.257	11.929
6.75	15.186	14.600	14.074	13.600	13.170	12.780	12.423	12.096
7	15.349	14.763	14.238	13.764	13.336	12.946	12.590	12.264
7.25	15.512	14.927	14.403	13.930	13.502	13.113	12.758	12.434
7.5	15.677	15.092	14.569	14.097	13.670	13.282	12.928	12.604
7.75	15.842	15.258	14.735	14.264	13.838	13.451	13.098	12.775
8	16.008	15.425	14.903	14.433	14.008	13.621	13.270	12.948
8.25	16.175	15.593	15.071	14.602	14.178	13.793	13.442	13.121
8.5	16.342	15.761	15.241	14.773	14.349	13.965	13.615	13.295
8.75	16.511	15.930	15.411	14.944	14.522	14.138	13.790	13.471
9	16.680	16.100	15.582	15.116	14.695	14.313	13.965	13.648
9.25	16.850	16.271	15.754	15.289	14.869	14.488	14.141	13.825
9.5	17.020	16.443	15.927	15.463	15.044	14.664	14.319	14.004
9.75	17.192	16.615	16.100	15.637	15.220	14.841	14.497	14.183
10	17.364	16.789	16.275	15.813	15.396	15.019	14.676	14.364
10.25	17.537	16.963	16.450	15.989	15.574	15.198	14.857	14.545
10.5	17.711	17.138	16.626	16.166	15.752	15.378	15.038	14.728
10.75	17.885	17.313	16.803	16.345	15.932	15.559	15.220	14.911
11	18.060	17.489	16.980	16.523	16.112	15.740	15.403	15.096
11.25	18.236	17.667	17.159	16.703	16.293	15.923	15.587	15.281
11.5	18.413	17.844	17.338	16.884	16.475	16.106	15.771	15.467
11.75	18.590	18.023	17.518	17.065	16.658	16.290	15.957	15.654
12	18.768	18.202	17.698	17.247	16.842	16.475	16.144	15.842
12.25	18.947	18.382	17.880	17.430	17.026	16.661	16.331	16.031
12.5	19.126	18.563	18.062	17.614	17.211	16.848	16.519	16.221
12.75	19.306	18.745	18.245	17.798	17.397	17.036	16.709	16.412
13	19.487	18.927	18.429	17.984	17.584	17.224	16.899	16.603
13.25	19.668	19.110	18.613	18.170	17.772	17.413	17.089	16.796
13.5	19.851	19.294	18.799	18.357	17.960	17.603	17.281	16.989
13.75	20.033	19.478	18.985	18.544	18.149	17.794	17.474	17.183
14	20.217	19.663	19.171	18.733	18.339	17.986	17.667	17.378
14.25	20.401	19.849	19.359	18.922	18.530	18.178	17.861	17.574
14.5	20.586	20.035	19.547	19.111	18.722	18.372	18.056	17.771
14.75	20.771	20.222	19.736	19.302	18.914	18.565	18.252	17.968
15	20.957	20.410	19.925	19.493	19.107	18.760	18.448	18.166
15.25	21.144	20.599	20.115	19.685	19.301	18.956	18.645	18.365
15.5	21.332	20.788	20.306	19.878	19.495	19.152	18.843	18.565
15.75	21.520	20.978	20.498	20.071	19.690	19.349	19.042	18.765
16	21.708	21.168	20.690	20.265	19.886	19.547	19.241	18.967
16.25	21.898	21.359	20.883	20.460	20.083	19.745	19.442	19.169
16.5	22.087	21.551	21.077	20.655	20.280	19.944	19.643	19.371
16.75	22.278	21.743	21.271	20.851	20.478	20.144	19.844	19.575
17	22.469	21.936	21.466	21.048	20.676	20.344	20.047	19.779
17.25	22.661	22.130	21.661	21.246	20.876	20.545	20.250	19.984
17.5	22.853	22.324	21.857	21.444	21.076	20.747	20.453	20.189
17.75	23.046	22.519	22.054	21.642	21.276	20.950	20.658	20.396
18	23.239	22.714	22.251	21.842	21.478	21.153	20.863	20.603
18.25	23.434	22.910	22.449	22.042	21.680	21.357	21.069	20.810
18.5	23.628	23.107	22.648	22.242	21.882	21.561	21.275	21.018
18.75	23.823	23.304	22.847	22.443	22.085	21.766	21.482	21.227
19	24.019	23.502	23.047	22.645	22.289	21.972	21.690	21.437
19.25	24.216	23.700	23.248	22.848	22.494	22.179	21.898	21.647
19.5	24.412	23.899	23.449	23.051	22.699	22.386	22.107	21.858
19.75	24.610	24.099	23.650	23.254	22.904	22.593	22.316	22.069
20	24.808	24.299	23.852	23.459	23.110	22.801	22.526	22.281

(continued)

635

Table B Amortizing Mortgages with One Equal Annual Payment

Percent	\multicolumn{8}{c}{Years}							
	13	13.5	14	14.5	15	15.5	16	16.5
5	10.646	10.364	10.102	9.860	9.634	9.424	9.227	9.043
5.25	10.806	10.525	10.265	10.023	9.798	9.588	9.392	9.208
5.5	10.968	10.688	10.428	10.187	9.963	9.754	9.558	9.376
5.75	11.132	10.852	10.593	10.352	10.129	9.920	9.726	9.544
6	11.296	11.017	10.758	10.519	10.296	10.089	9.895	9.714
6.25	11.462	11.183	10.926	10.687	10.465	10.259	10.066	9.886
6.5	11.628	11.351	11.094	10.856	10.635	10.430	10.238	10.058
6.75	11.796	11.519	11.264	11.027	10.807	10.602	10.411	10.233
7	11.965	11.689	11.434	11.199	10.979	10.776	10.586	10.408
7.25	12.135	11.860	11.607	11.372	11.153	10.951	10.762	10.585
7.5	12.306	12.033	11.780	11.546	11.329	11.127	10.939	10.764
7.75	12.479	12.206	11.954	11.721	11.505	11.305	11.118	10.944
8	12.652	12.380	12.130	11.898	11.683	11.483	11.298	11.125
8.25	12.827	12.556	12.306	12.076	11.862	11.663	11.479	11.307
8.5	13.002	12.733	12.484	12.255	12.042	11.845	11.661	11.491
8.75	13.179	12.911	12.663	12.435	12.223	12.027	11.845	11.675
9	13.357	13.089	12.843	12.616	12.406	12.211	12.030	11.862
9.25	13.535	13.269	13.025	12.799	12.590	12.396	12.216	12.049
9.5	13.715	13.450	13.207	12.982	12.774	12.582	12.403	12.238
9.75	13.896	13.633	13.390	13.167	12.960	12.769	12.592	12.427
10	14.078	13.816	13.575	13.352	13.147	12.958	12.782	12.618
10.25	14.261	14.000	13.760	13.539	13.336	13.147	12.972	12.810
10.5	14.445	14.185	13.947	13.727	13.525	13.338	13.164	13.004
10.75	14.629	14.371	14.134	13.916	13.715	13.529	13.358	13.198
11	14.815	14.558	14.323	14.106	13.907	13.722	13.552	13.394
11.25	15.002	14.747	14.512	14.297	14.099	13.916	13.747	13.590
11.5	15.190	14.936	14.703	14.489	14.292	14.111	13.943	13.788
11.75	15.378	15.126	14.895	14.682	14.487	14.307	14.141	13.987
12	15.568	15.317	15.087	14.876	14.682	14.504	14.339	14.187
12.25	15.758	15.509	15.281	15.071	14.879	14.702	14.538	14.388
12.5	15.950	15.702	15.475	15.267	15.076	14.901	14.739	14.589
12.75	16.142	15.896	15.670	15.464	15.275	15.101	14.940	14.792
13	16.335	16.090	15.867	15.662	15.474	15.302	15.143	14.996
13.25	16.529	16.286	16.064	15.861	15.674	15.503	15.346	15.201
13.5	16.724	16.482	16.262	16.060	15.876	15.706	15.550	15.407
13.75	16.920	16.680	16.461	16.261	16.078	15.910	15.755	15.613
14	17.116	16.878	16.661	16.462	16.281	16.114	15.962	15.821
14.25	17.314	17.077	16.862	16.665	16.485	16.320	16.169	16.029
14.5	17.512	17.277	17.063	16.868	16.690	16.526	16.376	16.239
14.75	17.711	17.478	17.266	17.072	16.895	16.733	16.585	16.449
15	17.911	17.679	17.469	17.277	17.102	16.941	16.795	16.660
15.25	18.112	17.882	17.673	17.483	17.309	17.150	17.005	16.872
15.5	18.313	18.085	17.878	17.689	17.517	17.360	17.216	17.085
15.75	18.515	18.289	18.083	17.896	17.726	17.571	17.429	17.299
16	18.718	18.494	18.290	18.104	17.936	17.782	17.641	17.513
16.25	18.922	18.699	18.497	18.313	18.146	17.994	17.855	17.728
16.5	19.127	18.905	18.705	18.523	18.357	18.207	18.069	17.944
16.75	19.332	19.112	18.914	18.733	18.569	18.420	18.285	18.161
17	19.538	19.320	19.123	18.944	18.782	18.635	18.500	18.378
17.25	19.744	19.528	19.333	19.156	18.996	18.850	18.717	18.596
17.5	19.952	19.738	19.544	19.369	19.210	19.066	18.934	18.815
17.75	20.160	19.947	19.756	19.582	19.425	19.282	19.152	19.034
18	20.369	20.158	19.968	19.796	19.640	19.499	19.371	19.255
18.25	20.578	20.369	20.181	20.011	19.857	19.717	19.590	19.475
18.5	20.788	20.581	20.394	20.226	20.073	19.935	19.810	19.697
18.75	20.999	20.793	20.609	20.442	20.291	20.155	20.031	19.919
19	21.210	21.007	20.823	20.658	20.509	20.374	20.252	20.142
19.25	21.422	21.220	21.039	20.876	20.728	20.595	20.474	20.365
19.5	21.635	21.435	21.255	21.093	20.947	20.816	20.697	20.589
19.75	21.848	21.650	21.472	21.312	21.168	21.037	20.920	20.814
20	22.062	21.866	21.689	21.531	21.388	21.260	21.144	21.039

(continued)

Table B Amortizing Mortgages with One Equal Annual Payment

Percent	Years							
	17	17.5	18	18.5	19	19.5	20	20.5
5	8.870	8.707	8.555	8.411	8.275	8.146	8.024	7.909
5.25	9.036	8.875	8.723	8.579	8.444	8.316	8.195	8.081
5.5	9.204	9.043	8.892	8.749	8.615	8.488	8.368	8.254
5.75	9.374	9.214	9.063	8.921	8.788	8.662	8.542	8.430
6	9.544	9.385	9.236	9.095	8.962	8.837	8.718	8.606
6.25	9.717	9.559	9.410	9.270	9.138	9.014	8.896	8.785
6.5	9.891	9.733	9.585	9.446	9.316	9.192	9.076	8.966
6.75	10.066	9.909	9.763	9.625	9.495	9.372	9.257	9.148
7	10.243	10.087	9.941	9.804	9.675	9.554	9.439	9.331
7.25	10.421	10.266	10.121	9.985	9.857	9.737	9.623	9.516
7.5	10.600	10.447	10.303	10.168	10.041	9.922	9.809	9.703
7.75	10.781	10.629	10.486	10.352	10.226	10.108	9.996	9.891
8	10.963	10.812	10.670	10.537	10.413	10.296	10.185	10.081
8.25	11.146	10.996	10.856	10.724	10.601	10.485	10.375	10.273
8.5	11.331	11.182	11.043	10.913	10.790	10.675	10.567	10.465
8.75	11.517	11.370	11.231	11.102	10.981	10.867	10.760	10.660
9	11.705	11.558	11.421	11.293	11.173	11.060	10.955	10.855
9.25	11.893	11.748	11.612	11.485	11.367	11.255	11.150	11.052
9.5	12.083	11.939	11.805	11.679	11.561	11.451	11.348	11.251
9.75	12.274	12.131	11.998	11.874	11.757	11.648	11.546	11.450
10	12.466	12.325	12.193	12.070	11.955	11.847	11.746	11.651
10.25	12.660	12.520	12.389	12.267	12.153	12.047	11.947	11.854
10.5	12.854	12.716	12.586	12.466	12.353	12.248	12.149	12.057
10.75	13.050	12.913	12.785	12.665	12.554	12.450	12.353	12.262
11	13.247	13.111	12.984	12.866	12.756	12.654	12.558	12.468
11.25	13.445	13.310	13.185	13.068	12.960	12.858	12.763	12.675
11.5	13.644	13.511	13.387	13.271	13.164	13.064	12.970	12.883
11.75	13.844	13.712	13.590	13.476	13.370	13.271	13.179	13.093
12	14.046	13.915	13.794	13.681	13.576	13.479	13.388	13.303
12.25	14.248	14.119	13.999	13.887	13.784	13.688	13.598	13.515
12.5	14.451	14.323	14.205	14.095	13.993	13.898	13.810	13.727
12.75	14.656	14.529	14.412	14.303	14.203	14.109	14.022	13.941
13	14.861	14.736	14.620	14.513	14.413	14.321	14.235	14.156
13.25	15.067	14.943	14.829	14.723	14.625	14.534	14.450	14.371
13.5	15.274	15.152	15.039	14.935	14.838	14.748	14.665	14.588
13.75	15.482	15.362	15.250	15.147	15.052	14.963	14.881	14.805
14	15.692	15.572	15.462	15.360	15.266	15.179	15.099	15.024
14.25	15.902	15.784	15.675	15.575	15.482	15.396	15.317	15.243
14.5	16.112	15.996	15.889	15.790	15.698	15.614	15.536	15.463
14.75	16.324	16.209	16.103	16.006	15.916	15.832	15.755	15.684
15	16.537	16.423	16.319	16.222	16.134	16.052	15.976	15.906
15.25	16.750	16.638	16.535	16.440	16.353	16.272	16.198	16.129
15.5	16.964	16.854	16.752	16.658	16.572	16.493	16.420	16.352
15.75	17.179	17.070	16.970	16.878	16.793	16.715	16.643	16.577
16	17.395	17.287	17.188	17.098	17.014	16.937	16.867	16.802
16.25	17.612	17.505	17.408	17.318	17.236	17.161	17.091	17.027
16.5	17.829	17.724	17.628	17.540	17.459	17.385	17.316	17.254
16.75	18.047	17.944	17.849	17.762	17.683	17.609	17.542	17.481
17	18.266	18.164	18.071	17.985	17.907	17.835	17.769	17.709
17.25	18.486	18.385	18.293	18.209	18.132	18.061	17.996	17.937
17.5	18.706	18.607	18.516	18.433	18.357	18.288	18.224	18.166
17.75	18.927	18.829	18.740	18.658	18.583	18.515	18.453	18.396
18	19.149	19.052	18.964	18.884	18.810	18.743	18.682	18.626
18.25	19.371	19.276	19.189	19.110	19.038	18.972	18.912	18.857
18.5	19.594	19.500	19.415	19.337	19.266	19.201	19.142	19.088
18.75	19.817	19.725	19.641	19.564	19.495	19.431	19.373	19.320
19	20.041	19.950	19.868	19.792	19.724	19.661	19.605	19.553
19.25	20.266	20.176	20.095	20.021	19.954	19.892	19.837	19.786
19.5	20.492	20.403	20.323	20.250	20.184	20.124	20.069	20.019
19.75	20.718	20.630	20.551	20.480	20.415	20.356	20.302	20.253
20	20.944	20.858	20.781	20.710	20.646	20.588	20.536	20.488

(continued)

Table B Amortizing Mortgages with One Equal Annual Payment

				Years				
Percent	21	21.5	22	22.5	23	23.5	24	24.5
5	7.800	7.696	7.597	7.503	7.414	7.328	7.247	7.169
5.25	7.972	7.869	7.771	7.678	7.589	7.505	7.424	7.347
5.5	8.146	8.044	7.947	7.855	7.767	7.683	7.604	7.528
5.75	8.323	8.221	8.125	8.033	7.946	7.864	7.785	7.710
6	8.500	8.400	8.305	8.214	8.128	8.046	7.968	7.894
6.25	8.680	8.580	8.486	8.396	8.311	8.230	8.153	8.079
6.5	8.861	8.763	8.669	8.580	8.496	8.416	8.340	8.267
6.75	9.044	8.947	8.854	8.766	8.683	8.604	8.528	8.457
7	9.229	9.132	9.041	8.954	8.871	8.793	8.719	8.648
7.25	9.415	9.319	9.229	9.143	9.062	8.984	8.911	8.841
7.5	9.603	9.508	9.419	9.334	9.254	9.177	9.105	9.036
7.75	9.792	9.699	9.610	9.526	9.447	9.372	9.301	9.233
8	9.983	9.891	9.803	9.720	9.642	9.568	9.498	9.431
8.25	10.176	10.084	9.998	9.916	9.839	9.766	9.697	9.631
8.5	10.370	10.279	10.194	10.113	10.037	9.965	9.897	9.832
8.75	10.565	10.476	10.391	10.312	10.237	10.166	10.099	10.035
9	10.762	10.674	10.590	10.512	10.438	10.368	10.302	10.240
9.25	10.960	10.873	10.791	10.714	10.641	10.572	10.507	10.446
9.5	11.159	11.074	10.993	10.917	10.845	10.777	10.713	10.653
9.75	11.360	11.276	11.196	11.121	11.050	10.984	10.921	10.862
10	11.562	11.479	11.401	11.327	11.257	11.192	11.130	11.072
10.25	11.766	11.684	11.606	11.534	11.465	11.401	11.340	11.283
10.5	11.971	11.890	11.813	11.742	11.675	11.611	11.552	11.496
10.75	12.177	12.097	12.022	11.951	11.885	11.823	11.765	11.710
11	12.384	12.305	12.231	12.162	12.097	12.036	11.979	11.925
11.25	12.592	12.515	12.442	12.374	12.310	12.250	12.194	12.141
11.5	12.802	12.725	12.654	12.587	12.524	12.465	12.410	12.358
11.75	13.012	12.937	12.867	12.801	12.740	12.682	12.628	12.577
12	13.224	13.150	13.081	13.016	12.956	12.899	12.846	12.797
12.25	13.437	13.364	13.296	13.233	13.173	13.118	13.066	13.017
12.5	13.651	13.579	13.512	13.450	13.392	13.338	13.287	13.239
12.75	13.866	13.795	13.730	13.669	13.611	13.558	13.508	13.462
13	14.081	14.012	13.948	13.888	13.832	13.780	13.731	13.685
13.25	14.298	14.230	14.167	14.108	14.053	14.002	13.954	13.910
13.5	14.516	14.449	14.387	14.330	14.276	14.226	14.179	14.135
13.75	14.735	14.669	14.608	14.552	14.499	14.450	14.404	14.361
14	14.954	14.890	14.830	14.775	14.723	14.675	14.630	14.589
14.25	15.175	15.112	15.053	14.999	14.948	14.901	14.857	14.817
14.5	15.396	15.334	15.277	15.223	15.174	15.128	15.085	15.045
14.75	15.619	15.558	15.501	15.449	15.400	15.355	15.314	15.275
15	15.842	15.782	15.727	15.675	15.628	15.584	15.543	15.505
15.25	16.066	16.007	15.953	15.902	15.856	15.813	15.773	15.736
15.5	16.290	16.233	16.179	16.130	16.085	16.043	16.004	15.968
15.75	16.516	16.459	16.407	16.359	16.314	16.273	16.235	16.200
16	16.742	16.686	16.635	16.588	16.545	16.504	16.467	16.433
16.25	16.968	16.914	16.864	16.818	16.776	16.736	16.700	16.667
16.5	17.196	17.143	17.094	17.049	17.007	16.969	16.933	16.901
16.75	17.424	17.372	17.324	17.280	17.239	17.202	17.167	17.136
17	17.653	17.602	17.555	17.512	17.472	17.436	17.402	17.371
17.25	17.882	17.832	17.787	17.744	17.706	17.670	17.637	17.607
17.5	18.113	18.064	18.019	17.977	17.939	17.905	17.873	17.843
17.75	18.343	18.295	18.251	18.211	18.174	18.140	18.109	18.080
18	18.575	18.528	18.485	18.445	18.409	18.376	18.345	18.318
18.25	18.807	18.761	18.718	18.680	18.645	18.612	18.583	18.555
18.5	19.039	18.994	18.953	18.915	18.881	18.849	18.820	18.794
18.75	19.272	19.228	19.188	19.151	19.117	19.086	19.058	19.032
19	19.505	19.462	19.423	19.387	19.354	19.324	19.297	19.272
19.25	19.739	19.697	19.659	19.624	19.592	19.562	19.536	19.511
19.5	19.974	19.933	19.895	19.861	19.829	19.801	19.775	19.751
19.75	20.209	20.169	20.132	20.098	20.068	20.040	20.015	19.992
20	20.444	20.405	20.369	20.336	20.307	20.279	20.255	20.232

(continued)

638

Table B   Amortizing Mortgages with One Equal Annual Payment

Percent	Years							
	25	25.5	26	26.5	27	27.5	28	28.5
5	7.095	7.024	6.956	6.891	6.829	6.770	6.712	6.657
5.25	7.274	7.204	7.137	7.073	7.011	6.952	6.896	6.842
5.5	7.455	7.386	7.319	7.256	7.195	7.137	7.081	7.028
5.75	7.638	7.569	7.504	7.441	7.381	7.324	7.269	7.217
6	7.823	7.755	7.690	7.629	7.570	7.513	7.459	7.408
6.25	8.009	7.943	7.879	7.818	7.760	7.704	7.651	7.600
6.5	8.198	8.132	8.069	8.010	7.952	7.898	7.845	7.795
6.75	8.389	8.324	8.262	8.203	8.146	8.093	8.041	7.992
7	8.581	8.517	8.456	8.398	8.343	8.290	8.239	8.191
7.25	8.775	8.712	8.652	8.595	8.540	8.489	8.439	8.392
7.5	8.971	8.909	8.850	8.794	8.740	8.689	8.641	8.594
7.75	9.169	9.108	9.049	8.994	8.942	8.892	8.844	8.798
8	9.368	9.308	9.251	9.196	9.145	9.096	9.049	9.004
8.25	9.569	9.510	9.454	9.400	9.350	9.301	9.256	9.212
8.5	9.771	9.713	9.658	9.606	9.556	9.509	9.464	9.421
8.75	9.975	9.918	9.864	9.813	9.764	9.718	9.674	9.632
9	10.181	10.125	10.072	10.021	9.973	9.928	9.885	9.844
9.25	10.388	10.333	10.281	10.231	10.184	10.140	10.098	10.058
9.5	10.596	10.542	10.491	10.443	10.397	10.353	10.312	10.273
9.75	10.806	10.753	10.703	10.655	10.611	10.568	10.528	10.490
10	11.017	10.965	10.916	10.870	10.826	10.784	10.745	10.708
10.25	11.229	11.178	11.130	11.085	11.042	11.002	10.963	10.927
10.5	11.443	11.393	11.346	11.302	11.260	11.220	11.183	11.148
10.75	11.658	11.609	11.563	11.520	11.479	11.440	11.404	11.369
11	11.874	11.826	11.781	11.739	11.699	11.661	11.626	11.592
11.25	12.091	12.045	12.001	11.959	11.920	11.883	11.849	11.816
11.5	12.310	12.264	12.221	12.181	12.143	12.107	12.073	12.041
11.75	12.529	12.485	12.443	12.403	12.366	12.331	12.298	12.267
12	12.750	12.706	12.665	12.627	12.590	12.556	12.524	12.494
12.25	12.972	12.929	12.889	12.851	12.816	12.783	12.752	12.722
12.5	13.194	13.153	13.113	13.077	13.042	13.010	12.980	12.951
12.75	13.418	13.377	13.339	13.303	13.270	13.238	13.209	13.181
13	13.643	13.603	13.565	13.531	13.498	13.467	13.439	13.412
13.25	13.868	13.829	13.793	13.759	13.727	13.697	13.669	13.643
13.5	14.095	14.057	14.021	13.988	13.957	13.928	13.901	13.876
13.75	14.322	14.285	14.250	14.218	14.188	14.160	14.133	14.109
14	14.550	14.514	14.480	14.449	14.419	14.392	14.366	14.343
14.25	14.779	14.743	14.711	14.680	14.652	14.625	14.600	14.577
14.5	15.008	14.974	14.942	14.912	14.885	14.859	14.835	14.812
14.75	15.239	15.205	15.174	15.145	15.118	15.093	15.070	15.048
15	15.470	15.437	15.407	15.379	15.353	15.328	15.306	15.285
15.25	15.702	15.670	15.640	15.613	15.588	15.564	15.542	15.522
15.5	15.934	15.903	15.875	15.848	15.823	15.800	15.779	15.759
15.75	16.167	16.137	16.109	16.083	16.060	16.037	16.017	15.998
16	16.401	16.372	16.345	16.320	16.296	16.275	16.255	16.236
16.25	16.636	16.607	16.581	16.556	16.534	16.513	16.493	16.475
16.5	16.871	16.843	16.817	16.793	16.772	16.751	16.733	16.715
16.75	17.106	17.079	17.054	17.031	17.010	16.990	16.972	16.955
17	17.342	17.316	17.292	17.269	17.249	17.230	17.212	17.196
17.25	17.579	17.553	17.530	17.508	17.488	17.470	17.453	17.437
17.5	17.816	17.791	17.768	17.747	17.728	17.710	17.694	17.678
17.75	18.054	18.030	18.007	17.987	17.968	17.951	17.935	17.920
18	18.292	18.268	18.247	18.227	18.209	18.192	18.177	18.162
18.25	18.530	18.508	18.487	18.467	18.450	18.433	18.419	18.405
18.5	18.769	18.747	18.727	18.708	18.691	18.675	18.661	18.648
18.75	19.009	18.987	18.968	18.949	18.933	18.918	18.904	18.891
19	19.249	19.228	19.209	19.191	19.175	19.160	19.147	19.135
19.25	19.489	19.469	19.450	19.433	19.417	19.403	19.390	19.378
19.5	19.730	19.710	19.692	19.675	19.660	19.646	19.634	19.622
19.75	19.971	19.951	19.934	19.918	19.903	19.890	19.878	19.867
20	20.212	20.193	20.176	20.161	20.147	20.134	20.122	20.111

(continued)

Table B   Amortizing Mortgages with One Equal Annual Payment

Percent	Years							
	29	29.5	30	30.5	31	31.5	32	32.5
5	6.605	6.554	6.505	6.458	6.413	6.370	6.328	6.288
5.25	6.790	6.740	6.692	6.646	6.601	6.559	6.518	6.478
5.5	6.977	6.928	6.881	6.835	6.792	6.750	6.710	6.671
5.75	7.166	7.118	7.072	7.027	6.984	6.943	6.904	6.866
6	7.358	7.310	7.265	7.221	7.179	7.139	7.100	7.063
6.25	7.552	7.505	7.460	7.417	7.376	7.337	7.299	7.263
6.5	7.747	7.702	7.658	7.616	7.575	7.537	7.500	7.464
6.75	7.945	7.900	7.857	7.816	7.777	7.739	7.702	7.668
7	8.145	8.101	8.059	8.018	7.980	7.943	7.907	7.873
7.25	8.346	8.303	8.262	8.222	8.185	8.149	8.114	8.081
7.5	8.550	8.508	8.467	8.429	8.392	8.356	8.323	8.290
7.75	8.755	8.714	8.674	8.636	8.600	8.566	8.533	8.502
8	8.962	8.921	8.883	8.846	8.811	8.777	8.745	8.714
8.25	9.170	9.131	9.093	9.057	9.023	8.990	8.959	8.929
8.5	9.381	9.342	9.305	9.270	9.237	9.205	9.174	9.145
8.75	9.592	9.555	9.519	9.484	9.452	9.421	9.391	9.363
9	9.806	9.769	9.734	9.700	9.669	9.638	9.610	9.582
9.25	10.020	9.984	9.950	9.918	9.887	9.857	9.829	9.803
9.5	10.236	10.201	10.168	10.136	10.106	10.078	10.051	10.025
9.75	10.454	10.420	10.387	10.357	10.327	10.300	10.273	10.248
10	10.673	10.639	10.608	10.578	10.550	10.523	10.497	10.473
10.25	10.893	10.860	10.830	10.801	10.773	10.747	10.722	10.699
10.5	11.114	11.083	11.053	11.025	10.998	10.972	10.948	10.926
10.75	11.337	11.306	11.277	11.250	11.224	11.199	11.176	11.154
11	11.561	11.531	11.502	11.476	11.451	11.427	11.404	11.383
11.25	11.785	11.756	11.729	11.703	11.679	11.656	11.634	11.613
11.5	12.011	11.983	11.956	11.931	11.908	11.885	11.864	11.844
11.75	12.238	12.211	12.185	12.161	12.138	12.116	12.096	12.077
12	12.466	12.439	12.414	12.391	12.369	12.348	12.328	12.309
12.25	12.695	12.669	12.645	12.622	12.600	12.580	12.561	12.543
12.5	12.925	12.900	12.876	12.854	12.833	12.814	12.795	12.778
12.75	13.155	13.131	13.108	13.087	13.067	13.048	13.030	13.013
13	13.387	13.363	13.341	13.320	13.301	13.283	13.266	13.250
13.25	13.619	13.596	13.575	13.555	13.536	13.518	13.502	13.486
13.5	13.852	13.830	13.809	13.790	13.772	13.755	13.739	13.724
13.75	14.086	14.064	14.044	14.026	14.008	13.992	13.976	13.962
14	14.320	14.300	14.280	14.262	14.245	14.229	14.215	14.201
14.25	14.556	14.536	14.517	14.499	14.483	14.468	14.454	14.440
14.5	14.792	14.772	14.754	14.737	14.721	14.707	14.693	14.680
14.75	15.028	15.009	14.992	14.975	14.960	14.946	14.933	14.921
15	15.265	15.247	15.230	15.214	15.200	15.186	15.173	15.161
15.25	15.503	15.485	15.469	15.454	15.440	15.426	15.414	15.403
15.5	15.741	15.724	15.708	15.694	15.680	15.667	15.656	15.645
15.75	15.980	15.963	15.948	15.934	15.921	15.909	15.897	15.887
16	16.219	16.203	16.189	16.175	16.162	16.151	16.140	16.130
16.25	16.459	16.444	16.429	16.416	16.404	16.393	16.382	16.373
16.5	16.699	16.684	16.671	16.658	16.646	16.635	16.625	16.616
16.75	16.940	16.926	16.912	16.900	16.889	16.878	16.869	16.860
17	17.181	17.167	17.154	17.143	17.132	17.122	17.113	17.104
17.25	17.423	17.409	17.397	17.386	17.375	17.366	17.357	17.348
17.5	17.664	17.652	17.640	17.629	17.619	17.610	17.601	17.593
17.75	17.907	17.894	17.883	17.872	17.863	17.854	17.846	17.838
18	18.149	18.137	18.126	18.116	18.107	18.098	18.091	18.083
18.25	18.392	18.381	18.370	18.361	18.352	18.343	18.336	18.329
18.5	18.636	18.625	18.614	18.605	18.596	18.589	18.581	18.575
18.75	18.879	18.869	18.859	18.850	18.842	18.834	18.827	18.821
19	19.123	19.113	19.103	19.095	19.087	19.080	19.073	19.067
19.25	19.367	19.357	19.348	19.340	19.332	19.325	19.319	19.313
19.5	19.612	19.602	19.594	19.586	19.578	19.572	19.565	19.560
19.75	19.857	19.847	19.839	19.831	19.824	19.818	19.812	19.807
20	20.102	20.093	20.085	20.077	20.070	20.064	20.059	20.054

(continued)

Table B Amortizing Mortgages with One Equal Annual Payment

Percent	33	33.5	34	34.5	35	35.5	36	36.5
5	6.249	6.212	6.176	6.141	6.107	6.075	6.043	6.013
5.25	6.440	6.403	6.368	6.334	6.301	6.269	6.239	6.209
5.5	6.633	6.598	6.563	6.530	6.497	6.467	6.437	6.408
5.75	6.829	6.794	6.760	6.728	6.696	6.666	6.637	6.609
6	7.027	6.993	6.960	6.928	6.897	6.868	6.839	6.812
6.25	7.228	7.194	7.162	7.131	7.101	7.072	7.044	7.018
6.5	7.430	7.397	7.366	7.335	7.306	7.278	7.251	7.225
6.75	7.634	7.602	7.572	7.542	7.514	7.487	7.460	7.435
7	7.841	7.810	7.780	7.751	7.723	7.697	7.672	7.647
7.25	8.049	8.019	7.990	7.962	7.935	7.909	7.885	7.861
7.5	8.259	8.230	8.201	8.174	8.148	8.123	8.099	8.077
7.75	8.471	8.443	8.415	8.389	8.363	8.339	8.316	8.294
8	8.685	8.657	8.630	8.605	8.580	8.557	8.534	8.513
8.25	8.901	8.873	8.847	8.823	8.799	8.776	8.754	8.734
8.5	9.118	9.091	9.066	9.042	9.019	8.997	8.976	8.956
8.75	9.336	9.311	9.286	9.263	9.241	9.219	9.199	9.180
9	9.556	9.531	9.508	9.485	9.464	9.443	9.424	9.405
9.25	9.778	9.754	9.731	9.709	9.688	9.668	9.649	9.631
9.5	10.000	9.977	9.955	9.934	9.914	9.895	9.876	9.859
9.75	10.225	10.202	10.181	10.160	10.141	10.122	10.105	10.088
10	10.450	10.428	10.407	10.388	10.369	10.351	10.334	10.318
10.25	10.677	10.655	10.635	10.616	10.598	10.581	10.565	10.550
10.5	10.904	10.884	10.864	10.846	10.829	10.812	10.797	10.782
10.75	11.133	11.113	11.095	11.077	11.060	11.044	11.029	11.015
11	11.363	11.344	11.326	11.309	11.293	11.277	11.263	11.249
11.25	11.594	11.575	11.558	11.542	11.526	11.512	11.498	11.485
11.5	11.826	11.808	11.791	11.775	11.760	11.746	11.733	11.721
11.75	12.058	12.041	12.025	12.010	11.996	11.982	11.969	11.957
12	12.292	12.276	12.260	12.245	12.232	12.219	12.206	12.195
12.25	12.526	12.511	12.496	12.482	12.468	12.456	12.444	12.433
12.5	12.762	12.746	12.732	12.719	12.706	12.694	12.683	12.672
12.75	12.998	12.983	12.969	12.956	12.944	12.933	12.922	12.912
13	13.234	13.220	13.207	13.195	13.183	13.172	13.162	13.152
13.25	13.472	13.458	13.446	13.434	13.422	13.412	13.402	13.393
13.5	13.710	13.697	13.685	13.673	13.662	13.652	13.643	13.634
13.75	13.949	13.936	13.924	13.913	13.903	13.893	13.884	13.876
14	14.188	14.176	14.165	14.154	14.144	14.135	14.126	14.118
14.25	14.428	14.416	14.405	14.395	14.386	14.377	14.369	14.361
14.5	14.668	14.657	14.647	14.637	14.628	14.619	14.612	14.604
14.75	14.909	14.898	14.888	14.879	14.870	14.862	14.855	14.848
15	15.150	15.140	15.131	15.122	15.113	15.106	15.099	15.092
15.25	15.392	15.382	15.373	15.365	15.357	15.350	15.343	15.336
15.5	15.635	15.625	15.616	15.608	15.601	15.594	15.587	15.581
15.75	15.877	15.868	15.860	15.852	15.845	15.838	15.832	15.826
16	16.120	16.112	16.104	16.096	16.089	16.083	16.077	16.071
16.25	16.364	16.355	16.348	16.341	16.334	16.328	16.322	16.317
16.5	16.608	16.600	16.592	16.585	16.579	16.573	16.568	16.563
16.75	16.852	16.844	16.837	16.830	16.824	16.819	16.814	16.809
17	17.096	17.089	17.082	17.076	17.070	17.065	17.060	17.055
17.25	17.341	17.334	17.327	17.321	17.316	17.311	17.306	17.302
17.5	17.586	17.579	17.573	17.567	17.562	17.557	17.553	17.549
17.75	17.831	17.825	17.819	17.813	17.808	17.804	17.800	17.796
18	18.077	18.071	18.065	18.060	18.055	18.051	18.047	18.043
18.25	18.323	18.317	18.311	18.306	18.302	18.298	18.294	18.290
18.5	18.569	18.563	18.558	18.553	18.549	18.545	18.541	18.538
18.75	18.815	18.809	18.805	18.800	18.796	18.792	18.789	18.785
19	19.061	19.056	19.051	19.047	19.043	19.040	19.036	19.033
19.25	19.308	19.303	19.299	19.294	19.291	19.287	19.284	19.281
19.5	19.555	19.550	19.546	19.542	19.538	19.535	19.532	19.529
19.75	19.802	19.797	19.793	19.789	19.786	19.783	19.780	19.777
20	20.049	20.045	20.041	20.037	20.034	20.031	20.028	20.026

(continued)

Table B Amortizing Mortgages with One Equal Annual Payment

				Years			
Percent	37	37.5	38	38.5	39	39.5	40
5	5.984	5.956	5.928	5.902	5.876	5.852	5.828
5.25	6.181	6.153	6.127	6.101	6.076	6.052	6.029
5.5	6.380	6.353	6.327	6.302	6.278	6.255	6.232
5.75	6.582	6.556	6.530	6.506	6.483	6.460	6.438
6	6.786	6.760	6.736	6.712	6.689	6.667	6.646
6.25	6.992	6.967	6.944	6.921	6.899	6.877	6.857
6.5	7.201	7.177	7.153	7.131	7.110	7.089	7.069
6.75	7.411	7.388	7.365	7.344	7.323	7.303	7.284
7	7.624	7.601	7.580	7.559	7.539	7.519	7.501
7.25	7.838	7.816	7.795	7.775	7.756	7.737	7.720
7.5	8.055	8.033	8.013	7.994	7.975	7.957	7.940
7.75	8.273	8.252	8.233	8.214	8.196	8.179	8.162
8	8.492	8.473	8.454	8.436	8.419	8.402	8.386
8.25	8.714	8.695	8.677	8.659	8.643	8.627	8.611
8.5	8.937	8.918	8.901	8.884	8.868	8.853	8.838
8.75	9.161	9.144	9.127	9.111	9.095	9.080	9.066
9	9.387	9.370	9.354	9.338	9.324	9.309	9.296
9.25	9.614	9.598	9.582	9.567	9.553	9.540	9.527
9.5	9.843	9.827	9.812	9.798	9.784	9.771	9.759
9.75	10.072	10.057	10.043	10.029	10.016	10.004	9.992
10	10.303	10.288	10.275	10.262	10.249	10.237	10.226
10.25	10.535	10.521	10.508	10.495	10.483	10.472	10.461
10.5	10.768	10.754	10.742	10.730	10.718	10.707	10.697
10.75	11.002	10.989	10.977	10.965	10.954	10.944	10.934
11	11.236	11.224	11.213	11.202	11.191	11.181	11.172
11.25	11.472	11.460	11.449	11.439	11.429	11.419	11.410
11.5	11.709	11.697	11.687	11.677	11.667	11.658	11.650
11.75	11.946	11.935	11.925	11.915	11.906	11.898	11.890
12	12.184	12.174	12.164	12.155	12.146	12.138	12.130
12.25	12.423	12.413	12.404	12.395	12.387	12.379	12.372
12.5	12.662	12.653	12.644	12.636	12.628	12.620	12.613
12.75	12.902	12.893	12.885	12.877	12.869	12.862	12.856
13	13.143	13.134	13.126	13.119	13.112	13.105	13.099
13.25	13.384	13.376	13.368	13.361	13.354	13.348	13.342
13.5	13.626	13.618	13.611	13.604	13.597	13.591	13.586
13.75	13.868	13.861	13.854	13.847	13.841	13.835	13.830
14	14.111	14.104	14.097	14.091	14.085	14.080	14.075
14.25	14.354	14.347	14.341	14.335	14.329	14.324	14.319
14.5	14.597	14.591	14.585	14.579	14.574	14.569	14.565
14.75	14.841	14.835	14.830	14.824	14.819	14.815	14.810
15	15.086	15.080	15.074	15.069	15.065	15.060	15.056
15.25	15.330	15.325	15.320	15.315	15.310	15.306	15.302
15.5	15.575	15.570	15.565	15.561	15.556	15.552	15.549
15.75	15.821	15.816	15.811	15.807	15.803	15.799	15.795
16	16.066	16.061	16.057	16.053	16.049	16.046	16.042
16.25	16.312	16.308	16.303	16.299	16.296	16.293	16.289
16.5	16.558	16.554	16.550	16.546	16.543	16.540	16.537
16.75	16.805	16.800	16.797	16.793	16.790	16.787	16.784
17	17.051	17.047	17.044	17.040	17.037	17.035	17.032
17.25	17.298	17.294	17.291	17.288	17.285	17.282	17.280
17.5	17.545	17.541	17.538	17.535	17.533	17.530	17.528
17.75	17.792	17.789	17.786	17.783	17.780	17.778	17.776
18	18.039	18.036	18.033	18.031	18.028	18.026	18.024
18.25	18.287	18.284	18.281	18.279	18.276	18.274	18.272
18.5	18.535	18.532	18.529	18.527	18.525	18.523	18.521
18.75	18.783	18.780	18.777	18.775	18.773	18.771	18.769
19	19.030	19.028	19.026	19.023	19.022	19.020	19.018
19.25	19.279	19.276	19.274	19.272	19.270	19.268	19.267
19.5	19.527	19.525	19.522	19.521	19.519	19.517	19.516
19.75	19.775	19.773	19.771	19.769	19.768	19.766	19.765
20	20.024	20.021	20.020	20.018	20.016	20.015	20.014

642

Table C Compounding Interest

Percent Per Period	1	2	3	4	5	6	7	8
2	1.02000	1.04040	1.06121	1.08243	1.10408	1.12616	1.14869	1.17166
2.25	1.02250	1.04551	1.06903	1.09308	1.11768	1.14283	1.16854	1.19483
2.5	1.02500	1.05063	1.07689	1.10381	1.13141	1.15969	1.18869	1.21840
2.75	1.02750	1.05576	1.08479	1.11462	1.14527	1.17677	1.20913	1.24238
3	1.03000	1.06090	1.09273	1.12551	1.15927	1.19405	1.22987	1.26677
3.25	1.03250	1.06606	1.10070	1.13648	1.17341	1.21155	1.25092	1.29158
3.5	1.03500	1.07123	1.10872	1.14752	1.18769	1.22926	1.27228	1.31681
3.75	1.03750	1.07641	1.11677	1.15865	1.20210	1.24718	1.29395	1.34247
4	1.04000	1.08160	1.12486	1.16986	1.21665	1.26532	1.31593	1.36857
4.25	1.04250	1.08681	1.13300	1.18115	1.23135	1.28368	1.33824	1.39511
4.5	1.04500	1.09203	1.14117	1.19252	1.24618	1.30226	1.36086	1.42210
4.75	1.04750	1.09726	1.14938	1.20397	1.26116	1.32107	1.38382	1.44955
5	1.05000	1.10250	1.15763	1.21551	1.27628	1.34010	1.40710	1.47746
5.25	1.05250	1.10776	1.16591	1.22712	1.29155	1.35935	1.43072	1.50583
5.5	1.05500	1.11303	1.17424	1.23882	1.30696	1.37884	1.45468	1.53469
5.75	1.05750	1.11831	1.18261	1.25061	1.32252	1.39856	1.47898	1.56402
6	1.06000	1.12360	1.19102	1.26248	1.33823	1.41852	1.50363	1.59385
6.25	1.06250	1.12891	1.19946	1.27443	1.35408	1.43871	1.52863	1.62417
6.5	1.06500	1.13423	1.20795	1.28647	1.37009	1.45914	1.55399	1.65500
6.75	1.06750	1.13956	1.21648	1.29859	1.38624	1.47981	1.57970	1.68633
7	1.07000	1.14490	1.22504	1.31080	1.40255	1.50073	1.60578	1.71819
7.25	1.07250	1.15026	1.23365	1.32309	1.41901	1.52189	1.63223	1.75057
7.5	1.07500	1.15563	1.24230	1.33547	1.43563	1.54330	1.65905	1.78348
7.75	1.07750	1.16101	1.25098	1.34794	1.45240	1.56496	1.68625	1.81693
8	1.08000	1.16640	1.25971	1.36049	1.46933	1.58687	1.71382	1.85093
8.25	1.08250	1.17181	1.26848	1.37313	1.48641	1.60904	1.74179	1.88549
8.5	1.08500	1.17723	1.27729	1.38586	1.50366	1.63147	1.77014	1.92060
8.75	1.08750	1.18266	1.28614	1.39868	1.52106	1.65415	1.79889	1.95629
9	1.09000	1.18810	1.29503	1.41158	1.53862	1.67710	1.82804	1.99256
9.25	1.09250	1.19356	1.30396	1.42458	1.55635	1.70031	1.85759	2.02942
9.5	1.09500	1.19903	1.31293	1.43766	1.57424	1.72379	1.88755	2.06687
9.75	1.09750	1.20451	1.32195	1.45084	1.59229	1.74754	1.91793	2.10492
10	1.10000	1.21000	1.33100	1.46410	1.61051	1.77156	1.94872	2.14359
10.25	1.10250	1.21551	1.34010	1.47746	1.62889	1.79586	1.97993	2.18287
10.5	1.10500	1.22103	1.34923	1.49090	1.64745	1.82043	2.01157	2.22279
10.75	1.10750	1.22656	1.35841	1.50444	1.66617	1.84528	2.04365	2.26334
11	1.11000	1.23210	1.36763	1.51807	1.68506	1.87041	2.07616	2.30454
11.25	1.11250	1.23766	1.37689	1.53179	1.70412	1.89583	2.10911	2.34639
11.5	1.11500	1.24323	1.38620	1.54561	1.72335	1.92154	2.14252	2.38891
11.75	1.11750	1.24881	1.39554	1.55952	1.74276	1.94753	2.17637	2.43209
12	1.12000	1.25440	1.40493	1.57352	1.76234	1.97382	2.21068	2.47596
12.25	1.12250	1.26001	1.41436	1.58762	1.78210	2.00041	2.24546	2.52052
12.5	1.12500	1.26563	1.42383	1.60181	1.80203	2.02729	2.28070	2.56578
12.75	1.12750	1.27126	1.43334	1.61609	1.82214	2.05447	2.31641	2.61175
13	1.13000	1.27690	1.44290	1.63047	1.84244	2.08195	2.35261	2.65844
13.25	1.13250	1.28256	1.45249	1.64495	1.86291	2.10974	2.38928	2.70586
13.5	1.13500	1.28823	1.46214	1.65952	1.88356	2.13784	2.42645	2.75402
13.75	1.13750	1.29391	1.47182	1.67419	1.90439	2.16625	2.46411	2.80292
14	1.14000	1.29960	1.48154	1.68896	1.92541	2.19497	2.50227	2.85259
14.25	1.14250	1.30531	1.49131	1.70382	1.94662	2.22401	2.54093	2.90302
14.5	1.14500	1.31103	1.50112	1.71879	1.96801	2.25337	2.58011	2.95423
14.75	1.14750	1.31676	1.51098	1.73385	1.98959	2.28305	2.61980	3.00623
15	1.15000	1.32250	1.52088	1.74901	2.01136	2.31306	2.66002	3.05902

(continued)

Table C   Compounding Interest

Percent Per Period	9	10	11	12	13	14	15	16
2	1.19509	1.21899	1.24337	1.26824	1.29361	1.31948	1.34587	1.37279
2.25	1.22171	1.24920	1.27731	1.30605	1.33544	1.36548	1.39621	1.42762
2.5	1.24886	1.28008	1.31209	1.34489	1.37851	1.41297	1.44830	1.48451
2.75	1.27655	1.31165	1.34772	1.38478	1.42287	1.46199	1.50220	1.54351
3	1.30477	1.34392	1.38423	1.42576	1.46853	1.51259	1.55797	1.60471
3.25	1.33355	1.37689	1.42164	1.46785	1.51555	1.56481	1.61566	1.66817
3.5	1.36290	1.41060	1.45997	1.51107	1.56396	1.61869	1.67535	1.73399
3.75	1.39281	1.44504	1.49923	1.55545	1.61378	1.67430	1.73709	1.00223
4	1.42331	1.48024	1.53945	1.60103	1.66507	1.73168	1.80094	1.87298
4.25	1.45440	1.51621	1.58065	1.64783	1.71786	1.79087	1.86699	1.94633
4.5	1.48610	1.55297	1.62285	1.69588	1.77220	1.85194	1.93528	2.02237
4.75	1.51840	1.59052	1.66607	1.74521	1.82811	1.91495	2.00591	2.10119
5	1.55133	1.62889	1.71034	1.79586	1.88565	1.97993	2.07893	2.18287
5.25	1.58489	1.66810	1.75567	1.84784	1.94486	2.04696	2.15443	2.26753
5.5	1.61909	1.70814	1.80209	1.90121	2.00577	2.11609	2.23248	2.35526
5.75	1.65395	1.74906	1.84963	1.95598	2.06845	2.18739	2.31316	2.44617
6	1.68948	1.79085	1.89830	2.01220	2.13293	2.26090	2.39656	2.54035
6.25	1.72568	1.83354	1.94813	2.06989	2.19926	2.33671	2.48276	2.63793
6.5	1.76257	1.87714	1.99915	2.12910	2.26749	2.41487	2.57184	2.73901
6.75	1.80016	1.92167	2.05138	2.18985	2.33767	2.49546	2.66390	2.84372
7	1.83846	1.96715	2.10485	2.25219	2.40985	2.57853	2.75903	2.95216
7.25	1.87748	2.01360	2.15959	2.31615	2.48408	2.66417	2.85732	3.06448
7.5	1.91724	2.06103	2.21561	2.38178	2.56041	2.75244	2.95888	3.18079
7.75	1.95774	2.10947	2.27295	2.44910	2.63891	2.84343	3.06379	3.30124
8	1.99900	2.15892	2.33164	2.51817	2.71962	2.93719	3.17217	3.42594
8.25	2.04104	2.20942	2.39170	2.58902	2.80261	3.03383	3.28412	3.55506
8.5	2.08386	2.26098	2.45317	2.66169	2.88793	3.13340	3.39974	3.68872
8.75	2.12747	2.31362	2.51607	2.73622	2.97564	3.23601	3.51916	3.82709
9	2.17189	2.36736	2.58043	2.81266	3.06580	3.34173	3.64248	3.97031
9.25	2.21714	2.42222	2.64628	2.89106	3.15848	3.45064	3.76983	4.11854
9.5	2.26322	2.47823	2.71366	2.97146	3.25375	3.56285	3.90132	4.27195
9.75	2.31015	2.53539	2.78259	3.05390	3.35165	3.67844	4.03709	4.43070
10	2.35795	2.59374	2.85312	3.13843	3.45227	3.79750	4.17725	4.59497
10.25	2.40662	2.65330	2.92526	3.22510	3.55567	3.92013	4.32194	4.76494
10.5	2.45618	2.71408	2.99906	3.31396	3.66193	4.04643	4.47130	4.94079
10.75	2.50665	2.77611	3.07455	3.40506	3.77110	4.17650	4.62547	5.12271
11	2.55804	2.83942	3.15176	3.49845	3.88328	4.31044	4.78459	5.31089
11.25	2.61036	2.90402	3.23073	3.59418	3.99853	4.44836	4.94880	5.50554
11.5	2.66363	2.96995	3.31149	3.69231	4.11693	4.59037	5.11827	5.70687
11.75	2.71786	3.03721	3.39409	3.79289	4.23856	4.73659	5.29314	5.91508
12	2.77308	3.10585	3.47855	3.89598	4.36349	4.88711	5.47357	6.13039
12.25	2.82929	3.17588	3.56492	4.00162	4.49182	5.04207	5.65972	6.35304
12.5	2.88651	3.24732	3.65324	4.10989	4.62363	5.20158	5.85178	6.58325
12.75	2.94475	3.32021	3.74354	4.22084	4.75899	5.36577	6.04990	6.82126
13	3.00404	3.39457	3.83586	4.33452	4.89801	5.53475	6.25427	7.06733
13.25	3.06439	3.47042	3.93025	4.45101	5.04077	5.70867	6.46507	7.32169
13.5	3.12581	3.54780	4.02675	4.57036	5.18736	5.88765	6.68248	7.58462
13.75	3.18833	3.62672	4.12539	4.69264	5.33787	6.07183	6.90671	7.85638
14	3.25195	3.70722	4.22623	4.81790	5.49241	6.26135	7.13794	8.13725
14.25	3.31670	3.78933	4.32931	4.94623	5.65107	6.45635	7.37638	8.42751
14.5	3.38259	3.87307	4.43466	5.07769	5.81395	6.65697	7.62223	8.72746
14.75	3.44964	3.95847	4.54234	5.21234	5.98115	6.86337	7.87572	9.03739
15	3.51788	4.04556	4.65239	5.35025	6.15279	7.07571	8.13706	9.35762

(continued)

644

Table C Compounding Interest

Percent Per Period	17	18	19	20	21	22	23	24
2	1.40024	1.42825	1.45681	1.48595	1.51567	1.54598	1.57690	1.60844
2.25	1.45974	1.49259	1.52617	1.56051	1.59562	1.63152	1.66823	1.70577
2.5	1.52162	1.55966	1.59865	1.63862	1.67958	1.72157	1.76461	1.80873
2.75	1.58596	1.62957	1.67438	1.72043	1.76774	1.81635	1.86630	1.91763
3	1.65285	1.70243	1.75351	1.80611	1.86029	1.91610	1.97359	2.03279
3.25	1.72239	1.77837	1.83616	1.89584	1.95745	2.02107	2.08675	2.15457
3.5	1.79468	1.85749	1.92250	1.98979	2.05943	2.13151	2.20611	2.28333
3.75	1.86981	1.93993	2.01268	2.08815	2.16646	2.24770	2.33199	2.41944
4	1.94790	2.02582	2.10685	2.19112	2.27877	2.36992	2.46472	2.56330
4.25	2.02905	2.11529	2.20519	2.29891	2.39661	2.49847	2.60465	2.71535
4.5	2.11338	2.20848	2.30786	2.41171	2.52024	2.63365	2.75217	2.87601
4.75	2.20099	2.30554	2.41505	2.52977	2.64993	2.77580	2.90765	3.04577
5	2.29202	2.40662	2.52695	2.65330	2.78596	2.92526	3.07152	3.22510
5.25	2.38658	2.51187	2.64375	2.78254	2.92863	3.08238	3.24421	3.41453
5.5	2.48480	2.62147	2.76565	2.91776	3.07823	3.24754	3.42615	3.61459
5.75	2.58682	2.73556	2.89286	3.05920	3.23510	3.42112	3.61783	3.82586
6	2.69277	2.85434	3.02560	3.20714	3.39956	3.60354	3.81975	4.04893
6.25	2.80280	2.97797	3.16410	3.36185	3.57197	3.79522	4.03242	4.28444
6.5	2.91705	3.10665	3.30859	3.52365	3.75268	3.99661	4.25639	4.53305
6.75	3.03567	3.24057	3.45931	3.69282	3.94208	4.20817	4.49222	4.79545
7	3.15882	3.37993	3.61653	3.86968	4.14056	4.43040	4.74053	5.07237
7.25	3.28665	3.52494	3.78050	4.05458	4.34854	4.66381	5.00193	5.36457
7.5	3.41935	3.67580	3.95149	4.24785	4.56644	4.90892	5.27709	5.67287
7.75	3.55708	3.83275	4.12979	4.44985	4.79472	5.16631	5.56669	5.99811
8	3.70002	3.99602	4.31570	4.66096	5.03383	5.43654	5.87146	6.34118
8.25	3.84835	4.16584	4.50952	4.88155	5.28428	5.72024	6.19215	6.70301
8.5	4.00226	4.34245	4.71156	5.11205	5.54657	6.01803	6.52956	7.08457
8.75	4.16196	4.52613	4.92216	5.35285	5.82123	6.33058	6.88451	7.48691
9	4.32763	4.71712	5.14166	5.60441	6.10881	6.65860	7.25787	7.91108
9.25	4.49950	4.91571	5.37041	5.86717	6.40997	7.00280	7.65056	8.35824
9.5	4.67778	5.12217	5.60878	6.14161	6.72507	7.36395	8.06352	8.82956
9.75	4.86269	5.33681	5.85715	6.42822	7.05497	7.74283	8.49775	9.32629
10	5.05447	5.55992	6.11591	6.72750	7.40025	8.14027	8.95430	9.84973
10.25	5.25335	5.79182	6.38548	7.03999	7.76159	8.55715	9.43426	10.40127
10.5	5.45957	6.03283	6.66628	7.36623	8.13969	8.99436	9.93876	10.98233
10.75	5.67340	6.28329	6.95875	7.70681	8.53529	9.45284	10.46902	11.59444
11	5.89509	6.54355	7.26334	8.06231	8.94917	9.93357	11.02627	12.23916
11.25	6.12492	6.81397	7.58054	8.43336	9.38211	10.43759	11.61182	12.91815
11.5	6.36316	7.09492	7.91084	8.82058	9.83495	10.96597	12.22706	13.63317
11.75	6.61010	7.38679	8.25473	9.22467	10.30856	11.51982	12.87340	14.38602
12	6.86604	7.68997	8.61276	9.64629	10.80385	12.10031	13.55235	15.17863
12.25	7.13129	8.00487	8.98540	10.08619	11.32174	12.70866	14.26547	16.01299
12.5	7.40616	8.33193	9.37342	10.54509	11.86323	13.34613	15.01440	16.89120
12.75	7.69097	8.67157	9.77720	11.02379	12.42933	14.01406	15.80086	17.81547
13	7.98608	9.02427	10.19742	11.52309	13.02109	14.71383	16.62663	18.78809
13.25	8.29181	9.39048	10.63472	12.04382	13.63962	15.44688	17.49359	19.81149
13.5	8.60854	9.77070	11.08974	12.58686	14.28608	16.21470	18.40369	20.88818
13.75	8.93663	10.16542	11.56316	13.15310	14.96165	17.01888	19.35897	22.02083
14	9.27646	10.57517	12.05569	13.74349	15.66758	17.86104	20.36158	23.21221
14.25	9.62843	11.00048	12.56805	14.35900	16.40516	18.74289	21.41375	24.46521
14.5	9.99294	11.44192	13.10099	15.00064	17.17573	19.66621	22.51781	25.78290
14.75	10.37041	11.90004	13.65530	15.66945	17.98070	20.63285	23.67620	27.16844
15	10.76126	12.37545	14.23177	16.36654	18.82152	21.64475	24.89146	28.62518

(continued)

Table C Compounding Interest

Percent Per Period	Periods							
	25	26	27	28	29	30	31	32
2	1.64061	1.67342	1.70689	1.74102	1.77584	1.81136	1.84759	1.88454
2.25	1.74415	1.78339	1.82352	1.86454	1.90650	1.94939	1.99325	2.03810
2.5	1.85394	1.90029	1.94780	1.99650	2.04641	2.09757	2.15001	2.20376
2.75	1.97036	2.02455	2.08022	2.13743	2.19621	2.25660	2.31866	2.38242
3	2.09378	2.15659	2.22129	2.28793	2.35657	2.42726	2.50008	2.57508
3.25	2.22460	2.29690	2.37155	2.44862	2.52820	2.61037	2.69521	2.78280
3.5	2.36324	2.44596	2.53157	2.62017	2.71188	2.80679	2.90503	3.00671
3.75	2.51017	2.60430	2.70196	2.80328	2.90841	3.01747	3.13063	3.24803
4	2.66584	2.77247	2.88337	2.99870	3.11865	3.24340	3.37313	3.50806
4.25	2.83075	2.95106	3.07648	3.20723	3.34353	3.48564	3.63377	3.78821
4.5	3.00543	3.14068	3.28201	3.42970	3.58404	3.74532	3.91386	4.08998
4.75	3.19044	3.34199	3.50073	3.66702	3.84120	4.02366	4.21478	4.41498
5	3.38635	3.55567	3.73346	3.92013	4.11614	4.32194	4.53804	4.76494
5.25	3.59379	3.78246	3.98104	4.19005	4.41002	4.64155	4.88523	5.14171
5.5	3.81339	4.02313	4.24440	4.47784	4.72412	4.98395	5.25807	5.54726
5.75	4.04585	4.27848	4.52450	4.78465	5.05977	5.35071	5.65837	5.98373
6	4.29187	4.54938	4.82235	5.11169	5.41839	5.74349	6.08810	6.45339
6.25	4.55222	4.83674	5.13903	5.46022	5.80149	6.16408	6.54933	6.95867
6.5	4.82770	5.14150	5.47570	5.83162	6.21067	6.61437	7.04430	7.50218
6.75	5.11914	5.46468	5.83355	6.22731	6.64766	7.09637	7.57538	8.08672
7	5.42743	5.80735	6.21387	6.64884	7.11426	7.61226	8.14511	8.71527
7.25	5.75351	6.17063	6.61801	7.09781	7.61240	8.16430	8.75621	9.39104
7.5	6.09834	6.55572	7.04739	7.57595	8.14414	8.75496	9.41158	10.11745
7.75	6.46297	6.96385	7.50355	8.08507	8.71166	9.38682	10.11430	10.89815
8	6.84848	7.39635	7.98806	8.62711	9.31727	10.06266	10.86767	11.73708
8.25	7.25601	7.85463	8.50263	9.20410	9.96344	10.78542	11.67522	12.63843
8.5	7.68676	8.34014	9.04905	9.81822	10.65277	11.55825	12.54070	13.60666
8.75	8.14201	8.85444	9.62920	10.47175	11.38803	12.38449	13.46813	14.64659
9	8.62308	9.39916	10.24508	11.16714	12.17218	13.26768	14.46177	15.76333
9.25	9.13137	9.97603	10.89881	11.90695	13.00834	14.21161	15.52619	16.96236
9.5	9.66836	10.58686	11.59261	12.69391	13.89983	15.22031	16.66624	18.24954
9.75	10.23560	11.23357	12.32884	13.53090	14.85017	16.29806	17.88712	19.63111
10	10.83471	11.91818	13.10999	14.42099	15.86309	17.44940	19.19434	21.11378
10.25	11.46740	12.64281	13.93870	15.36741	16.94257	18.67919	20.59380	22.70467
10.5	12.13548	13.40971	14.81772	16.37359	18.09281	19.99256	22.09178	24.41141
10.75	12.84084	14.22123	15.75001	17.44314	19.31827	21.39499	23.69495	26.24216
11	13.58546	15.07986	16.73865	18.57990	20.62369	22.89230	25.41045	28.20560
11.25	14.37145	15.98823	17.78691	19.78794	22.01408	24.49067	27.24587	30.31103
11.5	15.20098	16.94910	18.89824	21.07154	23.49477	26.19667	29.20928	32.56835
11.75	16.07638	17.96536	20.07629	22.43525	25.07139	28.01728	31.30931	34.98815
12	17.00006	19.04007	21.32488	23.88387	26.74993	29.95992	33.55511	37.58173
12.25	17.97458	20.17647	22.64808	25.42247	28.53673	32.03247	35.95645	40.36112
12.5	19.00260	21.37793	24.05017	27.05644	30.43849	34.24330	38.52372	43.33918
12.75	20.08694	22.64802	25.53565	28.79144	32.46235	36.60130	41.26797	46.52963
13	21.23054	23.99051	27.10928	30.63349	34.61584	39.11590	44.20096	49.94709
13.25	22.43651	25.40935	28.77608	32.58891	36.90695	41.79712	47.33523	53.60715
13.5	23.70809	26.90868	30.54135	34.66443	39.34413	44.65559	50.68410	57.52645
13.75	25.04870	28.49289	32.41067	36.86713	41.93636	47.70261	54.26172	61.72271
14	26.46192	30.16658	34.38991	39.20449	44.69312	50.95016	58.08318	66.21483
14.25	27.95151	31.93460	36.48528	41.68443	47.62446	54.41094	62.16450	71.02295
14.5	29.52141	33.80202	38.70331	44.31529	50.74101	58.09846	66.52273	76.16853
14.75	31.17578	35.77421	41.05091	47.10591	54.05404	62.02701	71.17599	81.67445
15	32.91895	37.85680	43.53531	50.06561	57.57545	66.21177	76.14354	87.56507

(continued)

Table C Compounding Interest

Percent Per Period	\multicolumn{8}{c}{Periods}							
	33	34	35	36	37	38	39	40
2	1.92223	1.96068	1.99989	1.42645	1.43657	1.44696	1.45764	1.46860
2.25	2.08396	2.13085	2.17879	1.42769	1.43911	1.45089	1.46302	1.47553
2.5	2.25885	2.31532	2.37321	1.42893	1.44167	1.45484	1.46847	1.48256
2.75	2.44794	2.51526	2.58443	1.43017	1.44423	1.45883	1.47397	1.48969
3	2.65234	2.73191	2.81386	1.43140	1.44681	1.46284	1.47953	1.49692
3.25	2.87324	2.96662	3.06304	1.43264	1.44939	1.46689	1.48516	1.50426
3.5	3.11194	3.22086	3.33359	1.43389	1.45199	1.47096	1.49085	1.51171
3.75	3.36983	3.49619	3.62730	1.43513	1.45460	1.47507	1.49660	1.51926
4	3.64838	3.79432	3.94609	1.43637	1.45722	1.47920	1.50242	1.52693
4.25	3.94921	4.11705	4.29202	1.43762	1.45984	1.48337	1.50829	1.53471
4.5	4.27403	4.46636	4.66735	1.43886	1.46248	1.48757	1.51424	1.54260
4.75	4.62469	4.84437	5.07447	1.44011	1.46514	1.49181	1.52025	1.55061
5	5.00319	5.25335	5.51602	1.44136	1.46780	1.49607	1.52632	1.55873
5.25	5.41165	5.69576	5.99479	1.44260	1.47047	1.50037	1.53247	1.56698
5.5	5.85236	6.17424	6.51383	1.44385	1.47316	1.50470	1.53868	1.57534
5.75	6.32780	6.69164	7.07641	1.44510	1.47585	1.50906	1.54496	1.58383
6	6.84059	7.25103	7.68609	1.44636	1.47856	1.51345	1.55131	1.59245
6.25	7.39358	7.85568	8.34666	1.44761	1.48128	1.51788	1.55773	1.60119
6.5	7.98982	8.50916	9.06225	1.44886	1.48400	1.52234	1.56423	1.61007
6.75	8.63257	9.21527	9.83730	1.45012	1.48675	1.52684	1.57079	1.61907
7	9.32534	9.97811	10.67658	1.45137	1.48950	1.53137	1.57743	1.62821
7.25	10.07189	10.80210	11.58525	1.45263	1.49226	1.53593	1.58414	1.63749
7.5	10.87625	11.69197	12.56887	1.45389	1.49503	1.54053	1.59093	1.64690
7.75	11.74276	12.65282	13.63342	1.45515	1.49782	1.54516	1.59780	1.65646
8	12.67605	13.69013	14.78534	1.45641	1.50062	1.54983	1.60474	1.66616
8.25	13.68110	14.80979	16.03159	1.45767	1.50343	1.55453	1.61176	1.67601
8.5	14.76323	16.01810	17.37964	1.45893	1.50625	1.55927	1.61886	1.68601
8.75	15.92817	17.32188	18.83754	1.46020	1.50908	1.56405	1.62604	1.69615
9	17.18203	18.72841	20.41397	1.46146	1.51193	1.56886	1.63329	1.70645
9.25	18.53138	20.24553	22.11824	1.46273	1.51478	1.57371	1.64064	1.71691
9.5	19.98324	21.88165	23.96041	1.46399	1.51765	1.57860	1.64806	1.72753
9.75	21.54515	23.64580	25.95126	1.46526	1.52053	1.58352	1.65557	1.73831
10	23.22515	25.54767	28.10244	1.46653	1.52342	1.58848	1.66316	1.74925
10.25	25.03190	27.59766	30.42643	1.46780	1.52632	1.59348	1.67084	1.76036
10.5	26.97461	29.80694	32.93667	1.46907	1.52924	1.59851	1.67861	1.77164
10.75	29.06319	32.18748	35.64763	1.47034	1.53217	1.60359	1.68646	1.78310
11	31.30821	34.75212	38.57485	1.47161	1.53511	1.60870	1.69441	1.79473
11.25	33.72102	37.51463	41.73503	1.47289	1.53806	1.61385	1.70244	1.80655
11.5	36.31371	40.48979	45.14611	1.47416	1.54102	1.61905	1.71057	1.81854
11.75	39.09926	43.69342	48.82740	1.47544	1.54400	1.62428	1.71879	1.83072
12	42.09153	47.14252	52.79962	1.47672	1.54699	1.62955	1.72710	1.84310
12.25	45.30536	50.85526	57.08503	1.47799	1.54999	1.63486	1.73551	1.85566
12.5	48.75658	54.85115	61.70755	1.47927	1.55300	1.64021	1.74401	1.86843
12.75	52.46216	59.15109	66.69285	1.48055	1.55603	1.64561	1.75262	1.88139
13	56.44021	63.77744	72.06851	1.48184	1.55906	1.65104	1.76132	1.89455
13.25	60.71010	68.75419	77.86412	1.48312	1.56211	1.65652	1.77012	1.90793
13.5	65.29252	74.10701	84.11146	1.48440	1.56518	1.66203	1.77903	1.92152
13.75	70.20958	79.86340	90.84461	1.48569	1.56825	1.66759	1.78803	1.93532
14	75.48490	86.05279	98.10018	1.48697	1.57134	1.67320	1.79715	1.94934
14.25	81.14372	92.70669	105.91740	1.48826	1.57444	1.67884	1.80636	1.96358
14.5	87.21297	99.85885	114.33838	1.48955	1.57756	1.68453	1.81569	1.97805
14.75	93.72143	107.54534	123.40828	1.49084	1.58068	1.69027	1.82512	1.99276
15	100.69983	115.80480	133.17552	1.49213	1.58382	1.69604	1.83466	2.00770

(continued)

Table C Compounding Interest

Percent Per Period	41	42	43	44	45	46	47	48
2	1.47987	1.49145	1.50335	1.51559	1.52817	1.54110	1.55441	1.56809
2.25	1.48843	1.50173	1.51545	1.52960	1.54421	1.55929	1.57485	1.59091
2.5	1.49714	1.51223	1.52785	1.54403	1.56078	1.57813	1.59612	1.61476
2.75	1.50601	1.52296	1.54057	1.55887	1.57790	1.59768	1.61826	1.63967
3	1.51504	1.53393	1.55362	1.57415	1.59558	1.61795	1.64131	1.66571
3.25	1.52424	1.54513	1.56699	1.58988	1.61385	1.63898	1.66531	1.69294
3.5	1.53360	1.55658	1.58071	1.60607	1.63274	1.66079	1.69032	1.72142
3.75	1.54313	1.56828	1.59478	1.62275	1.65226	1.68344	1.71630	1.75122
4	1.55284	1.58023	1.60922	1.63992	1.67245	1.70694	1.74355	1.78243
4.25	1.56272	1.59245	1.62404	1.65761	1.69332	1.73135	1.77188	1.81511
4.5	1.57279	1.60495	1.63923	1.67583	1.71491	1.75670	1.80143	1.84935
4.75	1.58304	1.61772	1.65483	1.69460	1.73725	1.78304	1.83227	1.88525
5	1.59348	1.63077	1.67084	1.71394	1.76036	1.81042	1.86446	1.92290
5.25	1.60411	1.64412	1.68727	1.73388	1.78428	1.83887	1.89808	1.96239
5.5	1.61494	1.65776	1.70414	1.75443	1.80905	1.86846	1.93320	2.00386
5.75	1.62597	1.67172	1.72146	1.77562	1.83469	1.89924	1.96990	2.04740
6	1.63721	1.68599	1.73924	1.79747	1.86125	1.93127	2.00828	2.09316
6.25	1.64866	1.70059	1.75750	1.82000	1.88877	1.96460	2.04841	2.14127
6.5	1.66032	1.71551	1.77626	1.84324	1.91728	1.99931	2.09041	2.19187
6.75	1.67220	1.73078	1.79552	1.86722	1.94683	2.03545	2.13438	2.24514
7	1.68431	1.74640	1.81531	1.89197	1.97747	2.07311	2.18043	2.30123
7.25	1.69664	1.76238	1.83565	1.91751	2.00924	2.11237	2.22868	2.36034
7.5	1.70921	1.77874	1.85654	1.94387	2.04220	2.15329	2.27926	2.42266
7.75	1.72201	1.79547	1.87802	1.97109	2.07640	2.19598	2.33231	2.48841
8	1.73507	1.81259	1.90009	1.99921	2.11189	2.24051	2.38797	2.55782
8.25	1.74837	1.83011	1.92279	2.02824	2.14874	2.28700	2.44642	2.63115
8.5	1.76192	1.84805	1.94612	2.05825	2.18700	2.33555	2.50781	2.70866
8.75	1.77574	1.86641	1.97011	2.08925	2.22675	2.38626	2.57232	2.79066
9	1.78982	1.88520	1.99479	2.12129	2.26805	2.43926	2.64017	2.87747
9.25	1.80418	1.90445	2.02018	2.15442	2.31099	2.49467	2.71155	2.96943
9.5	1.81882	1.92415	2.04629	2.18868	2.35563	2.55263	2.78670	3.06693
9.75	1.83374	1.94433	2.07317	2.22411	2.40206	2.61327	2.86586	3.17037
10	1.84895	1.96500	2.10082	2.26076	2.45036	2.67677	2.94929	3.28021
10.25	1.86446	1.98616	2.12929	2.29869	2.50064	2.74327	3.03729	3.39693
10.5	1.88028	2.00785	2.15859	2.33795	2.55299	2.81296	3.13015	3.52107
10.75	1.89641	2.03006	2.18876	2.37860	2.60751	2.88603	3.22822	3.65322
11	1.91286	2.05282	2.21984	2.42069	2.66432	2.96266	3.33184	3.79400
11.25	1.92963	2.07615	2.25184	2.46429	2.72353	3.04309	3.44142	3.94414
11.5	1.94674	2.10005	2.28482	2.50947	2.78527	3.12753	3.55737	4.10438
11.75	1.96420	2.12455	2.31879	2.55629	2.84966	3.21625	3.68016	4.27556
12	1.98200	2.14966	2.35380	2.60482	2.91686	3.30949	3.81027	4.45863
12.25	2.00017	2.17541	2.38989	2.65515	2.98700	3.40756	3.94823	4.65458
12.5	2.01870	2.20180	2.42710	2.70735	3.06026	3.51075	4.09468	4.86454
12.75	2.03761	2.22887	2.46547	2.76152	3.13679	3.61940	4.25020	5.08975
13	2.05690	2.25664	2.50503	2.81773	3.21677	3.73386	4.41551	5.33155
13.25	2.07659	2.28511	2.54585	2.87609	3.30041	3.85451	4.59137	5.59147
13.5	2.09669	2.31432	2.58797	2.93669	3.38790	3.98177	4.77860	5.87116
13.75	2.11719	2.34429	2.63143	2.99964	3.47946	4.11607	4.97811	6.17247
14	2.13813	2.37504	2.67629	3.06506	3.57532	4.25791	5.19089	6.49745
14.25	2.15950	2.40660	2.72260	3.13306	3.67574	4.40779	5.41801	6.84836
14.5	2.18131	2.43899	2.77043	3.20376	3.78097	4.56629	5.66067	7.22774
14.75	2.20358	2.47224	2.81982	3.27729	3.89130	4.73399	5.92016	7.63840
15	2.22632	2.50638	2.87085	3.35380	4.00704	4.91157	6.19791	8.08349

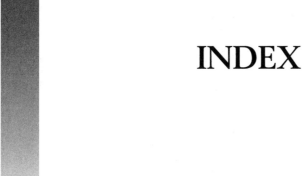

INDEX